Communications in Computer and Information Science 2934

Rationale
The CCIS series is devoted to the publication of proceedings of computer science conferences. Its aim is to efficiently disseminate original research results in informatics in printed and electronic form. While the focus is on publication of peer-reviewed full papers presenting mature work, inclusion of reviewed short papers reporting on work in progress is welcome, too. Besides globally relevant meetings with internationally representative program committees guaranteeing a strict peer-reviewing and paper selection process, conferences run by societies or of high regional or national relevance are also considered for publication.

Topics
The topical scope of CCIS spans the entire spectrum of informatics ranging from foundational topics in the theory of computing to information and communications science and technology and a broad variety of interdisciplinary application fields.

Information for Volume Editors and Authors
Publication in CCIS is free of charge. No royalties are paid, however, we offer registered conference participants temporary free access to the online version of the conference proceedings on SpringerLink (http://link.springer.com) by means of an http referrer from the conference website and/or a number of complimentary printed copies, as specified in the official acceptance email of the event.

CCIS proceedings can be published in time for distribution at conferences or as post-proceedings, and delivered in the form of printed books and/or electronically as USBs and/or e-content licenses for accessing proceedings at SpringerLink. Furthermore, CCIS proceedings are included in the CCIS electronic book series hosted in the SpringerLink digital library at http://link.springer.com/bookseries/7899. Conferences publishing in CCIS are allowed to use our online conference service (Meteor) for managing the whole proceedings lifecycle (from submission and reviewing to preparing for publication) free of charge.

Publication process
The language of publication is exclusively English. Authors publishing in CCIS have to sign the Springer CCIS copyright transfer form, however, they are free to use their material published in CCIS for substantially changed, more elaborate subsequent publications elsewhere. For the preparation of the camera-ready papers/files, authors have to strictly adhere to the Springer CCIS Authors' Instructions and are strongly encouraged to use the CCIS LaTeX style files or templates.

Abstracting/Indexing
CCIS is abstracted/indexed in DBLP, Google Scholar, EI-Compendex, Mathematical Reviews, SCImago, Scopus. CCIS volumes are also submitted for the inclusion in ISI Proceedings.

How to start

To start the evaluation of your proposal for inclusion in the CCIS series, please send an e-mail to ccis@springer.com

Hamid R. Arabnia · Leonidas Deligiannidis ·
Ken Ferens · Farid Ghareh Mohammadi ·
Farzan Shenavarmasouleh · Soheyla Amirian
Editors

Internet Computing, Internet of Things, Artificial Intelligence, and Applications

26th International Conference, ICOMP 2025, and 27th International Conference, ICAI 2025, Held as Part of the World Congress in Computer Science, Computer Engineering, and Applied Computing, CSCE 2025
Las Vegas, NV, USA, July 21–24, 2025
Revised Selected Papers

Springer

Editors
Hamid R. Arabnia
University of Georgia
Athens, GA, USA

Leonidas Deligiannidis
Wentworth Institute of Technology
Boston, MA, USA

Ken Ferens
University of Manitoba
Winnipeg, MB, Canada

Farid Ghareh Mohammadi
Verify Radiology Images Consultants
Athens, GA, USA

Farzan Shenavarmasouleh
MediaLab, Inc.
Lawrenceville, GA, USA

Soheyla Amirian
Pace University
New York, NY, USA

ISSN 1865-0929 ISSN 1865-0937 (electronic)
Communications in Computer and Information Science
ISBN 978-3-032-22189-6 ISBN 978-3-032-22190-2 (eBook)
https://doi.org/10.1007/978-3-032-22190-2

This Springer imprint is published by the registered company Springer Nature Switzerland AG
The registered company address is: Gewerbestrasse 11, 6330 Cham, Switzerland

Preface

It is our great pleasure to introduce this collection of selected papers presented at the 26th International Conference on Internet Computing & IoT (ICOMP 2025) and the 27th International Conference on Artificial Intelligence (ICAI 2025).

These conferences were held as part of the federated 2025 World Congress in Computer Science, Computer Engineering, and Applied Computing (CSCE 2025), which took place from July 21 to July 24, 2025, in Las Vegas, Nevada, USA.

The CSCE 2025 Congress brought together papers from a diverse array of communities, including researchers from universities, corporations, and government agencies. Accepted papers are published by Springer Nature, and the proceedings showcase solutions to key challenges in various critical areas of Computer Science, Computer Engineering, and Applied Computing.

Computer Science (CS) is the study of computational systems, data processing, information management, and automation. Many applications in CS focus on solving problems that would be impossible or extremely difficult to address without the use of computers. It serves as a bridge between computational science and other scientific fields. The interdisciplinary nature of CS involves leveraging computers to understand and solve complex challenges, making it the science of using computers to advance scientific discovery. Computer Engineering (CE), on the other hand, integrates aspects of computer science, electronic engineering, and electrical engineering. It encompasses the design and production of computer hardware, such as chips, servers, supercomputers, embedded systems, and communication systems, among others.

Considering the above broad outline, the CSCE 2025 Congress was composed of the following focused conferences:

Applied Cognitive Computing (ACC); Bioinformatics & Computational Biology (BIOCOMP); Biomedical Engineering (BIOENG); Scientific Computing (CSC); eLearning, e-Business, Enterprise Information Systems, & e-Government (EEE); Embedded Systems, Cyber-physical Systems, & Applications (ESCS); Foundations of Computer Science (FCS); Frontiers in Education (FECS); Grid, Cloud, & Cluster Computing (GCC); Health Informatics (HIMS); Artificial Intelligence (ICAI); Data Science (ICDATA); Emergent Quantum Technologies (ICEQT); Internet Computing & IoT (ICOMP); Wireless Networks (ICWN); Information & Knowledge Engineering (IKE); Image Processing, Computer Vision, & Pattern Recognition (IPCV); Modeling, Simulation & Visualization Methods (MSV); Parallel & Distributed Processing Techniques & Applications (PDPTA); Security & Management (SAM); and Software Engineering Research & Practice (SERP). The scope of each track can be found at: https://www.american-cse.org/csce2025/conferences.

The primary objective of the CSCE Congress and its associated conferences is to foster opportunities for cross-fertilization between the fields of Computer Science (CS) and Computer Engineering (CE). The CSCE Congress is deeply committed to promoting diversity and eliminating discrimination, both in its role as a conference organizer and as a service provider. Our goal is to create an inclusive culture that respects and values differences, promotes dignity, equality, and diversity, and encourages individuals to reach their full potential. We are also dedicated, wherever possible, to organizing a conference that represents the global community. We sincerely hope that we have succeeded in achieving these important objectives.

The Steering Committee and the Program Committees would like to extend their gratitude to all the authors who submitted papers for consideration. This year's conferences received submissions from 58 countries, with approximately 50% of them coming from outside the USA. Each submitted paper underwent a rigorous peer-review process, with at least two experts (an average of 2.4 referees per paper) evaluating the submissions based on originality, significance, clarity, impact, and soundness. In cases where reviewers' recommendations were contradictory, a program committee member was tasked with making the final decision, often consulting additional referees for further guidance. The Congress followed the guidelines of COPE (Committee on Publication Ethics):

Typical submissions underwent a single-blind peer review process, in which the authors remained unaware of the identities of the reviewers, while the reviewers were informed of the authors' identities.

Papers authored by one or more members of the program committee, including co-chairs, were subjected to a double-blind peer review process, ensuring that neither the authors nor the reviewers were aware of each other's identities or affiliations.

The ICAI 2025 Conference received a total of 293 submissions, of which 59 papers were accepted, resulting in a paper acceptance rate of 20%. For this volume we selected only 24 of the papers accepted at ICAI. The ICOMP 2025 Conference received 62 submissions, of which 14 papers were accepted, resulting in a paper acceptance rate of 23%.

This volume includes 35 of the accepted papers from ICAI 2025 and ICOMP 2025.

We are deeply grateful to the many colleagues who contributed their time and effort to organizing the Congress. In particular, we extend our thanks to the members of the Program Committees, the Steering Committee, the referees, and the Chairs and organizers of individual sessions and conferences. We would also like to express our appreciation to the primary sponsor of the conference, the American Council on Science & Education. The list of members of the Program Committee for each track can be found at: https://www.american-cse.org/csce2025/committees.

We extend our heartfelt gratitude to all the speakers and authors for their valuable contributions. We would also like to thank the following individuals and organizations for their support: the staff at the Luxor Hotel and the staff of Springer Nature for their assistance in various aspects of the event.

We are pleased to present a curated selection of papers from the ICAI 2025 and ICOMP 2025 conferences. These proceedings represent a collection of outstanding research contributions that reflect the diversity and depth of work in core areas of Internet Computing, Internet of Things (IoT), Artificial Intelligence, and Applications.

August 2025

Hamid R. Arabnia
Leonidas Deligiannidis
Ken Ferens
Farid Ghareh Mohammadi
Farzan Shenavarmasouleh
Soheyla Amirian

Organization

Steering Committee – Co-chairs (CSCE 2025)

Hamid R. Arabnia	University of Georgia, USA
Leonidas Deligiannidis	Wentworth Institute of Technology, USA
Fernando G. Tinetti	Universidad Nacional de La Plata, Argentina
Quoc-Nam Tran	Southeastern Louisiana University, USA

Co-editors of ICOMP 2025 and ICAI 2025 Proceedings – Publication Co-chairs

Hamid R. Arabnia	University of Georgia, USA
Leonidas Deligiannidis	Wentworth Institute of Technology, USA
Ken Ferens	University of Manitoba, Canada
Farid Ghareh Mohammadi	Verify Radiology Images Consultants, LLC, USA
Farzan Shenavarmasouleh	Medialab Inc., USA
Soheyla Amirian	Pace University, USA

Members of Steering Committee (CSCE 2025)

Babak Akhgar	Sheffield Hallam University, UK
Abbas M. Al-Bakry	University of IT & Communications, Iraq
Nizar Al-Holou	University of Detroit Mercy, USA
Hamid R. Arabnia	University of Georgia, USA
Rajab Challoo	Texas A&M University-Kingsville, USA
Chien-Fu Cheng	Tamkang University, Taiwan
Hyunseung Choo	Sungkyunkwan University, South Korea
Kevin Daimi	University of Detroit Mercy, USA
Leonidas Deligiannidis	Wentworth Institute of Technology, USA
Eman M. El-Sheikh	University of West Florida, USA
Mary Mehrnoosh Eshaghian-Wilner	University of California, Los Angeles, USA
David L. Foster	Kettering University, USA
Henry Hexmoor	Southern Illinois University at Carbondale, USA
Ching-Hsien (Robert) Hsu	Chung Hua University, Taiwan
James J. (Jong Hyuk) Park	SeoulTech, South Korea

Mohammad S. Obaidat	University of Jordan, Jordan
Marwan Omar	Illinois Institute of Technology, USA
Shahram Rahimi	University of Alabama, USA
Gerald Schaefer	Loughborough University, UK
Fernando G. Tinetti	Universidad Nacional de La Plata, Argentina
Quoc-Nam Tran	Southeastern Louisiana University, USA
Shiuh-Jeng Wang	Central Police University, Taiwan
Layne T. Watson	Virginia Polytechnic Institute & State University, USA
Chao-Tung Yang	Tunghai University, Taiwan
Mary Yang	University of Arkansas for Medical Sciences, USA

Research Tracks – Co-chairs (CSCE 2025)

Abeer Alsadoon (Co-chair, Health Informatics)	Charles Sturt University, Australia
Soheyla Amirian (Co-chair, Computer Vision & AI)	Pace University, USA
Hamid R. Arabnia (Co-chair, HPC)	University of Georgia, USA
Kevin Daimi (Co-chair, Security)	University of Detroit Mercy, USA
Leonidas Deligiannidis (Co-chair, Imaging Science, AI)	Wentworth Institute of Technology, USA
Richard Dill (Co-chair, Military and Defense Modeling)	US Air Force Institute of Technology, USA
Ken Ferens (Co-chair, Cognitive Computing & AI)	University of Manitoba, Canada
David de la Fuente (Co-chair, Information Management)	University of Oviedo, Spain
Shanzhen Gao (Co-chair, Artificial Intelligence, Education)	Virginia State University, USA
Farid Ghareh Mohammadi (Co-chair, Computer Vision & AI)	Verify Radiology Images Consultants, LLC, USA
Michael R. Grimaila (Co-chair, Military and Defense Modeling)	US Air Force Institute of Technology, USA
Douglas D. Hodson (Co-chair, Military and Defense Modeling)	US Air Force Institute of Technology, USA

Masahito Ohue (Co-chair, Mathematical Modeling)	Tokyo Institute of Technology, Japan
Peter M. Maurer (Co-chair, Theoretical Computer Science)	Baylor University, USA
Jose A. Olivas (Co-chair, Information Management)	University of Castilla - La Mancha, Spain
Javier Ordus (Co-chair, Quantum Computing & AI)	Earlham College, USA
Pablo Rivas (Chair, Quantum Computing & AI)	Baylor University, USA
Farzan Shenavarmasouleh (Co-chair, Computer Vision & AI)	MediaLab Inc., USA
Robert Stahlbock (Co-chair, Data Mining)	Universität Hamburg, Germany
Masami Takata (Co-chair, Mathematical Modeling)	Nara Women's University, Japan
Nazli Tekin (Co-chair, Energy Aware, Security)	Erciyes University, Turkey
Quoc-Nam Tran (Co-chair, Education & Bioinformatics)	Southeastern Louisiana University, USA
Torrey J. Wagner (Co-chair, Scientific Computing, Artificial Intelligence)	US Air Force Institute of Technology, USA
Troy Weingart (Co-chair, Military and Defense Modeling)	US Air Force Institute of Technology, USA
Nobuaki Yasuo (Co-chair, Mathematical Modeling)	Tokyo Institute of Technology, Japan
Tanwir Zaman (Co-chair, Artificial Intelligence)	Walmart Labs, USA
Chris Cheng Zhang (Co-chair, Artificial Intelligence, Robotics)	Canada Youth Robotics Club, Canada
Beilei Zhu (Co-chair, Supply Chain Management)	Intel Corporation, USA

Program Committees of ICOMP 2025 and ICAI 2025

Refer to the lists at: https://www.american-cse.org/csce2025/committees.

Contents

Internet Computing, Internet of Things, and Applications

A Framework for Improving Network Topology Based on Graph Theory in Software-Defined Networking

Datta Sai Krishna Naidu(✉) and Alex Modarresi

California State University, Northridge, CA, USA
datta-sai-krishna.naidu.929@my.csun.edu, alex.modarresi@csun.edu

Abstract. This paper presents a novel approach to network topology improvement in Software-Defined Networking (SDN) environments by developing a comprehensive mathematical framework for critical node identification. We introduce the Network Node Significance Index (NNSI), a new mathematical integration of multiple centrality metrics to provide a more accurate assessment of node criticality based on functional significance rather than topological scale. Through extensive experimental evaluation on 261 network topologies from the Internet Topology Zoo dataset, we demonstrate that NNSI consistently outperforms existing methods in identifying truly critical nodes, with an average improvement of 7.61% across all networks and up to 72% in very large networks. Building on this improved critical node identification capability, we develop a topology improvement framework that strategically reconfigures network connections to improve resilience, reduce latency, and improve network resource utilization. Our approach achieves significant improvements across multiple performance metrics, demonstrating its practical utility for network administrators seeking to optimize their infrastructure with minimal changes.

Keywords: Software-defined networking · Network resilience · Graph theory · Critical node identification · Network Topology · Network Node Significance Index

1 Introduction

Modern communication networks serve as the foundation of our digital society, facilitating a wide range of functions, from fundamental internet connectivity to essential services. With the expansion in scale and intricacy of these networks, the demands of effectively overseeing them have significantly intensified [1]. Network topology—the arrangement of nodes and links in a network—significantly influences performance attributes such as latency, throughput, reliability, and security [2]. Therefore, improving network topology has become a critical aspect of network management, particularly in large-scale enterprise and service provider environments.

H. R. Arabnia et al. (Eds.): CSCE 2025, CCIS 2934, pp. 3–18, 2026.
https://doi.org/10.1007/978-3-032-22190-2_1

Traditional network architectures have relied on distributed control protocols, where each network device makes routing and forwarding decisions based on limited local information [3]. While this approach is robust in some ways, it often leads to suboptimal resource utilization and makes network-wide improvement challenging. The inherent coupling of control and data planes in traditional networks constrains the ability to implement sophisticated topology management strategies [4].

Software-defined networking (SDN) embodies a fundamental change in network architecture by segregating the control plane, which determines traffic routing, from the data plane. This separation facilitates the forwarding of packets based on these determinations [5]. This separation enables centralized control and programmability of the network, providing unprecedented opportunities for dynamic topology management and improvement [6]. The centralized visibility and control offered by SDN create new possibilities for intelligent network management based on global knowledge rather than localized decision-making [7]. Graph theory provides a natural mathematical framework for analyzing and improving network topologies [8]. By representing networks as graphs, where devices are depicted as nodes and connections as edges, graph-theoretic principles and algorithms can be leveraged to improve comprehension of the network framework and pinpoint areas for improvement [9].

Identifying critical nodes—those whose failure or congestion would severely impact network performance—is a fundamental issue in network analysis and improvement [10]. By identifying these critical nodes, network administrators can prioritize resources, implement targeted redundancy, and optimize traffic routing to enhance overall network resilience and performance [11].

Recent developments in identifying critical nodes encompass the Integrated Value of Influence (IVI) technique [12]. This method integrates six centrality metrics to offer a thorough assessment of the significance of nodes in computer networks. While IVI represents a significant improvement over single-metric approaches, it still exhibits limitations in certain network topologies and fails to fully account for the functional significance of nodes in modern computer networks [13].

This research addresses these challenges by introducing a new mathematical framework for critical node identification that builds upon existing approaches while incorporating novel elements to enhance accuracy and applicability across diverse network structures. Our Network Node Significance Index (NNSI) reorganizes how centrality measures are combined to better capture the multifaceted nature of node criticality in network structures, focusing on functional significance rather than purely topological properties.

2 Background and Related Work

This section reviews the literature relevant to our research, exploring three interconnected areas: critical node identification, centrality measures in graph theory, and topology optimization in software-defined networking.

Research on identifying critical nodes in complex networks has spanned multiple domains, including telecommunications, transportation systems, and biological systems [14]. Critical nodes represent components whose failure would severely impact the functionality or performance of the entire network [15]. The importance of accurately identifying these nodes has grown with increasing network complexity and reliability requirements.

Early work by Albert et al. [16] laid the foundation for understanding network vulnerability by analyzing how node removal affects connectivity. Their study demonstrated that scale-free networks exhibit significant resilience to random failures but are highly vulnerable to targeted attacks on high-degree nodes. Building on this foundation, Cohen et al. [11] investigated Internet resilience to intentional attacks, finding that removing high-betweenness nodes caused more significant disruption than removing high-degree nodes in many real-world networks.

Graph theory provides the mathematical framework that enables systematic analysis of network topologies [8]. Within this framework, centrality measures form the foundation of critical node identification by quantifying node importance based on different topological properties [17]. These metrics can be categorized by their analytical scope.

Local centrality measures focus on a node's immediate vicinity, with degree centrality being the most fundamental metric [18]. These measures are computationally efficient but provide limited insight into a node's importance within the broader network context. In contrast, global centrality measures examine the complete network structure, with betweenness centrality measuring a node's position on shortest paths between other nodes [19]. While more comprehensive, these global measures often require significant computational resources.

Recent developments include the Integrated Value of Influence (IVI) technique [12], which integrates six centrality metrics to offer a more thorough assessment of node significance. While IVI represents an improvement over single-metric approaches, it still exhibits limitations, particularly in how it organizes centrality measures and addresses positional bias.

Software-defined networking has emerged as a revolutionary architecture, offering unprecedented centralized control opportunities [4] that create new possibilities for network topology optimization. The global view and programmability of SDN enable more sophisticated approaches to topology analysis and modification than previously possible with distributed control protocols.

Despite these advances, several challenges persist in SDN-based topology optimization. Muqaddas et al. [20] studied scale and complexity issues, showing that computational requirements increase dramatically with network size. Dixit et al. [21] addressed multi-objective optimization, demonstrating that networks must balance competing objectives like performance, reliability, and cost. Implementation concerns have been highlighted by Yeganeh et al. [22], who investigated overhead in SDN environments, while Yu et al. [23] explored the challenges of integrating SDN with legacy systems.

These three research areas—critical node identification, centrality measures, and SDN-based topology optimization—converge in our work as we develop a comprehensive framework that leverages centrality-based critical node identification to enable more effective topology optimization in SDN environments.

3 The Network Node Significance Index

This section introduces the Network Node Significance Index (NNSI), our novel approach to identifying critical nodes in network topologies. We first discuss the limitations of existing metrics, then present the mathematical foundations and components of NNSI.

3.1 Limitations of Existing Node Importance Metrics

Existing metrics for assessing node importance exhibit several limitations affecting their accuracy and practical utility. Traditional approaches often rely on individual centrality measures that capture only specific aspects of node importance [24]. Degree centrality focuses solely on direct connections, ignoring broader network position, while betweenness centrality assumes all communication follows shortest paths and exhibits significant positional bias [25].

This positional bias particularly affects global measures like betweenness centrality. Peripheral nodes often receive disproportionately high betweenness scores despite limited practical importance [26], while core nodes may be undervalued due to multiple alternative paths around them [27]. The Integrated Value of Influence (IVI) formula, while representing an advancement, still organizes centrality measures based on topological scale rather than functional significance, applies bias correction uniformly, and omits potentially valuable measures like closeness centrality and PageRank [12].

3.2 Components of NNSI

The Network Node Significance Index reorganizes centrality measures around functional significance rather than topological scale, providing a more intuitive and effective assessment of node criticality. While traditional approaches, including IVI, organize metrics based on topological scale (local, semi-local, global) [12], NNSI organizes centrality measures based on their functional significance in network operation [28], capturing three key dimensions.

The first dimension is the Connectivity Function, which measures how well a node connects to other nodes in the network, both directly and indirectly. The Connectivity Score (CS) is computed as the sum of normalized degree centrality and closeness centrality:

$$CS_i = DC'_i + CC'_i \tag{1}$$

where DC'_i is the normalized degree centrality of node i and CC'_i is the normalized closeness centrality of node i.

The second dimension is the Flow Control Function, which measures how much a node influences or controls the flow of traffic through the network [29]. The Flow Control Score (FCS) is computed as the sum of normalized betweenness centrality and K-core value:

$$FCS_i = BC'_i + K'_i \tag{2}$$

where BC'_i is the normalized betweenness centrality of node i and K'_i is the normalized K-core value of node i.

The third dimension is the Influence Propagation Function, which measures how effectively a node can spread information or influence through the network [30]. The Influence Propagation Score (IPS) is computed as the sum of normalized PageRank and collective influence:

$$IPS_i = PR'_i + CI'_i \tag{3}$$

where PR'_i is the normalized PageRank of node i and CI'_i is the normalized collective influence of node i.

These three functional components each capture different aspects of the importance of a node in network operation. To provide a comprehensive assessment of node criticality, these components are integrated using multiplication:

$$NNSI_i = CS_i \times FCS_i \times IPS_i \tag{4}$$

This integration approach ensures that nodes with high NNSI values are truly critical across multiple functional dimensions, providing a more comprehensive and balanced assessment of node importance than approaches that focus solely on topological scale.

4 Topology Improvement Framework

This section presents our framework for network topology improvement based on the NNSI critical node identification method. The framework follows a systematic approach to enhance network performance through targeted modifications, leveraging the capabilities of SDN environments for implementation.

4.1 Improvement Technique

Our improvement technique follows a systematic workflow designed to enhance network performance through targeted modifications based on critical node analysis. The improvement process begins with identifying critical nodes using NNSI. For each network, the NNSI values are calculated for all nodes, with normalization performed to enable fair comparison. The nodes are then ranked by their NNSI values, with the top 10–20% identified as critical to network operation. This threshold range is determined based on previous research showing that network performance is typically dominated by a relatively small percentage of nodes [11,16], and our empirical testing which demonstrated that focusing optimization efforts on more than 20% of nodes provides diminishing returns while increasing implementation complexity and cost.

Once critical nodes are identified, the algorithm performs a detailed analysis to detect potential bottlenecks. This process examines the network structure within a two-hop radius of each critical node, evaluating both direct and indirect connections. Specifically, we analyze the subgraph consisting of the critical node, its immediate neighbors, and their connections. For such a subgraph, we calculate the clustering coefficient, which measures how well neighbors are connected among themselves. A low clustering coefficient (below 0.3) indicates potential bottleneck conditions where traffic must funnel through the central critical node due to limited alternative paths between neighbors. A bottleneck is detected when a critical node has high betweenness centrality (exceeding 1.5 times the mean value), the node's neighbors have limited direct connections between themselves, and a significant proportion of network traffic must traverse the critical node. We established this 1.5 threshold through extensive experimental testing across our dataset, finding it strikes an optimal balance between sensitivity (identifying genuine bottlenecks) and specificity (avoiding false positives). Lower thresholds (e.g., 1.2) created too many potential intervention points, while higher thresholds (e.g., 2.0) missed important bottlenecks in several network types.

Based on the critical node and bottleneck analyses, the algorithm generates a prioritized list of recommended topology modifications. Our framework implements three strategic modification types based on bottleneck characteristics:

1. Redundant path creation: We systematically identify neighbor pairs around critical nodes that lack direct connections but share significant communication patterns. Using the SDN controller's global view, we calculate the traffic volume between each pair of critical node neighbors using historical flow statistics. Neighbor pairs with high traffic volume but no direct connection become candidates for new link creation. Each candidate is then evaluated based on physical proximity and implementation feasibility.
2. Direct link addition: Using flow statistics from the SDN controller, we identify node pairs that communicate heavily via a critical intermediate node. We calculate the ratio of traffic volume to path length, prioritizing connections that would yield the highest traffic-to-distance improvement. The controller then evaluates the physical feasibility of creating these direct connections.
3. Traffic distribution balancing: For each critical node, we identify alternative paths that could offload traffic. Using the SDN controller's flow management capabilities, we implement weighted multipath routing that distributes traffic across these alternatives while avoiding congestion on secondary paths.

For each recommended modification, the algorithm calculates an estimated impact score by measuring the NNSI reduction in critical nodes:

$$Impact = \frac{1}{|C|} \sum_{i \in C} (NNSI_{orig}(i) - NNSI_{new}(i)) \tag{5}$$

where $NNSI_{orig}(i)$ is the original NNSI value of critical node i, $NNSI_{new}(i)$ is the new NNSI value after implementing the proposed modification, and C is the set of critical nodes. This formula measures how much the criticality of important nodes is reduced by adding strategic links, with higher values indicating more effective modifications. The pseudocode for our impact calculation algorithm is:

Algorithm 1. Calculate Link Impact

```
procedure CalculateLinkImpact(G, source, target, criticalNodes)
    testGraph ← Copy of G
    Add edge (source, target) to testGraph
    originalNNSI ← CalculateNNSI(G)
    newNNSI ← CalculateNNSI(testGraph)
    reduction ← 0
    for each node in criticalNodes do
        reduction ← reduction + (originalNNSI[node] − newNNSI[node])
    end for
    if |criticalNodes| > 0 then
        avgReduction ← reduction/|criticalNodes|
    else
        avgReduction ← 0
    end if
    return avgReduction
end procedure
```

This approach effectively identifies modifications that most significantly reduce the strategic importance of critical nodes, thereby improving overall network resilience and performance. The algorithm prioritizes changes that create alternative paths around bottlenecks, distributing traffic more evenly throughout the network.

4.2 SDN Implementation

We implement our topology improvement technique, illustrated in Fig. 1, as a practical application for SDN environments. The system architecture consists of four primary components as follows:

NNSI Calculator Module. Performs network topology analysis by computing the six required centrality measures (degree centrality, closeness centrality, betweenness centrality, PageRank, K-core value, and collective influence) for each node. It normalizes these values, calculates the three functional component scores, and produces the final NNSI value for each node. The module includes optimization algorithms to handle large networks efficiently, dynamically switching to approximation methods when node count exceeds configurable thresholds.

Network Optimizer Module. Identifies potential network improvements, based on NNSI analysis. It analyzes the neighborhood structure around critical nodes,

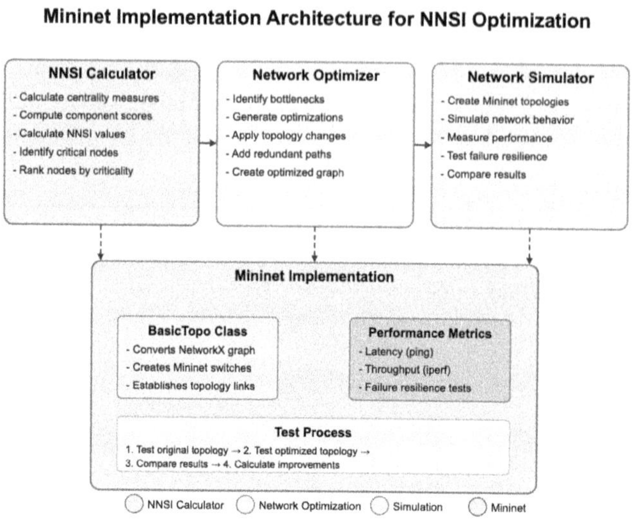

Fig. 1. Mininet implementation architecture.

detects bottlenecks, generates candidate modifications, and calculates their estimated impact scores. The module implements heuristic algorithms to find near-optimal solutions within computational constraints, maximizing improvement while minimizing implementation cost.

SDN Controller Integration. Translates abstract topology recommendations into concrete SDN controller instructions. It implements API connections to the controller, manages flow table modifications, handles network discovery and monitoring, and provides feedback mechanisms to verify changes. The module includes safety checks to prevent service disruption during topology changes.

Performance Evaluation Module. Measures the impact of optimizations through a comprehensive before-and-after analysis. It collects latency, throughput, and resilience metrics using both active probes and passive monitoring. The module implements statistical analysis to quantify improvements, generates reports, and provides visualization tools for network administrators.

The optimization framework is implemented in Python, utilizing Python NetworkX library for graph representation, NumPy for numerical computations, Mininet [31] for network emulation, Ryu [32] as the SDN controller framework, and OpenFlow 1.3 [33] as the southbound API protocol. The implementation includes optimizations for computational efficiency, such as approximation algorithms for betweenness centrality in large networks.

5 Experimental Evaluation

In this section, we describe our evaluation methodology for assessing the effectiveness of the Network Node Significance Index and the topology optimization framework, detailing the dataset used, metrics defined, and experimental design.

To evaluate the effectiveness of NNSI and compare it with other approaches, we used the Internet Topology Zoo [34], a collection of 261 network topologies from around the world. This dataset provides diverse real-world network structures representing various design principles, geographic constraints, and operational requirements, including networks of different types (research networks, commercial ISPs, university networks) and sizes (from small networks with fewer than 10 nodes to those with more than 100 nodes).

Our evaluation methodology enables rigorous assessment of NNSI's effectiveness in two key aspects: critical node identification accuracy and network improvement impact. We implement a systematic experimental framework that isolates and measures specific performance variables. Control variables (kept constant across experiments) include the network topology structures, simulated traffic patterns, and standardized performance measurement protocols. Independent variables (deliberately modified) include the node identification method (NNSI vs. IVI), network size categories, and specific improvement strategies applied. Dependent variables include quantifiable metrics such as connectivity degradation after node removal, computational processing time, and network performance improvements in terms of latency, throughput, and resilience. We define two key metrics to evaluate critical node identification methods. The Impact Score (IS) measures how much network connectivity degrades when a node is removed:

$$IS(i) = \frac{C(G) - C(G \setminus \{i\})}{C(G)} \tag{6}$$

where C(G) is a connectivity metric of the original graph G, and $C(G \setminus \{i\})$ is the connectivity after removing node i.

The Overlap Percentage (OP) measures the agreement between two methods in identifying top-k critical nodes:

$$OP(M_1, M_2; k) = \frac{|Top\text{-}k_{M_1} \cap Top\text{-}k_{M_2}|}{k} \times 100\% \tag{7}$$

where Top-k_M is the set of the k highest-ranked nodes by method M.

To understand the true criticality of nodes identified by different methods, we conduct detailed network impact assessments, including node removal simulation, traffic flow simulation, cascading failure analysis, and resilience scoring.

6 Results and Analysis

In this section, we present the results of our evaluation of the Network Node Significance Index and the topology optimization framework. We first compare

NNSI with IVI in identifying critical nodes, then present the results of our topology optimization framework.

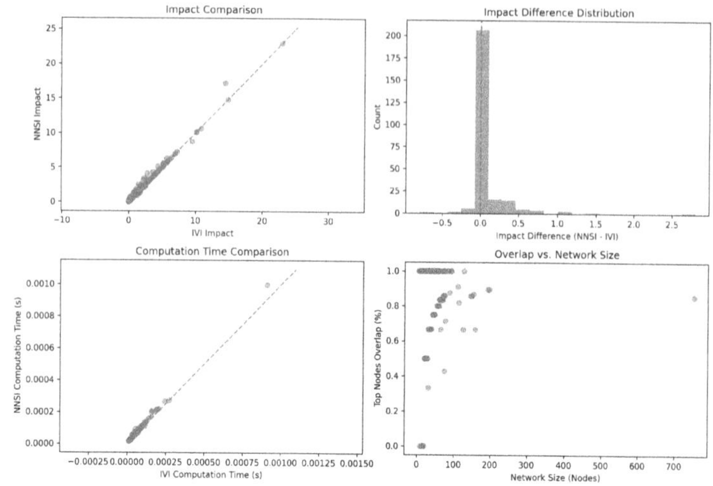

Fig. 2. Comparative analysis of NNSI and IVI performance.

From Fig. 2 we compare NNSI and IVI across the 261 network topologies. We introduce the *Impact Difference* (ID) metric to quantify NNSI's effectiveness compared to IVI. This metric measures the difference in network connectivity degradation when removing nodes identified by each method. Specifically, we calculate:

$$ID = \frac{1}{k}\sum_{i=1}^{k}(IS_{NNSI}(i) - IS_{IVI}(i)) \tag{8}$$

where $IS_{NNSI}(i)$ is the impact score of the i-th highest-ranked node according to NNSI, and $IS_{IVI}(i)$ is the impact score of the i-th highest-ranked node according to IVI. A positive ID indicates that NNSI identifies nodes with greater impact on network connectivity. Our analysis reveals that nodes identified by NNSI have, on average, an 8.04% greater impact on network connectivity when removed compared to nodes identified by IVI, demonstrating NNSI's superior effectiveness in identifying truly critical nodes.

To understand how NNSI's advantage varies across different networks, we perform performance distribution analysis, categorizing each network based on which method identifies more impactful critical nodes. This analysis examines the percentage of networks where each method outperforms the other, establishing a clear performance distribution pattern. The performance distribution analysis shows that NNSI outperforms IVI in 20.00% of networks, while IVI outperforms NNSI in 6.15% of networks. Both methods performed equally in

73.85% of networks, indicating substantial agreement in critical node identification across most network topologies. This distribution confirms NNSI's consistent advantage while highlighting that both methods identify similar nodes in many cases.

Figure 2 presents a multi-panel comparison of results. Panel (a) shows the impact comparison, demonstrating NNSI's superior performance in identifying critical nodes. Panel (b) displays the impact difference distribution with a positive skew, indicating NNSI's general advantage. Panel (c) shows computation time comparison, with most points falling below the diagonal reference line, indicating NNSI's computational efficiency advantage over IVI. This advantage becomes more pronounced in larger networks (points further right), where NNSI's streamlined approach delivers up to 16% faster processing. Panel (d) illustrates overlap percentage between critical nodes identified by both methods versus network size. The decreasing trend (from 95% overlap in small networks to 65% in very large networks) reveals that while both methods identify similar nodes in simpler networks, they increasingly diverge as network complexity grows, corresponding with NNSI's greater performance advantage in larger networks.

As shown in Fig. 3, the size-dependent performance analysis reveals a clear pattern where the advantage of NNSI increases dramatically with network size. For small networks (4–20 nodes), the mean Impact Difference is only 1.34%. For medium networks (21–50 nodes), this increases to 6.27%, and for large networks (51–100 nodes), to 6.39%. The most substantial advantage appears in very large networks (>100 nodes), where NNSI shows a 72.00% greater impact on network connectivity compared to IVI.

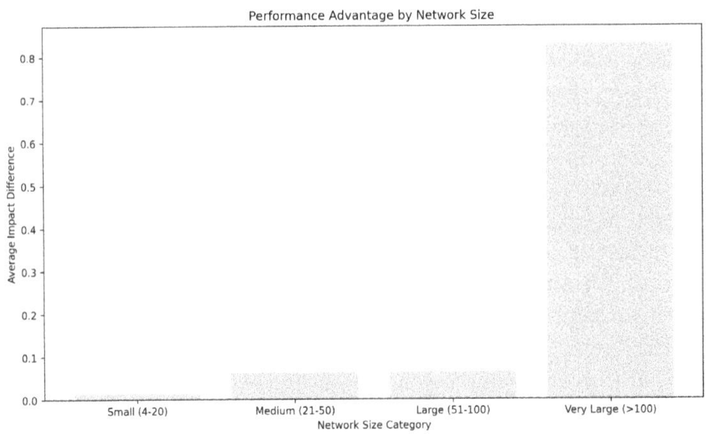

Fig. 3. Summary of performance improvements based on Network size

The Critical Node Overlap Analysis shows that the mean Overlap Percentage between the top nodes identified by NNSI and IVI is 90.15%, indicating very substantial agreement between the methods despite their different mathematical formulations.

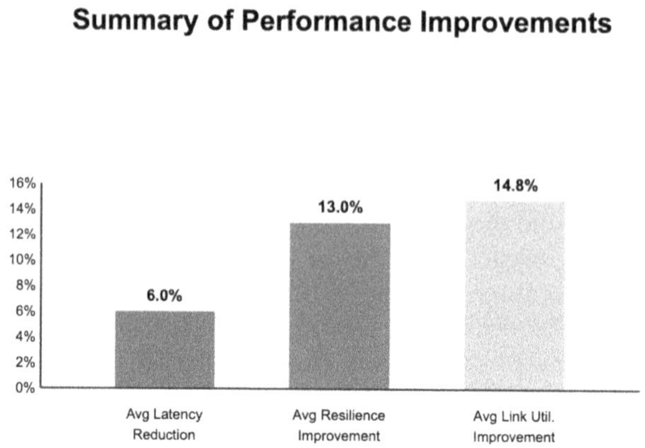

Fig. 4. Summary of performance improvements across all optimized networks.

Our framework demonstrates significant performance enhancements across multiple network metrics, as illustrated in Fig. 4, which presents the average improvement percentages across all optimized networks in the Internet Topology Zoo dataset.

1. Average Latency Reduction (6.0%) Our optimization framework achieves a 6.0% average reduction in network latency by strategically adding new connections that create shortcuts across the network topology. This improvement reduces the average path length between node pairs, translating to measurably decreased data transfer times in real-world implementations. For time-sensitive applications such as video conferencing, online gaming, and financial trading systems, this latency reduction results in tangible benefits, including reduced buffering, faster response times, and more reliable real-time communications, ultimately enhancing both application performance and user experience with minimal changes to the existing infrastructure.
2. Average Resilience Improvement (13.0%) The framework delivers a substantial 13.0% improvement in network resilience by reducing dependency on critical nodes and creating redundant paths around potential failure points. We measure this improvement through both a reduction in NNSI values of critical nodes (weighted at 70%) and decreased betweenness centrality (weighted at 30%), which together quantify how effectively the optimization distributes network traffic control across multiple nodes. This enhanced resilience significantly reduces the network's vulnerability to both targeted attacks and random failures, resulting in more reliable service, minimized downtime risk,

and improved business continuity—a critical consideration for enterprise and service provider networks where failures can have widespread operational impacts.

3. Average Link Utilization Improvement (14.8%) Our framework achieves a 14.8% improvement in link utilization efficiency by balancing traffic distribution across the network and reducing congestion on critical links. By strategically adding new connections that provide alternative routing options, the optimization reduces maximum edge betweenness centrality values, effectively redistributing traffic flows away from potential bottlenecks. This more balanced utilization translates directly to increased effective bandwidth, reduced packet loss during peak periods, and more consistent performance under varying traffic conditions—enabling networks to handle more traffic with existing infrastructure and postponing costly capacity upgrades while improving overall service quality.

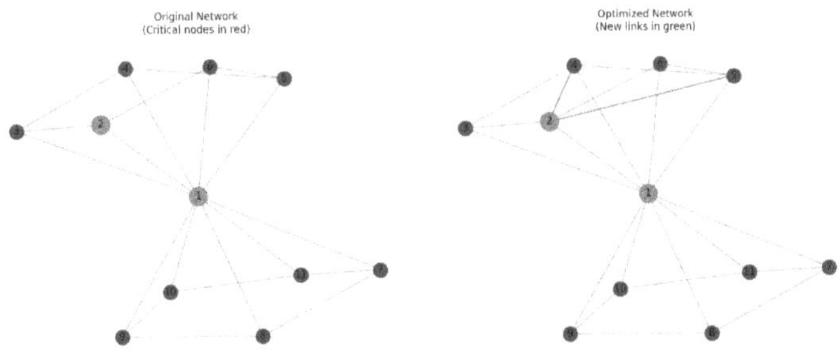

Fig. 5. Before and after optimization visualization.

Figure 5 provides a sample of a visual demonstration of our optimization approach. The left side shows the original network with critical nodes highlighted in red, while the right side displays the optimized network with new strategic links added in green. This dual-star topology consists of 11 nodes with two high-centrality nodes connecting separate clusters. After implementing these strategic modifications, measurements show significant performance improvements.

To validate our approach in a realistic SDN environment, we implemented a testing framework using Mininet. Figure 5 provides a visual example of our optimization approach, showing a test network consisting of 11 nodes in a dual-star topology. After implementing the optimizations in the Mininet environment, we measured significant improvements across all performance metrics. Latency was reduced by 21.1%, throughput increased by 28.3%, and resilience improved by 38.6%. This case study demonstrates how even a small number of strategic topology modifications can significantly improve network performance in a practical SDN environment.

7 Conclusion and Future Work

This research presented a novel approach to network topology improvement in SDN environments through the development of a comprehensive mathematical framework for critical node identification. We introduce the Network Node Significance Index (NNSI), which integrates multiple centrality measures to provide a more accurate assessment of node criticality based on functional significance rather than topological scale.

Through experimental evaluation on 261 network topologies, we demonstrate that NNSI consistently outperforms the IVI formula in identifying truly critical nodes, with an average improvement of 7.61% across all networks and up to 72% in very large networks. Building on this improved critical node identification capability, we develop a topology improvement framework that strategically reconfigures network connections to enhance resilience, reduce latency, and improve resource utilization.

Future research directions include extending the NNSI approach to dynamic networks where topology changes over time, developing specialized variants of NNSI for specific network domains and applications, and integrating machine learning techniques to further enhance critical node identification and topology optimization.

References

1. Jain, S., Kumar, A., Mandal, S., et al.: B4: experience with a globally-deployed software defined wan. ACM SIGCOMM Comput. Commun. Rev. **43**(4), 3–14 (2013)
2. Xia, W., Wen, Y., Foh, C.H., Niyato, D., Xie, H.: A survey on software-defined networking. IEEE Commun. Surv. Tutorials **17**(1), 27–51 (2015)
3. Thyagaturu, A.S., Mercian, A., McGarry, M.P., Reisslein, M., Kellerer, W.: Software defined optical networks (SDONs): a comprehensive survey. IEEE Commun. Surv. Tutorials **18**(4), 2738–2786 (2016)
4. Kreutz, D., Ramos, F.M.V., Veríssimo, P.E., et al.: Software-defined networking: a comprehensive survey. Proc. IEEE **103**(1), 14–76 (2015)
5. McKeown, N., Anderson, T., Balakrishnan, H., et al.: OpenFlow: enabling innovation in campus networks. ACM SIGCOMM Comput. Commun. Rev. **38**(2), 69–74 (2008)
6. Casado, M., Foster, N., Guha, A.: Abstractions for software-defined networks. Commun. ACM **57**(10), 86–95 (2014)
7. Sharma, S., Staessens, D., Colle, D., Pickavet, M., Demeester, P.: Enabling fast failure recovery in OpenFlow networks. In: Proceedings of the 8th International Workshop on the Design of Reliable Communication Networks, pp. 164–171. IEEE (2011)
8. Barabási, A.L., Albert, R.: Emergence of scaling in random networks. Science **286**(5439), 509–512 (1999)
9. Hage, P., Harary, F.: Eccentricity and centrality in networks. Soc. Netw. **17**(1), 57–63 (1995)
10. Callaway, D.S., Newman, M.E.J., Strogatz, S.H., Watts, D.J.: Network robustness and fragility: percolation on random graphs. Phys. Rev. Lett. **85**(25), 5468–5471 (2000)

11. Cohen, R., Erez, K., Ben-Avraham, D., Havlin, S.: Breakdown of the internet under intentional attack. Phys. Rev. Lett. **86**(16), 3682–3685 (2001)
12. Salavaty, A., Ramialison, M., Currie, P.D.: Integrated value of influence: an integrative method for the identification of the most influential nodes within networks. Patterns **1**(5), 100052 (2020)
13. Gao, C., Wei, D., Hu, Y., Mahadevan, S., Deng, Y.: A modified evidential methodology of identifying influential nodes in weighted networks. XXPhys. A **392**(21), 5490–5500 (2013)
14. Boccaletti, S., Latora, V., Moreno, Y., Chavez, M., Hwang, D.U.: Complex networks: structure and dynamics. Phys. Rep. **424**(4–5), 175–308 (2006)
15. Erdős, P., Rényi, A.: On random graphs. Publicationes Mathematicae Debrecen **6**, 290–297 (1959)
16. Albert, R., Jeong, H., Barabási, A.-L.: Error and attack tolerance of complex networks. Nature **406**(6794), 378–382 (2000)
17. Newman, M.E.J.: The structure and function of complex networks. SIAM Rev. **45**(2), 167–256 (2003)
18. Freeman, L.C.: Centrality in social networks conceptual clarification. Soc. Netw. **1**(3), 215–239 (1978)
19. Brandes, U.: A faster algorithm for betweenness centrality. J. Math. Sociol. **25**(2), 163–177 (2001)
20. Muqaddas, A.S., Bianco, A., Giaccone, P., Maier, G.: Inter-controller traffic in ONOS clusters for SDN networks. In: IEEE International Conference on Communications, pp. 1–6. IEEE (2016)
21. Dixit, A., Hao, F., Mukherjee, S., Lakshman, T.V., Kompella, R.: Towards an elastic distributed SDN controller. In: Proceedings of the Second ACM SIGCOMM Workshop on Hot Topics in Software Defined Networking, pp. 7–12. ACM (2013)
22. Yeganeh, S.H., Tootoonchian, A., Ganjali, Y.: On scalability of software-defined networking. IEEE Commun. Mag. **51**(2), 136–141 (2013)
23. Yu, M., Rexford, J., Freedman, M.J., Wang, J.: Scalable flow-based networking with DIFANE. In: ACM SIGCOMM Computer Communication Review, vol. 40, pp. 351–362. ACM (2010)
24. Lü, L., Chen, D., Ren, X., Zhang, Q., Zhang, Y., Zhou, T.: Vital nodes identification in complex networks. Phys. Rep. **650**, 1–63 (2016)
25. Guimerà, R., Amaral, L.A.N.: Functional cartography of complex metabolic networks. Nature **433**(7028), 895–900 (2005)
26. Oldham, S., Fulcher, B., Parkes, L., et al.: Consistency and differences between centrality measures across distinct classes of networks. PLoS ONE **14**(7), e0220061 (2019)
27. Chen, D., Lü, L., Shang, M.S., Zhang, Y.C., Zhou, T.: Identifying influential nodes in complex networks. XXPhys. A **391**(4), 1777–1787 (2012)
28. Borgatti, S.P.: Centrality and network flow. Soc. Netw. **27**(1), 55–71 (2005)
29. Freeman, L.C., Borgatti, S.P., White, D.R.: Centrality in valued graphs: a measure of betweenness based on network flow. Soc. Netw. **13**(2), 141–154 (1991)
30. Kempe, D., Kleinberg, J., Tardos, É.: Maximizing the spread of influence through a social network. In: Proceedings of the Ninth ACM SIGKDD International Conference on Knowledge Discovery and Data Mining, pp. 137–146. ACM (2003)
31. Lantz, B., Heller, B., McKeown, N.: A network in a laptop: rapid prototyping for software-defined networks (2010)
32. Ryu project team. Ryu SDN framework (2014)

33. Open Networking Foundation. OpenFlow switch specification version 1.3.0 (2013)
34. Knight, S., Nguyen, H.X., Falkner, N., Bowden, R., Roughan, M.: The internet topology zoo. IEEE J. Sel. Areas Commun. **29**(9), 1765–1775 (2011)

Visualization and Monitoring System for Autonomous Vehicles

Hassan Rajaei[1(✉)] and Akhil Kovuru[2]

[1] Bowling Green State University, Bowling Green, OH 43403, USA
rajaei@bgsu.edu
[2] Bowling Green State University, Bowling Green, OH 43403, USA

Abstract. The advent of Autonomous Vehicles (AV's) brought a new dimension to the field of automobile industry. The present-day technologies like IoT, Vehicular Ad Hoc Networks (VANET) are shaping the future of self-driving cars. Autonomous cars are aiming at navigating and drive through the cities and roads without drivers. Self-driving cars visualize the roads from the data images captured by the cameras and the sensors. However, weather conditions and obstacles where the vision is not clear can challenge the self-driving cars in harsh conditions. We propose using Inertial Navigation Systems (INS) to navigate safely and securely the AVs to manage most conditions. The INS technologies are used in the submarines and even in flights for navigation purposes where there are no visual images available. We propose using similar techniques for AVs. We investigated whether this approach could be used and be integrated with VANETs to communicate among other autonomous vehicles on the roads to achieve clear visualization of the traffic. The integration of IoT with VANETs in self-driving cars with INS monitoring could assist most potential scenarios on the roads, like accidents, traffic congestion, and sudden obstacles and share the information with the fleets of vehicles. This clustered sharing of data and diagnostics assists the control systems to navigate the self-driving cars safely under adverse conditions.

Keywords: Autonomous Vehicles · IoT · Smart Monitoring System · Visualization · Wireless Network

1 Introduction

Recent advances in technologies have led to extraordinary innovations particularly in the automobile sector. Autonomous Vehicles (AV) mandate new perspectives like high-speed communications and computation onboard the automobiles. Autonomous cars, aka self-driving cars, offer replacing traditional automobiles in near future. Internet of Things (IoT) has helped self-driving cars [1] to connect and share information to other vehicles and the participants on the roads. With IoT, self-driving cars share data about the path, road conditions, and other vital information to the vehicles connected in clustered network.

Primary goals of Autonomous Vehicles are to reduce traffics congestions and road accidents, thus significantly improving the safety of the vehicles, the passengers, and the

H. R. Arabnia et al. (Eds.): CSCE 2025, CCIS 2934, pp. 19–35, 2026.
https://doi.org/10.1007/978-3-032-22190-2_2

users. VANET (Vehicular Ad hoc Network) aims to secure overall safety by integrating IoT to vehicles achieving the objectives of self-driving. Using VANET, integration can provide wide ranges of applications starting from reducing traffic congestion, safety and monitoring tools, entertainment, and many more. Combining IoT and VANET in autonomous vehicles is the opening of transforming society into another informatic level.

Self-driving cars are meant to navigate on the roads and cities without human intervention. The Society of Autonomous Engineers (SAE) classified AVs into six levels of autonomous driving [2] starting from Level 0 to Level 5 (Fig. 1). Level 0 is traditional manual driving while Level 5 promotes Full Automation with no driver, and the system controls the vehicles under all conditions. Currently, most claimed smart cars are only at level 3 and thus long way to have highly automated of Level 4 and fully automated of Level 5.

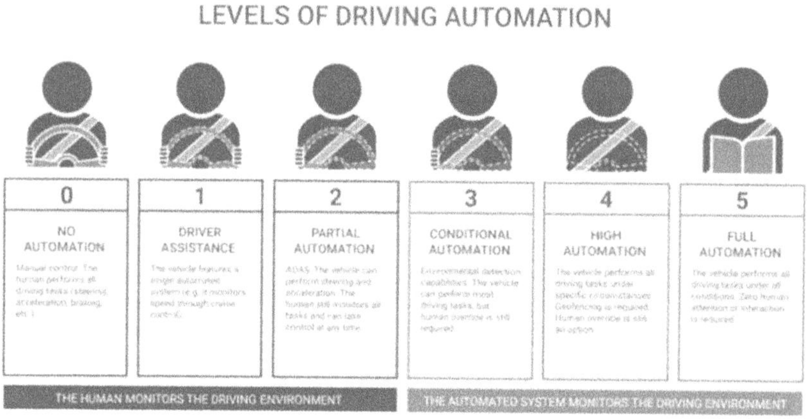

Fig. 1. Levels of cars automation according to SAE

Key issues crossing level 3 to full automation of level 5 can sufficient communication infrastructure, highspeed computing onboard at the edge, smart monitoring systems, and visualization in the cabin. Under normal weather conditions, self-driving cars can navigate and control the vehicles without major interruptions. They can identify obstacles, traffic lights, sign boards, pedestrians, and such. They rely on sensors such as LiDAR, RADAR, and cameras to perform operational activities. However, chief difficulty is the extreme weather conditions like heavy rain, snow, and fog. Performance of sensors and cameras in these cars worsens when they are not able to navigate safely under these conditions. As a result, recognizing and visualizing the path under these conditions becomes crucially important.

Main objective of current research is to find how autonomous cars could navigate and drive safely through extreme weather conditions. We investigated the navigation systems in submarines and airplanes which use monitoring and visualization techniques for their navigation. Further, our objective is to determine whether we can use similar technics integrating VANETs to navigate the car in such weather on the roads. To accomplish this goal, we imposed two research questions:

- How can self-driving cars detect and visualize the road under extreme weather conditions to navigate the vehicles safely?
- How to monitor the cars on the roads under harsh conditions and share the information to other vehicles in the clustered network?

This paper describes the results of the above questions. The rest of this paper is organized as follows: Sect. 2 presents related work. Section 3 describes IoT and Mobile Edge Computing (MEC) with 5G. Section 4 describes the needs for smart monitoring systems. Section 5 provides the relationship between visualization and smart monitoring system. Section 6 gives case studies and analysis. Section 7 gives conclusions and future work.

2 Related Work

Extensive research has been done on self-driving cars in recent years. Most research is focused on obstacle detection, pedestrian detection, traffic lights detection, and sensors. New techniques using detection methods include machine learning algorithms like CNN, fast RCNN, YOLO, and GAN. The work is focused on objects detections and efficiency improvements of images captured by the cameras under extreme weather conditions. Guang et al. in [3] used high resolution millimeter wave imaging for detecting the objects clearly. Ort et al. in [4] proposed Localizing Ground Penetrating Radar (LPGR) instead of normal RADAR in the vehicles. For extreme weather conditions, most of the related works are focused on image visualization techniques. Examples of the related work are described below

Ruotsalainen et al. [5] investigated use of navigation systems and optical sensors in arctic navigation of autonomous vehicles. The authors suggest that conventional fusion and map matching techniques are not sufficient under adverse conditions. They advocated that Global Navigation Satellite System (GNSS) alone cannot suffice and be reliable for extreme weather navigation. Using cameras and other optical sensors are also not sufficient either for navigation as they cannot produce accurate results, especially during low light conditions and roads covered with snow. The author proposed combining optical sensors, GNSS system, and INS to improve visualization of the roads.

Wang et al. in [6] proposed multi-sensor integrated navigation based on INS, Celestial Navigation System (CNS), and Doppler Velocity Log (DVL). The author suggested that the accuracy of the integrated system is better than INS alone. However, under extreme weather conditions, the accuracy of DVL and CNS are reduced. To mitigate the issue, they introduced Adaptive Information Sharing Factor Federated Filter (AISFF). Moreover, the authors conducted an experiment for harsh conditions and suggested that their integrated system perform accurately. They stated that the INS navigation error can be estimated and compensated by the fusion of INS, CNS and DVL using AISFF method.

Hnewa et al. [7] suggests that emerging technologies could reduce the influence of rainy conditions for self-driving cars. They targeted inspections and analyzed the performance of object detection methods using trained supervisor method testing the visual data collected during clear and rainy conditions. The authors examined efficiency and limitations with deep learning-based adaptation, and image translation frameworks.

They proposed an algorithm to improve the efficiency of the images. For object detection, they proposed a faster R-CNN algorithm which is based on two-stage deep learning and YOLO (You look only once) techniques. They proposed Attentive Generative Adversarial Network (GAN) Progressive Image Deraining system to remove the rain from the images iteratively.

Research on visualization techniques for Autonomous Vehicles is often focused about improving the efficiency of sensors and images with machine learning techniques. However, current results are not yet encouraging. There are still needs for extensive research on proper visualization techniques and integration with VANET such that the data could be shared securely and effectively with the autonomous vehicles connected in the network. Smart monitoring system and proper visualization method safeguard self-driving cars to safely navigate on the roads. Such a method could assist steering the cars and certify the safety of all onboard these vehicles. Such requires intelligent monitor systems to quickly share the data with all stakeholders in a nutshell, the infrastructure necessitates having more refreshing ideas out of the box.

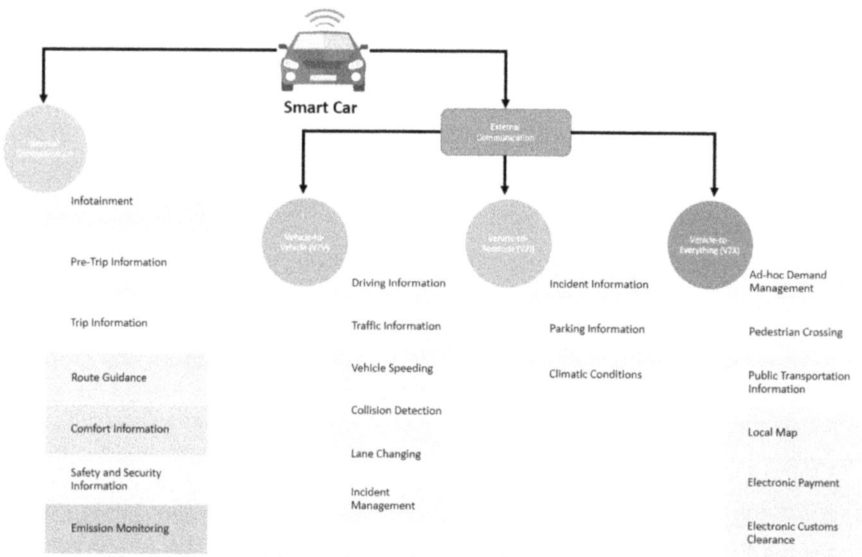

Fig. 2. Communications needs for autonomous vehicles

3 IoT, MEC, and 5G for Autonomous Vehicles

The Internet of Things (IoT) with its wide range of applications enabling transformation of traditional cars into a smart one. Autonomous vehicles are combination of smart automobiles and connected cars. Self-driving automobiles targeting to drive autonomously and share data with each other cars on the roads. IoT, VANET, sensors, and other devices integrated in smart cars can provide safety, security, and entertainment driving the transportation. Connect cars can form an Internet of Vehicle (IoV) with fleets of cars on the roads, forming clusters of networks to share data like the road conditions, traffic congestion, and other related updates in real-time. Autonomous cars are the future of transportation [8, 9] with advanced technologies and killer applications for smart cars to keep us safe on the roads. Figure 2 illustrates diverse communications needs for Autonomous cars.

3.1 VANET Communications

Vehicular Ad hoc Networks (VANETs) are key components of connected cars with the capabilities of reducing traffic congestion and improving safety and comforts on the roads. VANETs are extended future of mobile ad hoc networks with multiple sensors collecting data sharing between the vehicles. Main objective of VANET [10] is to offer fast communications between the vehicles in cluster (Fig. 3).

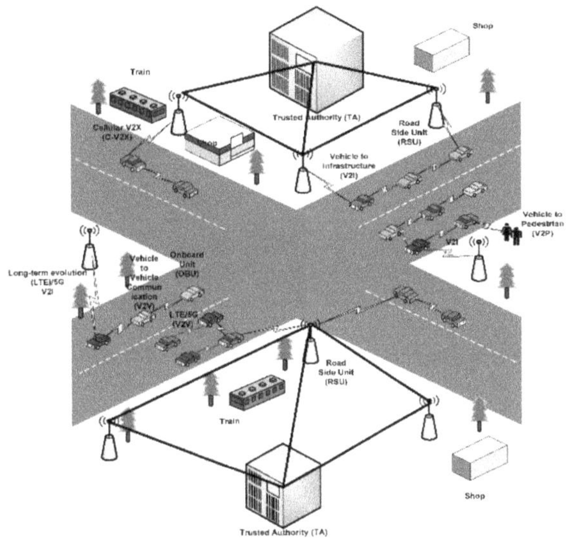

Fig. 3. An example of VANET [10]

Smart cars interact with others externally and communicate with diverse devices of the vehicle with the equipment installed in the cars. Smart cars have internal and external communications to improve safety, reduce congestion, and accidents via sharing data. High-speed communications and processing power are vitally important for autonomous cars. Advances in 5G networks furnish VANET with faster and secure data sharing. Internal communications are responsible for collecting and disseminating information like route guidance, safety and security, and camera images. Similarly, external communications between cars are Vehicle-to-Vehicle (V2V), Vehicle-to-Roadside (V2I), and Vehicle-to-everything (V2X). IoT vision, its key features, applications, and other issues are eloquently portrayed by Borgia [11].

3.2 IoT and 5G Support

IoT ecosystem has five layers [11, 12]. In the lowered layered, the sensors are located at the physical level collecting data, passing them to the communication layer to forward it to the desired destinations. Nevertheless, two additional top levels are still needed as data analytics and monitoring system [12]. For the intelligent part, data analytics with AI and machine learning are used. For monitoring techniques, visualization of the events with integrated intelligent monitoring methods interacting and supervising operations of the cars with the environment, the passengers and potentially remote centers.

The Fifth Generation (5G) of mobile networks and its successor 6G, undoubtedly can improve the external communications of the self-driving vehicles. Integration of 5G with IoT [13] makes the cars smarter, safer, and faster with less traffic congestion as well as few traffic accidents. With 5G and IoT integration, data sharing is transmitted quickly with internal units and other vehicles on the roads. Several features like connecting cars with specially designed applications, sending data from the cars to the control units, even with the manufacturers to improve the designs (Fig. 4).

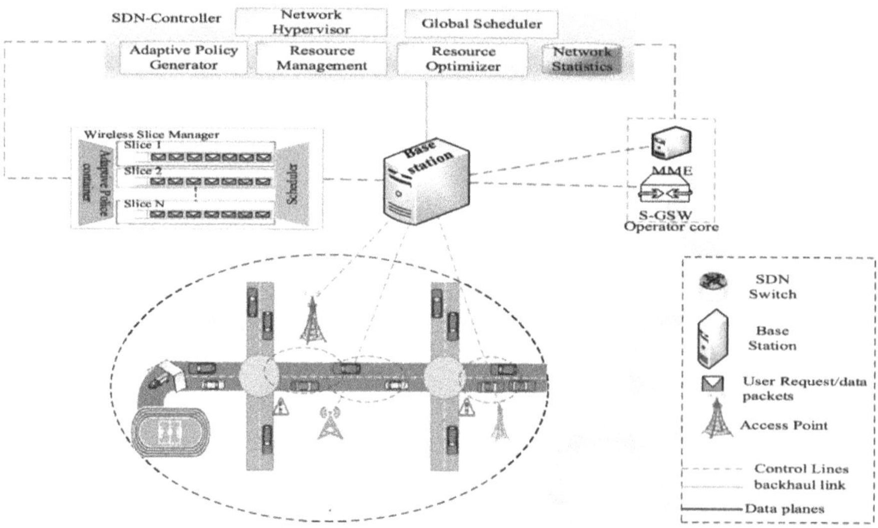

Fig. 4. SDN-based 5G architecture for VANET service using machine learning [14]

Major characteristics of 5G helpful smart cars include:

- *High bandwidth and Highspeed Data Rate*
- *Network slicing, application network virtualization with SDN and NFV*
- *Mobile Edge Computing and cloud-based infrastructure*
- *Security & Data Encryption*
- *Support for Detecting Attacks on Application Level*

The 5G wireless network is capable of hosting Edge Computing at the edge of the network closely interact with the onboard edge computing of the smart vehicles.

Connecting to the core of the network with Cloud can assist additional desirable resources when they are needed. In fact, Edge Computing balances the networking delay of the Cloud, and brings quickly the services to the edge device where it is needed. Combination of the Edge and 5G, assists IoT services to the next level to smart cars.

Major departure from traditional mobile networks comprises using multiple intelligent components and concepts. Examples include Cloud-Native, NFV/SDN Network Virtualization, Network Slicing, Mobile Edge Computing (MEC), trio support of 5G with LTE and WiFi, and Embedded Security Services. In addition to the above, ultrahigh bandwidth and ultrahigh speed processing power are desirable features.

With IoT and 5G/6G, the connected cars and machines onboard the vehicles are able to interact with each other and the environment. These devices are intelligent and capable of handling complex communications, computations with heterogeneous technologies. Machine to Machine (M2M), Device to Device (D2D), Vehicle to Vehicle (V2V), and Vehicle to Everything (V2X) communications are examples already being used for smart cares. Further, using 5G/6G the network would scale intensely to cover wider ranges and variety of equipment [15].

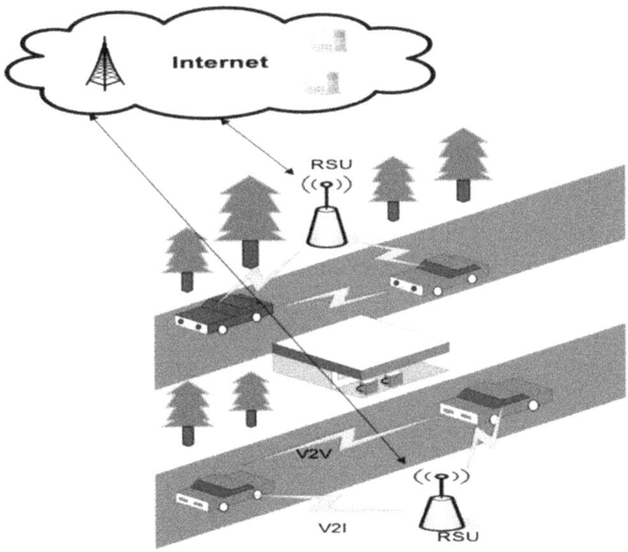

Fig. 5. Inter communication mechanisms for smart cars [16]

3.3 Inter- and Intra-Communications

Inter communications with the environment and the rest of the world are vitally important for self-driving cars. Safe operations and exchange of data with others need real-time communications with smart cars.

With speedy and reliable inter communication, connected cars can share their information with other vehicles, with the Road-Side Units (RSU) [16], traffic signals, and many more. 5G, IoT, and VANETs deliver the needed communications between the automobiles and the roadsides (Fig. 5). Accordingly, self-driving cars can achieve following activities between the car and other units:

- Inter-Vehicle Communications
- Vehicle-to-Roadside Communications
- Inter-Roadside Communications.

Smart cars can identify traffic congestion, detect and locate where accidents have happened, recognize the intensity of the traffic on the roads, just to name a few.

Advances in the hardware and processing capabilities led to several innovations for the automotive sectors. Intra-communications within the vehicle are significant since data collections and processing information from multiple devices are speedy computed and transferred to the needed units. The information is quickly sent to the control units to make on-time and correct decisions. Performance and dynamics of the vehicles and the surroundings assist navigation of cars to drive safely and efficiently. Numerous applications [17] can be added be each of which may have different communication requirements. Examples include passengers' assistance, infotainment data, safety and comfort applications. Figure 6 [18] describes use of ADAS and different sensors in autonomous vehicles.

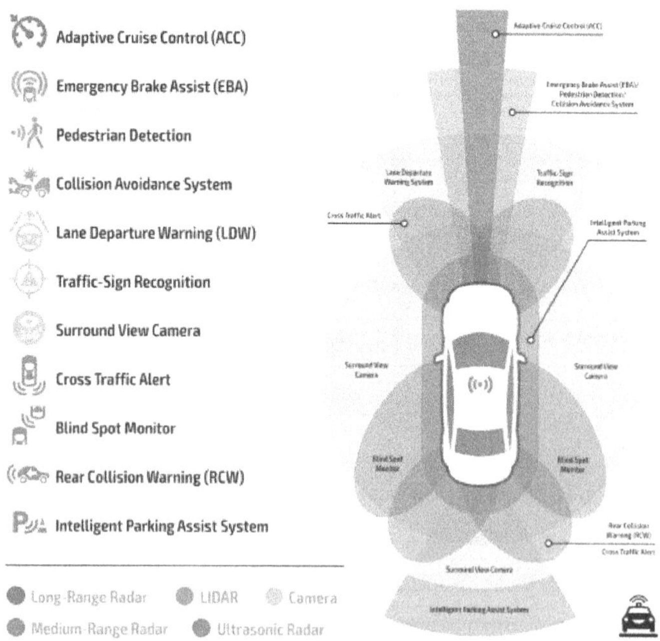

Fig. 6. ADAS sensors and applications communication for autonomous cars [18]

4 Monitoring Needs for Mart Cars

How to control an Autonomous Vehicle to perform its duties of correctly and navigate safely the drive of the car without the presents of a driver? This is a central issue for a driverless car, ensuring the passengers and the car are well like having an expert driver. While multiple answers are possible, our research focuses on the use of intelligent monitoring systems with smart visualization technics. This section further breaks down the answer, starting with another question: what are the needs for controlling the vehicles?

4.1 Safety and Reliability Requirements

The reliability and safety of autonomous vehicles are the prime need for such cars to become successful in the market and thus on the roads. Reliability depends on how safe and secure self-driving can be without a dependable driver. The data sharing with other cars should also be protected since the vehicles can have valuable information to safely navigate the cars bypassing traffic and road hazards. The shared data should not mislead others to create havoc on the roads. The shared information must be accurate and precise for the fleets of autonomous cars.

Technologies adapted to AVs demand highly efficient and reliable communication systems. Since minor flaws in the system could lead to accidents, the cars need intelligent monitoring systems to observe the operations and events surrounding cars in real-time. Moreover, we need a control system that could alleviate the unpredicted events both for people and cars. If needed, control should be passed to a reliable third party to interact with and avoid dangers situations. The very idea of smart and autonomous cars is to reduce the accidents and thus improve the safety of the people on the road. A reliable monitoring system could greatly convince the passengers that they are in good hands.

4.2 Remote and Onboard Monitoring

To fulfil the reliability and safety requirements, we propose having onboard monitoring and remote ones designed on multiple interconnect observatories similar to flight controller systems of aircraft in airports. While the interconnected remote monitoring systems are significantly in need, their complex operations and communication requirements suggest more investigations for robust architecture and standards. Meanwhile this paper focuses on onboard monitory techniques as a step toward that direction.

Internal monitoring systems employ combination of cameras, microphones, sensors, and other devices in the car surviving the car and its surroundings. The system should also recognize passengers' comfort or distress signals like weariness, drowsiness, or not feeling good. The system should also spot risk indicators like fires, collisions, errors, and other hazards. Exterior of the vehicle is also monitored by the systems using combinations of cameras, radar, and lidar. These devices can identify any pedestrians or other road users in the path of the vehicle, as well as obstacles like construction zones.

4.3 Data Monitoring and Management

Autonomous cars sense the surrounding environments from images captured by the built-in cameras of the cars together with sensors like LiDAR, RADAR, infrared, and other devices. Awareness of the surroundings is vital for autonomous vehicles to safely navigate on the roads. Monitoring the environment alone cannot suffice to classify it as fully autonomous. Intelligent monitoring systems should include supervision of the surroundings as well as the internal operations performed by autonomous cars. Perception of the surroundings include detections of objects, lanes, blind spots, and traffic signals just to name a few. Furthermore, monitoring should also include the health of passengers, engine, the tires and the brakes.

Figure 6 has illustrated use of ADAS [18] and diverse sensors and their applications which all generate large amount of data. The data collected from these sensors are sent to the Control Units which utilize the onboard Edge Computing to quickly process the data and extract the information needed for reliable decision making. Road conditions are often monitored by self-driving cars with additional help of nearby cars as well as the information that is forwarded by the remote monitoring centers. For example, based on the received data if the decision to choose an appropriate lane or root could be made for navigation purposes. Additionally, it is important that an autonomous car should quickly maneuver the vehicle to avoid detected obstruction. These observations mandate design of a Data Monitoring and Management System (DMS).

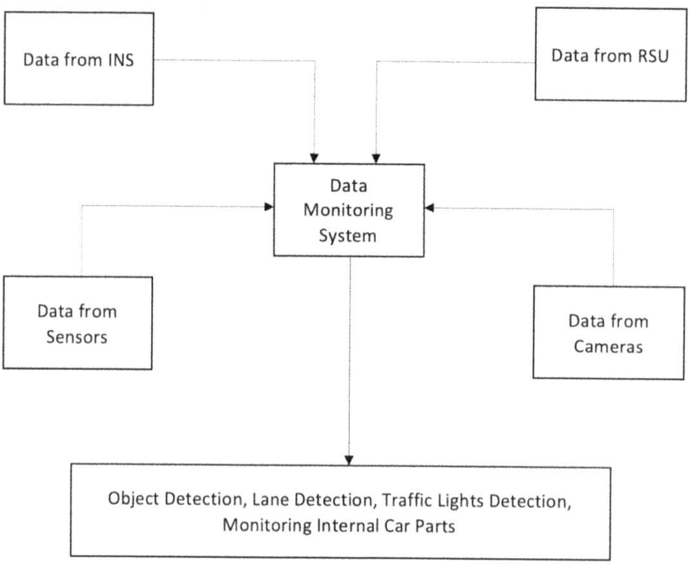

Fig. 7. Data Monitoring & Management System (DMS)

Figure 7 illustrates a schematic diagram of a DMS arrangement, without the details of system. The collects data from sensors, cameras, RSU, and Inertial Navigation System (INS) along with the road-side units is combined using a data fusion algorithm to take correct decisions for the safely navigation. The decision is forwarded to the action layer to perform the needed activities based on the interpreted data. The data from the INS (include position of the car), RSU (giving the AV position of the other vehicles), the sensors (RADAR, LiDAR), and the cameras are combined. To make any changes, DMS validates the information to safely navigate the automobile.

5 Visualization of Monitoring System

The need for intelligent monitory systems was introduced in the previous section. This section provides additional details focusing on visualization and navigation needs for rough weather like snow, fog, and heavy rain. Furthermore, we advocate use of INS similar to submarines as part of standard elements of all autonomous cars to clearly visualize the unclear roads to safely navigate the vehicle in those conditions. While the vision is clear, the paper launches preliminary works illustrating how to develop such methods.

5.1 Navigation and Monitoring

Navigation systems of AVs can be compared with Unman Aerial Vehicles (UAV) or drones, and robots used in warehouses. For AVs, the navigation system comprises several key components as illustrated in Fig. 8. Examples include Position navigation (e.g. GPS), Inertial Sensors, the accelerometers, gyroscopes, and the computational unit. The data from these sensing units is sent to an onboard Edge Computing Unit (ECU) [19] where the data is processed and sorted out to feed next designated units.

INS incorporates an Inertial Measurement Units (IMU) [20] to quantify the position of the vehicle, angular rates, and linear velocity of the vehicles. The measured data recorded from the accelerometers and gyroscopes is used to track the position and orientation of the object relative to the known starting point, orientation, and velocity [21]. The INS unit measures and reports the orientation as well as position of vehicles to the control unit of the self-driving car. The navigation system of the car is connected to the onboard monitoring system to furnish an accurate and safe direction-finding for the autonomous car in all weather conditions (Fig. 9).

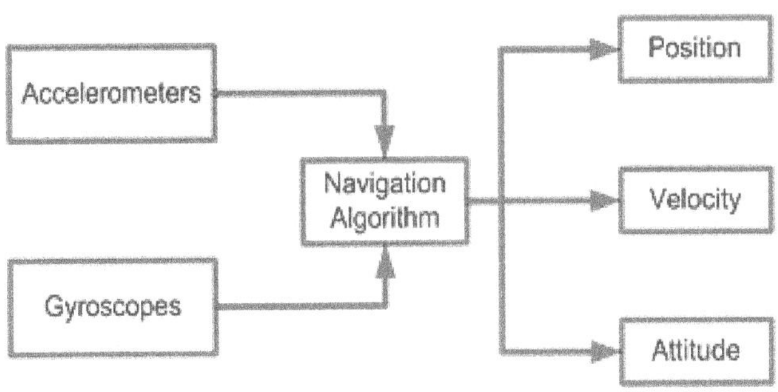

Fig. 8. An overview of Inertial Navigation System (INS) [22]

Under extreme weather conditions, where it is difficult to detect the lanes and the other cars in front and behind the vehicle, the INS unit can constantly give the position

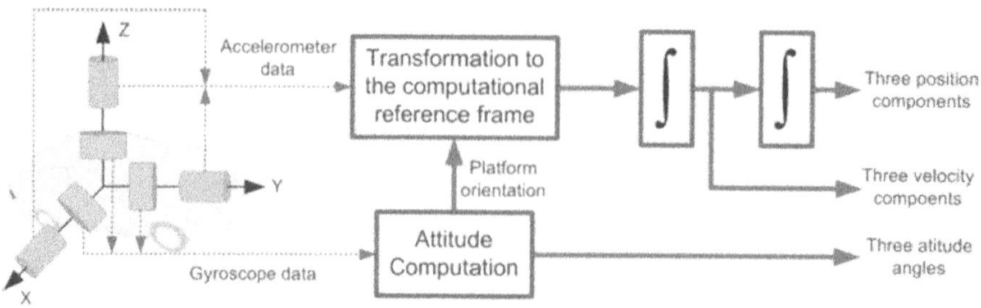

Fig. 9. Navigation with INS combines with Inertial Measurement Unit (IMU) [22]

of the vehicles and combine that with image processing to project a visual monitor that clearly shows the road for the passengers of the autonomous vehicle. The smart monitoring unit with RSU can either have stored information on the roads or acquire it from the positioning system to show the details of the road (e.g., lanes) under normal conditions. That image will be augmented and projected on the dashboard so that any passengers can clearly see the road in front of the car.

Fig. 10. A visual effect for AVs in a snowing condition and sharing the info with cars and RSU

5.2 Visualization of Activities

To visualize how AVs could navigate through rough weather, we developed several example scenarios to illustrate how visualization could add the smart monitoring system. However, due to spare limitations, we selected only one here.

Figure 10 describes the autonomous cars travelling during heavy snowfall. If no proper visualization, traffic lights and other obstacles could not be detected in time and thus cars can lead to accidents. Employing a smart navigation system, as advocated in this paper, self-driving car would detect the traffic light and the other objects in-time on the road. The AVs are connected to traffic lights and other RSU devices via IoT and other communication channels to help operate smart cars. Certainly, without a smart monitory system, the data from the images taken by cameras or even human eyes may not clearly detect traffic light and potentially other obstacles of the road and thus could cause accidents and traffic chaos.

5.3 Strength and Limitation

The main strength of the proposed system is that autonomous cars can navigate safely on the roads even during harsh weather with intelligent navigation and monitoring systems integrated into the ecosystem of the AVs. With the help of INS integrated with VANET, IoT, and other sensors, self-driving cars are empowered visualizing the path and thus drive safely the vehicle. Visualization and monitoring are key resources of autonomous cars. Position of the vehicle is constantly shared with RSU to help other cars notify the position of each other that are connected in the fleet. VANET, 5G/6G and other communication devices have vital roles in quick transmission of data between the vehicles and the road-side units.

Multiple limitations can be named for current methods about AVs, which are beyond the scope of this paper. For example, security of autonomous vehicles is an entire episode and needs to be discussed and developed. However, certain limitations on the system we mentioned can be named here. The data storage in road-side units, accuracy of the sensors, and quality of the images could limit the proposed idea. The RSU segments of the roads could involve expensive infrastructure and expenditure. In addition, communications between vehicles and RSUs must be secure since positions of the vehicle and other information are constantly shared between RSUs and vehicles in the network.

6 Case Studies and Discussions

For this research, multiple case studies have been done, two of which are selected and briefly discussed below, followed by some discussions.

6.1 Case Studies

Guan et al. in [23] proposed combing INS, GPS, and cameras to improve the accuracy, and reliability of the navigation of the cars. The Inertial Measurement Units were equipped with three accelerometers and three gyroscopes. The GPS receiver, IMU and the power systems were placed in the trunk of the car. Data Positioning acquired from GPS, INS, and IMP is illustrated in Fig. 11. Authors postulated that the position estimation from the integrated inertial-visual navigation system is more stable when compared to other navigation systems. This case study endorses our proposal of improving autonomous navigation with INS, IMU, and other related sensors to improve the accuracy of the AV navigation system.

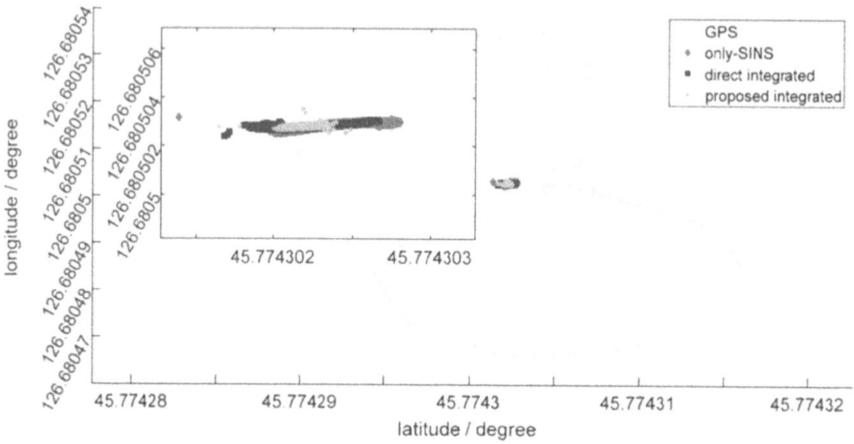

Fig. 11. Position estimation of GPS, SINS, INS-visual integrated architecture [23]

Hnewa et al. in [7] presented how emerging technologies could mitigating the influence of rainy conditions for AV. Smart cars cannot detect the objects clearly during adverse weather conditions. The authors proposed techniques to reduce the influence of rainy conditions to detect objects and analyze the detection methods that are trained and tested using visual data collected during clear and rainy conditions. Furthermore, they used deep learning-based adaptation and image translation frameworks by measuring and evaluating the data as shown in Fig. 12. For object detection, faster R-CNN is used with two stages of deep learning method. First stage is identifying the region proposals, and second stage is for refining and assigning class probabilities for corresponding regions, Input is fed into feature extractor which produces feature maps. RPN is used to predict regions. Major obstacle observed was lack of real training data for adverse weather conditions.

6.2 Analysis and Discussions

Multiple research projects clearly show that Autonomous Cars are the future of automobiles. However, countless additional work for research and development are needed to make AVs safe and trustworthy. Similar to the Internet and Smart Phones, future use will convince society that these technologies are here to assist certain needs to start with, then comes widespread use of the technology.

Smart Monitoring System as proposed in this paper can help to assure detection of the objects and visualization transparency of the operations. Integration of VANET, RSU,

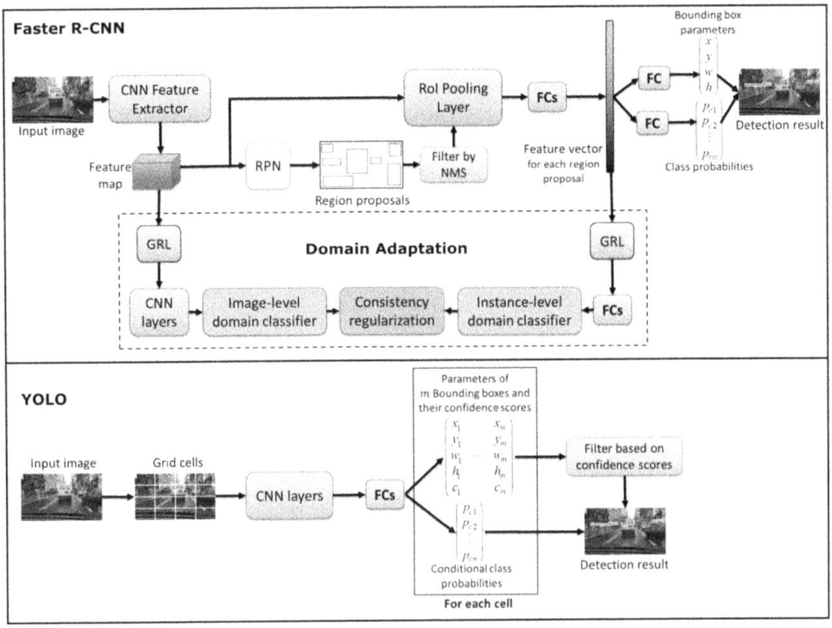

Fig. 12. High level architectures for detection methods [7].

and INS can improve navigation of AVs to safely drive the destination under adverse weather conditions. Multiple research projects suggest use of Artificial Intelligent with Machine Learning and Deep Larning meths which employ the data generated by sensors, images from the cameras, and other devises in the car to improve trajectory of the navigation.

The future will convince society that self-driving vehicles can be safe and convenient for the citizens. However, to promote worldwide use, two major constraints must be resolved: solutions for extreme weather conditions and safety of the passengers as well as the souring publics. While the visions and directions are clear, solutions thus far are in infancy phases.

7 Concluding Remarks and Future Work

Autonomous cars need some breakthrough similar to what 5G did for IoT, and Cloud Virtualization for 5G. The chain reactions of technological advances become clear by the widespread applications of that technology. Could visualization and smart monitoring system techniques make similar breakthroughs for driverless cars? This paper exhibited a path by integrations of key components such as IoT, 5G, INS, and VANET to the smart monitoring system to clearly visualize the road during harsh weathers.

We argued that a key issue of driverless is the lack of solid and safe navigation system for adverse weather. Since images from cameras and sensors degrade under these inclement conditions, we need solutions that could navigate carefully the vehicles even in adverse weather, assuring passengers their safety.

While our preliminary works and multiple others are convincing that the directions are clear, the roads appear to be long. In previous work, we proposed multiple techniques for AVs, whereas in this paper we sketched a smart monitoring and navigation system. Our future work includes further investigations and improvements with the details of the smart monitoring system adding precisions for the control system. Multiple supplementary features could be added further on safety mechanisms, specific security threads for AVs, and integration architecture with AI.

References

1. Krasniqi, X., Hajrizi, E.: Use of IoT technology to drive the automotive industry from connected to full autonomous vehicles. IFAC-PapersOnLine **49**(29), 269–274 (2016)
2. Mathur, G., Sharma, H., Pandey, R.: A study on self-driving car: an application of IoT. Int. J. Comput. Networking, Wireless Mobile Commun. (IJCNWMC). **9**, 25–34 (2019)
3. Guang, X., Gao, Y., Leung, H., Liu, P., Li, G.: An autonomous vehicle navigation system based on inertial and visual sensors. MDPI Sens. **18**(9), 2952 (2018)
4. Ort, T., Gilitschenski, I., Rus, D.: Autonomous navigation in inclement weather based on a localizing ground penetrating radar. IEEE Rob. Autom. Lett. **5**(2), 3267–3274 (2020)
5. Ruotsalainen, L., et al.: Toward autonomous driving in Arctic areas. IEEE Intell. Transp. Syst. Mag. **12**(3), 10–24 (2020)
6. Wang, Q., Cui, X., Li, Y., Ye, F.: Performance enhancement of a USV INS/CNS/DVL integration navigation system based on an adaptive information sharing factor federated filter. Sensors **17**(2), 239 (2017)
7. Hnewa, M., Radha, H.: Object detection under rainy conditions for autonomous vehicles: a review of state-of-the-art and emerging techniques. IEEE Signal Process. Mag. **38**(1), 53–67 (2020)
8. Arena, F., Pau, G., Severino, A.: An overview on the current status and future perspectives of smart cars. Infrastructures **5**(7), 53 (2020)
9. Yaqoob, I., Khan, L.U., Kazmi, S.A., Imran, M., Guizani, N., Hong, C.S.: Autonomous driving cars in smart cities: recent advances, requirements, and challenges. IEEE Netw. **34**(1), 174–181 (2019)
10. Shaikh, M., Liang, J., Wang, W.: A survey of security services, attacks, and applications for vehicular ad hoc networks (VANETs). MDPI Sens. **19**(16) (2019)
11. Boriga, E.: The internet of things: key features, applications, and open issues. Elsevier J. Comput. Commun. **54**(2014), 1–13 (2014)
12. Rajaei H.: IoT, from collection, to data processing, edge computing, to smart applications. In: The Proceeding of CSCE22 & ICOMP'22, Las Vegas, USA (2022)
13. Pisarov, J., Mester, G.: The impact of 5G technology on life in the 21st century. IPSI BgD Trans. Adv. Res. (TAR). **16**(2), 11–14 (2020)
14. Tayyaba, S., Khattak, H., Almogren, A., Shah, M., Guizani, H.: 5G vehicular network resource Management for Improving Radio Access through Machine Learning. IEEE Access **8** (2022)
15. Biral, A., Centenaro, M., Zanella, A.: The Challenges of M2M Massive Access in Wireless Cellular Networks. Univ of Padova, Padova, Italy (2015). http://www.telekomaustria.com/en/m2m
16. Khan, U.A., Lee, S.: Multi-layer problems and solutions in VANETs: a review. MDPI. J. Electron. **8**(2) (2019)
17. Tuohy, S., Glavin, M., Hughes, C., Jones, E., Trivedi, M., Kilmartin, L.: Intra-vehicle networks: a review. IEEE Trans. Intell. Transp. Syst. **16**(2), 534–545 (2014)

18. RSA Website: Road Safety, Advanced Driver Assistant Systems (ADAS) ant Autonomous vehicle sensors, https://www.rsa.ie/road-safety/road-users/assisted. Visited June (2025)
19. Rajaei, H., Kodali, S., Mulinti, N.: An edge computing architecture for autonomous vehicles. In: The Proceeding of CSCE24 & ICOMP'24, Las Vegas, USA (2024)
20. Wikipedia website: Inertial Measurement Units (IMU) (2025). Visited June 2025. https://en.wikipedia.org/wiki/Inertial_measurement_unit
21. Woodman, O.J.: An introduction to Inertial Navigation. (No. UCAM-CL-TR-696). University of Cambridge, Computer Laboratory (2007)
22. Noureldin, A., Karamat, T.B., Georgy, J.: Fundamentals of Inertial Navigation, Satellite-Based Positioning and their Integration. Springer (2013). https://link.springer.com/book/10.1007/978-3-642-30466-8. Accessed 24 Oct 2025
23. Guan, J., Madani, S., Jog, S., Hassanieh, H.: High Resolution Millimeter Wave Imaging for Self-Driving Cars (2019). arXiv preprint https://arxiv.org/abs/1912.09579

Carbon Flexing for Individual Households —A Study Based on Electrical Carbon Data—

Olaf Droegehorn[1(✉)] and Karolina Bargiel[2]

[1] Harz University of Applied Sciences, 38855 Wernigerode, Germany
odroegehorn@hs-harz.de

[2] Peer Carbon Ltd., Fitzrovia House, 153-157 Cleveland Street, London, UK

Abstract. De-carbonizing our electricity should be one of the leading steps to overcome climate changes and positively impact the environment in which we operate in the twenty-first century. This topic, which was widely explored by the production sector, has been outside the reach of individual households. Due to the high costs, de-carbonization could only happen through significant investments such as solar panels. This paper explores the possibility of reducing carbon usage not via high investments but via shifting the electricity load to less carbon-intensive grid electricity hours. Therefore, it enhances the fact that electricity on the grid can come from various sources at any given time, and it is better to use high-renewable intensive loads. The project explores both the social willingness to participate in such a shift, the response to automation, and the quantitative potential that could arise from such practices

The carbon reduction, that has been measured, is achieved by flexing user usage to times during the day when grid energy comes from primarily renewable sources.

The mixed method with user-centered study used data that was collected via questionnaire and quantitative assessment of pre-existed datasets. Carbon flexing potential quantified between 5–11%.

This study underscores the importance of integrating automated approaches to flexing energy consumption. By ensuring the convenience of automated adjustments, households can achieve significant carbon savings. The findings contribute valuable insights into the design of effective carbon reduction strategies and highlight the role of user participation in achieving sustainability goals.

Keywords: Building Automation · User Willingsness · Carbon flexing · User Intentions · Energy consumption

1 Introduction

The transition to sustainable energy systems is a critical component in mitigating climate change. In order to address this issue, we need to look not only at the high-level industry usages, such as airlines and data centers, but also at individual households. Carbon became one of the few measurable units that can be reported, assessed, and off-setted,

H. R. Arabnia et al. (Eds.): CSCE 2025, CCIS 2934, pp. 36–51, 2026.
https://doi.org/10.1007/978-3-032-22190-2_3

and therefore, it is on its way to becoming a global climate currency. We, as individuals, can participate in this carbon economy in various ways, for example, via choices that we make for our household, as well as the electrical load.

A transition to reusable energy sources for our homes can be a solution that will limit the impact of climate change across the whole globe. However, the process of de-carbonization is a transition that cannot happen overnight.

A significant aspect of this transition involves optimizing energy consumption patterns to align with periods of lower carbon intensity, referred to as "green hours." This concept, known as carbon flexing, seeks to shift energy usage to times when renewable energy sources are more used, and as an effect, it reduces overall carbon emissions.

The modern world empowers individuals to monitor and control their energy production and carbon footprint. One of the available technology is the Internet of Things (IoT) in our homes. Smart Homes provides an innovative solution for energy management by allowing homeowners to control and monitor their energy usage. While the industry offers various energy-saving solutions, it is essential to note that reducing energy consumption does not necessarily translate to reduced carbon emissions. Thus, there is a growing interest in IoT-software for Smart Homes that can limit the carbon footprint by regulating energy consumption and switching between energy sources.

The objective of the study described in this paper is to explore and evaluate the potential of carbon saving through energy-flexing practices in individual households. Additionally, the study proposes solutions that can empower individual household owners to take control of their carbon emissions. Ultimately, by empowering individuals to monitor and manage their carbon emissions, we can make significant strides toward a more sustainable future.

2 Introduction

Related works are divided in three sections: Potential for energy consumption flexing, the social willingness to participate and the investigation of the user satisfaction with automated adjustments and manual interventions. The last one shows details regarding the approach followed for implementation of the current work.

2.1 Potential for Energy Consumption Flexing

Research into energy consumption flexing suggests the potential for carbon savings when households adjust their energy use to coincide with "green hours". Steinberg [15] explores the impact of electrification on household energy use and carbon emissions, demonstrating that widespread electrification and power sector transformation can lead to significant carbon savings. Their findings suggest a 41% reduction in economy-wide fossil fuel combustion emissions when incorporating electrification without additional power sector carbon policies. This gives a high potential for flexing strategies if taken at the large scale of households, such as blocks of flats.

Additionally, Pickering [12] further supports this by discussing strategies for fossil fuel elimination and carbon neutrality, emphasizing the role of household energy consumption and flexibility. Their study shows that flexible energy demand, especially in residential sectors, can significantly contribute to achieving carbon neutrality across the European energy system.

The study by Fatih Issi and Orhan Kaplan [8] focuses on determining load profiles and power consumption of home appliances to enhance home energy management. Conducted in Çankırı, Turkey, the research collected high-resolution power consumption data from 12 home appliances in a two-person household over three months. Key findings include detailed consumption patterns, operational modes, and the impact of standby power use. Even though it was not targeted at carbon reduction, the research shows that around 15% of total home power consumption can be deferred based on energy tariffs, demonstrating the potential for significant load shifting in residential settings. This percentage can vary depending on specific household behaviors and the types of appliances used.

Lastly, the UK Power Network conducted The Low Carbon London (LCL) project. This initiative aimed at investigating the integration of low-carbon technologies (LCTs) in London's electricity distribution network from January 2011 to December 2014. One of the significant outcomes was the development of a comprehensive dataset, including the largest contiguous smart meter dataset in Great Britain that is used in this thesis to access the carbon limitation potential. The preliminary findings suggested a significant reduction in carbon, however, they work was not peer-reviewed. Nonetheless, the project underscored the importance of demand flexibility—adjusting power consumption patterns in response to supply conditions—which proved crucial for enhancing grid efficiency and reliability [3].

2.2 Social Willingness to Participate

The numbers by themselves might not be enough to make a real difference in carbon reduction. Understanding the social willingness to engage in carbon flexing is crucial for the success of such programs. Johnson [9] investigated household perspectives on electricity shifting and carbon reduction in low-income homes in the UK. The study reveals that approximately 60% of households are willing to participate in real-time energy use adjustments if provided with adequate information and incentives. The findings emphasize the importance of providing clear information and reliable notifications to encourage participation. This gives researchers two essential points. Primarily, a significant portion of the population is ready to engage in behaviors that flex their energy usage to off-peak times. Secondly, they directly contribute to decreased demand during high-load periods, thus reducing the need for energy production from carbon-intensive sources.

Bertoldi [6] adds to this by reviewing existing policies for energy conservation and recommending new policies that enhance household participation in carbon reduction efforts. This review highlights successful policy measures that have effectively engaged households in energy conservation and carbon reduction, such as dynamic pricing and educational campaigns. The authors' recommendations include personal carbon trading, energy taxation, and progressive appliance standards to shift consumer behavior and reduce overall energy demand. The creation of such policies could be the bridge to getting the integration described in this paper from academia all the way to industry people's Smart Homes.

2.3 User Satisfaction with Automated Adjustments and Manual Interventions

User satisfaction with automated smart device adjustments during high carbon intensity periods is a critical factor in the adoption of carbon flexing strategies. Nyborg [10] discusses the conflicting visions of energy impacts in Smart Homes, noting that while some users appreciate the convenience of automation, others express concerns over the loss of control and potential disruptions to their lifestyle. Their research indicates that user satisfaction is highly dependent on the perceived reliability and transparency of the automation systems.

Setlhaolo [13] further highlights the importance of balancing economic analysis with user convenience in residential demand-side management strategies. Their study shows that automated systems, while effective in reducing carbon emissions, need to be designed to minimize inconvenience and enhance user trust to achieve higher satisfaction levels.

Nicole D. Sintov and P. Wesley Schultz [14] in their research examine the role of adjustable green defaults in Smart Home technology and their impact on user satisfaction. They find that perceived control and trust in automation are significant factors influencing user satisfaction. Their study concludes that allowing users to adjust smart energy technologies while also providing automated options manually enhances user satisfaction and trust in the system. This finding underscores the importance of designing Smart Home technologies that balance automation with user control to improve satisfaction and adoption rates.

Collectively, these studies lay the ground for this work by showing the difficulty of the relationship between user satisfaction, control, and trust in the context of Smart Home automation.

3 Methodology

The research aims to evaluate the potential of carbon reduction for individual households by examining energy consumption patterns and carbon savings through the strategic use of Smart Home technology. The study is conducted in collaboration with PeerCo, a UK-based company, and their previous product "Yoyu App", which enables individual users to adjust their behavior based on carbon signals.

This research addresses the following research questions (RQs):

Main RQ: What is the potential for energy consumption flexing, and how much carbon savings can be realized by shifting energy usage to "green hours"?

- RQ1: What is the social willingness to participate in real-time notifications in prompting manual adjustments of smart device usage during high carbon intensity periods?
- RQ2: How satisfied are users with automated adjustments of their smart devices in response to high carbon intensity, and what is the perceived impact on convenience and lifestyle?
- RQ3: How do manual and automated interventions compare in terms of user satisfaction?

3.1 Goals and Metrics

The goal of this study is to evaluate how much and in what ways people are ready to participate in cutting their own carbon emissions. Two different approaches are used to accomplish this. The study conducts a user-centered experiment to evaluate the effectiveness of manual and automated interventions in reducing household carbon emissions and assess user satisfaction and willingness to participate in these interventions. To quantify the potential carbon savings from energy consumption flexing, the data analysis of pre-existing data sets is used. To achieve these goals, the study employs a variety of metrics, including:

- the reduction in carbon emissions measured in kilograms of CO2,
- user compliance rates with notifications assessed on a 1–5 scale
- user satisfaction scores accessed on a 1–5 scale
- energy consumption data collected from smart meters measured in kWh.

3.2 Methodology

To address the research issues, the study implements a mixed methodology approach. Mixed methods research involves collecting and analyzing both quantitative and qualitative data within the same study [7].

For the listed research questions, a controlled experiment is conducted. In this study, two groups are used to compare manual and automated adjustments to the system. Participants interact with the system within a controlled time-period and from the comfort of their homes. Data is collected via questionnaires administered to participants after their interaction with the system. This approach ensures that the experiment's conditions are standardized, which helps reduce biases and improve the results' reliability.

Later a series of simulations on data previously obtained through open-source channels [3] is applied. The data obtained depicts the electricity usage of London households throughout the year. This data is then multiplied by the grid's half-hourly carbon intensity to achieve quantifiable results for analysis. This is not described in this paper and will be explained in a follow-up report.

The combination of controlled experiments and simulations provided a comprehensive analysis, leveraging the strengths of both quantitative and qualitative data and fully answering the main research question.

4 Experiment Design

The experimental phase of the study involves two distinct groups, each comprising 10 participants. This phase is crucial for evaluating the effectiveness of manual and automated interventions in optimizing energy consumption and reducing carbon emissions. The notification group, therefore, serves as a control group to see the sentiments around the automation. The participants were asked to charge their personal devices, such as laptops, phones, etc., in accordance with carbon intensity within a span of min. 12 h.

4.1 Notification Group

Participants in this group receive real-time notifications via the Yoyu App when the cleanest energy is available. These notifications prompt manual adjustments to their devices during high carbon intensity periods. The Yoyu App serves as a tool for delivering timely notifications, enabling participants to make informed decisions about postponing the use of certain appliances or reducing energy consumption temporarily. The users can both have a display of the prediction of carbon intensity for the next 24 h, as well as subscribe to a notification that informs them at the exact hour that the carbon value is low. Figure 1 depicts the example display that user could interacted with. The horizontal line show the "cleanest" of each half hour, and the message on top informed participants, which time would be the best in the next 24 h, to charge the personal device.

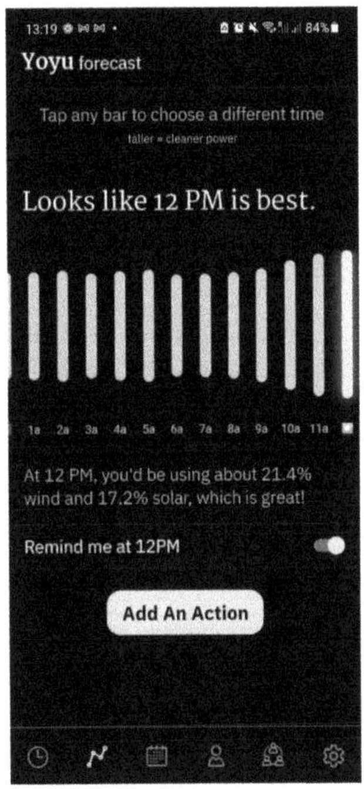

Fig. 1. Example of Yoyu App display

4.2 Automation Group

Participants in this group utilize an integrated IoT system that automatically adjusts their smart devices in response to high carbon intensity periods. The integrated IoT system was built on Home Assistant deployed within a UTM virtual environment or Smart Home Servers. Each participant was provided with at least one smart plug configured to automatically respond to carbon signals. In this phase of experiments, the participants in this group used the laptop of the researcher to monitor the visualization. The set up was done it their private home.

4.3 Data Collection

Both groups are tasked with using their respective systems for min. 12 h to charge their personal use devices, such as phones and laptops. This controlled period allows for consistent data collection across both groups. Following the experimental period, participants completed a questionnaire that captures the following data points:

- Demographic Information: Age, country, and typeof building.
- Group Allocation: Confirmation of participation in either the Notification Group or the Automation Group.
- Compliance with notifications/automations:
  Frequency and factors influencing compliance.
- Satisfaction Levels: Participants' satisfaction with the system, rated on a scale.
- Perceived Impact on Lifestyle: Whether the changes in device operation caused any inconvenience or noticeable reduction in electricity bills.
- Willingness to Continue: Participants' willingness to continue using CO_2 saving features post-study.
- Additional Comments and Suggestions: Open-ended feedback to gather qualitative insights.

5 System Set-Up

In order to enable an experiment the construction of an integrated IoT system that serves as an experimental environment is needed. The chapter details components required to construct an IoT ecosystem facilitated by a Home Assistant deployed within a Unified Threat Management (UTM) virtual environment. The chapter also details on integration of MQTT, API sensors, and automation mechanisms to the system.

5.1 System Overview

Figure 2 illustrates the overall architecture of the system. The Home Assistant ecosystem is hosted on macOS, which provides an environment for system management. Leveraging macOS's capabilities, the system benefits from hardware support and user interface interactions.

The system harnesses the capabilities of Home Assistant deployed within a UTM virtual environment. UTM serves as the platform for hosting and managing Home Assistant, ensuring a secure and scalable infrastructure for the system's operation. UTM was chosen for its simplicity of setup and compatibility with macOS, as Home Assistant has its limitations on the macOS system. For scalability of the solution, the HA can also be deployed on Smart Home Servers (typical small stand-alone Linux-based Mini-Systems). These mini-systems are designed to operate efficiently with minimal resources, making them ideal for integration into

Smart Home environments [4]. This allows for a more permanent and robust solution for deploying Home Assistant in Smart Homes, providing users with a dedicated and efficient system for managing their smart devices and home automation needs. These Smart Home Servers offer the advantage of being specifically designed for continuous operation, ensuring reliability and performance in a home environment.

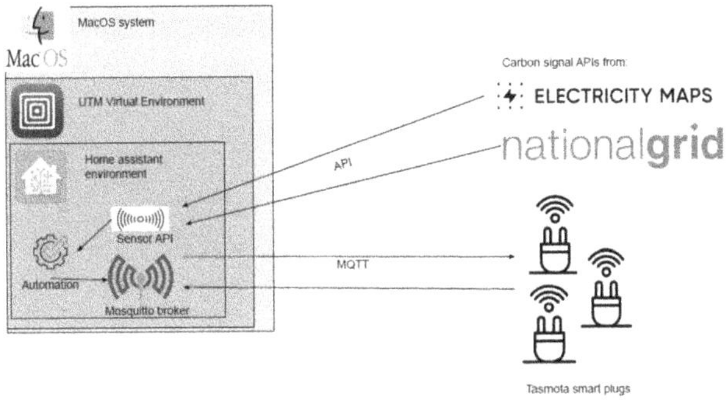

Fig. 2. IoT system design

Home Assistant was chosen due to its popularity. It is also a free Smart Home Management system available for all. Home Assistant is an open-source home automation platform that runs on local hardware, ensuring data privacy and security [4]. It supports thousands of integrations with various smart devices and services, allowing users to control and automate nearly every aspect of their home environment. Home Assistant offers robust automation capabilities, a customizable dashboard for data visualization, and mobile apps for remote access and notifications [4].

The primary IoT devices used in this setup are Tasmota smart plugs. Tasmota is a cloud-free, open-source firmware designed for a wide range of Smart Home devices, including plugs, bulbs, and switches. It ensures that communication stays local, enhancing privacy and reducing reliance on external cloud services. These smart plugs are configured to communicate via the MQTT protocol, which is a lightweight messaging protocol for small sensors and mobile devices. Tasmota Smart Plugs have built-in capabilities to listen to an MQTT broker, allowing for seamless remote control and monitoring of electrical appliances. On the Home Assistant side, the integration was facilitated by setting up a Mosquitto MQTT broker [5]. This involves creating a password-protected MQTT user to ensure secure communication between the Home Assistant and the Tasmota smart plugs.

The system incorporates API sensors to get real-time data from external sources. By interacting with National Grid and Electricity Map APIs, the system accesses up-to-date information regarding CO2 carbon emissions and grid predictions. This data, updated on a half-hourly basis, enables dynamic adjustments to energy consumption patterns. Below, the details of APIs are listed:

- National Grid API provides detailed CO2 emission data and grid status within the UK. This integration allows the system to make informed decisions based on real-time carbon intensity data specific to the UK energy market [2].
- Electricity Map API serves as an industry standard for carbon intensity data across various European markets. In this experiment, it was used to retrieve the data for Polish and Dutch markets. This API integration ensures that the system can operate effectively in different geographical contexts, providing relevant data for dynamic energy management [1].

Below is an example of JSON data showing energy intensity forecast and actual values:


```
{
  "data":[{
   "from": "2024-07-15T12:30Z",
   "to": "2024-07-15T13:00Z",
   "intensity": {
       "forecast": 168,
       "actual": 177,
       "index": "moderate"
}
   }]
}
```


The final component that brings all the elements together is the automation feature of Home Assistant. When carbon intensity exceeds predefined thresholds (180 gCO2/kwh), automation triggers actions to mitigate energy consumption. In this scenario, Smart Plug Control is dynamically managed by the system to switch off devices, toggling power states to optimize energy usage in response to environmental cues.

To enhance the user experience and facilitate intuitive data exploration the visualization board is also included in the system. Plotly Graph Card within Home Assistant is a visualization tool that allows users to dynamically analyze and interpret data trends. Plotly Graph Card enables users to interactively explore data points, zooming in on specific time intervals, and toggling between different data serves. Users can easily observe their progress and see how electricity usage changes during certain hours.

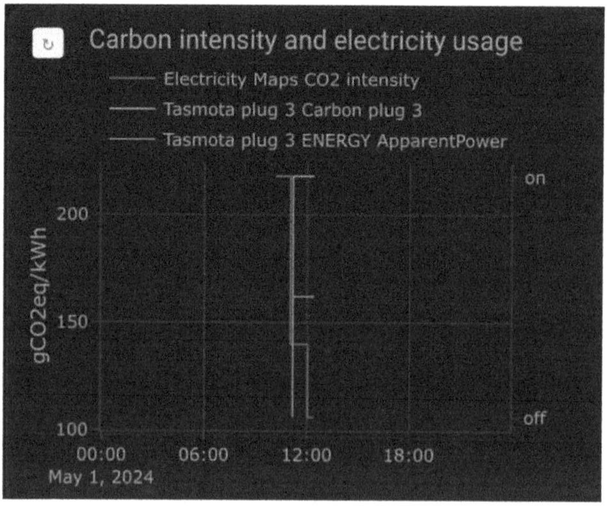

Fig. 3. Visualization in user dashboard

The above Fig. 3 is a snapshot of the integration capability within Home Assistant.

In order to enable an experiment the construction of an integrated IoT system that serves as an experimental environment is needed.

6 Experiment Results

The experimental phase of the study finished by collecting the data via a questionnaire. The main results are detailed in the following sub-subsections. Participants were divided into two groups: the Notification group and the Automation group. Each group utilizes different methods to manage their energy usage during periods of high carbon intensity.

6.1 Participants Demographics

The study involved 20 participants divided into two groups. The demographics of the participants are summarized as follows:

There were four age groups presented in the study, as seen in the Fig. 4 below. The youngest and biggest group was between the ages of 18–25 and contained 9 people. Following that, 7 participants were 35–45 years old. Finally, there were 2 people in the age group 35–45 as well as 45–55. No participants above the age of 55 were included in the study. This might affect the results as the demographic of the study was quite young and tech-fluent, which may have affected their enthusiastic response to the IoT solution.

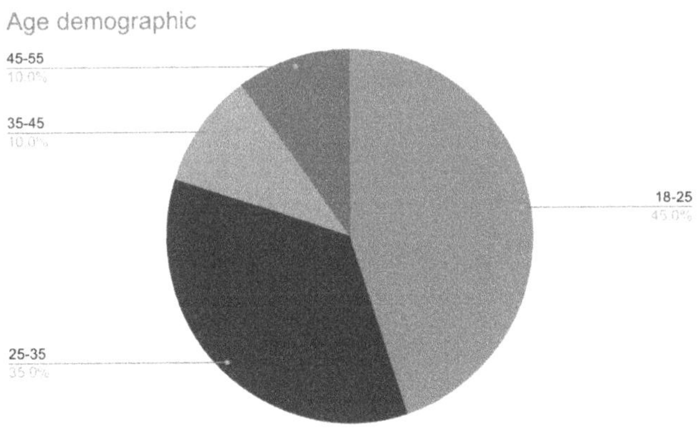

Fig. 4. Age demographic diagram

In terms of country demographic the biggest group came from UK, this is London based group, that is 9 participants, 5 came from Poland and 6 from the Netherlands, as shown in Fig. 5. The Automation group was present only in the UK and Netherlands, while the Notification group had its representation across all three countries.

The final demographic aspect of the study included Building Type of participants. This could be important as the type of house that participant live in can affect their energy provider and freedom in using renewable and alternative sources of energy.

Consequently, this can affect the willingness of participants to integrate carbon-flexing automations. As shown in Fig. 6, in this study the majority of participants live in Apartment/Flat: (11 participants). The other groups include Detached House (7 participants), Semi-detached House (1 participant) and Student Dormitory (3 participants).

These demographics provide an overall view of the participant pool, reflecting a diverse range of ages, countries, and residential settings. The majority of participants were younger adults from the UK, Netherlands, and Poland who lived in apartments or detached houses.

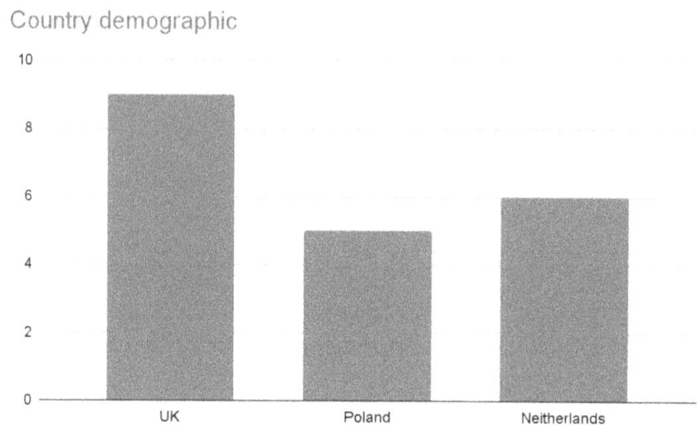

Fig. 5. Country demographic diagram

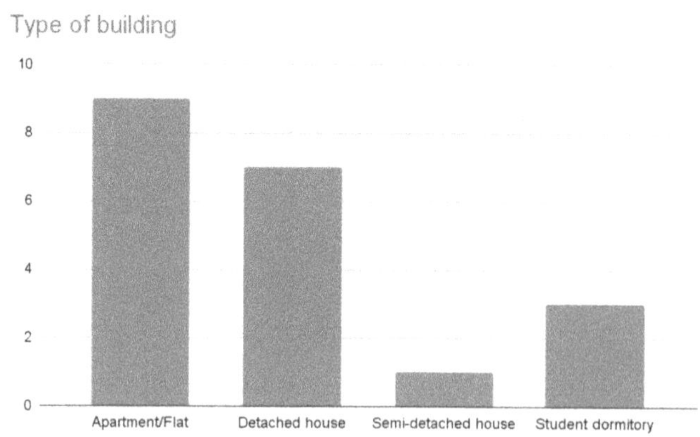

Fig. 6. Type of building demographic diagram

6.2 Group-Specific Analysis

Notification group: Participants in the Notification group received real-time notifications to manually adjust their smart devices during high carbon intensity periods through the

Yoyu App. This group was critical in evaluating whether active notifications could prompt behavior change and contribute to CO2 emission reductions. The compliance rate among the Notification group participants varied, indicating a mixed response to following the suggestions provided. Approximately 50% of participants complied regularly with the notifications, while others complied sporadically or not at all. The average compliance rating was 3.2 on a scale of 1 to 5 (1 not at all complied, 5 always complied), with the mode value 3. When it comes to factors influencing compliance, the primary reasons were convenience and forgetting. Convenience cited by 60% of respondents, indicating that most participants found it convenient to comply when it did not disrupt their routines. Forgetting was mentioned by 30% of respondents, highlighting the need for reminders or more engaging notification methods.

Automation Group: The Automation group experienced a different intervention where Smart Home systems automatically adjusted their settings during high carbon intensity periods. This approach tested the hypothesis that technology-driven adjustments could streamline energy usage reduction efforts. The satisfaction of the automation is rather height with 4.3 average on 1–5 scale and mode results 5 (5 participants responded with the highest score). Furthermore, the overall user trust for system autonomy also yelled positive results. Participants valued the hands-off approach of the automated system, although the necessity for occasional manual overrides indicated a gap in the system's ability to consistently accommodate individual preferences. It also reflects what was already mentioned in Literature review, that users do feel less empowered if left with automation only. Only two participants reported the need to overwrite the automation. The primary reasons for overrides included discomfort from adjustments and conflicts with personal schedules. Here, enhancing transparency and control options could potentially increase user satisfaction.

6.3 Perceived Impact on Energy Consumption and CO2 Emission Reduction

Participants from both groups reported increased awareness of their energy consumption, which often translated into more conscientious energy use. One participant noted, "I became more aware of my energy usage patterns and made an effort to adjust them, especially during peak hours." This suggests that both notification and automation strategies effectively raised awareness and prompted intentional energy management.

A participant from the Automation group reflected positively on the system's impact, saying, "The system made adjustments that I wouldn't have thought of, and it seemed to really help reduce my carbon use without much effort on my part." This indicates that automated interventions can successfully enhance carbon efficiency and contribute to CO2 reduction.

6.4 Satisfaction with the Initiative

Overall satisfaction with the CO2-saving initiative was high, with many participants expressing a willingness to continue using the features. In terms of quantitative comparison the Notification group has expressed their satisfaction with average of 4 points on 1–5 scale (1-low satisfaction, 5-high satisfaction), while the Automation group has ranked it higher with the average 4.6. This shows that automation has a higher potential for success, however, gives the notification also importance in the scenarios of Semi-Automated houses. The qualitative satisfaction in both groups was high, indicating a willingness to participate in further initiatives.

6.5 Willingness to Continue Using CO2 Saving Features and Suggestions and Recommendations

Many participants expressed a willingness to continue using CO2-saving technologies, driven by factors such as reduced energy costs and environmental benefits. One participant mentioned, "I would definitely continue with these features. It's easy once it's all setup, and knowing I'm saving carbon is a big plus."

Furthermore, participants provided several suggestions for improving the initiative:

- Customization and Flexibility: More options for personal settings adjustments based on individual preferences and schedules.
- Increased Transparency and Control: Enhanced transparency about how decisions are made and more control over those decisions.
- Enhanced Communication and Education: Better communication about the benefits and operations of the systems, as well as more educational resources to help users understand and effectively use the smart features.
- Financial gain: Some participants mentioned that the significant reduction in the bills could encourage them to use automation in the future.

6.6 F.Discussion on Experiment Results

The above study addressed the research questions.

For RQ1: What is the social willingness to participate in real-time notifications in prompting manual adjustments of smart device usage during high carbon intensity periods? The study revealed a moderate level of social willingness to participate in real-time notifications. Approximately 50% of the Notification group participants complied regularly with the notifications, with convenience and forgetting being the main factors influencing compliance. This indicates a potential for behavior change through notifications, though effectiveness is largely dependent on the practicality of integrating these alerts into daily routines. It is also noteworthy here that the notifications were tested on the users only for a certain amount of time, and the habits of responding to the notification might be weaker with the passing of time. Moreover, the study was conducted on young adults who might be more prompt in responding to phone notifications than the elderly generation.

Looking at RQ2: How satisfied are users with automated adjustments of their smart devices in response to high carbon intensity, and what is the perceived impact on convenience and lifestyle? Users in the Automation group reported high satisfaction with automated adjustments, with an average satisfaction rating of 4.3 out of 5. Participants appreciated the convenience and effectiveness of the system, though occasional manual overrides were necessary. The hands-off approach was valued, but the need for enhanced control and transparency was noted to better accommodate individual preferences and schedules. Furthermore, this group also reported a higher overall satisfaction of the study than their corresponding notification participants did.

Finally, in terms of RQ3: How do manual and automated interventions compare in terms of user satisfaction? Automated interventions generally resulted in higher user satisfaction compared to manual interventions. The Automation group reported an average satisfaction rating of 4.6, higher than the 4.0 rating from the Notification group. This suggests that automated systems, by reducing the need for manual intervention, can enhance user satisfaction and potentially lead to greater adoption of CO2-saving technologies. This might be particularly true if the experiment would extrapolate to week or month-long time-periods. The carbon intensity is not regular on a daily level, and adjusting the schedule to always respond to notifications can be challenging.

To sum up, the experiment demonstrated that both manual and automated interventions can effectively optimize energy consumption and reduce carbon emissions. Participants in the Notification group showed varying degrees of compliance, influenced by factors such as convenience and understanding of the impact. The Automation group generally reported higher satisfaction due to the convenience of automated adjustments. The overall willingness to continue using CO2-saving features was high, indicating a positive reception of the interventions.

7 Discussion and Future Studies

The results of this study highlight the significant potential of shifting energy usage to "green hours," offering a substantial reduction in carbon emissions through flexible energy consumption. The study aimed to explore this potential by an experimental setup.

This perspective examined social willingness and user readiness to implement such solutions, particularly comparing manual versus automated implementations. The findings were promising, showing high willingness and satisfaction among participants when engaging with real-time notifications and automated adjustments of smart devices during low carbon intensity periods. Automated interventions were more favorably received than manual adjustments due to their convenience and minimal disruption to users' lifestyles. Satisfaction ratings from the Automation Group underscored the effectiveness of integrating smart technologies in managing energy use, aligning with recent advancements and the acceptance of home automation systems.

These findings can serve as a starting point for an industry shift and a broader change towards de-carbonization through electrification. The study proved that there is market potential for such solutions and that society is ready to implement carbon reduction in households from both a technical and social willingness standpoint. The described solution is relatively simple in design, requiring only one type of automation. Given the current popularity of Smart Homes, such a solution could be adopted by many other systems and implemented across both small and large-scale projects.

The importance of such implementations is further supported by the introduction of various laws and regulations in the European market. For example, policies advocating for Building Automation Control Systems (BACS) in tertiary buildings by January 2025, as part of the EU Energy Performance of Buildings Directive (EPBD), highlight the timely relevance of this research [11]. These regulations not only promote energy efficiency but also encourage the commercialization of Smart Home solutions capable of supporting carbon flexing strategies.

Furthermore, this research can be seen as an extension of existing Smart Grid policies. Essentially, it examines similar patterns but empowers individual homes to "flex" - rather than the electricity provider. Smart grid policies aim to improve the efficiency, reliability, and sustainability of electricity services. By utilizing real-time data to balance electricity supply and demand more effectively, and incorporating energy consumption flexing, this system can dynamically reduce the grid's carbon footprint. The ability of smart grids to accommodate varying energy loads and integrate renewable energy sources seamlessly aligns with the objectives observed in this study. Implementing such strategies on both sides - grid and the home - can therefore enhance the functionality and environmental benefits of smart grid systems, providing a practical application of research findings within existing and future energy policies.

8 Conclusion

This study aimed to assess the potential for energy consumption flexing and the associated carbon savings by shifting energy usage to "green hours." The research explored the social willingness to participate in such initiatives by comparing real-time notifications prompting manual adjustments during high carbon intensity periods with automated adjustments enabled through Smart Home IoT technology.

The user-centered experiments revealed that real-time notifications and automated adjustments significantly affected users' energy consumption behaviors. The experiment resulted in the development of an IoT system for Home Assistant's open-source Smart Home Management System. This automation adjusts usage to low carbon intensive hours on the grid. The experiment involved two groups automation group that used the above-described system and the notification group that was manually informed to change the behavior via mobile application. Participants of both groups had a high willingness to engage in adjustments, indicating a strong social willingness to participate in carbon reduction efforts. However, the satisfaction with automated adjustments was higher, as when prompted by real-time notification, the notification group expressed concerns over the impact on their lifestyle and convenience.

The comparison between manual and automated interventions highlighted that while manual adjustments were perceived as more empowering and satisfying, automated interventions offered a seamless experience with less effort required from the users. This balance between manual and automated approaches suggests that a hybrid model could most effectively maximize user satisfaction and carbon savings. It also prompts further research that could be conducted on a wide range of participants from different tech-related backgrounds and over more extended periods of time.

By shifting energy usage to green hours, households could significantly reduce their carbon footprint. When aggregated across multiple households, this potential represents a meaningful contribution to broader carbon reduction goals.

In conclusion, this study underscores the importance of integrating automated approaches to flexing energy consumption. By ensuring the convenience of automated adjustments, households can achieve significant carbon savings. The findings contribute valuable insights into the design of effective carbon reduction strategies and highlight the role of user participation in achieving sustainability goals.

References

1. ElectricityMaps Methodology: (2024). https://www.electricitymaps.com/methodology?utm_source=app.electricitymaps.com&utm_medium=referral#carbon-intensity-and-emission-factors [Accessed 14 Jul 2024]
2. UK National Grid: Carbon Intensity. https://www.carbonintensity.org.uk/ [Accessed 14 Jul 2024]
3. UK Power Networks Open Data: (2024). https://ukpowernetworks.opendatasoft.com/pages/home/ [Accessed 14 Jul 2024]
4. Home Assistant: (2024). Home Assistant. https://www.home-assistant.io/. [Accessed 14 Jul 2024]
5. Home Assistant: (2024). Mosquitto Add-on Documentation. https://github.com/home-assistant/addons/blob /master/mosquitto/DOCS.md. [Accessed 14 Ju 2024]
6. Bertoldi, P.: Policies for energy conservation and sufficiency: review of existing policies and recommendations for new and effective policies in OECD countries. Energ. Buildings (2022)
7. Carswell, C., Reid, J., Walsh, I., et al.: A mixed-methods feasibility study of an arts-based intervention for patients receiving maintenance haemodialysis. BMC Nephrol. **21**(2020), 497 (2020). https://doi.org/10.1186/s12882-020-02162-4
8. Issi, F., Kaplan, O.: The determination of load profiles and power consumptions of home appliances. Energies **11**(3), 607 (2018). https://doi.org/10.3390/en11030607
9. Johnson, C.: Is demand side response a woman's work? Domestic labour and electricity shifting in low-income homes in the United Kingdom. Energy Res. Soc. Sci. (2020)
10. Nyborg, S., Røpke, I.: Energy impacts of the smart home - conflicting visions. In Energy Efficiency First: The Foundation of a Low-Carbon Society 1849–1860 (2011)
11. Romain Philipon. 2023. Building Automation Control Systems required in the EU. (1 August 2023). https://www.wattsense.com/blog/building-management/ bacsenergy-eu/ [Accessed 17 Jul 2024]
12. Pickering, B., Lombardi, F., Pfenninger, S.: Diversity of options to eliminate fossil fuels and reach carbon neutrality across the entire European energy system. Joule (2022)
13. Setlhaolo, D., Xia, X.: Combined residential demand side management strategies with coordination and economic analysis. Int. J. Electr. Power Energy Syst. (2016)
14. Sintov, N.D., Schultz, P.W.: Adjustable green defaults can help make smart homes more sustainable. Sustainability. **9**(4), 1–12 (2017). https://ideas.repec.org/a/gam/jsusta/v9y2017i4p622-d96017.html
15. D. Steinberg, D. Bielen, J. Eichman, and K. Eurek: Electrification and decarbonization: exploring US energy use and greenhouse gas emissions in scenarios with widespread electrification and power sector transformation (2017)
16. Droegehorn, O., Trenz, P., Brausse, B., Schwan, T., Voscort, C., Wemmer, M.: Capability Based Communication for Green Buildings and Homes - a REST-like API within the conex.io Project -. In: Proceedings of the 51st Hawaiian International Conference on System Sciences, ISBN 978–0–9981331-1-9, p.5767–5776 (2018). http://hdl.handle.net/10125/50612
17. Schrader, I., Droegehorn,O.: Transforming Business Moments into Business Models. Proceedings of the 17th International Conference on e-Learning, e-Business, Enterprise Information Systems, and e-Government, Ed. Hamid R. Arabnia, Azita Bahrami, Leonidas Deligiannidis, Fernando G. Tinetti, ISBN 1–60132-474-X, CSREA Press, pp. 87–93, USA, (2018)
18. Schrader, I., Droegehorn, O.: Digitization of companies - understanding IT as an enabler -. In: Proceedings of the 16th International Conference on e-Learning, e-Business, Enterprise Information Systems, and e-Government, ISBN: 1–60132–454-5, Ed. Hamid R. Arabnia, Leonidas Deligiannidis, Fernando G. Tinetti, pp. 83–87, LasVegas, Nevada, USA, (2017)

Deep Reinforcement Learning for Resource Management in 5G-Enabled IoT Networks: A Comprehensive Survey

Rahma Shahid[1], Logan Sherlock[1], Sagnika Ghosh[2], Kanwalinderjit Kaur[3], and Renu Balyan[1](✉)

[1] State University of New York at Old Westbury, Old Westbury, NY, USA
balyanr@oldwestbury.edu
[2] Tennessee State University, Nashville, TN, USA
[3] California State University, Bakersfield, CA, USA

Abstract. The rapid adoption of 5G-enabled Internet of Things (IoT) devices has created substantial challenges in resource management due to the diverse range of applications and massive connectivity requirements. Efficient resource allocation is crucial to ensure high-quality service, reduce latency, and maintain sustainable IoT network operations, especially in complex and dynamic environments. This paper explores how reinforcement learning (RL) techniques, particularly deep reinforcement learning (DRL), can address these challenges by optimizing resource allocation in 5G-enabled IoT networks. By reviewing existing research, this study identifies key challenges, evaluates current solutions, and proposes potential future directions. It highlights the significant potential of DRL to enhance resource efficiency and cater to the evolving demands of 5G-powered IoT ecosystems.

Keywords: 5G networks · Internet of Things (IoT) · Deep Reinforcement Learning (DRL) · **Regular Research Paper**

1 Introduction

The advent of 5G technology marks a transformative milestone in network capabilities, delivering substantial improvements in data transfer rates, ultra-low latency, and the capacity to connect billions of devices seamlessly. These advancements are critical for supporting the diverse and complex applications of the Internet of Things (IoT), including real-time analytics, autonomous systems, high-definition video streaming, and industrial automation (Shafi et al., 2017). However, the sheer scale and complexity of 5G networks, coupled with the heterogeneity of IoT devices, demand sophisticated resource management strategies to address these challenges effectively.

IoT networks within 5G ecosystems have varying requirements across applications. For instance, ultra-reliable low-latency communication (URLLC) is essential for autonomous vehicles, while massive machine-type communication (mMTC) supports

H. R. Arabnia et al. (Eds.): CSCE 2025, CCIS 2934, pp. 52–67, 2026.
https://doi.org/10.1007/978-3-032-22190-2_4

the large-scale connectivity needed for smart cities. Balancing these requirements while optimizing resource allocation, ensuring fairness, and maintaining network efficiency presents significant challenges. Traditional resource management approaches often lack the adaptability and intelligence required to handle these complexities (Andrews et al., 2014). Reinforcement learning (RL), particularly its deep learning-based variant DRL (Deep Reinforcement Learning), has emerged as a promising solution. By enabling systems to learn optimal strategies through interaction with their environment, DRL provides a robust framework for addressing complex resource management issues in 5G-enabled IoT networks.

This paper focuses on 5G-enabled IoT devices from RL perspective and examines how DRL can tackle the challenges encountered in these technologies and dynamic environments, offering insights into existing research and paving the way for future advancements in this domain. The main objective of this study is to identify strategies used in DRL to enhance resource management within the context of 5G network slicing. Managing resources across slices involves tackling several intricate challenges, such as dynamic allocation, maintaining Quality of Service (QoS), and optimizing network resource utilization (Li et al., 2017; Shafi et al., 2017; Andrews et al., 2014). Through this survey paper, we aim to connect theoretical DRL methodologies with practical applications in 5G network slicing.

1.1 Background

Traditional Approaches & their Challenges to Network Management. Traditional network management relies on static configurations and manual processes to maintain system performance and resolve operational issues. These methods are centered around rule-based systems where parameters like bandwidth allocation, priority rules, and resource thresholds are predefined by administrators. Fixed resource allocation strategies, such as pre-defined bandwidth or power limits, lack the flexibility to accommodate fluctuating traffic demands. This rigidity often results in resource wastage during low- demand periods or congestion during spikes, particularly in networks supporting heterogeneous applications like IoT devices and high-definition streaming (Toosi et al., 2019), hence failing to address proper ***resource allocation***.

While this approach was sufficient in earlier, less complex networks, it struggles to adapt to the dynamic demands of today's interconnected systems. Static configurations, often fail to accommodate rapid traffic surges or fluctuating user requirements, leading to resource inefficiencies and degraded service quality (Zhang et al., 2015). For example, during peak usage periods, high-priority users may monopolize resources, leaving other users with subpar service quality (Chinchali et al., 2018). Therefore, while simple, these traditional scheduling mechanisms, such as time-division multiplexing or fixed- priority systems result into challenges related to ***user scheduling***.

Moreover, traditional methods rely heavily on human intervention to address performance bottlenecks or outages. This reliance on manual adjustments not only increases the likelihood of errors but also ***slows response time*** in environments that require real-time adaptability (Ding et al., 2018). Another significant limitation of traditional approaches is their ***inability to scale effectively***. As networks grow more complex, accommodating an increasing number of devices and applications, static rules and configurations become impractical. Networks that support 5G technologies and IoT devices face additional challenges, as these systems demand ultra-low latency, high reliability, and the ability to handle diverse traffic types simultaneously (Park et al., 2017).

Finally, conventional network management often focuses on isolated optimization tasks and single objects, such as load balancing, energy efficiency or interference reduction, without considering or ignoring the interdependencies or broader interactions among different network parameters. This fragmented and siloed approach prevents the system from achieving holistic optimization, which is crucial for modern networks with interconnected dependencies (Ye et al., 2018; Wang et al., 2021) resulting into ***network optimization*** related challenges.

1.2 5G Network Slicing and IoT Resource Management

The exponential growth in user demands and diverse application requirements has rendered traditional one-size-fits-all network strategies inadequate. While 4G networks revolutionized global connectivity, 5G introduces significant advancements such as ultra-low latency, massive device connectivity, and high reliability. Looking beyond, 6G aims to build on this foundation, envisioning intelligent, hyper-connected ecosystems that leverage terahertz communication, AI-driven networks, and energy-efficient systems to support applications like holographic telepresence and real-time haptic communication (Karam et al., 2022). To meet these demands, the Next Generation Mobile Network Alliance (NGMN) advocates for a flexible, software-centric network architecture incorporating Network Slicing, Network Function Virtualization (NFV), Software-Defined Networking (SDN), and Cloud RAN (Foukas et al., 2017; Li et al., 2017; Shafi et al., 2017). Among these, network slicing has emerged as a pivotal technology, allowing networks to partition resources into virtual slices tailored to specific applications, such as enhanced mobile broadband (eMBB), massive machine-type communication (mMTC), and ultra-reliable low-latency communication (URLLC).

5G Network Slicing. Network slicing is a transformative technology that enables the creation of multiple virtual networks on a shared physical infrastructure. Each slice is tailored to meet specific service requirements, making it a key enabler for diverse IoT applications. For instance, network slices can provide ultra-reliable low-latency communications (URLLC) for autonomous vehicles and industrial automation, or support massive machine-type communications (mMTC) for large-scale IoT deployments like smart cities. High-bandwidth enhanced mobile broadband (eMBB) slices are well-suited for applications such as video streaming and augmented reality. The flexibility of network slicing is underpinned by advances in virtualization technologies, such as NFV and SDN, which allow dynamic provisioning and efficient resource allocation. Furthermore, the integration of artificial intelligence and machine learning is increasingly being leveraged to optimize slice management and predict network demands.

Recent research highlights the practical implementations of network slicing. For example, Zhao et al. (2021) demonstrated its application in smart grid networks to ensure reliable energy distribution, while Kaloxylos et al. (2018) explored its potential in ehealth systems for remote monitoring and emergency care. These examples underscore the adaptability of network slicing across verticals, supporting industry-specific quality-of-service (QoS) metrics and security requirements. Moreover, emerging 6G technologies promise to enhance network slicing capabilities further, enabling features like cross-domain slice orchestration and quantum security. Such advancements will drive new IoT paradigms and support applications requiring extreme reliability and scalability. Efficient resource allocation is critical to the success of network slicing in modern wireless networks. Imagine a system where a single physical network supports multiple virtual networks (slices), each with its own resource demand. The challenge is to allocate the total available network resource R among N slices (N = 3 in Fig. 1) so that each slice receives an amount S_i as close as possible to its demand d_i (see Fig. 1).

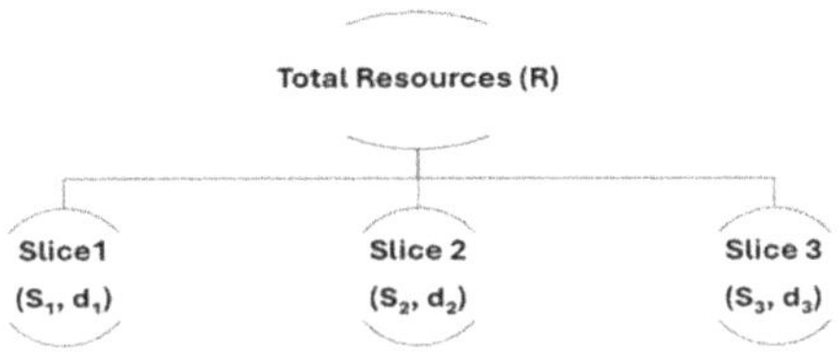

Fig. 1. Allocation (Si) to each slice is optimized to meet its demand (di)

IoT Resource Management. Managing resources within 5G networks requires the dynamic allocation of bandwidth, power, and computational resources to address the diverse demands of IoT devices. Effective resource management is crucial for maintaining Quality of Service (QoS) and ensuring the efficient use of network resources. The dynamic and heterogeneous nature of 5G networks complicates these tasks, necessitating advanced management techniques (Toosi et al., 2019; Ye et al., 2018).

1.3 Deep Reinforcement Learning in 5G IoT Management

To navigate the complexities of 5G networks and the varied needs of IoT applications, traditional management approaches often fall short. Deep Reinforcement Learning (DRL) provides a powerful framework for tackling these challenges due to its advanced learning and adaptability. By combining reinforcement learning with deep neural networks, DRL effectively manages high-dimensional state and action spaces (Troia et al., 2020; Hurtado Sánchez, 2022). DRL can significantly improve 5G network management by a) adjusting resources like bandwidth and power in real time based on network conditions and demands (Sivaganesan, 2019; Wang et al., 2021); b) developing intelligent scheduling policies to enhance user experience and network efficiency (Chinchali et al., 2018); and c) continuously improving load balancing, interference management, and energy efficiency (Gawłowicz and Zubow, 2018). By utilizing DRL, network operators can create more responsive and effective strategies, better manage the dynamic complexities of 5G networks, leading to more efficient resource and service management, ultimately boosting the performance and efficiency of 5G-enabled IoT networks (ITU 2018; ONF 2016; Alliance NGMN 2016; Hurtado Sánchez, 2022).

2 Reinforcement Learning

Reinforcement Learning (RL) is a subset of machine learning in which an agent learns to make optimal decisions by interacting with its environment. RL offers an adaptive alternative to traditional network management, transforming it into an intelligent system that meets the demands of modern 5G networks. Unlike static methods, RL continuously learns from network interactions, enabling dynamic decision-making for improved scalability, efficiency, and reliability. RL excels in user scheduling (Chinchali et al., 2018), resource allocation (Ye et al., 2018), and network optimization (Ordonez- Lucena et al., 2017) by analyzing real-time conditions, anticipating traffic surges, and adjusting resources accordingly. It balances loads, reduces interference, and cuts energy use while supporting emerging technologies like edge computing and network slicing, making it a future-ready solution.

2.1 Key Components

The key components of an RL algorithm in general and how these relate to our work are briefly explained below Sutton & Barto (2018).

Agent. Decision-making entity that interacts with the environment by using a policy to choose actions. RL agents are able to learn from their decisions with the help of other components listed below.

In a networking implementation, the ***agent*** *would be the software/program on a router or computer that adjusts the network or device parameters. The software works within the network (environment), to make changes (actions) and receives feedback from the system (reward).*

Environment. The world that an agent resides and acts within; where the agent receives its percepts. The environment also defines and contains the observation and action spaces; these are the possible values/data that the agent can observe, and the set/range of actions that can be chosen.

In a network implementation the ***environment*** *would be the network; the agent will use network information, reachable routers and switches, connected IoT devices, and other components within the environment's network to make decisions.*

States. Representations of the environment at a given time (step); the agent makes observations of states for decision-making.

In an IoT network ***states*** *could capture and contain data of network traffic levels, latency, bandwidth, packet loss, etc. It may also have IoT focused data such as BER values, power levels, bandwidth allocation levels and others.*

Actions. The options in decision-making that the agent has to choose from. This can be continuous or discrete; a range of values, or a finite set of options. Once an action is chosen and executed, the environment is updated and the cycle continues.

In an IoT RL environment, the agent's ***actions*** *will determine the number of resources to be allocated to a specific IoT device. The agent will base its choice of action on a policy. Other network environments may have actions such as dynamically redirecting traffic, or throttling controls.*

Rewards. Feedback that the environment returns to the agent after an action is executed. Rewards are determined by a reward function that may use probability to scale rewards to help the system converge. If the agent receives a positive reward, it can learn to repeat similar actions in comparable states, while negative rewards help it recognize and avoid unfavorable choices.

In networking, a ***positive reward*** *could be based on achieving lower latency or higher data throughput, while a* ***negative reward*** *might result from actions that cause congestion, increase packet loss, and degrade service quality.*

Policies. Policies guide an agent's decisions by mapping states to actions, either deterministically or through probability distributions. They balance exploitation (choosing known rewards) and exploration (trying new actions for potential gains). Some algorithms adapt policies over time to support convergence.

In a network management system, a ***policy*** *could dictate that if network congestion is detected, the agent should increase bandwidth for critical applications to maintain performance.*

Figure 2 shows the key RL components within the context of a 5G-enabled IoT network. The environment consists of the Radio Access Network (RAN), the 5G Core including the User Plane Function (UPF), Session Management Function (SMF), and Access and Mobility Management Function (AMF), as well as external data networks. The RL agent monitors network type, load, and QoS metrics to take actions like resource allocation, beamforming, and traffic offloading. Action effectiveness is measured by rewards based on QoS, spectral efficiency, and cost or profit. The system also supports multiple network slices eMBB, URLLC, and massive IoT (mIoT).

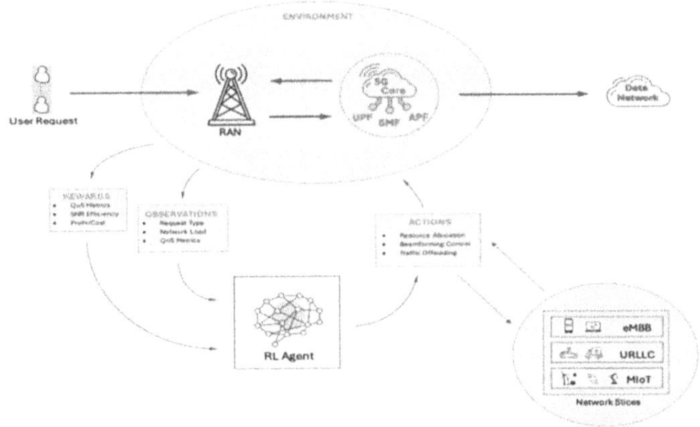

Fig. 2. RL components applied in a 5G-enabled IoT network.

2.2 Deep Reinforcement Learning

Deep Reinforcement Learning (DRL), which combines RL with deep learning, is a powerful tool for managing complex, high-dimensional environments such as 5G network systems (Troia et al., 2020; Ye et al., 2018). DRL excels in handling large state and action spaces where traditional RL struggles, enabling it to manage variables like network load, user demand, and resource allocation simultaneously (Chinchali et al., 2018; Wang et al., 2021). It also supports end-to-end learning, eliminating the need for manual feature extraction by mapping raw inputs directly to actions (Troia et al., 2020; Gawłowicz and Zubow, 2018). Moreover, DRL's ability to generalize policies and adapt to changing network conditions improves system robustness and flexibility (Si-vaganesan, 2019). The key components and techniques used in DRL are as follows:

Deep Neural Networks (DNNs). DNNs are central to DRL, which learn representations from large datasets. These networks are adept at identifying intricate patterns and features within high-dimensional state and action spaces, making them suitable for sophisticated decision-making tasks (Chinchali et al., 2018; Santos et al., 2018).

Value Functions and Q-Learning. DRL utilizes value functions to estimate expected cumulative rewards for states or state-action pairs. Techniques such as Deep Q-Learning (DQL) leverage deep neural networks to approximate the Q-value function, helping the agent identify actions that maximize long-term rewards (Troia et al., 2020; Alliance NGMN, 2016).

Policy Optimization. Some DRL methods focus on directly optimizing policies rather than learning value functions. Policy Gradient methods, including Proximal Policy Optimization (PPO) and Actor-Critic methods, use neural networks to represent and enhance the policy, determining the agent's actions across different states. This approach is beneficial in environments with continuous action spaces or where value function approximation is difficult (Troia et al., 2020; Ordonez-Lucena et al., 2017).

DRL has emerged as a promising approach for intelligent network management, offering adaptive solutions across multiple operational domains. In *dynamic resource allocation*, DRL facilitates real-time distribution of bandwidth and power, enhancing system performance while maintaining QoS (Ye et al., 2018; Chinchali et al., 2018). It also improves *user scheduling and traffic management* by learning optimal policies for prioritizing data flows under variable traffic conditions (Troia et al., 2020; Chinchali et al., 2018). Additionally, DRL contributes to *network-wide optimization* by addressing load balancing and interference mitigation through the analysis of network usage patterns (Ordonez-Lucena et al., 2017; Wang et al., 2021). From a sustainability perspective, DRL supports energy-efficient operations by developing strategies that minimize power consumption without compromising service quality—an increasingly critical requirement in 5G and IoT environments (Sivaganesan, 2019; Hurtado Sánchez, 2022).

3 Literature Review on DRL in 5G and IoT Networks

The interrelationships between the reviewed research papers and their primary areas of focus are systematically outlined in Table 1, which maps each paper to core topics like variants of RL, 5G/6G, IoT devices, and networking. This tabular overview offers valuable insights into the distribution of research efforts, revealing both prevailing trends and underexplored areas within the field.

3.1 Networks (5G/6G)

Javadpour et al. (2023); Lee & Qin (2019); Qian et al. (2019); Ssengonzi et al. (2022) & Zhang et al. (2021) explored mainly 5G networks. *Javadpour* et al. investigated network slicing in 5G and proposed a novel Actor-Critic RL model, called Slice Isolation, to protect slices from attacks. The proposed approach significantly improves acceptance ratios and mitigates the impact of DoS/DDoS attacks. *Lee & Qin* reviewed the applications of deep RL for resource management in 5G heterogeneous networks encompassing areas such as energy harvesting and network slicing, providing a comparative analysis and highlighting research gaps and future directions. *Qian et al* provided a comprehensive overview of the applications of RL and DRL in communication networks, in the context of 5G technology exploring mobile edge computing (MEC), SDN, and network virtualization. They emphasized on the potential of RL and DRL to enhance network efficiency, resource allocation, and overall system performance. *Ssengonzi* et al. addressed the goals and challenges of 5G networks, focusing on how deep RL can aid in managing network slices. They provided an overview of current research, discussed the principles of 5G network slicing and virtualization, and identified future research directions. Finally, *Zhang* et al. offered an extensive survey on DRL applications in network slicing, emphasizing challenges and solutions related to resource management, QoS provisioning, and network optimization. This paper surveys DRL techniques—covering theory, implementation, and performance—while highlighting research gaps and proposing future directions for DRL in network slicing.

Kaur et al. (2021). This paper explores how Machine Learning (ML), particularly Deep Learning (DL), can enhance 6G wireless networks by optimizing resource allocation and efficiency. It highlights key research challenges and emphasizes ML's role across both infrastructure and application layers.

Sánchez et al. (2022). Conducted a thorough survey on the applications of deep RL in network slicing. They explored various RL and DRL algorithms utilized in different phases of resource management, including admission control and scheduling, and identified key research challenges and future directions.

3.2 Networks (5G/6G) and IoT

Afrin (2024); Alzhrani (2024); Chavan et al. (2024); Chowdhury et al. (2019); Lafta (2024); Sharma et al. (2021) and Zamzami (2023) studied 5G and IoT devices. *Afrin* examined integrating 5G with IoT to build a scalable, high-speed, and cost-effective infrastructure for billions of devices, while also highlighting over- looked security issues. The study proposes cross-platform compatibility and open- source standardization to enhance security and privacy. *Alzhrani* investigated how 5G networks can bolster the security of IoT devices, which are vulnerable to Distributed Denial of Service (DDoS) attacks. They employed DL algorithms including Convolutional Neural Networks (CNN), Long Short-Term Memory (LSTM), and Deep Neural Networks (DNN), to identify DDoS threats for IoT devices operating in 5G environments. CNN achieved accuracy rates as high as 99%, while LSTM and DNN underper- formed. *Chavan* et al. examined how 5G enhances IoT through high speed, low latency, and dense connectivity, enabling real-time data processing across applications. They also address challenges like interoperability, security, and the need for edge computing and AI to realize 5G's full potential in IoT. *Chowdhury* et al. proposed a model-free, policy-gradient RL approach to enhance 5G network slicing. The algorithm dynamically allocates resources, detects malicious nodes, and strengthens slice security by reducing latency and blocking threats in real time. This method ensures optimal resource utilization while improving the reliability and adaptability of 5G networks.

Lafta et al. integrated 5G New Radio, network slicing, and reinforcement learning (RL) to optimize communications in increasingly dense intelligent object environments. The architecture uses slicing for service management and RL for efficient sub- channel and power allocation. Simulations in suburban settings demonstrate its ability to reduce interference and adapt to changing network conditions, showcasing its flexibility and responsiveness. *Sharma* et al. conducted a comprehensive review of how ML and DL can enhance the security of 5G-enabled Industrial IoT (IIoT) systems. The paper stresses the importance of strong encryption, authentication, and access control to protect data in applications like smart cities, healthcare, and industrial automation. It also highlights the promise of integrating blockchain and fog computing to build secure, scalable, and efficient IoT frameworks for future use. *Zamzami* investigated 5G adoption using deep learning models—DRL, LSTM, and CNN—to predict influencing factors, evaluated through mean squared error (MSE) and root MSE (RMSE). While LSTM shows high accuracy, it faces overfitting challenges. Unlike purely technical analyses, this work emphasizes predictive modeling, offering valuable insights for stakeholders planning 5G investments.

Gkagkas et al. (2024). This survey explores 5G's role in enabling IoT and how 6G will address its limitations. It reviews 5G challenges like scalability, latency, and slicing, and highlights how Control Plane and User Plane Separation (CUPS) and IPv6 aid efficient resource management. The paper concludes that 6G will be key to achieving the Internet of Everything (IoE).

3.3 Networks (5G/6G), IoT and RL

Yang et al. (2021). Discussed the application of a deep Q-network (DQN) based on DRL for joint resource allocation challenges in 5G IoT systems. The study focused on maximizing energy efficiency for communication and computation in MEC servers and sensors. The DQN approach outperformed other benchmark solutions, effectively lowering total energy consumption while maintaining accuracy in emotional computing.

Gupta et al. (2023). Explored integrating 5G with Multi-access Edge Computing (MEC) to support diverse resource demands, emphasizing network slicing for customizable virtual infrastructure. A DQN approach is proposed to optimize slicing at the RAN edge by modeling the problem as a Markov Decision Process (MDP). Simulations show improved computing performance and reduced network costs.

Wang et al. (2021). Examined the impact of cloud-native technology on 5G and future 6G networks, highlighting its benefits in automation, flexibility, and adaptability. The authors propose a container-based cloud-native wireless architecture, focusing on network slicing and MEC. Using DRL for resource allocation, experiments on a Free5GC testbed show improved network efficiency and highlight DRL's potential for future communication systems.

Tham et al. (2019). addresses resource allocation challenges in 5G Cloud RAN (C-RAN) systems, where traditional fixed-antenna setups lead to high costs and interference. C-RAN leverages distributed Remote Radio Heads (RRHs), creating complex optimization demands. The paper explores the use of DRL, modeling the problem as an MDP, and employing DNNs for system correction estimation. While effective, the approach faces challenges in identifying optimal DRL-based solutions.

El Boudani et al. (2020); Varga et al. (2020); Yadav et al. (2022); Zavyalova & Drozdova (2020) focused on 5G/6G, IoT and DNNs. *El Boudani* et al. presented DELTA, a deep learning-based cooperative architecture for enhancing 3D indoor positioning in 5G IoT networks. Using a real-world 5G testbed with C-RAN and diverse IoT devices, it builds a 3D multi-layer fingerprint radio map. DELTA outperforms traditional methods like K-Nearest Neighbor (KNN) and Support Vector Machine (SVM), proving effective for smart factories, indoor navigation, and large-scale asset tracking. *Varga* et al. reviews how 5G supports IIoT applications, emphasizing ultra-reliability, low latency, security, and flexibility. It surveys key areas like mobile edge cloud, NFV, blockchain-based security, AI-driven optimization, and private 5G networks. The study also identifies research gaps in scalability, AI integration in real-time processes, and securing decentralized IIoT systems. *Yadav* et al. proposes a deep learning-based intrusion detection system (IDS) for 5G-enabled IoT networks to counter escalating cyber threats targeting integrated IoT servers, applications, and communication layers. The IDS leverages neural networks and autoencoders to analyze network traffic in near real-time, enabling rapid and precise threat detection, demonstrating a significant reduction in detection latency and a high accuracy (99.76%). *Zavyalova & Drozdova* explored how DRL can optimize resource allocation in 5G networks to meet varying QoS requirements. The authors focus on IoT devices in large-scale systems and show how an RL agent (acting as a scheduler) learns to prioritize resources by maximizing through- put while minimizing latency.

Sreedevi (2019). Introduced RL-LCDC, a Q-learning-based approach to improve indoor 5G device-to-device (D2D) communication by dynamically discovering devices, establishing links, and adjusting communication ranges. It reduces end-to-end latency while enhancing connectivity and energy efficiency, outperforming conventional methods in convergence speed, delay, and energy usage.

Abba Ari et al. (2025). Reviews resource allocation and network slicing in 5G, B5G, and 6G networks, focusing on AI-driven methods like ML, DL, RL, DRL, and federated learning (FL). It highlights how these techniques enhance QoS, energy efficiency, and overall network performance, while addressing challenges such as dynamic conditions, real-time decisions, and scalability through multi-objective optimization.

Nieto et al. (2024). Proposes a distributed DRL-based task offloading strategy for the 5G edge-cloud continuum using an Actor-Critic (AC) algorithm on each User Equipment (UE). The model enables real-time, autonomous decisions on local processing, MEC, or cloud offloading without centralized control. Simulations show superior Quality of Experience (QoE) and battery efficiency compared to static and dynamic base- lines like Double Dueling DQN (DDDQN), demonstrating its effectiveness for 5G-enabled IoT environments.

Pinto Neto et al. (2023). Examined the use of federated reinforcement learning (FRL) in IoT, focusing on privacy-preserving offloading, resource allocation, and vehicular applications in 5G networks. By combining RL's adaptability with FL's privacy, FRL enables collaborative learning without data sharing. They categorize applications in security, IIoT, sustainability, and vehicular systems, identify research gaps and outline challenges for real-world deployment, for secure and efficient 5G IoT systems.

Saeed et al. (2020). Proposes UbiPriSEQ, a DRL-based framework for managing privacy, security, energy efficiency, and QoS in 5G IoT heterogeneous networks. Using a three-layer architecture, it learns optimal strategies for data processing, fog node selection, power control, and task prioritization. Evaluations show improved signal-to-interference-plus-noise ratio (SINR), lower latency, and increased system utility.

Iqbal et al. (2023). Proposed an RL-based multimedia content delivery framework using DDQN is proposed for 5G/6G networks, optimizing distribution by balancing congestion, bandwidth, and user preferences. It coordinates caching across buses, intersections, and base stations to improve quality and efficiency. Future directions include scalability, complex scenarios, and integration with blockchain and edge computing for enhanced security and performance.

Han et al. (2023). Proposed a twin-delayed deep deterministic (TD3)-based DRL strategy to optimize two-step random access in 5G-and-beyond Low Earth Orbit (LEO) satellite systems, addressing MsgA channel collisions and high-dimensional action spaces. By dynamically adjusting channel allocation using historical access data, the method enhances user-channel mapping improving access probability by 39.12%.

Saad et al. (2025). Proposed a TD3-based framework for intelligent edge server selection and collaborative load management in 5G-enabled industrial and Cooperative Intelligent Transportation System (C-ITS) environments. It tackles dynamic Edge Application Server (EAS) selection and overload handling in heterogeneous systems where latency-critical and high-throughput tasks coexist. The framework uses TD3 to assign tasks to optimal servers, balancing latency, bandwidth, and computation while distributing load across edge servers. Results demonstrate improved service delivery, resource efficiency, and QoS across diverse 5G applications.

Thakur et al. (2023). Explores how deep learning (DL) enhances IoT systems by

Table 1. Literature review on deep RL in 5G/6G IoT communication networks. A √ indicates that the paper addresses 5G networks, while a × signifies coverage of 6G networks

Survey Paper(s)	Networks		Reinforcement learning (RL)				
	5G/6G	IoT	DQN	TD3	DQL	PPO	DNN
Javadpour et al. (2023); Lee & Qin (2019); Qian et al. (2019); Ssengonzi et al. (2022); Zhang et al. (2021)	√						
Kaur et al. (2021)	×						
Sánchez et al. (2022)	√×						
Afrin (2024); Alzhrani (2024); Chavan et al. (2024); Chow-dhury et al. (2019); Lafta (2024); Sharma et al. (2021); Zamzami (2023)	√	√					
Gkagkas et al. (2024)	√ ×	√					
Yang et al. (2021)	√	√	√				
Gupta et al. (2023)	√		√		√		
Wang et al. (2021)	√		√	√	√		
Tham et al. (2019)	√						√
El Boudani et al. (2020); Varga et al. (2020); Yadav et al. (2022); Zavyalova & Drozdova (2020)	√	√					√
Sreedevi (2019)	√	√			√		
Abba Ari et al. (2025)	√ ×	√	√		√	√	√
Nieto et al. (2024)	√						√
Pinto Neto (2023)	√	√	√		√	√	√
Saeed et al. (2020)	√	√	√				√

(continued)

enabling efficient data processing, predictive analytics, and adaptive learning in smart devices. It covers IoT components, frameworks, connectivity protocols, and deep learning techniques, while addressing challenges like data privacy, computational limits, and scalability. The work provides a valuable foundation for understanding the synergy between DL and IoT, serving as a useful reference for researchers in data- driven IoT applications.

Table 1. (*continued*)

Survey Paper(s)	Networks		Reinforcement learning (RL)				
	5G/6G	IoT	DQN	TD3	DQL	PPO	DNN
Iqbal et al. (2023)	√×	√	√	√	√		√
Han et al. (2023)	√×			√			√
Saad et al. (2025)	√	√		√			√
Thakur et al. (2023)		√					√

4 Challenges and Future Directions in DRL

4.1 Open Challenges

Despite significant advancements in the application of DRL within 5G networks, several challenges including scalability, necessity for real-time decision-making, and integration of DRL with existing network infrastructures persist. Tackling these challenges is essential for the widespread adoption and success of DRL in network management.

Training Complexity. Training DRL models can be resource-intensive and may require significant computational power. Developing efficient training techniques and optimization algorithms is essential for applying DRL at scale (Foukas et al., 2017; Gawłowicz & Zubow, 2018).

Real-Time Decision-Making. For DRL to be effective in real-time network management, it must provide quick and reliable decision-making capabilities. Ensuring that DRL algorithms can function within the constraints of dynamic environments, poses a significant challenge (Alliance NGMN, 2016; ITU, 2018).

Integration with Existing Systems. Incorporating DRL solutions into current network management systems can be complex. Creating hybrid methods that combine DRL with traditional approaches may help bridge this gap (ONF, 2016; Santos et al., 2018).

4.2 Future Research Directions

Future research should prioritize the development of more efficient DRL algorithms and explore the integration of DRL with other machine learning techniques. Additionally, investigating new application domains, such as smart cities and autonomous vehicles, can broaden the impact of DRL. Advancing these areas will enhance the effectiveness and applicability of DRL in 5G networks, paving the way for innovative solutions.

Acknowledgments. This study was funded by the NSF (Award# 2318636). The opinions expressed are those of the authors and do not represent the views of the NSF.

Disclosure of Interests. The authors have no competing interests to declare that are relevant to the content of this article.

References

ONF: Applying SDN Architecture to 5G Slicing. Tech. Rep. TR, (2016).

Ordonez-Lucena, J., et al.: Network slicing for 5G with SDN/NFV: concepts, architectures, and challenges. IEEE Commun. Mag. **55**(5), 80–87 (2017)

Sivaganesan, D.: Design and development of AI-enabled edge computing for intelligent IoT applications. J. Trends Comput. Sci. Smart Technol. (TCSST) **1**(2), 84–94 (2019)

Toosi, A. N., et al.: Management and Orchestration of Network Slices in 5G, Fog, Edge, and Clouds. In: Fog Edge Computing: Principles and Paradigms, pp. 79–99 (2019)

Troia, S., et al.: On deep reinforcement learning for traffic engineering in SD-WAN. IEEE J Sel Areas Commun. **39**(7), 2198–2212 (2020)

Chinchali, S., et al.: Cellular Network Traffic Scheduling with Deep Reinforcement Learning. In: Proceedings of the Thirty-Second AAAI Conference on Artificial Intelligence (2018)

Alliance NGMN: Description of Network Slicing Concept. NGMN 5G P, (2016)

Gawłowicz, P., Zubow, A.: ns3-gym: Extending OpenAI Gym for Networking Research (2018). arXiv preprint https://arxiv.org/abs/1810.03943

Santos, J., et al.: Fog computing: enabling the management and orchestration of Smart City Applications in 5G networks. Entropy. **20**(1), 4 (2018)

Wang, M., et al.: Transfer learning promotes 6G wireless communications: recent advances and future challenges. IEEE Trans. Reliab. (2021)

Hurtado Sánchez, J. A.: Deep Reinforcement Learning for Resource Management in Network Slicing (2022)

Shafi, M., et al.: 5G: a tutorial overview of standards, trials, challenges, deployment, and practice. IEEE J Sel Areas Commun. **35**(6), 1201–1221 (2017)

Foukas, X., Patounas, G., Elmokashfi, A., Marina, M.K.: Network slicing in 5G: survey and Challenges. IEEE Commun. Mag. **55**(5), 94–100 (2017)

Andrews, J.G., et al.: What will 5G be? IEEE J Sel Areas Commun. **32**(6), 1065–1082 (2014)

Kaloxylos, A., et al.: E-Health Network Slicing in 5G: Innovations and Challenges (2018)

Sutton, R. S., Barto, A. G.: Reinforcement Learning: An Introduction, MIT Press, (2018)

Ding, S., et al.: Challenges in Modern Network Management. Int. J. Netw. Manag. (2018)

Park, J., et al.: Resource Management in Next-Generation Wireless Networks. IEEE Wirel. Commun. (2017)

Sharma, P., Jain, S., Gupta, S., Chamola, V.: Role of machine learning and deep learning in securing 5G-driven industrial IoT applications. Ad Hoc Netw. **123** (2021)

Zamzami, I.F.: Deep learning models applied to prediction of 5G technology adoption. Appl. Sci. **13**(1), 119 (2023)

Alzhrani, H.: Enhancing IoT security in 5G networks: mitigating DDoS attacks with deep learning. Arab J. Forensic Sci. Forensic Med. **7**(2), 155–166 (2024). https://doi.org/10.26735/MVMP8068

Lafta, A. J., Mahmood, A. F., Saeed, B. M.: 5G and internet of things: next-gen network architecture. J. Eng. Res. Accepted 28 Jul 2024

Karam, G.M., Gruber, M., Adam, I., Boutigny, F., Miche, Y., Mukherjee, S.: The evolution of networks and management in a 6G world: an inventor's view. IEEE Trans. Netw. Serv. Manag. **19**(4), 5395–5407 (2022). https://doi.org/10.1109/TNSM.2022.3188200

Sreedevi, A.G.: Reinforcement learning algorithm for 5G indoor device-to-device communications. Trans. Emerg. Telecommun. Technol. **30**(4) (2019). https://doi.org/10.1002/ett.3670

Abba Ari, A.A., Samafou, F., Ndam Njoya, A., Djedouboum, A.C., Aboubakar, M., Mohamadou, A.: IoT-5G and B5G/6G resource allocation and network slicing orchestration using learning algorithms. IET Networks, e70002 (2025). https://doi.org/10.1049/ntw2.70002

Nieto, G., de la Iglesia, I., Lopez-Novoa, U., Perfecto, C.: Deep reinforcement learning techniques for dynamic task offloading in the 5G edge-cloud continuum. J. Cloud Comput. **13**(94) (2024). https://doi.org/10.1186/s13677-024-00658-0

Pinto Neto, E.C., Sadeghi, S., Zhang, X., Dadkhah, S.: Federated reinforcement learning in IoT: applications, opportunities and open challenges. Appl. Sci. **13**(11), 6497 (2023). https://doi.org/10.3390/app13116497

Qian, Y., Wu, J., Wang, R., Zhu, F., Zhang, W.: Survey on reinforcement learning applications in communication networks. IEEE Xplore, PTP J. Magazine. (2019). https://doi.org/10.1109/MNET.2019.1800221

Chowdhury, M.Z., Hossan, M.T., Jang, Y.M.: Applying model-free reinforcement learning algorithm in network slicing for 5G. In: 2019 1st International Conference on Advances in Science, Engineering and Robotics Technology (ICASERT), pp. 1–4. IEEE (2019)

Zavyalova, D., Drozdova, V.: 5G scheduling using reinforcement learning. In: 2020 International Multi-Conference on Industrial Engineering and Modern Technologies (FarEastCon), pp. 1–5. Vladivostok, Russia (2020). https://doi.org/10.1109/FarEastCon49939.2020.9271421

Kaur, J., Khan, M.A., Iftikhar, M., Imran, M., Emad Ul Haq, Q.: Machine learning techniques for 5G and beyond. IEEE Access. **9**, 23472–23488 (2021). https://doi.org/10.1109/ACCESS.2021.3051557

Tham, M.-L., Iqbal, A., Chang, Y. C.: Deep Reinforcement Learning for Resource Allocation in 5G Communications. In: 2019 Asia-Pacific Signal and Information Processing Association Annual Summit and Conference (APSIPA ASC), Lanzhou, China, pp. 1852–1855 (2019). https://doi.org/10.1109/APSIPAASC47483.2019.9023112.

Javadpour, A., Ja'fari, F., Taleb, T., Benzaïd, C.: Enhancing 5G Network Slicing: Slice Isolation Via Actor-Critic Reinforcement Learning with Optimal Graph Features. In: GLOBECOM 2023–2023 IEEE Global Communications Conference, Kuala Lumpur, Malaysia, pp. 31–37 (2023). https://doi.org/10.1109/GLOBECOM54140.2023.10437687.

Varga, P., et al.: 5G support for industrial IoT applications—challenges, solutions, and research gaps. Sensors. **20**(3), 828 (2020). https://doi.org/10.3390/s20030828

Gkagkas, G., Vergados, D.J., Michalas, A., Dossis, M.: The advantage of the 5G network for enhancing the internet of things and the evolution of the 6G network. Sensors. **24**(6), 2612 (2024). https://doi.org/10.3390/s24062612

El Boudani, B., et al.: Implementing deep learning techniques in 5G IoT networks for 3D indoor positioning: DELTA (DeEp learning-based co-operaTive architecture). Sensors. **20**(19), 5568 (2020). https://doi.org/10.3390/s20195568

Yadav, N., Pande, S., Khamparia, A., Gupta, D.: Intrusion detection system on IoT with 5G network using deep learning. Wirel. Commun. Mob. Comput., 9304689 (2022). https://doi.org/10.1155/2022/9304689

Iqbal, M.J., Farhan, M., Ullah, F., Srivastava, G., Jabbar, S.: Intelligent multimedia content delivery in 5G/6G networks: a reinforcement learning approach. Trans. Emerg. Telecommun. Technol., e4842 (2023). https://doi.org/10.1002/ett.4842

Han, X., Li, Z., Xie, Z.: Two-step random access optimization for 5G-and-beyond LEO satel- lite communication system: a TD3-based MsgA channel allocation strategy. IEEE Commun. Lett. **27**(6), 1514–1518 (2023). https://doi.org/10.1109/LCOMM.2023.3270465

Saad, M., Jamshed, M.A., Adedamola, A.I., Nauman, A.: Twin delayed DDPG (TD3)-based edge server selection for 5G-enabled industrial and C-ITS applications. IEEE Open J. Commun. Soc. **99**, 1–1 (2025). https://doi.org/10.1109/OJCOMS.2025.3545566

Chavan, S. S., Ingole, P. P., More, Y. K., Kajale, S. G., Musale, J., Gaikwad,R.: The impact of 5G networks on IoT devices. In: Proceedings of the 3rd International Conference on Optimization Techniques in the Field of Engineering (ICOFE-2024), (2024). https://doi.org/10.2139/ssrn.4316289.

Thakur, D., Saini, J.K., Srinivasan, S.: DeepThink IoT: the strength of deep learning in internet of things. Artif. Intell. Rev. **56**, 14663–14730 (2023). https://doi.org/10.1007/s10462-023-10444-6

Express Dialer 2

Dwight Deugo(✉)

The School of Computer Science, Carleton University, Ottawa, ON, Canada
dwightdeugo@cunet.carleton.ca

Abstract. As we age, our cognitive abilities can both improve and decline. Declines can include the abilities of reasoning, attention span, memory and processing speed, each having different impacts on how we are able to complete tasks. Older mobile devices users often find these declines make it difficult to use their devices. Given a major use of mobile devices is the ability to call other people, the goal of this work is to simplify the mobile dialing application and hardware to enable an aging population to make a call quickly and easily.

Keywords: Express Dialer · Android · iOS · Complexity Metric · Aging

1 Introduction

Our cognitive abilities change as part of the aging process. Some abilities improve and others decline. These changes to our abilities as we age have been well documented [7, 13]. While our vocabulary may improve, other abilities like reasoning, attention, memory and processing speed decline. Depending on the combination and severity of our declines, they can lead to significant changes in how well we are able to complete our daily tasks.

The combination of declining abilities can impact how older individuals are able to interact and use their applications on their mobile devices. Applications that have time-outs can be difficult for this group of users, especially when the declining abilities include memory recall. For example, users can be asked to quickly remember and provide user ids and passwords, which can prove to be difficult as there are no specific cues to work from. In general, older individuals experience a decline in the spontaneous retrieval of information. This lack of retrieval can also impair one's ability to perform other required tasks and actions, as the precise sequence of steps may not be remembered. One's memory can also be impacted with aging with the inability to store new information. The result is that we may not be able to remember ids, passwords, or process steps because we can't store them away. How many times have you heard someone use a pen and paper to write things down as their secondary storage and retrieval mechanism? Memory issues for mobile device users result in not being able to enter the correct information or not being able to navigate to the correct screen to perform a task.

In addition to one's cognitive abilities, one's motor abilities are also impacted by the process of aging [12]. Studies have shown increases in uncontrolled movement on a variety of tasks, such as tremors [14]. In addition to uncontrolled movements, the

H. R. Arabnia et al. (Eds.): CSCE 2025, CCIS 2934, pp. 68–80, 2026.
https://doi.org/10.1007/978-3-032-22190-2_5

movements can be less smooth and temporal and special deficits can also be present [12]. indicates, "Motor performance impairments with aging are likely due in part to changes in peripheral structures such as sensory receptors, muscles, peripheral nerves, joints, etc., as well as central nervous system changes". Declining motor abilities in mobile device users result in difficulties with hand-eye coordination when users are asked to work with small widgets, font sizes and dark screens.

A major use of mobile devices is the ability to call other people. We call those in our contacts lists and we call on demand. Calling applications are available on all mobile device platforms making calling a simple task for many. Go to one's contact list, select a contact, select one of the potentially many numbers for the desired person and then click call. It all sounds easy. However, the contact information had to be entered previously. It had to be located by the user and multiple screens had to be navigated to find the number. This is not easy for an older user. Declines in reasoning, attention span, memory and processing make the task much more difficult.

The goal of this and our previous work [15] was to create a simplified dialing application for the aging population and be able to objectively measure its complexity and compare it with the complexity of the standard Android and iOS dialing applications.

To meet the goal, we set the following objectives for our work:

1. Build a dialing application that considers the declines seen in an aging population. Knowing from the onset that memory is one of the declining attributes. We will use a "What you see is what you get" as guiding principle for the application.
2. Use an objective metric to measure the complexity of a mobile application.

In the following section, we discuss prior research and work done on a simple mobile dialing applications and complexity issues for an aging population. Section 3 covers the design of our updated Express Dialer 2 application, including a discussion on why we made our decisions for the design. In Sect. 4, we present our conclusions drawn from the work.

2 Background

2.1 Mobile Applications

Several dialing apps claim to be simple. On such application is the Simple Dialer [1]. This app has large keys that can be customized to any color and size. The app's description claims that the app is "Perfect for people with bad eyesight or elderly people!'. However, this statement is a bit of a contraction. Application customization is something that is not done often, and the process is easily forgotten. The implication is that the mere ability to customize, especially if there are other views with more widgets that themselves do not change in size or color, can be problematic. The app also allows for the manipulation and selection of contacts, but these are done on separate screens. For the elderly, the required memory of these operations can be problematic.

Another app is the Dialer Widget [2]. This app provides three main views: a dialling pad, a list of contacts and a call log. A configuration view is also available to enable one to configure colors, date format, text size, icon sizes and other configuration parameters.

One nice feature of the app is that it operates as a resizable widget that can be added to your lockscreen.

A third app is the Telephone - Right Dialer [3]. This app provides numerous customization options letting you personalize your interface with different colors and themes.

2.2 Complexity Analysis

Developing user interfaces (UIs) that are intuitive to use and enhance a user's experience is difficult. In work done by [6], several general principles are proposed that the authors' claim are "fundamental to the design and implementation of effective interfaces". While their work focuses on web interfaces the principles carry over to other interfaces, such as those for mobile applications. The first principle indicates a UI should have a visual composition that is attractive to the eye. The second principle is the UI "must be clear in visual appearance, concept, and wording". A third is compatibility, where the UI should be compatible with the user, tasks and job, and the product. Another is comprehensibility, where the operation on the objects in the UI to complete the task (s) should be obvious. The UI should also be configurable and consistent. Customization leads to user satisfaction and consistency is important to minimize the amount of learning that a user must do as understanding in one situation can transfer to another. User control and directness are important to help one take charge and perform tasks directly rather than having negative feelings towards a machine controlling activities. Efficiency of hand and eye movement, familiarity, flexibility, forgiveness, predictability and responsiveness are principles that most designers already take for granted. Of interest to the work here are the principles of recovery, simplicity, groupings and focus. Their notion of simplicity comes from [9]. Helping users by grouping screen elements to form meaningful structure, while maintaining focus and allowing users to recover from mistakes is always important, but even more important to my work is when you consider the cognitive abilities of older adults using mobile apps.

The work of [5] compiled several recommendations regarding navigation, interaction and visual design aspects of mobile UIs targeted at older adults. For navigation, they advised against using hidden screens and controls and stated using a home screen menu as a point of return. For interactions, they recommended always providing a back button, using scrolling when needed, minimizing the use of the keyboard, and using words in the UI the correspond to the vocabulary of older adults. For the visual design side, the found providing generous space between UI items advisable, using Icons with text labels, and being cautious about locating interactive elements towards the edge of the screen.

Guidelines and recommendations towards designing UIs for older adults have existed for years, [8, 11]. More recent work [4, 10] has discussed how "one of the main reasons why older adults experience problems with mobile phone use is that there is a discrepancy between the design of devices and users' needs". The question that remains is, how to measure simplicity based on needs?

2.3 Original Express Dialer Approach

With the principles mentioned previously in mind, we developed a mobile dialing application named Express Dialer. Figure 1 shows the main and only screen for the application. The screen includes the typical twelve buttons of any dialing application, for the numbers 0 to 9 and * and #. Once a user pushes a button, the corresponding number is shown in the dialing area. If there are numbers shown in the dialing area, the delete button is enabled for the user to delete the last number entered. When pressed, the call button initiates a call with the current phone number entered. The four buttons at the bottom of the screen are for storing and fast dialing of saved numbers. When the application first starts, any of the four buttons is configured by holding the button until a dialog, like the one shown in Fig. 4, is presented. Once the names and numbers are entered, the user clicks "OK" to save them, or has the option to cancel the dialog with no updating. After selecting "OK", the name and number are shown on the button. To perform fast dialing, a user simply clicks the button to put the number in the dialing area and start the calling process. The calling process uses the standard calling screen, as in the Pixel's Android dialer, for the corresponding device. After a call disconnects from either person ending the call, the user is presented with the previous screen.

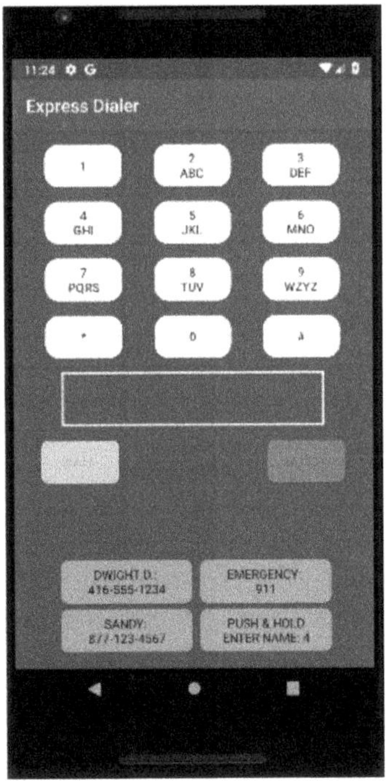

Fig. 1. Original Express Dialer Main Screen

Express Dialer's single screen dialing application, attempts to simplify the calling process for a user. Compared to both the standard Android and iOS calling applications the application had fewer screens, menus and opportunities for the user to click on a widget and start a new function or transition to a new screen and/or task. This is an important distinction. Elderly mobile users just want to make a call. That is the single most important task they use a dialling application for. Fewer screens imply fewer functions and tasks available to complete. In addition, fewer screens imply fewer widgets, decreasing the number of possible wrong clicks that can lead to unwanted or unknown transitions.

Fewer transitions make it easier for those with memory issues to understand where they are in an application and relieves them of remembering how to navigate back to the location where they can complete their intended task, e.g. calling someone. Fewer screens, fewer widgets, fewer tasks, fewer functions, fewer menus all contributed to making it easier for those users that are cognitively disadvantages complete their desired task without getting sidetracked into a different part of an application. How many times have you yourself transition to an area of an application where you don't know how the transition was made and why? Often it is simply a slip of the finger clicking something you didn't mean to select. For those with shaky hands, this situation is exaggerated by one's inability to select the desired button or field.

We showed that the complexity of using Express Dialer was better than the that of the standard Android or iPhone applications. The question now is, can we do better?

3 Express Dialer 2

With the principles and objectives considered in the original Express Dialer in mind, we developed a second version of the dialing application. Figure 2 shows our modification to the main and one of only two screens of the application. The two areas modified of notice are shown in Fig. 2. One is where it says, "No Pads", The other modification is an extra number or the word "PAD?" in one of the four dialing buttons. The dialing buttons are configured as before, by doing a long touch on them to raise the configuration screen shown in Fig. 4. Enter the name and phone number in this screen, hit okay and the button is now ready to use. Click any button and you enter into a call as in the previous application.

As before our goal was to simplify the calling process for a user. The configuration step was and is still required, but after that we believed we could simplify the call initiation even further by having the end user not even use the phone application, but how? The answer was to consider our application as a MIDI phone application. MIDI [16] stands for Musical Instrument Digital Interface and is a standard that permits musical instruments and devices to communicate with one other using messages. MIDI messages do not transmit sounds. They transmit notes, timings system and pitch information, which receiving devices use to typical play music. However, our approach was to have our application receive MIDI messages and make phone calls based on those messages.

Our MIDI implementation uses Android's android.media.midi package [17]. This package provides classes for sending and receiving messages MIDI messages over USB, Bluetooth LE, and virtual (inter-app) transports. Among its many functions, the packages allow us to connect MIDI controllers and MIDI keyboards to our application to help drive its function. The MIDI packages help us to enumerate connect devices that includes the

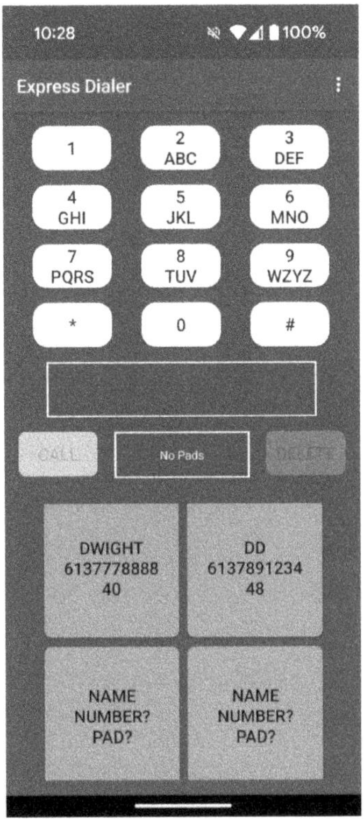

Fig. 2. Express Dialer 2 Main Screen

name, vendor and other capabilities. In particular, we make use of the following MIDI classes:

- import android.media.midi.MidiManager;
- import android.media.midi.MidiDevice;
- import android.media.midi.MidiDeviceInfo;
- import android.media.midi.MidiReceiver;

The MidiManager class is the public application interface to the Android MIDI service. We access an instance of the MidiManager by executing the following:

```
MidiManager midiManager =
    (MidiManager)getSystemService(Context.MIDI_SERVICE);
```

Once we have a MidiManager, we can gain access to the information about the connected MIDI devices by executing the following code. In Fig. 3, we have placed the manufacture string, "AKAI PROFESSIONAL, LP", in the text box were it had, "No Pads" before when no MIDI device. was connected.

```
Set<MidiDeviceInfo> information =
      midiManager.getDevicesForTransport(
      MidiManager.TRANSPORT_MIDI_BYTE_STREAM);
Iterator<MidiDeviceInfo> iterator = information.iterator();
```

Once having access to an iterator of MidiDeviceInfo information, we can access the specific device information, such as the manufacture by executing the following:

```
String result;
MidiDeviceInfo midiDeviceInfo;
android.os.Bundle.properties properties;

while(iterator.hasNext()) {
   midiDeviceInfo = (MidiDeviceInfo)iterator.next();
   result = midiDeviceInfo.toString();
   properties = midiDeviceInfo.getProperties();
   manufacturer = properties.getString(
      MidiDeviceInfo.PROPERTY_MANUFACTURER);
}
```

Having found the MIDI device we desire, we open the device by executing the following:

```
// this being the MainActivity
MyReceiver myReceiver = new MyReceiver(this);
midiManager.openDevice(midiDeviceInfo,
      new MidiManager.OnDeviceOpenedListener() {
      @Override
      public void onDeviceOpened(MidiDevice device) {

            if (device == null) {
               showToast("Device Null");
            }
            else {
               showToast("Device Open");
               MidiDeviceInfo.PortInfo[] portInfos =
                        device.getInfo().getPorts();
               String portName = portInfos[0].getName();
               if (portInfos[0].getType() ==
                  MidiDeviceInfo.PortInfo.TYPE_INPUT) {
                   showToast("Info on Port 0");
               }
               outputPort = device.openOutputPort(0);
               outputPort.connect(myReceiver);
            }
      }}, new Handler(Looper.getMainLooper()));
```

Using MIDI in an Android application assumes the features have been enabled in the AndroidManifest.xlm file by adding the following line:

```
<uses-feature android:name="android.software.midi" android:required="true"/>
```

This feature's presence can be test by executing the following in the MainActivity class:

```
import android.content.pm.PackageManager;

if (getApplicationContext().getPackageManager().hasSystemFeature(
        PackageManager.FEATURE_MIDI)) {
    ....
}
```

The final required class to receive the MIDI messages is the MyReceiver class used above when the device was opened. It extends the MidiReceiver class and enables us to receive and process messages. Here is the skeleton of the class:

```
import android.media.midi.MidiReceiver;
import com.example.midiphone.MainActivity;
import java.io.IOException;
import android.os.Handler;
import android.os.Looper;

public class MyReceiver extends MidiReceiver {
     MainActivity topLevelWindow;

public  MyReceiver(MainActivity topLevelWindow) {
     this();
     this.topLevelWindow = topLevelWindow;
}

public  MyReceiver(){
     super();
}

public synchronized void onSend(byte[] data, int offset,
          int count, long timestamp) throws IOException {

     new Handler(Looper.getMainLooper()).post(new Runnable() {
     @Override
     public  synchronized  void run() {
     ...
     // data, offset, count, and timestamp contain the midi message.
     }
}
```

The final piece to the puzzle is how to close the MIDI device. This action is simply a matter of executing the following:

```
outputPort.close();
```

We gained access to this port when we opened the device. It is a matter to either storing a reference to the port or the device to get access to the port when the opening is done. We wrapped the opening and closing functionality into two methods: connectToMidi()

and closeMidi(). These methods were run in our onResume() and onPause() methods respectively.

Looking at the onSend(…) method above, we access the contents of the MIDI message by executing the following:

```
if ((data[offset] & 0xF0) == 144)
```

In this case we are checking to see if the message is a Note On message on MIDI channel 0, indicating a key or pad has been pushed on the MIDI device. MIDI messages have many forms of messages [18] on 16 different channels. Here is a simplification of the list:

Message	Status(hex)	Data 1	Data 2
Note Off	8n	Note Number	Velocity
Note On	9n	Note Number	Velocity
Polyphonic Aftertouch	An	Note Number	Pressure
Control Change	Bn	Controller Number	Data
Program Change	Cn	Program Number	Unused
Channel Aftertouch	Dn	Pressure	Unused
Pitch Wheel	En	LSB	MSB

Term	Meaning
n	MIDI Channel Number (0-F)
LSB	Least Significant Byte
MSB	Most Significant Byte

In [15], we considered the question of what were the differences in complexity between our application and the standard Android and iOS call applications? Given our proposed complexity measure and assumptions, we produced the following measurements for the different approaches:

1. Express Dialer: 35
2. Android Dialer: 94
3. iOS Dialer: 83

Our new version of Express Dialer has a similar complexity measure than the previous version. The difference being that when one enters a number for one of the dialing pads, as shown in Fig. 4, one has the option to also input a Pad Number. This number is the MIDI note-on number (in decimal) from the connected device, through the mobile device's USB connector, that will trigger the dialing of the corresponding number when it is pushed. Figures 5, 6, and 7 show different devices we have used to trigger MIDI note-on messages. The first device is the AKAI LPD 8. This MIDI pad controller features 8 velocity-sensitive RGB pads for connecting to any general MIDI-based application using

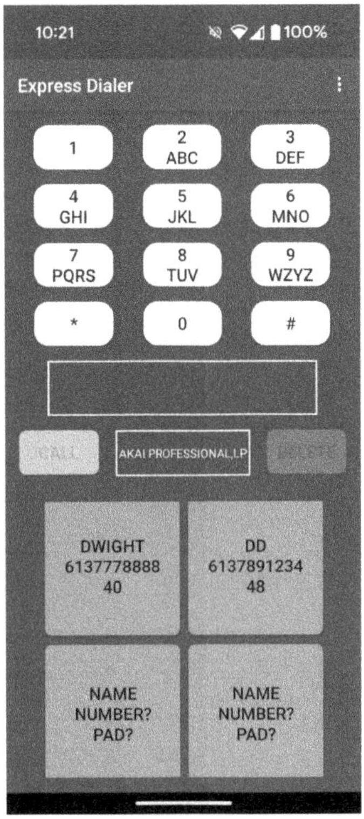

Fig. 3. Making a call through MIDI

a USB-C connector. The second device is the M-Audio Oxygen 25. This USB MIDI controller has eight assignable knobs, transport and track select buttons and Velocity-sensitive keys. The third device, shown in Fig. 7, is the Novation Launchpad Pro MK3. This MIDI grid controller has 64 large, RGB velocity and pressure-sensitive pads. What all devices have in common is the pressing of a pad or key will generate a MIDI note-on message. Once our Express Dialer receives theses message and dials the associate number.

Some devices, such as the Novation Launchpad Pro MK3, generate MIDI Sync messages, particularly MIDI Clock messages, that are used to support the synchronizing of multiple MIDI devices. When connected to these types of devices, the application must ignore these messages otherwise it will not be able to process the note-on messages fast enough.

Fig. 4. Creating a contact entry

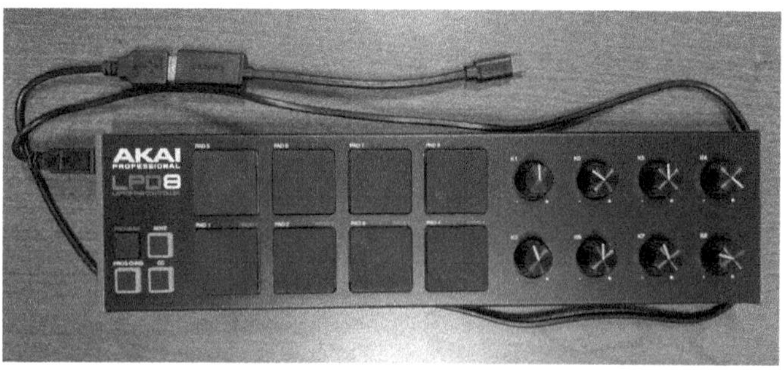

Fig. 5. AKAI LPD 8

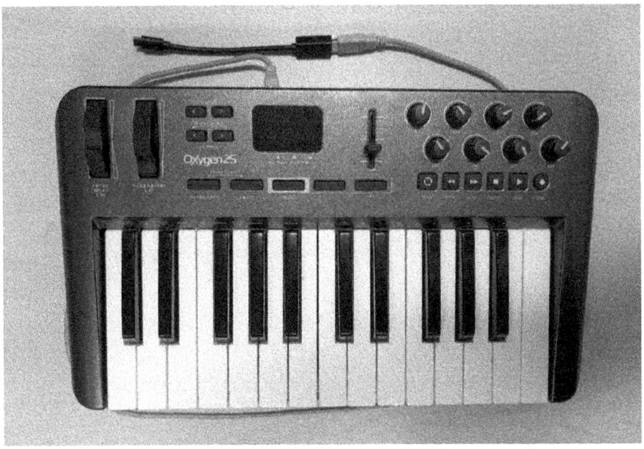

Fig. 6. M-Audio Oxygen 25

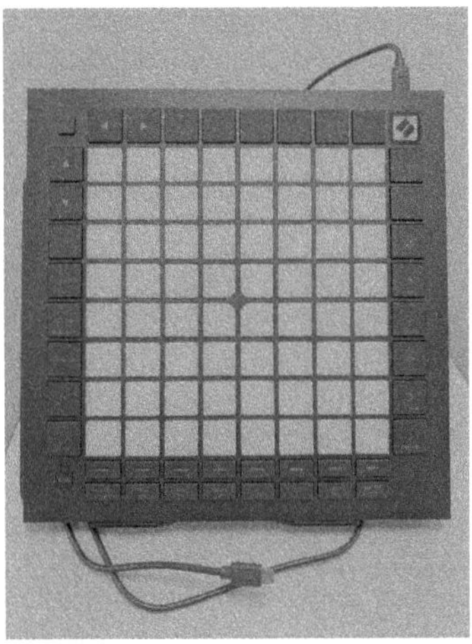

Fig. 7. Novation Launchpad Pro MK3

4 Conclusion

The goal this work was to create a simplified dialing application for an ageing population. To meet this goal, we enhanced the Express Dialer application to make use of MIDI controllers for call activation. Compared to our previous application, the contact entry screen, shown in Fig. 4, contains one more field to enable a contact number to be associated with a MIDI pad/note number. After making this association, other than starting the application on the calling device, all users need to do to make a call is hit the corresponding pad on the associated MIDI device. There are no screens or buttons to navigate through making it a complexity measure of 1 operation. Our belief is that the application's number and pad configuration portion can be done once in advance by a more tech savvy induvial.

The result is that users have no screens to navigate through and no small buttons to push when making a call. What they do have is larger tactile devices with corresponding buttons making the overall task of making a call both physical and mentally easier.

Our future work will continue to look for methods, techniques and devices to simplify the call process of mobile devices.

References

1. Google Play App Store.: https://play.google.com/store/apps/details?id=com.simplemobiletools.dialer&hl=en_CA. Accessed 12 Oct 2025
2. Google Play App Store.: https://play.google.com/store/apps/details?id=com.kuma.dialerwidget&hl=en_CA. Accessed 12 Oct 2025
3. Google Play App Store.: https://play.google.com/store/apps/details?id=com.goodwy.dialer&hl=en_CA. Accessed 12 Oct 2025
4. Petrovčič, A., Taipale, S., Rogelj, A., Dolničar, V.: Design of Mobile phones for older adults: an empirical analysis of design guidelines and checklists for feature phones and smartphones. Int. J. Hum.–Comput. Interact. **34**(3), 251–264 (2018)
5. de Barros, A.C., Leitao, R., Ribeiro, J.: Design and evaluation of a mobile user interface for older adults: navigation, interaction and visual design recommendations. Procedia Comput. Sci. **27**, 369–378 (2014)
6. Bhaskar, U., et al.: General principles of user Interface design and websites. Int. J. Softw. Eng. (IJSE) **2**(3), 45–60 (2011)
7. Wisdom, N.M., Mignogna, J., Collins, R.L.: Variability in Wechsler adult intelligence scale-IV subtest performance across age. Arch. Clin. Neuropsychol. **27**(4), 389–397 (2012)
8. Fisk, A.D., Rogers, W.A., Charness, N., Czaja, S.J., Sharit, J.: Designing for Older Adults: Principles and Creative Human Factors Approaches. CRC Press, Boca Raton (2009)
9. Galitz, W.O.: The Essential Guide to User Interface Design Second Edition. Wiley India Edition (2002)
10. Hwangbo, H., Yoon, S.H., Jin, B.S., Han, Y.S., Ji, Y.G.: A study of pointing performance of elderly users on smartphones. Int. J. Hum.-Comput. Interact. **29**(9), 604–618 (2013)
11. Pak, R., McLaughlin, A.: Designing displays for older adults. CRC Press, Boca Raton (2011)
12. Seidler, R.D., et al.: Motor control and aging: links to age-related brain structural, functional, and biochemical effects. Neurosci. Biobehav. Rev. **34**(5), 721–733 (2010). https://doi.org/10.1016/j.neubiorev
13. Selective review of cognitive aging. Salthouse TA, J Int Neuropsychol Soc. 16(5), 754–760, (2010)
14. Lacritz, L.H., Dewey Jr., R., Giller, C., Cullum, C.M.: Cognitive functioning in individuals with "benign" essential tremor. J. Int. Neuropsychol. Soc. **8**, 125–129 (2002)
15. Deugo, D.: Express Dialer. InL: The 2019 International Conference on Internet Computing and Internet of Things (ICOMP'19), 38–44, (2019)
16. MIDI 1.0: (2025). https://midi.org/midi-1-0. Accessed 12 Oct 2025
17. android.media.midi: https://developer.android.com/reference/android/media/midi/package-summary. Accessed 12 Oct 2025
18. Expanded MIDI 1.0 Messages List: https://midi.org/expanded-midi-1-0-messages-list. Accessed 12 Oct 2025

Societal Impact of Technology on Wellbeing and Cohesion

Rotimi-Williams Bello(✉), Pius A. Owolawi, Etienne A. van Wyk, and Chunling Tu

Department of Computer Systems Engineering, Faculty of Information and Communication Technology, Tshwane University of Technology, Pretoria 0152, South Africa
{bellorw,owolawipa,vanwykea,duc}@tut.ac.za

Abstract. Several challenges such as cyberbullying, digital divides, and erosion of traditional community structures are introduced by digital advancements in the enhancement of information connectivity and accessibility. The multifaceted effects of technological advancement on societal wellbeing and cohesion were explored in this paper. Likewise, both the positive and negative impacts of technological advancement on individual wellbeing and social dynamics were examined in the paper by drawing on specific insights and global studies from Africa. Moreover, this paper is prepared and intended as a foundational summary of the societal impact of technology on wellbeing and cohesion.

Keywords: Cohesion · Cyberbullying · Digital divides · Societal impact · Technology · Wellbeing

1 Introduction

The interaction, information accessibility, and community perception of individuals have been transformed by rapid technological integration into daily life [1]. However, unintended implications have been introduced by these significant benefits and changes, affecting individual wellbeing and social cohesion [2]. The multifaceted effects of technological advancements on societal wellbeing and cohesion have been addressed in several publications [3]. The identification of key opportunities and challenges that technological transformation and digital advancements offer within Africa and the potential risks involved have been presented in several conferences [4]. Also, some researchers have discussed important issues related to development and governance of technology, including digital sovereignty and participation, privacy concerns, ethical AI practices, democratic processes, development of equitable systems, and economic impact of digital platforms tailored to an African context [5]. Strategies have been analyzed and developed to help in shaping technology and digital policy and foster research and innovation in Africa, with emphasis and focus on how diversity, inclusion and ethical governance can be promoted [6]. Therefore, this paper is prepared and intended as a foundational summary of the societal impact of technology on wellbeing and cohesion.

H. R. Arabnia et al. (Eds.): CSCE 2025, CCIS 2934, pp. 81–87, 2026.
https://doi.org/10.1007/978-3-032-22190-2_6

2 Technology and Its Positive Impacts

2.1 Enhancement of Wellbeing by Connectivity

A global study and research led by Oxford University discovered that the use of the internet is usually associated with higher wellbeing. Analyzing the data collected from about 2.4 million participants across one hundred and sixty-eight countries, the study showed that the accessibility of internet has positive correlation with various aspects of wellbeing, such as social life and life satisfaction, for 84.9% of the associations [7]. Further study and research indicate that digital technologies like video calls and online communities can reduce feelings of social isolation and loneliness, particularly among older adults. The social ties maintenance is facilitated by these technologies, which are essential for mental health and overall wellbeing.

2.1.1 The Role of Connectivity in Wellbeing Enhancement

(a) Mental health and emotional support: by using digital platforms, individuals can relate to others to seek support and share experiences, through which feelings of loneliness and depression can be alleviated. Spaces for emotional expression and validation are provided by social networks and online communities, contributing to improved mental health outcomes, (b) access to information and resources: through connectivity, access to a wealth of information related to social services, health, and education is made possible for individuals. People are empowered by this access for informed decision making, assistance seeking when needed, and lifelong learning engagement, all of which contribute to overall wellbeing, (c) community engagement and social cohesion: community building is facilitated by digital connectivity in that it allows the participation of individuals in virtual forum, events, and discussions. A sense of belonging and collective identity is fostered by this engagement, strengthening cohesion and social bonds within communities [8].

2.2 Social Cohesion Facilitation

In South Africa and some other regions of Africa, social media has greatly contributed and played positive roles in bridging ethnic, racial, and geographical divides, most especially during the lockdown period. Different platforms have become necessary tools for uninterrupted and daily communication, fostering and promoting unity among diverse people and populations [9]. Social cohesion facilitation is crucial for developing communities that are resilient, inclusive, and harmonious. The two effective strategies for promoting social cohesion are discussed in the next sub-sections.

2.2.1 Promoting Shared Values and Inclusive Dialogue

(a) The establishment of common values and the encouragement of open communication are the basis on which social cohesion is grounded. There are several key approaches, including (i) identification and promotion of shared values: highlighting shared beliefs and principles, such as empathy, respect, and tolerance, can foster and promote unity among community people, (ii) dialogue and discussion encouragement: enabling and facilitating conversations through different community activities, events, meetings, forums, and online platforms allow understanding of diverse perspectives by individuals, moreover, this also allows finding of common ground, and building relationships, (iii) encouraging and supporting diversity and inclusivity: embracing and practicing religious, cultural, and political diversity by celebrating and allowing different traditions and promoting equal opportunities strengthens the fabric of a cohesive society [10].

2.2.2 Implementing Community Engagement and Empowerment Initiatives

(a) Social bonds are fostered by active empowerment and participation of community members. There are various effective strategies for achieving this, including (i) different programs for developing the community: engaging community members on identification of common concerns and collaboration for solutions to common problems enhances mutual respect and collective action, (ii) facilitating and encouraging inclusion of groups that are marginalized: giving voice to all the voiceless and underrepresented groups in decision making is a gateway to promoting equity and strengthening social ties, (iii) leveraging arts and culture: employing creative expressions such as theater, music, and visual arts can bridge divides, embrace diversity, and build communal identities within communities [11]. The integration of these approaches facilitates the communities in enhancing social cohesion, resulting in improved wellbeing and a more inclusive society.

3 Challenges and Negative Impacts of Digital Technological Advancements

3.1 Digital Divide and Inequality

The digital divide is a term used in referring to the gap between individuals and communities that have access to digital devices, and information and communication technologies (ICT) and those that do not have such privilege. This digital divide (disparity) drastically contributes to socioeconomic inequalities, thereby negatively impacting healthcare, education, employment, and civic participation [12].

3.1.1 Global Impact of the Digital Divide

Digital divide has severe global impacts on the people worldwide, among which are (a) lack of internet access: as of 2025, nearly 2.6 billion people worldwide go about their daily activity without access to internet, predominantly in underdeveloped and remote regions. This lack of internet and connectivity has limited the access of people to essential services like healthcare, education, and financial systems, (b) economic disparities: there are disparities in economy and economic growth among the people due to lack of digital infrastructure in many developing nations which exacerbates poverty and hampers developmental growth. When there is no access to online markets and resources, communities find it difficult to take part in the global economy [13].

3.1.2 Digital Divide in South Africa

Digital divide presents several challenges to the unprivileged people, including (a) educational inequities: In South Africa, there are significant educational disparities with the digital divide, particularly during the COVID-19 pandemic, where nearly 750,000 children were dropped out of school because of their inability to access remote learning platforms, (b) employment challenges: job opportunities were restricted due to lack of internet access and limited digital skills, particularly in rural and remote areas, thereby perpetuating unemployment, underdevelopment, and hindering economic mobility, (c) age and digital literacy: older populations are frequently confronted with challenges in adopting digital technologies in an increasingly digital society, resulting in their marginalization [14].

3.1.3 Digital-Divide Contributory Factors

There are many factors that contribute to the digital divide, including (a) infrastructure deficits: inadequate or lack of investment in digital infrastructure, especially in remote, underserved, and rural areas, limits ICT's connectivity and access by the people, (b) affordability: digital access by low-income households becomes unattainable with high costs of internet services and devices, (c) digital literacy: the available technologies are not effectively utilized by individuals due to their lack of education and training in digital skills [15].

3.1.4 Strategies for Bridging the Digital Divide

Several strategies have been proposed for bridging the digital divide, including (a) infrastructure development, which involves investing in broadband and mobile networks for connectivity extension to remote and rural regions, (b) affordable access, which is by implementation of programs and policies that reduce or subsidize cost of digital devices and internet services for low-income populations, (c) digital education, which is by providing training and resources for the digital literacy enhancement across all age groups, (d) public-private partnerships, which is by working in partnership with private sector entities for the support and funding of digital inclusion initiatives [16].

Addressing this digital divide is essential for promoting and encouraging equitable access to opportunities, information, and services in the digital age. Implementation of comprehensive strategies that embrace equitable access to affordable infrastructure, education, and collaboration, by societies would facilitate such societies to work towards mitigating digital inequalities, thereby fostering inclusive development and growth.

3.2 Cyberbullying and Online Harassment

Cyberbullying and online harassment are permeative issues in today's digital world, affecting individuals across the world and leading to significant social, economic, and psychological consequences. Likewise, the rise of digital platforms also contributes to the increase of cyberbullying and online harassment, which in turn affect mental health and social wellbeing of individuals. Studies high spot the need for adaptive strategies to tackle cyberbully and online harassment to promote online environments that are safe [17].

3.2.1 Prevalence and Forms of Cyberbullying

A range of dangerous and harmful behaviors that are conducted via digital platforms are embraced by cyberbullying, including (a) harassment, which is referred to as the persistent, hurtful and threat-filled messages, (b) cyberstalking, which is referred to as the use of electronic communications to stalk or harass someone by monitoring their online activities, (c) outing, which is referred to as sharing private information of someone without their consent, (d) exclusion, which is referred to as the deliberate acts of leaving someone out of online conversations or group. Deliberate acts can happen across any digital communication platforms, such as messaging apps, online forums, and social media [18].

3.2.2 Mental Health Implications

The psychological effect of cyberbullying on the victims is profound, and this include (a) increased stress and trauma: about 32% victims of cyberbullying give account of stress-related symptoms they experience, (b) emotional distress: around 38% of teenagers subjected to online harassment become highly upset, resulting in issues like anxiety and depression, (c) academic and behavioral consequences, where victims may be confronted with challenges like substance abuse, dropping out of school, and becoming a juvenile delinquent [19].

3.2.3 Prevention and Intervention Strategies

There are multifaceted approaches for addressing cyberbullying, including (a) education and awareness, which is by implementing educative programs and activities in schools to teach and understand digital citizenship and the penalties for online harassment, (b) reporting mechanisms, which require and encourage victims to report cyberbullying incidents to social media platform moderators and, if necessary, to the law enforcement agencies, (c) parental involvement, which requires that parents and guardians monitor their children and wards online activities and ensure that open communication is maintained with them about their digital experiences, (d) legal frameworks, which requires the development and enforcement of laws that address and tackle cyberbullying for the protection of victims' rights [20].

Cyberbullying is a difficult and complex issue that demands collective action from everybody, including individuals, communities, and governments. By creating and fostering awareness, encouraging and promoting digital morals, and providing robust and reliable support systems, a safer online environment is possible for all.

4 Conclusions

The societal impact of technology on wellbeing and cohesion has been presented in this paper. Technology has the potential to considerably enhance the wellbeing and cohesion of society. However, there is a need to address the associated challenges to ensure positive contributions are derived from digital advancements to all segments of society. Assistance is offered by several organizations to the victims of cyberbullying, including (a) StopBullying.gov [21], which provides undiluted information on how cyberbullying can be identified, prevented, and responded to, (b) the United Nations Children's Fund (UNICEF) [22], which provides guidance on how to handle cyberbullying and protect personal information online, (c) find a helpline [23], which is for finding and connecting individuals in South Africa to support services and awareness for bullying and other mental health concerns.

This paper recommends (a) that digital literacy be promoted, and this is by implementing educational programs for the enhancement of digital skills across all age groups [24], (b) the infrastructure improvement, and this is by investing in technological and digital infrastructure to ensure equitable access to technological and digital resources, (c) support systems development, and this is by establishing mechanisms to address and tackle online harassment while giving support to the affected individuals, (d) encourage community engagement, and this is by leveraging technology to ease the building activities of the community and reinforce traditional social structures.

Acknowledgement. The authors received funding from the Tshwane University of Technology, South Africa.

References

1. Newman, N., Fletcher, R., Robertson, C.T., Ross Arguedas, A., Nielsen, R.K.: Reuters Institute digital news report 2024. Reuters Institute for the Study of Journalism (2024)
2. Matema, T., Kariuki, P.: The impact of social media on social cohesion in South Africa. J. Econ. Behav. Stud. **14**(2), 1–12 (2022)
3. Magida, A.: The Nexus Between the Digital Divide and Social Cohesion and Their Socio-Economic Drivers in South Africa (Doctoral dissertation), pp. 1–297. University of the Witwatersrand, Johannesburg (2023)
4. Kulkarni, M., Durve, S., Jia, B.: Cyberbully and online harassment: Issues associated with digital wellbeing (2024). arXiv:2404.18989
5. Blezard, E.: Cohesive communities and segregated estates: values and challenges. In: Social Work, Housing, and Homelessness, pp. 61–81. Routledge (2025)
6. Petersen, I.H., Kruss, G.: Promoting alignment between innovation policy and inclusive development in South Africa. Dev. South. Afr. **36**(3), 351–375 (2019)
7. Vuorre, M., Przybylski, A.K.: Global well-being and mental health in the internet age. Clin. Psychol. Sci. **12**(5), 917–935 (2024)
8. Vela, A., Kamsickas, L.: Happiness and social connectivity. In: Lifestyle Nursing, pp. 99–111. CRC Press (2022)
9. Sabbe, S., Bradt, L., Roose, R.: Facilitating conditions for establishing social cohesion through structural approaches in community sport. In: Community Sport and Social Inclusion, pp. 83–100. Routledge (2021)
10. Roberge, M.É., Alokha, Y.O.: Establishing an effective dialogue to support diversity, inclusion, and the learning outcomes. J. Bus. Divers. **22**(2), 1–10 (2022)
11. Russell, K., Rosenbaum, S., Varela, S., Stanton, R., Barnett, F.: Fostering community engagement, participation and empowerment for mental health of adults living in rural communities: a systematic review. Rural Remote Health **23**(1), 1–13 (2023)

12. Cornejo Müller, A., Wachtler, B., Lampert, T.: Digital divide—Social inequalities in the utilisation of digital healthcare. Bundesgesundheitsblatt-Gesundheitsforschung-Gesundheitsschutz **63**, 185–191 (2020)
13. Tiene, D.: Addressing the global digital divide and its impact on educational opportunity. Educ. Media Int. **39**(3–4), 212–222 (2002)
14. Global Citizen (2025). https://www.globalcitizen.org/en/content/south-africa-digital-divide-makes-inequality-worse/retrieved
15. Hustad, E., Hansen, J.L., Skaiaa, A., Vassilakopoulou, P.: Digital inequalities: a review of contributing factors and measures for crossing the divide. In: Digital Transformation for a Sustainable Society in the 21st Century: 18th IFIP WG 6.11 Conference on e-Business, e-Services, and e-Society, I3E 2019, Trondheim, Norway, Proceedings 18, pp. 505–519. Springer International Publishing (2019)
16. Pokrovskaia, N.N., Garin, A.K.: Strategies for bridging the digital divide by enhancing communication competence. In: 2022 Communication Strategies in Digital Society Seminar (ComSDS), pp. 166–170. IEEE (2022)
17. Slaughter, A., Newman, E.: New frontiers: moving beyond cyberbullying to define online harassment. J. Online Trust Saf. **1**(2) (2022)
18. Trbojević, F., Šikuten, L.: Prevalence, forms, and predictors of cyberbullying perpetration. Medijska istraživanja **28**(1), 133–154 (2022)
19. Ali, S.I., Shahbuddin, N.B.: The relationship between cyberbullying and mental health among university students. Sustainability **14**(11), 6881 (2022)
20. Vandebosch, H.: Cyberbullying prevention, detection and intervention. Narratives in research and interventions on cyberbullying among young people, pp. 29–44 (2019)
21. StopBullying.gov/retrieved on May 28 (2025)
22. UNICEF (2025). https://www.unicef.org/stories/how-to-stop-cyberbullying
23. Find a Helpline (2025). https://findahelpline.com/countries/za/topics/bullying
24. Bello, R.W., Akpojaro, J.: Application of social networking and cloud-based services to smart education. Int. J. Adv. Res. Comput. Sci. Softw. Eng. **9**(1), 6–13 (2019)

Internet of Things, Security, Distributed Processing, and Applications

Efficient Non-linear Primitives for Secure Multi-party Computation Among IoT Devices

Zhaohong Wang[1] and Jing Guo[2(✉)]

[1] EECE, California State University, Chico, CA 95929, USA
zwang25@csuchico.edu
[2] MATH, California State University, Chico, CA 95929, USA
jguo2@csuchico.edu

Abstract. Secure multi-party computation (secure MPC) has indeed sparked considerable interest, leading to the development of various algorithms and application ideas. However, its deployment remains limited primarily due to performance bottlenecks inherent in its distributed nature and the associated overhead of data encryption. With the proliferation of Internet of Things (IoT) devices–many of which are resource-constrained–there is an urgent need to revisit secure MPC for practical applications in IoT and edge environments. This paper proposes lightweight and simplified secure MPC primitives specifically designed for these resource-constrained devices, aiming to serve as foundational building blocks for more complex algorithms in the future. We focus on baseline primitives that address critical non-linear operations, including comparison and equality testing, which are known to be significant bottlenecks in secure MPC. Through theoretical analysis, we demonstrate that our proposed protocols exhibit substantial improvements in efficiency, making them suitable for deployment in resource-constrained settings while ensuring security against semi-honest adversaries. The results indicate that these lightweight primitives not only mitigate performance limitations but also enable secure computations across a variety of applications in IoT and edge environments. We envision that this work will pave the way for the broader adoption of secure MPC in scenarios where computational resources are limited, making secure collaborative computation a viable option for a diverse range of IoT uses.

Keywords: non-linear operations · Internet-of-Things · information-theoretic secure multiparty computation (ITS-MPC)

1 Introduction

Secure Multiparty Computation (Secure MPC) is a cryptographic paradigm that enables a group of mutually distrusting parties to jointly compute a function over their private inputs while preserving the confidentiality of those inputs. A powerful foundation for building secure MPC protocols is *linear secret sharing schemes*, which allow individual secrets to be distributed among participants in a way that enables collaborative computation without revealing private data.

H. R. Arabnia et al. (Eds.): CSCE 2025, CCIS 2934, pp. 91–100, 2026.
https://doi.org/10.1007/978-3-032-22190-2_7

In a typical secure MPC setting, there are n participants $(A_1, A_2, ..., A_n)$, each holding a private input $(x_1, x_2, ..., x_n)$. The goal is to compute a vector of outputs $(y_1, y_2, ..., y_n) = F(x_1, x_2, ..., x_n)$ such that each party A_i learns only their respective output y_i, while learning nothing about the inputs or outputs of others. This strong privacy guarantee makes secure MPC a compelling solution for distributed computing in untrusted environments.

Over the past decades, a variety of secure MPC protocols have been developed, leveraging different cryptographic primitives such as oblivious transfer [1], garbled circuits [8], homomorphic encryption [6], and linear secret sharing [5]. Among these, a particularly promising line of work focuses on *information-theoretic security (ITS)* — a setting where security does not rely on computational hardness assumptions. One of the most widely used techniques in ITS-MPC is *ShamirâĂŹs Secret Sharing (SSS)*, a threshold linear secret sharing scheme known for its efficiency and robustness.

Despite its advantages, ITS-MPC faces significant challenges when handling non-linear operations, which are essential for many real-world applications. Operations such as comparison, equality testing, and interval membership are particularly difficult to implement efficiently under ITS constraints, often becoming bottlenecks in practical deployments.

This paper addresses these challenges in the context of resource-constrained environments, such as Internet-of-Things (IoT) systems deployed at the network edge. These devices are typically limited in both computational power and memory capacity, making the design of lightweight, efficient protocols a necessity. We propose novel protocols for non-linear primitives — specifically, secure comparison and equality testing — that are tailored for such constrained devices. Through rigorous mathematical analysis and performance evaluation, we demonstrate that our protocols maintain strong security guarantees while significantly reducing computational overhead, making them suitable for deployment in real-world edge computing scenarios.

The paper is structured as follows: Sect. 2 reviews related work and key building blocks. Section 3 details our algorithm and Sect. 4 concludes the paper.

2 Related Works and Concepts

In this section, we provide brief descriptions about related work that is in secure MPC, and the building blocks of our proposed protocol, for necessary background to understand our protocol in Sect. 3.

2.1 Secure Multiparty Computation

Secure Multiparty Computation (secure MPC) addresses a setting in which n parties $(A_1, A_2, ..., A_n)$ each hold a private input $(x_1, x_2, ..., x_n)$ and collaboratively compute a function $(y_1, y_2, ..., y_n) = F(x_1, x_2, ..., x_n)$. During the computation, each party A_i learns only their own inputs x_i and outputs y_i, without gaining access to othersâĂŹ data. A variety of secure MPC protocols have been developed, including oblivious transfer [1], garbled circuits [8], homomorphic encryption [6], and linear secret sharing schemes [5].

Secure MPC enables many practical applications. One such domain is blockchain, where smart contracts often require access to usersâĂŹ private data. Using secure MPC to safeguard this data has become a prominent research direction. For example, Hyperledger Fabric has been extended with secure MPC to support private computations directly on-chain [4], embedding the protocols within smart contracts instead of relying on off-chain execution. Another application in Hyperledger Fabric utilizes the Paillier cryptosystem to preserve data privacy while enforcing access control list policies for ledger protection [7].

Information-Theoretic Secure Multiparty Computation. We now summarize the building blocks and notation involved in the algorithms we propose. The foundational primitive is information-theoretic secure MPC (ITS-MPC), based on ShamirâĂŹs Secret Sharing (SSS), which offers superior efficiency relative to encrypted-domain methods [11,13]. In a (t,n) SSS scheme, a secret x from a finite field F_m (where m denotes the field size) is divided into n shares $\{[x]_i^t, i=1,\dots,n\}$. The scheme ensures that any collection of fewer than $t \leq \lceil n/2 \rceil$ shares provides no information about x. The procedures for secret sharing and reconstruction are given in Eqs. (1) and (2), respectively [3].

$$[x]_i^t \triangleq \sum_{j=1}^{t-1} \alpha_j i^j + x \bmod m, \tag{1}$$

$$x = \sum_{i \in K} \gamma_i [x]_i^t \bmod m, \tag{2}$$

Here, the share generator randomly selects the α_j's, and the reconstruction coefficients are given by $\gamma_i \triangleq \prod_{j \in K, j \neq i} \frac{-j}{i-j}$, where K is any subset of $\{1,\dots,n\}$ containing at least t elements.

In this finite field setting, more complex operations can be constructed from basic addition and multiplication. For instance, to compute $x+y$—with x and y being private inputs from U and V—the parties first generate and distribute n secret shares of each input. Then, each agent locally computes a share of $x+y$ homomorphically, without needing communication:

$$[x + y \bmod m]_i^t = [x]_i^t + [y]_i^t \bmod m. \tag{3}$$

For multiplication, although the product of the two secret polynomials yields xy as its constant term, the degree of the resulting polynomial becomes $2t-2$. Repeated multiplications may increase the degree beyond what n can support for reconstruction. To address this, either more agents must be added, or a âĂIJrenormalizationâĂİ technique can be used to reduce the degree back to threshold t. In this method, each agent decomposes their product share into n parts and sends one to each agent. The agents then compute the final share collectively. This process preserves secrecy and requires at least 3 agents. Compared to increasing the number of agents, it offers lower computational cost.

$$[xy \bmod m]_i^t = \sum_{j=1}^{n} \gamma_j [[xy \bmod m]_j^{2t-1}]_i^t \bmod m. \tag{4}$$

3 Non-linear Primitives

In this section, we present our core primitive protocols for non-linear operations, comparison and equality test. They are lightweight, measured by their cryptographic complexity, suitable for resource-constrained IoT devices.

3.1 Protocol: COMPARE-PARALLEL

We first consider determining whether $u \geq v$ using a parallel algorithm in the encrypted (or secret-shared) domain. This protocol compares two secret values u and v represented in binary form by their bits $(u_0, u_1, \ldots, u_{l-1})$ and $(v_0, v_1, \ldots, v_{l-1})$, with u_0 and v_0 being the most significant bits (MSBs).

Protocol 1, COMPARE-PARALLEL, is presented below. The main idea is to:

1. Compute per-bit equality, greater-than, and less-than flags.
2. Identify the first position where u and v differ using prefix equality.
3. Aggregate these differences to determine whether $u \geq v$.

Initially, all agents receive shares of the two secret numbers, u and v, from the Dealer. In Steps 2 and 3, all agents compute three variables, $[eq_j]$, $[gt_j]$, and $[lt_j]$, on all bits, all in the encrypted domain. Each of them require a secure multiplication through renormalization, but all variables and all bits are independent, so they can be computed in a single round parallelly. Step 4's computation is also done in the encrypted domain and should be done in $(l-1)$ rounds, because the prefixes depends on their previous iteration's value. Each multiplication requires a renormalization. In Step 5, the agents first find the diference between $[gt_j]$ and $[lt_j]$, and then multiply the difference with $[prefix_e q_j]$. The renormalization inherited within the secure multiplication can be done in a single round of networking for all bits because all bits can be processed in parallel in an array. In Step 6, the agents compute the encrypted domain variable, $[cmp]$. In Step 7, agents send their $[cmp]$ to the agents. The last step is done at the dealer. The dealer will learn from the comparison result by looking at the c value. $cmp \in [0, \lfloor \frac{m}{2} \rfloor]$ tells that $u \geq v$, leading to $c = 1$. In contrast, $cmp \in [0, \lceil \frac{m}{2} \rceil]$ tells that $u < v$, giving $c = 0$. $c > 0$ tells that $u > v$, all without revealing the exact difference between u and v if they are not equal. Furthermore, $cmp = 0$ will give $e = 1$, telling that $u = v$. Otherwise, $e = 0$. In summary,

$$c = \begin{cases} 1 & u \geq v \\ 0 & u < v \end{cases}$$

and

$$e = \begin{cases} 1 & u = v \\ 0 & u \neq v \end{cases}$$

In total, the complexity measured by the number of secure multiplication in rounds is $1 + l - 1 + 1 = l + 1$. The number of secure multiplications is $3l + l - 1 + l = 5l - 1$. Protocol 1 is better in efficiency than most existing protocols using the number of secure multiplication as a measurement. For example, the complexity of [9] is $188l \log l + 205l$. The complexity of [12] is $279l + 5$. The complexity of [10] is about $53l$.

Algorithm 1. COMPARE-PARALLEL

Require: Secrets $u, v \in \{0,1\}^l$ shared bit-wisely: $[u_j]_i^t, [v_j]_i^t$, for $i \in 1,\dots,n$ and $j \in 0,\dots,l-1$.

Ensure: Share $[c]_i^t$ where $c = 1$ if $u \geq v$, else $c = 0$, and share $[e]_i^t$ where $e = 1$ if $u = v$, else $e = 0$.

1: Dealer: $[u_j]_i^t, [v_j]_i^t \longrightarrow A_i$ for $i \in 1,\dots,n$ and $j \in 0,\dots,l-1$.

2: **for all** $j = 0$ to $l-1$ (in parallel) **do**

3: All A_i's compute:
- $[eq_j] := 1 - ([u_j] \oplus [v_j]) \mod m$ (1 if bits are equal)
- $[gt_j] := [u_j] \cdot (1 - [v_j]) \mod m$ (1 if $u_j = 1, v_j = 0$)
- $[lt_j] := (1 - [u_j]) \cdot [v_j] \mod m$ (1 if $u_j = 0, v_j = 1$)

4: All A_i's compute prefix equalities for all j:

$$[prefix\_eq_0] = 1$$

$$[prefix\_eq_j] = \prod_{k=0}^{j-1} [eq_k] \mod m \quad \text{for } j \geq 1$$

5: For all j, A_i's compute the flags:

$$[flag_j] = [prefix\_eq_j] \cdot ([gt_j] - [lt_j]) \mod m$$

6: A_i's aggregate result:

$$[cmp] = \sum_{j=0}^{l-1} [flag_j] \mod m$$

7: A_i: $[cmp] \longrightarrow U$ for $i \in 1,\dots,n$.

8: Outputs reconstructed at Dealer: $c = 1$ if $cmp \in [0, \lfloor \frac{m}{2} \rfloor]$, else $c = 0$; $e = 1$ if $cmp = 0$, else $e = 0$.

We give some examples to illustrate the correctness of the protocol, using $l = 4$ for simplicity.

3.2 Example 1: $u = 9, v = 6$

Binary representation:

$$u = 1001_2, \quad v = 0110_2$$

j	u_j	v_j	eq_j	gt_j	lt_j
0	1	0	0	$1 \cdot 1 = 1$	$0 \cdot 0 = 0$
1	0	1	0	$0 \cdot 0 = 0$	$1 \cdot 1 = 1$
2	0	1	0	$0 \cdot 0 = 0$	$1 \cdot 1 = 1$
3	1	0	0	$1 \cdot 1 = 1$	$0 \cdot 0 = 0$

Step 1: Bitwise Comparison

Step 2: Prefix Equality

$$prefix\_eq_0 = 1, \quad prefix\_eq_j = 0 \text{ for } j \geq 1 \text{ (since } eq_0 = 0)$$

Step 3: Flag Computation

$$flag_0 = 1 \cdot (1 - 0) = 1, \quad \text{all others } = 0$$

Result

$$cmp = 1 \Rightarrow c = 1 \Rightarrow u \geq v$$

3.3 Example 2: $u = 8, v = 9$

Binary:

$$u = 1000_2, \quad v = 1001_2$$

j	u_j	v_j	eq_j	gt_j	lt_j
0	1	1	1	$1 \cdot 0 = 0$	$0 \cdot 1 = 0$
1	0	0	1	$0 \cdot 1 = 0$	$1 \cdot 0 = 0$
2	0	0	1	$0 \cdot 1 = 0$	$1 \cdot 0 = 0$
3	0	1	0	$0 \cdot 0 = 0$	$1 \cdot 1 = 1$

Step 1: Bitwise Comparison

Step 2: Prefix Equality

$$prefix\_eq_0 = 1, \quad prefix\_eq_1 = 1, \quad prefix\_eq_2 = 1, \quad prefix\_eq_3 = 1$$

Step 3: Flag Computation

$$flag_3 = 1 \cdot (0 - 1) = -1, \quad \text{all others } = 0$$

Result

$$cmp = -1 \Rightarrow c = 0 \Rightarrow u < v$$

3.4 Example 3: $u = 5, v = 5$

Binary:

$$u = 0101_2, \quad v = 0101_2$$

j	u_j	v_j	eq_j	gt_j	lt_j
0	0	0	1	0	0
1	1	1	1	0	0
2	0	0	1	0	0
3	1	1	1	0	0

Step 1: Bitwise Comparison

Step 2: Prefix Equality

$$prefix\_eq_j = 1 \quad \text{for all } j$$

Step 3: Flag Computation

$$\text{All } flag_j = 0$$

Result

$$cmp = 0 \Rightarrow c = 1 \Rightarrow u = v$$

3.5 Protocol: EQUAL

There are situations where we are only interested in determining whether two secret values u and v are equal, i.e., testing if $u = v$. A simple protocol suitable for resource-constrained devices can be constructed under a secure multiparty computation framework using linear secret sharing. We first need a building block of agents collectively generating an unknown random number x, to be used in the equality test protocol [2]. We call the building block DRAND, standing for "distributed random number generator," presented in Protocol 2.

Step 1 of DRAND is for each agent to secretly pick its own random number x_i and hide it in a polynomial ready to share, according to Eq. (1). In Step 2, each agent sends the shares of its secret x_i to every other agent. In Step 3, each agent locally adds all shares that it has received, including its own share, to compute $x = \sum_{i=1}^{n} x_i$. Because each agent only sees the share of x, so it has $[x]_i^t$ as the output of the DRAND protocol.

Next, the problem of equality test is addressed by Protocol 3, which achieves this goal with a single round of secure multiplication and ensures that no sensitive information is leaked during the process.

Protocol 2. DRAND – Generate a random number unknown to agents

Require: A_i: randomly selects a secret x_i, for $i = 1, \dots, n$;
Ensure: A_i: obtains $[x]_i^t$ where $x = \sum_{i=1}^{n} x_i$, for $i = 1, \dots, n$;
A_i computes $p_i(i) = \sum_{j=1}^{t-1} \alpha_j i^j + x_i \bmod m$;
A_i: $p_i(j) \longrightarrow A_j$ for all $i, j \in 1, \dots, n$;
A_i: $[x]_i^t = q(i) = \sum_{i=1}^{n} p_j(i)$ for all $j \in 1, \dots, n$;

Protocol 3. EQUAL – Test if u equals v in the encrypted domain

Require: Dealer U has its secret u, V has its secret v;
Ensure: $[c]_i^t$ at dealers U and V where $c := (u = v)$.
for $k = 1$ to 3 **do**
  A_i: $[x]_{i(k)}^t = \text{DRAND}(x_i)$, for $i = 1, \dots, n$;
U, V share $[u]_i^t, [v]_i^t \longrightarrow A_i$ for $i = 1, \dots, n$;
A_i: $[w]_i^t = [u]_i^t - [v]_i^t$;
for $k = 1$ to 3 **do**
  A_i: $[c]_{i(k)}^{2t-1} = [x]_{i(k)}^t \times [w]_i^t$;
  A_i: $[c]_{i(k)}^{2t-1} \longrightarrow A_i : [c]_{i(k)}^t$
A_i: $\longrightarrow U, V : [c]_{i(k)}^t$
U, V: $c_{i_{(k)}} = \sum_{i \in K} \gamma_i [c]_{i_{(k)}}^t \bmod m$
U, V: $c = \sum c_{i_{(k)}} \bmod m$

Let $u, v \in \mathbb{F}_m$ be two secret values held respectively by parties U and V, where $\mathbb{F}_m$ denotes a finite field of size m. The goal is to determine whether $u = v$ without revealing any additional information beyond the outcome of this comparison.

The basic idea of the protocol is to compute the difference $w = u - v$. Clearly, $u = v$ if and only if $w = 0$. However, directly revealing w would compromise the privacy of u and v. Therefore, the protocol employs a masking strategy: each party computes a shared value $[w]_i^t$, and this value is then masked with a random value $x \in \mathbb{F}_m$, resulting in $x \cdot w$. If $x \cdot w = 0$, then with high probability $w = 0$, and hence $u = v$. Conversely, if $w \neq 0$, then $x \cdot w = 0$ only when $x = 0$.

To mitigate the risk of false positives due to the random mask x being zero, the protocol performs this masking operation three times using independently generated random values $x_{(1)}, x_{(2)}, x_{(3)}$. The parties then evaluate:

$$c_{(k)} = x_{(k)} \cdot w \quad \text{for } k = 1, 2, 3.$$

If all three results $c_{(1)}, c_{(2)}, c_{(3)}$ equal zero, then the protocol concludes $u = v$. Otherwise, $u \neq v$.

Let us analyze the soundness of the protocol when $w \neq 0$, i.e., the case where $u \neq v$. Since $w \neq 0$, the correctness of the test relies on at least one of the products $x_k \cdot w$ being non-zero. Assume that each random value $x_{(k)}$ is sampled independently and uniformly at random from $\mathbb{F}_m$. The probability that a single $x_k = 0$ is exactly $1/m$. Therefore, the probability that all three independently sampled random values are zero is:

$$\Pr[x_{(1)} = 0 \wedge x_{(2)} = 0 \wedge x_{(3)} = 0] = \left(\frac{1}{m}\right)^3.$$

Thus, the probability of a false positive, i.e., incorrectly concluding $u = v$ when $u \neq v$, is bounded above by $1/m^3$. In typical cryptographic settings where m is large (e.g., a 128-bit field), this probability is negligible.

Each round of random masking and secure multiplication requires one multiplication per party. Although three such rounds are executed, the protocol optimizes performance by vectorizing the operations: all masked products $[c_{i_{(k)}}^{2t-1}]_i^t$ can be renormalized in a single round. Hence, the overall communication complexity remains equivalent to one round of secure multiplication, which is highly efficient in practice, especially for those resource-constrained IoT devices.

3.6 Security Analysis

The proposed primitive protocols relies on ITS-MPC employing Shamir's Secret Sharing (SSS) scheme. At its core is Protocol 1, with communications taking place in Steps 2 through 7. Step 2 involves the initial share distribution, while subsequent steps entail renormalization, offering no additional information. These messages represent secret shares from a (t, n)-SSS scheme, ensuring information-theoretic security against semi-honest adversaries controlling $(t-1)$ or fewer agents. A similar analysis can be applied to the equality test protocol.

4 Conclusion

This paper presents lightweight and streamlined secure MPC primitives tailored for constrained devices commonly found in IoT and edge computing scenarios. We concentrate on foundational non-linear operations—specifically, comparison and equality testing—which are known to constitute major performance bottlenecks in existing MPC systems. Our proposed protocols are designed with efficiency in mind, leveraging mathematical simplifications and minimal communication rounds. Through formal analysis, we demonstrate that these constructions maintain security under the semi-honest model while significantly improving performance.

Acknowledgment. Research reported in this paper was supported by AMMTO of the Department of Energy under award number W911SR24F0070.

References

1. Badrinarayanan, S., Masny, D., Mukherjee, P., Patranabis, S., Raghuraman, S., Sarkar, P.: Round-optimal oblivious transfer and MPC from computational CSIDH. In: IACR International Conference on Public-Key Cryptography, pp. 376–405. Springer (2023)
2. Bar-Ilan, J., Beaver, D.: Non-cryptographic fault-tolerant computing in constant number of rounds of interaction. In: Proceedings of the eighth annual ACM Symposium on Principles of distributed computing, pp. 201–209 (1989)

3. Benaloh, J.C.: Secret sharing homomorphisms: Keeping shares of a secret secret. In: Conference on the theory and application of cryptographic techniques, pp. 251–260. Springer (1986)
4. Benhamouda, F., Halevi, S., Halevi, T.: Supporting private data on hyperledger fabric with secure multiparty computation. IBM J. Res. Dev. **63**(2/3), 3–1 (2019)
5. Cramer, R., Damgård, I., Maurer, U.: General secure multi-party computation from any linear secret-sharing scheme. In: Advances in Cryptology—EUROCRYPT 2000, pp. 316–334. Springer (2000)
6. Das, D.: Secure cloud computing algorithm using homomorphic encryption and multi-party computation. In: 2018 International Conference on Information Networking (ICOIN), pp. 391–396. IEEE (2018)
7. Ghadamyari, M., Samet, S.: Privacy-preserving statistical analysis of health data using Paillier homomorphic encryption and permissioned blockchain. In: 2019 IEEE International Conference on Big Data (Big Data), pp. 5474–5479. IEEE (2019)
8. Hastings, M., Hemenway, B., Noble, D., Zdancewic, S.: SoK: general purpose compilers for secure multi-party computation. In: 2019 IEEE Symposium on Security and Privacy (SP), pp. 1220–1237. IEEE (2019)
9. Kiltz, E.: Unconditionally secure constant round multi-party computation for equality, comparison, bits and exponentiation. Cryptology ePrint Archive (2005)
10. Makri, E., Rotaru, D., Vercauteren, F., Wagh, S.: Rabbit: efficient comparison for secure multi-party computation, pp. 249–270 (2021)
11. Mohanty, M., Ooi, W.T., Atrey, P.K.: Scale me, crop me, knowme not: supporting scaling and cropping in secret image sharing. In: 2013 IEEE International Conference on Multimedia and Expo (ICME), pp. 1–6. IEEE (2013)
12. Nishide, T., Ohta, K.: Multiparty computation for interval, equality, and comparison without bit-decomposition protocol. In: International Workshop on Public Key Cryptography, pp. 343–360. Springer (2007)
13. Resende, A., Railsback, D., Dowsley, R., Nascimento, A.C., Aranha, D.F.: Fast privacy-preserving text classification based on secure multiparty computation. IEEE Trans. Inf. Forensics Secur. **17**, 428–442 (2022)

Placement of Distributed Machine Learning Services for AI and Smart Grid-Enabled IoT Platforms

Jérémie Rodez[1](✉), Patricia Stolf[1], and Thierry Monteil[1,2]

[1] University of Toulouse, IRIT, CNRS, Toulouse, France
{jeremie.rodez,patricia.stolf,thierry.monteil}@irit.fr
[2] INSA, Toulouse, France

Abstract. Artificial intelligence, fog computing, and smart grids allow for better energy management and personal data control. However, such heterogeneous platforms complexify service placement due to hardware and network heterogeneity. This paper proposes a distributed machine learning service for fog computing platforms model, and two new algorithms that aim to reduce time and energy consumption. The first algorithm groups services geographically, while the second places services vertically in the topology to reduce network usage. The Batsim simulator have been used to deploy distributed AI applications for measuring their duration and energy usage of the fog architecture. Results show that the first algorithm induces higher time and energy consumption than the second one, which outperforms multiple baseline algorithms for both metrics.

Keywords: Service placement · Internet of Things · Fog Computing · Distributed Learning · Smart Grids

1 Introduction

Recent advances in artificial intelligence (AI), particularly in deep learning, have paved the way for cutting-edge, sector-specific applications in fields such as medicine, finance, industry or energy. Artificial intelligence raises new challenges, such as preserving privacy over data collections and learning processes based on these data. A solution is to be as close as possible to the user while improving QoS and data confidentiality. In parallel, numerous studies demonstrate the value of fog computing architecture for managing smart grid infrastructures, especially for energy management from the production to the consumption. For example, distributed learning use cases, such as weather or energy production forecasting, make the smart grid more efficient at controlling both small- and large-scale power loads. The combination of fog computing, smart grids, and distributed AI opens new possibilities for energy management in the context of climate change and data privacy issues.

Moreover, due to the need for hardware acceleration for certain components (e.g., training and inference), deployment is more complex than for standard

H. R. Arabnia et al. (Eds.): CSCE 2025, CCIS 2934, pp. 101–115, 2026.
https://doi.org/10.1007/978-3-032-22190-2_8

CPU-only IoT services. While some studies classify distributed artificial intelligence for edge, fog, and cloud deployment, others cover the interest of overlaying fog networks over smart grids [14,15]. The intersection of these fields leads to new approaches and constraints for service placement.

To address these challenges, we propose a distributed learning service placement model over a fog computing platform, along with algorithms that solve the service placement problem while minimizing time consumption and indirectly energy. The evaluations of the proposed algorithms were conducted through simulations of distributed AI on the continuum of fog-cloud architecture.

This paper will first summarize the state of the literature on subjects related to smart grid, fog computing, distributed learning and the placement in Sect. 2. Then, the placement model including a service workflow model and a platform model will be formalized in Sect. 3. Afterward, Sect. 4 will propose algorithms for placing distributed learning services on a smart grid-enabled fog computing platform. The algorithms presented will be evaluated in Sect. 5 through simulations. Finally, we conclude this paper with a discussion on the results and open perspectives, in Sect. 6.

2 Related Work

Distributed artificial intelligence (AI) refers to the deployment of AI services across multiple devices. These technologies, such as federated learning, can be distributed in different ways within an IoT continuum. Distributed AI is classified into several levels corresponding to the distance of its services from the end user. Full use of AI services on end-devices corresponds to a level where the services are the closest to the user. Intermediate levels correspond to a hybrid use of AI services deployed on edge or fog computing. Another level corresponds to full use of the AI application on cloud [15].

At least three types of part of distributed AI services can be identified. The part of the application that generate data, the part that learns from the data, and the part that aggregates the results of the learning services. These three parts can be considered as services. [3,15]

As of machine learning, the decentralization of machine learning can limit network data transferred when slow or congested. Federated learning is a commonly distributed ML technology. It uses the same machine that provides the data to train it, thereby increasing privacy. [3,15]. However, not updating local models regularly with the global model can lead to concept drift. [11]

As for the use of hardware, resource usage will depend on the implementation. Among the most common frameworks (e.g. TensorFlow, Apache MXNet), the use of hardware accelerators is possible and can lead to significant performance improvements [10]. These hardware accelerators are generally GPUs, but can also be other types of hardware acceleration architectures such as TPUs or NPUs, sometimes implemented over an FPGA [15].

Fog computing is a distributed computing paradigm that extends edge computing by providing an unlimited number of layers between end-devices and the cloud [5]. One primary objective is to bring services closer to the data source, which is particularly useful for applications that require privacy preservation, such as federated learning [12]. Fog computing is used in various IoT domains, including smart cities and smart grids [14].

Distributed learning is known to cause performances issues when used over a fog computing platform. These challenges include the heterogeneity of devices and networks, that needs a non-negligible effort on the machine selection when placing the services [3]. Additionally, studies focus on the placement of AI services on Mobile Edge Computing (MEC) platforms or others IoT paradigms [6,11]. Some of these studies examine the use of hardware accelerators in the Edge-Cloud continuum and demonstrate their importance in the deployment of machine learning services [6,11]. It is important to keep in mind that the local models of each learning service must be updated regularly to avoid concept drift. Therefore, when placing services, it is essential to consider bidirectional communication between the learning services and the aggregation service [6,11]. [8] shows that using the edge layer is more time- and energy-efficient for federated learning deployment. However, the authors consider the lowest layers of the network to have the same bandwidth and performance as the fog layer, and do not explore multi-layer placement. The state of the literature lacks sufficient approaches to optimize the deployment of contemporary distributed learning applications on a fog computing platform.

Smart grids introduce intelligence to the electrical network, making it more flexible and resistant to outages. One key benefit of smart grids is their ability to collect data on energy consumption and production. Data is then used to improve energy production and distribution management.

Several studies have evaluated the use of fog computing architecture for organizing smart grid intelligence. Advantages include reduced latency, scalability, confidentiality, security, and energy efficiency [14].

In terms of architecture, various means of communication have been proposed to connect smart grid elements, including power line communication, 5G, and traditional methods such as optical fibers [9]. A case study of the city of Toulouse revealed that the average number of buildings (condominium) per medium-voltage to low-voltage transformers is 3.4 buildings. Moreover, Toulouse has an average of 33.6 apartments per condominium[1]. This is an indication of the number of equipments in the fog architecture.

3 Model

Distributed AI Machine Learning is used through a set of entities that will be called services. These entities will communicate with each other to perform a succession of distributed machine learning rounds, where each round is divided into several phases. Each round begins with a learning phase, during which data

[1] Data on French electrical infrastructure and condominium immatriculation from *Agence ORE* and *Agence Nationale de l'Habitat*
www.data.gouv.fr/datasets/postes-de-distribution-publique-postes-hta-bt-1
www.data.gouv.fr/datasets/registre-national-dimmatriculation-des-coproprietes.

is received. This is followed by a computation phase, during which a local model is computed. Finally, an aggregation phase reconstructs a global model. At the end of each round, the global model is distributed to the learning services to improve the model that will ultimately be used for inference. This service chain requires initial modeling, which must be supplemented by modeling the execution platform. Indeed, the latter uses different computing machines interconnected by networks of varying characteristics within the framework of a fog architecture. The ultimate goal is to meet the needs of the target application as quickly as possible while ensuring reasonable energy consumption.

3.1 Services Workflow Model

A **service** s_j is a code execution entity which requires different resources such as CPU, GPU, memory, I/O or network. In the case of distributed AI machine learning, the class s_j^{cl} of a service could be either *Learning*, *Aggregation*, or data *Generation*. Each class of service has its own behavior, as specified earlier.

An execution of a service can be made when the machine hosting the service has the data required to process, this i^{th} execution is called an invocation of a service s_j and is noted s_j^i. These invocations will occur over time, involving computations and communications before being completed. The interactions between services form a directed graph called a service workflow. However, succession of invocations creates a directed acyclic graph in which a same service is called several times. This graph is called an invocation trace.

An example of a service workflow containing 3 *Generation* services, 3 *Learning* services and 1 *Aggregation* service is shown in the Fig. 1a. The Fig. 1b shows the data exchanges between the service invocations of the trace.

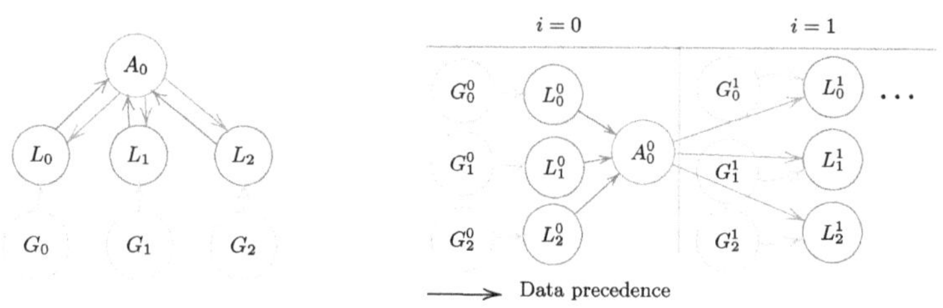

(a) Service workflow (b) Invocation trace

Fig. 1. Example of a service workflow and its invocation trace

$\mathbb{S}^{inv}$ is the set of all service invocations and $\mathbb{S}^{wf}$ the set of all services. $\mathcal{A}_i$ represents an application, which gathers services at least weakly connected in the service workflow graph. $\mathcal{A}_i \subset \mathbb{S}^{wf}$ and $\mathbb{A}$ being the set of all applications such that $\mathcal{A}_i \in \mathbb{A}$. A set of properties is defined to extract the characteristics of a service invocation s_j^i and its corresponding service s_j:

- $\mathbb{S}^c$ the set of all service classes such that $\forall s_j \in \mathbb{S}^{wf} : s_j^{cl} \in \mathbb{S}^c$.

- $s_j^{cops}, s_j^{gops} \in \mathbb{N}$ respectively the amount of CPU and GPU operations to make for each invocation of the service s_j. All invocations of a service s_j are supposed to require the same amount of CPU and GPU operations.
- $s_j^{cmem}, s_j^{gmem} \in \mathbb{N}$ respectively the amount of CPU and GPU memory needed by the service s_j. All invocations of a service s_j are supposed to require the same amount of memory.
- $data_{j,j'}^{i,i'}$ the amount of data to be sent from the invocation s_j^i to the invocation $s_{j'}^{i'}$ (in *Bytes*).
- $succ_j^i \subset \mathbb{S}^{inv}$ and $pred_j^i \subset \mathbb{S}^{inv}$ respectively the set of service invocations that are direct successors and predecessors of the invocation s_j^i.
- $state^t(s_j^i) \rightarrow \{waiting, ready, executing, finished\}$ the function that for a service invocation returns its state at time t. The *waiting* state corresponds to a state in which the service invocation is waiting for its dependencies to be satisfied (i.e. all predecessors are in the *finished* state). The *ready* state is when the service invocation is ready to be executed (i.e. all predecessors are in the *finished* state). The *executing* state indicates that the service invocation is currently being executed, and the *finished* state corresponds to a state in which the service invocation has been executed.
- $sent^t(s_j^i, s_{j'}^{i'}) \rightarrow \{true, false\}$ the function that returns *true* when a service $s_{j'}$ received the data $data_{j,j'}^{i,i'}$ sent by s_j^i, needed for the invocation of $s_{j'}^{i'}$. It is associated with the properties : $state^t(s_{j'}^{i'}) = ready \implies (\forall s_j^i \in pred_{j'}^{i'} : sent^t(s_j^i, s_{j'}^{i'}) = true)$ and $(\forall s_{j'}^{i'} \in succ_j^i : sent^t(s_j^i, s_{j'}^{i'}) = true) \Leftrightarrow state^t(s_j^i) = finished$.
- $starttime(s_j^i)$ and $invocduration(s_j^i)$ the functions that return respectively the moment when the invocation was made (i.e. entered in the *executing* state) and the duration that the invocation has taken to achieve its computations then all its communications. The result of $starttime(s_j^i)$ is defined if and only if $state^t(s_j^i) \in \{executing, finished\}$, and $invocduration(s_j^i)$ if and only if $state^t(s_j^i) = finished$ at time t.

The makespan can be computed when all service invocations are in *finished* state at a time t. It corresponds to the last invocation completion time, as defined in Eq. (1).

$$makespan = \max_{s_j^i \in \mathbb{S}^{inv}} \left(starttime(s_j^i) + invocduration(s_j^i) \right) \tag{1}$$

This paper compares algorithms for placing services over a fog platform with the objective of minimizing the *makespan*, that is, the time needed to execute all the service invocations of all services from all applications.

3.2 Platform Model

According to the National Institute of Standards and Technology (NIST), fog computing is the set of computing resources between sensors or effectors and the cloud [5]. In this paper, the first layer is called the mist layer, and contains the least powerful machines. This layer differs from the other two layers of more powerful machines due to its extreme proximity to sensors and effectors, as well as its low computing and memory capacity (e.g. single-board computers). Machines that serve as gateways to the mist layer are called edge machines, as they connect to mist nodes using edge communication technologies, such as 5G. The most powerful machines, called fog machines, constitute the fog layer.

According to [7], a fog based smart gridcan be modelized as a 3-level infrastructure, including a layer containing smart meters, a fog layer and a cloud layer. The layer corresponding to smart meters is named smart gridlayer in [7], and will be called mistlayer in this paper. In [14], the authors have shown that fog machines can be localized in electrical substations. In this paper, each of the mist, edge, and fog layers corresponds to fog computing and smart grid elements. The mist layer corresponds to apartments, homes, and offices where smart meters are located, while the edge layer corresponds to buildings or groups of homes. The fog layer corresponds to electrical substations.

The physical locations of the machines are called localities. A locality contains a set of machines of the same type, i.e. mist, edge, fog or cloud. There is always a unique mist machine in each mist locality. However, as the edge and fog machines form clusters that act as gateways, there can be several either edge or fog machines in the same locality.

We represent a building as either a PLC or 5G network that connects the mist machines (apartments) and the edge cluster gateway. The cluster of machines composing each edge locality acts as a gateway. These gateways connect the bellowing mist localities and their upper fog locality (substation). The fog localities are connected to their bellowing edgelocalities by dedicated links as a star topology, and fog machines compose gateways between the edgeand the cloud. The fog localities are connected to the cloud in a star topology network representing a wide or metropolitan area network.

The number of fog localities is noted $\mathcal{X}$ and the xth fog locality is noted $fogcluster_x$. Each $fogcluster_x$ has a number $\mathcal{Y}$ of edge cluster below and has a dedicated number $\mathcal{Z}$ of mistlocalities underneath all its $edgecluster_{x,y}$. Further in this paper, the notion of group will be used to represent a set of localities. For example, an edge-mist group is a set of an $edgecluster_{x,y}$ and all the $\{mist_{x,y,1}, \dots, mist_{x,y,Z}\}$ localities below it. Layers differ from groups in that they represent all the machines of a given locality type (i.e. mist, edge, fog or cloud). We present an overview on how the localities are connected in the Fig. 2.

A **machine** is a physically located node in the infrastructure, which contains some computing units (i.e. CPU or GPU). Let $\mathbb{M}$ be the set of physical machines. For each kth physical machine in the computing infrastructure, noted $m_k \in \mathbb{M}$, we define the following properties:

- $lay_k \in \{Mist, Edge, Fog, Cloud\}$ the layer of the machine m_k.
- ram_k^{max} the total amount of main memory (RAM) on the machine m_k
- ram_k^t the available main memory (RAM) on the machine m_k at the time t.
- $\mathbb{U}_k$ the set of all computing units of the machine m_k.
  - $u_{k,l}^{ded} \in \{true, false\}$ the boolean that indicates if the lth computing unit has a dedicated memory or uses the RAM of m_k as a shared memory.

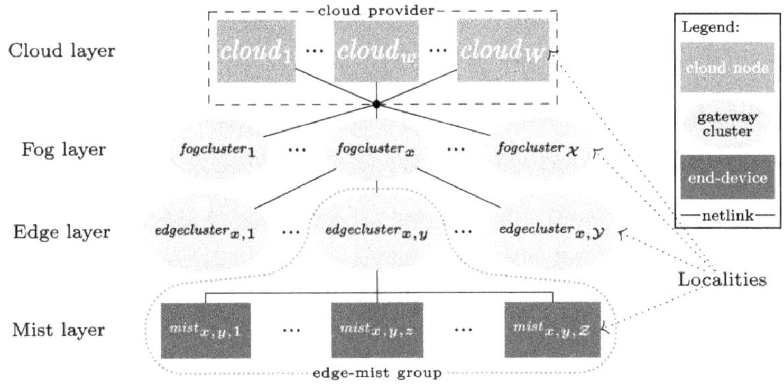

Fig. 2. General topology of a platform

- $u_{k,l} \in \mathbb{U}_k$ the lth computing unit of a machine $m_k \in \mathbb{M}$.
- $u^c_{k,l} \in \mathbb{U}^c$ the class of the computing unit $u_{k,l}$ with $\mathbb{U}^c = \{CPU, GPU\}$ the set of all classes of computing units.
- $speed^{max}_{k,l}$ and $mem^{max}_{k,l}$ respectively the maximum speed and the maximum memory of the computing unit $u_{k,l}$. Please note that $mem^{max}_{k,l}$ can be equal to ram^{max}_k if the computing unit shares its memory with the machine to which it belongs.
- $speed^t_{k,l}$ and $mem^t_{k,l}$ respectively the speed and the memory of the computing unit $u_{k,l}$ at the time t. If $u^{ded}_{k,l} = true$ then $mem^t_{k,l} \equiv ram^t_k$.
- $pcu^{min}_{k,l}$ the minimum power consumption of the computing unit, $pcu^{max}_{k,l}$ the maximum power consumption of the computing unit and $pcu^t_{k,l}$ the power consumption of the computing unit at the time t.

Service Placement. Is the process of assigning a service s_j to some computing units of a machine m_k. It is noted $\upsilon_{j,k}$ with $\upsilon_{j,k} \subset \mathbb{U}_k$. The set of all service placements defined at a time t is noted $\mathbb{P}^t$. A service can only be placed on a machine if the machine has enough resources available to execute the service. We suppose that there is no migration of a service already placed.

4 Proposed Algorithms

All algorithms in this paper assume that *Generation* services are randomly placed on mistmachines before they start. The algorithms aim to place the services of other classes. Indeed, the selection of the data providers are not the subject of this paper, as the data source quality is addressed in dedicated works such as [11].

Functions and variables common to all algorithms are the following:

- $get\_allocation(s_j, m_k, t)$ returns $\upsilon_{j,k}$, an allocation of available units at time t of a machine m_k for the service s_j.

- *sort_applications*($\mathbb{A}$) returns a sorted set of applications. The sorting algorithm is specific to each algorithm.
- *has_resources*(s_j, m_k, t) returns *true* if the machine m_k has enough resources to host the service s_j at time t. It checks the available RAM and GPU memory by verifying whether some GPU units use dedicated memory or share the machine's RAM. If the memory is shared, it is important to account for s_j^{cmem}, in order to not allocate more memory than available. It doesn't take cores into account, so it always allows the cores to time-share and run s_j.

4.1 Most Processing Time First (MPTF) Algorithms

The proposed MPTF algorithms consist of placing service by the service with the most processing time first. In the Algorithm 1, we propose a Machine-Grouping MPTF (MG-MPTF) algorithm that groups machines as explained in Sect. 3.2. All the machines in the localities constituting the fog layer are in a dedicated group, as well of cloudmachines. The first objective of this algorithm is to be aware of the GPU needs of every service, and to ignore GPUs in machine selection if a service does not need them. The second objective is to place the services of a same application in the same group if possible, so that the services can communicate with each other without going through the network.

The first step is the creation of two sorted lists of machine groups, one for CPUs and one for GPUs. Depending on whether the service requires a GPU, the algorithm uses either the CPU or GPU machine group list to iterate through the groups. While iterating through the groups, the algorithm searches for a machine that is available to host the service, taking into account a time-sharing factor.

Two lists of machine groups are built from the set of machines, with one corresponding to CPU speeds and one to GPU speeds respectively *cpuSortedGroups* and *gpuSortedGroups*. There are two variants of this algorithm that will differ on the sorting order, which will be either by putting the fastest machines first (*FastestFirstMG*) or the slowest machines first (*SlowestFirstMG*). In order to sort the machines in all groups of *cpuSortedGroups*, using the variant order, the machines are compared by the total amount of computation speeds of their computing units corresponding to the *CPU* class. The groups are then sorted among themselves by the sum of CPU speed of their machines. Then, the *gpuSortedGroups* is formed by reproducing the same logic but for units of the *GPU* class. These two lists of machine groups are obtained using the *sort_groups* function in lines 4 and 5 of Algorithm 1. *sort_groups* sorts the machines into groups depending on the provided machine set and the computing units class. The applications are sorted from the one containing the most services to the least. The services in each application $\mathcal{A}_i$ are sorted with *sort_services*($\mathcal{A}_i$). This function returns a set of services, where services are sorted by their total computational needs index, from the most to the least. The computational needs index of a service s_j is defined in Eq. (2) using the most CPU and the most GPU computationally intensive values among all services in $\mathcal{A}_i$.

$$\frac{s_j^{cops}}{\max_{s_j \in \mathcal{A}_i}(s_j^{cops})} + \frac{s_j^{gops}}{\max_{s_j \in \mathcal{A}_i}(s_j^{gops})} \tag{2}$$

```
Function MG-MPTF :
    Input: 𝕄 ,𝕊^wf ,t ∈ ℝ+
    ℙ^t ← ∅
    cpuSortedGroups ← sort_groups(𝕄, CPU)
    gpuSortedGroups ← sort_groups(𝕄, GPU)
    for A_i ∈ sort_applications(𝔸) do
        for s_j ∈ A_i do
            selectedGroupSet ← ∅
            if s_j^gops > 0 then
                selectedGroupSet ← gpuSortedGroups
            else
                selectedGroupSet ← cpuSortedGroups
            end
            m_k ← get_first_machine(s_j,
             selectedGroupSet, t)
            υ_j,k ← get_allocation(s_j, m_k, t)
            ℙ^t ← ℙ^t ∪ {(υ_j,k)}
        end
    end
    return ℙ^t
```

Algorithm 1: Machine-Grouping MPTF

```
Function get_first_machine :
    tsFactor ← 1
    while tsFactor ≤ MAX_FACTOR do
        for group ∈ selectedGroupSet do
            for m_k ∈ group do
                if is_viable(t, tsFactor, s_j, m_k) then
                    return m_k
                end
            end
        end
        tsFactor ← tsFactor + 1
    end
```

Algorithm 2: *get_first_machine*

The function $is\_viable(t, tsFactor, s_j, m_k)$ checks if the machine m_k has enough memory at a time t, using $has\_resources(s_j, m_k, t)$. It also checks if there is enough GPU count and CPU cores to host the service s_j, considering a time-sharing factor *tsFactor*. The time-sharing factor is applied to the number of GPU and CPU cores, allowing the cores to be shared among the services. This factor is incremented each time no machine has enough resources to host the service s_j, with a limit of *MAX_FACTOR*, reaching this limit means that the platform is unsuitable. The intended behavior of this factor is to limit the cores time-sharing in the platform without blocking the placement of the services.

4.2 Data and Learning Grouping (DLG) Algorithm

The *data and learning grouping* algorithm (DLG) aims to place learning services the nearest possible from their data provider. In this algorithm, the applications are sorted among them by their total computational needs index, which is the sum of the normalized sums of the CPU and GPU computational needs of their services. The computational needs index of an application $\mathcal{A}_i$ is defined in Eq. (3). As a result, applications are iterated from the one with the most normalized computational needs to the least.

$$\frac{\sum_{s_j \in \mathcal{A}_i} s_j^{cops}}{\max_{\mathcal{A}_{i'} \in \mathbb{A}} \sum_{s_j \in \mathcal{A}_{i'}} s_j^{cops}} + \frac{\sum_{s_j \in \mathcal{A}_i} s_j^{gops}}{\max_{\mathcal{A}_{i'} \in \mathbb{A}} \sum_{s_j \in \mathcal{A}_{i'}} s_j^{gops}} \tag{3}$$

Different functions are used in this algorithm. $get\_data\_gen(s_j)$ returns the unique service $s_{j'}$ with $s_{j'}^{cl} = Generation$ that for each invocation $s_{j'}^{i'} \in \mathbb{S}^{inv}, \exists s_j^i \in succ_{j'}^{i'}$.
$get\_learning\_services(\mathcal{A}_i)$ and $get\_aggregation\_service(\mathcal{A}_i)$ returns the set of learning services and the aggregation service of the application $\mathcal{A}_i$.
$sort\_machines(M)$ returns a sorted set of the machines of M.
$get\_placement(s_j, t)$ returns the machine m_k such that $\exists! \upsilon_{j,k} \in \mathbb{P}^t$.
$get\_edge\_cluster(m_k)$ returns, for machine m_k in locality $mist_{x,y,z}$, the set of machines in the edgecluster above m_k, corresponding to locality $edgecluster_{x,y}$.
$try\_placing\_in\_machine\_set(s_j, M, t)$ returns the first possible placement of the service s_j in the set of machines M at a time t, with machines being sorted using $sort\_machines$.

The objective of this algorithm is to minimize the communication time by trying to place the learning services as close as possible to their data generation service while placing the aggregation service preferably on the fog layer. Placing the aggregation service on the fog layer aims to limit the model update impact on the slowest networks. While iterating over the applications, the services are placed over 2 phases. The first phase, presented in Algorithm 3, places the learning services by considering the data generation service placement location for each learning service. DLG first tries to place the learning service on the same machine as its data generation service, if it is not possible, it tries to place it on an upper machine in the topology.

The second phase, as shown in Algorithm 4, places the aggregation service, which is placed considering the placement of the learning services. The aggregation service will be preferably placed on the fog machines. The fog locality with the most learning services below it will be selected first and, inside the cluster corresponding to this locality, the fog machine with the fewest services placed on will be preferred. This list of fog clusters sorted by the number of learning services below is noted $layer\_fog\_clusters$. The machines inside a fog cluster are sorted from the least service placed on using the function $sort\_machines(M)$. If no fog machine has enough resources to host the aggregation service, the service is preferably placed inside the mist-edge group that has the most machines. The list of mist-edge groups sorted by the number of machines is noted $mist\_edge\_groups$. Inside a group, the machines will be iterated over the returned list of $sort\_machines(M)$.

5 Experimental Results

5.1 Methodology and Environment

We used a simulation-based methodology to evaluate the proposed algorithms. The simulator that we used is Batsim [2], which is well-known in the literature. It focuses on resource management and scheduling while taking energy consumption into account, which is why it was a good choice for our experiments.

An experimental campaign comprises a series of experiments that test multiple algorithms across various numbers of service workflows. Each experiment, defined by a specific algorithm and service-count pair, consists of many samples—simulations that share the same algorithm and service count but differ in the randomized properties (e.g., memory consumption) of each service to ensure statistical accuracy. For each sample, randomization of service properties (normal distribution) on the base workflows as specified in the campaign and input files (repeated per workflow) is performed at first. Next, the simulation is run. Using the algorithm, Batsim simulates the service placements on the machines and their invocations. After all samples complete, a post-processing step analyzes network time and energy consumption. Once every experiment finishes, the pipeline aggregates results and generates plots.

```
Function place_learning_services :
  Input: 𝕄 ,𝒜_i ,t ∈ ℝ⁺
  Output: 𝒫
  𝒫 ← ∅
  for s_l ∈ get_learning_services(𝒜_i) do
    s_g ← get_data_gen(s_l)
    m_k ← get_placement(s_g, t)
    p ← ∅
    if has_resources(s_l, m_k, t) then
      υ_{l,k} ← get_allocation(s_l, m_k, t)
      p ← {υ_{l,k}}
    end
    if p = ∅ then
      edge_cluster ← get_edge_cluster(m_k)
      p ← try_placing_in_machine_set(s_l,
        edge_cluster, t)
    end
    if p = ∅ then
      fog_machines ← {m_f | m_f ∈ 𝕄 ∧ lay_f = Fog}
      p ← try_placing_in_machine_set(s_l,
        fog_machines, t)
    end
    if p = ∅ then
      cloud_machines ← {m_c | m_c ∈ 𝕄 ∧ lay_c = Cloud}
      p ← try_placing_in_machine_set(s_l,
        cloud_machines, t)
    end
    𝒫 ← 𝒫 ∪ p
  end
  return 𝒫
```

Algorithm 3: DLG learning placement phase

```
Function place_aggregation_service :
  Input: 𝒜_i
  Output: 𝒫
  s_a ← get_aggregation_service(𝒜_i)
  𝒫 ← ∅
  while 𝒫 = ∅ and
   layer_fog_clusters ≠ ∅ do
    fog_cluster ← pop_first(
      layer_fog_clusters)
    𝒫 ←
      try_placing_in_machine_set(s_a,
      fog_cluster, t)
  end
  while 𝒫 = ∅ and
   mist_edge_groups ≠ ∅ do
    group ← pop_first(
      mist_edge_groups)
    𝒫 ←
      try_placing_in_machine_set(s_a,
      group, t)
  end
  if 𝒫 = ∅ then
    𝒫 ←
      try_placing_in_machine_set(s_a,
      cloud_machines, t)
  end
  return 𝒫
```

Algorithm 4: *DLG* aggregation placement phase

The entire experimental workflow is implemented in Snakemake and executed in a Nix-defined environment (including Snakemake, Batsim, etc.). This environment is fully specified for recursive reproducibility, isolated from the host system, and ensures that results depend solely on the Nix configuration. A single, fixed random-number-generator seed for the entire campaign guarantees deterministic, reproducible outcomes and controls random statistical biases.

In order to compare the studied algorithms to naive ones, different algorithms have been implemented. The *AllInCloud* algorithm places all services in the cloud. The machines are initially shuffled, and the services are placed with a round-robin distribution. If the machine does not have enough resources to host the service, it is skipped. On the other hand, the *IoTFirst* algorithm shuffles the machines and sorts them by computation speed in ascending or descending order. The services iterate over the machines until they find a machine that has enough resources to host them. There are two variants, which are named according to the sorting order (i.e. *FastestIoTFirst* and *SlowestIoTFirst*).

For both algorithms, the services are sorted using the *sort_services* function from Sect. 4.1. All of these algorithms iterate on the services by starting with the service with the most amount of operations per invocation.

5.2 Input Data

The specifications of the machines, in terms of speed (flops for CPU and TOPs for GPU), memory (RAM and GPU memory), and power consumption, are extracted from the manufacturer or from literature specifications. Each cloud machine is composed of 2 *AMD EPYC 9654*,256 *GB* of RAM and 8 *NVIDIA Tesla A100*. The mist machines are *Nvidia Jetson Orin Nano (8GB)*, the edge machines are *Nvidia Jetson Orin NX (16GB)*, and the fog machines are *Nvidia Jetson AGX Orin (32GB)*.

The number of machines per locality is 1 mistmachine, 8 edgemachines, 8 fog machines, and 1 cloud machine. The minimum power consumption (pmin) of the GPUs is counted as 0, since we consider that the system can disable the GPU when it is not used. As for the number of localities, there are $\mathcal{X} = 5$ fog localities. There is also an average of $\mathcal{Y} = 3.4$ edgeper fog localities, and each edgelocality has an average of $\mathcal{Z} = 33.6$ mistlocalities underneath. The count of cloud localities is 10 (i.e. 10 cloud machines).

PLC or 5G links are used between the mistmachines and their edgegateways. The PLC values are extracted from the Broadcom BCM60500 module presented in [1], along with an energy consumption model. The 5G base-stations corresponds to an indoor *RAKwireless All In One 5G* base-station. The bandwidth of the 5G links are defined as a 1.25 Gb/s network between the mistmachines and their edgelocality. The edgelocalities are connected to their fog locality through an optical fiber link, which uses a *Cisco CGP-ONT-1P* optical network terminal and a *Cisco CGP-OLT-16T* optical line terminal. The network between the cloud and fog layers is a wide area network (WAN). Since it is not managed by the smart grid or cloud provider, we do not account for the energy consumption of this part of the network. A *Dell PowerSwitch S5200-ON* ethernet switch is used to connect the cloud machines between them. A factor of 0.8 is applied to the speeds of the links to account for network loss.

Each service workflow is based on a distributed learning application, based on MobileNetV2 architecture and the CIFAR-10 dataset. This application is used in the literature for smart grid use-cases [4,13]. We extracted the service properties by measuring the resource usage of the different services of this application when being distributed into 10 *Learning* services for 1 *Aggregation* server. The measurements were done using the *Gres* cluster on the Grid'5000 platform. When measuring a service, it is run on a different machine in the cluster to avoid any interference. The size of the data used to train the local model at each round was also measured. This corresponds to the data exchanged from a *Generation* service to a *Learning* service.

The size of the data sent by each *Generation* service invocations is set to 49.152 MB. *Learning* services are set to use 3.01 GB of RAM and 1.536 GB of GPU RAM. Each invocation of *Learning* costs 15.47 GFLOPs of CPU and 338.6 TOPs of GPU. The *Aggregation* service uses 1.01 GB of RAM and 694.7 MFLOPs of CPU (FedAvg). The size of the model exchanged by the *Aggregation* and *Learning* services is 8.8 MB. The base service workflow is so composed of 10 *Generation* services, 10 *Learning* services and 1 *Aggregation* service. There is 50 rounds for each application (i.e. 50 invocations for each service).

For the MG-MPTF algorithms (i.e. *SlowestFirstMG* and *FastestFirstMG*), the MAX_FACTOR value is set to 10.

5.3 Results

Algorithm were compared by simulating a variable number of applications. The number of applications tested is 1, 20, 40, 60, 80, and 100. Since there are 21 services per application, these numbers correspond to a total of 21, 420, 840, 1260, 1680, and 2100 services, respectively. There are 60 samples (simulations) per experiment, and there is an experiment for each algorithm (6) and application number (6). The total number of simulations is $6 \times 6 \times 60 = 2160$.

The Fig. 3 shows how the metric results vary as the number of services increases. The result metrics are the makespan (3a), the energy consumed by the network (3b), energy consumption by the machines (3c) and total energy consumption (3d). Each point in these plots represents the mean value of a given metric (y-axis) for a particular combination of an algorithm (color) and a number of services (x-axis). As shown in Fig. 3a, *DLG*, *FastestIoTFirst*, *FastestFirstMG* and *AllInCloud* algorithms present the best mean makespan results. On the other hand, *SlowestFirstMG* and *SlowestIoTFirst* diverge from the other algorithms, as their respective mean makespans are 29.8% and 41.1% higher than those of *DLG*, *AllInCloud*, *FastestIoTFirst* and *FastestFirstMG*.

As for the energy consumption, the results in Fig. 3d show that the *DLG* algorithm consumes the least total energy (network and machines), with a mean energy consumption 1.9 times lower than the second lowest algorithm, *FastestIoTFirst*. *FastestFirstMG* tends to consume less energy as the number of applications increases, but it is still 2.9 times more energy consuming than *DLG*. With respectively 5.2 times and 6.1 times more energy consumed than *DLG*, *SlowestIoTFirst* and *SlowestFirstMG* are the most energy consuming algorithms when reaching 2100 services (100 applications).

A more detailed view of the energy consumption of the network and machines in Figs. 3b and 3c shows additional insights. It appears that *DLG* and *AllInCloud* energy consumptions are mainly due to the machines (i.e. 76.9% and 74.7% for 2100 services). The other algorithms consume more energy in the network with 60.2% for *FastestIoTFirst*, 66.7% for *FastestFirstMG*, 68.9% for *SlowestIoTFirst* and 78.4% for *SlowestFirstMG*.

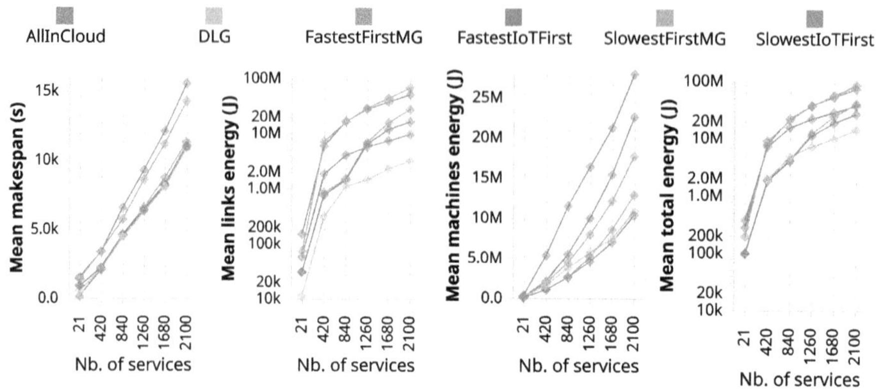

(a) (b) (c) (d)

Fig. 3. Mean makespan, links energy, machine energy and total energy for each algorithm and number of services

It seems that the *DLG* algorithm is able to reduce the network energy consumption by placing *Learning* services preferably with the *Generation* ones, and the *Aggregation* service upper in the topology (meaning faster networks). In contrary, *SlowestFirstMG* aims to regroup the *Learning* and *Aggregation* services of an application as close as possible to each other, discarding the location of the *Generation* services. The results demonstrate the feasibility of efficiently deploying distributed learning services on a fog computing platform at the smart grid scale. However, this is possible when the service placement algorithm focuses on reducing the transfer time of learning data and model exchange, as *DLG* does. The *DLG* algorithm significantly outperforms others in terms of platform energy consumption, particularly with regard to network energy. *DLG* also reduces the makespan to the level of *AllInCloud*, which uses faster computational machines.

6 Conclusion and Future Work

In this paper, we focus on the problem of placing distributed learning services in a fog computing platform adapted to AI and scaled for smart grids.

We presented a model for the placement of distributed learning services, as well as a model for a smart grid-dimensioned fog computing platform. A set of algorithms was also proposed to minimize the makespan, and indirectly, the energy consumption of the machines and network, when placing the services.

We evaluated the proposed algorithms using a simulation-based methodology and a large number of samples. The results demonstrate that network usage inherent to distributed machine learning significantly impacts energy consumption, and that *DLG* is able to greatly reduce the energy consumption while not sacrificing the makespan. Future work may focus on replacement strategies for services in cases where machines become unavailable due to failure.

Acknowledgments. This work was supported by the French State through the National Research Agency (ANR) under the France 2030 program, reference 22-PETA-0004 - AI-NRGY project. Experiments presented in this paper were carried out using the Grid'5000 testbed, supported by a scientific interest group hosted by Inria and including CNRS, RENATER and several Universities as well as other organizations (see https://www.grid5000.fr).

References

1. Bakkali, W., Pagani, P., Chonavel, T.: Experimental analysis and modeling of energy consumption behaviour for MIMO PLC Modems. In: 2015 IEEE Global Communications Conference (GLOBECOM), pp. 1–5 (2015)
2. Dutot, P.F., Mercier, M., Poquet, M., Richard, O.: Batsim: a realistic language-independent resources and jobs management systems simulator. In: 20th Workshop on Job Scheduling Strategies for Parallel Processing (2016)
3. Hosseinalipour, S., Brinton, C.G., Aggarwal, V., Dai, H., Chiang, M.: From federated to fog learning: distributed machine learning over heterogeneous wireless networks. IEEE Commun. Mag. **58**(12), 41–47 (2020)
4. Huang, J., Wan, Q.: Smart grid line fault detection based on deep learning image recognition algorithm. Int. J. Low-Carbon Technol. **19**, 2174–2180 (2024)
5. Iorga, M., Feldman, L., Barton, R., Martin, M.J., Goren, N.S., Mahmoudi, C.: Fog Computing Conceptual Model. Tech. rep., Michaela Iorga, Larry Feldman, Robert Barton, Michael J. Martin, Nedim S. Goren, Charif Mahmoudi (2018)
6. Lin, Z., Bi, S., Zhang, Y.J.A.: Optimizing AI service placement and resource allocation in mobile edge intelligence systems. IEEE Trans. Wireless Commun. **20**(11), 7257–7271 (2021)
7. Okay, F., Ozdemir, S.: A fog computing based smart grid model (2016)
8. Rajagopal, S.M., M., S., Buyya, R.: FedSDM: federated learning based smart decision making module for ECG data in IoT integrated edge–fog–cloud computing environments. Internet Things **22**, 100784 (2023)
9. Saadatmand, M., Ramezy, b., Mozafari, B.: Review of Communication Technologies for Smart Grid applications (2017)
10. Shi, S., Wang, Q., Chu, X.: Performance modeling and evaluation of distributed deep learning frameworks on GPUs. In: 2018 IEEE International Conference on Dependable, Autonomic and Secure Computing, International Conference on Pervasive Intelligence and Computing, International Conference on Big Data Intelligence and Computing and Cyber Science and Technology Congress(DASC/PiCom/DataCom/CyberSciTech) (2018)
11. Yellas, N.E.H., Addis, B., Boumerdassi, S., Riggio, R., Secci, S.: Function placement for in-network federated learning. Comput. Netw. **256** (2025)
12. Yi, S., Li, C., Li, Q.: A survey of fog computing: concepts, applications and issues. In: Proceedings of the 2015 Workshop on Mobile Big Data, pp. 37–42. Association for Computing Machinery, New York (2015)
13. Zhao, R., et al.: A Federated-learning algorithm based on client sampling and gradient projection for the smart grid. Electronics **13**(11), 2023 (2024)
14. Zhao, S., et al.: Smart and practical privacy-preserving data aggregation for fog-based smart grids. IEEE Trans. Inf. Forensics Secur. **16**, 521–536 (2021)
15. Zhou, Z., Chen, X., Li, E., Zeng, L., Luo, K., Zhang, J.: Edge intelligence: paving the last mile of artificial intelligence with edge computing. Proc. IEEE **107**(8), 1738–1762 (2019)

SLO-FEI: A Novel Secure and Lightweight Offloading Approach for Fog–Edge Federation-Based IoT

Yashar Salami(✉)

Faculty of Computer and Information Technologies, Cappadocia University, Ürgüp, Nevşehir, Turkey
Yashar.salami@kapadokya.edu.tr

Abstract. The Internet of Things (IoT) has rapidly evolved into a fundamental technology in modern life. However, IoT devices often struggle with computationally intensive tasks due to limited processing capabilities. Offloading such tasks to fog or edge nodes can alleviate this burden,s but introduces significant computational and communication costs. Moreover, the inherent vulnerabilities of wireless communication channels expose IoT systems to active and passive security threats during the offloading process. We propose SLO-FEI, a lightweight and secure offloading approach designed for IoT environments to address these issues. The approach utilises Elliptic Curve Cryptography (ECC) to provide mutual authentication and secure session key establishment between communicating entities, ensuring data confidentiality and integrity during task delegation. We evaluate the security of the SLO-FEI approach using both formal methods and informal analysis. The results demonstrate strong resistance to a wide range of potential attacks. Additionally, we compare SLO-FEI with a related existing approach in terms of computational and communication overhead, as well as security features. Our findings indicate that SLO-FEI achieves enhanced security with reduced overhead, making it a cost-effective and reliable solution for secure offloading in resource-constrained and wireless-vulnerable IoT scenarios.

Keywords: Lightweight · Offloading · Secure · IOT

1 Introduction

The IoT, a key enabler of the Fourth Industrial Revolution, integrates billions of devices for real-time data processing and intelligent decision-making empowered by AI and optimization [1, 2]. Its applications span transportation, healthcare, energy, and urban infrastructure, including smart vehicles and drones that enhance mobility, monitoring, and automation [3, 4]. However, large-scale connectivity introduces challenges in security, privacy, and data management. Blockchain technology addresses these concerns through decentralisation, immutability, and transparent authentication, enabling secure collaboration via smart contracts [5–8]. The integration of IoT and blockchain promotes

H. R. Arabnia et al. (Eds.): CSCE 2025, CCIS 2934, pp. 116–131, 2026.
https://doi.org/10.1007/978-3-032-22190-2_9

reliable, tamper-resistant, and transparent systems [9, 10]. Yet, IoT devices remain constrained by limited computation and energy, necessitating lightweight, energy-efficient, and fog-assisted offloading mechanisms for secure and effective real-time operations [11]. Khashan et al. (2020) proposed a method that fails to eliminate processing latency due to re-encryption at fog nodes and lacks support for lightweight offloading [12]. Michailidis et al. (2022) introduced an approach that does not adequately address the energy and computational limitations of unmanned aerial vehicles, nor does it support lightweight offloading [13]. Benisha Chris et al. (2025) presented a method that falls short in optimizing resources in heterogeneous IoT scenarios and cannot support lightweight secure offloading. Chakraborty et al. (2023) proposed a solution that is ineffective in mitigating execution delays in dynamic fog environments and does not support lightweight offloading [14]. Gong et al. (2024) offered a method that does not ensure scalability in large-scale IoT systems and is unable to support lightweight secure offloading [15]. Irshad et al. (2022) proposed a solution that inadequately mitigates sophisticated insider threats in MEC environments and fails to support lightweight secure offloading [16]. Al-Daraiseh et al. (2022) introduced a method that lacks robust user access control to sensitive data in smart home settings and does not support lightweight secure offloading [17]. Kenioua et al. (2024) presented an approach that cannot effectively prevent advanced threats such as impersonation in edge computing and lacks lightweight secure offloading capabilities [18]. Tanveer et al. (2025) introduced a solution that falls short in ensuring scalability in dense 6G IoT networks and lacks support for lightweight secure offloading [19]. Ravindra et al. (2024) offered a method that fails to mitigate man-in-the-middle attacks in device-dense IoT environments and is incapable of lightweight secure offloading [20]. Hou et al. (2025) proposed a solution that does not reduce computational overhead for lightweight IoT devices and lacks support for lightweight secure offloading [21]. Yashar et al. (2024) proposed a secure offloading approach in IoT, which does not support lightweight secure offloading [22]. Given that the absence of lightweight secure offloading in IoT environments has been recognized as a research gap in prior studies, this paper proposes a novel lightweight secure offloading method for IoT environments based on fog and cloud computing.

1.1 Paper Contribution

We propose SLO-FEI, a lightweight and secure offloading scheme designed for IoT environments. It ensures mutual authentication between entities, supports secure session key generation, and enables trusted device selection for efficient task offloading, all while maintaining security. Comprehensive evaluations demonstrate its superiority in communication, computation, and security compared with existing schemes, while both formal and informal analyses confirm its robustness against common attacks.

1.2 Paper Organisation

The remainder of this paper is structured as follows: Sect. 2 introduces the network model, underlying assumptions, and problem statement. Section 3 details the SLO-FEI approach. Section 4 provides a comprehensive security analysis, employing both formal and informal methods. Section 5 presents the performance evaluation, including computational and communication costs, as well as additional security features. Finally, Sect. 6 concludes the paper with a summary of findings and future research directions.

2 Network Model and Problem Statement

This section presents the network model, outlines the underlying assumptions, adversarial model, and defines the problem statement.

2.1 Network Model

Network models play a vital role in modern data communication and processing. The proposed SLO-FEI network model comprises three main layers: cloud, fog, and end. The cloud layer, positioned at the top, offers extensive storage and powerful computational resources, acting as a central data hub that communicates with the fog layer. The fog layer, serving as an intermediate bridge, has lower processing and storage capabilities than the cloud but exceeds the end layer. It interacts with both the cloud and blockchain networks to process data closer to its source, thereby reducing latency and improving system efficiency. The end layer consists of vehicles, roadside stations, and drones with limited energy and computing capacity, yet capable of local data collection and communication with fog nodes. Together, these layers enable hierarchical data processing: the cloud manages large-scale computation, the fog handles intermediate operations and latency optimisation, and the end layer focuses on edge-level data acquisition. Figure 1 illustrates the overall network model.

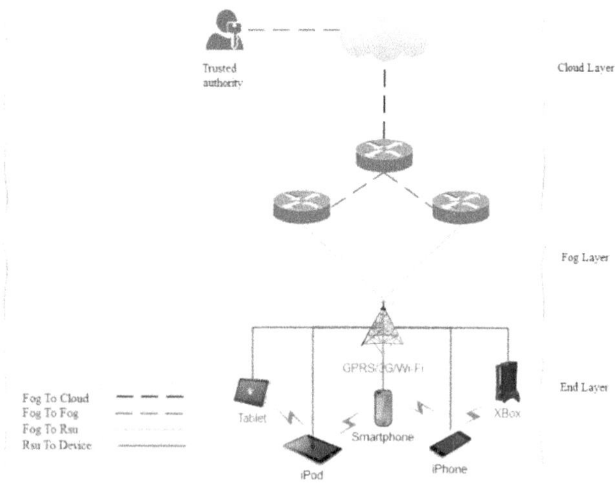

Fig. 1. Network model [22].

2.2 Assumption Model

The network model assumes that all vehicles and fog nodes are synchronised and operate uniformly. In reality, their environments are heterogeneous, with differences in computational power, processing capabilities, and communication quality. The fog and cloud layers are mutually aware and maintain secure, coordinated communication through their resilient design. The fog layer also interacts securely with the blockchain network to ensure reliable data exchange, while fog nodes within this layer can identify and communicate effectively with each other. However, newly joined vehicles lack prior knowledge of existing fog nodes, facing an unfamiliar environment during offloading. At the edge layer, communication security remains insufficient, and nodes with limited processing and storage resources are more vulnerable to potential threats, reducing their efficiency in managing data.

2.3 Adversarial Model

This research adopts the Dolev–Yao (D&Y) adversarial model to systematically analyze potential security vulnerabilities within the network's communication infrastructure. The model assumes an adversary capable of intercepting, observing, and manipulating messages exchanged between legitimate entities at the edge layer. Acting as a man-in-the-middle, the attacker may access confidential information without detection. The D&Y framework distinguishes between passive eavesdropping, where the adversary silently monitors communications to extract sensitive data, and active interference, which involves modifying, injecting, or blocking messages to disrupt or deceive participants. Using this framework, the network's vulnerabilities are identified, and the SLO-FEI scheme is evaluated against threats such as impersonation, replay, and man-in-the-middle attacks through both formal and informal analyses, including model-based evaluations and simulated attack scenarios.

2.4 Problem Statement

IoT devices at the edge layer face limited computational power and energy capacity, necessitating the offloading of intensive tasks to fog or cloud nodes with higher processing capabilities. While this task offloading improves efficiency, it also introduces critical security challenges such as data interception, manipulation, and eavesdropping. To address these risks, mutual authentication between entities is essential before data exchange. Recognising the lack of lightweight and secure offloading mechanisms in IoT environments, this study proposes a hybrid fog-cloud-based lightweight offloading scheme that minimises computational overhead while preserving data integrity and confidentiality. The proposed solution utilises robust authentication and encryption techniques to ensure authorised access and secure data transmission, thereby enhancing the integrity, reliability, and trustworthiness of IoT ecosystems.

3 SLO-FEI

This section presents an SLO-FEI approach that includes the Notations and Initialisation Phase, Register phase, Login and Authentication Phase, and final Offloading phase.

3.1 Notation

Table 1 shows the Notation used in the SLO-FEI approach.

Table 1. Notation SLO-FEI approach.

Notation	Description
Cs	*Cloud*
Fs	*Fog*
R	*RSU or Fog node*
Ii, Ij	*IoT device*
TA	*Trusted authority*
IdCs, IdFi, IdRi, IdIi, IdIj,	*Cs, Fi, Ri, Ii, Ij*
r1, r2	*Random number for Ecc*
R1	*Random number by IdRi*
Pow	*Processing power of an IoT device*
Pr	*Processing requirements*
RO	*Result Offloading*
Pwi	*Password Hash function of IdIi*
TCs, TFi, TRi, TIi, TIj	*Timestamp Cs, R, Fs, Ii, Ij*
ΔT	*The maximum delay*
$h(\cdot)$	*The Hash function*
$\oplus$	*XOR*
$\Vert$	*Concatenation operation*

3.2 Initialization

Initially, IdRi, IdIj, and IdFi agree on an elliptic curve defined by the equation. $y^2 = x^3 + ax + b$ Over a finite field Zp. They each select parameters ∊ Zp such that the equation. $y^2 = x^3 + ax + bmodp$ Defines a valid elliptic curve. On this curve, G is chosen as a base point of prime order n, where $n > 2^{160}$. The point at infinity is denoted as O, satisfying the equation. $n.G = O$. Next, IdRi, IdIj, and IdFi each randomly select secret keys, denoted as Pr and PfJ, respectively. A summary of the initialization phase is shown in Fig. 2.

Initialization
IdRi, IdIj, IdFi Chooses: $(y^2 = x^3 + ax + b)\ (mod\ p)$
where $4a^3 + 27b^2(mod\ p) \neq 0$, *voer* $Zp\ (P > 2^{160})$
Pr: IdRi secret key; $P = (Pr.G)$: *IdRi public key*
PfJ: IdIj, IdFi, and secret key; $P = (Pfj.G)$: *IdIj public key*
G: generator point; $r.G = O, r > 2^{160}$

Fig. 2. Initialisation phase.

3.3 Register Phase

Step 1: Registration phase. First step in IdIi Computing S1 = h(Pwi ⊕ IdIi)||(IdIi ⊕ TIi) and sends {S1, Pwi, IdIi, TIi} to IdRi.

Step 2: After receiving the message IdRi, the first step is to check if TIi < ΔT and compute S1′ = h(Pwi ⊕ IdIi)||(IdIi ⊕ TIi) and check if S1 = S1′Computing Rr = ((IdRi||IdFi||IdCs||TRi) ⊕ (S1)), inpub = h(IdRi||IdFi||IdCs||Rr||TRi) and Select a random number R1 computing pub = h((IdRi ⊕ Pr)||(IdRi ⊕ IdFi ⊕ IdCs) ⊕ R1), IdIi(pub) = pub. G, Pk = h(IdRi||Rr||inpub||IdIi(pub)), Pki = Pk. G,S2 = h(Rr, inpub, IdIi(pub), TRi),Storage Pki, IdIi(pub), pub, S1, in memory and Send {Rr, IdIi(pub), pub, S2, TRi} to the IdIi.

Step 3: After receiving the message IdIi check if TRi < ΔT Computing Rr′ = ((IdRi||IdFi||IdCs||TRi) ⊕ (S1)) and Check if Rr = Rr′, S2′ = h(Rr, inpub, IdIi(pub), Rr, TRi). Check if S2 = S2′, Storge {IdIi(pub), Rr, inpub} in memory. Figure 3 shows the Register phase.

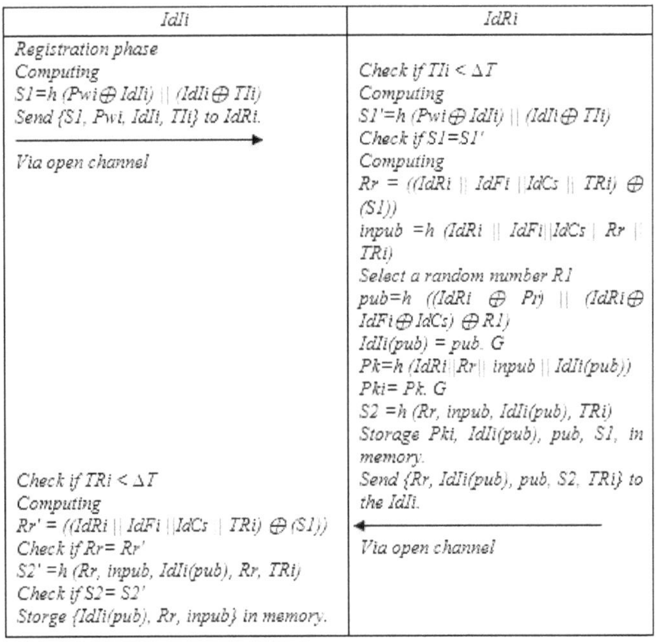

Fig. 3. Register phase.

3.4 Login and Authentication Phase

Step 1: IdIi first step Select a random number r1 and compute x1 = (r1.G), x2 = h(r1. IdIi(pub)), x3 = h((x1 ⊕ x2 ⊕ TIi)||(IdRi ⊕ IdIi)), and Send {x1, x2, x3, TIi, IdIi, IdIi(pub), IdRi} to IdRi.

Step 2: After receiving the message IdRi, check if TIi < ΔT and compute x3′ = h((P1 ⊕ P2 ⊕ TIi)||(IdRi ⊕ IdIi)), and check if x3 = x3′. Compute pub =

h((IdRi ⊕ Pr)||(IdRi ⊕ IdFi ⊕ IdCs) ⊕ R1), Checking IdIi(pub), from the database, Check if IdIi(pub) = IdIi(pub), x2* = h(x1. IdIi(pub)), Verify x2* = x2, if true, then select a random number r2 and compute, x4 = r2.G; x5 = r2. Pki, x6 = h((x4 ⊕ x5)||(IdRi ⊕ TRi)), Sends {x4, x5, x6, IdRi, TRi} to IdIi.

Step 3: First, check if TRi < ΔT and Computing x6′ = h((x4 ⊕ x5)||(IdRi ⊕ TRi)), Check if x6 = x6′, Pk = h(IdRi||Rr||inpub||IdIi(pub)), Pki* = Pk.G, x5* = x4.Pki*, Verify x5* = x5 Computing SIR = r1.x7 = r1. r2.G, S3 = h((r1.IdIi(pub))||SIR)), S4 = h((S3 ⊕ Pow ⊕ TIi)||(IdRi ⊕ IdIi)), Send {S3, S4, Pow, TIi, IdRi, IdIi} to IdRi.

Step 4: IdRi first, Check if TIi < ΔT and computing S4′ = h ((S3 ⊕ Pow ⊕ TIi)||(IdRi ⊕ IdIi)), Computing SIR* = r2.x8 = r2. r1.G; S3* = h ((x8. IdIi′)||SK*)), Verify S3* = S3, if true, RSU authentication IOT; Otherwise, S3 rejected. After mutual authentication, the session key SIR = r1.x7 = r1. r2. G = r2. x8 SIR* is shared. Storage Pow in memory. St = h ((IdIi(pub)) ⊕ IdIi)||(Pow ⊕ TRi)||(IdRi ⊕ IdFi)), Sends {IdIi(pub), IdIi, Pow, TRi, IdRi, IdFi, St} to IdFi.

Step5: IdFi after receiving massage first Check if TRi < ΔT, St′ = h((IdIi′ ⊕ IdIi)||(Pow ⊕ TRi)||(IdRi ⊕ IdFi)), Check if St = St′., Storage {IdIi(pub)*, IdIi, IdRi, Pow} in database. Figure 4 shows the Login and Authentication Phase.

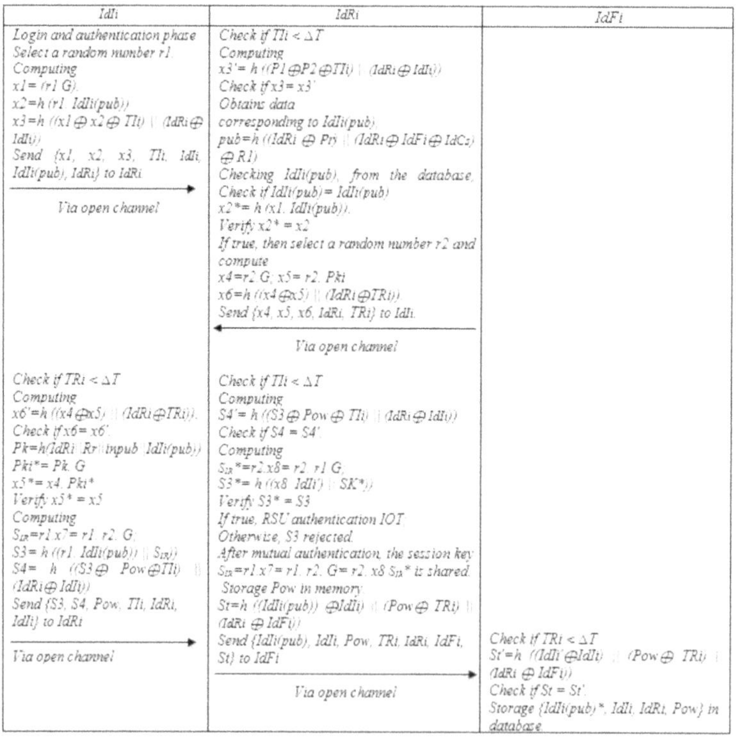

Fig. 4. Login and Authentication phase.

3.5 Offloading Phase

Step 1: First step IdIi sends {IdIi(pub), Pr, TIi} to IdRi for Request Offloading.

Step2: IdRi Check if TIi $< \Delta T$ and Computing, pub $= h((\text{IdRi} \oplus \text{pr})||(\text{IdRi} \oplus \text{IdFi}) \oplus \text{R1})$, Checking IdIi(pub), from the database, Verify IdIi(pub) = IdIi(pub)′ and Send {IdIi(pub), Pr, TRi} to IdFi.

Step 3: IdFi, after receiving IdRi, check if TRi $< \Delta T$. Check if IdIi(pub), from the database, Check if Verify IdIi(pub)′* = IdIi(pub) = IdIi(pub)*, Search for required processing power. If available S4 $= h((\text{IdIi(pub)}'^{*} \oplus \text{PfJ})||(\text{Pow}, \oplus \text{Pr})||(\text{IdIi} \oplus \text{TFi}) \oplus \text{IdRi}) \oplus (\text{PfJ}||\text{IdIj})$, Rf = S4. G Send {IdIi, IdIi(pub)′*, Pow, Pr, IdIisf′, TFi, IdRi, Rf, S4, IdIj} to IdIj.

Step 4: IdIj first Check if TFi $< \Delta T$ Computing S4′ $= h((\text{IdIi(pub)}'^{*} \oplus \text{PfJ})||(\text{Pow}, \oplus \text{Pr})||(\text{IdIi} \oplus \text{TFi}) \oplus \text{IdRi}) \oplus (\text{PfJ}||\text{IdIj})$ Check if S4 = S4′ Computing Rf′ = S4. G Check if Verify Rf = Rf ′Computing Offloading for processing IdIi and sending the result. (RO) sends to IdFi.

Step 5: IdFi Receive RO and Send {RO} to IdRi, IdRi Receive RO and Send {RO} to IdIi, IdIi Receive RO and compilation offloading. Figure 5 shows the Offloading phase. Figure 5 shows the Offloading phase.

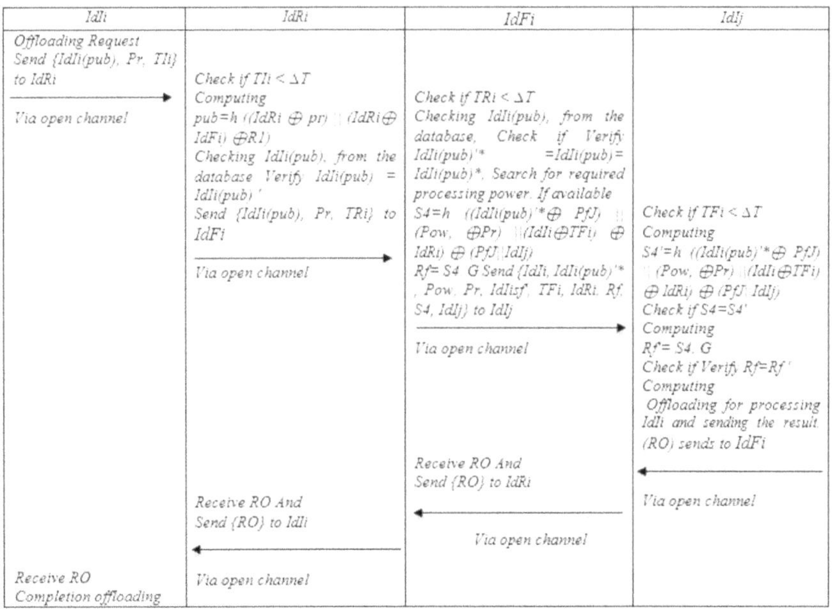

Fig. 5. Offloading phase.

4 Security Analysis

This section presents a formal analysis and an informal analysis-based DY threat model.

4.1 Formal Analysis

Avispa is a security-sensitive tool widely used to validate security protocols against active or passive adversaries. Its primary goal is to ensure resistance to Man-in-the-middle and Replay attacks. Avispa employs the High-Level Protocol Specification Language (HLPSL), a role-oriented language for describing participant roles and protocol execution scenarios. Protocols are tested using one of four backends: OFMC, CL-AtSe, SATMC, or TA4SP. HLPSL code is converted to an Intermediate Format (IF), processed by a backend, and produces an Output Format (OF).

4.2 Formal Result

The Avispa tool validated the security of the Lightweight Offloading protocol through two backends, CL-AtSe and OFMC, both confirming the protocol as SAFE within a bounded session model, demonstrating resilience against attacks such as Man-in-the-middle and Replay. Figs. 6 and 7 show the CL-AtSe and OFMC results. CL-AtSe Analysis: The backend explored 44 states (16 reachable) using a typed model, ensuring robust type-checking. Translation to Intermediate Format (IF) required 0.17s, with constraint-solving computation at 0.8s. The bounded session model constrained the state space, enabling efficient security validation. OFMC Analysis: OFMC examined 14 nodes across a 12-ply search depth, completing in 0.27s (parse time: 0.00s). It's an optimized on-the-fly model-checking that minimizes node exploration, enhancing verification speed. Comparative Insights: Both backends affirm the protocol's security, with CL-AtSe's extensive state analysis (44 states) offering thorough coverage and OFMC's leaner exploration (14 nodes, 0.27s) prioritizing efficiency. The consistent SAFE outcomes across backends reinforce the protocol's robustness. While limiting scalability analysis, the bounded session model ensures computational tractability, making the protocol ideal for lightweight, security-critical applications.

4.3 In Formal Analysis

Replay Attack: In a replay attack, an adversary resends previously intercepted messages to deceive the system. The SLO-FEI approach mitigates this threat by incorporating timestamps (e.g., TIi, TRi) in each message, which are verified against a predefined time window (ΔT). During the login phase, if an attacker replays a message such as {x1, x2, x3, TIi}, the roadside unit (IdRi) checks whether TIi falls within the allowed ΔT. If it does not, the message is discarded, rendering replay attacks ineffective.

Man-in-the-Middle Attack: This attack involves intercepting and modifying messages during transmission. The approach employs ECC-based private (e.g., Pr, PfJ) and public keys (e.g., IdIi(pub)), protected by secure hash functions such as h ((IdRi $\oplus$ Pr)||). During the authentication phase, values like x3 and S4 are generated using session-specific random numbers (r1, r2) and hash operations. Without access to Pr or r1, an attacker cannot generate valid messages, thus preventing this type of attack.

Impersonation Attack: In this scenario, an attacker attempts to masquerade as a legitimate participant (e.g., IdIi or IdRi). The approach authenticates entities using public keys like IdIi(pub) and values derived from private keys and hashes (e.g., Pki). In

```
% OFMC
% Version of 2006/02/13
SUMMARY
 SAFE
DETAILS
 OUNDED_NUMBER_OF_SESSIONS
PROTOCOL
/home/span/span/testsuite/results/Lightwe
ight Offloading. If
GOAL
 as_specified
BACKEND
 OFMC
COMMENTS
STATISTICS
 parseTime: 0.00s
 searchTime: 0.27s
 visited Nodes: 14 nodes
depth: 12 plies
```

Fig. 6. CL-AtSe results.

```
SUMMARY
 SAFE
DETAILS
BOUNDED_NUMBER_OF_SESSIONS
 TYPED_MODEL
PROTOCOL
/home/span/span/testsuite/results/
Lightweight Offloading. If
GOAL
 as_Specified
BACKEND
 CL-AtSe

STATISTICS
 Analysed: 44 states
 Reachable: 16 states
 Translation: 0.17 seconds
 Computation: 0.8 seconds
```

Fig. 7. OFMC results.

the login phase, IdRi verifies whether x2 = h(r1. IdIi(pub)) matches the received x2*. Without knowledge of r1 or Pr, it is computationally infeasible for an adversary to forge a valid identity, thereby thwarting impersonation attempts.

Brute-force Attack: Brute-force attacks require exhaustive searching over all possible combinations of security parameters such as Pr, R1, and R2. Given that ECC key lengths exceed 2^{160} bits and random numbers are protected via hash functions, the keyspace is astronomically large. Consequently, guessing secret values like XR, Xisf, or r1 becomes computationally infeasible.

Stolen Verifier Attack: In this attack, an adversary gains access to stored verification data (e.g., Pki, IdIi(pub)) and attempts to misuse it. However, in the SLO-FEI approach, such values are useless without the associated private keys (Pr, PfJ) or session-specific random numbers (r1, r2). For example, generating valid x2 or S3 during authentication requires r1, which is never stored. Thus, the stolen verifier attack is effectively neutralized.

Session Key Leakage Attack: The session key (SIR = r1·r2·G) is established during the authentication phase. Since r1 and r2 are randomly generated and never directly transmitted, but instead embedded within hashes such as S3 and S4, adversaries cannot derive SIR. ECC-based key generation further strengthens the resistance to key leakage.

Guessing Attack: This attack targets passwords (Pwi) or secret keys through educated guessing. In the registration phase, Pwi is secured using S1 = h (Pwi ⊕ IdIi)||(IdIi ⊕ TIi), and is never transmitted in plaintext. Furthermore, private keys (Pr) and random values (R1, r1) are of high entropy (greater than 2^{160}) and are hashed, making successful guessing attacks practically impossible.

Rainbow Table Attack: Rainbow tables use precomputed hash values to reverse-engineer hashed data. The SLO-FEI approach employs dynamic inputs (e.g., TIi, TRi, r1, r2) in its hash functions, ensuring that values like S2 or x3 are unique for each session. As a result, precomputed hash tables are ineffective against this approach.

Sniffer Attack: In a sniffer attack, an adversary passively listens to network communications to extract confidential data. The approach secures messages (e.g., x1, x2, S3) using ECC encryption and cryptographic hashes. Sensitive parameters (e.g., Pr, r1) are never transmitted explicitly. For instance, x2 = h(r1·IdIi(pub)) cannot be reverse-engineered without knowing r1, making intercepted data useless.

Session Key Agreement: The approach ensures secure session key establishment through SIR = r1·r2·G during the authentication phase, with verification via S3 and S4. Because r1 and r2 are random, independently generated, and protected by hashes, adversaries cannot tamper with or forge the session key, ensuring robust key agreement.

Mutual Authentication: Mutual authentication is guaranteed as both entities (IdIi and IdRi) validate each other's identity. During the authentication phase, IdIi provides x2 and x3, while IdRi responds with x5 and x6. Verification, such as confirming S3* = S3, ensures that both parties are genuine and communication remains secure.

Confidentiality: The confidentiality of transmitted data is preserved using ECC and hash-based encryption. Messages such as S3 and S4 are protected using private keys and random values. Since critical parameters like Pr and r1 are never revealed, attackers cannot decrypt the data. Additionally, in the offloading phase, result data (RO) is only shared among authenticated and verified nodes, maintaining data privacy.

The strength of the SLO-FEI approach lies in its comprehensive use of ECC (with key sizes exceeding 2^{160} bits), session-specific random numbers (r1, r2, R1), secure hash functions, and timestamp validation (ΔT). This layered security architecture forms a robust defense against a wide range of attacks. Any successful intrusion attempt would require breaking cryptographic primitives or predicting high-entropy random values, both of which are computationally infeasible with current technology.

5 Performance Analysis

This section presents evaluation performance analysis, including computation, communication, and security Features. We used the closest existing work in the field of IoT offloading in fog and cloud environments for comparison. We phase the following in the SLO-FEI approach: Scenario 1: Login and Authentication Phase, Scenario 2: Register Phase and Scenario 3: Offloading Phase. In evaluating the communication overhead of the SLO-FEI approach, we assume that all random numbers (r1, r2) are 160 bits in length, and the hash function employed is SHA-1, which also produces a 160-bit output. Our approach utilizes ECC with a key size of 160 bits, offering a security level comparable to a 1024-bit RSA key. Accordingly, all parameters associated with the elliptic curve are 160 bits each. Hence, a point on the elliptic curve, represented as P = (Px, Py), requires a total of 320 bits (160 bits for Px and 160 bits for Py).

5.1 Communication and Total Bits

In Scenario 1, the SLO-FEI approach of exchanged messages: {S1, Pwi, IdIi, TIi} {Rr, IdIi(pub), pub, S2, Tri} is between IdIi and IdRi, and is used. Scenario 1 requires (32

+ 320 + 160 + 160 + 32) + 160 + 32 + 32 + 32) = 960 bits, and in Scenario 2, the exchanged messages. {x1, x2, x3, TIi, IdIi, IdIi(pub), IdRi}, {x4, x5, x6, IdRi, Tri}, {S3, S4, Pow, TIi, IdRi, IdIi}, IdIi(pub), IdIi, Pow, TRi, IdRi, IdFi, St} is between IdIi and IdRi, IdFi and is used. Scenario 2 requires, (320 + 160 + 160 + 32 + 32 + 320 + 160) + (320 + 320 + 160 + 32 + 32) + (160 + 160 + 32 + 32 + 32 + 32) + (320 + 32 + 32 + 32 + 32 + 32 + 160) = 3136 bits. In Scenario 3, the exchanged messages {IdIi(pub), Pr, TIi}, {IdIi(pub), Pr, TRi}, {IdIi, IdIi(pub)′*, Pow, Pr, IdIisf′, TFi, IdRi, Rf, S4, IdIj}, {Ro + Ro + RO} are between IdIi and IdRi, IdFi, and are used. Scenario 3 requires (320 + 32 + 32) + (320 + 32 + 32) + (32 + 320 + 32 + 32 + 32 + 32 + 32 + 32 + 32 + 160) + (32 + 32 + 32) = 1600 bits. Compared to the SOS-FCI approach, which is made up of 5 Scenarios, and in the first Scenario 1024 bits, in the second Scenario 2884 bits, in the third Scenario 256 bits, and the fourth and fifth Scenarios 2208 bits and 3040 bits are used, respectively. The SOS-FCI approach has a total of 24 messages, while the SLO-FEI Approach has 12 messages, meaning the SOS-FCI approach has 12 more messages, and the SLO-FEI Approach is lighter. The total cost of SOS-FCI is 9412 bits, and the Approach is 5696 bits, meaning SOS-FCI is 3716 bits more costly, and the SLO-FEI Approach is lighter. Table 2 shows a comparison of the number of messages and total bits.

Table 2. Comparison of the number of messages and total bits.

Scheme	*No. of messages*	*Total cost (in bits)*
SOS-FCI (Scenario 1)	*2*	*1024*
SOS-FCI (Scenario 2)	*4*	*2884*
SOS-FCI (Scenario 3)	*3*	*256*
SOS-FCI (Scenario 4)	*5*	*2208*
SOS-FCI (Scenario 5)	*10*	*3040*
SLO-FEI (Scenario 1)	*2*	*960*
SLO-FEI (Scenario 2)	*4*	*3136*
SLO-FEI (Scenario 3)	*6*	*1600*

5.2 Computation

Symbols Th, Tecm, and TR have been used to compute the computational cost of the SLO-FEI approach. These symbols represent the One-way hash function, Elliptic curve point multiplication, and random number selection, respectively. The arithmetic mean of the symbols is Th = 0.0023 ms, Tecm = 2.226 ms, and TR = 0.539 ms, as derived from reference [23]. The SLO-FEI approach consists of three Scenarios with the following computational costs: Scenario 1: The functions used are Th7 + TR1 + Tecm2. The total cost is calculated as (Th7 × 0.0023) + (TR1 × 0.539) + (Tecm2 × 2.226) = (7 × 0.0023) + (1 × 0.539) + (2 × 2.226) = 0.0161 + 0.539 + 4.452 = 5.0071 ms. Scenario 2: The functions used are Th14 + TR2 + Tecm5. The total cost is calculated as (Th14 ×

0.0023) + (TR2 × 0.539) + (Tecm5 × 2.226) = (14 × 0.0023) + (2 × 0.539) + (5 × 2.226) = 0.0322 + 1.078 + 11.130 = 12.2402 ms. Scenario 3: The functions used are Th3 + Tecm2. The total cost is calculated as (Th3 × 0.0023) + (Tecm2 × 2.226) = (3 × 0.0023) + (2 × 2.226) = 0.0069 + 4.452 = 4.4589 ms. Table 3 shows the comparison of computational costs. Comparison Between the SLO-FEI Approach and the SOS-FCI Approach. In terms of structural complexity, the newly SLO-FEI approach, comprising 3 Scenarios, is simpler than the SOS-FCI approach, which involves 5 Scenarios. This reduction in the number of Scenarios suggests a more streamlined design focused on specific scenarios and a potential simplification of computational processes. Regarding total computational cost, the SLO-FEI approach demonstrates superior performance, with a total cost of 21.7062 ms, compared to 30.0495 ms for the SOS-FCI approach—a difference of 8.3433 ms, representing an improvement of approximately 27.8%. This efficiency gain can be attributed to two primary factors: Reduced number of Scenarios, which decreases the overall computational load. Utilization of more efficient functions, such as replacing Tecm6 with the less computationally expensive Tecm5 in Scenario 2, results in significant cost savings.

Table 3. Comparison of computational costs.

Approach	*Total cost*	*Total cost (in milliseconds)*
SOS-FCI (Scenario 1)	*Th9 + TR1 + Tecm2*	*5.0117 ms*
SOS-FCI (Scenario 2)	*Th14 + TR2 + Tecm6*	*14.4662 ms*
SOS-FCI (Scenario 3)	*Th2*	*0.0046 ms*
SOS-FCI (Scenario 4)	*Th4 + TR1*	*0.5482 ms*
SOS-FCI (Scenario 5)	*Th16 + TR2 + Tecm4*	*10.0188 ms*
SLO-FEI (Scenario 1)	*Th7 + TR1 + Tecm2*	*5.0071 ms*
SLO-FEI (Scenario 2)	*Th14 + TR2 + Tecm5*	*12.2402 ms*
SLO-FEI (Scenario 3)	*Th3 + Tecm2*	*4.4589 ms*

5.3 Comparison of Security Features

Table 4 compares the security features of the SLO-FEI and SOS-FCI approaches, emphasising their strengths and capabilities. Both frameworks fulfill the essential security requirements (FST1–FST16), demonstrating resilience against replay, man-in-the-middle, impersonation, and guessing attacks. They also ensure secure session key generation, mutual authentication, confidentiality, and reliable offloading, verified through formal (AVISPA) and informal analyses. The key distinction lies in FST16, where SLO-FEI achieves superior lightweight performance by minimising computational and communication overhead using elliptic curve cryptography, lightweight hashing, and timestamp validation. This makes it more suitable for resource-constrained IoT environments, while SOS-FCI exhibits higher resource consumption, limiting its efficiency in such settings.

Table 4. Comparison of security features.

Features	*SOS-FCI*	*SLO-FEI*
FST1	*Approved*	*Approved*
FST2	*Approved*	*Approved*
FST3	*Approved*	*Approved*
FST4	*Approved*	*Approved*
FST5	*Approved*	*Approved*
FST6	*Approved*	*Approved*
FST7	*Approved*	*Approved*
FST8	*Approved*	*Approved*
FST9	*Approved*	*Approved*
FST10	*Approved*	*Approved*
FST11	*Approved*	*Approved*
FST12	*Approved*	*Approved*
FST13	*Approved*	*Approved*
FST14	*Approved*	*Approved*
FST15	*Approved*	*Approved*
FST16	*Denied*	*Approved*

FST1: Replay attack, FST2: Man-in-the-middle attack, FST3: Impersonation attack, FST4: Brute-force attack, FST5: Stolen verifier attack, FST6: Session key leakage attack, FST7: guessing attack, FST8: Rainbow table attack, FST9: Sniffer attack, FST10: Session key agreement, FST11 mutual authentication, FST12: Provides confidentiality, FST13: formal security verification using AVISPA, FST14: Informal Security Analysis, FST15: Secure offloading, FST16: Lightweight.

6 Conclusion

In this work, we proposed SLO-FEI, a lightweight and secure offloading approach designed for IoT environments. The approach ensures mutual authentication and the establishment of a secure session key, thereby preserving the confidentiality and integrity of communications between devices. Furthermore, it enables the safe and efficient selection of offloading targets, addressing the challenges posed by limited resources and wireless vulnerabilities in IoT systems. Through a detailed comparative analysis, we demonstrated that SLO-FEI outperforms existing approaches in terms of communication and computation efficiency, while offering enhanced security features. The approach's robustness was further validated using both formal methods, including AVISPA-based verification, and informal analysis, confirming its resistance to active and passive attacks. Overall, SLO-FEI provides a cost-effective and secure solution for task offloading in resource-constrained IoT environments, making it a strong candidate for real-world deployment in next-generation IoT systems. However, like many lightweight approaches, its scalability in large-scale networks with thousands of devices remains a potential limitation and warrants further investigation.

References

1. Sun, P., Wan, Y., Wu, Z., Fang, Z., Li, Q.: A survey on privacy and security issues in IoT-based environments: technologies, protection measures and future directions. Comput. Secur. **148**, 104097 (2025)

2. Salami, Y.: Dialectic optimization algorithm (DOA): a novel metaheuristic inspired by dialectical philosophy. J. Supercomput. **81**(15) (2025). https://doi.org/10.1007/s11227-025-07879-3
3. Salami, Y.: SOBT-UF: secure offloading in blockchain infrastructure for intelligent transportation systems using 5G-enabled UAVs within a Fog-edge computing federation. In: 2024 19th Iranian Conference on Intelligent Systems (ICIS), pp. 217–222. IEEE (2024). https://doi.org/10.1109/ICIS64839.2024.10887460
4. Salami, Y., Khajehvand, V., Zeinali, E.: LSMAK-IOV: lightweight secure mutual AKE scheme in Fog-based IoV. In: 2024 10th International Conference on Artificial Intelligence and Robotics (QICAR), pp. 1–5. IEEE (2024). https://doi.org/10.1109/QICAR61538.2024.10496659
5. Salami, Y., Khajehvand, V., Zeinali, E.: Efficiency simultaneous key exchange-cryptography extraction from public key in Fog-cloud federation-based secure offloading for automatic weather stations observing systems. Nivar **47**(120–121), 153–165 (2023). https://doi.org/10.30467/nivar.2023.416270.1261
6. Salami, Y., Hosseini, S.: BSAMS: blockchain-based secure authentication scheme in meteorological systems. Nivar **47**(120–121), 181–197 (2023). https://doi.org/10.30467/nivar.2023.415722.1260
7. Salami, Y., Khajehvand, V.: LSKE: lightweight secure key exchange scheme in Fog federation. Complexity **2021**, 4667586 (2021). https://doi.org/10.1155/2021/4667586
8. salami, Y., Ebazadeh, Y., Khajehvand, V.: CE-SKE: cost-effective secure key exchange scheme in Fog Federation. Iran J. Comput. Sci. **4**(4), 305–317 (2021). https://doi.org/10.1007/s42044-021-00086-2
9. Salami, Y.: SO-ITS: a secure offloading scheme for intelligent transportation systems in federated fog-cloud. Iran J. Comput. Sci. (2025). https://doi.org/10.1007/s42044-025-00318-9
10. Salami, Y., Khajehvand, V., Zeinali, E.: SAIFC: a secure authentication scheme for IOV based on fog-cloud federation. Secur. Commun. Netw. **1**, 1–19 (2023). https://doi.org/10.1155/2023/9143563
11. Salami, Y., Khajehvand, V., Zeinali, E.: A new secure offloading approach for internet of vehicles in fog-cloud federation. Sci. Rep. **14**(1), 5576 (2024). https://doi.org/10.1038/s41598-024-56141-y
12. Khashan, O.A.: Hybrid lightweight proxy re-encryption scheme for secure fog-to-things environment. IEEE Access **8**, 66878–66887 (2020). https://doi.org/10.1109/ACCESS.2020.2984317
13. Michailidis, E.T., Maliatsos, K., Skoutas, D.N., Vouyioukas, D., Skianis, C.: Secure UAV-aided mobile edge computing for IoT: a review. IEEE Access **10**, 86353–86383 (2022). https://doi.org/10.1109/ACCESS.2022.3199408
14. Chakraborty, A., Kumar, M., Chaurasia, N.: Secure framework for IoT applications using deep learning in fog computing. J. Inf. Secur. Appl. **77** (2023). https://doi.org/10.1016/j.jisa.2023.103569
15. Gong, B., et al.: SLIM: a secure and lightweight multi-authority attribute-based signcryption scheme for IoT. IEEE Trans. Inf. Forensics Secur. **19**, 1299–1312 (2024). https://doi.org/10.1109/TIFS.2023.3331566
16. Irshad, A., Chaudhry, S.A., Ghani, A., Mallah, G.A., Bilal, M., Alzahrani, B.A.: A low-cost privacy preserving user access in mobile edge computing framework. Comput. Electr. Eng. **98** (2022). https://doi.org/10.1016/j.compeleceng.2022.107692
17. Al-daraiseh, A.A., Chowdhury, R., Ould-Slimane, H., Talhi, C., Taha, M.B.: Lightweight scheme for smart home environments using offloading technique. Int. J. Commun. Netw. Inf. Secur. **14**(1), 11–18 (2022). https://doi.org/10.54039/ijcnis.v14i1.5065

18. Kenioua, L., Lejdel, B., Alamri, S., Ramadan, Q.: A password-based authentication approach for edge computing architectures. Egypt. Inform. J. **28** (2024). https://doi.org/10.1016/j.eij.2024.100543
19. Tanveer, M., Aldossari, S.A.: RAM-MEN: robust authentication mechanism for IoT-enabled edge networks. Alexandria Eng. J. **112**, 436–447 (2025). https://doi.org/10.1016/j.aej.2024.10.116
20. Ravindra, K.S., Rao, M.V.P.: A novel secured open standard framework for internet of things applications integrating elliptic curve cryptography and fog computing. Int. J. Electr. Comput. Eng. **14**(6), 7224–7235 (2024). https://doi.org/10.11591/ijece.v14i6.pp7224-7235
21. Hou, G., et al.: Cross-cloud associated multi-replica auditing for lightweight devices in the IoT. IEEE Internet Things J. (2025). https://doi.org/10.1109/JIOT.2025.3552169
22. Salami, Y., Khajehvand, V., Zeinali, E.: SOS-FCI: a secure offloading scheme in fog–cloud-based IoT. J. Supercomput. **80**(1), 570–600 (2024). https://doi.org/10.1007/s11227-023-05499-3
23. Salami, Y., Khajehvand, V., Zeinali, E.: E3C: a tool for evaluating communication and computation costs in authentication and key exchange protocol. Iran J. Comput. Sci. 1–11 (2024). https://doi.org/10.1007/s42044-024-00176-x

A Systematic Literature Review on Secure Extraction of Multiple Features for Privacy Protection in Wearable Medical Devices

Kwame Bell-Dzide[1(✉)], Forgor Lempogo[2], Martin Mabeifam Ujakpa[3], Stephen Asunka[1,2,3], Hillary Kwame Ofori[1,2,3], Emmanuel Akwah Kyei[1,2,3], and Justice Williams Asare[1,2,3]

[1] Faculty of Computing and Information Systems, Ghana Communication Technology University, Accra, Ghana
kbell-dzide@gctu.edu.gh

[2] School of Governance, IT and Management, University of KwaZulu-Natal, Durban, South Africa

[3] Faculty of Applied Science and Technology, Koforidua Technical University, Koforidua, Ghana

Abstract. Wearable medical devices have revolutionised modern healthcare through continuous physiological monitoring and authentication. This paper presents a systematic review of multi-feature extraction and privacy-preserving approaches in ECG-based biometric authentication for wearable devices. Emphasising deep learning, federated learning, and TinyML integration, the review analyses developments from 2015 to 2025, focusing on works between 2021 and 2024. The study adheres to PRISMA guidelines and draws on databases from IEEE Xplore, MDPI, and Google Scholar. Results indicate significant advancements in model accuracy and computational efficiency; however, privacy leakage, inconsistent datasets, and limited real-world validation remain challenges. The findings underscore the need for robust, privacy-preserving frameworks that strike a balance between accuracy, efficiency, and security in resource-constrained environments.

Keywords: Wearable · Medical · Electrocardiograms · Biometric · Privacy · healthcare IoT

1 Introduction

Wearable medical devices have become integral to modern healthcare systems, enabling continuous, non-invasive monitoring of physiological and behavioural signals such as the electrocardiogram (ECG) and electroencephalogram (EEG) [1, 2]. These devices capture vital parameters, including heart rate, neurological activity, and blood pressure, facilitating preventive care, telemedicine, and personalised health monitoring without prolonged clinical supervision [3]. The growing ubiquity of these devices has promoted biometric authentication, especially through ECG-based recognition, which leverages individual electrophysiological traits for continuous and secure identification [4].

H. R. Arabnia et al. (Eds.): CSCE 2025, CCIS 2934, pp. 132–144, 2026.
https://doi.org/10.1007/978-3-032-22190-2_10

Wearable medical devices usually consist of sensing, processing, and communication layers that gather, analyse, and securely transmit biomedical data. Among the acquired signals, ECG and EEG are especially valuable for authentication because they encode both physiological and behavioural individuality. Extracting distinctive features—whether temporal, spectral, or morphological—is crucial for accurate and energy-efficient functioning in environments with limited resources [5, 6]. Figure 1 illustrates a typical wearable architecture showing how signals are acquired, processed, and transmitted.

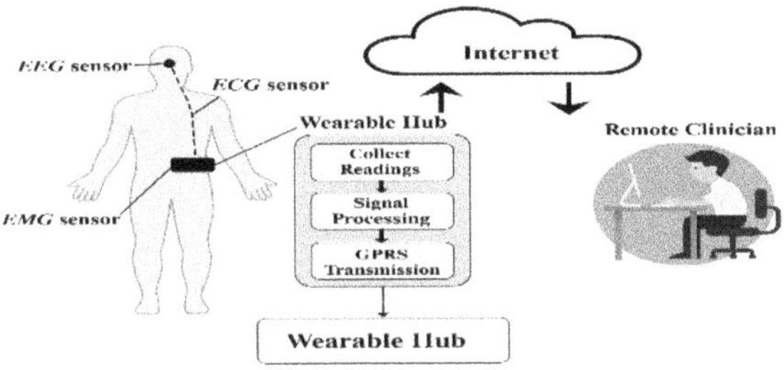

Fig. 1. Typical architecture of a wearable medical device showing three functional layers: (a) sensing for physiological signal acquisition; (b) processing for local feature extraction; and (c) communication for secure data transmission to edge or cloud servers.

Since such systems process highly sensitive health information, privacy and security are of paramount importance [7, 8]. Regulations, including the Health Insurance Portability and Accountability Act (HIPAA) and the General Data Protection Regulation (GDPR), as well as standards such as ISO/IEC 27001 and ISO/IEC 27701, mandate robust controls over the confidentiality, integrity, and availability of data. Implementing privacy-by-design principles alongside encryption and access management mitigates exposure risks in distributed healthcare IoT environments [9–12].

Recent advances—Federated Learning (FL), Tiny Machine Learning (TinyML), and Blockchain—offer decentralised, low-power, and verifiable mechanisms that preserve user privacy without degrading analytical performance [13]. FL allows distributed model training without sharing raw data; TinyML enables efficient on-device inference; and Blockchain ensures immutable audit trails for secure collaboration [14, 15]. Integrating these techniques enables the development of privacy-preserving multi-feature extraction frameworks that balance accuracy, efficiency, and data protection within wearable healthcare ecosystems [16, 17].

Despite these advances, existing reviews remain fragmented, often presenting either algorithmic or privacy perspectives instead of presenting unified frameworks. Many reported models depend on idealised datasets that overlook practical constraints such as hardware variability, connectivity limitations, and power consumption [18]. These issues limit scalability and real-world applicability, leaving open questions about how privacy, computational efficiency, and diagnostic utility can coexist in constrained environments.

Accordingly, this study presents a systematic review of multi-feature extraction and privacy-preserving methods for wearable medical devices, with a focus on ECG and

EEG signals. The review follows the PRISMA framework to ensure methodological transparency and reproducibility. By synthesising research across deep learning, federated learning, TinyML, and blockchain-assisted privacy mechanisms, the paper identifies emerging trends, limitations, and future directions for developing secure and efficient biometric authentication systems in healthcare IoT.

The main contributions of this review are as follows:

- It analyses recent studies (2015–2025) on feature extraction for ECG- and EEG-based authentication, with emphasis on privacy-preserving frameworks.
- It evaluates the trade-offs among privacy, data utility, energy efficiency, and real-time feasibility in wearable medical environments.
- It identifies significant research gaps and proposes design recommendations for developing generalisable, privacy-enhancing frameworks for next-generation healthcare systems.

In line with these objectives, the review is guided by the following research questions (RQs):

- RQ1: What are the current limitations of feature extraction techniques in protecting privacy within wearable medical devices, particularly when processing ECG and EEG signals?
- RQ2: How can a multi-feature extraction framework that integrates model pruning, quantisation, TinyML, and federated learning enhance both privacy and computational efficiency?
- RQ3: What performance metrics (e.g., speed, energy consumption, data quality) have been adopted in evaluating resource-constrained wearable environments?
- RQ4: What frameworks effectively balance privacy preservation and data utility in healthcare IoT systems?

These research questions form the analytical foundation of this review and guide the subsequent sections on methodology, literature synthesis, and identified research gaps.

2 Methodology

This systematic review was conducted in accordance with the PRISMA guidelines to ensure transparency, reproducibility, and completeness of the results. The process involved structured identification, screening, and selection of studies related to privacy-preserving multi-feature extraction for wearable medical devices, particularly those using electrocardiogram (ECG) and electroencephalogram (EEG) signals for biometric authentication.

A comprehensive search was conducted across IEEE Xplore, SpringerLink, ScienceDirect, MDPI, and Google Scholar, encompassing publications from 2015 to 2025, with a particular emphasis on the most recent developments between 2021 and 2024. Boolean operators and keyword combinations were used to refine the results, including: ("ECG biometrics" OR "EEG biometrics" OR "wearable authentication") AND ("feature extraction" OR "deep learning" OR "TinyML" OR "federated learning") AND ("privacy" OR "security" OR "blockchain" OR "healthcare IoT").

Only peer-reviewed journal or conference papers that focused on ECG/EEG-based authentication, privacy-preserving computation, or lightweight learning models for healthcare IoT were included. Materials such as editorials, theses, non-peer-reviewed sources, purely cryptographic studies without a biometric focus, and papers published before 2015 were excluded. The inclusion and exclusion criteria are summarised in Table 1.

Table 1. Inclusion and exclusion criteria

Criterion	Inclusion	Exclusion
Publication Type	Peer-reviewed journal or conference papers	Editorials, theses, or non-reviewed sources
Time Frame	Studies published 2015–2024	Studies published before 2015
Domain Focus	ECG/EEG-based authentication, wearable medical or healthcare IoT systems	Non-biometric or unrelated IoT studies
Technical Scope	Feature extraction, deep learning, federated learning, TinyML, or blockchain-based privacy frameworks	Cryptography-only or theoretical works without biometric context
Data Availability	Studies reporting model accuracy, dataset details, or performance metrics	Works lacking quantitative evaluation or inaccessible data
Privacy Consideration	Explicit discussion of data privacy, security, or compliance mechanisms	Studies with no privacy or security relevance

The initial search yielded 264 records (88 from IEEE Xplore, 33 from MDPI, and 143 from Google Scholar), from which 56 duplicates were removed. Titles and abstracts of the remaining 133 papers were screened for relevance, and 33 full texts were reviewed in detail. After applying the inclusion criteria, 20 primary studies were retained for synthesis. The process followed the PRISMA four-phase protocol—identification, screening, eligibility, and inclusion—as illustrated in Fig. 2.

For each included study, relevant information was extracted, including bibliographic details, methodology, model type, reported accuracy, privacy mechanisms, and observed limitations. Due to methodological heterogeneity across studies, a narrative and comparative synthesis was adopted instead of a meta-analysis. This approach facilitated cross-comparison of algorithmic trends, privacy-preserving strategies, and trade-offs between computational efficiency and data utility.

Each selected study was further appraised for methodological clarity, reproducibility, privacy consideration, and applicability to real-world wearable environments. Studies that met at least half of these quality criteria were retained for analysis. The final corpus of twenty studies, as summarised in Table 2, formed the empirical base for identifying

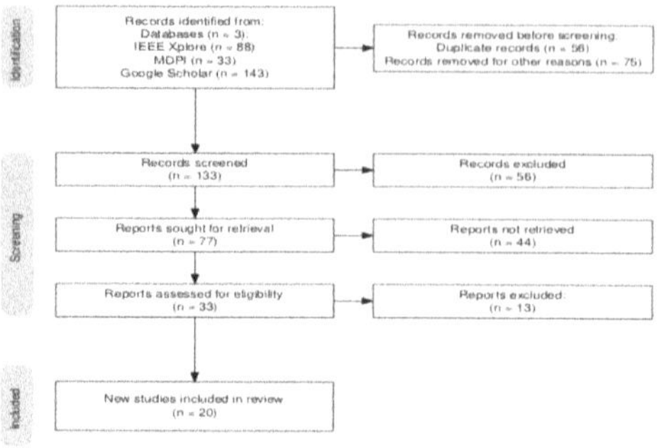

Fig. 2. PRISMA Flow Diagram for Literature Selection.

current trends, performance benchmarks, and open research gaps in privacy-preserving feature extraction for wearable healthcare systems.

2.1 Contributions to Knowledge

This study contributes to the expanding research on privacy-preserving biometric authentication in wearable medical systems by providing a structured synthesis of multi-feature extraction methods using ECG and EEG signals. Unlike previous fragmented reviews that focused on isolated mechanisms, this work integrates insights across deep learning, TinyML, Federated Learning, and Blockchain-based privacy frameworks, presenting a unified perspective on how these technologies can jointly enhance data security and computational efficiency.

The review extends the body of knowledge by:

- Systematically identifying and analysing twenty key experimental studies published between 2015 and 2025.
- Comparing privacy levels, accuracy, and resource trade-offs across models, offering a benchmark for evaluating lightweight biometric frameworks.
- Highlighting research priorities such as dataset diversity, standardised metrics, and privacy–utility trade-off optimisation, which remain underexplored in existing studies.

Collectively, these contributions provide both researchers and practitioners with a roadmap for developing secure, efficient, and ethically aligned biometric systems for next-generation healthcare IoT environments.

2.2 Review of Related Works

Research on ECG- and EEG-based biometric authentication has expanded significantly with advances in signal processing and machine learning. Early studies focused on leveraging the inherent uniqueness and liveness of ECG signals for continuous authentication, demonstrating that cardiac dynamics offer higher resistance to spoofing and physiological mimicry than traditional traits such as fingerprints or facial images. [39].

Table 2. Summary of Reviewed Studies on Privacy-Preserving ECG/EEG Feature Extraction.

References	Method Used	Accuracy (%)	Privacy Consideration	Limitation
Safie et al. [19]	SqueezeNet	84	No	Resource-constrained wearable devices limit their practical applicability
Lynn et al. [20]	RNN, GRU	96.1–98.5	No	No privacy focus. Data-dependent acquisition, where only ECG-I type data are suitable for the pre-processing phase before training
Aminifar et al. [21]	FL Base Model	80–84	High	Lacks a robust threat model to address stronger adversarial models
Huang et al. [22]	Not Specified	Not Specified	High	Reduction in data utility and model accuracy
Agrawal et al. [23]	CNN	96.8	Yes	Improve ECG data quality
Kim et al. [24]	DT, SVM	Not Specified	No	The framework was not tested or validated on real-world wearable devices, making its practical effectiveness uncertain
Chen et al. [25]	FL Framework	Not Specified	High	FedHealth has only been tested on human activity recognition and has not yet been validated for clinical applications
Ihsanto et al. [26]	CNN	97.92 and 98.89	Yes	Not validated on diverse datasets
Kim et al. [27]	Not Specified	95	No	The proposed system was evaluated on a small dataset of only 60 ECG samples, which may not reflect real-world performance
Kim et al. [28]	CNN	96	No	The system was not designed to handle large-scale training data for detecting multiple types of heart diseases
Baucas et al. [29]	FL	90.43	High	The platform has not yet been tested using multiple neural network designs, diverse datasets, or metrics like propagation delay and power consumption
Waheed et al. [30]	FedBlockHealth based CNN Model	99.03	High	The system has only been tested on a low-dimensional dataset (EMNIST) and with a relatively simple neural network

(*continued*)

Table 2. (*continued*)

References	Method Used	Accuracy (%)	Privacy Consideration	Limitation
Chen et al. [31]	FL	92	High	Focuses only on membership inference attack
Wang et al. [32]	CNN	98.67	Low	The system was only tested under certain conditions and resource constraints
Ammour et al. [33]	DL	98.02	No	The system's performance across different sessions and time intervals may be inconsistent due to session variability
Aleidan et al. [34]	VGG16	98.7	No	The system's effectiveness has only been tested on a selected dataset, so its generalizability to larger and more diverse populations remains unverified
Ku et al. [35]	CNN	96.8	No	The system requires a 5-s verification time and depends on expensive Edge-AI boards
Khan et al. [36]	FL Framework, SNN	Not Specified	High	The HNFL framework is the trade-off between energy efficiency and accuracy when using random participant selection
Kabel et al. [37]	Not Specified	99.96	Yes	Dependency on ECG signal quality
Prakash et al. [38]	DL	99.85	No	Reliance on custom datasets derived from a single public ECG database (ECGID v1.0.0)

Several studies have investigated the potential of deep learning methods such as Convolutional Neural Networks (CNNs), Recurrent Neural Networks (RNNs), and hybrid architectures, to enhance the assessment and performance of ECG-based biometric systems [31, 41, 46]. For example, Madan et al. [40] introduced a hybrid deep learning classification framework that automates the detection and categorisation of arrhythmias from ECG signals, capable of managing complex signal transformations. Their results highlighted the importance of training models on ECG datasets gathered under varying temporal conditions and physical states. The framework demonstrated notable improvements over existing methods, reducing the frequency of medical interventions required.

Similarly, Ihsanto et al. [26] addressed key issues such as processing speed and accuracy by introducing the Residual Depthwise Separable Convolutional Neural Network (RDSCNN). Their model achieved 100% accuracy on the MIT-BIH and ECG-ID databases while avoiding intensive pre-processing steps, demonstrating the feasibility of lightweight, real-time models for deployment in wearable medical devices. Lynn et al. [20] also enhanced traditional recurrent architectures by proposing a bidirectional deep Recurrent Neural Network based on Gated Recurrent Units for ECG-based human identification, while Agrawal et al. [23] highlighted the broader potential of deep learning in developing secure and convenient ECG-based authentication systems.

Beyond classification, some studies have also explored the integration of self-supervised and transfer learning techniques. Ding and Wu [41] reviewed ECG and photoplethysmogram (PPG) analysis, focusing on the use of self-supervised learning to enhance representation learning and transferability across various clinical tasks, including arrhythmia and anomaly detection, as well as heart rate variability analysis. Their work highlighted challenges in translating high-performance biometric models to embedded platforms suitable for wearable devices. Similarly, Ullah et al. [42] proposed a two-dimensional CNN architecture for ECG classification using reduced feature sets, demonstrating that competitive performance can be achieved with minimal input, which is a crucial step for lightweight biometric applications.

Privacy preservation remains a key concern in biometric systems, particularly in distributed or IoT environments. Rivadeneira et al. [43] highlighted the importance of privacy considerations, while Aminifar et al. [21] proposed a privacy-preserving federated learning framework for seizure detection in wearable devices, demonstrating its viability on cloud platforms such as Amazon AWS. Although federated learning offers a promising approach by enabling distributed training without sharing raw data, Chen et al. [31] revealed its susceptibility to membership inference attacks, exposing a gap between theoretical privacy assurances and practical security. Furthermore, Safie et al. [19] explored the use of Continuous Morse Wavelet Transform coefficients as CNN inputs, showing enhanced performance with architectures such as SqueezeNet and underscoring the potential of hybrid feature extraction methods for dependable ECG authentication.

Overall, the literature highlights substantial progress but persistent challenges: limited dataset diversity, insufficient real-world validation, incomplete privacy guarantees in decentralised learning frameworks, and difficulty balancing accuracy, energy efficiency, and data protection. These gaps highlight the need for integrated, privacy-preserving multi-feature extraction frameworks specifically designed for resource-constrained wearable medical devices.

2.3 Discussions and Research Gaps

The findings of this review show that ECG- and EEG-based biometrics have matured significantly as viable modalities for continuous authentication in wearable medical systems. Deep learning models—particularly CNNs, RNNs, and hybrid architectures—have achieved high accuracy across benchmark datasets, confirming their capacity to extract robust morphological and temporal features. However, these models often struggle under real-world conditions [44]. Motion artefacts, physiological variability, and sensor inconsistencies degrade performance, revealing the need for adaptive feature extraction techniques that account for dynamic and noisy environments typically encountered in wearable use [45, 46].

A recurring theme across the reviewed studies is the tension between computational efficiency and authentication accuracy. Lightweight approaches, such as TinyML, pruning, and quantisation, reduce energy consumption and enable on-device inference; however, they may compromise model generalisability. Conversely, high-capacity deep networks perform well in controlled conditions but exceed the processing and memory capabilities of most wearable platforms. This trade-off highlights the need for hardware-aware optimisation strategies that maintain accuracy without surpassing device limitations.

Privacy preservation remains crucial in deploying biometric systems within healthcare IoT. Federated Learning (FL) has become a promising approach by allowing distributed training without sharing raw data [47]. However, FL frameworks are still vulnerable to reconstruction and inference attacks, and they demand significant communication resources that many wearables cannot handle. Blockchain-based methods enhance transparency and auditability, but they also introduce additional computational overhead. These limitations suggest that privacy-protecting mechanisms should include multi-layered defences—such as differential privacy, secure aggregation, and encrypted computation—to ensure robust protection in constrained environments.

A key challenge pointed out in this review is the limited range of datasets used for training and evaluating models. Most studies rely on controlled datasets, such as MIT-BIH and ECG-ID, which do not capture within-person variability, multi-day recordings, or the wide demographic diversity required for real-world use. The lack of standardised benchmarks also makes it harder to compare models across studies, especially in terms of energy efficiency, latency, and privacy metrics. Without comprehensive datasets and evaluation frameworks, it remains difficult to accurately assess the reliability, scalability, and fairness of proposed biometric systems.

Together, these observations highlight several research gaps. First, there is a need for multi-feature extraction frameworks that combine morphological, spectral, and time–frequency characteristics while remaining computationally feasible on wearable devices. Second, existing privacy-preserving techniques need to be enhanced through combined methods that protect both raw data and model updates. Third, future research requires more realistic evaluation pipelines that reflect real-world noise, demographic diversity, and scenarios of continuous use. Lastly, the lack of standardised performance and privacy metrics limits the field's ability to establish baseline benchmarks for wearable biometric authentication.

Addressing these gaps will be vital for developing secure, energy-efficient, and reliable biometric systems that can function effectively in next-generation wearable medical and healthcare IoT environments.

2.4 Limitations of the Study

This review provides significant and critical insights into biometric authentication using electrocardiograms (ECG) and electroencephalograms (EEG) signals, as well as privacy protection in wearable medical devices. It highlights several limitations that could impact the scalability and usability of its findings. Many experimental evaluation studies heavily depend on publicly available electrocardiogram datasets, including the MIT-BIH, PTB-XL, and Kaggle datasets. However, these datasets, despite being publicly accessible, do not fully represent the diversity and complexity of real-time biometric scenarios. They mostly lack key factors such as demographic diversity and environmental noise, which are necessary to thoroughly test and evaluate the robustness of various models across behavioural and physiological states.

Another limitation pertains to the lack of a formal user-centred evaluation. The system's usability, acceptance, and interaction with actual users were not examined. Continuous biometric systems require assessment not only of algorithmic performance but also of how they integrate into user routines, maintain reliability during various daily activities, and accommodate user variability over time. The federated learning and privacy-preserving methods cited in related work are not implemented in the current study. Although the proposed system suggests compatibility with such frameworks, a practical demonstration of secure distributed training and privacy risk reduction is missing. This restricts the claims regarding privacy-preserving deployment in multi-device environments.

3 Conclusion and Future Work

The review in this study demonstrates significant progress in developing ECG-based biometric authentication systems, particularly through the application of deep learning, self-supervised learning, and lightweight models for IoT edge deployments. Current advances also show positive results in improving authentication accuracy and resilience under various physiological and environmental conditions. Furthermore, the implementation of federated learning and blockchain has promoted new paradigms for data privacy and security in decentralised healthcare systems. These developments highlight a growing interest in creating secure, energy-efficient, and privacy-protecting authentication frameworks for wearable healthcare technologies.

Future research should focus on tackling privacy risks and vulnerabilities, as well as incorporating privacy-preserving authentication frameworks in wearable healthcare devices. This is essential, considering the sensitive health and vital information of patients and wearable device users. Additionally, studies should aim to expand and differentiate datasets for ECG to encompass a wider array of physiological and demographic variations, supporting the testing and evaluation of methods and techniques. Moreover, there should be increased deployment of biometric authentication models on wearable platforms for ongoing performance assessment and monitoring of effectiveness and stability. Addressing these gaps will improve the reliability, security, and user-friendliness of biometric authentication solutions within healthcare systems.

References

1. Lu, L., et al.: Wearable health devices in health care: narrative systematic review. JMIR Mhealth Uhealth **8**(11), e18907 (2020). https://mhealth.jmir.org/2020/11/e18907. https://doi.org/10.2196/18907
2. Neri, L., et al.: Electrocardiogram monitoring wearable devices and artificial-intelligence-enabled diagnostic capabilities: a review. Sensors **23**(10), 4805 (2023). https://doi.org/10.3390/S23104805

3. Iqbal, S.M.A., Mahgoub, I., Du, E., Leavitt, M.A., Asghar, W.: Advances in healthcare wearable devices. npj Flexible Electron. **5**(1), 1–14 (2021). https://doi.org/10.1038/s41528-021-00107-x
4. Uwaechia, A.N., Ramli, D.A.: A comprehensive survey on ECG signals as new biometric modality for human authentication: recent advances and future challenges. IEEE Access **9**, 97760–97802 (2021). https://doi.org/10.1109/ACCESS.2021.3095248
5. Jayaram, R., Prabakaran, S.: Onboard disease prediction and rehabilitation monitoring on secure edge-cloud integrated privacy preserving healthcare system. Egypt. Inform. J. **22**(4), 401–410 (2021). https://doi.org/10.1016/J.EIJ.2020.12.003
6. Al-Harrasi, A., Shaikh, A.K., Al-Badi, A.: Towards protecting organisations' data by preventing data theft by malicious insiders. Int. J. Organ. Anal. **31**(3), 875–888 (2023). https://doi.org/10.1108/IJOA-01-2021-2598/FULL/XML
7. Lu, L., et al.: Wearable health devices in health care: narrative systematic review. jmir.org (2020). https://doi.org/10.2196/18907
8. Neal Joshua, E.S., Rao, N.T., Bhattacharyya, D.: Managing information security risk and Internet of Things (IoT) impact on challenges of medicinal problems with complex settings: a complete systematic approach In: Multi-Chaos, Fractal and Multi-Fractional Artificial Intelligence of Different Complex Systems, pp. 291–310 (2022). https://doi.org/10.1016/B978-0-323-90032-4.00007-9
9. Cui, Y., Gu, Z., Sun, L., Tang, H., Cui, L.: The security and privacy protection framework for wearable devices. In: Lecture Notes in Computer Science (including subseries Lecture Notes in Artificial Intelligence and Lecture Notes in Bioinformatics), vol. 13337 LNCS, pp. 203–210 (2022). https://doi.org/10.1007/978-3-031-05014-5_16
10. Gagandeep, A., Sharma, A.: Securing the future of healthcare: ensuring privacy and security in wearable and implantable medical devices. In: Security, Privacy, and Trust in WBANs and E-Healthcare, pp. 105–125 (2024). https://doi.org/10.1201/9781032635101-8/SECURING-FUTURE-HEALTHCARE-GAGANDEEP-ANJALI-SHARMA
11. Schmidt, A.: Regulatory challenges in healthcare IT: ensuring compliance with HIPAA and GDPR. acadexpinnara.com (2020). https://acadexpinnara.com/index.php/ajst/article/view/82. Accessed 04 June 2025
12. Kalloniatis, C., Lambrinoudakis, C., Musahl, M., Kanatas, A., Gritzalis, S.: Incorporating privacy by design in body sensor networks for medical applications: a privacy and data protection framework. serbia.nb.rs **18**(1), 323–350 (2021). https://doi.org/10.2298/CSIS200922057K
13. Kumar Myakala, P., Naayini, P., Kamatala, S.: A survey on federated learning for TinyML: challenges, techniques, and future directions. puiij.com (2025). https://doi.org/10.5281/zenodo.15240508
14. Li, H., Li, C., Wang, J., Yang, A., Ma, Z.: Review on Security of Federated Learning and Its Application in Healthcare. Elsevier (2023). https://www.sciencedirect.com/science/article/pii/S0167739X23000626. Accessed 31 May 2025
15. Ali, M., Naeem, F., Tariq, M.: Federated learning for privacy preservation in smart healthcare systems: a comprehensive survey. ieeexplore.ieee.org (2022). https://ieeexplore.ieee.org/abstract/document/9794622/?casa_token=8Gb0hBqiWisAAAAA:IsJcpilt1uqv9VWK8USAsRiHTen3KNRSLFB8bC1ZnBM-1T7FKudYYAli_bv4YyHEgIC2_uJnt4NoWA. Accessed 31 May 2025
16. Elhanashi, A., Dini, P., Saponara, S., Zheng, Q.: Advancements in TinyML: applications, limitations, and impact on IoT devices. mdpi.com (2024). https://www.mdpi.com/2079-9292/13/17/3562. Accessed 31 May 2025
17. Alajlan, N., Ibrahim, D.M.: TinyML: enabling of inference deep learning models on ultra-low-power IoT edge devices for AI applications. mdpi.com (2022). https://www.mdpi.com/2072-666X/13/6/851. Accessed 31 May 2025

18. Zhao, J., Qu, X., Wu, Y., Fowler, M.: Artificial Intelligence-Driven Real-World Battery Diagnostics. Elsevier (2024). https://www.sciencedirect.com/science/article/pii/S2666546824000855. Accessed: May 31, 2025
19. Safie, S.I., Ja'afar, N.H., Johari, A., Ismail, M.A.: ECG biometric authentication using deep CNN feature learning from analytic wavelet-transformed signals. Int. J. Online Biomed. Eng. **20**(15), 4–18 (2024). https://doi.org/10.3991/ijoe.v20i15.51041
20. Lynn, H.M., Pan, S.B., Kim, P.: A deep bidirectional GRU network model for biometric electrocardiogram classification based on recurrent neural networks. IEEE Access **7**, 145395–145405 (2019). https://doi.org/10.1109/ACCESS.2019.2939947
21. Aminifar, A., Shokri, M., Aminifar, A.: Privacy-preserving edge federated learning for intelligent mobile-health systems. Futur. Gener. Comput. Syst. **161**, 625–637 (2024). https://doi.org/10.1016/j.future.2024.07.035
22. Huang, P., Guo, L., Li, M., Fang, Y.: Practical privacy-preserving ECG-based authentication for IoT-based healthcare. IEEE **6**(5), 9200–9210 (2029). https://doi.org/10.1109/JIOT.2019.2929087
23. Agrawal, V., Hazratifard, M., Elmiligi, H., Gebali, F.: Electrocardiogram (ECG)-based user authentication using deep learning algorithms. Diagnostics **13**(3) (2023). https://doi.org/10.3390/diagnostics13030439
24. Kim, S.K., Yeun, C.Y., Damiani, E., Lo, N.W.: A machine learning framework for biometric authentication using electrocardiogram. IEEE Access **7**, 94858–94868 (2019). https://doi.org/10.1109/ACCESS.2019.2927079
25. Chen, Y., Wang, J., Yu, C., Gao, W., Qin, X.: FedHealth: A Federated Transfer Learning Framework for Wearable Healthcare (2019). http://arxiv.org/abs/1907.09173
26. Ihsanto, E., Ramli, K., Sudiana, D., Gunawan, T.S.: Fast and accurate algorithm for ECG authentication using residual depthwise separable convolutional neural networks. Appl. Sci. (Switzerland) **10**(9) (2020). https://doi.org/10.3390/app10093304
27. Kim, S.K., Yeun, C.Y., Yoo, P.D.: An enhanced machine learning-based biometric authentication system using RR-interval framed electrocardiograms. IEEE Access **7**, 168669–168674 (2019). https://doi.org/10.1109/ACCESS.2019.2954576
28. Kim, S.-K., Yeob Yeun, C., Yoo, P.D., Lo, N.-W., Damiani, E.: Deep Learning-Based Arrhythmia Detection Using RR-Interval Framed Electrocardiograms
29. Baucas, M., Spachos, P., Plataniotis, K.: Federated Learning and Blockchain-enabled Fog-IoT Platform for Wearables in Predictive Healthcare (2023). http://arxiv.org/abs/2301.04511
30. Waheed, N., et al.: FedBlockHealth: A Synergistic Approach to Privacy and Security in IoT-Enabled Healthcare through Federated Learning and Blockchain (2023). http://arxiv.org/abs/2304.07668
31. Chen, K., Zhang, D., Guan, S., Mi, B., Shen, J., Wang, G.: Private Data Leakage in Federated Human Activity Recognition for Wearable Healthcare Devices (2024). http://arxiv.org/abs/2405.10979
32. Wang, G., Shanker, S., Nag, A., Lian, Y., John, D.: ECG Biometric Authentication Using Self-Supervised Learning for IoT Edge Sensors (2024). https://doi.org/10.1109/JBHI.2024.3455803
33. Ammour, N., Jomaa, R.M., Islam, M.S., Bazi, Y., Alhichri, H., Alajlan, N.: Deep contrastive learning-based model for ECG biometrics. Appl. Sci. (Switzerland) **13**(5) (2023). https://doi.org/10.3390/app13053070
34. Aleidan, A.A., et al.: Biometric-based human identification using ensemble-based technique and ECG signals. Appl. Sci. (Switzerland) **13**(16) (2023). https://doi.org/10.3390/app13169454
35. Ku, G., et al.: Electrocardiogram-based driver authentication using autocorrelation and convolutional neural network techniques. Electronics (Switzerland) **13**(24) (2024). https://doi.org/10.3390/electronics13244974

36. Khan, A.R., Manzoor, H.U., Ayaz, F., Imran, M.A., Zoha, A.: A privacy and energy-aware federated framework for human activity recognition. Sensors **23** (2023). https://doi.org/10.3390/s23239339
37. El-Moneim Kabel, S.A., et al.: Securing Internet-of-Medical-Things networks using cancellable ECG recognition. Sci. Rep. **14**(1) (2024). https://doi.org/10.1038/s41598-024-54830-2
38. Prakash, A.J., Patro, K.K., Samantray, S., Pławiak, P., Hammad, M.: A deep learning technique for biometric authentication using ECG beat template matching. Information (Switzerland) **14**(2) (2023). https://doi.org/10.3390/info14020065
39. Asadianfam, S., Talebi, M.J., Nikougoftar, E.: ECG-based authentication systems: a comprehensive and systematic review. Springer **83**(9), 27647–27701 (2024). https://doi.org/10.1007/S11042-023-16506-3
40. Madan, P., Singh, V., Singh, D.P., Diwakar, M., Pant, B., Kishor, A.: A hybrid deep learning approach for ECG-based arrhythmia classification. Bioengineering **9**(4), 152 (2022). https://doi.org/10.3390/BIOENGINEERING9040152
41. Ding, C., Wu, C.: Self-supervised learning for biomedical signal processing: a systematic review on ECG and PPG signals. Springer Nat. (2024). https://doi.org/10.1101/2024.09.30.24314588.ABSTRACT
42. Ullah, A., Anwar, S.M., Bilal, M., Mehmood, R.M.: Classification of arrhythmia by using deep learning with 2-D ECG spectral image representation. Remote Sens. **12**(10), 1685 (2020). https://doi.org/10.3390/RS12101685
43. Rivadeneira, J.E., Sá Silva, J., Colomo-Palacios, R., Rodrigues, A., Boavida, F.: User-centric privacy preserving models for a new era of the Internet of Things. J. Netw. Comput. Appl. **217**, 103695 (2023). https://doi.org/10.1016/J.JNCA.2023.103695
44. SHaker, I.H.: Machine learning: algorithms, real-world applications and research directions. Springer **2**(3) (2021). https://doi.org/10.1007/S42979-021-00592-X
45. Dargan, S., Kumar, M.: A comprehensive survey on the biometric recognition systems based on physiological and behavioral modalities. Expert Syst. Appl. **143**, 113114 (2020). https://doi.org/10.1016/J.ESWA.2019.113114
46. Lien, C.-W., Vhaduri, S., Dibbo, S.V., Shaheed, M.: Explaining vulnerabilities of heart rate biometric models securing IoT wearables. Mach. Learn. Appl. **16**, 100559 (2024). https://doi.org/10.1016/J.MLWA.2024.100559
47. Li, Z., Sharma, V., Mohanty, S.P.: Preserving data privacy via federated learning: challenges and solutions. IEEE Consum. Electron. Mag. **9**(3), 8–16 (2020). https://doi.org/10.1109/MCE.2019.2959108

Artificial Intelligence and Health Informatics

A Multimodal Multi-agent Framework for Radiology Report Generation

Ziruo Yi[1], Jinyu Liu[2], Ting Xiao[1,3,4](✉), and Mark V. Albert[1,2,4]

[1] Department of Computer Science and Engineering, University of North Texas, Denton, TX, USA
ziruoyi@my.unt.edu, mark.albert@unt.edu

[2] Department of Information Science, University of North Texas, Denton, TX, USA
jinyuliu@my.unt.edu

[3] Department of Data Science, University of North Texas, Denton, TX, USA

[4] Center of Computational Life Sciences, University of North Texas, Denton, TX, USA
ting.xiao@unt.edu

Abstract. As an essential task in medical imaging, radiology report generation (RRG) aims to automatically generate diagnostic reports from chest X-ray images, thereby improving the efficiency of clinical workflows and alleviating the workload of radiologists. Recent methods using multimodal large language models (MLLMs) and retrieval-augmented generation (RAG) have achieved notable progress in combining visual and textual information for automated report generation, but they still face challenges of factual inconsistency, hallucination, and cross-modal misalignment. To address these limitations, we propose a multi-agent framework with specialized agents that handle distinct tasks including retrieval, drafting, refinement, visual analysis, and synthesis. This design enables structured collaboration that aligns with the clinical reasoning process of radiologists. Experimental results demonstrate that our approach consistently outperforms strong baselines in both automatic metrics and LLM-based evaluations, producing more accurate, structured, and interpretable reports. This work highlights the potential of clinically aligned multi-agent frameworks to support explainable and trustworthy clinical AI applications, enhancing transparency and reliability in medical decision-making.

Keywords: Radiology Report Generation · Multimodal Large Language Models · Multi-Agent Systems · Retrieval-Augmented Generation

1 Introduction

Radiology plays an essential role in modern healthcare, supporting diagnosis, treatment planning, and outcome prediction. It involves diverse data sources such as chest X-ray images, laboratory results, and clinical notes. Among multimodal

H. R. Arabnia et al. (Eds.): CSCE 2025, CCIS 2934, pp. 147–161, 2026.
https://doi.org/10.1007/978-3-032-22190-2_11

tasks in radiology, radiology report generation (RRG) is particularly impactful as it directly supports clinical workflows and decision-making. Recent studies further emphasize the importance of RRG as it aligns closely with radiologists' documentation [1,2]. RRG typically involves two key modalities: chest X-ray images that provide visual evidence of patient conditions, and corresponding radiology reports that capture clinical details in natural language. However, increasing demand for radiological exams and a shortage of radiologists have led to delays, forcing clinicians to make critical decisions without radiological guidance, which may result in errors or conclusions that differ from those of experienced radiologists [3,4].

With advancements in artificial intelligence (AI), computer vision (CV), and natural language processing (NLP), multimodal learning has emerged as a powerful paradigm for integrating and analyzing diverse data sources [5,6]. Recently, large language models (LLMs) and large vision models (LVMs), including GPT-4V [7], LLaMA 3 [8], and DALL·E 3 [9], have gained substantial attention. Building on these advances, multimodal large language models (MLLMs) have demonstrated strong performance on tasks like image captioning [10] and visual-language dialogue [11]. In the medical domain, MLLMs such as Med-PaLM 2 [12] and LLaVA-Med [13] have made notable progress in pharmaceutical research [14] and clinical support [15]. For RRG, MLLMs integrate visual and textual information to generate detailed and clinically accurate reports [16,17], facilitating structured documentation and supporting clinical decision-making. These applications extend the capabilities of radiologists, reduce workload, and assist less experienced clinicians. Despite this progress, existing MLLM-based approaches face key limitations in RRG. First, although MLLMs can process visual inputs effectively, they often struggle when essential information is textual or requires cross-modal reasoning. Second, most existing systems lack a unified architecture that flexibly integrates techniques such as prompt engineering. This limits their adaptability to new requirements in RRG. Third, current methods typically lack intermediate validation or refinement stages, making them prone to factual inconsistencies and hallucinations.

Retrieval-augmented generation (RAG) [18–20] has emerged as a promising method to enhance the factual accuracy of medical MLLMs. By integrating external and reliable sources, RAG enriches the model's knowledge and supports more grounded generation. It has been applied to tasks such as visual question answering (VQA) [21] and report generation [22,23]. However, applying RAG to medical MLLMs introduces several new challenges. While retrieving too few contexts may miss relevant information, retrieving too many can introduce noise and redundancy, making it harder for the model to identify relevant content and ultimately degrading output quality. Given the complexity of RRG, which requires accurate retrieval, clinical reasoning, and multimodal synthesis, a single model often struggles to meet all demands. This motivates a multi-agent design in which specialized agents collaborate within a clinically aligned, stepwise workflow.

To address the limitations of existing MLLM and RAG approaches, we propose a multimodal multi-agent framework for RRG that decomposes the task into five specialized agents: retrieval, drafting, refinement, visual analysis, and synthesis. This design aligns with clinical reasoning and enables modular and interpretable generation. By combining RAG with collaboration among task-specific agents, our system jointly processes visual and textual information to improve factual consistency and clinical relevance. The main contributions of our work are: (1) A clinically aligned multi-agent framework that introduces modular and stepwise reasoning into RRG, improving interpretability and factuality; (2) Extensive experiments showing that our method consistently outperforms strong baselines across both automatic and LLM-based evaluation metrics; (3) Detailed ablation studies and agent-level analyses that examine alternative model configurations and assess each agent's contribution.

2 Related Work

MLLMs for RRG. MLLMs have recently emerged as a promising solution for automating RRG [24–28]. Models such as R2GenGPT [29], XrayGPT [30], and MAIRA-1 [31] combine visual encoders (e.g., Swin Transformer [32], MedCLIP [33]) with LLMs (e.g., LLaMA [8], Vicuna [34]) to align visual features with textual representations, demonstrating strong performance on benchmark datasets. Despite their success, these models still suffer from key limitations including factual inconsistency [35,36], hallucination [37], and catastrophic forgetting [38,39]. These issues are particularly critical in RRG, which demands high factual accuracy and clinical reliability. In contrast to these single-stage designs, our multi-agent framework introduces modular decomposition with explicit retrieval and refinement stages, enhancing factual control, interpretability, and alignment with clinical workflows.

Retrieval-Augmented Generation. RAG has been widely adopted to enhance factual accuracy by incorporating contextual information from external datasets [18,40]. It has been applied to RRG to reduce hallucinations and enhance content relevance [41–45]. Despite these benefits, current RAG techniques still face critical challenges: the number and quality of retrieved contexts, and the risk of over-reliance on these references, both of which may degrade model performance or introduce factual errors [46]. Moreover, existing RAG methods often retrieve and process text and image information independently, limiting their ability to perform integrated multimodal reasoning [47]. These limitations are particularly problematic in RRG, which depends on fine-grained alignment between retrieved knowledge and visual evidence. To address these challenges, our framework embeds retrieval into a multi-agent workflow, where a fine-tuned retrieval agent selects semantically aligned references for downstream agents to distill and validate using both textual and visual inputs. This design enables stronger factual control and integrated multimodal reasoning, better suited to the demands of RRG.

Multi-Agent Systems. Multi-agent systems have gained increasing attention in NLP and healthcare AI [48–53]. They assign different tasks to specialized agents, which collaborate to accomplish complex goals that single models often struggle with. Preliminary attempts have explored multi-agent paradigms for RRG [54,55], showing promising results. However, applying multi-agent systems to multimodal tasks introduces new challenges. In particular, simply combining outputs from isolated vision and text agents often fails to capture the cross-modal relationships required for accurate interpretation. Moreover, aligning agent interactions with domain-specific workflows such as stepwise clinical reasoning remains a key challenge in current systems. To address these limitations, we propose a multimodal multi-agent framework aligned with stepwise clinical reasoning, where specialized agents handle retrieval, drafting, refinement, visual analysis, and synthesis in a modular and interpretable pipeline. This design better aligns with real-world clinical workflows and enables tighter integration across modalities than previous multi-agent systems.

3 Method

We propose a modular multi-agent framework for RRG, designed to emulate the clinical workflow by combining case retrieval, visual interpretation, and structured textual synthesis. Given a chest X-ray image, the system sequentially activates five specialized agents: a retrieval agent, a draft agent, a refiner agent, a vision agent, and a synthesis agent. Each agent fulfills a distinct functional role and operates independently, using either task-specific prompts (for LLM/VLM agents) or embedding-based retrieval (for the retrieval module). As shown in Fig. 1, agents communicate via structured intermediate outputs that progressively refine radiological observations into a final, coherent impression. This modular design not only enables clear task decomposition but also facilitates the assignment of different LLMs to individual agents, leveraging their respective strengths in fluency, abstraction, and semantic precision.

3.1 Retrieval Agent

The retrieval agent performs cross-modal retrieval by identifying prior radiology reports that are semantically similar to a given chest X-ray image. Inspired by the design of CLIP [56], the agent encodes the input image into a visual embedding and compares it against report embeddings using cosine similarity. The top-k most similar reports are selected based on similarity scores, where k is a predefined parameter balancing retrieval coverage and efficiency. These reports provide relevant diagnostic context, such as clinical findings and report style, which serve as guidance for downstream generation.

3.2 Draft Agent

The draft agent composes a preliminary radiology report by synthesizing information from the top-k reports selected by the retrieval agent. Inspired by how

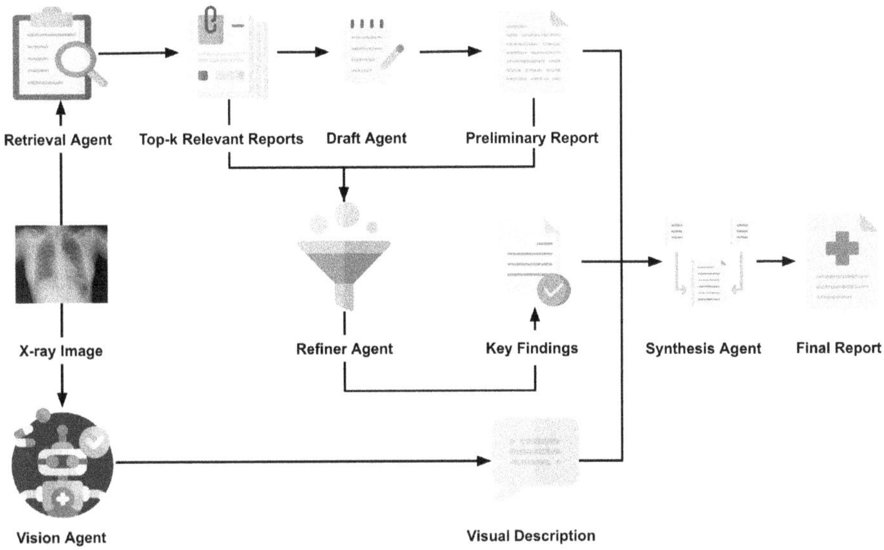

Fig. 1. Overview of the proposed multi-agent framework. The pipeline includes: (1) Retrieval agent for top-k report retrieval, (2) Draft agent for generating a preliminary report, (3) Refiner agent for key clinical findings, (4) Vision agent for visual description, and (5) Synthesis agent for final report generation.

radiologists review prior similar cases, the agent identifies shared findings, prioritizes relevant observations, and organizes them into a clinically focused preliminary report. This intermediate output provides a structured textual basis for downstream processing by subsequent agents.

3.3 Refiner Agent

The refiner agent distills key clinical findings from the outputs of the draft and retrieval agents. It identifies clinically important observations that are consistently supported by the input. Unlike the draft agent, which generates a broad preliminary report, the refiner agent focuses solely on findings-level content. It takes the preliminary report and retrieved reports as input and produces a concise summary of essential findings. To ensure factuality, the agent enforces retrieval-grounded constraints: every sentence must be directly supported by the input, with no speculation or paraphrasing beyond factual rewriting. The output serves as a structured clinical signal for downstream synthesis.

3.4 Vision Agent

The vision agent generates a visual description of the chest X-ray image to complement textual information from previous agents. It uses a medical MLLM to generate image-grounded descriptions based on visible observations. The output is a caption describing key chest regions, such as the lungs and mediastinum. The agent is designed to avoid unclear statements and irrelevant content, ensuring that the caption is grounded in visible evidence and written in a radiology report style. This step introduces visual cues from the input image to support the final synthesis.

3.5 Synthesis Agent

The synthesis agent produces the final radiology report by integrating a preliminary report, critical findings, and a visual caption from the previous agents. To ensure factual consistency and stylistic coherence, the final report includes only observations explicitly supported by the inputs. The agent avoids unsupported content and unnecessary rewriting, preserving key clinical information while maintaining logical consistency. This final step concludes the multi-agent pipeline by generating a clinically grounded and well-structured radiology report. The agent architecture is model-agnostic and flexibly supports different LLMs to balance fluency and factual precision. We explore this design choice in detail in our experiments.

4 Experiments

In this section, we evaluate our multimodal multi-agent framework by addressing the following questions: (1) Does our multi-agent design improve the clinical accuracy of generated radiology reports compared to strong baselines? (2) What contributions do individual agents make to the generation process? (3) How does the overall framework enhance report quality and clinical reliability?

4.1 Experimental Setup

Implementation Details. Our framework consists of five agents: a retrieval agent, a draft agent, a refiner agent, a vision agent, and a synthesis agent. We follow the retrieval setup of RULE [46] to construct the retrieval agent, which fine-tunes CLIP on MIMIC-CXR using contrastive learning to adapt to the medical domain. LLaVA-Med 1.5 (7B) [13] serves as the backbone for the vision agent, while GPT-4o [7] is used for the draft and refiner agents, and GPT-o1 [57] powers the synthesis agent. The retrieval agent selects the top-k most similar reports ($k = 5$ by default), which are then passed to the draft agent as input.

Datasets. We utilize two publicly available chest X-ray datasets: MIMIC-CXR [58] and IU X-ray [59]. We fine-tune the retrieval agent using 3,000 imageâĂŞreport pairs from MIMIC-CXR, a large-scale dataset of chest X-rays with associated radiology reports. For evaluation, we use the IU X-ray dataset, which includes chest radiographs and corresponding diagnostic reports. Following the data split from [60], the IU X-ray dataset contains 2,068 training and

590 test imageâĂŞreport pairs after filtering. We use the training set to construct the retrieval database and the test set to evaluate the performance of our framework.

Evaluation Metrics. The performance of our multi-agent framework is evaluated using standard metrics for text generation, including BLEU [61], ROUGE-1, ROUGE-2, ROUGE-L [62], METEOR [63], and BERTScore [64]. These metrics focus on surface-level similarity between generated and reference impressions, primarily based on lexical or token overlap. To complement these automatic metrics, we adopt the LLM-as-a-Judge paradigm [65] and employ Claude-3 Opus [66], a state-of-the-art LLM developed by Anthropic, to assess both the semantic accuracy and clinical relevance of the generated reports.

4.2 Results

In this section, we present a comprehensive evaluation of our multimodal multi-agent framework on the IU X-ray dataset. The analysis includes comparisons with strong baselines, evaluations of different language models within the synthesis agent, and ablation studies assessing the contribution of each agent. Both automatic metrics and LLM-based evaluation are used to examine factual accuracy, coherence, and clinical alignment.

Quantitative Analysis Standard Metrics. We evaluate our multi-agent framework using conventional natural language generation (NLG) metrics, including BLEU, ROUGE (1/2/L), METEOR, and BERTScore. The results are presented in Table 1, comparing our system against recent state-of-the-art (SOTA) medical MLLMs: CheXagent [67], MiniGPT-Med [68], and LLaVA-Med. Our framework achieves the highest scores across all metrics, indicating consistent superiority in both lexical and semantic quality. Specifically, our model achieves a BLEU score of 0.0522, outperforming CheXagent (0.0422), MiniGPT-Med (0.0242), and LLaVA-Med (0.0036). ROUGE-1, ROUGE-2 and ROUGE-L scores improve to 0.3742, 0.1408 and 0.2612 respectively, indicating stronger alignment with reference texts over all baselines. On METEOR, our score of 0.3496 notably surpasses that of MiniGPT-Med (0.2904), CheXagent (0.2471), and LLaVA-Med (0.1437), suggesting enhanced lexical diversity and content richness. Furthermore, our framework achieves the highest BERTScore at 0.8870, reflecting stronger semantic alignment and factual consistency. These results highlight the effectiveness of our multi-agent design in generating clinically relevant and coherent radiology reports.

LLM-as-a-Judge. To complement standard metrics, we further assess the clinical and linguistic quality of the generated reports using Claude-3 Opus [66], focusing on five key aspects: coverage of key findings, consistency with original reports, diagnostic accuracy, stylistic alignment, and conciseness. Each aspect is rated from 1 to 10, with higher scores indicating better quality. As summarized in Table 2, our multi-agent framework outperforms LLaVA-Med on four of the

Table 1. Quantitative comparison between our multi-agent framework and SOTA medical MLLMs.

Model	BLEU	ROUGE-1	ROUGE-2	ROUGE-L	METEOR	BERTScore
CheXagent	0.0422	0.2658	0.0987	0.1937	0.2471	0.8501
MiniGPT-Med	0.0242	0.3061	0.0798	0.1989	0.2904	0.8751
LLaVA-Med	0.0036	0.2398	0.0278	0.1537	0.1437	0.8617
Ours	**0.0522**	**0.3742**	**0.1408**	**0.2612**	**0.3496**	**0.8870**

five evaluation dimensions. It achieves a diagnostic accuracy score of 8.26 compared to 7.78, demonstrating stronger clinical reasoning. Our framework scores 8.16 in style alignment and 7.26 in conciseness, surpassing the baseline scores of 7.98 and 6.98. These improvements reflect stronger alignment with clinical report writing standards. Key finding coverage also improves from 5.86 to 6.36, showing a clearer presentation of clinically relevant information. Although LLaVA-Med slightly leads in consistency (6.94 vs. 6.74), the overall results highlight the effectiveness of our multi-agent design in enhancing clinical reliability and writing quality.

Table 2. Qualitative performance comparison between our multi-agent framework and a single MLLM.

Model	Findings	Consistency	Diagnosis	Style	Conciseness
LLaVA-Med	5.86	**6.94**	7.78	7.98	6.98
Ours	**6.36**	6.74	**8.26**	**8.16**	**7.26**

Qualitative Analysis. Figure 2 presents a representative example comparing the report generated by the vision agent only with that of our full multi-agent framework. This case highlights the benefit of incorporating retrieved reports and extracted key findings through our multi-agent pipeline. The vision-only output, while stylistically reasonable, lacks specificity and misses important observations. In contrast, the multi-agent output offers a more complete and clinically aligned summary. It follows terminology and structure commonly seen in prior reports, such as the inclusion of "pleural effusion" and "Degenerative changes are noted in the spine," better aligning with the original report. These improvements are enabled by structured agent collaboration: the retrieval agent supplies relevant contextual examples, the refiner agent extracts key clinical findings, and the synthesis agent combines them with the visual caption into a structured report. The final output is more concise, better organized, and clinically reliable, illustrating how retrieval grounding and agent collaboration lead to higher-quality reports than those produced by a vision-only agent.

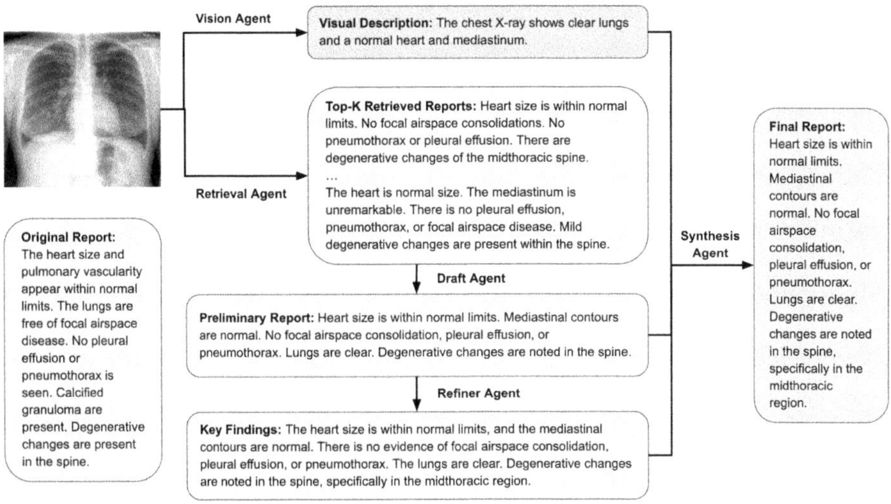

Fig. 2. A case study showing that retrieval and key findings help overcome the limitations of a vision-only agent.

4.3 Ablation Study

Impact of LLM Selection in the Synthesis Agent. To investigate how different language models affect the synthesis process, we experiment with six LLMs, including GPT-4o, GPT-o1, Claude-3, Mistral [69], DeepSeek-R1 [70], and Command-R [71]. Evaluation is conducted on the IU X-ray test set using BLEU, ROUGE (1/2/L), METEOR, and BERTScore.

As shown in Table 3, GPT-o1 achieves the best overall performance, leading in BLEU (0.0522), ROUGE-2 (0.1408), ROUGE-L (0.2612), and BERTScore (0.8870), indicating strong semantic alignment and coherence. DeepSeek-R1 obtains the highest METEOR score (0.3778), suggesting greater lexical diversity and fluency. GPT-4o achieves the highest ROUGE-1 score (0.3762) but underperforms in ROUGE-2, ROUGE-L, and BERTScore compared to GPT-o1, reflecting weaker capability in capturing longer dependencies and semantic alignment. Considering both quantitative and qualitative performance, we adopt GPT-4o in the earlier stages of the pipeline (draft and refiner agents) for its fluency, and GPT-o1 in the synthesis agent to ensure semantic completeness and diagnostic precision in the final report.

Contribution of Agents in the Full Framework. We further analyze the role of each agent in our pipeline by progressively enabling key components. Specifically, we compare three configurations:

1. **Vision-only**: The synthesis agent generates reports using only visual features extracted from LLaVA-Med, without incorporating any retrieved textual context.

Table 3. Performance of different LLMs within the synthesis agent.

Model	BLEU	ROUGE-1	ROUGE-2	ROUGE-L	METEOR	BERTScore
GPT-4o	0.0479	**0.3762**	0.1360	0.2544	0.3620	0.8818
GPT-o1	**0.0522**	0.3742	**0.1408**	**0.2612**	0.3496	**0.8870**
Claude-3	0.0465	0.3641	0.1293	0.2489	0.3600	0.8818
Mistral	0.0363	0.3608	0.1230	0.2426	0.3644	0.8801
DeepSeek-R1	0.0506	0.3463	0.1476	0.2322	**0.3778**	0.8803
Command-R	0.0318	0.3522	0.1155	0.2303	0.3613	0.8762

2. **Retrieval + Draft**: Retrieved reports are used by the draft agent to generate a preliminary report, which is then passed to the synthesis agent along with the visual features to produce the final report.
3. **Full Framework (Retrieval + Draft + Refiner)**: A refiner agent further extracts key findings from the retrieved reports, which are incorporated into the synthesis agent to enhance final report generation.

The performance of each configuration is evaluated using BLEU, ROUGE (1/2/L), METEOR, and BERTScore, as shown in Table 4. When using only image features, performance degrades significantly across all metrics (e.g., BLEU: 0.0032, ROUGE-2: 0.0324, METEOR: 0.1623), indicating that visual information alone is insufficient for generating detailed and semantically rich radiology reports. The absence of textual context limits the model's capacity to produce semantically complete and clinically grounded text. Introducing preliminary reports substantially boosts performance: BLEU increases from 0.0032 to 0.0519, ROUGE-2 from 0.0324 to 0.1379, and BERTScore from 0.8791 to 0.8851. These results highlight the value of retrieved context in providing essential clinical cues and linguistic grounding, enabling the model to generate more structured and fluent outputs. Adding a refiner agent further improves performance, with notable gains in BLEU (0.0522), ROUGE-1 (0.3742), ROUGE-2 (0.1408), METEOR (0.3496), and BERTScore (0.8870). This suggests that using key findings strengthens semantic guidance, leading to more accurate and coherent reports. Overall, we confirm that textual context is essential for generating high-quality radiology reports. While image-only inputs lead to poor performance, incorporating preliminary reports and key findings progressively enhances content relevance, semantic precision, and overall coherence.

4.4 Discussion

Our results show that the proposed multi-agent framework consistently enhances RRG across both standard automatic metrics and LLM-based clinical assessment. By decomposing the report generation process into specialized agents

Table 4. Performance comparison of different agent configurations.

Agents	BLEU	ROUGE-1	ROUGE-2	ROUGE-L	METEOR	BERTScore
Vision only	0.0032	0.3161	0.0324	0.1833	0.1623	0.8791
Retrieval + Draft	0.0519	0.3593	0.1379	0.2552	0.3357	0.8851
Full Framework	**0.0522**	**0.3742**	**0.1408**	**0.2612**	**0.3496**	**0.8870**

responsible for retrieval, abstraction, refinement, visual captioning, and synthesis, the framework introduces modularity and a clear separation of functional responsibilities, enabling controllable, interpretable, and clinically aligned generation.

Beyond agent modularity, our experiments reveal that model choice significantly affects output quality. GPT-o1 leads in semantic metrics while GPT-4o excels in fluency, combining both leverages their complementary strengths. The ablation study further highlights that preliminary reports provide strong clinical grounding, and that the refiner agent enhances semantic coherence and diagnostic specificity, validating our staged pipeline design.

One limitation is a slight drop in consistency, likely due to the complexity introduced by combining retrieved context, refined findings, and visual input. This aligns with prior findings [55] showing that RAG may introduce redundant or irrelevant content that reduces coherence. Nevertheless, both automatic and LLM-based evaluations confirm that our framework outperforms strong baselines. The case study further illustrates how individual agents contribute to improving factual accuracy and structure. Future work will focus on enhancing inter-agent communication and output alignment to improve robustness across diverse cases and ensure clinical reliability.

5 Conclusion

We present a multimodal multi-agent framework for RRG that breaks down the task into specialized agents for retrieval, drafting, refinement, visual interpretation, and synthesis. Our approach follows the diagnostic reasoning process and consistently outperforms strong baselines, as demonstrated by both automatic metrics and LLM-based evaluations. Agent-level analyses and ablation studies highlight the individual contributions of each component and how their collaboration improves factuality, coherence, and stylistic alignment. This modular design provides a generalizable approach for other multimodal medical tasks that require diagnostic reasoning and clinical precision.

Acknowledgments. This work was supported by the Center for Computational Life Sciences (CCLS) at the University of North Texas.

Disclosure of Interests. The authors declare no competing interests.

References

1. Yi, Z., Xiao, T., Albert, M.V.: A survey on multimodal large language models in radiology for report generation and visual question answering. Information **16**(2), 136 (2025)
2. Yildirim, N., et al.: Multimodal healthcare AI: identifying and designing clinically relevant vision-language applications for radiology. In: Proceedings of the 2024 CHI Conference on Human Factors in Computing Systems, pp. 1–22 (2024)
3. McDonald, R.J., et al.: The effects of changes in utilization and technological advancements of cross-sectional imaging on radiologist workload. Acad. Radiol. **22**(9), 1191–1198 (2015)
4. Petinaux, B., Bhat, R., Boniface, K., Aristizabal, J.: Accuracy of radiographic readings in the emergency department. Am. J. Emerg. Med. **29**(1), 18–25 (2011)
5. Huang, Y., Du, C., Xue, Z., Chen, X., Zhao, H., Huang, L.: What makes multimodal learning better than single (provably). In: Advances in Neural Information Processing Systems, vol. 34, pp. 10944–10956 (2021)
6. Waqas, A., Tripathi, A., Ramachandran, R.P., Stewart, P.A., Rasool, G.: Multimodal data integration for oncology in the era of deep neural networks: a review. Front. Artif. Intell. **7**, 1408843 (2024)
7. Achiam, J., et al.: GPT-4 technical report. arXiv preprint: arXiv:2303.08774 (2023)
8. Meta AI: Introducing meta llama 3: The most capable openly available LLM to date (2024). https://ai.meta.com/blog/meta-llama-3/. Accessed 13 Nov 2025
9. OpenAI: DALL-E3 (2023). https://openai.com/index/dall-e-3/. Accessed 13 Nov 2025
10. Li, J., Li, D., Savarese, S., Hoi, S.: BLIP-2: bootstrapping language-image pre-training with frozen image encoders and large language models. In: International Conference on Machine Learning, pp. 19730–19742. PMLR (2023)
11. Huang, Y., Meng, Z., Liu, F., Su, Y., Collier, N., Lu, Y.: Sparkles: unlocking chats across multiple images for multimodal instruction-following models. arXiv preprint: arXiv:2308.16463 (2023)
12. Singhal, K., et al.: Toward expert-level medical question answering with large language models. Nat. Med., 1–8 (2025)
13. Li, C., et al.: LLaVA-med: training a large language-and-vision assistant for biomedicine in one day. In: Advances in Neural Information Processing Systems, vol. 36, pp. 28541–28564 (2023)
14. Grisoni, F.: Chemical language models for de novo drug design: challenges and opportunities. Curr. Opin. Struct. Biol. **79**, 102527 (2023)
15. Ali, S.R., Dobbs, T.D., Hutchings, H.A., Whitaker, I.S.: Using ChatGPT to write patient clinic letters. Lancet Digit. Health **5**(4), e179–e181 (2023)
16. Danu, M.D., et al.: Generation of radiology findings in chest X-Ray by leveraging collaborative knowledge. Procedia Comput. Sci. **221**, 1102–1109 (2023)
17. Liu, Z., et al.: Radiology-Llama2: best-in-class large language model for radiology. arXiv preprint: arXiv:2309.06419 (2023)
18. Gao, Y., et al.: Retrieval-augmented generation for large language models: a survey **2**, 1. arXiv preprint: arXiv:2312.10997 (2023)
19. Qu, X., Chen, Q., Wei, W., Sun, J., Dong, J.: Alleviating hallucination in large vision-language models with active retrieval augmentation. arXiv preprint: arXiv:2408.00555 (2024)
20. Qu, X., Sun, J., Wei, W., Cheng, Y.: Look, compare, decide: alleviating hallucination in large vision-language models via multi-view multi-path reasoning. arXiv preprint: arXiv:2408.17150 (2024)

21. Yuan, Z., et al.: RAMM: retrieval-augmented biomedical visual question answering with multi-modal pre-training. In: Proceedings of the 31st ACM International Conference on Multimedia, pp. 547–556 (2023)
22. Kumar, Y., Marttinen, P.: Improving medical multi-modal contrastive learning with expert annotations. In: European Conference on Computer Vision, pp. 468–486. Springer (2024)
23. Tao, Y., Ma, L., Yu, J., Zhang, H.: Memory-based cross-modal semantic alignment network for radiology report generation. IEEE J. Biomed. Health Inform. (2024)
24. Ji, J., Hou, Y., Chen, X., Pan, Y., Xiang, Y.: Vision-language model for generating textual descriptions from clinical images: model development and validation study. JMIR Formative Res. **8**, e32690 (2024)
25. Liu, C., Tian, Y., Chen, W., Song, Y., Zhang, Y.: Bootstrapping large language models for radiology report generation. In: Proceedings of the AAAI Conference on Artificial Intelligence, vol. 38, pp. 18635–18643 (2024)
26. Lu, Y., Hong, S., Shah, Y., Xu, P.: Effectively fine-tune to improve large multimodal models for radiology report generation. arXiv preprint: arXiv:2312.01504 (2023)
27. Wang, Y., et al.: TRRG: towards truthful radiology report generation with cross-modal disease clue enhanced large language model. arXiv preprint: arXiv:2408.12141 (2024)
28. Zhou, Z., Shi, M., Wei, M., Alabi, O., Yue, Z., Vercauteren, T.: Large model driven radiology report generation with clinical quality reinforcement learning. arXiv preprint: arXiv:2403.06728 (2024)
29. Wang, Z., Liu, L., Wang, L., Zhou, L.: R2GenGPT: radiology report generation with frozen LLMs. Meta-Radiol. **1**(3), 100033 (2023)
30. Thawkar, O., et al.: XrayGPT: chest radiographs summarization using medical vision-language models. arXiv preprint: arXiv:2306.07971 (2023)
31. Hyland, S.L., et al.: MAIRA-1: a specialised large multimodal model for radiology report generation. arXiv preprint: arXiv:2311.13668 (2023)
32. Liu, Z., et al.: Swin transformer: hierarchical vision transformer using shifted windows. In: Proceedings of the IEEE/CVF International Conference on Computer Vision, pp. 10012–10022 (2021)
33. Wang, Z., Wu, Z., Agarwal, D., Sun, J.: MedCLIP: contrastive learning from unpaired medical images and text. In: Proceedings of the Conference on Empirical Methods in Natural Language Processing. Conference on Empirical Methods in Natural Language Processing, vol. 2022, p. 3876 (2022)
34. The Vicuna Team: Vicuna: An open-source chatbot impressing GPT-4 with 90%* ChatGPT quality (2023). https://lmsys.org/blog/2023-03-30-vicuna/. Accessed 13 Nov 2025
35. Su, Z., et al.: ConflictBank: a benchmark for evaluating the influence of knowledge conflicts in LLM. arXiv preprint: arXiv:2408.12076 (2024)
36. Xia, P., et al.: CARES: a comprehensive benchmark of trustworthiness in medical vision language models. In: Advances in Neural Information Processing Systems, vol. 37, pp. 140334–140365 (2024)
37. Liu, H., et al.: A survey on hallucination in large vision-language models. arXiv preprint: arXiv:2402.00253 (2024)
38. Khan, H., Bouaynaya, N.C., Rasool, G.: The importance of robust features in mitigating catastrophic forgetting. In: 2023 IEEE Symposium on Computers and Communications (ISCC), pp. 752–757. IEEE (2023)
39. Zhai, Y., et al.: Investigating the catastrophic forgetting in multimodal large language models. arXiv preprint: arXiv:2309.10313 (2023)

40. Sun, J., Zhang, J., Zhou, Y., Su, Z., Qu, X., Cheng, Y.: SURf: teaching large vision-language models to selectively utilize retrieved information. arXiv preprint: arXiv:2409.14083 (2024)
41. Bernardi, M.L., Cimitile, M.: Report generation from X-Ray imaging by retrieval-augmented generation and improved image-text matching. In: 2024 International Joint Conference on Neural Networks (IJCNN), pp. 1–8. IEEE (2024)
42. Liang, S., Sánchez, P., Sonntag, D.: Optimizing relation extraction in medical texts through active learning: a comparative analysis of trade-offs. In: Proceedings of the 1st Workshop on Uncertainty-Aware NLP (UncertaiNLP 2024), pp. 23–34 (2024)
43. Ranjit, M., Ganapathy, G., Manuel, R., Ganu, T.: Retrieval augmented chest X-Ray report generation using OpenAI GPT models. In: Machine Learning for Healthcare Conference, pp. 650–666 (2023) PMLR
44. Sun, L., Zhao, J., Han, M., Xiong, C.: Fact-aware multimodal retrieval augmentation for accurate medical radiology report generation. arXiv preprint: arXiv:2407.15268 (2024)
45. Xia, P., et al.: MMed-RAG: versatile multimodal rag system for medical vision language models. arXiv preprint: arXiv:2410.13085 (2024)
46. Xia, P., et al.: RULE: reliable multimodal rag for factuality in medical vision language models. In: Proceedings of the 2024 Conference on Empirical Methods in Natural Language Processing, pp. 1081–1093 (2024)
47. Han, S., et al.: MDocAgent: a multi-modal multi-agent framework for document understanding. arXiv preprint: arXiv:2503.13964 (2025)
48. Ke, Y.H., et al.: Enhancing diagnostic accuracy through multi-agent conversations: using large language models to mitigate cognitive bias. arXiv preprint: arXiv:2401.14589 (2024)
49. Smit, A.P., Duckworth, P., Grinsztajn, N., Tessera, K.a., Barrett, T.D., Pretorius, A.: Are we going mad? benchmarking multi-agent debate between language models for medical q&a. In: Deep Generative Models for Health Workshop NeurIPS 2023 (2023)
50. Tang, X., et al.: MedAgents: large language models as collaborators for zero-shot medical reasoning. arXiv preprint: arXiv:2311.10537 (2023)
51. Wang, L., et al.: A survey on large language model based autonomous agents. Front. Comp. Sci. **18**(6), 186345 (2024)
52. Wei, H., Qiu, J., Yu, H., Yuan, W.: MEDCO: medical education copilots based on a multi-agent framework. arXiv preprint: arXiv:2408.12496 (2024)
53. Yue, L., Fu, T.: CT-Agent: clinical trial multi-agent with large language model-based reasoning. arXiv e-prints pp. arXiv–2404 (2024)
54. Alam, H.M.T., Srivastav, D., Kadir, M.A., Sonntag, D.: Towards interpretable radiology report generation via concept bottlenecks using a multi-agentic RAG. In: European Conference on Information Retrieval, pp. 201–209. Springer (2025)
55. Zeng, F., Lyu, Z., Li, Q., Li, X.: Enhancing LLMs for impression generation in radiology reports through a multi-agent system. arXiv preprint: arXiv:2412.06828 (2024)
56. Radford, A., et al.: Learning transferable visual models from natural language supervision. In: International Conference on Machine Learning, pp. 8748–8763. PmLR (2021)
57. Jaech, A., et al.: OpenAI o1 system card. arXiv preprint: arXiv:2412.16720 (2024)
58. Johnson, A.E., et al.: MIMIC-CXR-JPG, a large publicly available database of labeled chest radiographs. arXiv preprint: arXiv:1901.07042 (2019)

59. Demner-Fushman, D., Kohli, M.D., Rosenman, M.B., Shooshan, S.E., Rodriguez, L., Antani, S., Thoma, G.R., McDonald, C.J.: Preparing a collection of radiology examinations for distribution and retrieval. J. Am. Med. Inform. Assoc. **23**(2), 304–310 (2016)
60. Liu, K., et al.: Factual serialization enhancement: a key innovation for chest X-Ray report generation. arXiv preprint: arXiv:2405.09586 (2024)
61. Papineni, K., Roukos, S., Ward, T., Zhu, W.J.: BLEU: a method for automatic evaluation of machine translation. In: Proceedings of the 40th Annual Meeting of the Association for Computational Linguistics, pp. 311–318 (2002)
62. Lin, C.Y.: ROUGE: a package for automatic evaluation of summaries. In: Text Summarization Branches Out, pp. 74–81 (2004)
63. Banerjee, S., Lavie, A.: METEOR: an automatic metric for mt evaluation with improved correlation with human judgments. In: Proceedings of the ACL Workshop on Intrinsic and Extrinsic Evaluation Measures for Machine Translation And/Or Summarization, pp. 65–72 (2005)
64. Zhang, T., Kishore, V., Wu, F., Weinberger, K.Q., Artzi, Y.: BERTScore: evaluating text generation with BERT. arXiv preprint: arXiv:1904.09675 (2019)
65. Zheng, L., et al.: Judging LLM-as-a-Judge with mt-bench and chatbot arena. In: Advances in Neural Information Processing Systems, vol. 36, pp. 46595–46623 (2023)
66. Anthropic: Claude 3 Haiku: Our fastest model yet (2024). https://www.anthropic.com/news/claude-3-haiku. Accessed 13 Nov 2025
67. Chen, Z., et al.: CheXagent: Towards a foundation model for chest X-Ray interpretation. arXiv preprint: arXiv:2401.12208 (2024)
68. Alkhaldi, A., et al.: MiniGPT-Med: large language model as a general interface for radiology diagnosis. arXiv preprint: arXiv:2407.04106 (2024)
69. Jiang, A.Q., et al.: Mistral 7B (2023). https://arxiv.org/abs/2310.06825
70. Guo, D., et al.: DeepSeek-R1: incentivizing reasoning capability in LLMs via reinforcement learning. arXiv preprint: arXiv:2501.12948 (2025)
71. Cohere: Command R+ documentation (2024). https://docs.cohere.com/docs/command-r. Accessed 13 Nov 2025

SensTrans: An AI Model for Generating Wearable Sensor Time-Series Signals to Improve Human Activity Detection

HyungKyun Kim and Sayma Akther(✉)

San Jose State University, California, USA
{hyungkyun.kim,sayma.akther}@sjsu.edu

Abstract. Wearable devices like smartwatches offer great promise for real-time activity tracking and personalized healthcare. However, small organizations often lack access to large-scale, high-quality sensor data. This paper addresses this challenge by leveraging a Sensor Transformer model for synthetic time-series data generation. By learning temporal patterns, the model generates additional data to augment training for activity recognition tasks. Experiments using benchmark datasets-WISDM, HARTH, and PAMAP2 - demonstrate that synthetic data improves classification performance across models such as SVMs, CNNs, and LSTMs. This approach enhances model robustness and generalization, enabling accurate recognition even with limited data. Future work includes real-time generation, dynamic validation, and scaling to more complex activities and sensors, offering an accessible path for startups in health monitoring innovation.

Keywords: Synthetic sensor data · wearable devices · human activity recognition · sensor transformer · data augmentation · time-series modeling

1 Introduction

Human Activity Recognition (HAR) using wearable sensors has gained significant attention due to its potential in healthcare, fitness monitoring, assisted living, and smart environments. By leveraging motion data from sensors such as accelerometers and gyroscopes, HAR models can classify human activities, enabling applications like fall detection, rehabilitation tracking, personalized fitness recommendations, and early diagnosis of movement disorders. The effectiveness of HAR systems, however, depends heavily on the availability of high-quality, diverse, and large-scale labeled datasets, which are crucial for training robust machine learning models.

This work was completed in partial fulfillment of the requirements for the M.S. degree of HyungKyun Kim[1] in Computer Science at San José State University. Sayma Akther[2] is the corresponding author.

H. R. Arabnia et al. (Eds.): CSCE 2025, CCIS 2934, pp. 162–175, 2026.
https://doi.org/10.1007/978-3-032-22190-2_12

Despite advances in sensor technology and data-driven modeling, current HAR datasets suffer from several limitations. Many publicly available datasets have *small sample sizes, restricted activity classes, and variations in sensor placement, device configurations, and sampling rates*, all of which hinder model generalization. Moreover, collecting large-scale HAR data is a *time-consuming and resource-intensive* process that requires participants to wear multiple sensors for extended durations. Labeling this data is equally challenging, often relying on *manual annotation methods*, which introduce errors and inconsistencies. Additionally, *privacy concerns* limit the sharing of HAR datasets, as continuous sensor monitoring raises ethical and security challenges.

Given these constraints, *synthetic data generation* has emerged as a promising solution to *enhance existing HAR datasets, improve model generalization, and reduce the dependency on extensive real-world data collection.* By employing advanced generative models, synthetic HAR data can mimic *realistic motion patterns*, introduce *greater diversity*, and address issues like *class imbalance*, ultimately leading to improved activity recognition performance.

1.1 Our Contributions

To overcome the limitations of existing HAR datasets, we propose a *Transformer-based synthetic data generation* approach that enhances HAR model performance. Our key contributions include:

- Introducing a *Transformer-based generative model* for synthesizing HAR data that accurately preserves real-world motion characteristics.
- Augmenting three widely used HAR datasets (WISDM, HARTH, and PAMAP2) with synthetic data to enhance model training.
- Evaluating the impact of synthetic data on both traditional machine learning models (Decision Trees, Random Forest, SVM, and XGBoost) and deep learning architectures (CNN, RNN, and LSTM).
- Demonstrating how synthetic data mitigates class imbalance, increases dataset diversity and enhances model generalization without the need for additional real-world data collection.
- Validating our approach by conducting extensive experiments to quantify improvements in classification accuracy and robustness across multiple datasets.

By leveraging synthetic HAR data, our approach aims to bridge the gap between data scarcity and model robustness, ensuring more scalable, diverse, and privacy-preserving activity recognition systems.

2 Related Works

Researchers have extensively explored Human Activity Recognition (HAR) through wearable sensors by applying traditional machine learning as well as deep learning methods. The performance of these models relies heavily on the presence of well-maintained labeled datasets. The majority of publicly available datasets originate from controlled environments with scripted settings and feature limited activity data. This data usually proves inadequate for deep learning model training which results in common problems such as overfitting. This section analyzes prior research on HAR datasets followed by a discussion about synthetic data generation methods.

2.1 HAR Datasets and Challenges

The field of biomarker detection of health and recognition of human activities was made easier by the presence of a number of public human activity recognition datasets. The PAMAP2 [15], HARTH [2], and WISDM [3] datasets contain inertial sensor data from magnetometers, gyroscopes, and accelerometers and physiological data such as heart rate and ECG readings from wearable sensors such as smartwatches to ease human activity classification. These results indicate some of the limitations that include limited sample sizes and variable sensor locations as well as restricted activity range. The controlled or laboratory conditions under which these experiments take place pose difficulties in trying to extrapolate models.

The aggregation of large HAR datasets is very demanding due to the need for accurate activity annotations which are normally sourced from self-reports or video recordings liable to human errorss [19]. The existence of numerous datasets necessary for solid model training is limited by privacy concerns which restrain data gathering and sharing.

2.2 Machine Learning and Deep Learning for HAR

Decision Trees [14], Random Forest [5], Support Vector Machines (SVM) [7], and XGBoost [6] represent traditional machine learning techniques that have found widespread application in both health biomarker detection and human activity monitoring [8]. Traditional machine learning methods depend on manually extracted features from raw sensor data. Researchers face major obstacles when they attempt to discover unique features that enable them to distinguish between activities that are very similar. The detection of rare and brief activities presents significant difficulties because positive examples make up less than 1% of the entire dataset.

Deep learning architectures such as Convolutional Neural Networks (CNNs) [11], Recurrent Neural Networks (RNNs) [17], and Long Short-Term Memory (LSTM) networks [9] have demonstrated outstanding results through their ability to automatically derive hierarchical feature representations from raw sensor signals [4]. Although deep learning models demonstrate high effectiveness they need extensive labeled datasets to both prevent overfitting and improve generalization capabilities according to [16]. The performance of models is negatively impacted by both data scarcity and class imbalance, making it essential to implement sophisticated data augmentation methods and create synthetic data.

2.3 Synthetic Time-Series Data Generation

Researchers investigated different methods of data augmentation and synthetic data generation to overcome the constraints of real-world datasets. Researchers utilized traditional augmentation methods like jittering and scaling along with time warping to artificially increase training datasets according to [13]. The traditional techniques for expanding datasets do not effectively address the intricate temporal relationships found in multimodal sensor data.

The main research focus of recent generative models such as Variational Autoencoders (VAEs), Generative Adversarial Networks (GANs), and Transformer-based models has been natural language processing (NLP). Kumar et al. [10] used GPT-2, BERT, and BART to perform data augmentation in NLP and demonstrated successful results for text generation, classification and translation tasks. These models demonstrate effectiveness when they assign class labels to text sequences during augmentation processes. Transformer models have primarily served natural language processing applications, yet this study investigates their potential use with time-series data which exhibits different properties from text data. The objective of this research project is to create a method that enables transformer models to generate time-series data which will expand their use beyond natural language processing applications.

Building upon these advancements, our work introduces a Transformer-based approach for generating synthetic Human Activity Recognition (HAR) data. Unlike conventional augmentation methods, our approach generates realistic motion patterns that maintain temporal dependencies, effectively addressing class imbalance and enhancing model generalization.

3 Proposed Method

3.1 System Architecture Overview

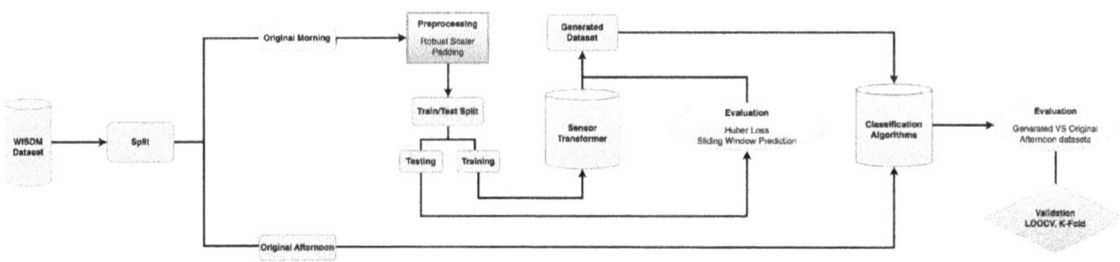

Fig. 1. System Architecture of Modeling.

The overall workflow of our proposed system is shown in Fig. 1. The workflow begins with data splitting, where the dataset is divided into morning and afternoon sessions. Then, we preprocessed the morning data, including outlier handling using RobustScaler and sequence length adjustment through padding.

Next, the preprocessed data is split into training and testing sets. The proposed model called **SensTrans**, is designed for time-series data generation and is then trained using the training subset. Since the sensor data is multimodal, this transformer-based model captures temporal dependencies and generates synthetic data to augment the existing dataset.

To assess the quality and stability of the generated data, the model is evaluated using Huber loss and a sliding window prediction approach. Huber loss provides robustness against outliers, while the sliding window technique ensures temporal coherence in the generated sequences. Finally, model performance is validated using both Leave-One-Out Cross-Validation (LOOCV) and K-Fold Cross-Validation. LOOCV iteratively selects one sample as test data while training on the remaining dataset, which makes it particularly effective for small datasets.

This architecture ensures a robust pipeline for evaluating synthetic data generation and its impact on activity recognition models, ultimately improving classification performance with limited original data (Fig. 2).

3.2 SensTrans: Proposed Synthetic Data Generator

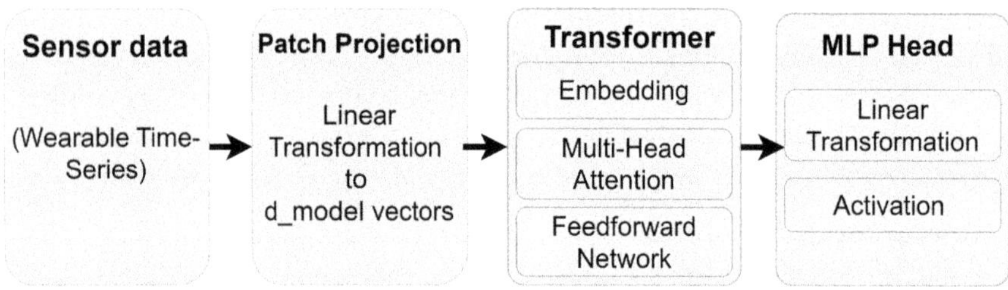

Fig. 2. Architecture of the Sensor Transformer Model for Synthetic Time-Series Data Generation.

We propose a Transformer-based model, referred to as the *SensTrans*, to generate synthetic time-series data from wearable sensors. Compared with traditional time-series models like RNN, LSTM, and GRU, the transformer model has several advantages. Its parallel processing capabilities allow it to handle large datasets efficiently, overcoming the sequential nature of RNN-based models that can slow down the learning process [18]. Unlike those models, the transformer doesn't have to process each piece of data in order to make sense of it and learn from it (i.e., it's not forced to be sequential). For another example of an advantage, let's take a look at the attention mechanism. The way RNNs work is that they use a hidden state vector to represent the information processed at a given time step.

To generate synthetic wearable sensor time-series data, we propose a *Transformer based* model, referred to as the *SensTrans*. There are several advantages of the transformer model compared to traditional time-series models such as RNN, LSTM, and GRU. Its parallel processing capabilities allow for efficient handling of large datasets [18], overcoming the sequential nature of RNN-based models, which can slow down the learning process. Also, positional embedding is needed to maintain the time-series data in its natural temporal order through reasonably effective learning, even if using long sequences [1]. The use of multi-head attention in the transformer model embeds the data in parallel from multiple perspectives, thus capturing many high-order dependencies and interactions [12]. We present an overview of our model in this section.

Step 1: Patch projection : First, the model divides the incoming sensor data into fixed-size patches, i.e., fixed-size time-series segments. in this step, each fixed-size patch is converted to a *d_ model*-dimensional vector to serve as the input to the transformer model.

The patch-based approach enhances the model's ability to learn spatial as well as temporal relationships in time-series data. The patches are passed through a linear layer and positional embeddings are added to keep the sequential data intact. Through this, the model is able to preserve temporal relationships in time-series data to learn useful long-term patterns over time.

$$\text{Patch Projection: } z_0 = [x_1P; x_2P; \ldots; x_NP] + E \tag{1}$$

where x_i is each patch input, P is a linear projection mapping the patches into embedding space, and E is the positional embedding vector.

Step 2: Transformer Layer: The heart of our proposed *SensTrans* model lies in its encoder layer, which takes the form of a multi-block Transformer architecture. The Transformer block in each has multi-head self-attention and feedforward network. These layers are able to capture complex interactions and patterns in the input data. The multi-head attention layer allows the model to focus on multiple parts of the input data simultaneously, allowing it to capture complex relationships and correlations among the various inputs. The feedforward network layer then fine-tunes these representations by converting the embedding vectors of every patch.

$$\text{Attention Output: Attention}(Q, K, V) = \text{softmax}\left(\frac{QK^T}{\sqrt{d_k}}\right)V \tag{2}$$

where Q is the query matrix, K is the key matrix, V is the value matrix, and d_k is the query and key vector dimension.

We employ the GELU activation function to introduce non-linearity. Additionally, we include LayerNorm and dropout after each transformer block to provide stability in learning and reduce risk of overfitting. Finally, the output of the transformer layer is a feature vector.

Step-3: Multi-layer Perceptron (MLP) Head: Then the output of the Transformer model is passed through a multi-layer perceptron (MLP) head. The MLP head accepts the feature vector from the Transformer block and produces the final prediction. The MLP is a deep linear layer, followed by an activation function, to map the feature vector to the output space.

This is the final representation of all the time-series segments that permit training multiple classification or time-series prediction models.

The proposed *SensTrans* represents temporal trends and complex sensor data interactions efficiently, thus fitting wearable sensor application.

4 Experiment Setup

This section outlines the experimental setup used to evaluate the performance of various machine learning and deep learning models for Human Activity Recognition (HAR) tasks. The setup includes details about the datasets, preprocessing procedures, models, and evaluation protocol.

4.1 Dataset Description

Table 1. Summary of the datasets used for evaluation

	WISDM [3]	HARTH [2]	PAMAP2 [15]
# of Participants	51	22	9
# of Activities	18	12	12
# of Observations	659,563	982,162	1,024,752
Sampling Rate	20 Hz	50 Hz	100 Hz

The datasets used in this study are summarized in Table 1. We utilized three publicly available Human Activity Recognition (HAR) datasets: WISDM, HARTH, and PAMAP2. These datasets consist of sensor data collected from wearable devices, such as accelerometers and gyroscopes, to classify various human activities. A high-level summary of these three datasets is shown in Table 1. The key characteristics of each dataset are as follows:

- **WISDM** (Wireless Sensor Data Mining): This dataset includes sensor data collected from smartphones worn by users performing 18 different activities. The data includes time-series accelerometer readings sampled at 20 Hz, a total of 659,563 datapoints [3].
- **HARTH** (Human Activity Recognition using Smartphones): The HARTH dataset consists of data from 22 participants performing 12 activities, using two 3-axis accelerometers sampled at 50 Hz with total of 982,162 datapoints, which includes a notable class imbalance [2].
- **PAMAP2** (Physical Activity Monitoring for Aging People): The PAMAP2 dataset consists of data from 9 participants performing 12 activities using three IMU sensors, sampled at 100 Hz, amounting to 1,024,752 datapoints [15].

4.2 Data Pre-processing

To ensure that the models received consistent and standardized input, the following preprocessing steps were applied to the datasets:

- **Outlier removal**: We remove the outliers from the sensor signal. Also, segments of the sensor data are removed when the participant did not wear the sensor but data was collected.
- **Normalization**: The sensor data was normalized using the StandardScaler to ensure each datapoint has a mean of 0 and a standard deviation of 1.
- **Imputation of missing data**: In the real-world setting there is a lot of missing data, so we interpolate the missing sensor data.
- **Activity label encoding**: Activity labels were encoded as integer values using Label Encoding to convert categorical target variables into numerical form.

4.3 Evaluation Method

We evaluated the models using different approaches to determine the stability and effectiveness of the synthetic data. We employed Huber loss for robustness against outliers and sliding window for temporal coherence in the generated time-series data.

To measure model generalization, we employed both Leave-One-Out Cross-Validation (LOOCV) and K-Fold Cross-Validation. LOOCV iterates over every data point once, training on the remaining data, and is extremely valuable for limited datasets. K-Fold Cross-Validation splits the data into K folds, training on $K - 1$ folds and testing on the hold-out fold. These cross-validation methods provide consistent performance metrics so that the models become stable and generalize efficiently to fresh data.

4.4 Evaluation Metrics

The performance of the models was evaluated using the following metrics:

- **Accuracy**: The proportion of correctly classified instances out of the total instances.
- **Cross-Validation Accuracy**: To ensure reliable results, 5-fold cross-validation was employed to evaluate the models across different data splits.

We report the average accuracy of the models on both the original and augmented datasets for each of the three datasets (WISDM, HARTH, and PAMAP2).

4.5 Computational Resources

All experiments were conducted on a system with the following specifications:

- CPU: Intel Core i7-9700K
- RAM: 16 GB
- GPU: NVIDIA GeForce GTX 1080 Ti (for deep learning models)

The experiments were implemented in Python, using libraries such as scikit-learn for traditional machine learning models and TensorFlow/PyTorch for deep learning models.

5 Evaluation and Experiment Results

This section presents the evaluation of various machine learning (ML) and deep learning models for Human Activity Recognition (HAR) using the PAMAP2, WISDM, and HARTH datasets. The models were trained using both original and synthetic datasets, generated by the Sensor Transformer model. The results are categorized into two groups: traditional Machine Learning (ML) models and Deep Learning models (Figs. 3).

5.1 Traditional Machine Learning Models

First, we discuss the performance of detecting human daily activities using both original data and synthetic data using the traditional machine learning models. For this experiment, we trained decision tree (DT), random forest (RF), support vector machine (SVM), and gradient-boosting (XGBoost) classifiers.

Decision Tree (DT). Through grid search, the Decision Tree (DT) classifier is fine-tuned during the training procedure to achieve an accuracy range of 0.7–0.8 in detecting human daily behaviors on the original three datasets; however, accuracy improved and was above 0.9 with respect to each of the datasets when trained using synthetic data. This shows the advantages of data augmentation in boosting models' performance for simpler classifiers like Decision Trees.

Random Forest (RF). This Random Forest was trained with 100 trees and surpassed an accuracy of 0.8 with the base trained dataset. Overall accuracy with the synthetic dataset increased to above 0.96. The ensemble nature of Random Forest, along with the availability of augmented data, helped improve its generalization ability and performance over the single decision tree.

Support Vector Machine (SVM). The SVM model, when trained using synthetic data, subsequently improved its performance above 0.97 accuracy on all datasets likelihoods against the original datasets, thus suggesting that SVM later benefited from the increased variation of the augmented data which allowed SVM to fit the underlying relationships of the sensor data more robustly.

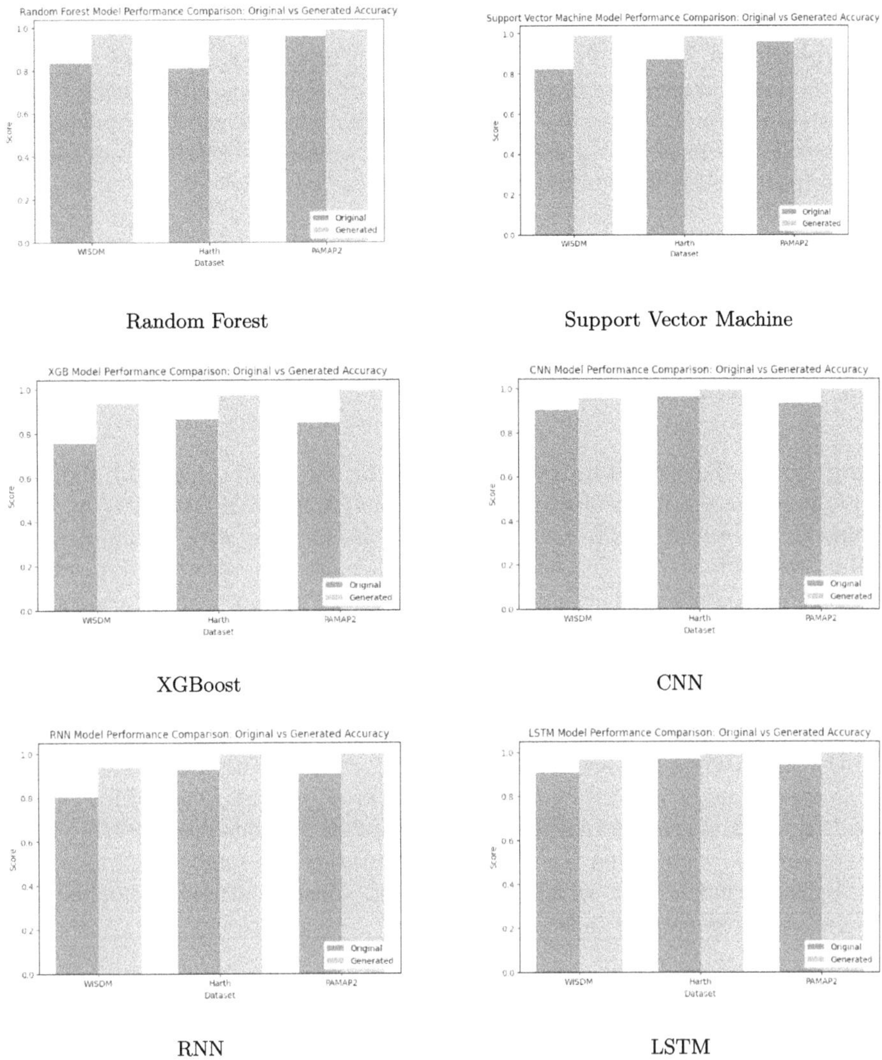

Fig. 3. Human activity detection accuracy of different ML models on three datasets.

XGBoost. Synthetic data also makes an impact on the performance of XGBoost, which, being a gradient-boosting algorithm, seems to be benefiting as well. The accuracy achieved on the PAMAP2 dataset far exceeded 0.99, thus showcasing the effectiveness of synthetic data in enabling the model to enhance prediction accuracy.

5.2 Deep Learning Models

Convolutional Neural Network (CNN). The CNN model performed well with original datasets, with accuracy above 0.9. Training with synthetic data enhanced accuracy to over 0.96 on all datasets. This shows the robustness of CNNs to learn effectively spatial hierarchies in sensor observations and the positive impact of augmented data on performance.

Recurrent Neural Network (RNN). The RNN model showed considerable performance gains when it was trained using synthetic data, and performance on all datasets was enhanced. The model's capability to learn temporal dependencies in the data was enhanced by the introduced diversity of the synthetic data, and its generalization was boosted.

Long Short-Term Memory (LSTM). LSTM model achieved the highest improvements, particularly on PAMAP2 and WISDM datasets. Accuracy improved to over 0.99 when trained on synthetic data, with a sample showcasing its ability to handle long-term dependencies. The enriched data allowed the LSTM model to further optimize performance by more effectively learning sequential patterns of activity.

5.3 Result Summary

Table 2 summarizes the classification accuracy results of each model using both the original and generated datasets across three datasets: WISDM, HARTH, and PAMAP2. As shown in Table 2, the generated datasets consistently yielded higher accuracy compared to the original datasets, especially for models like SVM, CNN, and LSTM, which demonstrated substantial improvements when trained on the generated data.

Table 2. Model Accuracy: Original Dataset vs Generated Dataset across Models and Datasets

	WISDM		HARTH		PAMAP2	
	Original	Generated	Original	Generated	Original	Generated
DT	0.684	**0.934**	0.804	**0.949**	0.827	**0.959**
RF	0.836	**0.974**	0.812	**0.964**	0.960	**0.989**
SVM	0.824	**0.990**	0.872	**0.988**	0.959	**0.980**
Xgb	0.755	**0.937**	0.865	**0.973**	0.847	**0.994**
CNN	0.903	**0.957**	0.963	**0.994**	0.933	**0.997**
RNN	0.802	**0.938**	0.925	**0.999**	0.905	**0.998**
LSTM	0.907	**0.966**	0.971	**0.991**	0.944	**0.999**

The results presented in Table 2 show that synthetic data generated using the Sensor Transformer model consistently led to improved model performance across all evaluated models. Notably, traditional ML models showed significant improvements in classification accuracy when trained on the generated data, highlighting the effectiveness of data augmentation in enhancing model generalization.

6 Discussion

This study explored the use of data augmentation techniques to enhance user activity classification models using smartwatch sensor data. By augmenting the dataset, we addressed the challenge posed by limited data, which often degrades the generalization performance of machine learning models. The results demonstrated that the augmented dataset significantly improved classification accuracy compared to the original dataset. Notably, models such as SVM, CNN, and LSTM showed considerable performance gains, highlighting the value of data augmentation in boosting predictive accuracy for wearable sensor-based activity recognition. This reinforces the critical role of data augmentation in improving model performance, especially in situations where real-world data is sparse.

The practical implications of this study are significant. In real-world applications, wearable devices like smartwatches often collect limited sensor data, which can hinder model performance. By applying data augmentation, more training data can be generated, improving the model's ability to make accurate predictions. This approach can benefit a wide range of applications, including health monitoring and activity recognition, where collecting large amounts of real-time data may not always be feasible. This research also lays the foundation for future work in expanding datasets and models to recognize a broader range of activities, such as complex, mixed, or transitional activities.

6.1 Limitations and Future Directions

One significant limitation of this study is the high computational cost associated with processing large-scale sensor datasets, such as PAMAP2, WISDM, and HARTH. As the size of these datasets increases, both the time required for learning and resource consumption also rise, making it challenging to work with the entire dataset. To address this issue, data sampling was utilized in some experiments; however, this approach may have resulted in the loss of important patterns, potentially affecting the model's ability to generalize.

Furthermore, the Leave-One-Subject-Out (LOSO) method used for personalized performance evaluation was time-consuming, which restricted the ability to obtain results within the study's timeframe. To tackle these computational challenges, future research should consider utilizing high-performance computing resources and optimization techniques to streamline data preprocessing and training. Exploring distributed learning or parallel processing methods could offer more efficient approaches for managing large datasets, enhancing the practicality of the system for real-world applications. This would lead to faster processing of sensor data and more efficient model training.

7 Conclusion

The results of this study confirm that data augmentation boosts the performance of models used for activity classification. The model accuracy showed significant improvement after we applied data augmentation techniques specifically for SVM, CNN, and LSTM models. The results demonstrate that data augmentation serves as an essential technique for recognizing activities through wearable sensor technology. Our future plans include enlarging the dataset with varied sensor data to build models capable of identifying complex daily activities. Developing models to detect mixed or transitional activities will enable applications to explore new functional capabilities.

The evaluation of the model took place in a static environment but additional development work is necessary before it can be applied to real-time settings. The next phase of research will aim to create systems that generate and predict real-time data which stay highly efficient in wearable devices such as smartwatches. Our goal includes evaluating generated data to verify its accuracy when compared to real-world data. Through the enhancement of data augmentation methods and the improvement of model reliability during real-world applications we expect to boost both system performance and its practical usability.

References

1. Ahmed, S., Nielsen, I.E., Tripathi, A.: Transformers in time-series analysis: a tutorial. Circ. Syst. Signal Process. **42**, 7433–7466 (2023). https://doi.org/10.1007/s00034-023-02454-8
2. Anguita, D., et al.: The harth dataset: a collection of sensor data for human activity recognition. Inter. J. Comput. Intell. Syst. **7**(5), 735–744 (2014)
3. Anguita, D., Ghio, A., Oneto, L., Parra, X., Reyes Ortiz, J.L.: A public domain dataset for human activity recognition using smartphones. In: 21st European Symposium on Artificial Neural Networks, Computational Intelligence and Machine Learning, pp. 437–442 (2013)
4. Aydın, E., Arslan, G.: Deep learning-based approaches for human activity recognition: a survey. J. Electr. Eng. Technol. **13**(4), 1310–1318 (2018)
5. Breiman, L.: Random forests. Mach. Learn. **45**(1), 5–32 (2001)
6. Chen, T., Guestrin, C.: Xgboost: a scalable tree boosting system. In: Proceedings of the 22nd ACM SIGKDD International Conference on Knowledge Discovery and Data Mining, pp. 785–794 (2016)
7. Cortes, C., Vapnik, V.: Support-vector networks. Mach. Learn. **20**(3), 273–297 (1995)
8. He, Z., Wu, Y.: A survey of machine learning methods for human activity recognition using wearable sensors. J. Comput. Sci. Technol. **32**(3), 445–462 (2017)
9. Hochreiter, S., Schmidhuber, J.: Long short-term memory. Neural Comput. **9**(8), 1735–1780 (1997)

10. Kumar, V., Choudhary, A., Cho, E.: Data augmentation using pre-trained transformer models. arXiv preprint arXiv:2003.02245 (2020), https://doi.org/10.48550/arXiv.2003.02245, in Proceedings of the 2nd Workshop on Life-long Learning for Spoken Language Systems @ AACL 2020
11. LeCun, Y., Bottou, L., Bengio, Y., Haffner, P.: Gradient-based learning applied to document recognition. Proc. IEEE **86**(11), 2278–2324 (1998)
12. Nino, S.: Transformers and time series forecasting. Princeton University Senior Theses (2020). http://arks.princeton.edu/ark:/88435/dsp01kk91fp583
13. Ordóñez, F.J., Roggen, D.: Deep convolutional and lstm recurrent neural networks for multimodal wearable activity recognition, pp. 465–472 (2016)
14. Quinlan, J.R.: Induction of decision trees. Mach. Learn. **1**(1), 81–106 (1986)
15. Reinders, M.: Pamap2: A large-scale dataset for physical activity recognition (2013)
16. Ribeiro, F., et al.: Overfitting in deep learning models for har: solutions and recommendations. Neural Comput. Appl. **32**(15), 11861–11874 (2020)
17. Rumelhart, D.E., Hinton, G.E., Williams, R.J.: Learning representations by back-propagating errors. Nature **323**, 533–536 (1986)
18. Vaswani, A., et al.: Attention is all you need. In: Advances in Neural Information Processing Systems (2017)
19. Zhang, S., et al.: Challenges in collecting human activity recognition datasets and possible solutions. J. Ambient. Intell. Humaniz. Comput. **10**(7), 2553–2568 (2019)

Unveiling Gender Disparities in Neurodegenerative Disease Diagnosis on Microblogs

Ahmed Isam Al-Hatem[1], Samer Muthana Sarsam[2(✉)], Abdul Samad Shibghatullah[3], Chit Su Mon[4], Abd Aziz Alias[5], and Lubna A. Hussein[6]

[1] College of Arts, Al Iraqia University, Baghdad, Iraq
ahmed.i.khaleel@aliraqia.edu.iq

[2] School of Management, Coventry University, Coventry, UK
samer.sarsam@coventry.ac.uk

[3] College of Computing and Informatics (CCI), Universiti Tenaga Nasional, Kajang, Selangor, Malaysia
abdul.samad@uniten.edu.my

[4] Wentworth Institute of Higher Education, Sydney, NSW, Australia
chit.mon@win.edu.au

[5] Department of Oral and Craniofacial Sciences, Faculty of Dentistry, Universiti Malaya, 50603 Kuala Lumpur, Malaysia
alias123@um.edu.my

[6] Department of Computing and Information Sciences, University of Technology and Applied Sciences (UTAS), Suhar 311, Sultanate of Oman
lubnafatlawi@gmail.com

Abstract. Recent research highlights how biological sex may influence the development of neurodegenerative conditions such as Parkinson's disease (PD). Early and accurate diagnosis of PD symptoms can play a key role in extending life expectancy and enhancing quality of life. This study presents a novel model to predict PD using gendered data from X (Twitter). We analyzed PD-related tweets to identify user gender, extract hidden topics and sentiments, and applied multi-label classification. The classification results showed the potential of gender-based sentiment in predicting PD at 85.64% accuracy. Emotional patterns differed by gender, with males showing anger and surprise, and females expressing disgust, fear, sadness, and trust. The proposed approach offers new possibilities for enhancing online PD diagnosis and personalized healthcare.

Keywords: Neurodegenerative disorders · Parkinson's disease · Gender · Sentiment analysis · X/Twitter · Machine learning

1 Introduction

Many previous studies have identified neurodegenerative diseases as disorders that affects individual motor and/or cognitive functions. They are usually accompanied by psychiatric disorders, mainly in the form of Alzheimer's disease (AD) and Parkinson's

H. R. Arabnia et al. (Eds.): CSCE 2025, CCIS 2934, pp. 176–188, 2026.
https://doi.org/10.1007/978-3-032-22190-2_13

disease (PD). Despite many clinical successes, the treatment of these diseases is not well established. Neurodegenerative diseases are driven by different factors such as age, genetics, and injuries [1]. The increasing incidences of these disorders have been known as the major cause of death and disability worldwide [2]. These diseases directly contribute to the quality of life. Affected individuals are likely to experience neurological symptoms after the middle age, which get more severe throughout the disease course [3]. Although current research on neurodegenerative diseases is progressively developing, several studies are looking at the potential of big data in preventing and diagnosing these diseases. This includes exploring new prevention mechanisms and surveillance directions [4]. Since neurodegenerative diseases can be classified into several sub diseases, the main focus of this study was on the recognition and prediction of PD.

Several previous studies on public perception have argued that people's expression of pain and emotions can help develop future predictive models. Stories associated with PD that user shares on social media sites can be useful in establishing a prediction model of the disease in a specific population. There have been a number of attempts to facilitate the prediction and surveillance of PD using various ways. Current classical methods (e.g., clinical survey) can be useful for surveying and monitoring PD in a population periodically. However, these methods require long time, coordination, and resource. Therefore, this work explored the possibility of diagnosing the main symptoms of PD using shared messages on social media sites rather than focusing on its treatment and palliation. The main aim of this work was to develop a gender-based machine learning model capable at predicting PD using users' sentimental features posted/shared on X. Precisely, this study attempts to answer three key questions: 1) What topics being shared by PD male and female users on X? 2) What types of emotions do PD male and female users tend to express? and 3) How to use these topics and emotions to diagnose PD among male and female users? The proposed approach has potential to help in the development of diagnosing strategies and speed efforts to discern new directions for PD tailored treatment and management. Outcomes from this work can help speed up health interventions and provide healthcare organizations the means to better understand, monitor, manage, and prevent PD in population.

2 Literature Review

Among the neurodegenerative diseases, PD is considered the second most common disease, which can increasingly affect the older population [5]. The progressive rise of PD cases among people is a key concern for many developed and developing countries due to the health cost implications.

Previous studies on PD have heavily relied on clinical assessment to diagnose and predict disease progress in patients [6]. Another study by Mandal and Sairam [7] developed a machine learning model to help prevent the delay and misdiagnosis of PD patients. The authors emphasized on the potential of using Bayesian network during the feature selection and ranking processes of PD. The conclusion made by the authors is somehow relevant to the previous work of Wingate, Kollia, Bidaut and Kollias [8] who proposed the use of deep learning in order to diagnose PD through the use of medical imaging. The authors claimed that such approach can offer a unified framework for the prediction of PD in different medical settings. Furthermore, Shahid and Singh [9] developed a deep neural network (DNN) model based on the characteristics of PD's telemonitoring dataset in an attempt to monitor the progression of the disease.

Our review of the literature on PD prediction has also revealed the potential of developing machine learning models based on voice data of PD patients to predict the severity of the disease. For example, Aich, Kim, Hui, Al-Absi and Sain [10] used voice data to predict PD progress in the affected patients. The authors applied principal component analysis in order to improve the process of feature reduction which they then compared using a set of individual performance metrics. It was concluded that voice data can provide clues to monitor PD severity in patients. On the same line Hemmerling and Wojcik-Pedziwiatr (2022) presents the possibilities of using speech signal processing and regression methods to help clinicians to assess PD state in patients after taking medication. Despite these efforts, there seems to be a limited understanding on how non-clinical data gathered from PD patients can be used to diagnose and predict the disease. In addition, previous techniques were heavily designed based on various imaginary and voice datasets collected from PD patients.

With that said, there is a rational to consider the development of more agile and cost-effective methods to assess the diagnosing and prediction of PD in a population. Big data has been widely used to extract, analyze, and understand human behavior in recent years. Social media sites or microblogs have been identified as one of the main sources of big data. The use of social media big data in characterizing and predicting diseases is a recent trend that still needs establishing (Galetsi & Katsaliaki, 2020). And since PD is classified as a chronic and progressive nervous system disorder that affects body movement [11], it is assumed that this will lead affected individuals to express their sense of pain and emotions on social media sites. Individuals with other PD symptoms (e.g., muscle rigidity, resting tremors, loss of facial expression, hypophonia, and diminished blinking) are also likely to express them with others [12]. This type of behavior is considered typical among social media users who actively get involved in sharing and seeking advises from others as a way to manage their pain. The literature also showed that the severity of PD symptoms varies among male and female patients, both from clinical and behavioral perspectives [13, 14]. The next section explains the role of gender in disease prediction and justifying its potential in facilitating the prediction of PD online.

3 The Role of Gender in Disease Prediction

Gender differences have been widely considered by previous scholars and linked to individual brain structure and function, which are shaped based on sex determining genes and fetal hormonal programming [14]. Understanding how gender differences drive disease progression can help in the development of future prediction models, especially of brain-diseases. Brain-related diseases have been commonly linked to sex-specific genetic and hormonal factors, which contributed to the expression of PD [15]. The literature reported that some health effects associated with PD may likely be found in men more often than women. For example, men are likely to experience rigidity and rapid eye movement behavior disorder, whereas women are likely to experience dyskinesias and depression [16]. Picillo, Nicoletti, Fetoni, Garavaglia, Barone and Pellecchia [14] stated that gender differences in PD clinical phenotype do exist. Yet, there is still more work needed to investigate the interaction between gender and genetics in assessing the PD risk and various clinical characteristics [17].

4 Method

The main stages followed in this study are summarized in Fig. 1. The research process was organized as follows: data collection, gender extraction, data pre-processing, topic modeling, emotion extraction, part-of-speech tagging, association rules mining, and classification task.

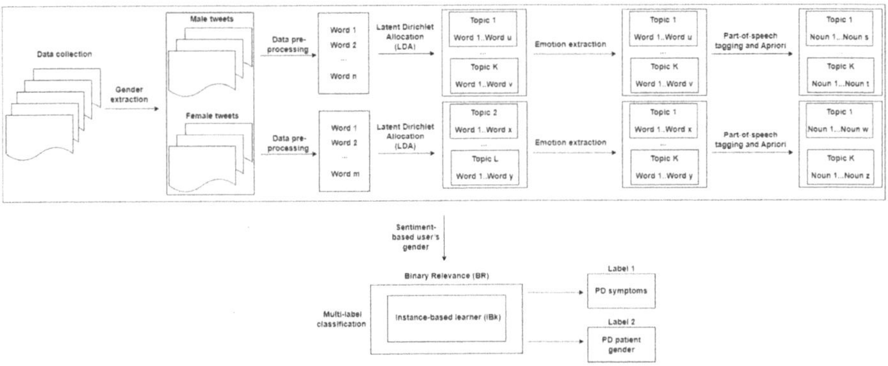

Fig. 1. The research process.

4.1 Data Collection

The data for this study was collected from the X Application Programming Interface (API) using keywords such as 'Parkinson's disease' and 'neurodegenerative disorders. Our search was performed for six months period (from March to October 2024). The search resulted in a total of 1,575,943 English tweets. We applied several data preparation procedures to improve the quality of the collected data.

4.2 Gender Extraction

We identified users' genders from their tweets following the recommendations of Thelwall, Thelwall and Fairclough [18]. The gender extraction process was initiated by obtaining the first names of male and female users from the public US census 1990 (contains tables of popular first names by gender that was supplemented with Gender-API.com). In this sense, a particular name can be gendered if at least 90% of the time the same name was used by the same male or female user. Hence, in this study, X users were classified as male or female if the first part of their username matches either male or female names list, otherwise they were classified as unknown.

4.3 Data Pre-processing

We prepared the collected data using several pre-processing tools to enhance the quality of data and make it more reliable for the next analysis step. Here we extracted the bag-of-words model from the collected data using the "Tokenization" approach. This model facilitated the words extraction from each tweet, which were then used to build the dataset (corpus) features. All the extracted words were then converted into a lowercase form to generate data with a standard dictionary. This process allowed us to eliminate unnecessary words from the generated corpus using the Stopwords list approach. The length of the tweets was also normalized using the L2 norm method.

4.4 Topic Modeling

At this stage we applied the Latent Dirichlet Allocation (LDA) algorithm to retrieve the embedded topics in the collected tweets based on the classification of users' gender (Shurrab, Shannak, Almshnanah, Khazaleh, & Najadat, 2021). LDA is a commonly used unsupervised generative probabilistic technique that models the collection of documents. These documents are generally characterized as random mixtures over hidden topics, where a topic is defined by its distribution over words.

To get an overview of the general distribution of the discussed PD topics, we extended the LDA in order to generate a heatmap presentation using a density-based method. The color was estimated based on the number of items within the textual content as well as the importance of neighboring items. The intensity of the color was based on the item density. The larger the number of neighboring words and the smaller the distances between them and the point of interest, the higher the density of the words. In the context of this study, words with high density were associated with the weights of the neighboring words.

After having all the topics extracted, three neurologists were asked to independently assess the contents of the identified topics and provide a theme label that can properly define these topics. The kappa statistic value of 0.93 was obtained which indicate a high agreement between the assessors in relation to the classification of PD topics. To effectively diagnose PD topics on X, we applied a multi-label classification to predict PD symptoms in association with users' genders. For this purpose, a new dataset was constructed based on two labeling classes in an attempt to diagnose PD on X (see Sects. 4.8 and 5.3).

4.5 Emotion Extraction

Users' sentimental features were extracted from their tweets using NRC Affect Intensity Lexicon and SentiStrength, as recommended by [19]. NRC scores words from 0 to 1 based on their association with six emotions. Tweet scores were calculated by summing word intensities.

4.6 Part-of-Speech Tagging

In this study, the part-of-speech (POS) tagging method was applied on each topic to obtain the necessary features related to PD. Part-of-speech tagging is a popular method that can be used to extract different parts of speech from a text [20]. It works by assigning a unique tag to the extracted words. In this study, we applied POS via the Penn State Treebank tokenizer in conjunction with the Document Pre-processor approach. Then, the Penn State Treebank tokenizer was utilized again to create a set of relevant words before applying the Probabilistic context-free grammar parser. Such a process facilitated the extraction of the 'noun' words from the collected tweets, which we then used to predict possible associations via the association rules mining approach.

4.7 Association Rules Mining

To predict PD-related words that are commonly linked to a specific users' gender (male or female), the association rules mining technique was applied through the Apriori method [21]. The Apriori method was configured by setting the delta value to 0.05, mainly to reduce the support value until reaching its minimum value. In addition, the minimum metric score was set to 0.9 and both upper and lower bounds of the support were set to 1.0. The Apriori scheme performs the process of counting item occurrence that is necessary for determining the large 1-itemsets.

4.8 Classification Task

After constructing the dataset, we attempted to diagnose PD from the collected X messages. For this we used a multi-label classification method. We used the Meka framework (an extension of the Weka tool) to facilitate the process of performing the multi-label classification task. To understand the role of users' emotions in diagnosing PD, we considered two scenarios: 1) gender-based PD sentiment and 2) non-gender-based PD sentiment.

Gender-based sentiment consisted of PD tweets that can be linked to a specific gender (male/female), while non-gender-based sentiment consisted of either motor or non-motor PD symptoms and containing no identification of gender. We used various multi-label classification algorithms to predict both scenarios (gender-based and non-gender-based) at the same time. In this way we can understand the role of gender in predicting PD among X users.

For the classification purpose, we used the following algorithms based on the recommendations of previous studies: instance-based learner (IBk) [22], boosting algorithm (AdaBoostM1) [23], Sequential Minimal Optimization (SMO) classifier [24], and RandomForest [25]. We applied multi-label classification by invoking each of these classifiers independently in conjunction with the "Binary Relevance" (BR) technique [26], which separates the binary classifier per label. Finally, the algorithm with the highest prediction results (accuracy and hamming loss) was selected and validated using stratified tenfold cross-validation.

5 Results

5.1 Topic Modeling Results

In this study, the LDA approach was configured by conducting several experiments. The number of topics was determined first with the consideration of the trade-off between information loss and information overload. After multiple experiments, the number of topics to be investigated was confirmed.

The extracted topics from the LDA phase were classified based on the classification of users' gender (the gender extraction process was explained in Sect. 4.2). This step enabled us to further understand the topics in the collected tweets by male and female users. The generated LDA heatmap (see Fig. 2) shows some interesting insights about the main PD topics and words discussed by male and female users on X. The intensity of the topics was largely depending on the number of neighboring items and their importance. Important topics in this study represent high dense and frequently repeated tweets. We

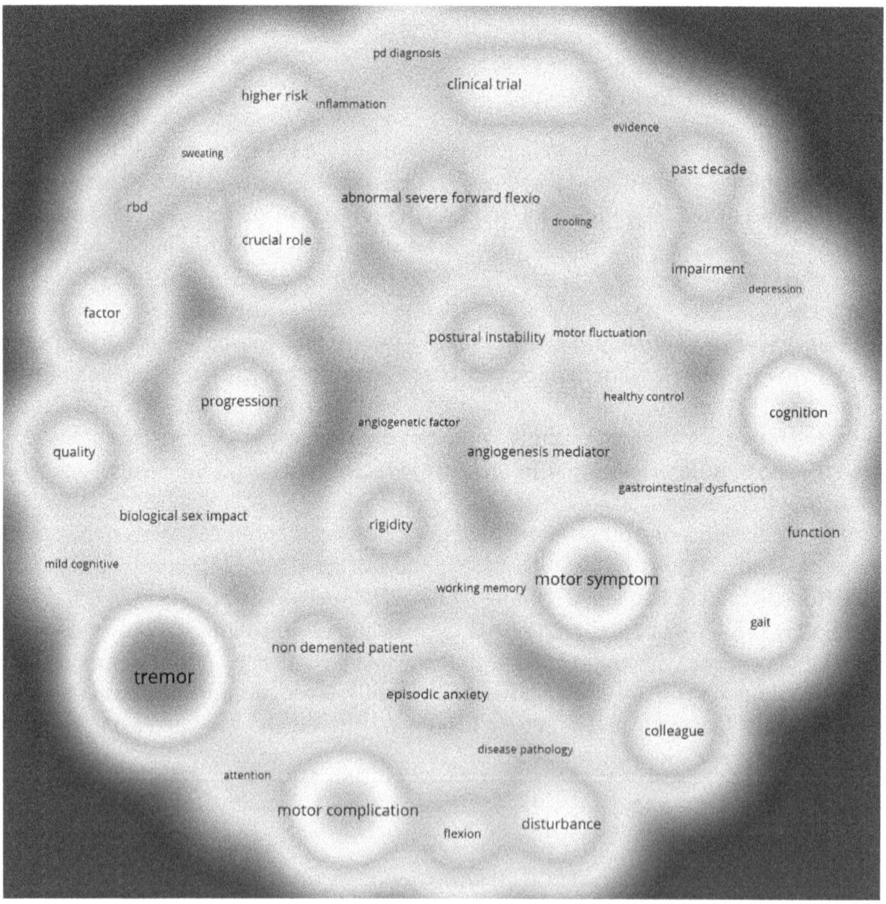

Fig. 2. Heatmap of PD topics among male and female users.

involved three assessors (see Sect. 4.4) to assess the labeling of the topics. The LDA results exhibited three male-related topics. The first male topic (MT-1) discussed the camptocormia and freezing of gait (a motor symptom), which were considered to be the most disabling motor complication of PD among men. The second male topic (MT-2) and the third male topic (MT-3) were related to non-motor symptoms. In MT-2, it was found that impulse control disorders, e.g., pathological gambling and hypersexuality, were commonly discussed by male users. In MT-3, REM sleep behavior disorder (RBD)– a parasomnia characterized by recurrent dream enactment with excessive motor activity– was mainly observed among male users. PD-related topics associated with female users covered two main areas. The first female topic (FT-1) discussed some of the popular motor symptoms that can be observed among female patients, including reduced rigidity, tremor, and elevated risk for levodopa-related motor complications. The second female topic (FT-2) discussed some of the non-motor symptoms such as fatigue, depression, restless legs, constipation, pain, loss of taste or smell, and excessive sweating.

5.2 Sentiment Analysis and Association Rules Mining Results

The result shows the NRC Affect Intensity Lexicon results where PD male users were found to exhibit a higher proportion of anger ($\boldsymbol{M} = 1.71$, $\boldsymbol{SD} = 1.23$) and surprise emotions ($\boldsymbol{M} = 0.19$, $\boldsymbol{SD} = 0.05$) than PD female users who exhibited a higher proportion of anger ($\boldsymbol{M} = 1.62$, $\boldsymbol{SD} = 1.14$) and surprise ($\boldsymbol{M} = 0.16$, $\boldsymbol{SD} = 0.07$) emotions. Our observation of the results also leads us to assert that female tweets on PD contained a higher level of disgust ($\boldsymbol{M} = 1.14$, $\boldsymbol{SD} = 1.09$), fear ($\boldsymbol{M} = 1.45$, $\boldsymbol{SD} = 1.18$), sadness ($\boldsymbol{M} = 1.57$, $\boldsymbol{SD} = 0.21$), and trust ($\boldsymbol{M} = 0\ .75$, $\boldsymbol{SD} = 0.29$) emotions than these found in the male tweets (disgust: $\boldsymbol{M} = 1.07$, $\boldsymbol{SD} = 0.80$; fear: $\boldsymbol{M} = 1.41$, $\boldsymbol{SD} = 1.18$; sadness: $\boldsymbol{M} = 1.53$, $\boldsymbol{SD} = 1.25$; and trust: $\boldsymbol{M} = 0.73$, $\boldsymbol{SD} = 0.55$). The SentiStrength results showed a high presence of negative sentiments among male (86%) and female (92%) users. From these results, it can be observed that emotions of anger and surprise were mostly expressed by PD male users, while disgust, fear, sadness, and trust were mostly expressed by PD female users. The Apriori results are summarized in Fig. 3. From the figure, it can be observed that PD terms, such as Gait, Camptocormia, Flexion, Drooling, and Stress, were highly associated with male users (see Fig. 3a) at confidence (accuracy) values of 95%, 92%, 87%, 81%, and 75%, respectively. Furthermore, PD terms like Tremor, Depression, Fatigue, Sweating, and Rigidity (accuracy of 97%, 93%, 85%, 85%, and 72%, respectively) were highly associated with female users, see Fig. 3b. The association of these terms can be explained by the differences in gender which are believed to provoke certain users' emotional states. When PD users share or express their experience online, they also tend to convey certain emotions/feelings that can help in the development of effective prediction models.

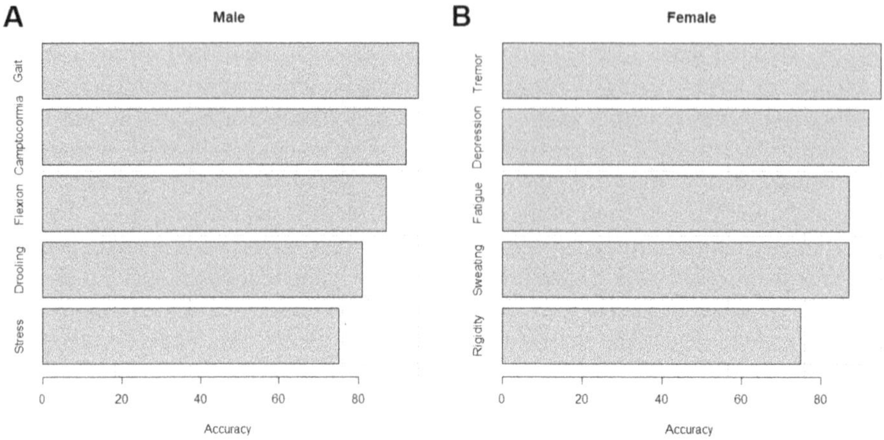

Fig. 3. Frequent words expressed by PD male and female users on X.

5.3 Classification Results

To evaluate the prediction capability of the proposed machine learning model, we used and compared the performance of multi-label classifier algorithms using accuracy and hamming loss metrics [27]. The evaluation results are summarized in Table 1. The result of the first scenario (gender-based PD sentiment) indicates that the IBk classifier produced the highest accuracy value (85.64%), followed by AdaBoostM1 (72.13%), SMO (55.67%), and RandomForest (43.23%), respectively. In addition, RandomForest produced the highest hamming loss value (61%), compared with SMO (49%), AdaBoostM1 (23%), and IBk (5%), respectively. The result of the second scenario (non-gender-based PD sentiment) showed that IBk produced the highest accuracy (74.22%), followed by AdaBoostM1 (63.49%), SMO (41.19%), and RandomForest (28.15%), respectively. In contrast, RandomForest produced the highest hamming loss value (77%), compared with SMO (69%), AdaBoostM1(62%), and IBk (14%), respectively. Figure 4 demonstrates the evaluation metrics results.

Table 1. Classification results.

Classifier	PD sentiment	Accuracy (%)	Hamming loss (%)
IBk	*With gender*	85.64	5
	Without gender	74.22	14
AdaBoostM1	*With gender*	72.13	23
	Without gender	63.49	62
SMO	*With gender*	55.67	49
	Without gender	41.19	69
RandomForest	*With gender*	43.23	61
	Without gender	28.15	77

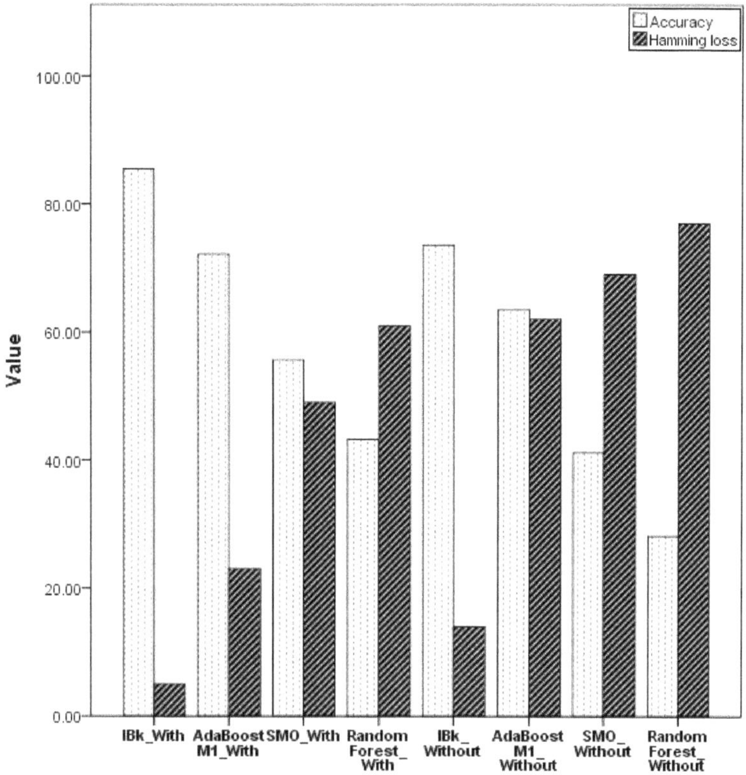

Fig. 4. Classification results of PD using multi-label classifier algorithms.

6 Discussion and Implications

This study proposed a machine learning model for the prediction of PD based on a mix of users' gender sentimental features on X. Two scenarios were predicted by the IBk classifier: gender-based PD sentiment and non-gender-based PD sentiment. The results showed a high prediction accuracy of PD when using gender-based sentiment (85.64%) as compared to non-gender-sentiment (74.22%). The use of sentiment indicators (e.g., emotions and message polarity) for each gender can significantly increase the diagnosis and prediction capability of PD on X. The literature supports the role of gender in characterizing and predicting the severity of various diseases in human patients. The topic modeling results revealed the presence of different PD topics discussed by male and female users on X. For example, women were likely to experience positive PD outcomes that were usually expressed in the form of emotion processing, non-motor symptoms, and cognitive functions. Crispino, Gino, Barbagelata, Ciarambino, Politi, Ambrosino, Ragusa, Marranzano, Biondi and Vacante [28] reported that female PD patients might experience poor quality of life that are usually reflected in reduced physical functioning and socioemotional health, while PD male patients tend to experience the cognitive domain of health-related quality of life. The same has been reported by Solla, Cannas, Ibba, Loi, Corona, Orofino, Marrosu and Marrosu [29] who highlighted the relationship between gender differences and the occurrence of motor and non-motor disorders in PD patients.

Our findings indicate that the spectrum and severity of PD symptoms can be shaped based on the gender classification of PD patients. These may also explain why affected men had a higher tendency to express and share their feelings about gait, camptocormia, flexion, drooling, and stress. PD female users, however, had a higher tendency to express their feeling of tremor, depression, fatigue, sweating, and rigidity. According to Abraham, Bay, Ni, Schindler, Singh, Leeth, Bozorg, Hart and Hackney [30] men might exhibit worse PD-specific health-related quality of life related to mobility, activities of daily living, emotional well-being, cognitive impairment, communication, and more depressive symptoms than women. The results showed a high presence of motor symptoms in PD male tweets such as camptocormia. The discussion and sharing of PD symptoms by male users on social media sites can be justified by the fact that men are likely to experience different levels of motor disturbance [31], which may lead them to look for possible coping strategies to deal with these symptoms.

In addition, it is believed that the use of users' specific emotions (e.g., anger, disgust, fear, sadness, surprise, and trust) helped increase the prediction capability of the proposed machine learning model. This can be reasoned to that certain emotions expressed in tweets can reflect people's actual thoughts, emotional states, and behaviors caused by PD. This finding is supported by previous works (e.g., [32, 33]) which have shown the effectiveness of using users' emotions to predict various health-related events. Findings from this study can be useful at facilitating the diagnosis and prediction of PD in a population. This study provides a first attempt to use gender in the prediction of PD online. It is hoped that the proposed model can increase knowledge about the impact of gender differences in characterizing and predicting PD severity and occurrence in a population, thus leading to better personalized management. In addition, the proposed model offers a timely PD surveillance strategy in which health organizations and monitoring agencies can use to recognize and identify men and women at risk. The proposed model can also advance the development of intelligent health systems and prompt timely PD interventions. Understanding the main topics discussed by PD male and female users can also help healthcare providers and agencies in tailoring healthcare facilities to specific gender needs.

7 Limitations and Future Work

This study has several limitations that future research could address. First, we focused on PD and explored the role of gender in predicting it through Twitter data. Future studies could test our model on other neurodegenerative conditions. Second, we used only English tweets due to compatibility with current sentiment tools; analyzing tweets in other languages could offer broader insights. Third, we examined a limited set of emotions found in our dataset—future work might explore additional sentiments. Lastly, we applied the Apriori method for finding gender-related disease terms; other association rule mining techniques may yield further valuable patterns.

8 Conclusion

This study examined how gendered sentiment features can help diagnose and predict Parkinson's disease (PD) on X. We analyzed 1,575,943 tweets, identifying users' gender and extracting hidden topics and sentiments using LDA, the NRC Affect Intensity Lexicon, and SentiStrength. A multi-label classification model was used to predict PD sentiment based on gender. The model achieved 85.64% accuracy when using gendered sentiment. Emotions like anger, fear, sadness, and negative sentiment were strongly linked to PD, with anger and surprise more common in male tweets, and disgust, fear, sadness, and trust more frequent in female tweets. This approach offers a promising method for online PD prediction using emotion and polarity patterns tied to gender.

References

1. Mason, H.D., McGavern, D.B.: How the immune system shapes neurodegenerative diseases. Trends Neurosci. (2022)
2. Mazon, J.N., de Mello, A.H., Ferreira, G.K., Rezin, G.T.: The impact of obesity on neurodegenerative diseases. Life Sci. **182**, 22–28 (2017)
3. Katsuno, M., Sahashi, K., Iguchi, Y., Hashizume, A.: Preclinical progression of neurodegenerative diseases. Nagoya J. Med. Sci. **80**, 289 (2018)
4. Hong, S., Han, K., Kim, K.-S., Park, C.-Y.: Risk of neurodegenerative diseases in patients with acromegaly: a cohort study. Neurology **99**, e1875–e1885 (2022)
5. Lu, J., Wu, M., Yue, Z.: Autophagy and Parkinson's disease. Autophagy: biology and diseases. Clin. Sci. 21–51 (2020)
6. Ali, L., Zhu, C., Zhang, Z., Liu, Y.: Automated detection of Parkinson's disease based on multiple types of sustained phonations using linear discriminant analysis and genetically optimized neural network. IEEE J. Transl. Eng. Health Med. **7**, 1–10 (2019)
7. Mandal, I., Sairam, N.: New machine-learning algorithms for prediction of Parkinson's disease. Int. J. Syst. Sci. **45**, 647–666 (2014)
8. Wingate, J., Kollia, I., Bidaut, L., Kollias, S.: Unified deep learning approach for prediction of Parkinson's disease. IET Image Proc. **14**, 1980–1989 (2020)
9. Shahid, A.H., Singh, M.P.: A deep learning approach for prediction of Parkinson's disease progression. Biomed. Eng. Lett. **10**, 227–239 (2020)
10. Aich, S., Kim, H.-C., Hui, K.L., Al-Absi, A.A., Sain, M.: A supervised machine learning approach using different feature selection techniques on voice datasets for prediction of Parkinson's disease. In: 2019 21st International Conference on Advanced Communication Technology (ICACT), pp. 1116–1121. IEEE (2019)
11. Bárcenas, R., Fuentes-García, R., Naranjo, L.: Mixed kernel SVR addressing Parkinson's progression from voice features. PLoS ONE **17**, e0275721 (2022)
12. Meenakshi, S., Umayaparvathi, S., Saravanan, R., Manivasagam, T., Balasubramanian, T.: Neuroprotective effect of fucoidan from Turbinaria decurrens in MPTP intoxicated Parkinsonic mice. Int. J. Biol. Macromol. **86**, 425–433 (2016)
13. Georgiev, D., Hamberg, K., Hariz, M., Forsgren, L., Hariz, G.M.: Gender differences in Parkinson's disease: a clinical perspective. Acta Neurol. Scand. **136**, 570–584 (2017)
14. Picillo, M., Nicoletti, A., Fetoni, V., Garavaglia, B., Barone, P., Pellecchia, M.T.: The relevance of gender in Parkinson's disease: a review. J. Neurol. **264**, 1583–1607 (2017)
15. Pardue, M.-L., Wizemann, T.M. (eds.): Exploring the Biological Contributions to Human Health: Does Sex Matter? Institute of Medicine (2001)

16. Miller, I.N., Cronin-Golomb, A.: Gender differences in Parkinson's disease: clinical characteristics and cognition. Mov. Disord. **25**, 2695–2703 (2010)
17. Cerri, S., Mus, L., Blandini, F.: Parkinson's disease in women and men: what's the difference? J. Parkinson's Dis. **9**, 501–515 (2019)
18. Thelwall, M., Thelwall, S., Fairclough, R.: Male, female, and nonbinary differences in UK Twitter self-descriptions: a fine-grained systematic exploration. J. Data Inf. Sci. **6**, 1–27 (2021)
19. Mohammad, S.M.: Word affect intensities (2017). arXiv:1704.08798
20. Wang, B., Meng, B., Wang, J., Chen, S., Liu, J.: Perceiving residents' festival activities based on social media data: a case study in Beijing, China. ISPRS Int. J. Geo-Inf. **10**, 474 (2021)
21. Chen, S., Xue, Y., Cui, X.J.S.C.: Information literacy of college students from library education in smart classrooms: based on big data exploring data mining patterns using Apriori algorithm. Appl. Soft Comput. **28**, 3571–3589 (2024)
22. Kanwal, N., Bostanci, E.: Comparative Study of Instance Based Learning and Back Propagation for Classification Problems (2016). arXiv:1604.05429
23. Ahmed, U., Lin, J.C.-W., Srivastava, G.: Mitigating adversarial evasion attacks of ransomware using ensemble learning. Comput. Electr. Eng. **100**, 107903 (2022)
24. Sarsam, S.M., Al-Samarraie, H., Alzahrani, A.: Influence of personality traits on users' viewing behaviour. ResearchGate **49**, 233–247 (2023)
25. Palimkar, P., Shaw, R.N., Ghosh, A.: Machine learning technique to prognosis diabetes disease: random forest classifier approach. In: Advanced Computing and Intelligent Technologies, pp. 219–244. Springer (2022)
26. Tanaka, E.A., Nozawa, S.R., Macedo, A.A., Baranauskas, J.A.: A multi-label approach using binary relevance and decision trees applied to functional genomics. J. Biomed. Inform. **54**, 85–95 (2015)
27. Muhammad, N.A., Rehman, A., Shoaib, U.: Applications: Accuracy based feature ranking metric for multi-label text classification. Int. J. Adv. Comput. Sci. Appl. **8** (2017)
28. Crispino, P., et al.: Gender differences and quality of life in Parkinson's disease. Int. J. Environ. Res. Public Health **18**, 198 (2021)
29. Solla, P., et al.: Gender differences in motor and non-motor symptoms among Sardinian patients with Parkinson's disease. J. Neurol. Sci. **323**, 33–39 (2012)
30. Abraham, A., et al.: Gender differences in motor and non-motor symptoms in individuals with mild-moderate Parkinson's disease. PLoS ONE **18**, e0272952 (2023)
31. Lee, J.Y., Shin, C.M.: Sex Differences and Gut Microbiota Changes in Parkinson's Disease. Sex/Gender-Specific Medicine in the Gastrointestinal Diseases, pp. 393–403. Springer (2022)
32. Alamoodi, A.H., et al.: Sentiment analysis and its applications in fighting COVID-19 and infectious diseases: a systematic review. Expert Syst. Appl. **167**, 114155 (2021)
33. Edo-Osagie, O., Smith, G., Lake, I., Edeghere, O., De La Iglesia, B.: Twitter mining using semi-supervised classification for relevance filtering in syndromic surveillance. PLoS ONE **14**, e0210689 (2019)

Artificial Intelligence, Security, Power-Aware Methods, and Applications

A Unified Framework Incorporating AW-TRBAC and Semantic Variational Autoencoders for Dynamic Threat Detection and Access Control

Abaniseniolwa K. Orojo[1(✉)], Emmanuelli El-Mahmoud[1], Shaun Hutton[1], Michael J. Donahoo[1], and Webster Elumelu[2]

[1] Baylor University, Waco, TX, USA
{abaniseniolwa_orojl,emmanuelli_elmahmou1,shaun_hutton, jeff_donahoo}@baylor.edu

[2] Webster University, St. Louis, MO, USA
webster_elumelu@labackdoor.com

Abstract. This paper presents a composite framework to enhance cyber resilience in Cyber-Physical Systems (CPS) against advanced persistent threats. It integrates Dynamic Access Control, specifically Authorizing Workflow and Task-Role-Based Access Control (AW-TRBAC), with Semantic Variational Autoencoders (SVAEs) for Intrusion Detection Systems (IDSs). AW-TRBAC offers context-aware access control with dynamic Segregation of Duties, while SVAEs improve anomaly detection. This multi-layered approach focuses on preventing threats and enabling real-time adjustments to access policies. The framework's probabilistic learning allows in-depth analysis of CPS access flows. Simulations in water treatment CPS scenarios validated its effectiveness, demonstrating improved security with minimal false positives and enhanced access control. This research contributes a proactive, adaptable security solution for the unique challenges in CPS environments.

Keywords: Cyber-Physical Systems · Intrusion Detection Systems · Task-Role-Based Access Control · Variational Autoencoder · Authorizing Workflows

1 Introduction

The evolution and preponderate integration of Cyber-Physical Systems (CPS) into critical infrastructure have ushered in a new era of complexity in cybersecurity challenges [12]. As these systems become more embedded in essential services, their vulnerability to increasingly sophisticated cyber threats has become a paramount concern. This vulnerability underscores a critical gap in current security paradigms, which primarily rely on static, rule-based defenses that are ill-equipped to adapt to the landscape of cyber threats. Recognizing this inadequacy, our research seeks to pivot towards a more resilient framework, drawing

H. R. Arabnia et al. (Eds.): CSCE 2025, CCIS 2934, pp. 191–206, 2026.
https://doi.org/10.1007/978-3-032-22190-2_14

upon the principles of cyber resilience as outlined by the National Institute of Standards and Technology (NIST) [9].

The concept of cyber resilience, as advocated by the NIST, offers a strategic framework to address these challenges. Cyber resilience emphasizes the ability to anticipate, withstand, recover from, and adapt to adverse conditions, stresses, attacks, or compromises on systems. Of these requirements, our model is trying to address the issues of withstanding and adaptation. It advocates for a holistic approach that incorporates anticipating potential threats, protecting critical assets, detecting unauthorized actions, responding to incidents, and recovering from attacks to maintain essential functions. Therefore, integrating cyber resilience techniques into the security architecture of CPS is paramount to ensuring their robustness and sustainability [9]. Acknowledging the limitations of existing security measures, it becomes evident that a successful solution must fulfill several key requirements. It must be adaptable, capable of changing with the threat landscape, and it must integrate real-time decision-making capabilities and ensure the continuity of critical functions even in the event of successful attacks. These requirements form the basis of our proposed solution, aiming to address the gaps in current security practices and enhance the resilience of CPS.

Our research introduces a composite framework that synergizes Dynamic Access Control with Intrusion Detection Systems (IDSs), incorporating Authorizing Workflow and Task-Role-Based Access Control (AW-TRBAC) alongside Variational Autoencoders (VAEs). This framework is designed to meet the outlined requirements by embedding adaptability and probabilistic intelligence into the security mechanisms of CPS. AW-TRBAC enhances traditional access control models by integrating real-time decision-making and dynamic segregation of duties at the task level, thereby enabling flexible adjustments in access permissions in response to evolving operational contexts [2,5,13]. Concurrently, VAEs, through their advanced machine learning capabilities, enhance the detection and prediction of anomalies and threats, ensuring a proactive and intelligent response to emerging cyber challenges.

To substantiate our claims and the necessity of our proposed solution, we refer to a review of related work and existing security limitations in CPS. This not only provides a foundation for our research but also emphasizes key aspects of our approach in addressing the resilience requirements advocated by NIST. In conclusion, our paper aims to contribute an adaptive, and intelligent security solution for CPS, addressing the complex and dynamic nature of cyber threats. Through this research, we aspire to align with NIST's cyber resilience principles, offering a framework that not only anticipates and mitigates threats but also ensures the continuity and integrity of CPS in the face of adversity.

2 Related Works

The intersection of dynamic access control and intrusion detection in Cyber-Physical Systems (CPS) is an area of research that deserves more focus. This section reviews the relevant literature, highlighting key developments and identifying gaps that our framework addresses.

2.1 Dynamic Access Control

Dynamic access control mechanisms play a pivotal role in safeguarding complex and evolving network environments. This section critically evaluates several contemporary methodologies aimed at enhancing the dynamism and granularity of access control, with a focus on their applicability to Cyber-Physical Systems (CPS), particularly in the context of water treatment facilities.

The Authorising Workflow and Task-Role-Based Access Control (AW-TRBAC) model, proposed by Uddin et al. [13], emerges as a salient advancement in addressing the inherent limitations of conventional static models. By integrating task-level dynamic Segregation of Duties (SoD) alongside real-time decision-making capabilities, AW-TRBAC offers nuanced control over access permissions, adapting swiftly to changing user roles and access requirements. Such adaptability is crucial in environments experiencing frequent role variability, underscoring AW-TRBAC's relevance to CPS where the interplay between operational efficiency and security is critical. Despite CPS's traditionally static user roles, the escalating integration with the Internet necessitates a more granular and intelligent access control approach, a demand unmet by existing models like RBAC and ABAC. The detailed granularity provided by AW-TRBAC, absent in current research within the CPS domain, presents a novel avenue for enhancing security protocols in these systems without the need for frequent role reconfigurations.

In contrast, blockchain-based solutions, while robust, fall short in offering the required granularity for effective CPS management. Song et al. [10] showcased the potential of blockchain in achieving distributed and fine-grained access control through smart contracts. However, the inherent characteristics of blockchain technologies prioritize decentralization and immutability over dynamic, role-based access control, thereby limiting their direct applicability to the nuanced requirements of CPS. The exploration of adapting blockchain technologies to emulate the granularity offered by AW-TRBAC remains an open research avenue, potentially addressed in future work.

The landscape of dynamic access control is thus marked by a transition from static, rigid frameworks [7] to more adaptable, intelligent, and decentralized models. This evolution reflects the growing complexity of network environments and the imperative for security mechanisms to be both flexible and context-aware. However, the application of such advanced models to the specific needs of CPS, especially in sectors as critical as water treatment, necessitates further investigation. The integration of AW-TRBAC into CPS domains represents a promising yet underexplored frontier, highlighting the need for targeted research to fully leverage its potential in enhancing the resilience and security of these vital systems.

2.2 Intrusion Detection Systems and Semantic Variational Autoencoders

Intrusion Detection Systems (IDS) constitute a critical component in safeguarding information systems against cyber threats. The integration of machine learning techniques, ranging from Convolutional Neural Networks (CNNs) [8] to

Semantic Variational Autoencoders (SVAEs), has marked a significant advancement in IDS by enhancing their anomaly detection capabilities within intricate network landscapes.

VAEs, as introduced by Kingma and Welling [4], offer a probabilistic framework for encoding and decoding data, thereby facilitating the detection of outliers in network traffic. The application of VAEs in IDS, highlighted by An and Cho [1], underscores the utility of reconstruction probability as a metric for identifying anomalous activities, surpassing traditional detection methodologies in efficacy.

Despite these advancements, the application of standard VAEs in IDS encounters limitations, particularly in capturing semantic relationships within data. This shortfall is addressed by the development of Semantic Variational Autoencoders (SVAEs), which refine the encoding process by incorporating semantic information into the data representation. By semantically re-encoding input data, SVAEs enhance the model's ability to discern probabilistic insights, thus improving anomaly detection performance in IDS.

The key differentiation between Semantic Variational Autoencoders (SVAEs) and conventional Variational Autoencoders (VAEs) centers around the SVAEs' capability to encode semantic information into the data representation process. Unlike traditional VAEs that primarily focus on input reconstruction, SVAEs enrich the encoding phase with semantic representation, thereby enhancing the model's interpretative depth. This semantic enrichment provides a better analysis of network activities, improving the detection of cyber threats. By semantically re-encoding the input, SVAEs equip VAEs with a richer probabilistic understanding of the data, enabling a more effective anomaly detection mechanism.

3 Methodology

3.1 Implementing AW-TRBAC in a CPS Context

This section outlines the methodology for adapting and implementing the Authorising Workflow and Task-Role-Based Access Control (AW-TRBAC) model within a Cyber-Physical System (CPS) environment. We introduce specific changes to the model to address the needs of CPS. Figure 1 shows an overview of our approach.

Dynamic Environment Adaptation. Contrary to the perception that CPS environments are static, they exhibit dynamic characteristics, particularly in their operational contexts. This dynamism arises from:

- Environmental fluctuations: Changes in physical conditions that affect system operations.
- Variable system loads: Differing demands on system resources based on time or external factors.

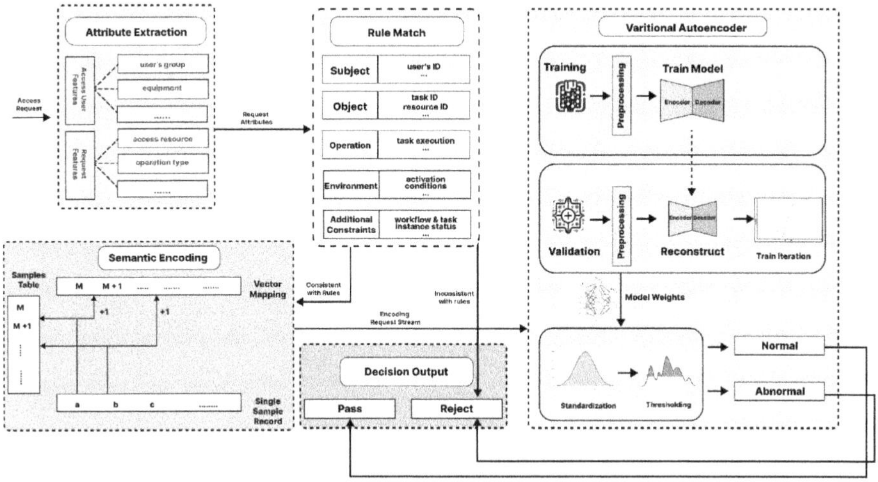

Fig. 1. Composite Framework Employing AW-TRBAC and Semantic Variational Autoencoders.

- Evolving security landscapes: The need to adapt to new threats and vulnerabilities.
- Shifting operational priorities: Adjustments in system goals based on real-world requirements.

To navigate these challenges, we enhance the AW-TRBAC model with dynamic Segregation of Duties (SoD) and Binding of Duties (BoD), enabling real-time adjustments to access controls based on the current operational context. This dynamic adaptation is critical for maintaining both security and operational efficiency in the face of changing conditions within CPS environments.

Dynamic SoD and BoD in Action. Operational contexts within a Cyber-Physical System (CPS) can impact system behavior and requirements. For example, a smart grid system during peak electricity demand faces different challenges and priorities compared to off-peak periods [6]. Such variability necessitates adaptable access control policies. In response, our algorithm dynamically adjusts Segregation of Duties (SoD) and Binding of Duties (BoD) policies to align with current operational scenarios, enhancing both system flexibility and security [13]. This approach ensures that access controls are contextually appropriate, mitigating risks while accommodating operational needs.

By implementing dynamic SoD and BoD, the Authorising Workflow and Task-Role-Based Access Control (AW-TRBAC) model offers granular access control tailored to the specific dynamics of CPS environments [13]. This granularity and adaptability contrast with traditional access control models, which may not fully account for the fluid operational contexts characteristic of CPS, thereby underscoring the goal of our approach.

Algorithm 1. Dynamic SoD and BoD Adjustment Algorithm

```
Require: SystemState, UserRoles, TaskAssignments
Ensure: Secure and Efficient operation in CPS environment
while System is operational do
    CurrentContext ← GetCurrentOperationalContext()
    for each user in UserRoles do
        AssignedTasks ← GetTasksAssignedToUser(user)
        for each task in AssignedTasks do
            TaskReassigned ← FALSE
            if IsSoDViolation(task, user, CurrentContext) then
                ReassignTask(task, user)
                TaskReassigned ← TRUE
            end if
            if NOT TaskReassigned AND IsBoDRequirement(task, user, CurrentContext) then
                BindTask(task, user)
            end if
        end for
    end for
    AdjustRolesAndPermissions(UserRoles, TaskAssignments, CurrentContext)
    LogChanges(SystemState, UserRoles, TaskAssignments)
    WaitForNextCycle()
end while
```

Role Change Functionality. Considering the fluidity of roles in CPS, we have implemented enhanced role change functionalities:

- *Automated Role Validation*: A mechanism to automatically validate role changes while ensuring compliance with SoD and BoD policies.
- *Real-time Role Adaptation*: Roles are adapted in real-time based on system status, operational needs, and security policies.

Workflow and Task Integration. We integrate CPS workflows into the AW-TRBAC model as follows:

- *Task-based Access Control*: Access rights are assigned based on the tasks aligned with user roles and business processes.
- *Workflow Compliance*: Ensuring access control policies are in harmony with defined business processes and workflow sequences.

Resource and Business Process Management. In the CPS context, resources and business processes are managed through:

- *Resource-Role Linkage*: Linking CPS resources to roles and tasks, ensuring appropriate access based on operational requirements.
- *Business Process Alignment*: Aligning access control policies with business process objectives and security requirements.

Technology Integration. For seamless integration into CPS infrastructure, we employ:

- *Java-based Technologies*: Utilizing Java Open-Source balana policy engine technologies for backend development.

This approach ensures that the AW-TRBAC model is effectively adapted and implemented in a CPS context, addressing the unique challenges and requirements of such systems.

3.2 Semantic Re-encoding of Request Data

In the context of Cyber-Physical Systems (CPS), handling and analyzing access control requests efficiently is crucial. The XACML (eXtensible Access Control Markup Language) standard, used for defining access control policies, produces complex and nuanced XML-based requests. To process these requests more effectively, we introduce a semantic re-encoding algorithm tailored for this data. This algorithm enhances the interpret-ability and processing efficiency of requests.

Algorithm Overview. The Semantic Re-encoding Algorithm transforms the structure and content of requests into a format that is more amenable for analysis. The algorithm consists of two main pathways: one for processing actual XACML request data and the other for handling vector-based transformations for access flows.

Algorithm 2. Semantic Re-encoding Algorithm

Require: RequestData
Ensure: Semantically re-encoded data for efficient processing

CharacterStream $\leftarrow$ TransformToCharacterStream(XACMLRequestData)
WordSegments $\leftarrow$ PerformWordSegmentation(CharacterStream)
WordTable $\leftarrow$ BuildWordTable(WordSegments)
ReconstructedRecords $\leftarrow$ RearrangeXACMLIntoRecords(WordTable)
SampleRecordSet $\leftarrow$ ExtractSamples(ReconstructedRecords)
SortedWordTable $\leftarrow$ SortWordTable(WordTable)
ReencodedWordList $\leftarrow$ ReencodeWordList(SortedWordTable)
MappedSamples $\leftarrow$ RemapSamples(SampleRecordSet, ReencodedWordList)
ReducedDimensionData $\leftarrow$ PerformDimensionReduction(MappedSamples)

The core idea behind 'semantic re-encoding' is to transform the verbose and structurally complex XACML requests into a format that not only reduces dimensionality but also captures the inherent meaning and intent of an access attempt. Standard XACML requests define who (Subject) is attempting what action (Action) on what resource (Resource), often under specific conditions (Environment). Simply processing the raw XML might lead the VAE to focus on superficial syntactic variations rather than the underlying purpose. Our algorithm aims to preserve these fundamental semantic relationships, which is crucial for distinguishing legitimate variations from genuine anomalies in a CPS context. Specifically, the RearrangeXACMLIntoRecords step (Algorithm 2, line 4) moves beyond a linear parse by restructuring the request data into a consistent record format, ensuring that attributes related to 'Subject', 'Action', and 'Resource' are always placed in corresponding fields. Furthermore, the ReencodeWordList step (line 7) establishes a structured vocabulary and encoding scheme where functionally similar terms—even if textually different—are mapped into a numerical space reflecting these functional roles. For example, consider a request for 'Operator A' to 'Read' 'PressureSensor_1' and another for 'Engineer B' to 'View' 'FlowMeter_3'. Our semantic re-encoding aims to represent both such that 'Operator A' and 'Engineer B' are recognized as 'Human_Subject_Roles', 'Read' and 'View' fall under 'Observation_Actions', and 'PressureSensor_1' and 'FlowMeter_3' are classified as 'Sensor_Resources'. This semantically richer representation allows the VAE to learn a more meaningful latent space, improving its ability to distinguish subtle, yet potentially malicious, deviations in access patterns from benign operational variations.

Processing Request Data. The initial steps involve transforming the XACML request data into a character stream, segmenting it into discrete words or terms, and then constructing a word table from these segments. This table forms the basis for reconstructing the XACML requests into a more structured record format. Subsequently, the algorithm extracts samples from these records, sorts the word table for consistency, and applies a new encoding scheme to optimize the data for semantic relevance. The final step involves reducing the dimensionality of the data, retaining key features for subsequent analysis.

3.3 Variational Autoencoding

Table 1. Model Structures and Neuron Counts

Model Structure	Number of Neurons for Each Layer
(5,32)	input – 32 – 16 – latent layer – 16 – 32 – output
(5,64)	input – 64 – 32 – latent layer – 32 – 64 – output
(7,64)	input – 64 – 32 – 16 – latent layer – 16 – 32 – 64 – output

This subsection introduces our approach to leveraging a Variational Autoencoder (VAE) for processing semantically re-encoded request data. A critical component of our methodology is the configuration of the VAE model, which directly influences its effectiveness in identifying anomalous access requests. Table 1 outlines various model structures and neuron counts that we explore in our study. Each row in the table represents a different configuration of the VAE, detailing the depth and size of the model alongside the specific neuron counts for each layer, from the input to the latent layer, and then back to the output. These configurations are pivotal in understanding how the model's complexity and capacity for feature representation affect its performance in anomaly detection tasks. By examining these structures, we aim to identify the optimal model configuration that balances the ability to capture complex data patterns with computational efficiency, thereby ensuring high accuracy in detecting deviations from typical access request patterns.

Preprocessing. The first step involves preprocessing the request data. After semantic re-encoding, the data is vectorized, converting feature values into numerical vectors using min-max normalization. The normalization is based on the minimum and maximum values obtained from the training dataset.

Training the Autoencoder. The autoencoder model is trained exclusively with normal requests. The training objective is to minimize the L2 norm reconstruction loss, enabling the model to learn typical access patterns. Theoretically, the VAE trained on normal patterns should poorly reconstruct anomalous requests, creating a significant difference between the input and its output.

Model Selection. During training, the performance of the model is evaluated at each epoch using the Area under the Curve (AuC) score of the Receiver Operating Characteristic (ROC) curve. The model weights corresponding to the highest AuC score are recorded for later use. This process ensures that we select the best-performing model configuration for intrusion detection.

$$\text{ROC Curve} = \text{Plot of TPR vs. FPR} \tag{1}$$

at various threshold settings

$$\text{AUC} = \int_0^1 \text{ROC(FPR)}\, d(\text{FPR}) \tag{2}$$

Threshold Selection. The threshold for differentiating between normal and abnormal requests is determined based on the reconstruction error. We employ the Z-score metric derived from the standard normal distribution to set the threshold. The Z-score is calculated using the mean and variance of the reconstruction errors from the normal samples in the validation dataset. The optimal threshold is the Z-score that best separates normal and abnormal classes. The Z-score is calculated as follows:

$$Z = \frac{x - \mu}{\sigma} \tag{3}$$

where x is the reconstruction error of a request, μ is the mean of reconstruction errors from normal samples, and σ is the standard deviation.

Evaluation of the Model. For the final evaluation, each request's reconstruction error is converted into a Z-score. A request is classified as an attack if its Z-score exceeds the predetermined threshold. The model's effectiveness is then assessed using standard metrics such as accuracy, True Positive Rate (TPR), False Positive Rate (FPR), and Matthews Correlation Coefficient (MCC).

Model Structure and Latent Size Variations. We experiment with various autoencoder configurations, altering the model structure (depth and width) and the latent size. The models comprise fully connected hidden layers with ReLU activation functions and a sigmoid output layer. The decoder mirrors the encoder's structure. We test different latent layer sizes to find the optimal balance between data representation and model generalization. Table 1 represents the models we tested [11].

4 Results and Discussion

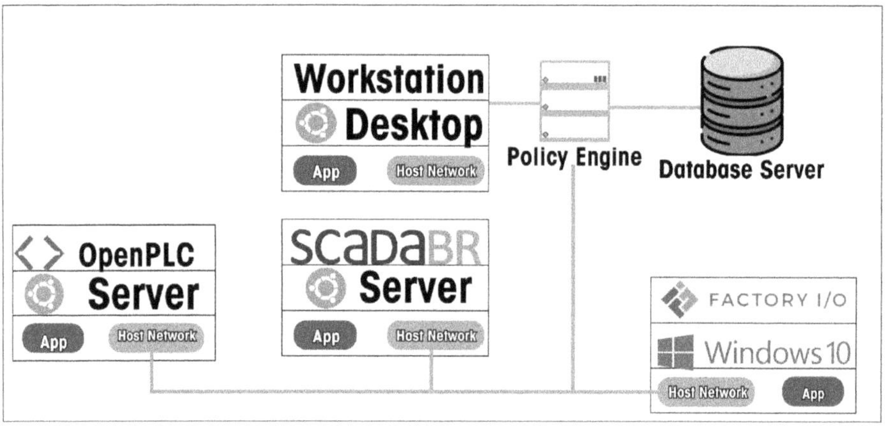

Fig. 2. Cyber Physical System Test Network.

This study evaluated the performance and efficacy of the proposed composite framework using a small-scale simulated CPS network on VMware vSphere in Fig. 2. The CPS network architecture designed for the simulation consists of a SCADA Server for data acquisition and process control, an OpenPLC Server functioning as a programmable logic controller, and a Workstation Desktop providing the user interface for system interaction. These components are equipped with application layers and network interfaces, indicating their roles in the network's communication framework. Additionally, a Factory I/O module running on Windows 10 simulates the physical processes, interfacing with the SCADA system for real-time automation. Central to the network's security is the Policy Engine, connected to a Database Server that stores policy and operational data. This architecture models a cohesive, secure network environment where the Policy Engine enforces access control measures. In the vSphere simulation environment, each machine was provisioned with 4 GB of RAM and 2 CPU cores to ensure adequate resources for stable system operation and effective simulation execution. Our results provide important insights into the framework's impact on system performance and its ability to accurately detect security threats.

Table 2. Model Performance Metrics

Model	Latent	Threshold	Accuracy	TPR	FPR	MCC	F1
(5,32)	7	1.926	89.04%	88.06%	9.86%	78.09%	89.48%
(5,64)	4	2.856	84.61%	83.26%	13.86%	69.27%	85.20%
(7,64)	13	2.340	84.04%	78.90%	9.69%	68.95%	84.45%

4.1 System Performance Evaluation

An assessment of the system's performance was conducted, focusing on the processing times of security-related requests within the CPS environment. To ensure reproducibility of our results, we defined two categories of requests: simple end-to-end security requests and Role Change requests. The former pertains to routine authentication and authorization operations, while the latter involves modifications to user roles within the AW-TRBAC framework, necessitating a re-evaluation of access permissions. We employed a consistent set of procedures to measure the processing time for each request type. Simple end-to-end security requests yielded an average processing time of 0.54 ± 0.084 seconds, indicating the system's capability to handle routine security tasks. The Role Change requests, given their complexity due to the re-calibration of access controls, exhibited a slightly higher mean processing time of 0.86 s. The results demonstrate that the integration of AW-TRBAC and the Semantic Variational Autoencoder imposes a moderate computational overhead. However, the system retains a level of efficiency that is conducive to real-time operations in a CPS environment. The average processing times, within the sub-second range, affirm the practicality of our security framework.

4.2 Intrusion Detection Performance

The framework's intrusion detection capabilities were evaluated using a dataset derived from 43,644 normal XACML requests formatted according to the AW-TRBAC model. Following the principle that models trained solely on normal data should poorly reconstruct anomalies [3], we trained the Semantic Variational Autoencoder (SVAE) models using 80% of these normal requests (34,915 data points). To evaluate the models' performance (Table 2), we constructed a dedicated test set. This test set comprised the remaining 20% of normal requests (8,729 data points) combined with 5,000 anomalous requests. These anomalous requests were synthetically crafted by violating established AW-TRBAC policies and simulating known water treatment CPS attack vectors, such as those targeting control logic and sensor inputs. These simulated attacks included unauthorized attempts to change chemical dosing levels, efforts to bypass safety interlocks for pump operations, the injection of spoofed sensor readings, and attempts to issue critical commands outside permitted operational parameters. The final test set, thus comprising 13,729 requests with approximately 63.6% normal and 36.4% anomalous distribution, was then used to assess performance on this mixed test set using standard metrics: Accuracy, True Positive Rate (TPR), False Positive Rate (FPR), Matthews Correlation Coefficient (MCC), and F1 Score. The results for three different model structures are summarized in the Table 2.

The comparative analysis depicted in Fig. 3 provides a view of the model performance across various metrics. The results show how the (5,32) model average compared to several models of similar size on the same dataset. The Variational Autoencoder (VAE) and the Semantic Variational Autoencoder (SVAE) both exhibit high accuracy, registering a score of 0.85. This suggests that these models are effective in classifying instances correctly. However, the Support Vector Machine (SVM) model, while not reaching the same level of accuracy, shows a significantly high recall of 0.95. This indicates the SVM's strength in identifying positive cases, but it also implies a potential for a higher false positive rate, as evidenced by its lower precision. In this regard, SVAE with a score of 0.90, suggesting it is well-suited for applications where it is crucial to minimize incorrect anomaly detections. Conversely, the Autoencoder (AE) shows balanced performance across all metrics, which may make it a reliable choice for scenarios where both the detection of anomalies and the reduction of false alarms are important. Both VAE and SVAE have achieved the highest F1-score of 0.90, indicating their robustness in a scenario where it is equally important to identify all relevant instances and to minimize false positives. These findings demonstrate the strengths and potential applications of each model.

5 Understanding Principal Components and SHAP Values

To gain insight into the decision-making process of our SVAE model, we employed post-hoc explainability techniques. It is important to clarify that Principal Component Analysis (PCA) and SHAP (SHapley Additive exPlanations) were not used during the training or pre-processing stages of the SVAE model itself. Instead, they were applied after the model was trained, solely for the purpose of interpreting its behavior. We utilized PCA on the semantically re-encoded data to identify the principal components (PCA1 and PCA2) capturing the most significant variance. Subsequently, we applied SHAP analysis to understand and visualize how these dominant components influence the SVAE model's reconstruction error, which forms the basis for anomaly detection.

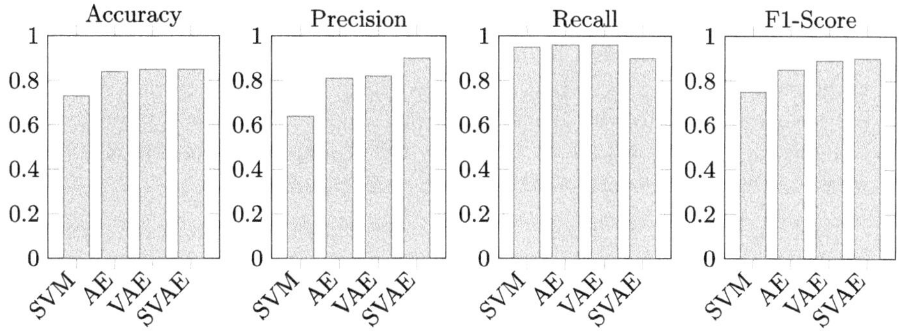

Fig. 3. Comparison of SVM, AE, VAE, and SVAE models across four performance metrics (Y axis is %).

The SHAP summary plot, depicted in Fig. 4, visualizes this relationship. Each point on the plot represents an individual access request. Its position on the horizontal axis indicates its SHAP value—quantifying its contribution to the model's output (positive values push towards a higher anomaly score, while negative values push towards a lower score, indicating normality). The color of each point signifies the magnitude of the principal component's value for that specific request, with red indicating high values and blue indicating low values.

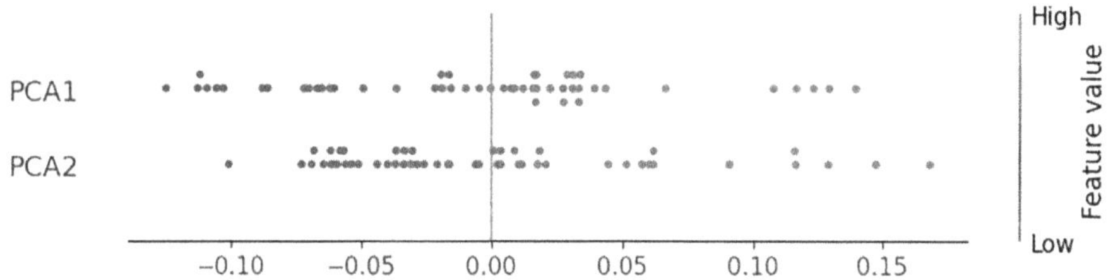

Fig. 4. SHAP value plot illustrating the impact of PCA1 and PCA2 on the model's predictions.

Observing Fig. 4, we can interpret the influence of the principal components:

1. PCA1: There is a distinct trend where high values of PCA1 (red points) predominantly result in positive SHAP values. This suggests that requests exhibiting characteristics strong in PCA1 are more likely to be considered anomalous by the model. Conversely, low values of PCA1 (blue/purple points) tend to have negative SHAP values, aligning them with normal behavior.
2. PCA2: Low values of PCA2 (blue/purple points) show a strong tendency towards negative SHAP values, indicating that these features significantly contribute to a request being classified as normal. High PCA2 values (red points), while less numerous, generally correlate with positive SHAP values,

suggesting they push towards an anomaly classification, albeit with some spread. This visualization, by linking the most significant dimensions of data variance (PCA1 and PCA2) to their predictive impact, offers valuable, interpretable insights into why the SVAE model flags certain access requests while considering others normal. It enhances the transparency of our framework, which is crucial in security-critical CPS environments.

This visualization, by linking the most significant dimensions of data variance (PCA1 and PCA2) to their predictive impact, offers valuable, interpretable insights into why the SVAE model flags certain access requests while considering others normal. It enhances the transparency of our framework, which is crucial in security-critical CPS environments.

5.1 Comparative Analysis Against Existing Framework

In the realm of dynamic access control for teleworking systems, the ABAC-IntroVAE model presents a robust solution integrating attribute-based control with introspective variational autoencoders for anomaly detection. Our proposed framework, while conceptually similar, diverges in its employment of Semantic Variational Autoencoders (SVAEs) to enhance intrusion detection capabilities within CPS environments. The ABAC-IntroVAE model excels in its use of rule matching combined with behavioral analysis to determine access control decisions. It boasts an impressive anomaly detection accuracy of 97.2%, and maintains this high accuracy through continual learning despite the introduction of new user behaviors. This model's strength lies in its requirement for only normal behavior samples during training, sidestepping the challenge of accumulating a comprehensive dataset of attack behaviors. In contrast, our framework leverages the adaptability and semantic understanding of SVAEs to provide nuanced insights into CPS data flows. While our model structure configurations, such as (5,32), (5,64), and (7,64), demonstrate lower anomaly detection accuracies ranging from 84.04% to 89.04%, they offer valuable explainability through SHAP values and also offers a greater range of granular access control, which is crucial for transparent decision-making processes in security-critical applications. Additionally, our framework's design considers the complex and heterogeneous nature of CPS networks as there is a diversity of protocols and proprietary systems, ensuring a high degree of flexibility and real-time responsiveness to emerging threats. Both models prioritize the adaptability to new behaviors, an essential feature given the dynamic nature of access patterns in teleworking and CPS environments. However, our model emphasizes explainability, granular access and the ability to integrate seamlessly with existing CPS infrastructure, utilizing Java-based technologies for backend development.

6 Conclusion

This paper introduced a unified framework enhancing Cyber-Physical Systems (CPS) security by integrating Authorising Workflow and Task-Role-Based Access Control (AW-TRBAC) with Semantic Variational Autoencoders

(SVAEs). AW-TRBAC provides adaptive, real-time access control, while SVAEs offer semantic anomaly detection. Simulations in a water treatment CPS confirmed the framework's ability to improve security posture while maintaining system performance. Crucially, our approach incorporates Explainable AI (XAI) via SHAP values, affording transparency into the model's decision-making. While its accuracy is currently lower than some existing models, our framework distinguishes itself through its emphasis on explainability, granular access control, and integration capabilities—vital aspects for operational trust in CPS. Future research will focus on enhancing detection accuracy, exploring scalability, and adapting the framework to other CPS domains, striving for a dynamic, intelligent, and transparent security solution against evolving threats.

References

1. An, J., Cho, S.: Variational autoencoder based anomaly detection using reconstruction probability. SNUDataMiningCenter (2015), Accessed 06 Jan 2024
2. Chen, L., Gasparini, L., Norman, T.J.: Xacml and risk-aware access control. In: 10th International Workshop on Security in Information Systems, pp. 66–75. SCITEPRESS (2013). https://doi.org/10.5220/0004609200660075
3. Hu, X., et al.: A dynamic access control model based on attributes and intro vae. Conference Paper (2020), Accessed 05 Jan 2024
4. Kingma, D.P., Welling, M.: An introduction to variational autoencoders. Foundat. Trends Mach. Learn. **12**(4), 307–392 (2019). https://doi.org/10.1561/2200000056
5. Ma, G., Wu, K., Zhang, T., Li, W.: A flexible policy-based access control model for workflow management systems. In: Proceedings of the IEEE International Conference on Computer Science and Automation Engineering. p. Volume and Page Numbers. IEEE (2011). https://www.semanticscholar.org/paper/A-flexible-policy-based-access-control-model-for-Ma-Wu/e5d1dbf4de86bde66fcd2a9c97e1b2f5b8219645, accessed: 2024-01-06
6. Meliani, M., Barkany, A.E., Abbassi, I.E., Darcherif, A.M., Mahmoudi, M.: Energy management in the smart grid: State-of-the-art and future trends. Inter. J. Eng. Bus. Manag. **13** (2021). https://doi.org/10.1177/18479790211032920
7. Orojo, A., El-Mahmoud, E., Speegle, G.: Assessing the impact of access control policies on data accessibility in distributed nosql environments. In: The Twenty Fourth International Conference on Security & Management (SAM 2025) (2025)
8. Orojo, A.: Advancing network intrusion detection with a sliding window-based cnn and cfs-ba feature selection. ResearchGate (2023). https://doi.org/10.13140/RG.2.2.22967.84648
9. Ross, R., Pillitteri, V., Graubart, R., Bodeau, D., McQuaid, R.: Developing cyber resilient systems: A systems security engineering approach. Special Publication 800-160 Volume 2, Revision 1, National Institute of Standards and Technology (NIST), Gaithersburg, MD (2021)
10. Song, H., Tu, Z., Qin, Y.: Blockchain-based access control and behavior regulation system for iot. Sensors **22**(21), 8339 (2022). https://doi.org/10.3390/s22218339, https://www.mdpi.com/1424-8220/22/21/8339
11. Song, Y., Hyun, S., Cheong, Y.G.: Analysis of autoencoders for network intrusion detection. Sensors **21**(13), 4294 (2021). https://doi.org/10.3390/s21134294, https://www.mdpi.com/1424-8220/21/13/4294

12. Tyagi, A.K., Sreenath, N.: Cyber physical systems: analyses, challenges and possible solutions. Internet of Things and Cyber-Physical Systems **1**, 22–33 (2021). https://doi.org/10.1016/j.iotcps.2021.12.002, https://www.sciencedirect.com/science/article/pii/S2667345221000055
13. Uddin, M., Islam, S., Al-Nemrat, A.: A dynamic access control model using authorising workflow and task-role-based access control. IEEE Access **7**, 166676–166689 (2019). https://doi.org/10.1109/ACCESS.2019.2947377, https://ieeexplore.ieee.org/document/8890335

A Power Control Scheme for Artificial Intelligence and IoT (AIoT) ProSe-Enabled Sensors

Weston Mwashita[1](✉) and Marcel Ohanga Odhiambo[2]

[1] Internation University of Management, Windhoek, Namibia
w.mwashita@ium.edu.na

[2] Mangosuthu University of Technology, Durban, South Africa
ohanga.marcel@mut.ac.za

Abstract. The Internet of Things (IoT) and Artificial Intelligence (AI) are influential technologies. When Artificial Intelligence (AI) and Internet of Things (IoT) are combined, the result is AIoT, or Artificial Intelligence of Things. Artificial intelligence can be thought of as the brain of a system, while IoT devices can be thought of as the digital nervous system. The combination of AI and IoT allows systems to be predictive, prescriptive and autonomous. IoT sensors on one hand, allow for the collection of massive quantity of data, while AI on the other hand aids in the development of smarter applications for a smarter world. AIoT sensors are crucial in the Internet of Things. A power control approach involving two power control mechanisms is presented in this study: an open loop power control (OLPC) mechanism that can be used by a ProSe-enabled sensor to establish communication with a base station (BS) and a closed loop power control (CLPC) mechanism that can be used by a ProSe-Enabled sensor to establish communication with a base station (BS). Several researchers have proposed power control schemes to mitigate interference in mobile networks, but none has attempted to deal with the interference caused by ProSe-enabled sensors communicating with smart phones and 5G BSs. Simulation results showed that the proposed strategy performed well when compared to an optimal solution when it came to evaluating it. The proposed approach does not have a negative impact on the quality of service (QoS) of a 5G mobile network, according to a simulator created using the MATLAB high-level programming language.

Keywords: Artificial Intelligence · Internet of Things · Artificial Intelligence of Things · power control · Device to device

1 Introduction

One of the most eagerly awaited new technologies is the fifth-generation wireless technology. According to a poll conducted by Ericsson in 2017, 92% of executives in charge of at least 100 of the world's largest telecommunications companies agree that 5G will pave the way for a significant number of new technologies. The 5G infrastructure mainly

H. R. Arabnia et al. (Eds.): CSCE 2025, CCIS 2934, pp. 207–221, 2026.
https://doi.org/10.1007/978-3-032-22190-2_15

serves as a foundation for heterogeneous wireless networks and AI systems and gadgets, allowing for seamless connectivity that will spur the growth of smart cities around the world. Figure 1 shows ProSe-enabled devices that are running ProSe applications.

ProSe-enabled devices can interact with a ProSe Function by using PC3 to retrieve information for network-related actions, as shown in Fig. 1. ProSe-enabled devices use PC3 to request permission from a BS to participate in a D2D session. However, this direct communication comes at a cost to the overall 5G QoS. When external devices, such as ProSe sensors (3GPP, 2014), interact directly within an underlying 5G network, the following types of interference occur, according to Mach, Becvar, and Vanek (2015):

(i) Cellular interference due to D2D.
(ii) Interference between D2D and D2D.
(iii) Interference between cells and D2D.

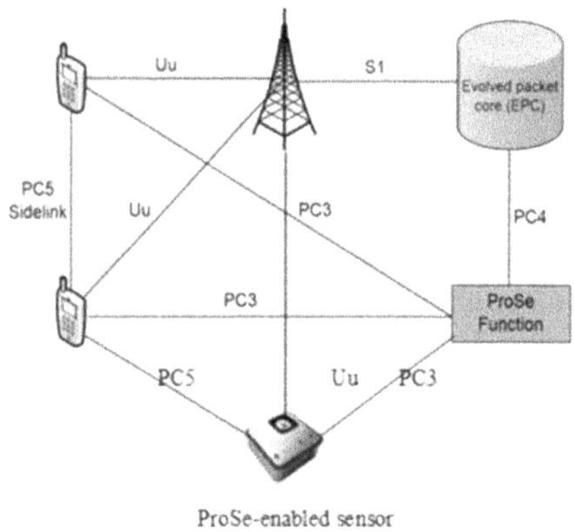

Fig. 1. Adding a ProSe-enabled sensor to the architecture. Adapted from 3rd Generation Partnership Project (3GPP) Organisational Partners (2017)

These types of interference pose a significant threat to cellular networks, prompting many researchers to seek solutions to the resulting interference. The following interference management schemes have been identified, according to Mwashita and Odhiambo (2021):

(i) Resource allocation interference management schemes.
(ii) Power control interference management schemes.
(iii) Retransmission interference management schemes.

2 Related Work

Several researchers have worked on power control schemes to mitigate interference caused by D2D communications in cellular networks (Song, Niyato, Han, & Hossain, 2015; D. Feng, Lu, Yuan-Wu, Li & G. Feng, 2013; Chen, Liu, H. Li, X. Li, & S. Li, 2016). Fodor, Penda, Belleschi, Johansson, and Abrardo (2013) investigated how power control schemes perform in D2D-enabled cellular networks in terms of interference mitigation. The researchers looked at power control mechanisms based on a fixed signal-to-interference-plus-noise-ratio (SINR) target, fixed transmit power, and open and closed loops.

To compensate for large-scale pathloss effects, Abdallah, Mansour, and Chehab (2017) proposed a distributed power control scheme that uses distance-based parameters existing between the BS and the D2D link. D2D transmitters can choose their transmit powers based on the current channel conditions under the proposed scheme. Without involving the BS, the D2D pairs settle on their transmit powers on their own. The scheme captures the randomness of BS-D2D distances perfectly. The proposed system, on the other hand, did not account for the versatility of D2D pairs and CUEs. This is particularly relevant in mobile networks because users seldom remain stationary when making or receiving calls. While ProSe-enabled sensors are usually fixed, the CUEs with which they must communicate are usually mobile. Using this proposed scheme with devices like ProSe-enabled sensors may be problematic because the network QoS is likely to be compromised because the BS is not included in the equation.

According to Safdar, Ur-Rehman, Muhammad, Imran, and Tafazolli (2016), power management systems, whether centralised or distributed, are incapable of effectively dealing with network interference levied on devices participating in D2D. When it comes to interference from CUEs to devices involved in D2D communication, the researchers found that power control schemes do not help much. According to Xing and Hakola (2010), power control schemes must be used in conjunction with other interference mitigation schemes to be efficient.

In D2D-enabled cellular networks where D2D may have been implemented to improve cellular network throughput, most power control schemes that have appeared in literature are designed to deal with cross-tier as well as co-tier interference. According to Mahdi (2016), the power control schemes are intended to help D2D improve overall network throughput. The main goal of these proposed D2D schemes is to offload mobile data traffic to nearby devices through resource sharing rather than the use of the BS. This is done to make better use of the frequency spectrum, resulting in higher average throughput in each cell. According to Lopez (2016) and Lin, Andrews, Ghosh, and Ratasuk (2014), D2D has piqued the interest of many researchers, but there has been very little research on power control schemes for potential immobile D2D-enabled devices such as ProSe-enabled sensors that are fixed in one place harvesting Artificial Intelligence information for onward transmission to the relevant devices via the Internet. This is what has motivated this research work.

3 The Proposed Scheme

For the purposes of this study, it is suggested that a ProSe-enabled sensor link to a BS through the OLPC first. The maximum transmit power that the sensor can use, according to 3GPP (2014), is:

$$P_{Tx} = \min\left(P_{CMAX} , P_{target} + \mathrm{PL}\right) \text{ [dBm]}. \tag{1}$$

Where:

P_{CMAX} =The maximum allowable transmit power for the ProSe-enabled sensor.
P_{target} = target reception power.
PL = the pathloss between the BS and the ProSe-enabled sensor and is calculated in the ProSe-enabled sensor.

This transmit power is then corrected by the sensor after getting feedback from the BS to Eq. 2:

$$P\_Tx = min\begin{cases} P_{CMAX\,(i)}, \\ P_0\,(j) + 10\log_{10}\left(2^{\mu}\,.\,M_{RB}\,(i)\right) + \acute{\alpha}\,(j)\,.\,PL + \Delta_{TF} + f(i) \end{cases} \tag{2}$$

Where:

$\boldsymbol{P_{CMAX}}$=Configured UE maximum power.
$\boldsymbol{P_0}$=The power to be contained in one RB. It is a cell specific parameter that is determined using higher layer parameters and measured in dBm/RB.
M = The number of allocated RBs per user.
μ = A 5G New Radio parameter which changes the sub-carrier spacing (SCS).
$\acute{\alpha}$=This is a pathloss compensation factor which is a cell specific parameter in the range [0, 1].
$\boldsymbol{\Delta_{TF}}$=A correction function from the BS to the UE for fine tuning the in UE's transmission power.
PL = Downlink path-loss estimate in dB calculated by the UE using a reference signal.
$f(i)$ = Power control adjustment function.

Combining the power control adjustment and correction functions simplifies Eq. 2 to:

$$\boldsymbol{P_{Tx} = \min\begin{cases} P_{CMAX\,(i)}, \\ P_0\,(j) + 10\log_{10}(2^{\mu}.M_{RB}\,(i)) + \alpha\,(j).\ PL + \Delta_j \end{cases}} \tag{3}$$

Taking a subcarrier spacing of 15 kHz and using 1 RB, ($2^{\mu} = 1$ ($for\ \mu = 0$) , M = 1) simplifies Eq. 3 to:

$$\boldsymbol{P_{Tx} = \min\begin{cases} P_{CMAX\,(i)}, \\ P_0\,(j) + \alpha\,(j).\ PL + \Delta_j \end{cases}} \tag{4}$$

Where Δ_j is the Transmit Power Command (TPC) generated by BS. The TPC value is a feedback value from the BS that is used to fix errors. It is proposed that the TPC value be calculated using the received SINR and a SINR target for this research project. If P_{CMAX} is less than the calculated power, $P_0\,(j) + \alpha\,(j).\ PL + \Delta_j$, the sensor transmits to the BS using the calculated power, if it is more, then the sensor transmits at P_{CMAX}. According to 3GPP (2018), P_{CMAX} is 23 dBm ± 2 which is Power Class 3 (PC3). High Performance User Equipment (HPUE) which are devices with a capability of transmitting in the uplink with power higher than 23 dBm are being considered for 5G (MediaTek, 2018). This increase in uplink transmit power is most welcome as ProSe sensors will be able to have a wider coverage area, thus reducing the number of sensors that must be deployed.

Once the transmit power that a sensor must use when communicating with a BS has been determined, the sensor and a nearby CUE must determine the transmit power that they must use once a BS has approved D2D communication. The maximum transmit power of devices communicating directly with one another should be strictly regulated, not only to avoid interference but also to ensure effective D2D communication. The objective of the proposed power control is to ensure that a network-prescribed SINR target for CUEs, $SINR_{ue}^{target}$, and a network prescribed SINR target for UE-Sensor (DUEs), $SINR_{due}^{target}$ are met. For a sensor that has to share an uplink resource with a CUE, the SINR over RB r at the BS is given by:

$$SINR_{ue}^{r} = \frac{G_{ueBS}.p_{ue}}{Ga + p_{D2D}G_{D_t.BS}} \tag{5}$$

And for the downlink, the SINR over resource block (RB) r at the CUE is given by:

$$SINR_{ue}^{r} = \frac{G_{ueD2D}.p_{D2D}}{Ga + p_{D2D}G_{D_t.BS}} \tag{6}$$

To meet pre-defined QoS requirements, this SINR over RB r should be equal to/or higher than a target SINR, $SINR_{ue}^{target}$ that is required at the BS for successful communication.

$$\frac{G_{ueBS}.p_{ue}}{Ga + p_{D2D}G_{D_t.BS}} \geq SINR_{ue}^{target} \tag{7}$$

If the interference that a sensor adds on RB r over subframe s is given by:

$$I_s^r = p_{D2D}G_{D_t.BS} \tag{8}$$

Then:

$$G_{D_t\ D_r}p_{D2D} \leq \frac{G_{cueBS}.p_{ue}}{SINR_{ue}^{target}} - Ga \tag{9}$$

$$p_{D2D} \leq \frac{G_{cueBS}.p_{ue}}{SINR_{ue}^{target}G_{D_t\ D_r}} - \frac{Ga}{G_{D_t\ D_r}} \tag{10}$$

Where:

Ga Represents the Gaussian noise power on a specific link.
p_{ue} Represents the transmit power of UE.
p_{D2D} Represents the transmit power of D2D (ProSe-enabled sensor to UE transmission).
$G_{D_t\ D_r}$ Represents channel gain between D2D transmitter *(Dt)* and D2D receiver *(Dr)*.
G_{ueBS} Represents the channel gain between UE and the BS.
$G_{UE.D_r}$ Represents channel gain between UE and D2D receiver.
$G_{D_t.BS}$ Represents channel gain between D2D transmitter and the BS.
$SINR_{ue}^{r}$ SINR for any arbitrary UE in a cell over RB r.

$SINR^{r}_{D2D}$ SINR for any arbitrary D2D in a cell over RB r.
$P_{BS}\,G_{CU}$ Represents macro tier interference.

In a D2D communication, Algorithm 1 is used to control the transmit powers of the devices involved.

Algorithm 1: Power Control Algorithm

1: Input: Matrix P // Paired UE- ProSe-enabled sensor devices
2: Output: A set of transmit powers, $p = (p1, p2, \ldots, pL)$;
3: for all pairs,
3.1 calculate transmit powers for the D2D transmitters using the equation:

$$p_{D2D\,Tx} = \frac{G_{ueBS}.p_{ue}}{SINR_{ue}^{target} G_{D_t D_r}} - \frac{Ga}{G_{D_t D_r}}$$

3.2 allocate powers accordingly
4: end for
5: $P = (p1, p2, \ldots, pL)$

4 Simulation and Discussion of Results

Radio propagation effects should always be correctly modelled, according to the research community since these effects can easily degrade the system efficiency of any radio system. The propagation environment, noise, and interference are all factors that affect wireless communication networks. Signal attenuation is caused by large barriers, as well as the distance between devices and multi-path fading. Pathloss, shadowing, and multipath fading are all factors that are considered in this study.

Deployment of Network Elements

For this project, 5 CUEs are dropped at random near an immobile ProSe-enabled sensor at a random distance from a BS. CUE positioning and results collection are repeated several times before representative results are collected. Figure 2 shows five CUEs that have been randomly placed in a 300 m-by-300 m field. The proposed algorithm takes a snapshot of the CUEs' exact locations, as well as the BS and ProSe-enabled sensors' positions. The BS is presumed to be capable of receiving channel quality and geolocation data. Since the 5 CUEs are so close to a ProSe-enabled sensor, they may be permitted to engage in D2D communication with it. Permission to participate in D2D contact is first requested from the BS, which grants permission if resources are available and the QoS conditions are met

Figure 6 shows a 180 m by 200 m area with 50 CUEs dropped randomly 10 times around an immobile BS and a fixed ProSe-enabled sensor. As shown in Fig. 3, the simulation is run for many UE droppings in various locations. Convergence and statistically meaningful results can only be achieved with a large enough number of droppings.

Path Loss Model

Sun et al. (2017) proposed a path loss model for a 5G micro cellular scenario, which was used to test the power control scheme proposed in this report. The alpha-beta-gamma

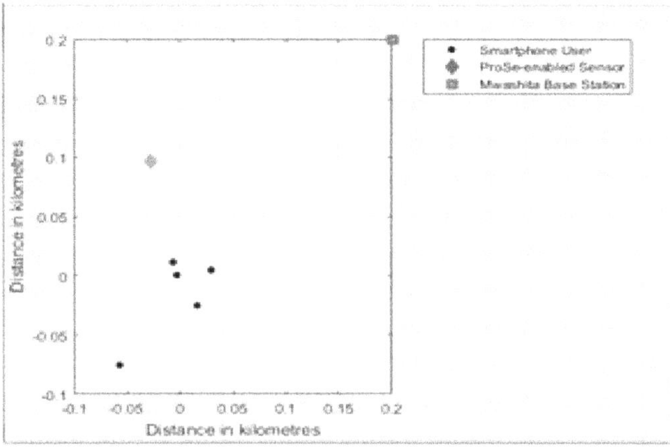

Fig. 2. 5 CUEs, 1 ProSe-enabled sensor and a BS

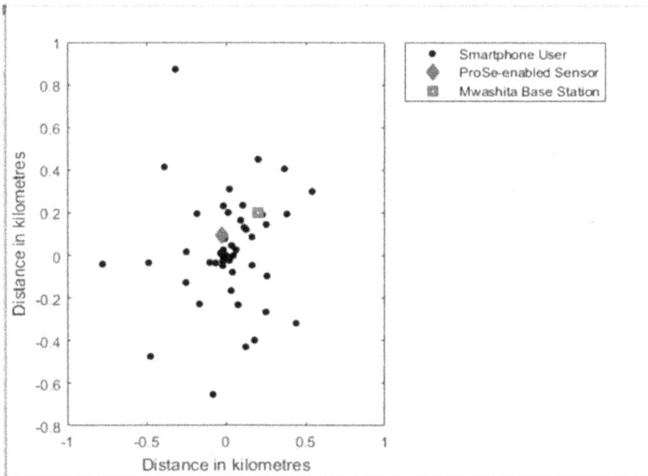

Fig. 3. 50 CUEs randomly dropped, 1 ProSe-enabled sensor and a BS

(ABG) model was used first, followed by the close-in (CI) free space reference distance model. This is because the CI model is very similar to the current 3GPP path loss model in terms of structure. A floating constant is replaced by a frequency dependent free space path loss in the CI model, which is based on a one-meter standard CI reference distance. This minor modification streamlines the analysis process, resulting in improved accuracy over a broad range of mmWave and microwave frequencies. Table 1 presents the parameters of the ABG and the CI models.

The traffic model proposed by Hossain (2013) is used in this study because it produces a realistic traffic profile like that of a real cellular network. The traffic generation in practical mobile networks is inhomogeneous, with the arrival rate varying both in space and time. CUEs generate and forward high-quality level video streams to one

Table 1. Parameters in the ABG and CI path loss models in UMi and UMa scenarios (Sun et al., 2016)

Scenario	Env.	Freq.	Dist.	Model	PLE	β(dB)
UMi SC	LOS	Range (GHz)	Range (m)	ABG	2.0	31.4
				CI	2.0	–
	NLOS	2–73.5	5–121	ABG	3.5	24.4
				CI	3.1	–
UMi OS	LOS	2–73.5	19–272	ABG	2.6	24.0
				CI	1.9	–
	NLOS	2–60	5–88	ABG	4.4	2.4
				CI	2.8	–
UMa	LOS	2–60	8–235	ABG	2.8	11.4
				CI	2.0	–
	NLOS	2–73.5	58–930	ABG	3.3	17.6
				CI	2.7	–

another through the BS in this research project, while ProSe-enabled sensors compete for resources for D2D communication with SUEs.

Simulation Parameters

The proper parameters for the simulation system were chosen for the proper evaluation of the established strategy for interference management. The simulation parameters recommended by the 3GPP in 2017 and 2018 for use with 5G D2D systems were used. Table 2 lists the parameters.

Variation of ProSe-enabled Sensor Transmit Power with Distance

Figure 7 depicts the transmit power that a ProSe-enabled sensor can use at various distances from the BS for various degrees of power control. It can be seen that for $\alpha = 0$, the sensor transmits at full power to the BS, and that as α increases, the transmit power needed to transmit to the BS for the same distances decreases. This implies that as α increases, the level of interference between cells using the same resources decreases. Figure 4 also shows that as the distance between the BS increases, sensors must transmit at higher power.

Reusable distance

Figure 8 depicts the distance from the BS at which uplink (UL) services currently in use by a specific CUE can be reused by a ProSe-enabled sensor without compromising cellular network QoS. The reusable distance decreases rapidly as the power control level rises in both non-line of sight (NLOS) and line of sight (LOS) propagation settings, as shown in Fig. 5. It is also worth noting that in an NLOS propagation environment, the reusable distance decreases significantly faster than in a LOS propagation environment. It is also clear that ProSe-enabled sensors should never be allowed to share UL resources with CUEs that are more than 160 m away from the BS in an NLOS environment and 150 m away in a LOS environment.

Table 2. Simulation parameters

Parameter	Value
System bandwidth	100 MHz
Carrier frequency	4 GHz
Maximum smartphone transmission power	23 dBm
Maximum BS transmission power	24 dBm
Maximum ProSe-enabled sensor transmission power	26 dBm
Shadowing Standard Deviation	10 dB
Noise Spectral Density	−174 dBm /Hz
Total number of available RBs	50
D2D transmission power	Proposed power control scheme to meet a specified SINR
Monte Carlo simulation runs	1000
Bit rate requirement for prioritised CUEs	2Mbps
Bit rate requirement for non-prioritised CUEs	1.0Mbps

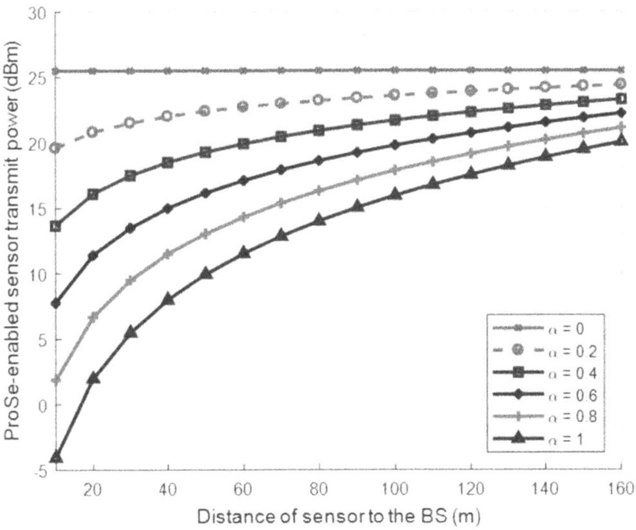

Fig. 4. Variation of power with distance

Maximum Allowed Transmit Power

Figures 6 and 7 show that as the CUE gets closer to the BS, the maximum permissible power increases faster towards the maximum power. Reusing subchannels at distances

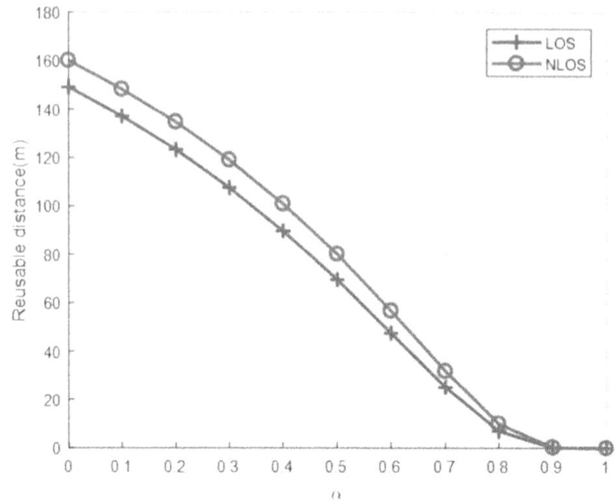

Fig. 5. Reusable distance from BS vs. power control levels

greater than 115 m from the BS for an NLOS environment should be prohibited for CUEs that are quite close to the BS.

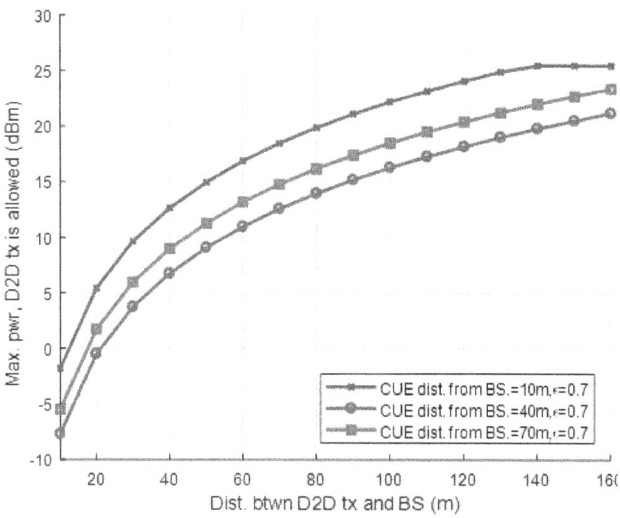

Fig. 6. Maximum transmit power vs. distance for LOS

*G. ProSe-enabled sensor SINR variation with distanc*e

Figure 8 depicts the SINR of a ProSe-enabled sensor as a function of distance from a BS. SINR is high when a sensor is close to a BS and decreases exponentially as the distance from the BS increases for a power control of 0.7. It can also be shown that at distances of up to 120 m from the BS, LOS propagation loses its advantage over NLOS propagation in terms of SINR. This is a strange phenomenon that can be explained by the fact that, according to Rappaport, Xing, MacCartney, Molisch, Mellios, and Zhang (2016), many reflections and scatterings from ceilings and walls, which are abundant in densely populated areas like shopping malls, as well as the waveguiding effects of hallways, corridors, and alleys, all lead to an increased received power.

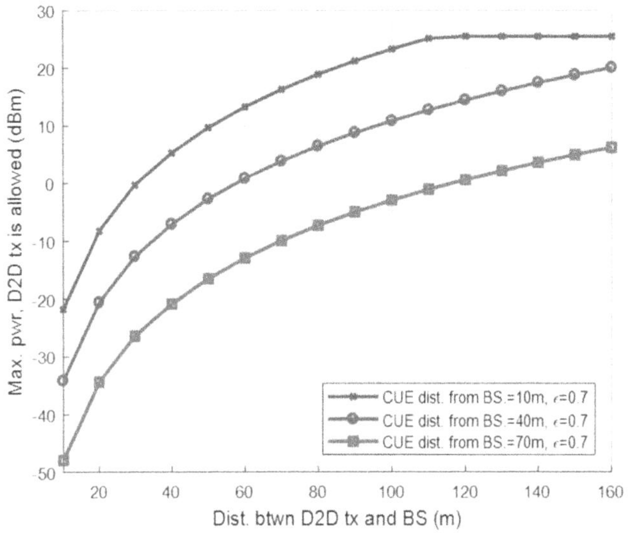

Fig. 7. Maximum transmit power vs. distance for NLOS

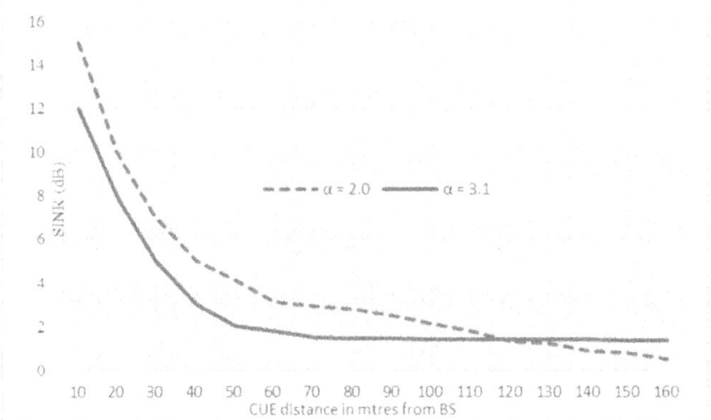

Fig. 8. Variation of a CUE's throughput with distance from BS for (α = 2.0) LOS and (α = 3.1) NLOS

H Impact of D2D Communication on CUE Throughput

Figures 9 and 10 depict the difference in throughput of one CUE. Figure 9 depicts how the CUE's throughput varies as it travels around the cell. The CUE's throughput is then monitored again after a ProSe-enabled sensor is permitted to reuse the CUE's UL resources. The reuse of resources by the ProSe-enabled does not appear to have affected the CUE's throughput, as shown in Fig. 10. The small improvement in throughput at 4.8 m from the BS can be attributed to the high SINR that signals enjoy for short distances from the BS, as shown in Fig. 11.

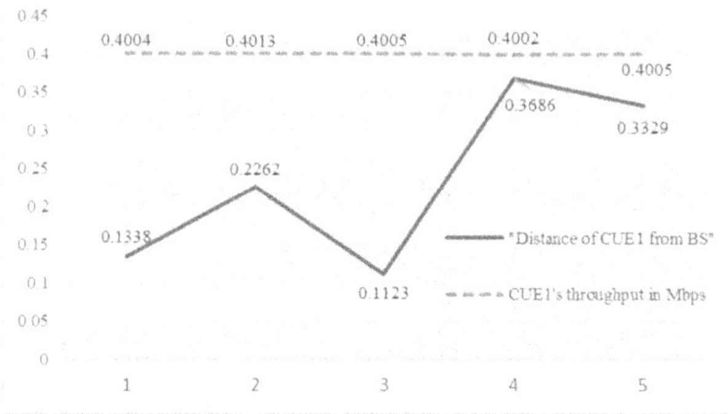

Fig. 9. CUE 1's throughput before introducing D2D communication

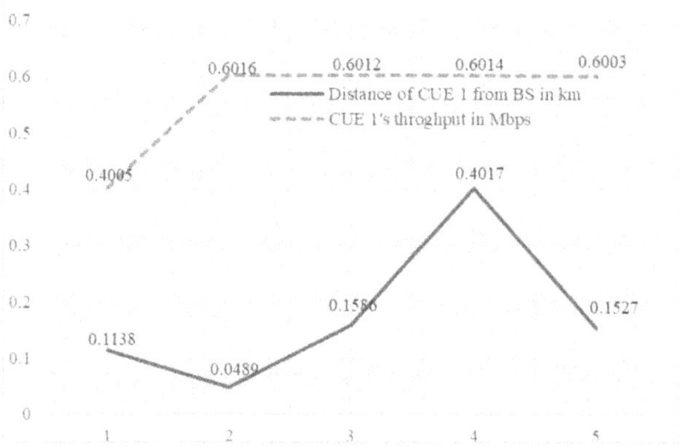

Fig. 10. CUE 1's throughput after introducing D2D communication

I. Impact of resource sharing on the SINR of one CUE

The effect of allowing ProSe-enabled sensors to share UL resources on the CUE SINR is investigated by computing the variation of the CUE SINR with cell distance before UL resources are shared. The CUE SINR obtained before D2D communication is compared to the CUE SINR obtained after D2D communication is added. As shown in Fig. 11, the negative effect is so minor that it can be safely overlooked. The proposed scheme only allows a ProSe-enabled sensor to communicate with cellular network elements in D2D mode when the operation does not degrade the cellular network elements' SINR.

Even when D2D is allowed, the power at which ProSe-enabled sensors communicate with cellular network elements is strictly controlled to ensure that the cellular network elements maintain the minimum network Quality of Service requirements (QoS).

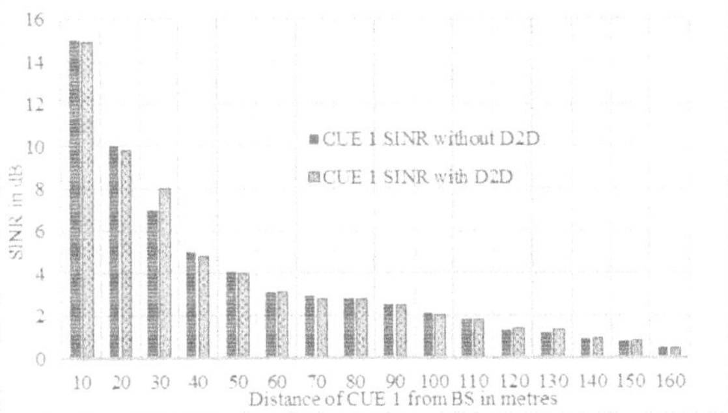

Fig. 11. SINR of one CUE with and without resources being shared

5 Conclusion

A power control strategy for ProSe-enabled sensors deployed to harvest Artificial Intelligence information, and smart phones connected to these sensors in a D2D fashion was developed in this research work. A fractional power technique with pathloss compensation is used in the proposed strategy. The ability of ProSe-enabled sensors to connect directly to smartphones and BSs is not likely to degrade a cellular network's QoS. The proposed strategy uses a target SINR to set the transmit powers of D2D devices, ensuring that the QoS of a cellular network is not jeopardized. There has not been a state-of-the-art scheme that considers interference reduction in 5G networks where smartphones interact with ProSe-enabled sensors directly. To test the strategy, a compact system-level MATLAB simulator specifically designed for 5G networks was developed. The system-level simulator could do the following:

(i) The capturing of the randomness of the distance between a ProSe enabled sensor and the BS.
(ii) The capturing of the mobility of the CUEs.
(iii) Capturing the randomness of the location of ProSe-enabled sensors.

Six experiments were performed on the device level simulator to determine the efficacy of the proposed strategy, and the results indicate that the proposed strategy is capable of adequately managing interference levels that are known to cause problems in D2D-enabled networks. According to simulation results, allowing ProSe-enabled sensors to communicate directly with nearby UEs will result in a 3.6% reduction in overall user throughput. This figure is modest, and both network users and network providers are likely to embrace it. According to Ramasamy (2017:45), a reduction of up to 5% is appropriate to both consumers and network providers and is often reflected in service level agreements between network providers and their clients. As compared to conventional power control systems, the power control strategy described in this paper results in a reasonable reduction in a cellular network's overall QoS. The results show that the overall network QoS is not affected by controlling the power at which ProSe-enabled devices transmit to the BSs and the power at which D2D devices communicate with each other. This is relevant because cellular network operators are less likely to consider schemes that compromise network quality of service

References

Generation Partnership Project Organisational Partners: Proximity-based services (ProSe), 3GPP TS 23.303 V15.0.0. Valbonne: 3GPP Organisational Partners' Publications Offices (2017)

Generation Partnership Project Organisational Partners: Physical layer procedures for control, (3GPP TS 38.213 version 15.2.0 Release 15), Valbonne: 3GPP Organisational Partners' Publications Offices, 1–101 (2018)

Generation Partnership Project Organizational Partners: Technical Specification Group Services and System Aspects; Study on architecture enhancements to support Proximity-based Services (ProSe) (Release 12)," 3GPP TR 23.703 V12.0.0 (2014–02). Valbonne: 3GPP Organizational Partners' Publications Offices (2014)

Abdallah, A., Mansour, M. M., Chehab, A. (2017). A Distance-Based Power Control Scheme for D2D Communications Using Stochastic Geometry. In: Proceedings of the 2017 IEEE 86th Vehicular Technology Conference (VTC-Fall), Toronto: IEEE, 1–6.

Bhushan, B., Sahoo, G.: Recent advances in attacks, technical challenges, vulnerabilities and their countermeasures in wireless sensor networks. Wireless Pers. Commun. **98**, 2037–2077 (2018)

Chen, J., Liu, C., Li, H., Li, X., Li, S.: A categorized resource sharing mechanism for device-to-device communications in cellular networks. Mob. Inf. Syst., 1–10 (2016)

Cho, S., Choi, J.W., You, C.: Adaptive multi-node multiple input and multiple output (MIMO) transmission for mobile wireless multimedia sensor networks. Sensors, 3382–3401 (2013)

Ericsson.: 5G Readiness Survey 2017: an Assessment of Operators' Progress on the Road to 5G. Ericsson, Stockholm (2017)

Feng, D., Lu, L., Yuan-Wu, Y., Li, G.Y., Feng, Y., Li, S.: Device-to-device communications Underlaying cellular networks. IEEE Trans. Commun. **61**(8), 3541–3551 (2013)

Fodor, G., Penda, D. D., Belleschi, M., Johansson, M., & Abrardo, A. (2013). A comparative study of power control approaches for device-to-device communications. In: Proceedings of 2013 IEEE International Conference on Communications (ICC), Budapest: IEEE, 6008–6013.

Hossain, M. F.: Traffic-driven energy efficient operational mechanisms in cellular access networks. (Doctoral dissertation), The University of Sydney, Sydney (2013)

Institute of Electrical and Electronics Engineers: Multi-hop relay system evaluation methodology (channel model and performance metric), IEEE C802.16j-06/013r3, New York: IEEE, 1–38 (2006)

Lin, X., Andrews, J., Ghosh, A., Ratasuk, R.: An overview of 3GPP device-to-device proximity services. IEEE Commun. Mag. **52**(4), 40–48 (2014)

Lopez, S. M. (2016). An overview of D2D in 3GPP LTE standard. http://d2d-4-5g.gforge.inria.fr/Workshop-June2016/slides/Overview_LTE_D2D.pdf

Mach, P., Becvar, Z., Vanek, T.: In-band device-to-device communication in OFDMA cellular networks: a survey and challenges. IEEE Commun. Surv. Tutor. **17**(4), 1885–1922 (2015)

Mahdi, A. H.: The integration of device-to-device communication in future cellular systems. (Doctoral dissertation), Technischen Universität, Berlin (2016)

MediaTek: 5G NR Uplink enhancements better cell coverage & user experience, 1–13 (2018)

Mwashita, W., Odhiambo, M. O.: Interference Management Techniques for Device-to-Device Communications. In Management Association, I. (Ed.), Research Anthology on Developing and Optimizing 5G Networks and the Impact on Society (pp. 383–409). IGI Global (2021). https://doi.org/10.4018/978-1-7998-7708-0.ch016

Rappaport, T., et al.: Overview of millimetre wave Communications for Fifth Generation (5G) wireless networks-with a focus on propagation models. IEEE Trans. Antennas Propag. **65**(12), 6213–6230 (2017)

Rathee, D., Ahuja, K., Nayyar, A.: Sustainable Future IoT Services with Touch-Enabled Handheld devices' (Healthcare Technologies, 2019), pp. 131–152. Concepts, paradigms, and solutions, Security and Privacy of Electronic Healthcare Records (2019)

Safdar, G.A., Ur-Rehman, M., Muhammad, M., Imran, M.A., Tafazolli, R.: Interference mitigation in D2D communication Underlaying LTE-A network. IEEE Access **4**, 7967–7987 (2016)

Song, L., Niyato, D., Han, Z., Hossain, E.: Wireless Device-to-Device Communications and Networks. Cambridge University Press, New York (2015)

Sun, S., et al.: Propagation path loss models for 5G urban micro- and macro-cellular scenarios. In: Proceedings of the IEEE 83rd Vehicular Technology Conference (VTC Spring), pp. 1–6. Nanjing, IEEE (2016)

Xing, H., Hakola, S.: The investigation of power control schemes for a device-to-device communication integrated into OFDMA cellular system. In: Proceedings of 21st Annual IEEE International Symposium on Personal, Indoor and Mobile Radio Communications, pp. 1775–1780. Instanbul, IEEE (2010)

Leveraging Transformer Models for Extractive Question Answering in Criminal Report Analysis

Lenin G. Falconi(✉), Lorena Isabel Barona López, and Myriam Hernandez-Alvarez

Escuela Politécnica Nacional, Quito 170525, Ecuador
{lenin.falconi,lorena.barona,myriam.hernandez}@epn.edu.ec
https://www.epn.edu.ec

Abstract. Transformer-based models have greatly advanced extractive question answering (EQA) in NLP, but their application to legal document analysis remains underexplored. This paper introduces a domain-adapted BERT model for EQA on Spanish-language robbery case reports from Ecuador's Prosecutor's Office (*Fiscalía General del Estado*). We used generative artificial intelligence to synthesize a SQuAD-format dataset tailored to robbery cases. The pre-trained BERT model was first evaluated in a zero-shot setting on this dataset, then further fine-tuned for the specific domain. The fine-tuned model outperformed the base version, achieving a final F1-score of 82.88. Our results demonstrate the effectiveness of transformer-based models, both in zero-shot and fine-tuned settings, for EQA tasks in legal language processing. These advancements highlight the potential to enhance information retrieval and optimize workloads in judicial systems, ultimately improving service delivery to communities.

Keywords: Legal Natural Language Processing · NLP · Natural Language Processing · transformers · LNLP · law

1 Introduction

Transformer-based models have emerged as powerful tools in Natural Language Processing (NLP), enabling more accurate and efficient extraction of relevant information from complex texts such as criminal reports. These models utilize self-attention mechanisms to weigh the importance of different words in a sentence, allowing for better context understanding and improved performance in tasks like Question Answering (QA). By fine-tuning these models on domain-specific datasets, researchers can enhance their ability to discern pertinent details and provide precise answers to inquiries related to criminal incidents.

The implementation of Extractive Question Answering (EQA) systems in legal contexts not only enhances the efficiency of information retrieval but also

H. R. Arabnia et al. (Eds.): CSCE 2025, CCIS 2934, pp. 222–233, 2026.
https://doi.org/10.1007/978-3-032-22190-2_16

addresses challenges related to data variability and complexity inherent in criminal reports. As these models are fine-tuned on diverse datasets, they can improve their generalizability across different types of legal documents, ensuring that critical details are accurately captured regardless of nuances in language or structure [9]. Moreover, recent advancements in model architectures, such as the integration of dynamic masking techniques, have shown promise in further refining performance by enabling models to better adapt to varying levels of difficulty in questions posed about complex narratives [14]. This evolution highlights the potential for transformer-based models to facilitate more informed decision-making processes within the justice system, ultimately contributing to enhanced outcomes for legal practitioners and stakeholders alike.

The Prosecutor's Office of Ecuador is responsible for handling a wide range of cases, including criminal investigations and public safety matters. Among these, robbery poses a significant challenge, with 67,705 reported incidents in 2024[1] (equivalent to 376 robberies per 1,00,000 inhabitants). The comprehensive analysis of these crime reports serves multiple critical functions: (1) it enables more effective investigations by revealing criminal patterns, (2) supports victims' insurance claims for stolen property, and (3) provides essential data for public safety planning. Artificial Intelligence (AI) is particularly valuable in this context, as automated systems can enhance the efficiency of processing case information, alleviate backlogs, and ultimately improve service delivery to citizens.

Our previous research investigated robbery classification using state-of-the-art neural architectures, with a focus on fine-tuned language models. Extending this work, the current study investigates the application of EQA systems for processing criminal reports. The proposed methodology demonstrates significant potential to assist legal authorities by: (1) extracting actionable insights for criminal investigations, and (2) enabling comprehensive crime statistics analysis. To our knowledge, this represents the first application of transformer-based models utilizing a specially curated Spanish-language Spanish-language Stanford Question Answering Dataset (SQuAD) dataset derived from Ecuadorian legal documents.

This paper is organized as follows: Sect. 2 surveys existing applications of AI in legal domains, with a focus on question answering (QA) tasks and discusses important concepts such as Generative Artificial Intelligence (GAI) and ZeroShot Learning (ZSL). Section 3 describes our methodology, including dataset construction and model training. Section 4 presents the comparative results of the ZSL model and the fine-tuned model. Finally, Sect. 5 summarizes our main findings and outlines opportunities for future work.

2 Literature Review

Large Language Models (LLMs) represent a category of Deep Learning (DL) models that integrate transformer architectures with large-scale pre-training on

[1] Statistics reported by FGE with data cut-off date June 13, 2025.

extensive text corpora. Trained in a self-supervised fashion, these models capture detailed linguistic patterns and can subsequently be fine-tuned to address domain-specific challenges in Legal NLP (LNLP). For instance, one influential model is described in [4], and another is presented in [16], where OpenAI reported that the model achieved performance at the 90th percentile on the Uniform Bar Exam, a standardized examination used to evaluate the competency of prospective attorneys. However, subsequent analysis by [12] indicates that GPT-4's actual performance ranges from the 48th to the 62nd percentile. These authors critique the imprecision and lack of transparency in OpenAI's report, arguing that such shortcomings may hinder the development of safe AI and lead to misconceptions regarding the model's true capabilities in handling complex legal tasks.

Legal Question Answering (LQA) is a complex task that entails addressing queries related to legal issues, necessitating not only the analysis of extensive legal corpora but also their nuanced interpretation [2]. A wide range of models and algorithms have been explored for QA in NLP, such as *Recurrent Neural Networks (RNNs)*, *Long Short-Term Memory (LSTM)*, and *Convolutional Neural Networks (CNN)*. Additionally, information retrieval approaches, including *Term Frequency-Inverse Document Frequency (TF-IDF)*, are frequently utilized. Both extractive and generative methodologies have demonstrated effectiveness in addressing NLP-based QA tasks [11].

It is important to clarify the primary distinction between these two approaches. EQA identifies and retrieves a span of text directly from the given context: Given a tuple composed of the question q and the context c, the model predicts the start and end positions of the answer. In contrast, Generative Question Answering (GQA) synthesizes responses using encoder-decoder architectures, generating answers in an autoregressive manner [11]. According to a systematic evaluation of QA models by [11], generative readers generally outperform extractive readers with longer contexts, providing more fluent and comprehensive answers, whereas extractive readers are more effective when the context is limited and exhibit better out-of-domain generalization.

2.1 Large Language Models and Generative AI

GAI refers to a class of AI models that learn the underlying data distribution $p_{data}(\mathbf{x})$ to generate novel samples (e.g., text, images, or audio) through an estimated model distribution $p_{model}(\mathbf{x})$ [5]. Modern AI models are considered Foundational Models, which represent a class of general-purpose models capable of handling diverse data modalities and supporting multiple AI tasks [7]. Notable examples include the Llama 3 family of models, which are foundational language models featuring multilingual capabilities, programming proficiency, reasoning skills, and tool integration [7]. Equation (1) represents the goal of GAI, which is to learn a model distribution $p_{model}(\mathbf{x})$ that approximates the true data distribution $p_{data}(\mathbf{x})$, where $\mathbf{x}$ represents observations from the data domain.

$$p_{model}(\mathbf{x}) \approx p_{data}(\mathbf{x}) \tag{1}$$

LLMs are a specialized subset of foundational AI and GAI models, with a primary focus on text-based tasks. These models leverage transformer architectures [7,13] and undergo extensive pre-training on textual corpora. Notably, LLMs exhibit exceptional capabilities in natural language understanding and complex problem-solving (i.e., General Purpose Task Solver) [22], rendering them particularly effective for sophisticated linguistic tasks. The basic working of an LLMs can be thought of as a next-word prediction problem, where given a sequence of tokens $\mathbf{x}_{1:t} = (x_1, \ldots, x_t)$, an LLM defines a conditional probability distribution over the vocabulary $\mathcal{V}$:

$$P(x_{t+1}|\mathbf{x}_{1:t};\theta) = \text{softmax}(\mathbf{W} \cdot \mathbf{h}_t + \mathbf{b}) \quad (2)$$

θ denotes the model parameters, and $\mathbf{h}_t$ is obtained by several layers of transformer blocks that process an embedded representation of the tokenized text:

$$\mathbf{h}_t = \text{Transformer}(\mathbf{x}_{1:t};\theta) \quad (3)$$

2.2 Zero-Shot Learning

Traditional supervised learning in DL requires large labeled datasets, which can be difficult and expensive to obtain [19]. For instance, the SQuAD 2.0 benchmark dataset for EQA contains approximately 1,50,000 samples (1,00,000 answerable and 50,000 unanswerable) [17]. In this context, ZSL establishes a new paradigm in machine learning, where models trained on a subset of classes are expected to recognize new classes not seen during training [18]. Consequently, ZSL addresses the challenge posed by unlabeled data [19]. Moreover, pre-trained language models (e.g., BERT) that are trained on large-scale corpora achieve strong performance in ZSL by encoding linguistic patterns.

Transfer learning aims to utilize knowledge from a source domain to improve performance in a target domain with limited labeled data, typically through fine-tuning pre-trained language models [18]. However, this fine-tuning process can lead to catastrophic forgetting, where the model loses its original capabilities while adapting to new tasks. In contrast, ZSL does not require explicit labeling [8], thereby preserving the model's original knowledge while enabling generalization to unseen classes.

In this research, we explore ZSL on the Legal EQA domain using a new set of samples from our dataset. Traditional applications in NLP include text classification, sentiment analysis, and Named Entity Recognition (NER) [19]. Our approach relies on the use of pre-trained language models such as BERT, which are powerful tools for ZSL. However, other ZSL techniques are: semantic embedding, attribute-based approaches, and generative [18,19]

2.3 Related Works

There is significant interest within both the scientific community and legal institutions in studying the applications of AI in this expansive field. The current state of the art in NLP with DL primarily focuses on the use of transformer-based architectures, which have demonstrated superior performance across various NLP tasks. However, improvements over this architecture are discussed in [20], where a Bidirectional Long Short-Term Memory (BiLSTM) layer is integrated with the transformer to capture both global and sequential features. Although, their work is limited to natural language domain, the authors show that hybrid architectures with varied pooling strategies may improve state-of-the-art performance in QA.

In [21], the deployment of a RoBERTa Base QA classification model specifically for legal questions is discussed. It compares the performance of this transformer model against a traditional linear Support Vector Machine (SVM) in the legal domain, using the PRIVACYQA dataset. The results indicate that RoBERTa significantly outperforms the SVM, achieving a 31% improvement in F1-score and a 41% improvement in Mean Reciprocal Rank, demonstrating the effectiveness of transformers in enhancing answer retrieval for legal inquiries.

For information retrieval, [10] discuss the use of transformer-based approaches for legal information retrieval and entailment, specifically in the context of the COLIEE competition. For case law retrieval, a sentence-transformer model was employed to create numeric representations of case paragraphs, facilitating similarity assessments. As for the entailment task, a fine-tuned DeBERTa large language model was utilized, achieving third place among eight teams. These methods demonstrate the effectiveness of transformers in addressing LQA challenges.

Another area of interest is predicting legal judgments. In [6] six transformer-based models (BERT, XLNet, RoBERTa, DeBERTa, ELECTRA, and BigBird) are evaluated in predicting legal judgments using the ILDC dataset. It highlights the potential of these models in automating legal decision-making, with newer models achieving up to 80% accuracy compared to 76% for older models. This comparative analysis underscores the advancements in NLP technology and its applicability in the legal domain, suggesting a promising future for QA in law through transformer models.

Finally, in [15] the use of transformers to generate legal text is addressed, indicating their potential to assist in legal practice. The findings suggest that these models can effectively generate judicial opinions and help differentiate between human and machine-generated legal texts, which could be beneficial for tasks like drafting contracts and briefs, although direct application to QA is not discussed.

The reviewed studies indicate that transformer-based architectures have become the dominant approach in LNLP, either through fine-tuning or architectural modifications. Applications include information retrieval, judgment prediction, and legal text generation. These trends highlight the relevance of the present work in addressing the LQA.

3 Methodology

In this paper, we present a BERT-based model fine-tuned for EQA on Spanish-language criminal reports. We started from a Spanish BERT architecture already pre-trained and optimized for QA tasks, then fine-tuned it to extract information from robbery crime narratives. Our methodology consists of three phases: (1) dataset generation, (2) ZSL pre-trained model performance, and (3) model fine-tuning.

3.1 Phase 1: Robbery Crime QA Dataset Generation

Data Collection and Preprocessing. We constructed our dataset using a set of unlabeled robbery crime reports. The text preprocessing pipeline involved removing non-alphanumeric characters and converting all text to lowercase. Statistical analysis of the collected reports revealed an average length (mean) of 112 words, and an upper bound of 150 words. Consequently, we included reports x_i satisfying $82 \leq \Gamma(x_i) \leq 150$, where $\Gamma : x_i \rightarrow \mathbb{N}$ denotes the word count function for report x_i. This filtering criterion effectively removed statistical outliers while maintaining the core distribution. Figure 1 illustrates the word count distribution across the original dataset of 1,74,594 samples, presented through both histogram and box plot visualizations. Finally, we transformed this dataset into a QA format compatible with SQuAD using GAI.

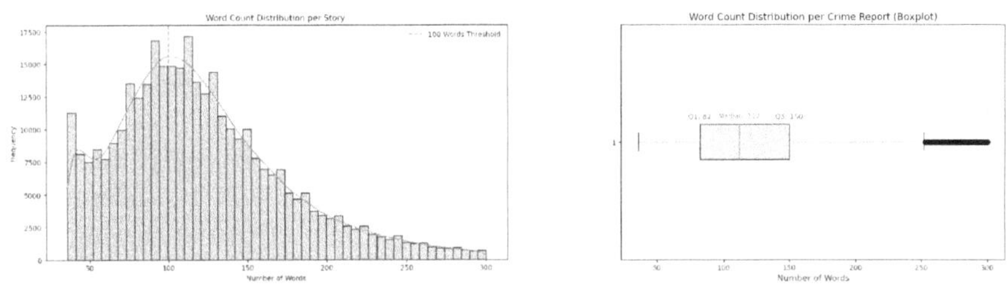

(a) Original Dataset Histogram (b) Box Plot of word counts

Fig. 1. Distribution of word counts in collected data presented as (a) histogram and (b) boxplot. The histogram shows a right-skewed distribution of crime reports. The interquartile range spans from 82 to 150 words, with a median of 112 words.

Generative AI Prompt Engineering. For this research, we used Meta-Llama-3-8B-Instruct [1], an instruction-tuned variant of Meta's Llama 3 8B parameter language model, optimized for conversational and task-oriented interactions with multilingual capabilities. Built on a decoder-only Transformer architecture, it leverages supervised fine-tuning (SFT) and reinforcement learning from human feedback (RLHF) to align responses with user intent. The model is pre-trained on a diverse corpus of publicly available text data, with enhancements in reasoning, coding, and safety mitigation compared to its predecessors.

Prompt engineering is the process of crafting a suitable prompt to drive the LLMs to solve a complex task, using natural language text [22]. In this work, the LLM functions as an expert data science assistant with the goal of constructing a dataset in the SQuAD format in Spanish. For this purpose, the prompt receives the content of the crime report as the `context` and each of the questions from Table 1 as the `question`. The LLM was also instructed to retrieve a `json` format output with the variables: `context`, `question`, `answer_text`, `answer_start`, `answer_end`, and `impossible_find_answer`. The latter was calculated by finding the `answer_text` in the context. In the case that no answer was possible to be retrieved, either because there is no answer or because the LLM failed, the variable `impossible_find_answer` was set to True.

Table 1. Proposed Questions for the Dataset

Question
What objects were stolen?
On what date did the incident occur?
At what time did the robbery happen?
At what address or between which streets did the robbery/incident occur?
What was the dollar value of the stolen or taken objects?

Hugging Face's Inference API processed samples at a speed of 6.4 samples per minute. A total of 1,544 samples were obtained after four hours. Our evaluation revealed two key limitations of the LLM: (1) incomplete retrieval of answers for certain queries, and (2) sporadic generation of irrelevant content. These results suggest that manual verification of the generated dataset can aid in improving quality. However, the engineered prompt allowed for the identification of problems in generated samples.

Dataset Quality. After collecting the initial 1,544 samples, which generated 7,705 question-answer pairs at five questions per context, we conducted quality assessment using the `impossible_find_answer` flag. This process identified approximately 3,000 invalid cases, leading us to retain only samples where `impossible_find_answer` is `False`. Through histogram and box plot analysis of answer lengths, we established an upper limit of 17 words for valid responses. The final curated dataset consisted of 4,572 samples, all containing at least one word and meeting our validity criteria, suitable for model training and evaluation.

Dataset Train and Test Split. The dataset was partitioned into training and testing sets, with 20% of the samples allocated for evaluation. The remaining

80% were used for training. This approach is a fundamental machine learning technique that helps to evaluate the model's performance and generalization capability. Table 2 summarizes the sample sizes for each subset. The split was performed randomly.

Table 2. Dataset Train and Test Split

Partition	# Samples
Train	3,657
Test	915
Total	4,572

3.2 Phase 2: Zero Shot Learning Pre-trained Model Performance

We selected the `mrm8488/bert-base-spanish-wwm-cased-finetuned-spa-squad2-es` model as the baseline pre-trained model due to its specialization for Spanish language processing in QA tasks. This model represents a distilled version of BETO (Spanish BERT) [3] that was further fine-tuned on the SQuAD-es-v2.0 dataset. The architecture follows the standard BERT-base [4] configuration, featuring:

- 12 Transformer blocks
- 768-dimensional hidden states
- 12 self-attention heads
- 384 tokens of sequence length

BETO was pretrained on an extensive Spanish corpus using Whole Word Masking. In preliminary testing without additional fine-tuning, the model achieved an F1-score of 81.70, demonstrating strong baseline performance for Spanish QA tasks.

3.3 Phase 3: Model Fine-Tuning

To fine-tune the pre-trained model, both the question and the answer need to be tokenized. As a result of this process, the indices indicating the start and end of the answer must be recalculated based on the tokenized embedding. In the case of long text, truncation should be applied only to the context, and a window of 128 tokens was used to avoid losing the answer during truncation. However, in this scenario, since most of the current samples have no more than 100 words in the context, this issue is unlikely to occur; nonetheless, it has been addressed in the program.

In order to train the model, the parameters shown in Table 3 were used. A small learning rate is recommended for fine-tuning in order to reuse the pre-training from the original model and adapt the new model to the target dataset.

Our results prove that it is possible to achieve a better performance on the target domain with the fine-tuned model rather than using the pre-trained model. Although the difference in performance is small, it could be related to the fact that we were not able to use the whole dataset.

Table 3. Training Parameters

Parameter	Value
Strategy	epoch
Learning rate	2×10^{-5}
Batch Size	64
Epochs	10
Weight Decay	0.01
FP16	True
Metric for best model	F1 (eval)

4 Results

In this section, we present the results of fine-tuning the model, along with the performance of the pre-trained model on the test set. This comparison was conducted to determine whether the fine-tuned model demonstrates any improvement over ZSL. Table 4 shows the performance of each learning approach used in this research.

Fine-tuning improves upon ZSL in terms of F1 score and exact match, with values of 82.88 and 81.70, respectively, indicating higher accuracy. The exact match metric measures the percentage of predictions that match any ground truth answer exactly. However, the pre-trained model used in ZSL shows lower evaluation loss and higher steps per second, suggesting less error and greater throughput. Thus, while fine-tuning yields better accuracy, the ZSL model is slightly less accurate but faster.

Our results suggest that increasing the number of samples for the fine-tuning approach may improve model performance. It is also important to note that the use of GAI enabled the synthesis of a training dataset through prompt engineering. According to [18] and [19], this represents another application of ZSL.

Table 4. Comparison of Pre-trained and Fine-tuned Model Performance

Metric	Zero Shot	Fine-tuning
eval_loss	0.9102	1.0088
eval_model_preparation_time	0.0077	0.0077
eval_exact	53.5519	55.7377
eval_f1	81.7041	82.8805
eval_total	915.0000	915.0000
eval_HasAns_exact	53.5519	55.7377
eval_HasAns_f1	81.7041	82.8805
eval_HasAns_total	915.0000	915.0000
eval_best_exact	53.5519	55.7377
eval_best_exact_thresh	0.0000	0.0000
eval_best_f1	81.7041	82.8805
eval_best_f1_thresh	0.0000	0.0000
eval_runtime	12.3982	12.8109
eval_samples_per_second	73.8010	71.4240
eval_steps_per_second	1.2100	1.1710
epoch	–	10.0000

5 Conclusions and Future Works

In this study, we demonstrated the effectiveness of transformer-based models for EQA within the context of criminal report analysis. Our fine-tuned model showed achieved an F1 score of 82.88, improving upon the pre-trained model's zero-shot score of 81.70. This indicates the potential for enhanced performance through domain-specific fine-tuning. It also shows that ZSL can achieve a reasonable performance with a higher throughput.

The proposed methodology could be extended to other legal contexts in other countries, provided a pre-trained QA model in the target language is available. According to our results, a zero-shot approach achieves good performance. However, based on our experience, fine-tuning the model increases performance. Additionally, using GAI to create a SQuAD dataset can be adapted to the new target.

The application of our model to robbery crime reports could facilitate the extraction of crucial information, supporting legal practitioners in their investigations and reporting. However, the study also highlighted some limitations, including the model's occasional inability to retrieve accurate answers and the need for manual verification of results.

Future work will address current limitations by exploring advanced techniques and incorporating manual dataset labeling by expert peers. Additional computational resources will be necessary for larger datasets. Integrating AI into the legal domain offers significant potential for improved case management and resource allocation, promoting a safer community. Further research should assess the impact of AI in the legal field, particularly regarding data and methodological biases. Exploring other NLP approaches, such as Legal NER and Document Summarization (LDS), within the Ecuadorian context is also recommended. Continued research and collaboration are encouraged to refine these methods and maximize AI's benefits in supporting the justice system.

Acknowledgments. The authors would like to thank to the Faculty of Systems Engineering at Escuela Politécnica Nacional in Quito, Ecuador, for providing both academic guidance and financial support. We are equally indebted to the Fiscalía General del Estado for their cooperation in the development of this research.

Disclosure of Interests. The authors have no competing interests to declare that are relevant to the content of this article.

References

1. AI@Meta: Llama 3 model card (2024). https://github.com/meta-llama/llama3/blob/main/MODEL_CARD.md
2. Ariai, F. and Demartini, G.: Natural language processing for the legal domain: a survey of tasks, datasets, models, and challenges. ACM Comput. Surv. **1** (10 2024). https://doi.org/10.1145/nnnnnnn.nnnnnnn, https://arxiv.org/abs/2410.21306v2
3. Cañete, J., Chaperon, G., Fuentes, R., Ho, J.H., Kang, H., Pérez, J.: Spanish pre-trained bert model and evaluation data. In: PML4DC at ICLR 2020 (2020)
4. Devlin, J., Chang, M.W., Lee, K., and Toutanova, K.: BERT: Pre-training of deep bidirectional transformers for language understanding. In: Burstein, J., Doran, C., and Solorio, T. (eds.) Proceedings of the 2019 Conference of the North American Chapter of the Association for Computational Linguistics: Human Language Technologies, Volume 1 (Long and Short Papers), pp. 4171–4186. Association for Computational Linguistics, Minneapolis, Minnesota (Jun 2019). https://doi.org/10.18653/v1/N19-1423, https://aclanthology.org/N19-1423/
5. Foster, D.: Generative deep learning. " O'Reilly Media, Inc." (2022)
6. Ghosh, T., Kumar, S.: Evaluating transformer models for legal judgement prediction: a comparative study, pp. 1–4 (Jun 2024). https://doi.org/10.1109/icccnt61001.2024.10725043
7. Grattafiori, A., Dubey, A., Jauhri, A., Pandey, A., Kadian, A., et al.: The llama 3 herd of models (July 2024). https://arxiv.org/pdf/2407.21783
8. Guo, Y., Ding, G., Han, J., Tang, S.: Zero-shot learning with attribute selection (2018). www.aaai.org
9. Jha, R., Devi, V.S.: Extractive question answering using transformer-based lm. In: International Conference on Neural Information Processing, pp. 373–384. Springer (2022). https://doi.org/10.1007/978-981-99-1642-9_32
10. Kim, M.Y., Rabelo, J., Babiker, H.K.B., Rahman, M.A., Goebel, R.: Legal information retrieval and entailment using transformer-based approaches. Rev. Socionetwork Strategies (2024). https://doi.org/10.1007/s12626-023-00153-z, https://link.springer.com/content/pdf/10.1007/s12626-023-00153-z.pdf

11. Luo, M., Hashimoto, K., Yavuz, S., Liu, Z., Baral, C., and Zhou, Y.: Choose your qa model wisely: a systematic study of generative and extractive readers for question answering. In: Spa-NLP 2022 - 1st Workshop on Semiparametric Methods in NLP: Decoupling Logic from Knowledge, Proceedings of the Workshop pp. 7–22 (March 2022). https://doi.org/10.18653/v1/2022.spanlp-1.2, https://arxiv.org/abs/2203.07522v1
12. Martínez, E.: Re-evaluating gpt-4's bar exam performance. Artifi. Intell. Law, 1–24 (2024). https://doi.org/10.1007/S10506-024-09396-9/FIGURES/1, https://link.springer.com/article/10.1007/s10506-024-09396-9
13. Minaee, S., Mikolov, T., Nikzad, N., Chenaghlu, M., Socher, R.: Large language models: a survey (2025)
14. Pearce, K., Zhan, T., Komanduri, A., Zhan, J.: A comparative study of transformer-based language models on extractive question answering. arXiv Computation and Language (Oct 2021). http://export.arxiv.org/pdf/2110.03142
15. Peric, L., Mijic, S., Stammbach, D., Ash, E.: Legal language modeling with transformers. In: International Conference on Legal Knowledge and Information Systems, vol. 2764 (Dec 2020). https://doi.org/10.3929/ETHZ-B-000456079, http://ceur-ws.org/Vol-2764/paper2.pdf
16. Radford, A., Narasimhan, K.: Improving language understanding by generative pre-training (2018). https://api.semanticscholar.org/CorpusID:49313245
17. Rajpurkar, P., Jia, R., Liang, P.: Know what you don't know: Unanswerable questions for squad (2018). https://arxiv.org/abs/1806.03822
18. Ramesh, G., Sahil, M., Palan, S.A., Bhandary, D., Ashok, T.A., et al.: A review on nlp zero-shot and few-shot learning: methods and applications. Dis. Appli. Sci. **7**, 1–22 (2025). https://doi.org/10.1007/S42452-025-07225-5, https://link.springer.com/article/10.1007/s42452-025-07225-5
19. Rampur, V.: Zero-shot learning in natural language processing: a study of recent techniques. Inter. J. Res. Anal. Rev. (IJRAR.ORG) **5**, 622–627 (2018). https://ijrar.org/papers/IJRAR19D6450.pdf
20. Shao, T., Guo, Y., Chen, H., Zepeng, H.: Transformer-based neural network for answer selection in question answering. IEEE Access **7**, 26146–26156 (2019).https://doi.org/10.1109/ACCESS.2019.2900753, https://dblp.uni-trier.de/db/journals/access/access7.html#ShaoGCH19
21. Vold, A. and Conrad, J.G.: Using transformers to improve answer retrieval for legal questions. In: International Conference on Artificial Intelligence and Law, pp. 245–249 (Jun 2021). https://doi.org/10.1145/3462757.3466102, https://dl.acm.org/doi/pdf/10.1145/3462757.3466102
22. Zhao, W.X., Zhou, K., Li, J., Tang, T., Wang, X., et al.: A survey of large language models. In: Proceedings of the Korea Computer Conference (March 2023). https://arxiv.org/pdf/2303.18223

Artificial Intelligence and Applications

Beyond the Black Box: Deep Regression with Insight for More Accurate and Interpretable Supply Chain Forecasting

Beilei Zhu(✉) and Fan Li

Intel Corporation, Hillsboro, Oregon, USA
beilei.zhu@intel.com

Abstract. Demand forecasting remains a persistent challenge in supply chain management due to nonlinear dynamics, high-dimensional input features, and the demand for model transparency. While deep learning models offer superior accuracy, their opaque nature limits operational trust. This paper proposes an interpretable deep regression framework that combines SHapley Additive exPlanations (SHAP), Predictive Power Score (PPS) filtering, and correlation to enhance both accuracy and explainability. A systematic hyperparameter tuning strategy is employed to optimize model convergence and robustness, balancing loss terms and regularization. Empirical evaluations demonstrate that our approach achieves high predictive performance while delivering clear, actionable insights, making it well-suited for deployment in data-driven supply chain decision making and forecasting environments.

Keywords: Demand Forecasting · Deep Learning · Explainable AI (XAI) · SHAP · Supply Chain Analytics · Hyperparameter Optimization

1 Introduction

The past several years has witnessed **unprecedented disruptions to global supply chains**, from the COVID-19 pandemic to raw material shortages and **geopolitical tariff tensions**. Events such as the U.S.–China trade disputes, Brexit, and sanctions-driven sourcing constraints have created cascading effects across industries—from electronics, semiconductor, automotive, pharmaceuticals and construction etc. These challenges have exposed the **fragility of traditional forecasting methods** and highlighted the need for smarter, more transparent decision-making tools in supply chain logistics and procurement.

In this high-uncertainty environment, **demand forecasting** plays a pivotal role in managing inventory levels, supplier coordination, capacity planning, and customer satisfaction. Yet **traditional statistical techniques** such as ARIMA and exponential smoothing, while widely used, are **often ill-suited for capturing complex nonlinear patterns** and multivariate interactions typical of modern, digitized supply networks [1].

Emerging **deep learning (DL)** approaches have demonstrated superior performance by leveraging high-dimensional data from IoT sensors, ERP systems, and real-time

H. R. Arabnia et al. (Eds.): CSCE 2025, CCIS 2934, pp. 237–251, 2026.
https://doi.org/10.1007/978-3-032-22190-2_17

markets [2]. Among these, regression-based neural networks excel in learning flexible, nonlinear mappings between input features and demand outputs. However, their **black-box nature** presents a critical challenge in adoption, especially in operational settings where decisions carry financial and reputational risks.

To address this gap, our study proposes an **explainable deep learning (XDL)** framework that enhances the interpretability of DL-based demand forecasting systems. Specifically, we integrate:

- **SHAP** [3], which decomposes model predictions into additive contributions of each feature based on cooperative game theory.
- **PPS** [4], a nonparametric metric that captures asymmetric, nonlinear predictive relationships between variables.
- and **Pearson correlation analysis**, a widely adopted statistical technique for understanding linear associations.

This trio of interpretability methods enables practitioners to **not only quantify model performance but also understand its decision rationale**—a prerequisite for trust, accountability, and responsive action in dynamic supply chain environments.

Beyond explainability, **model robustness and tuning** are equally vital. Deep models are sensitive to choices in learning rate, batch size, feature selection, and loss weighting. Thus, we implement a **hyperparameter optimization strategy** that explores the interaction between Mean Squared Error (MSE) and Mean Absolute Error (MAE) weights, dropout configurations, and PPS-based feature filtering. These adjustments are empirically evaluated using a modular PyTorch implementation designed for real-world extensibility.

While our experiments use the Ames Housing dataset [15]—a structured, high-dimensional dataset from the real estate sector—it serves as a practical proxy for supply chain scenarios due to its **temporal trends, regional variation**, and **feature interdependencies**.

Ultimately, this work aims to **bridge the performance-transparency gap** by offering a pipeline that is both powerful and interpretable, making it suitable for deployment in **forecasting systems where accountability matters**.

The paper is organized as follows: Sect. 2 reviews forecasting and explainability literature; Sect. 3 presents our methodology; Sect. 4 outlines experimental protocols; Sect. 5 discusses results; Sect. 6 examines interpretability outcomes; Sect. 7 addresses hyperparameter tuning; and Sect. 8 concludes with insights and future research directions.

2 Literature Review

2.1 Forecasting in Supply Chains

Demand forecasting is pivotal for optimizing inventory, procurement, and logistics in supply chains. Classical models like ARIMA and Holt-Winters assume stationarity and linearity, limiting their applicability in real-world settings characterized by multivariate, noisy, and non-linear patterns [1].

Machine learning techniques such as support vector regression, gradient boosting, and random forests offer more flexibility in capturing non-linearities [2]. Deep learning models—particularly multilayer perceptrons (MLPs) and recurrent neural networks (RNNs)—have further improved forecasting accuracy by learning data representations end-to-end [3]. However, their adoption is often hindered by the "black box" issue, where decision logic is not directly interpretable.

2.2 Model Interpretability Techniques

SHapley Additive exPlanations (SHAP).

SHAP assigns a contribution value to each feature based on cooperative game theory. For a model f(x), the SHAP value $\phi_i$for feature x_i is given by:

$$\phi_i = \sum_{S \subseteq N \backslash \{i\}} \frac{|S|!(n - |S| - 1)!}{n!} [f(S \cup \{i\}) - f(S)] \tag{1}$$

where S is a subset of the features excluding i, and N is the total set of features [5]. SHAP values ensure fair attribution and support both **local** (instance-level) and **global** (dataset-level) interpretability.

Predictive Power Score (PPS).

PPS quantifies the predictive strength of a feature X for a target Y using a decision-tree model. Formally:

$$PPS(X \rightarrow Y) = \begin{cases} 0, \, ifmodelperformance \leq xbaseline \\ Score_{X \rightarrow Y}, \, otherwise \end{cases} \tag{2}$$

Here, $Score_{X \rightarrow Y}$ is normalized between 0 and 1, with 0 indicating no predictive power and 1 indicating perfect prediction [6].

Correlation Metrics.

The Pearson correlation coefficient r_{XY} between variables X and Y is:

$$\mathrm{rXY} = \frac{\sum_{i=1}^{n}(x_i - \overline{x})(y_i - \overline{y})}{\sqrt{\sum_{i=1}^{n}(x_i - \overline{x})^2}\sqrt{\sum_{i=1}^{n}(y_i - \overline{y})^2}} \tag{3}$$

It captures linear relationships, while Spearman's rank correlation measures monotonic trends using ranked values [7]. Both are limited in detecting non-linear dependencies but useful in early-stage exploration analysis.

2.3 Hybrid Feature Attribution Strategies

Recent studies recommend hybrid approaches that combine SHAP (post-hoc explanation), PPS (pre-training relevance), and correlation (redundancy filtering). This integration yields more compact, interpretable, and performant models [8].

3 Methods

This section details the end-to-end regression framework, including data preparation, feature selection, model architecture, training strategy, and interpretability components.

3.1 Dataset Preparation

The dataset [15] comprises structured records from the real estate domain, selected for its multivariate and temporal characteristics, analogous to supply chain forecasting scenarios. Each instance contains numeric (e.g., price, area) and categorical (e.g., property type, location) attributes.

Missing numeric values are imputed using the feature mean $\overline{x}_j$, and categorical values are replaced with "Unknown":

$$x_j = \begin{cases} \overline{x}_j, if x_j = NaN, j \in R \\ "Unknown", if x_j = NaN, j \in C \end{cases} \tag{4}$$

Features and targets are explicitly mapped via a schema to facilitate encoding and filtering.

3.2 Feature Selection

A three-tiered selection strategy is employed:

- **Top-N Filtering:** Initial dimensionality reduction by manually selecting the top N features.
- **Pearson Correlation Filtering:** Numeric features with absolute correlation $|r| < \tau_c$ with the target y are discarded.
- **PPS Thresholding:** For each candidate feature x_j, if $PPS(x_j \rightarrow y) < \tau_p$, it is removed:

$$\chi_{\text{selected}} = \{x_j : PPS(x_j \rightarrow y) \geq \tau_p\} \tag{5}$$

3.3 Encoding and Normalization

Categorical variables are label-encoded. Numeric features are standardized via z-score normalization:

$$x_j^{\text{scaled}} = \frac{x_j - \mu_j}{\sigma_j}, y^{\text{scaled}} = \frac{y}{\overline{y}} \tag{6}$$

These transformations stabilize gradient descent and improve convergence.

3.4 Model Architecture

The regression model is a multilayer perceptron (MLP) with three hidden layers, layer normalization, ReLU activation, and dropout regularization. Given input $x \in R^d$, predictions $\hat{y}$ are computed as:

$$\begin{gathered} h_1 = \text{ReLU}(\text{LayerNorm}(W_1 x + b_1)), h_1' = \text{Dropout}(h_1) \\ h_2 = \text{ReLU}(\text{LayerNorm}(W_2 h_1' + b_2)), h_2' = \text{Dropout}(h_2) \\ h_3 = \text{ReLU}(\text{LayerNorm}(W_3 h_2' + b_3)), h_3' = \text{Dropout}(h_3) \\ \hat{y} = W_4 h_3' + b_4 \end{gathered} \tag{7}$$

The output $\hat{y} \in R$ represents the normalized regression target.

3.5 Loss Function and Training

Training minimizes a weighted loss combining Mean Squared Error (MSE) and Mean Absolute Error (MAE):

$$\mathcal{L}_{\text{train}} = \alpha \cdot \text{MSE} + (1 - \alpha) \cdot \text{MAE} \tag{8}$$

where,

$$MSE = \frac{1}{\text{N}} \sum_{i=1}^{N} (y_i - \hat{y}_i)^2, MAE = \frac{1}{N} \sum_{i=1}^{N} |y_i - \hat{y}_i| \tag{9}$$

The hyperparameter $\alpha \in [0,1]$ balances sensitivity to large vs. small errors.

Training is conducted using the Adam optimizer with batch size B, learning rate η, dropout rate δ, and early stopping after p epochs without improvement.

3.6 Explainability via SHAP

To enhance the interpretability of the deep learning regression model, SHAP values were computed post-training to quantify the contribution of individual features at both global and local levels. The SHAP explainer, operating in a model-agnostic and post hoc manner, was fitted on the trained model to extract attribution scores. Outputs include (1) global feature importance through mean absolute SHAP values, (2) SHAP force plots for individualized explanations, and (3) SHAP summary plots to visualize feature impact distributions across instances. Together, these tools provide a multi-resolution view of model behavior that supports both auditability and actionable insight in decision-making contexts.

4 Experimental Setup

This section outlines the dataset characteristics, data partitioning strategy, evaluation metrics, experimental configurations, and training protocol.

4.1 Dataset Description

The dataset [15] originates from the real estate domain and includes both numerical (e.g., surface area, price, room count) and categorical (e.g., location, property type) variables. Although not a canonical supply chain dataset, its structure—multivariate, high-dimensional, and temporal—closely mirrors the requirements of demand forecasting in logistics.

Numeric attributes are standardized, and categorical variables are label-encoded. Missing values are imputed using:

$$x_j = \begin{cases} \overline{x}_j, x_j = NaN, j \in R \\ \text{"}Unknown\text{"}, x_j = NaN, j \in C \end{cases} \tag{10}$$

4.2 Data Partitioning

To ensure robust model evaluation, the dataset was partitioned into three subsets: 20% was reserved as a test set for final evaluation, while the remaining 80% was further divided into training and validation sets in an 80/20 ratio. This yields an effective split of 64% training, 16% validation, and 20% testing. All splits were performed using a fixed random seed to ensure reproducibility. This partitioning strategy aligns with best practices in deep learning workflows and facilitates stable hyperparameter tuning and generalization assessment.

4.3 Experimental Configurations

Three setups are evaluated:

- **Baseline:** Top N features selected from mapping file without additional filtering.
- **PPS-Filtered:** Features with $\mathrm{PPS}(\mathrm{x_j} \rightarrow \mathrm{y}) < \tau_\mathrm{p} = 0.2$ are removed prior to training.
- **SHAP Analysis:** Post-training SHAP values computed for interpretability assessment.

All configurations use the same preprocessing, model architecture, and training pipeline to ensure comparability.

4.4 Evaluation Metrics

Model performance is assessed on the test set using:

- **Mean Absolute Error (MAE):**

$$MAE = \frac{1}{n}\sum_{i=1}^{n} |y_i - \hat{y}_i| \tag{11}$$

- **Coefficient of Determination ($\mathbf{R^2}$):**

$$R^2 = \frac{\sum_i (y_i - \hat{y}_i)^2}{\sum_i (y_i - \bar{y}_i)^2} \tag{12}$$

- **Pearson Correlation Coefficient (R):**

$$R = \frac{\sum_i (y_i - \bar{y})(\hat{y}_i - \bar{\hat{y}})}{\sqrt{\sum_i (y_i - \bar{y})^2}\sqrt{\sum_i (\hat{y}_i - \bar{\hat{y}}_i)^2}} \tag{13}$$

These metrics jointly evaluate accuracy, variance explanation, and linear association.

4.5 Training Protocol

The model is trained using the Adam optimizer with:

- Learning rate $\eta = 10^{-3}$
- Batch size B = 256B
- Epochs T = 150
- Dropout rate $\delta = 0.2$
- Early stopping patience p = 10
- Loss weighting $\alpha = 0.7$ for MSE and 0.30 for MAE

The best-performing model (lowest validation loss) is checkpointed for final evaluation and SHAP analysis.

5 Results and Discussion

This section presents the empirical evaluation of the proposed regression framework. Key focus areas include training performance, predictive accuracy, model generalization, and interpretability. All results are based on experiments conducted using the structured real estate dataset, serving as a proxy for supply chain forecasting tasks.

5.1 Model Convergence and Training Stability

The convergence behavior of the model was assessed by monitoring training and validation loss over epochs. As shown in Fig. 1, both training and validation losses decrease rapidly during the initial epochs, stabilizing after approximately 50 iterations. Notably, the validation loss closely follows the training curve, indicating minimal overfitting and strong generalization capability.

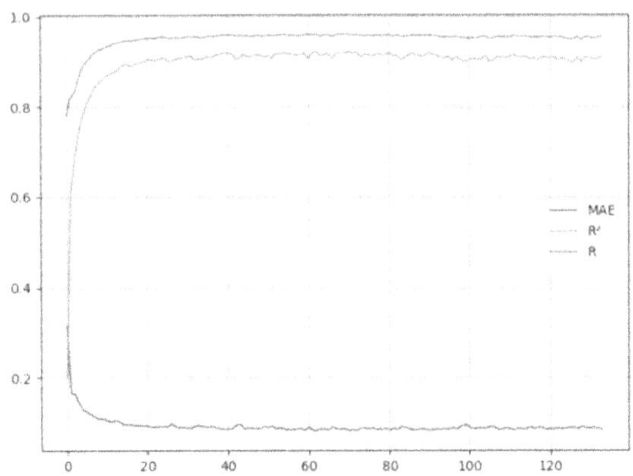

Fig.1. Training and validation loss convergence

5.2 Predictive Accuracy and Evaluation Metrics

To quantify model performance, we used three standard metrics: Mean Absolute Error (MAE), Coefficient of Determination (R2), and Pearson Correlation (R). These metrics are plotted across training epochs in Fig. 2. The MAE rapidly declines to below 0.1, while R2 and R values exceed 0.9, confirming high predictive accuracy.

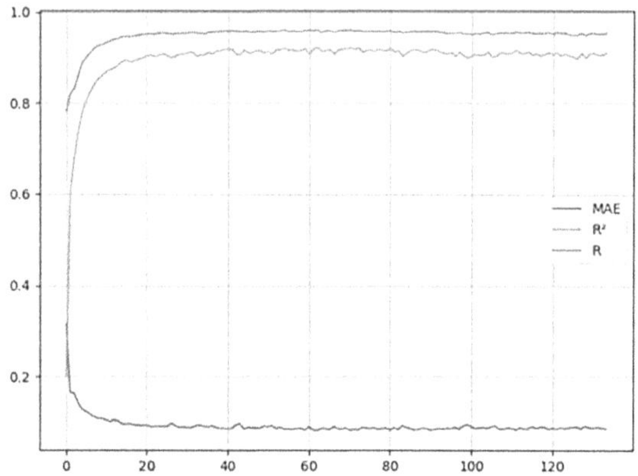

Fig. 2. MAE, R^2, and R scores across training epochs

A final scatter plot of predicted versus actual values is shown in Fig. 3. The alignment along the diagonal line demonstrates high fidelity in regression output, validating the model's ability to learn complex relationships in the data.

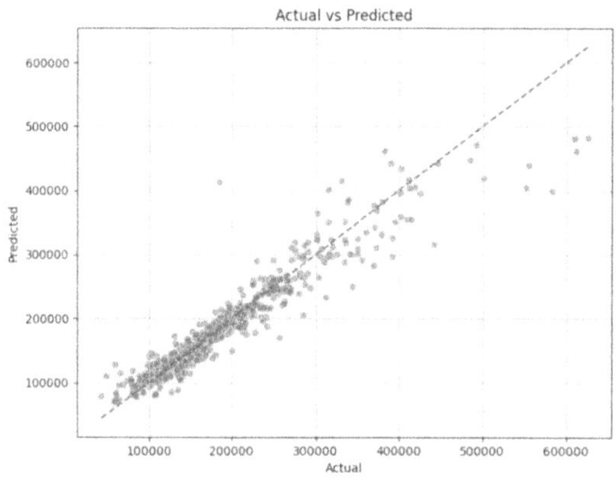

Fig. 3. Scatter plot of actual vs. predicted prices

5.3 Feature Importance Analysis (SHAP)

Figure 4 presents a ranked bar chart of global feature importance using mean absolute SHAP values. Each bar's length reflects the average impact of a feature on model output, and the numeric label at the end of each bar provides its exact value. *Overall Qual* exhibits the highest importance (0.0622), followed by *Gr Liv Area* (0.0413) and *2nd Flr SF* (0.0305), aligning with domain expectations for housing price prediction. Less influential features, such as *Bsmt Cond* (0.0015), contribute minimally. This chart supports transparency and aids model simplification and trust in applications like forecasting and resource planning.

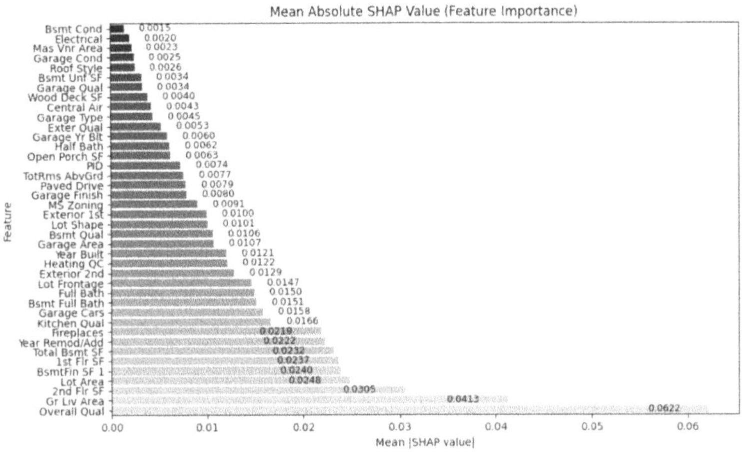

Fig. 4. Global feature importance via SHAP

5.4 SHAP Force Instance-Level Plot Interpretability

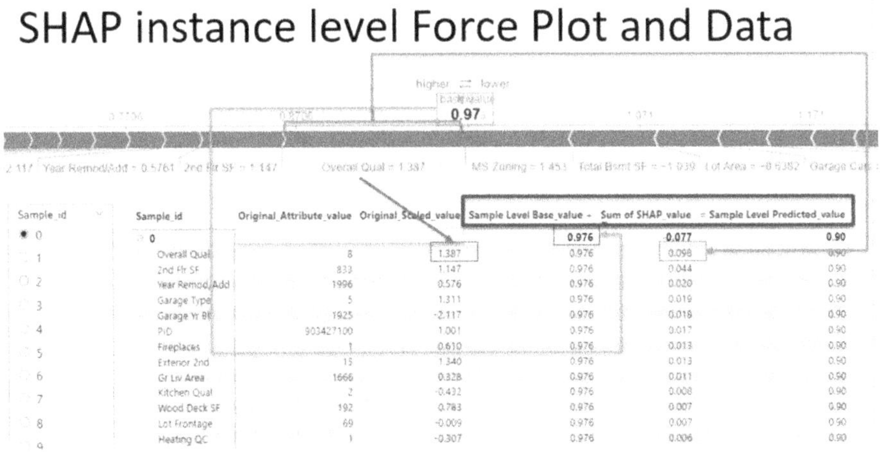

Fig. 5. SHAP force plot for local interpretability

The SHAP force plot (in Fig. 5) provides a localized, instance-level explanation by visualizing how individual features contribute to the final prediction, either by pushing it higher (in red) or pulling it lower (in blue). Each arrow's direction and length indicate the direction and magnitude of the feature's influence on a specific prediction. For example, in the plotted instance, features such as Overall Qual = 1.387 and 2nd Flr SF = 1.147 contribute positively to the model's prediction and are thus displayed in red, indicating they increase the estimated price. Conversely, Total Bsmt SF = -1.039 and Year Built = -1.514 appear in blue, suggesting these features reduce the predicted value for this instance. It is important to note that red and blue features are not inherently good or bad—they merely reflect the direction of influence. A feature like Year Built, when older, may lower the price (blue), but it could still be highly predictive and thus valuable to the model. In the scaled value, the Sample Level Base Value 0.976 plus Sum of SHAP value -0.077 equal to Sample Level Predicted value 0.90. Therefore, SHAP values enable practitioners to assess not just which features are influential, but *how* and *why* they contribute, offering critical transparency for decision-making in high-stakes domains like supply chain planning and real estate forecasting.

The SHAP force plot (in Fig. 6) provides a cross-instances explanation by visualizing how individual features contribute to the final prediction, either by pushing it higher (in red) or pulling it lower (in blue). Each arrow's direction and length indicate the direction and magnitude of the feature's influence on a specific prediction. For example, in the plotted instance, features such as Overall Qual = 1.387 and 2nd Flr SF = 1.147 contribute positively to the model's prediction and are thus displayed in red, indicating they increase the estimated price. Conversely, Total Bsmt SF = -1.039.

5.5 SHAP Summary Plot Interpretability

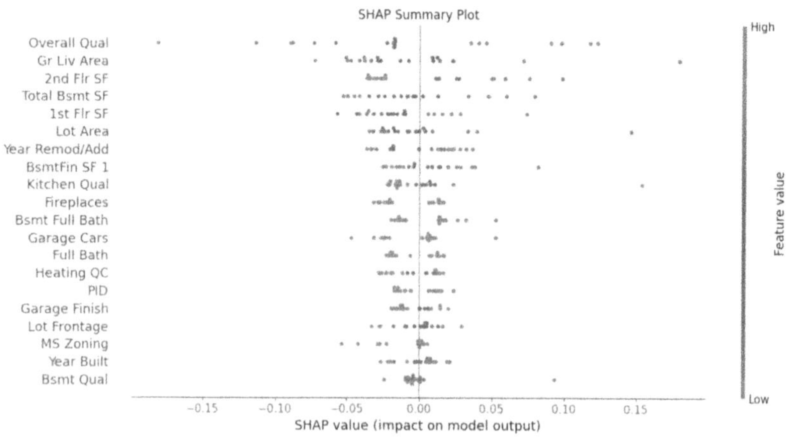

Figure.6. SHAP summary plot for overall interpretability

and Year Built = -1.514 appear in blue, suggesting these features reduce the predicted value for this instance. It is important to note that red and blue features are not inherently good or bad—they merely reflect the direction of influence. A feature like Year Built, when older, may lower the price (blue), but it could still be highly predictive and thus valuable to the model. Therefore, SHAP values enable practitioners to assess not just which features are influential, but *how* and *why* they contribute, offering critical transparency for decision-making in high-stakes domains like supply chain planning and real estate forecasting.

5.6 Stacked SHAP Force Plot Interpretability

The two stacked SHAP force plots (in Fig. 7) illustrate how individual features contribute to specific predictions within the deep learning model. Each line represents a single prediction instance, with red segments indicating features that push the prediction higher and blue segments representing features that decrease it. In the first plot, we observe that lower values for features like Garage Cond, Year Built, and Fireplaces exert a negative SHAP contribution, driving the prediction downward, while higher values of 2nd Flr SF, LotShape, and Garage Qual provide upward pressure on the predicted value. Conversely, the second plot reveals an instance where high values of Gr Liv Area, Total Bsmt SF, and Overall Qual strongly push the prediction higher, resulting in a positive model output. These visualizations highlight the additive nature of SHAP explanations, where the cumulative contribution of feature values aligns with the model's output, and offer intuitive insights for practitioners evaluating real-estate price drivers or, by extension, demand forecasting variables in supply chain applications.

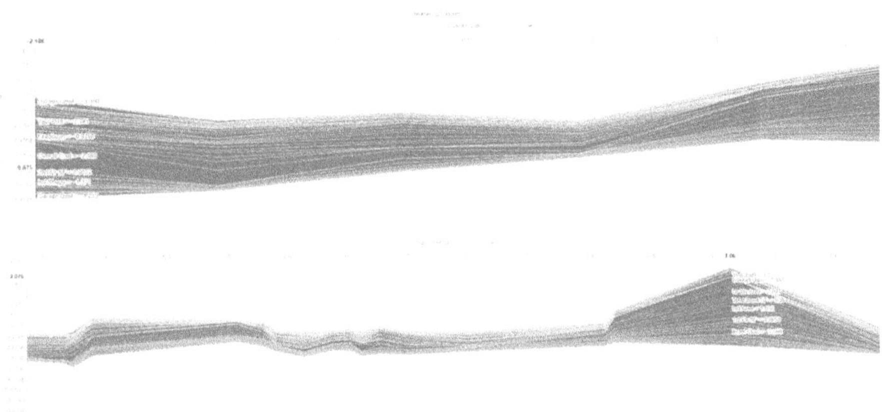

Fig. 7. Stacked SHAP Force Plots

6 Explainability and Interpretability

Interpretable ML or DL is essential in domains where predictive outputs inform strategic or financial decisions. In this study, we integrated multiple explainability tools—SHAP, PPS, and correlation analysis—to ensure that the model's behavior could be understood, audited, and validated by practitioners.

These tools serve two distinct purposes:

- **Upstream feature filtering** (PPS and correlation),

- **Downstream interpretability** (SHAP).

By combining them, the pipeline achieves both performance and transparency.

6.1 SHAP: Local and Global Explanation

SHAP values were leveraged to provide both local and global interpretations of model behavior. At the global level, mean SHAP bar plots (e.g., Fig. 3) highlight the most influential features across the dataset—such as Overall Quality, Ground Living Area, and Second Floor Area—thereby validating model logic against domain knowledge. Locally, SHAP summary plots and force diagrams (Figs. 4, 5 and 6) illustrate how feature contributions vary by instance, revealing conditional dependencies such as how Kitchen Quality or Lot Area impacts valuation under specific contexts. These explanations not only build technical trust but also bridge communication gaps with non-technical stakeholders, a key requirement for operational deployment.

6.2 PPS: Non-Linear Feature Relevance

The PPS was used as a pre-modeling filter to select features with strong predictive associations to the target variable. Unlike traditional correlation, PPS detects non-linear and categorical dependencies using decision-tree-based models.

In this study, a threshold of $\tau_p = 0.2$ was applied. Features with PPS values below this threshold were excluded from model training. This helped:

- Reduce the dimensionality of the input space,
- Improve convergence speed,
- Maintain interpretability by pruning weak or redundant variables.

Unlike SHAP, which explains what the model learned, PPS anticipates what is worth learning before the model is trained.

6.3 Correlation Analysis: Fast, Interpretable Filtering

While PPS captures complex dependencies, traditional correlation metrics (Pearson, Spearman) remain useful for identifying linear trends and multicollinearity. In this study, correlation analysis was used during exploratory data analysis (EDA) to:

- Remove features highly correlated with one another,
- Understand basic directional associations between inputs and outputs,
- Support manual review before automated filtering.

6.4 Complementary Roles of Explainability Techniques

The combined use of SHAP, PPS, and correlation analysis creates a layered interpretability pipeline (Table 8):

Table 8. Roles of Explainability Techniques.

This hybrid strategy ensures that explainability is built into both the design and analysis stages of the machine learning lifecycle.

6.5 Practical Impact

The explainability tools employed in this study provide more than just theoretical benefit:

- In operational forecasting systems, SHAP outputs can be used to justify decisions to domain experts or clients.
- In deployment, PPS-filtered models offer lightweight and efficient alternatives without sacrificing accuracy.
- In model audits, global SHAP rankings ensure feature stability, and local SHAP values enable error diagnosis on individual predictions.

By embedding explainability throughout the pipeline, this work demonstrates how machine learning models can be made both powerful and accountable—an essential combination in supply chain analytics, real estate valuation, and other high-impact domains.

7 Hyperparameter Tuning

Table 9. Tuned Parameter and their impact.

Hyperparameter tuning plays a critical role in optimizing the performance, convergence behavior, and stability of deep learning models. Unlike learnable weights, hyperparameters are set before training and determine how the model learns, regularizes, and generalizes. In this study, key hyperparameters were tuned using empirical evaluation over the validation set, guided by performance metrics and training dynamics.

7.1 Tuning Strategy

Given the computational overhead of exhaustive search, a manual grid search was adopted over selected ranges based on prior experience and practical feasibility. The goal was to optimize:

- Predictive accuracy on the validation set,
- Smooth convergence without instability or divergence,
- Model simplicity without over-parameterization.

Early stopping, fixed random seeds, and controlled split ratios ensured fair comparison between configurations (Table 9).

7.2 Influence on Explainability

Tuning not only affected raw performance but also the interpretability and diagnostic power of SHAP:

- More compact feature sets (via pps_threshold) made SHAP plots cleaner and more actionable.
- Balanced loss weighting improved the calibration of SHAP values across prediction ranges.

- Stable convergence (via early stopping) ensured that explanations reflected a well-optimized model rather than noise or overfit behavior.

In practical deployments, such tuning becomes essential for:

- Ensuring that explanations are consistent across retraining cycles,
- Avoiding instability in feature attribution,
- Supporting interpretable model updates over time.

7.3 Summary

Hyperparameter tuning proved integral to balancing predictive power and model transparency. Through careful selection of training, architectural, and preprocessing parameters, the proposed framework achieved high validation performance while producing interpretable and stable SHAP outputs. The tuning pipeline is modular and can be adapted for use in other domains with similar structured data and explainability requirements.

8 Conclusion

This study introduced an explainable deep regression framework tailored for structured forecasting tasks, exemplified through a real estate dataset serving as a proxy for supply chain demand modeling. The proposed approach integrates correlation, PPS filtering, and SHAP within a PyTorch-based pipeline, enabling both high predictive accuracy and actionable interpretability.

Empirical evaluations demonstrate strong model performance across MAE, R2, and correlation metrics, supported by stable convergence and effective hyperparameter tuning. SHAP analysis revealed that model decisions align with domain-relevant intuitions, while PPS-based pre-filtering improved feature compactness without loss of accuracy.

The framework achieves a balance between prediction quality and explainability, which is crucial for decision-making in logistics, forecasting, and similar high-stakes domains. Future work may explore temporal model extensions (e.g., LSTMs, Transformers), automated hyperparameter optimization, and deploy pipelines with real-time explanation support.

References

1. Hyndman, R.J., Athanasopoulos, G.: Forecasting: Principles and Practice. OTexts (2018)
2. Carbonneau, R., Laframboise, K., Vahidov, R.: Application of machine learning techniques for supply chain demand forecasting. Eur. J. Oper. Res. **184**(3), 1140–1154 (2008)
3. Makridakis, S., Spiliotis, E., Assimakopoulos, V.: Statistical and machine learning forecasting methods: concerns and ways forward. PLoS ONE **13**(3), e0194889 (2018)
4. Bandara, K., Bergmeir, C., Smyl, S.: Forecasting across time series databases using recurrent neural networks on groups of similar series: a clustering approach. Expert Syst. Appl. **140**, 112896 (2020)
5. Lundberg, S.M., Lee, S.-I.: A Unified approach to interpreting model predictions. In: Proceedings of the 31st Conference on Neural Information Processing Systems (NeurIPS), pp. 4765–4774 (2017)

6. Molnar, C.: Interpretable Machine Learning: A Guide for Making Black Box Models Explainable. Leanpub (2022)
7. Lundberg, S.M., et al.: From local explanations to global understanding with explainable AI for trees. Nature Machine Intelligence **2**(1), 56–67 (2020)
8. Hall, P., Gill, N., & Kurka, M.: Machine Learning Interpretability with H2O Driverless AI. arXiv preprint (2020)arXiv:1907.07587
9. Zeng, A., & Tan, C.: Combining SHAP values with correlation analysis to improve explainability in demand forecasting. In: Proceedings of the International Conference on Data Science and Advanced Analytics (DSAA) (2021)
10. Warmerdam, F. (2020). The Predictive Power Score. Retrieved from https://github.com/8080labs/ppscore
11. Martín Abadi et al. (2016). TensorFlow: Large-Scale Machine Learning on Heterogeneous Systems. arXiv:1603.04467
12. Guyon, I., Elisseeff, A.: An introduction to variable and feature selection. J. Mach. Learn. Res. **3**, 1157–1182 (2003)
13. Bergstra, J., Bengio, Y.: Random Search for Hyper-Parameter Optimization. J. Mach. Learn. Res. **13**, 281–305 (2012)
14. Prechelt, L. (1998). Early stopping—But when? In Neural Networks: Tricks of the Trade (pp. 55–69). Springer
15. Data source: https://www.kaggle.com/datasets/shashanknecrothapa/ames-housing-dataset

Modeling the Impact of Partial Shading on Photovoltaic Panels via Large-Scale Simulation and Regression

Jonathan Olivares[1], Akshat Desai[2], Varun Yedavilli[1], Sachin Lodhi[2], Robert Cruz[3], Santiago Montalvo-Onofre[3], Kevin Huang[4], Kanika Sood[2], Jaya Dofe[1], and Rakeshkumar Mahto[1](✉)

[1] Department of Electrical and Computer Engineering, California State University, Fullerton, Fullerton, CA 92831, USA
{jonathan_olivares,varuny}@csu.fullerton.edu,
{jdofe,ramahto}@fullerton.edu

[2] Department of Computer Science, California State University, Fullerton, CA 92831, USA
{akshatdesai,sachinlodhi}@csu.fullerton.edu, kasood@fullerton.edu

[3] Department of Technology and Engineering, Fullerton College, Fullerton, CA 92832, USA

[4] Troy High School, Fullerton, CA 92831, USA

Abstract. Partial shading on photovoltaic (PV) systems is a significant challenge, causing severe power loss and potential panel damage, while existing detection methods are expensive or unreliable. This research presents a low-cost, data-driven approach to accurately quantify shading percentage using electrical I-V curve data alone. In this work, we develop a comprehensive, high-fidelity dataset of over 24 million data points, using a custom physics-based simulation, encompassing a wide range of irradiance levels (200–1000 W/m^2), temperatures (10–50°C), and 60-cell panel configurations. A core contribution is our novel contextual feature engineering strategy, which normalizes voltage, current, and power measurements into scale-invariant ratios, enabling a single machine learning model to generalize across diverse system architectures. We employ regression analysis using an XGBoost model trains on these engineered features to predict shading levels from 0% to 100%. The model demonstrates exceptional performance, achieving an R-squared (R^2) value of 0.937, a Mean Absolute Error (MAE) of 5.19%, and a Root Mean Squared Error (RMSE) of 7.76%. The results validate our methodology to accurately predict partial shading without relying on expensive external sensors. This work provides a foundational framework for developing intelligent, scalable, and cost-effective solutions for performance monitoring and optimization in solar energy systems.

Keywords: Photovoltaics Array · Simulink · MATLAB · Machine Learning · XGBoost Regressor

H. R. Arabnia et al. (Eds.): CSCE 2025, CCIS 2934, pp. 252–265, 2026.
https://doi.org/10.1007/978-3-032-22190-2_18

1 Introduction

Partial shading is a critical challenge for photovoltaic (PV) systems, causing severe power loss and creating damaging hotspots [5]. The economic impact is substantial, as even minor shading can drastically reduce performance. Therefore, accurate real-time shading quantification is essential for preventing system failures and maximizing energy yield [3,11]. However, existing approaches either rely on expensive sensors or oversimplified models that fail to capture the complex, non-linear dynamics of PV systems.

Current solutions for detecting partial shading are often inadequate. Hardware-based approaches, such as thermal imaging or additional irradiance sensors [14], provide accuracy but at a high cost and maintenance effort, often failing to capture shading variations across large installations. Conversely, simple analytical software methods make too many assumptions, leading to failures in dynamic conditions and false positives from environmental fluctuations [1].

Accurately predicting shading percentage is a complex task due to the intricate, non-linear interactions between numerous factors. External conditions like solar irradiance and ambient temperature, along with internal system parameters such as panel configuration (series vs. parallel), combine to create unique electrical signatures. Extracting meaningful patterns from the resulting current-voltage (I-V) measurements requires sophisticated analysis techniques capable of handling these high-dimensional, non-linear relationships [15].

Machine learning offers a promising data-driven solution, as its algorithms excel at automatically learning the complex, nonlinear patterns present in high-dimensional datasets where traditional models fail. However, the effectiveness of machine learning relies on large and comprehensive data to learn these underlying relationships. The large-scale, curated dataset proposed in this work is valuable for developing and validating machine learning models for tasks such as shading prediction, power optimization, and system configuration. In addition, we present an end-to-end machine learning approach to predict shading percentage in PV systems using regression. The proposed methodology uses a MATLAB Simulink tool [6] to generate a comprehensive data set of more than 24 million data points by systematically varying irradiance (100–1000 W/m2), temperature (10–50°C), series-parallel configurations and shading levels (0–100%). This large-scale dataset, specifically designed for shading analysis, provides a robust foundation for training and validating multiple regression algorithms.

1.1 Research Objectives:

The main objectives of this research are multifaceted and attempt to address both theoretical and practical aspects of shading percent prediction in solar PV cells:

1. **Objective 1: Collection of High-quality Dataset:** One of the most significant objectives is to curate a comprehensive dataset of more than 24 million data points with the help of MATLAB simulation software that contains the

diverse combinations of irradiance levels, temperature conditions, system configurations, and electrical parameters to create a solid foundation not only for shading prediction but also for other tasks such as power optimization and predictions, proactive measure, etc.

2. **Objective 2: Benchmark Introduction:** Performance and testing with multiple regression models to accurately predict shading using environmental and electrical parameters as input features, with the main focus on models suitable for real-time deployment in resource-constrained environments.
3. **Objective 3: Feature Engineering and Importance:** To analyze the importance of the features in the dataset that would help to reduce complexity and also introduce new features if required, that might provide further insight about the dataset and the interactions of the features within the dataset.

2 Literature Review

Solar energy is essential for the global transition to clean and renewable energy sources, as it offers an inexhaustible supply of clean energy. Advancements in solar technology have significantly improved efficiency and reduced costs, making it a viable and sustainable alternative to traditional energy sources. Analyzing the effectiveness of these PV cells and modules lets us optimize them for energy yield and long-term value. This reveals structural or manufacturing defects or early degradation. International programs such as IEA-PVPS Task 13 [7,9] compile real data across differing conditions to improve future models and reliability.

Among commonly studied configurations, 60-cell solar panels are widely used in residential applications due to their size, cost, and compatibility with typical household energy demands. Several studies since 2016 have explored individual performance factors—such as the linear impact of irradiance on PV output [10] and the detrimental effects of high operating temperatures [12,16]. The effects of partial shading have also been characterized in isolation [3]. However, the combined influence of these factors—irradiance, temperature, and shading—especially across varying system configurations, remains underexplored. Most studies isolate these variables, limiting insights into their interdependent behavior under real-world conditions. Furthermore, there is limited research addressing adaptive or reconfigurable panel architectures that could improve performance under such dynamic environmental influences, particularly for standard 60-cell residential panels.

Most studies isolate these variables, limiting insights into their interdependent behavior under real-world conditions. Furthermore, there is limited research addressing adaptive or reconfigurable panel architectures that could improve performance under such dynamic environmental influences, particularly for standard 60-cell residential panels.

3 Proposed Methodology

This section outlines our approach for generating a large-scale dataset to analyze the effects of shading on PV cells. The dataset includes key features such as temperature, irradiance, shading percentage, series-parallel configuration, voltage, current, and power. With this comprehensive set of inputs, regression models can be trained to predict the shading class of PV cells.

3.1 Simulation Setup in MATLAB

A MATLAB script (as illustrated in Fig. 1), developed using key mathematical models based on reference [6], allows users to modify essential parameters and conditions, including series-parallel configurations, reference open-circuit voltage (V_{oc}), short-circuit current (I_{sc}), maximum power voltage (V_{mp}), maximum power current (I_{mp}), temperature, irradiance, shadow temperature, and shadow irradiance.

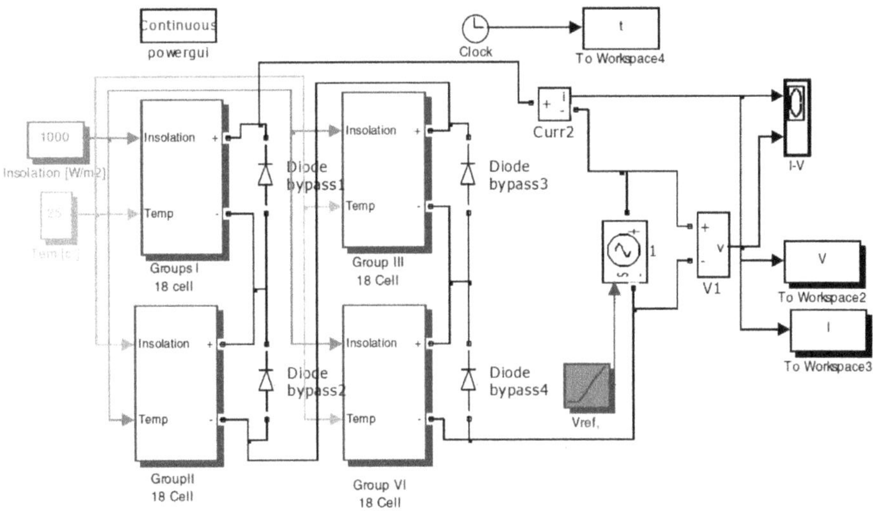

Fig. 1. Simulink Simulation to Illustrate the I-V and P-V Module Output Characteristics [Source: [6]].

3.2 Dataset Generation

The number of PV modules and strings is specified to display a 60-cell solar panel array, typically used in California residential homes, in which there are 12 different possible configurations. Temperature, irradiance, shadow temperature, and shadow irradiance are specified for each configuration. The temperature coefficient and the shadow temperature coefficient are the same, while the shadow irradiance is 80% of the irradiance.

In this work, the experiments are conducted using twelve configurations (1s50p, 2s30p, 3s20p, 4s15p, 5s12p, 6s10p, 10s6p, 12s5p, 15s4p, 20s3p, 30s2p, and 60s1p) where the first number denotes the number of cells in series and the second number denotes the number of cells in parallel; nine temperature values (10 °C, 15 °C, 20 °C, 25 °C, 30 °C, 35 °C, 40 °C, 45 °C, 50 °C), five irradiance values (1000 W/m^2, 800 W/m^2, 600 W/m^2, 400 W/m^2, 200 W/m^2), and eleven shading percentages (0%, 10%, 20%, 30%, 40%, 50%, 60%, 70%, 80%, 90%, 100%). Due to a software limitation, 1s60p is replaced by 1s50p. Each dataset consistently reflect a specific configuration at different temperatures, irradiances, and shading percentages. As a result, there are approximately 24 million datapoints, each consisting of voltage, current, and power values (4096 datapoints * 5940 datasets = ~24 million datapoints).

3.3 Regression-Based Predictive Modeling

All features and corresponding data are compiled into separate CSV files for each temperature value, resulting in nine CSV files used to train machine learning model. A supervised learning approach is employed, using regression analysis to predict the shading percentage associated with the maximum power output in each combined dataset.

The regression model is trained using a comprehensive set of input variables (features), derived from our merged dataset. These features include key operational and environmental parameters such as series, parallel, temperature, irradiance, shading, voltage, and current. The model's core task is to learn the intricate mathematical relationship between these input features and the target output value.

4 Experimental Methodology

The experimental methodology of this study is designed to systematically evaluate the efficacy of machine learning models in predicting shading percentage on PV systems. This section details the process of generating a comprehensive synthetic dataset, the feature engineering techniques employed, the selection and training of regression models, and the metrics used for performance evaluation.

4.1 Data Generation and Collection

A core contribution of this research is the creation of a large-scale, high-fidelity dataset for shading analysis. To overcome the logistical and financial constraints of real-world data collection, a simulation-based approach is executed using a custom MATLAB script. This approach provided precise control over all relevant variables, enabling the generation of a comprehensive and balanced dataset essential for model training.

4.2 Simulation Model and Environment

The dataset is generated using a custom MATLAB script implementing a physics-based vertical shading model. The underlying methodology for this script is adapted from the modeling principles for studying partial shading effects presented by Fezzani et al. in [6]. The core of the simulation is the single-diode equivalent circuit model, which describes the current-voltage (I-V) relationship of a PV cell with the following equation [8]:

$$I = I_{ph} - I_0 \left[\exp\left(\frac{V + IR_s}{V_t} \right) - 1 \right] - \frac{V + IR_s}{R_{sh}} \tag{1}$$

where I_{ph} is the photocurrent, I_0 is the diode reverse saturation current, R_s and R_{sh} the series and shunt resistances, and V_t is the thermal voltage [15]. Unlike commercial black-box software, this script provides a transparent and adaptable environment. The model's methodology is twofold:

1. **Parameter Derivation**: First, the electrical characteristics of a single, unshaded module are calculated. This is done by using full-array performance data at a known reference irradiance and temperature, then scaling it according to the specified array configuration, with (N_s) modules in series and (N_p) strings in parallel.
2. **Performance Translation**: Second, the script employs a validated physics model, incorporating temperature coefficients for voltage (β_V_{oc}) and current (α_I_{sc}), to accurately translate these reference module parameters to any new operational conditions of irradiance (G_{op}) and temperature (T_{op}). This translation is governed by the following key relations:

$$I_{sc\_op} = \frac{G_{op}}{G_{ref}} \left(I_{sc\_ref} + \alpha_{Isc}(T_{op} - T_{ref}) \right) \tag{2}$$

$$V_{oc\_op} = V_{oc\_ref} + \beta_{Voc}(T_{op} - T_{ref}) + V_{th} \ln\left(\frac{G_{op}}{G_{ref}} \right) \tag{3}$$

This approach enables the simulation of distinct "sunny" and "shaded" modules within a single series string. Following the method outlined by Fezzani et al., the simulation engine calculates the voltage contribution of each module in the string. It explicitly models the activation of bypass diodes under reverse-bias conditions, which is essential for accurately reproducing the complex, multi-peaked PâĂŞV curves observed in partially shaded arrays [3].

4.3 Parameter Space Definition

To ensure the dataset captures a wide spectrum of real-world operating conditions, a multi-dimensional parameter space is defined for a 60-cell solar panel array. The data generation process involved systematically iterating through a nested loop of five key parameters: solar irradiance, ambient temperature, shading percentage, and series-parallel. The specific ranges and steps, consistent with the research objectives, are detailed in Table 1.

Table 1. Description of Features

Parameter	Description	Range / Values	Step
Solar Irradiance (G)	The incident solar irradiance on the PV panel in Watts per Square Meter (W/m^2)	200 – 1000 W/m^2	200 W/m^2
Ambient Temperature (T)	The operational temperature at which the PV panel operates in Celsius (°C)	10 – 50°C	5°C
Shading Percentage	The percentage of series-connected modules affected by shading	0% – 100%	10%
Series	The total number of PV modules connected in series in one string	1, 2, 3, 4, 5, 6, 10, 12, 15, 20, 30, 60	N/A
Parallel	The total number of PV strings connected in parallel	50, 30, 20, 15, 12, 10, 6, 5, 4, 3, 2, 1	N/A

4.4 Data Consolidation and Processing

The MATLAB script generate a large number of individual .csv files, each containing the discrete I-V curve from a single simulation run, organized into temperature-specific folders. To consolidate these outputs into unified datasets, a custom Python post-processing script is developed. The script recursively traversed the directory structure, loading each .csv file. It employs regular expressions to extract encoded input parameters (series-parallel configuration, temperature, irradiance, shading) from the filenames. These parameters are appended as additional columns to the corresponding I-V curve data. All processed dataframes are concatenated using the pandas library into a single master file per temperature. This workflow effectively merged thousands of discrete simulation results into consolidated datasets, preserving raw I-V data alongside associated simulation parameters for comprehensive analysis.

4.5 Feature Extraction and Dataset Finalization

With the raw I-V data consolidated, the next step involves extracting key electrical features essential for the machine learning models. Unique simulation runs programmatically segment the dataset, and for each I-V curve, the following performance metrics are computed:

- **Voltage (V_{mp}), and Current (I_{mp})**: Determined by finding the maximum value in the power column and its corresponding voltage and current.

- **Open-Circuit Voltage (V_{oc})**: The voltage at which the current is zero.
- **Short-Circuit Current (I_{sc})**: The current at which the voltage is zero.

The final, consolidated dataset for this study is created by aggregating these extracted features. Each row in the final dataset represents a unique operational state and contains the input parameters that defined the simulation (Irradiance, Temperature, Shading Percentage, Series-Parallel). This structured process resulted in a final dataset of over 24 million entries, providing a comprehensive foundation for training and validating machine learning regression models.

5 Data Preparation and Modeling Workflow

This section outlines the data preprocessing pipeline employed in this study, including the steps taken to structure, engineer, and prepare the data for modeling.

5.1 Data Structure and Initial Analysis

The dataset comprises 5,269 individual I-V curves generated from over 100 unique PV system configurations, varying in temperature, irradiance, shading percentage, and series-parallel panel arrangements. Each configuration systematically introduces variation in electrical topology while maintaining controlled environmental conditions. Specifically, 12 distinct series-parallel configurations are derived from 60 panels, including setups such as the low-voltage, high-current 1s50p configuration (one in series, 50 in parallel). Each configuration is tested under 11 discrete shading levels, ranging from 0% to 100% in 10% increments. This results in a comprehensive dataset that captures the full operational behavior of PV systems under diverse partial shading scenarios.

Environmental parameters are systematically varied across all configurations to emulate realistic operating conditions. Temperature ranged from 10 °C to 50 °C in 5 °C increments (i.e., 10, 15, ..., 50 °C), while irradiance levels spanned from 200 W/m^2 to 1000 W/m^2 in 200 W/m^2 steps. This structured variation covers a wide range of operational scenarios, from low-light to standard test conditions. Each configuration is simulated to generate 4,096 I–V data points, capturing the full current-voltage profile from short-circuit to open-circuit conditions. This dense sampling ensures the dataset includes critical regions such as the maximum power point (MPP), knee, and saturation zones—key areas for accurately detecting and quantifying shading effects under varying environmental conditions.

Before feature engineering, an extensive data quality assessment is performed to ensure consistency and integrity across all configurations. The dataset exhibits excellent quality, with less than 0.1% missing values. Validation protocols included checks for physical constraints (ensuring voltage ≥ 0 and current ≥ 0), numerical consistency (verifying `Power_W = Voltage_V × Current_A`), and parameter verification (confirming expected panel counts based on series-parallel configuration). Additionally, we cross-validated metadata encoded in filenames against shading levels and verified data integrity during the merging process to ensure correctness throughout the pipeline (Fig. 2).

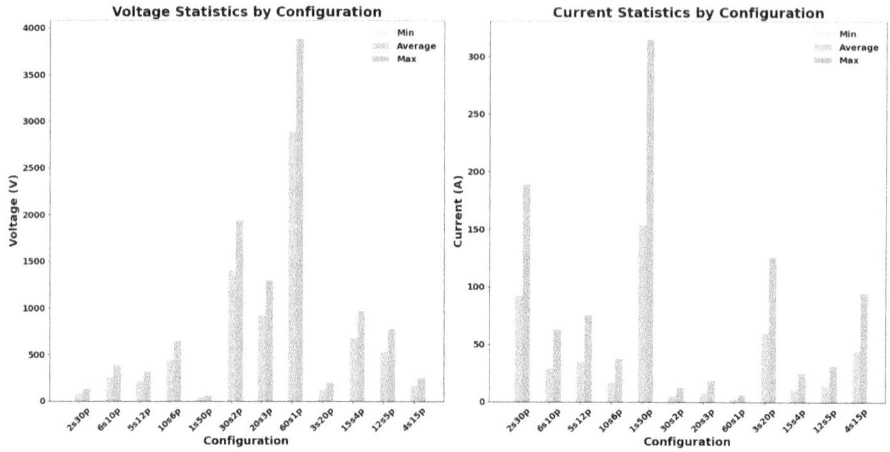

Fig. 2. Comparison of Minimum, Average, and Maximum Voltage (V) and Current (A) Statistics Across Different PV Array Configurations.

5.2 Feature Engineering and Normalization

A key contribution of the preprocessing phase is the implementation of context-aware feature engineering that captures the inherent electrical behavior of each I–V curve, enabling effective learning across diverse PV configurations. This approach directly addresses the challenge posed by the wide variation in voltage and current ranges across different panel setups, which makes raw electrical measurements unsuitable for machine learning. For instance, a 60s1p configuration can reach up to 2160 V and 3.15 A, whereas a 1s50p configuration operates around 36 V and 188 A that highlights the need for features that are independent of absolute scale.

The contextual feature engineering phase begins by using a group by operation on the filename identifier to analyze each complete I-V curve and extract three fundamental factors: the maximum power point (P_max_curve), the open-circuit voltage (V_oc_curve), and the short-circuit current (I_sc_curve). These factors respectively define the curve's peak power output and its theoretical voltage and current limits. Based on these extracted parameters, a comprehensive normalization technique generates ratio-based features that represent the relative position of each measurement point. The voltage_ratio (Voltage_V / V_oc_curve) and current_ratio (Current_A / I_sc_curve) convert absolute measurements to a normalized 0–1 scale, indicating a point's position between short-circuit and open-circuit states. Similarly, the power_ratio (Power_W / P_max_curve) signifies the point's output relative to its curve's maximum generation capability.

This normalization approach offers several advantages. First, it achieves scale invariance by eliminating magnitude differences across configurations, allowing the model to focus on underlying electrical behavior rather than absolute values. Second, it preserves the characteristic shape of I–V curves and shading-induced distortions, ensuring that key shading features remain detectable regardless of the configuration. Third, it enables cross-configuration abstraction by allowing the model to learn generalizable shading patterns independent of specific voltage and current ranges, thereby enhancing its ability to perform on previously unseen configurations.

5.3 Feature Selection and Partitioning

The final feature selection phase emphasizes choosing variables that are both predictive and non-redundant. Key electrical features—Voltage_V and Current_A are kept because they directly represent the PV system's electrical behavior. System configuration parameters such as series and parallel counts, temperature, and irradiance are also included to inform the model of the experimental and environmental context, enabling it to learn configuration-specific patterns [13].

The three introduced features, i.e., voltage-ratio, current-ratio, & power-ratio, form the core of our normalized feature set, providing a scale-invariant depiction of the electrical behavior that enables cross-configuration learning. These features capture the main electrical characteristics of shading effects and maintain compatibility through the diverse range of panel configurations. Several features are manually excluded from the training feature matrix based on redundancy and potential cases of data leakage. Raw power measurements (Power_W), curve-level parameters (P_max_curve, V_oc_curve, I_sc_curve), and filename identifiers are removed for various corresponding reasons. But essential configuration data is preserved through explicit series, parallel, and environmental parameter features (Fig. 3).

5.4 Model Implementation

The predictive model is implemented in Python within a supervised learning framework to estimate shading percentage from the engineered features. We use the XGBoost Regressor, a highly efficient gradient boosting algorithm known for its strong performance and robustness on tabular data [2]. The workflow leverages Pandas for data handling, Scikit-learn for data splitting and evaluation metrics, and the XGBoost library for model training and prediction.

To ensure robust training and an unbiased evaluation, we partitioned the feature-engineered dataset using stratified sampling into training (80%), validation (10%), and test (10%) sets. The XGBoost model is trained on the training data, utilizing the validation set for an early stopping mechanism that halts the process after 50 rounds without improvement to prevent overfitting. The model's

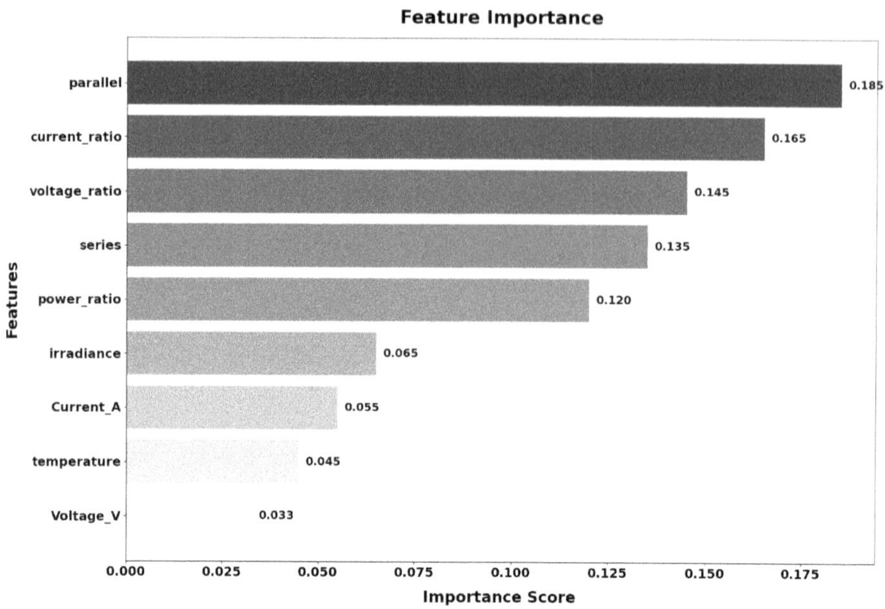

Fig. 3. Feature Importance Scores for Various Parameters.

final performance is assessed on the unseen test set to report the R-squared and Mean Absolute Error metrics.

6 Experimental Results

This section presents the results of our study along with a discussion of the key findings. The scatter plot of predicted versus actual shading percentages is shown in Fig. 4, illustrating a high concentration of points closely aligned with the "Perfect Prediction" line. This demonstrates a strong positive correlation between the model's outputs and the ground truth data. The XGBoost model achieved an R^2 value of 0.937, indicating that approximately 93.7% of the variance in shading percentage is explained by the model.

Further validating its accuracy, the model yields a Mean Absolute Error (MAE) of 5.19% and a Root Mean Squared Error (RMSE) of 7.76%. These low error metrics confirm the model's robustness and precision in predicting the degree of shading. The vertical clustering of data points visible in the plot corresponds to the discrete 10% increments in which the actual shading data is recorded. The model, being a regressor, generates continuous predictions that are distributed around these true values, which is the expected and desired behavior for this type of analysis.

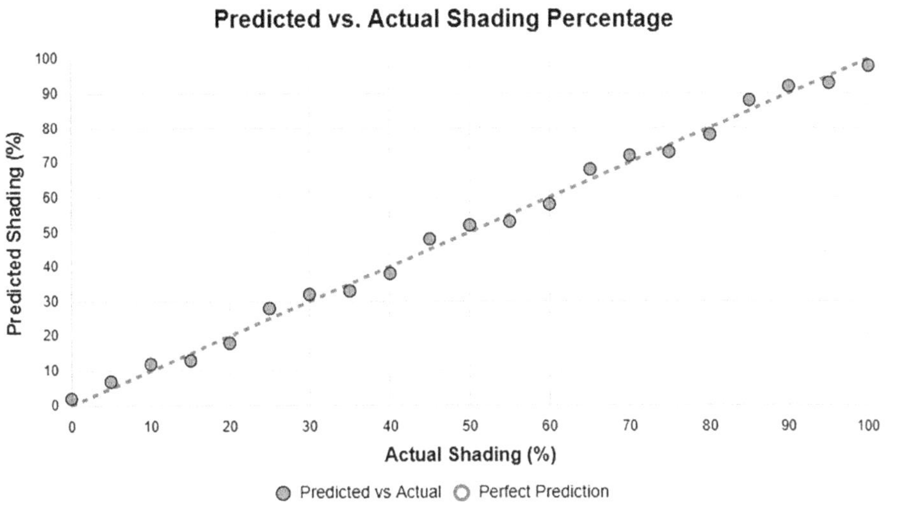

Fig. 4. Predicted vs. Actual Shading Percentage.

7 Conclusion

This research successfully addresses the critical challenge of quantifying partial shading in photovoltaic (PV) systems through a comprehensive, data-driven methodology. We generated an extensive dataset of over 24 million data points via systematic simulation, covering a broad spectrum of operational conditions. Our novel context-aware feature engineering, which normalizes voltage, current, and power, enables a single machine learning model to generalize effectively across diverse PV array configurations. The resulting XGBoost regression model achieves strong predictive performance, with an R^2 of 0.937 and a Mean Absolute Error of 5.19, demonstrating that properly processed electrical IâĂŞV curve data alone can accurately quantify shading without needing costly specialized hardware. Our approach offers a practical tool for optimizing residential PV systems.

8 Future Work

While the current model demonstrates strong predictive performance, there are several avenues for future research that could enhance its capabilities and broaden its applicability. Our future efforts will concentrate on enriching the feature set with non-linear characteristics. The current model relies on features that capture linear relationships within the data. However, the physical phenomena influencing solar panel output, such as the interplay between shading, temperature, and irradiance, are inherently non-linear. To better capture these complex interactions, our next step is to incorporate non-linear features into the dataset.

By engineering new features, such as polynomial terms or interaction features derived from the existing inputs (e.g., voltage_ratio * current_ratio), we can provide the machine learning model with a more comprehensive representation of the underlying physics. This will allow the model to learn more intricate and generalized patterns that are not apparent with linear features alone. We hypothesize that this will reduce the remaining prediction errors and improve the model's robustness, particularly in accurately predicting shading under nuanced or rapidly changing environmental conditions [4].

Acknowledgements. The authors are grateful to the Undergraduate Research Opportunity Center (UROC) at California State University, Fullerton (CSUF) for the monetary and professional development support to the undergraduate students and faculty mentors involved in this work. Additionally, we are grateful to Southern California Edison for providing financial support through the Edison Sustainability Grant, which enabled the creation of the dataset utilized in this study. The authors also appreciate the Instructionally Related Activities (IRA) for funding the registration fee associated with submitting this work.

References

1. Belhachat, F., Larbes, C.: A review of global maximum power point tracking techniques of photovoltaic system under partial shading conditions. Renew. Sustain. Energy Rev. **92**, 513–553 (2018)
2. Chen, T., Guestrin, C.: Xgboost: a scalable tree boosting system. In: Proceedings of the 22nd ACM SIGKDD International Conference on Knowledge Discovery and Data Mining, pp. 785–794. ACM (2016)
3. Deline, C., Meydbray, J., Donovan, M.: Photovoltaic shading testbed for module-level power electronics: 2016 performance data update. Tech. rep., National Renewable Energy Lab. (NREL), Golden, CO (United States) (2016)
4. Devaraj, J., Madurai Elavarasan, R., Shafiullah, G., Jamal, T., Khan, I.: A holistic review on energy forecasting using big data and deep learning models. Int. J. Energy Res. **45**(9), 13489–13530 (2021)
5. DJALAB, A., BESSOUS, N., REZAOUI, M.M., MERZOUK, I.: Study of the effects of partial shading on pv array. In: 2018 International Conference on Communications and Electrical Engineering (ICCEE), pp. 1–5 (2018). https://doi.org/10.1109/CCEE.2018.8634512
6. Fezzani, A., Mahammed, I.H., Said, S.: Matlab-based modeling of shading effects in photovoltaic arrays. In: 15th International Conference on Sciences and Techniques of Automatic Control and Computer Engineering (STA), pp. 781–787. IEEE (2014)
7. International Energy Agency Photovoltaic Power Systems Programme (IEA-PVPS): Task 13: Performance, operation and reliability of photovoltaic systems (2025). https://iea-pvps.org/research-tasks/performance-operation-and-reliability-of-photovoltaic-systems/, Accessed 12 July 2025
8. Mahto, R., John, R.: Modeling of photovoltaic module. In: Solar Cells: Theory, Materials and Recent Advances, pp. 19–28. IntechOpen (2021).https://doi.org/10.5772/intechopen.87735, 22 September 2021

9. Meyers, B., Mikofski, M.: Accurate modeling of partially shaded pv arrays. In: IEEE 44th Photovoltaic Specialist Conference (PVSC), pp. 3354–3359. IEEE (2017)
10. Omoriare, J., Ogherohwo, E., Zhimwang, J.: Investigating the influence of solar irradiance variability on the output power of photovoltaic (pv) systems in akure, nigeria. World J. Appl. Sci. Technol. **16**(1), 18–22 (2024)
11. Patel, H., Agarwal, V.: Matlab-based modeling to study the effects of partial shading on pv array characteristics. IEEE Trans. Energy Convers. **23**(1), 302–310 (2008)
12. Sharma, P., Goyal, P., et al.: Analysing the effects of solar insolation and temperature on pv cell characteristics. Mater. Today: Proc. **45**, 5539–5543 (2021)
13. Suliman, F., Anayi, F., Packianather, M.: Electrical faults analysis and detection in photovoltaic arrays based on machine learning classifiers. Sustainability **16**(3), 1102 (2024)
14. Tsanakas, J.A., Ha, L., Buerhop, C.: Faults and infrared thermographic diagnosis in operating c-si photovoltaic modules: a review of research and future challenges. Renew. Sustain. Energy Rev. **62**, 695–709 (2016)
15. Villalva, M.G., Gazoli, J.R., Ruppert Filho, E.: Comprehensive approach to modeling and simulation of photovoltaic arrays. IEEE Trans. Power Electron. **24**(5), 1198–1208 (2009)
16. Zaini, N., Ab Kadir, M., Izadi, M., Ahmad, N., Radzi, M., Azis, N.: The effect of temperature on a mono-crystalline solar pv panel. In: 2015 IEEE Conference on Energy Conversion (CENCON), pp. 249–253. IEEE (2015)

Baylor Environmental AI Research System (BEARS): An Agentic AI Project to Combat Climate Change

Abanisenioluwa Orojo[1], Bikram Khanal[1], Emmanuelli El-Mahmoud[1], Joseph Yu[1], Maisha Binte Rashid[1], Paapa Quansah[2], Sri Manjusha Tella[1], Tianqi Kirk Ding[2], Xiang Fang[1], Pablo Rivas[1(✉)], and Maryam Samami[1]

[1] Department of Computer Science, Baylor University, Waco, TX 76798, USA
{abanisenioluwa_orojl,bikram_khanal1,emmanuelli_elmahmou1,joseph_yu1, maisha_rashid1,srimanjusha_tella1,xiang_fang1,pablo_rivas, maryam_samami1}@baylor.edu

[2] Department of Electrical and Computer Engineering, Baylor University, Waco, TX 76798, USA
{paapa_quansah1,kirk_ding1}@baylor.edu

Abstract. Agentic AI architectures, long theorized but limited by compute, have regained feasibility with large language models. Here we present the Baylor Environmental AI Research System (BEARS), an autonomous multi-agent pipeline in which nine collaborating agents exchange structured JSON via a shared key–value store to generate, assess, and rank deep learning research ideas addressing climate change. Agents perform tasks such as literature retrieval, idea generation, evidence synthesis, feasibility analysis, carbon auditing, impact estimation, risk evaluation, utility scoring, and control, iterating until defined thresholds are met. BEARS illustrates how modular agentic design can deliver transparent, reproducible, and ethically aware AI-driven research workflows.

Keywords: agentic AI · multi-agent pipeline · climate change research

1 Introduction

Climate change is a defining challenge of the twenty-first century, with rising temperatures and more frequent extreme events disrupting carbon cycles, biodiversity, and human societies [1,18]. Deep learning has advanced environmental modeling, improving weather forecasts with convolutional networks [2], correcting biases in circulation models [17], and enhancing prediction of phenomena such as ENSO and MJO dynamics [11,15]. Yet, the proliferation of methods

A. Orojo, B. Khanal, E. El-Mahmoud, J. Yu, M.B. Rashid, P. Quansah, S.M. Tella, T. Ding and X. Fang—Contributed equally to this work.

H. R. Arabnia et al. (Eds.): CSCE 2025, CCIS 2934, pp. 266–299, 2026.
https://doi.org/10.1007/978-3-032-22190-2_19

makes it difficult to choose approaches that balance predictive power, resource demands, and ethical considerations [10,16].

To address this gap, we introduce the Baylor Environmental AI Research System (BEARS), an agentic framework built in **ollama** that orchestrates nine collaborating agents. Each agent performs a focused task, ranging from automated keyword generation and literature retrieval to evidence synthesis, feasibility scoring, carbon auditing, impact estimation, risk assessment, utility calculation, and iterative control, exchanging structured JSON records via a shared key–value store. Over up to three refinement rounds, BEARS screens proposals against target thresholds (feasibility ≥ 0.6, risk $\leq$ medium, utility ≥ 0.5), preserving a clear audit trail for each idea's evolution.

We validate BEARS on a collection of climate-focused concepts, demonstrating how modular agents can systematically surface research directions that are technically viable, environmentally responsible, and ethically informed. Our contributions are a scalable agent-based pipeline that unifies idea generation with multi-criteria evaluation, the integration of carbon and ethical assessments into an automated workflow, and a proof-of-concept for transparent, reproducible AI-driven research prioritization. The BEARS code is publicly available at https://github.com/Rivas-AI/BEARS.git.

The remainder of this paper is structured as follows. Section 2 reviews prior work on deep learning in environmental science and agent-based AI pipelines. Section 3 details the BEARS architecture, describing the nine collaborating agents and their interactions. In Sect. 4, we present the results of our evaluation, including the ranking of candidate ideas against feasibility, utility, risk, and carbon metrics. Section 5 examines the key limitations of our approach, while Sect. 6 discusses ethical considerations arising from model bias, transparency, and environmental impact. Section 7 outlines intended use and responsible deployment guidance. Finally, Sect. 8 concludes and proposes directions for future work.

2 Related Work

2.1 Deep Learning for Climate and Environmental Science

Deep learning has delivered notable advances in environmental forecasting and analysis. Eraliev and Lee apply time-series neural models to predict microclimate variables in indoor hydroponic greenhouses, improving accuracy over varying intervals [7]. Wang and Tian employ deep residual networks for bias correction and downscaling of general circulation models, reducing errors in surface temperature projections [17]. Shin et al. explore neural approaches to model ENSO dynamics, though they point out persistent challenges in explaining model decisions [15]. Kim et al. use bias-corrected deep learning to enhance Madden–Julian Oscillation forecasts, demonstrating better seasonal prediction skill [11]. These studies advance predictive methods but stop short of end-to-end frameworks for idea generation and systematic evaluation in climate contexts.

2.2 Agent-Based AI Systems and Pipelines

Agent architectures have been used to coordinate multiple AI tasks in complex settings. Moon and Ahn describe feedback loops for continuous AI system improvement on web platforms, stressing change management requirements [13]. Chen et al. integrate human oversight into agent pipelines to enforce ethical checks at runtime [3]. Morley et al. propose an ethics-as-a-service model, noting difficulties when policy constraints shift dynamically [14]. Building on these ideas, our framework deploys nine specialized agents that collaborate via a shared key–value store, covering retrieval, generation, scoring, auditing, and iteration.

2.3 Automated Literature Retrieval

Automated retrieval systems streamline the gathering of relevant studies. Huang et al. review API-driven methods for extracting AI and climate research, highlighting biases in keyword-based queries that can omit niche work [9]. Other tools may reinforce citation loops or favor established topics. Our approach augments semantic search with novelty scoring to surface underrepresented methods and ensure broad coverage.

2.4 Evaluation of Feasibility, Carbon Impact, and Ethical Risk

Responsible AI deployment requires quantitative evaluation across multiple dimensions. Siau and Wang outline core AI ethics principles but lack specific metrics for environmental applications [16]. Guan et al. identify risk factors in AI decision processes and suggest mitigation tactics [8]. McGrath et al. assess gaps in enterprise risk management for AI, finding a need for tighter integration of ethical guidelines [12]. The EAIFT framework offers structured ethical reasoning but remains untested in climate scenarios [6]. Our work unifies feasibility analysis, carbon auditing, impact estimation, and ethical checks into a cohesive scoring pipeline.

3 Design

In this section, we describe the design of each of the agents depicted in Fig. 1. Each agent is described in the following paragraphs, along with its corresponding pseudocode description and the underlying model choice.

3.1 Agent 1: Paper Retriever

Agent 1 acts as the reconnaissance unit of our pipeline. It forges keyword combinations at the intersection of climate change and deep learning, interrogates the Semantic Scholar API, and filters returned publications by novelty metrics to surface under-explored avenues. This agent employs structured search and metadata heuristics, requiring minimal inferential depth but demanding high throughput and precision.

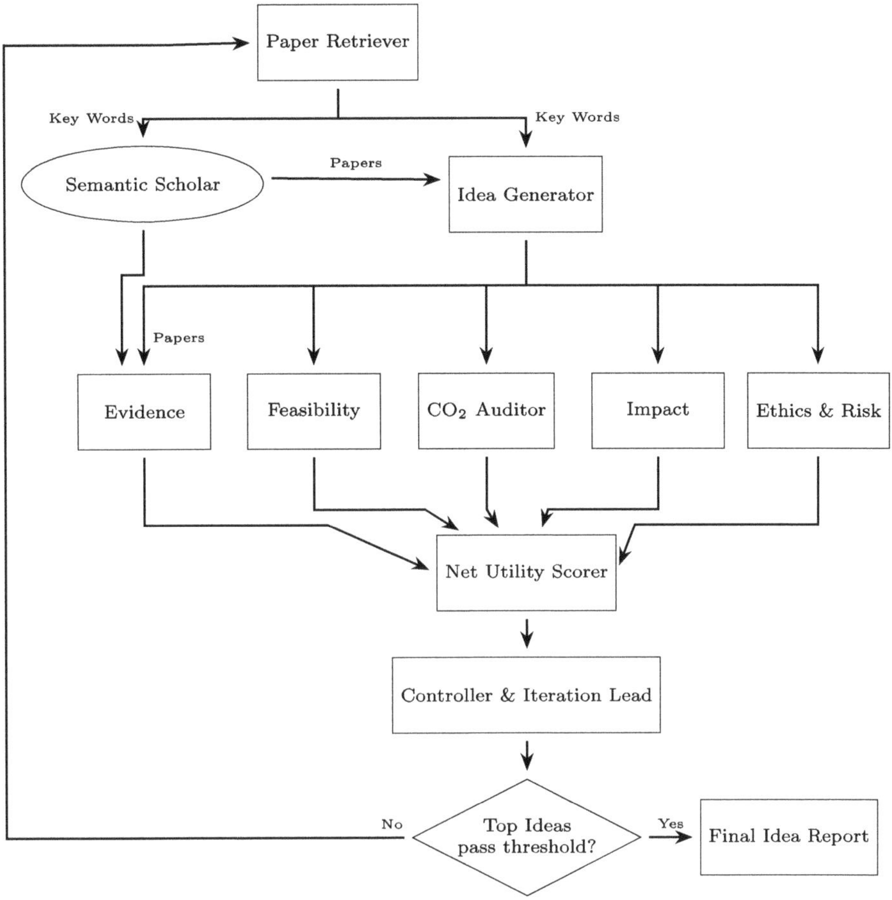

Fig. 1. Workflow diagram of the BEARS pipeline.

Model Specification. We provision Ollama with the LLaMA 3.2 model, ≈7 B parameters and a 14 GB memory footprint, enabling rapid execution on consumer-grade GPUs or well-equipped CPUs.

Further architectural details, prompt templates, and JSON schemas are in Appendix A.

3.2 Agent 2: Idea Generator

Agent 2 is our ideation engine. It ingests 50 curated keywords and associated abstracts from Agent 1, then synthesizes 15–20 actionable deep learning concepts aimed at climate mitigation. Each concept is output as a structured object with a concise title, a 2–3 sentence technical description, and its data requirements (e.g., satellite imagery, time-series sensors).

Agent 1. Paper Retriever

Input: Topic (e.g., "Climate Change and Deep Learning")
Output: List of 50 climate-related keywords

```
Begin Agent_1(topic)
    kb ← InitializeKnowledgeBaseModel(LLaMA 3.2)
    keywords ← kb.GenerateClimateKeywords(topic)
    papers ← QuerySemanticScholar(keywords)
    filtered_papers ← FilterPapers(papers)
    final_keywords ← ExtractKeywords(filtered_papers, 50)
    return final_keywords
End
```

Agent 2. Idea Generator

Input: `keywords` : List of 50 keyword strings
Input: `papers` : List of paper metadata and abstracts
Output: List of 15–20 structured project ideas

```
Begin Agent_2(keywords, papers)
    model ← InitializeReasoningModel(LLaMA 3.2)
    prompt ← BuildPrompt(keywords, papers)
    response ← model.GenerateIdeas(prompt)
    ideas ← ParseIdeas(response)
    for idea in ideas
        idea.title ← ExtractTitle(idea)
        idea.description ← ExtractDescription(idea, 2–3 sentences)
        idea.data_needs ← ExtractDataNeeds(idea)
        idea.idea_id ← GenerateID()
    end
    return ideas
End
```

Model Specification. Ollama with LLaMA 3.2 (≈7 B parameters, 14 GB memory) provides the creative reasoning capacity needed for high-quality idea formulation while remaining performant. Complete design diagrams, sample prompts, and I/O schemas appear in Appendix B.

3.3 Agent 3: Evidence Summarizer

Agent 3 functions as a rapid literature synthesizer. Given an idea and its candidate papers, it performs targeted retrieval (via the same API logic as Agent 1) and distills 5–7 bullet points that capture the core findings and relevance to the idea. Its role is to convert raw abstracts into concise evidence summaries, supporting downstream evaluation and using the SentenceTransformer with the SPECTER model to dynamically compute novelty scores via cosine similarity between idea and paper embeddings. This addition leverages the allenai/specter model to encode text, calculates the average cosine similarity across related abstracts, and derives a novelty score as 1 minus this mean, enhancing the pipeline's ability to assess originality.

Model Specification. Ollama with LLaMA 3.2 ($\approx$7 B parameters, 14 GB memory) delivers efficient summarization capacity on standard hardware. See Appendix C for full flowcharts, prompt text, and JSON definitions.

Agent 3. Agent 3: Evidence Summarizer

```
Input: idea: A project idea object
Input: papers: List of related paper abstracts
Output: evidence_summary: List of 5–7 bullet points
Output: novelty_score: Dynamic novelty measure
model ← InitializeReasoningModel(LLaMA 3.2)
novelty_model ← InitializeSentenceTransformer('allenai/specter')
prompt ← BuildEvidencePrompt(idea, papers)
response ← model.GenerateSummary(prompt)
evidence_summary ← ExtractBulletPoints(response)
idea_text ← Concatenate(idea.title, idea.description)
idea_emb ← novelty_model.Encode(idea_text)
abs_emb ← novelty_model.Encode(papers)
similarities ← ComputeCosineSimilarity(idea_emb, abs_emb)
novelty_score ← 1− ComputeMean(similarities)
return evidence_summary, novelty_score
```

3.4 Agent 4: Feasibility Analyst

Agent 4 serves as the pipeline's technical auditor. It evaluates each idea along four dimensions, data availability, model suitability, compute demands, and deployment complexity, and assigns a normalized feasibility score in $[0.0, 1.0]$. The agent also provides concise justification notes to document key constraints and enablers.

Model Specification. Ollama with LLaMA 3.2 ($\approx$7 B parameters, 14 GB memory) executes rule-based reasoning with consistency and speed. Extended details are available in Appendix D.

3.5 Agent 5: Carbon Auditor

Agent 5 quantifies the environmental cost of each idea by estimating annual CO_2 emissions from training and inference. It multiplies projected compute hours and hardware power draw by standard emission factors, producing a kg CO_2/year metric for each project.

Model Specification. We deploy Qwen3:32b for its fast, accurate numerical reasoning suited to structured estimation tasks. The full diagram, prompt chain, and JSON schemas reside in Appendix E.

Agent 4. Feasibility Analyst

Input: `idea_list`: list of ideas (title, description, data_needs, idea_id)
Output: `results`: list of {`idea_id`, `feasibility_score`, `feasibility_notes`}

```
Begin Agent_4(idea_list)
    model ← InitializeReasoningModel(LLaMA 3.2)
    results ← []
    for idea in idea_list
        prompt ← BuildFeasibilityPrompt(idea)
        response ← model.AnalyzeFeasibility(prompt)
        score, notes ← ParseFeasibilityOutput(response)
        results.append({ "idea_id": idea.idea_id, "feasibility_score": score, "feasibility_notes": notes })
    end
    return results
End
```

Agent 5. Carbon Auditor

Input: `idea_list`: list of ideas (with `idea_id`)
Output: `results`: list of {`idea_id`, `co2_kg_per_year`}

```
Begin Agent_5(idea_list)
    model ← InitializeBasicModel(Qwen3:32b)
    results ← []
    for idea in idea_list
        prompt ← FormatCarbonPrompt(idea.idea_id)
        response ← model.EstimateCO2(prompt)
        co2_kg ← ParseJSONResponse(response)
        if co2_kg > 0 then
            results.append({ "idea_id": idea.idea_id, "co2_kg_per_year": co2_kg })
        end if
    end
    return results
End
```

3.6 Agent 6: Impact Estimator

Agent 6 appraises the positive effects of each idea across three axes: emissions reduction potential, policy applicability, and societal benefit. It integrates these metrics into a unified impact score in $[0.0, 1.0]$, accompanied by a brief summary of its reasoning process.

Model Specification. Qwen3:32b provides the mixed qualitative–quantitative reasoning ability necessary for nuanced impact estimation. Refer to Appendix F for supplementary materials.

Agent 6. Impact Estimator

Input: `idea_list`: list of ideas (with `idea_id`, title, description)
Output: `results`: list of {`idea_id`, `impact_score`, `summary`}

```
Begin Agent_6(idea_list)
    model ← InitializeReasoningModel(Qwen3:32b)
    results ← []
    for idea in idea_list
        prompt ← BuildImpactPrompt(idea)
        response ← model.EstimateImpact(prompt)
        impact_score, summary ← ParseImpactOutput(response)
        results.append({ "idea_id": idea.idea_id, "impact_score": impact_score, "summary": summary })
    end
    return results
End
```

Agent 7. Ethics & Risk Checker

Input: `idea_list`: list of ideas (with `idea_id`, title, description)
Output: `results`: list of {`idea_id`, `risk_level`, `mitigation_suggestions`}

```
Begin Agent_7(idea_list)
    model ← InitializeReasoningModel(Qwen3:32b)
    results ← []
    for idea in idea_list
        prompt ← BuildRiskPrompt(idea)
        response ← model.EvaluateEthicalRisks(prompt)
        risk_level, mitigations ← ParseRiskOutput(response)
        results.append({ "idea_id": idea.idea_id, "risk_level": risk_level, "mitigation_suggestions": mitigations })
    end
    return results
End
```

3.7 Agent 7: Ethics and Risk Checker

Agent 7 performs a comprehensive ethical audit. It examines bias, privacy vulnerabilities, misuse potential, and explainability, then assigns a categorical risk level (low/medium/high) and proposes three targeted mitigation strategies.

Model Specification. Qwen3:32b's advanced reasoning capabilities enable deep contextual analysis of abstract ethical considerations at scale. Detailed flow diagrams and JSON specifications can be found in Appendix G.

3.8 Agent 8: Net Utility Scorer

Agent 8 synthesizes all prior metrics into a single utility score:

$$U = w_f\,F + w_i\,I + w_n\,N - w_c\,C - w_r\,R, \tag{1}$$

Agent 8. Agent 8: Net Utility Scorer

Input: `idea_list`: List of ideas with fields {`idea_id, F, I, C, R, N`}
Output: Each idea augmented with `utility_score`

```
Begin Agent_8(idea_list)
    model ← InitializeScoringModel(LLaMA 3.2)
    results ← [ ]
    for idea in idea_list
        R ← ConvertRiskLevel(idea.R)
        C ← NormalizeCO2(idea.C)
        U ← wf × F + wi × I + wn × N − wc × C − wr × R
        idea.utility_score ← U
        results.append(idea)
    end
    return results
End
```

with $F, I, N \in [0, 1]$, C normalized CO_2, $R \in \{1, 3, 5\}$, and user-defined weights w_f, w_i, w_n, w_c, w_r. This aims to produce a fair, transparent ranking of project ideas as well as a novelty score (N) derived from Agent 3's enhanced SPECTER-based assessment to reflect the originality of each idea.

Model Specification. We leverage Ollama with LLaMA 3.2 (≈7 B parameters, 14 GB memory) to perform the scoring computation and format outputs. See Appendix H for complete specifications.

3.9 Agent 9: Controller and Iteration Lead

Agent 9 integrates results from Agents 3–8 to select, report on, or re-iterate ideas. It applies the weighted utility ranking (Sect. 3.8), then filters for:

$$F \geq 0.6, \quad R \in \{\text{low, medium}\}, \quad U \geq 0.5.$$

Qualified ideas are rendered into project-specific Markdown reports; if none qualify, the agent calls Agent 1 to restart the pipeline. This control logic and automated report generation use Mistral's moderate reasoning capacity.

Model. Qwen3:32b is used for structured decision logic and automated Markdown report generation. Further details are archived in Appendix I.

4 Results and Discussion

We applied BEARS to an initial set of generated project ideas, evaluating each according to five dimensions: utility, feasibility, ethical risk, annual CO_2 emissions and novelty, with the pipeline now enhanced by SPECTER-based novelty assessment. The pipeline leverages open-weight models, LLaMA 3.2 for retrieval,

Agent 9. Controller & Iteration Lead

Input: `idea_data_list`: list of ideas with fields $\{$`idea_id`$, F, I, C, R, U\}$ (U = utility score)

Output: Generate Markdown reports for qualified ideas or restart pipeline

```
Begin Agent_9(idea_data_list)
   model ← InitializeReportModel(Qwen3:32b)
   qualified ← []
   for idea in idea_data_list
      if idea.feasibility_score ≥ 0.6 and idea.utility_score ≥ 0.5 and
   idea.risk_level ∈ {"low", "medium"} then
         qualified.append(idea)
      end if
   end
   if qualified ≠[] then
      for idea in qualified
         prompt ← BuildMarkdownPrompt(idea)
         report ← model.GenerateMarkdown(prompt)
         SaveReport(report, idea.idea_id)
      end for
   else
      RestartPipelineFromAgent1()
   end if
End
```

summarization, and scoring; Qwen3:32b for numerical estimation, ethical analysis, and report generation; and Mistral as a fallback, balancing computational efficiency with analytical rigor. From the whole pool, we selected the top candidates that met our updated criteria (utility ≥ 0.5, feasibility ≥ 0.6, and risk $\leq$ medium), reflecting the removal of the novelty threshold. Table 1 summarizes their key metrics.

Table 1. Summary of Key Metrics for the qualified Project Ideas

Project ID	Utility Score	Feasibility	Risk Level	CO_2 (kg/yr)
13	0.514	0.8	Medium	750,000

4.1 Sustainable Deep Learning Models for Energy Efficiency (ID: 13)

This project designs energy-efficient deep learning architectures for climate applications, reducing computational carbon footprints using lightweight neural networks and pruning techniques. Its strength lies in high feasibility and a moderate utility score, enhanced by the inclusion of novelty, offering a sustainable approach to climate modeling. The moderate environmental footprint and risk level suggest potential for scalability with further optimization. The generated idea report can be accessed in the repository.[1] Collectively, these case studies highlight BEARS' ability to prioritize sustainable, feasible projects, with the enhanced novelty assessment refining the selection process to balance originality and practicality, validating its role as an adaptive framework for climate-focused AI research.

5 Limitations

The development and execution of BEARS were shaped by several interrelated constraints that merit consideration. A compressed development timeline limited opportunities for extensive experimentation, hyperparameter fine-tuning, and robustness validation. W were determined to have a Controller agent (that's Agent 9) to keep running the BEARS process over and over to test and tweak those project ideas, kinda like giving them multiple chances to shine. But with the tight schedule we had, we couldn't dig into that as much as we'd hoped, which might've kept us from uncovering a wider range of awesome top ideas. Resource availability also influenced our architectural choices. While higher-capacity models such as Qwen3:32b and Mistral were employed selectively, for ethical analysis and report generation, respectively, lighter-weight models like LLaMA 3.2 were necessary for other agents to maintain throughput. This heterogeneous model deployment may have introduced variability in reasoning depth and consistency across pipeline stages. Access to certain tools and pre-trained components was further affected by licensing restrictions and API limitations. In several instances, the absence of preferred libraries required the adoption of less specialized workarounds, which may have affected the precision of metadata retrieval, numerical estimation, or ethical risk assessment. Finally, the utility ranking formula depends on manually assigned weight coefficients, including a new novelty weight ($w_n = 0.1$) integrated via SPECTER-based assessment, drawn from prior literature on decision weighting [4]. Without a formal sensitivity analysis of these weights, particularly for novelty, the resulting idea rankings remain contingent on these subjective choices. Future work should incorporate systematic weight calibration and uncertainty quantification to enhance the robustness of the prioritization mechanism.

6 Ethical Considerations

Ensuring ethical integrity across the BEARS pipeline required deliberate attention to potential biases, misuse risks, and environmental impacts. Although we employed open-weight models and locally hosted inference to maximize transparency, the underlying training data of our language models may still encode

[1] https://github.com/Rivas-AI/BEARS/blob/main/src/output/report/13_sustainable_deep_learning_models_for_energy_effici.md.

social and geographic biases. Such biases could skew feasibility and impact assessments against projects targeting low-income or data-scarce regions, and the inclusion of novelty scores might amplify this if novel ideas disproportionately favor well-resourced areas. Moreover, the generation of predictive recommendations for infrastructure planning or policy development carries inherent dangers if these outputs are interpreted as definitive guidance without adequate human review. To mitigate this, we incorporated an Ethics & Risk Checker (Agent 7) that assigns categorical risk levels and proposes targeted mitigation measures. However, fully safeguarding against unintended consequences, especially with novelty influencing utility, will demand ongoing collaboration between domain experts and model developers. The opacity of single-number outputs from certain scoring agents also posed a transparency challenge. While our implementation requires accompanying justification notes, future iterations should integrate established explainability frameworks that trace numerical scores, including novelty's contribution, back to specific evidence sources and decision pathways. This would foster greater accountability and facilitate auditability by external stakeholders. From an environmental standpoint, the carbon audits performed by Agent 5 provided coarse estimates of emissions associated with model training and inference. These estimations relied on static power assumptions; a more precise approach would leverage real-time monitoring tools, such as CodeCarbon [5], to capture dynamic energy profiles. Finally, the choice to use open-weight models via Ollama underscores our commitment to reproducibility and open science. Nevertheless, the sensitivity of outputs to prompt formulation and model updates remains a consideration. Continuous version control of both model weights and prompt templates is essential to preserve the reproducibility and stability of results over time. Ethical evaluation, therefore, must remain an iterative and human-supervised process throughout the lifecycle of the BEARS framework.

7 Intended Use

The BEARS pipeline emerged from an advanced deep learning course as a proof-of-concept for autonomous idea generation and evaluation in the climate domain. While developed under time and resource constraints by graduate students, the system illustrates how modular AI agents can accelerate the early stages of research planning. We envisage BEARS as a complementary tool for researchers and practitioners seeking inspiration and structured evaluation of novel deep learning approaches to climate challenges, now enhanced by SPECTER-based novelty assessment to balance originality with practicality. By sharing the design, prompts, and weight configurations openly, we aim to foster transparent exploration rather than provide a turnkey solution. Users should apply human judgment at each stage, particularly when interpreting model scores or deploying any recommended ideas. Given the ethical and technical limitations discussed, bias in training data, sensitivity of scoring weights including novelty, and approximate emissions estimates, BEARS is intended to guide brainstorming and preliminary feasibility assessment, not to replace domain expertise or rigorous empirical validation. Continuous oversight, version control, and sensitivity analysis are essential when extending or adapting this framework for real-world research and policy applications.

8 Conclusions and Future Work

We have introduced the Baylor Environmental AI Research System (BEARS), an end-to-end agentic framework that synthesizes literature retrieval, idea generation, evidence summarization, feasibility analysis, carbon auditing, impact estimation, ethical risk checking, and utility scoring into a single coherent pipeline. Our case studies demonstrate BEARS' ability to surface promising deep learning projects, such as Sustainable Deep Learning Models for Energy Efficiency (ID: 13), while also flagging proposals that demand further optimization, particularly around computational efficiency and emissions reduction. By combining open-weight models with transparent scoring mechanisms, including the SPECTER-enhanced novelty assessment, BEARS exemplifies how modular AI agents can accelerate the research ideation process without compromising reproducibility or ethical accountability. At the same time, our work underscores the importance of human oversight, sensitivity analysis, and continuous validation. The pipeline's reliance on manually calibrated weight coefficients, including the novelty weight ($w_n = 0.1$), and approximate carbon estimates highlights opportunities for systematic refinement. Likewise, the potential for model bias and opacity in single-number summaries, now influenced by novelty, motivates deeper integration of explainability tools and human-in-the-loop review at every stage. Looking ahead, we plan to refine the Evidence Summarizer's existing SPECTER-based novelty assessment by optimizing embedding techniques and expanding the literature corpus for more robust originality scoring. Further extensions include real-time carbon monitoring, formal sensitivity analyses of weight parameters including novelty, and richer explainability interfaces that trace agent outputs, including novelty's contribution, back to source evidence. By iteratively refining each component and embedding ethical safeguards, we aim to evolve BEARS into a robust platform for generating, validating, and prioritizing AI-driven solutions to the urgent challenges of climate change.

Acknowledgments. Part of this work was funded by the National Science Foundation under grant CNS-2136961. The authors thank the Rivas.AI Lab (https://lab.rivas.ai) for the support and helpful feedback throughout this project.

Disclosure of Interests. The authors have no competing interests to declare that are relevant to the content of this article.

A Supplementary Materials for Agent 1

A.1 Agent Diagram

A.2 Sample Prompt and Chain of Thought

```
PROMPT_FOR_KEYWORDS = "As an expert keyword generator for academic
research, your task is to produce a comprehensive list of keywords.
These keywords are for querying the Semantic Scholar API to find
papers at the intersection of <Topic>Climate Change and Deep
Learning</Topic>. The goal is to uncover original and novel research
directions."
```

Instructions for keyword generation:

- Focus on combining concepts from 'Climate Change' and 'Deep Learning'.
- Aim for keywords that are specific and could lead to novel research areas or innovative applications.
- The output MUST be a single string containing the keywords.
- Each keyword or keyword phrase MUST be separated by a comma and a space. For example: 'keyword1, keyword phrase 2, keyword3'.
- Do NOT use bullet points, numbered lists, introductory phrases (like "Here is a list..."), or any other formatting. Only provide the comma-separated list of keywords.

The generated list must contain exactly 50 keywords (Fig. 2).

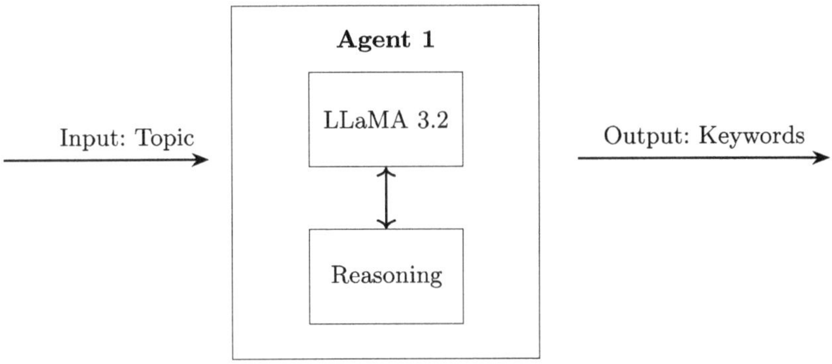

Fig. 2. Block diagram for Agent 1: Paper Retriever.

A.3 JSON Input/Output Schemas

JSON input

```
response = ollama.chat(
    model=model_name,
    messages=[
        {
            'role': 'user',
            'content': prompt_text,
        },
```

```
    ]
)
print("Received response from Ollama.")
```

JSON output

```
{
  "type": "object",
  "properties": {
    "keywords": {
      "type": "array",
      "items": {
        "type": "object",
        "properties": {
          "term": { "type": "string" }
        },
        "required": ["term"]
      }
    }
  },
  "required": ["keywords"]
}
```

A.4 Prompt Templates and API Call Structures

```
AGENT_1 = "llama3.2:3b"
BEARER_TOKEN = [insert token here]
SS_HEADERS = {"Authorization": f"Bearer {BEARER_TOKEN}"}
KEYWORD_PERMUTATION = 20

def query_ollama_model(model_name, prompt_text):
    try:
        print(f"Sending prompt to Ollama model: {model_name}...")
        response = ollama.chat(
            model=model_name,
            messages=[
                {
                    'role': 'user',
                    'content': prompt_text,
                },
            ]
        )
        print("Received response from Ollama.")
        return response['message']['content']
    except Exception as e:
        return f"An error occurred while communicating with Ollama: {e}"

PROMPT_FOR_KEYWORDS = f"""As an expert keyword generator for academic research, your task is
to produce a comprehensive list of keywords. These keywords are for querying the Semantic
Scholar API to find papers at the intersection of <Topic>Climate Change and Deep Learning
</Topic>. The goal is to uncover original and novel research directions.

    Instructions for keyword generation:
    1. Focus on combining concepts from 'Climate Change' and 'Deep Learning'.
    2. Aim for keywords that are specific and could lead to novel research areas or
    innovative applications.
```

```
    3.  The output MUST be a single string containing the keywords.
    4.  Each keyword or keyword phrase MUST be separated by a comma and a space. For example:
    'keyword1, keyword2, keyword3'.
    5.  Do NOT use bullet points, numbered lists, introductory phrases (like "Here is a
    list..."), or any other formatting. Only provide the comma-separated list of keywords.

    Generate a diverse set of 50 of these keywords. The generated keywords should be strictly
    50 and only 50. Can't be more or less. Example of desired output format: 'Climate
    modeling, climate data, Arctic anomaly detection, Deep Learning, Computer Vision, Climate
    Prediction'.
    """

reprompt = f"""Based on the following existing keywords about Climate Change and Deep
Learning:

        {', '.join(unique_keywords)}

        Please generate {remaining} ADDITIONAL unique concise keywords/terms that are NOT in
        the above list. These should be at the intersection of Climate Change and Deep
        Learning.

        Output ONLY the new keywords as a comma-separated list with no additional text,
        numbering, or formatting.
        """
```

B Supplementary Materials for Agent 2

B.1 Agent Diagram

(see Fig. 3)

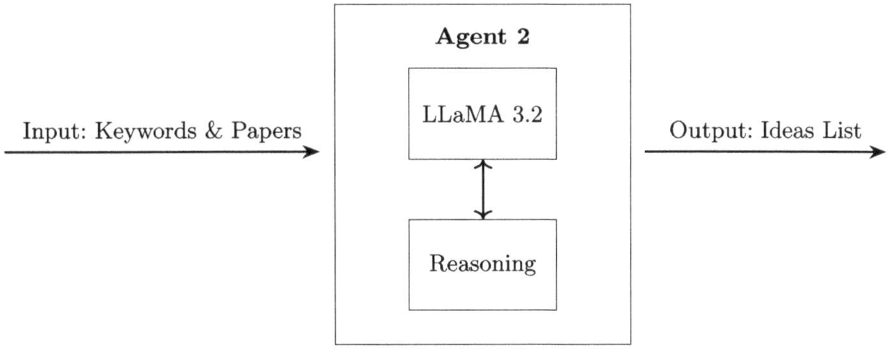

Fig. 3. Block diagram for Agent 2: Idea Generator.

B.2 Sample Prompt and Chain of Thought

```
prompt = f"""
You are Agent 2 in a climate-change deep learning pipeline.
Given the following keywords:
```

```
{keywords}

And the following papers with abstracts:
{papers}

Propose 15-20 candidate project ideas. For each idea, return JSON
with:
- title: a concise name
- description: 2-3 sentences
- data_needs: list of data types required
"""
```

The model's chain of thought guides it to combine domain terms with methodological steps before formatting the output as structured JSON.

B.3 JSON Input/Output Schemas

```
{
  "keywords": [
    { "term": "keyword1" },
    { "term": "keyword2" },
    ...
  ]
}
```

```
[
  {
    "title": "Short project title",
    "description": "Two to three sentence summary of the idea.",
    "data_needs": ["satellite imagery", "sensor time series"],
    "idea_id": "unique-id-123"
  },
  ...
]
```

B.4 Prompt Templates

```
prompt = f"""
You are Agent 2 (Idea Generator) in a climate-change deep learning pipeline.

Given the following keywords:
{keywords}

Given the following papers:
{paper}

Propose 15-20 candidate deep learning project ideas to combat climate change.
```

```
RESPONSE FORMAT:
Return your response as a simple formatted list with TITLE and DESCRIPTION for each
idea, separated by blank lines. For example:

TITLE: Climate Tipping Point Prediction System
DESCRIPTION: A deep learning system that identifies potential climate tipping points by
analyzing historical climate data and current trends. Uses recurrent neural networks to
process time series data from multiple sources to predict non-linear climate transitions.
DATA NEEDS: Historical climate records, current sensor data, satellite imagery

TITLE: Carbon Sequestration Optimization Network
DESCRIPTION: An ML algorithm that determines optimal locations and methods for carbon
sequestration based on geographical and atmospheric conditions. Combines computer vision
analysis of terrain with climate models to maximize carbon capture efficiency.
DATA NEEDS: Historical climate records, current sensor data, satellite imagery

Do not include any additional text, explanations, introductions, or conclusions. Start
directly with the first TITLE and end with the last DESCRIPTION. Ensure each project idea
is separated by exactly one blank line from the next idea.

Now, generate 15-20 creative and technically feasible project ideas based on the provided
keywords and papers.
"""
```

C Supplementary Materials for Agent 3

C.1 Agent Diagram

(see Fig. 4)

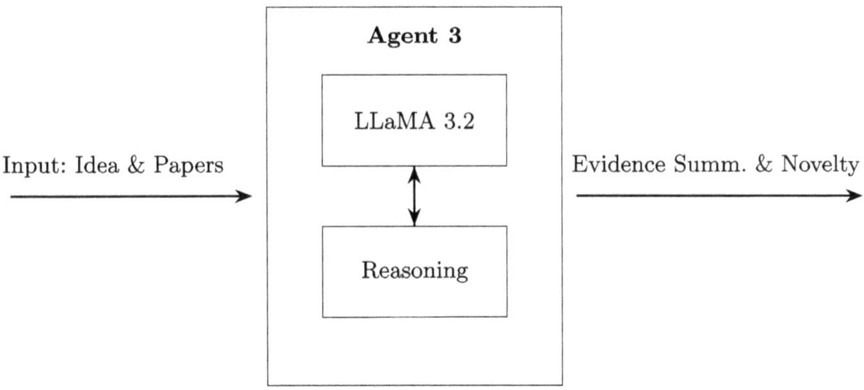

Fig. 4. Block diagram for Agent 3: Evidence Summarizer.

C.2 Sample Prompt and Chain of Thought

```
key_ideas_generation_prompt_1 =
```

```
You are an AI Research Synthesizer. Given a project idea and a set of related
paper abstracts, distill the core findings into 5-7 concise bullet points
that capture the main themes and evidence across all sources.

Instructions:
1. Analyze all abstracts jointly to identify common methods, results, and gaps.
2. Formulate new summary points reflecting the combined insights.
3. Produce a unified list of bullet points without any framing text.
4. Use standard bullet characters (e.g., '-', '*').
5. Return exactly 5-7 points.

Input:
idea: {"title", "description", "data_needs", "idea_id"}
papers: [{"title", "abstract"}, ...]
```

key_ideas_generation_prompt_2 =

```
**Your Task:**
Generate a single, unified list of 5-7 key bullet points that synthesize the core gist and
holistic picture from ALL 'n' abstracts provided above. Adhere strictly to all instructions,
especially regarding the synthesis approach and output formatting.
```

C.3 JSON Input/Output Schemas

Input:

```
{
  "idea": {
    "title": "Project Title",
    "description": "Description of the idea",
    "data_needs": "...",
    "idea_id": "unique-id"
  },
  "papers": [
    {"title": "Paper 1 Title", "abstract": "Abstract text here"},
    {"title": "Paper 2 Title", "abstract": "Abstract text here"},
    ...
  ]
}
```

Output:

```
{
  "evidence_summary": [
    "* Summary point 1",
    "* Summary point 2",
    ...
    "* Summary point 5-7"
  ],
  "novelty_score": 0.73
}
```

C.4 Prompt Templates

Prompt Instructions:

```
You are an AI Research Synthesizer. Your primary objective is to analyze a collection of 'n'
research paper abstracts, all related to a common theme or a specific research idea within
<Topic>Climate Change and Deep Learning</Topic>. Your task is to distill these abstracts into
a single, unified set of key bullet points that capture the holistic picture and core gist of
the combined information. These points should highlight the most significant, recurring, or
foundational insights that emerge when considering all abstracts together.

**Instructions for Synthesizing Collective Key Points:**
1. **Comprehensive Review:** Thoroughly read and analyze ALL 'n' provided abstracts.
2. **Identify Overarching Themes & Connections:** Look for:
   - Common research questions, objectives, or problems.
   - Recurring methodologies or datasets.
   - Converging findings or consistent conclusions.
   - Complementary insights across papers.
   - The overall narrative these abstracts support.
3. **Synthesize, Don't Aggregate:** Formulate new bullet points that represent
   synergistic understanding-not per-abstract summaries.
4. **Focus on the Core Gist:** Include the most critical and impactful insights.
5. **Conciseness and Clarity:** Each point should be a clear and concise phrase or sentence.
6. **Number of Points:** Provide exactly 5-7 bullet points.
7. **Holistic Perspective:** Ensure the list reads as a coherent synthesis.
8. **Output Formatting (CRUCIAL):**
   - Use standard bullet characters (*, -, or •)
   - DO NOT include separate summaries per abstract
   - DO NOT include intro or closing remarks
```

C.5 Paper Search API (Semantic Scholar)

Function:

```
def search_papers(query: str, limit: int = 3) -> List[Dict]:
    """Search for papers using the given query."""
    SEARCH_URL = "https://api.semanticscholar.org/graph/v1/paper/search"
    search_params = {
        "query": query,
        "limit": limit,
        "fields": "paperId,title,externalIds,abstract"
    }
    try:
        resp = requests.get(SEARCH_URL, params=search_params, headers=SS_HEADERS)
        resp.raise_for_status()
        return resp.json().get("data", [])
    except requests.exceptions.RequestException as e:
        print(f"Search error for query '{query}': {e}")
```

D Supplementary Materials for Agent 4

D.1 Agent Diagram

(see Fig. 5)

D.2 Sample Prompt and Chain of Thought

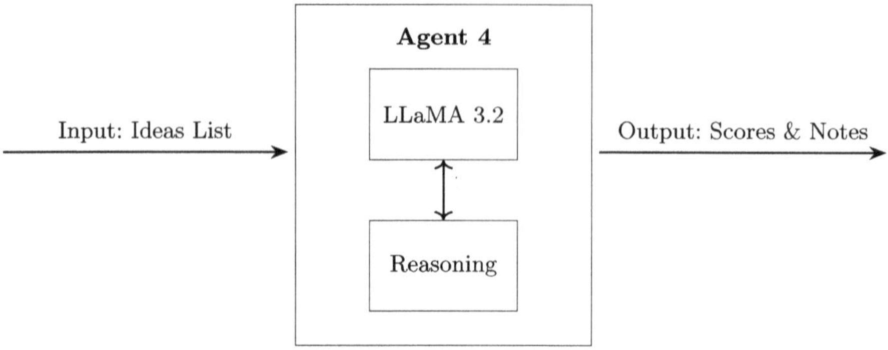

Fig. 5. Block diagram for Agent 4: Feasibility Analyst.

```
You are an AI Feasibility Analyst. Your task is to evaluate the
practical viability of a proposed research idea in Climate Change
and Deep Learning. You will receive the idea's title, description,
and data requirements.

1. Assess:
   - Data Volume & Availability (e.g., public vs. proprietary, labeling)
   - Model Fit & Complexity (standard vs. novel architectures)
   - Compute Needs (GPU, HPC, specialized hardware)
   - Deployment Path & Scalability (integration, maintenance)
2. Assign Feasibility Score: x in [0.0,1.0]
3. Provide 2-4 concise justification notes.
4. Format exactly:
   Feasibility Score: x, Notes: [note1; note2; ...]
Input:
{ "title": ..., "description": ..., "data_needs": [...],
"idea_id": "..." }
```

D.3 JSON Input/Output Schemas

```
[
  {
    "title": "...",
    "description": "...",
    "data_needs": ["..."],
    "idea_id": "..."
  },
  ...
]
```

```
[
```

```
  {
    "idea_id": "...",
    "feasibility_score": 0.0-1.0,
    "feasibility_notes": "Concise notes explaining score"
  },
  ...
]
```

D.4 Prompt Templates

```
    prompt1 = f"""
You are an AI Feasibility Analyst. Your task is to meticulously evaluate the practical
viability of a proposed research idea related to <Topic>Climate Change and Deep Learning
</Topic>. You will be provided with the idea's title, description, and data requirements.

Based on this information, you must:
1.  **Evaluate Feasibility Dimensions:** Thoroughly assess the idea against the following
dimensions, making internal notes on each:
    *   **Data Volume & Availability:** Consider the scale, accessibility, and preparation
    challenges of the required data. Note any significant hurdles (e.g., "requires petabytes
    of proprietary data," "extensive manual labeling needed") or facilitators (e.g., "uses
    readily available public datasets").
    *   **Model Fit & Complexity:** Evaluate the suitability of deep learning. Note if
    standard models apply or if it requires novel, highly complex, or exceptionally resource-
    intensive models. Consider the technical risk associated with the proposed modeling
    approach.
    *   **Compute Needs:** Estimate the computational resources. Note if it implies standard
    GPU usage, high-performance computing, or specialized hardware, and whether this is a
    significant barrier.
    *   **Deployment Path & Scalability:** Assess the complexity of real-world implementation
    if successful. Note potential challenges in scalability, maintenance, or integration.

2.  **Synthesize into a Feasibility Score:** Based on your detailed assessment of the
dimensions above, assign a single numerical Feasibility Score.
    *   The score MUST be a value between 0.0 and 1.0, inclusive.
    *   0.0 indicates extreme unfeasibility; 1.0 indicates high feasibility.

3.  **Formulate Justification Notes:** Based on your evaluation of the dimensions, compose
concise notes that clearly justify the assigned Feasibility Score. These notes should
highlight the primary factors (both positive and negative) that influenced your scoring
across the different feasibility dimensions. Aim for 2-4 key points in your notes.

4.  **Provide Output in Specified Format:** Your response must contain both the Feasibility
Score and the Notes.

**Input Research Idea Details:**
---
"""
promp2 = f"""
**Output Requirement:**

Your response MUST be formatted *strictly* as follows, with no other text, explanations, or
characters outside this structure on a single line:
'Feasibility Score: x, Notes: [Your concise notes explaining the score, highlighting key
factors from data, model, compute, and deployment considerations]'

**Example of desired output format:**
'Feasibility Score: 0.65, Notes: Moderate data acquisition challenges due to specificity, but
utilizes established model architectures. Compute needs are manageable with standard GPUs.
Deployment path requires integration with existing sensor networks which could be complex.'

OR
```

```
'Feasibility Score: 0.3, Notes: Relies on extremely large, currently unavailable datasets.
Proposed model is highly experimental with significant technical risk. Deployment would
require substantial new infrastructure.'

Now, analyze the provided idea details and output the Feasibility Score and corresponding
Notes in the specified format.

"""
```

E Supplementary Materials for Agent 5

E.1 Agent Diagram

(see Fig. 6)

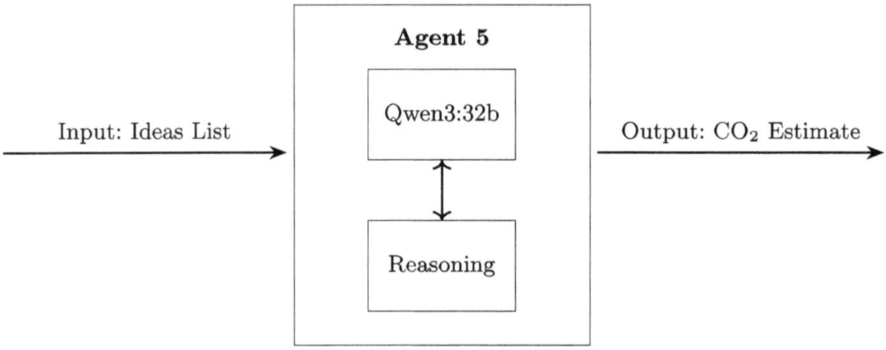

Fig. 6. Block diagram for Agent 5: Carbon Auditor.

E.2 Sample Prompt and Chain of Thought

```
PROMPT_TEMPLATE = """
You are Agent 5: Carbon Auditor for climate-change AI projects.

Input:
  "idea_id": "<project ID>"

Task:
  Estimate annual CO2 emissions (kg/year) for training and inference,
  using standard emission factors. Do not return zero.

Output:
  A JSON object with exactly:
    "idea_id": string,
    "co2_kg_per_year": number
"""
```

The model's chain of thought multiplies estimated compute hours by hardware power draw and applies the CO_2/kWh factor before formatting the JSON.

E.3 JSON Input/Output Schemas

```
[
  { "idea_id": "..." },
  ...
]
```

```
[
  {
    "idea_id": "...",
    "co2_kg_per_year": 12345.67
  },
  ...
]
```

E.4 Prompt Templates

```
    PROMPT_TEMPLATE = """
You are Agent 5: a Carbon Auditor for climate-change AI projects.

Project idea ID: {idea_id}

Based solely on this ID (which concisely represents the project title), estimate the annual
CO2 emissions (in kilograms per year) associated with training and inference of this deep
learning project.
Do not let the CO2 emissions be 0, as that would not be realistic for any deep learning
project.
Also, please return the exactly same idea_id in the output, as it is used in downstream tasks.

RESPONSE FORMAT:
Return your response in this exact format (just these two lines):

IDEA_ID: {idea_id}
CO2_KG_PER_YEAR: [your estimated number]

Do not include any additional text, explanations, introductions, or conclusions. Your entire
response should be exactly two lines that follow the format above.
"""
```

F Supplementary Materials for Agent 6

F.1 Agent Diagram

(see Fig. 7)

F.2 Sample Prompt and Chain of Thought

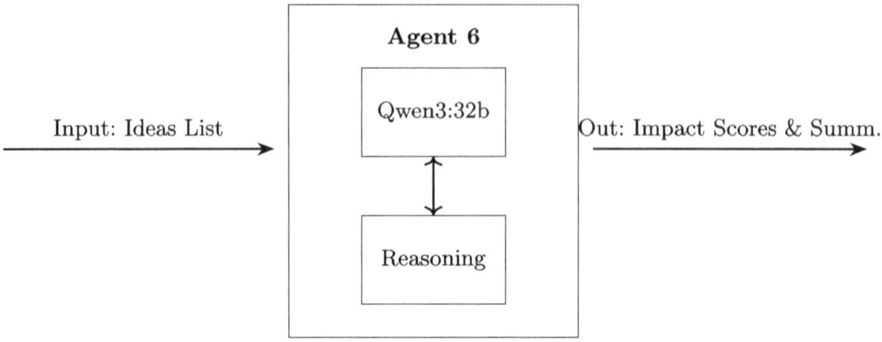

Fig. 7. Block diagram for Agent 6: Impact Estimator.

```
prompt = f"""
You are Agent 6: Impact Estimator for climate-change AI projects.

Project idea:
  Title: {idea['title']}
  Description: {idea['description']}

Estimate on a 0-1 scale:
  - emissions_reduction
  - policy_applicability
  - social_benefit

Include a 2-sentence summary under "summary". Return only a JSON array:
[
  {
    "idea_id": "...",
    "impact_score": number,
    "summary": "Two-sentence reasoning"
  },
  ...
]
"""
```

F.3 JSON Input/Output Schemas

```
[
  {
    "idea_id": "unique-id",
    "title": "Project title",
    "description": "Brief description"
  },
  ...
]
```

```
[
  {
    "idea_id": "unique-id",
    "impact_score": 0.0-1.0,
    "summary": "Concise explanation of score"
  },
  ...
]
```

F.4 Prompt Templates

```
    prompt = f"""
You are Agent 6: an Impact Estimator for climate-change deep learning projects.

Project idea:
Title: {idea['title']}
Description: {idea['description']}
ID: {idea.get('idea_id', '')}

Your task is to estimate the potential impact of this project on three metrics, each on a
scale of 0.0 to 1.0:
1. EMISSIONS_REDUCTION: How effectively will this project reduce greenhouse gas emissions?
2. POLICY_APPLICABILITY: How useful will this project be for climate policy decisions?
3. SOCIAL_BENEFIT: How much will this project benefit society and communities?

RESPONSE FORMAT:
You must use this exact format with these exact headings:

IDEA_ID: {idea.get('idea_id', '')}
EMISSIONS_REDUCTION: [value between 0.0 and 1.0]
POLICY_APPLICABILITY: [value between 0.0 and 1.0]
SOCIAL_BENEFIT: [value between 0.0 and 1.0]
SUMMARY: [2-3 sentences explaining your reasoning]
"""
```

G Supplementary Materials for Agent 7

G.1 Agent Diagram

(see Fig. 8)

G.2 Sample Prompt and Chain of Thought

```
PROMPT_TEMPLATE = """
You are Agent 7: an Ethics & Risk Checker for climate-change AI projects.

Input:
  "idea_id": "<ID>",
  "title": "<Project Title>",
  "description": "<Project Description>"

Task:
  1. Assess bias, privacy, misuse risk, and explainability.
```

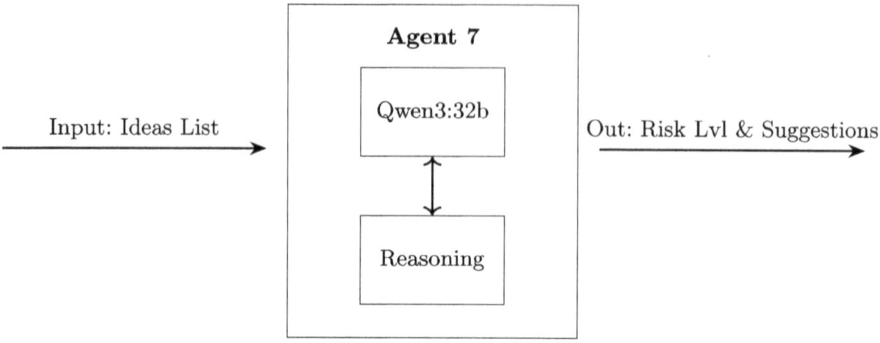

Fig. 8. Block diagram for Agent 7: Ethics & Risk Checker.

```
  2. Assign overall risk level: "low", "medium", or "high".
  3. Suggest exactly 3 mitigation steps (one per line).

Output:
  A JSON object with:
    "idea_id": string,
    "risk_level": "low"|"medium"|"high",
    "mitigation_suggestions": [string]
"""
```

The model's chain of thought reviews each dimension in turn, identifying potential harms, privacy gaps, and explainability issues, then composes the risk level and mitigation list.

G.3 JSON Input/Output Schemas

```
[
  {
    "idea_id": "unique-id",
    "title": "Project title",
    "description": "Brief description"
  },
  ...
]
```

```
[
  {
    "idea_id": "unique-id",
    "risk_level": "low",  // or "medium" or "high"
    "mitigation_suggestions": [
      "First mitigation step",
```

```
      "Second mitigation step",
      "Third mitigation step"
    ]
  },
  ...
]
```

G.4 Prompt Templates

```
    PROMPT_TEMPLATE = """
You are Agent 7: an Ethics & Risk Checker for climate-change AI projects.

Project idea:
Title: {title}
Description: {description}
ID: {idea_id}

Considering the following potential risks in AI systems:
- BIAS: Does the system risk reinforcing existing inequities or disadvantaging certain
groups?
- MISUSE: Could bad actors exploit this system for harmful purposes?
- PRIVACY: Does the system collect, process, or generate sensitive data about individuals or
groups?
- EXPLAINABILITY: Are the system's decisions transparent and interpretable to users and
stakeholders?
- ECOLOGICAL IMPACT: Could the system directly or indirectly cause environmental harm?

First, identify the TWO MOST SIGNIFICANT risks specific to this particular project.
Then, assign an overall risk level (low, medium, or high) based on your analysis.
Finally, provide 3 HIGHLY SPECIFIC mitigation suggestions that directly address the
identified risks for THIS PROJECT.

RESPONSE FORMAT:
Return your response in this exact format:

IDEA_ID: {idea_id}
RISK_LEVEL: [low/medium/high]
MITIGATION_SUGGESTIONS:
1. [First project-specific mitigation suggestion that addresses a concrete risk]
2. [Second project-specific mitigation suggestion with technical or procedural detail]
3. [Third project-specific mitigation suggestion with measurable outcomes]

Your mitigation suggestions must be SPECIFIC to this project, ACTIONABLE, and DIVERSE. Do not
use generic solutions that could apply to any AI system. Each suggestion should be
substantially different from the others.
"""
```

H Supplementary Materials for Agent 8

H.1 Agent Diagram

(see Fig. 9)

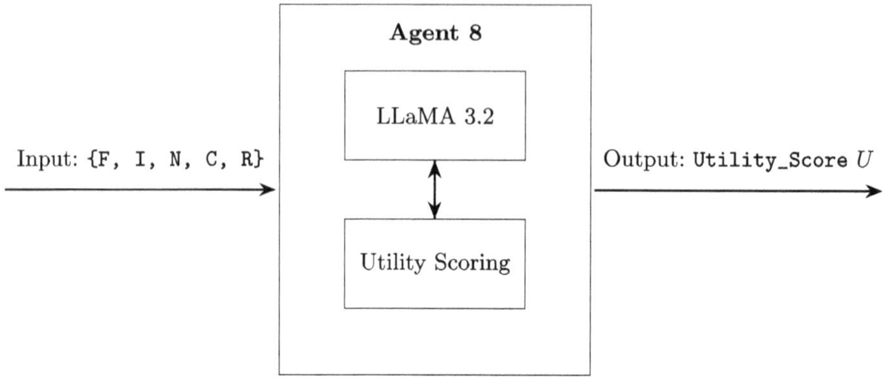

Fig. 9. Block diagram for Agent 8: Net Utility Scorer.

H.2 Prompt Chain and Inference Steps

```
You are Agent 8: Net Utility Scorer.
Input: list of ideas with fields F (feasibility), I (impact),
       C (co2_kg_per_year), R (risk_level), N (novelty_score).

Steps:
1. Convert risk_level: low → 1, medium → 3, high → 5.
2. Normalize CO2: C_norm = C/CO2_MAX.
3. Compute U = wf * F + wi * I + wn * N - wc * C_norm - wr * R.
4. Output JSON list with idea_id and utility_score.
```

H.3 JSON Input/Output Schemas


```
[
  {
    "idea_id": "id123",
    "feasibility_score": 0.75,
    "impact_score": 0.82,
```

```
    "novelty_score": 0.67,
    "co2_kg_per_year": 1200.0,
    "risk_level": "medium"
  },
  ...
]
```

```
[
  {
    "idea_id": "id123",
    "feasibility_score": 0.75,
    "impact_score": 0.82,
    "novelty_score": 0.67,
    "co2_kg_per_year": 1200.0,
    "risk_level": "medium",
    "utility_score": 0.58
  },
  ...
]
```

H.4 Prompt Template (Used Internally)

```
You are an AI utility scorer. Your task is to compute a 'Utility Score' for each idea.

Inputs:
- feasibility_score (0.0-1.0)
- impact_score (0.0-1.0)
- novelty_score (0.0-1.0)
- co2_kg_per_year (positive float)
- risk_level (low / medium / high)

Steps:
1. Convert risk_level:
   'low' → 1, 'medium' → 3, 'high' → 5

2. Normalize CO2:
   C_norm = co2_kg_per_year / CO2_MAX

3. Compute Utility Score:
   U = wf * F + wi * I + wn * N - wc * C_norm - wr * R

Weights (example):
   wf = 0.3   (feasibility)
   wi = 0.3   (impact)
   wn = 0.2   (novelty)
   wc = 0.001 (CO2)
   wr = 0.2   (risk)

Output:
JSON array of ideas with their computed utility_score.
```

I Supplementary Materials for Agent 9

I.1 Agent Diagram

(see Fig. 10)

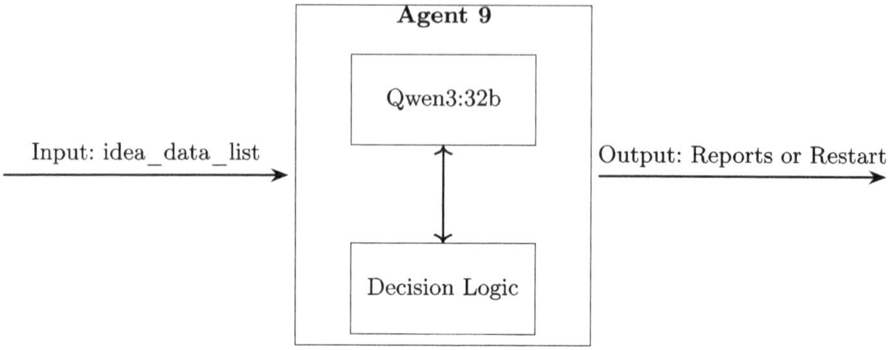

Fig. 10. Block diagram for Agent 9: Controller & Iteration Lead.

I.2 Sample Prompt and Chain of Thought

```
prompt = f"""
You are Agent 9: Controller & Iteration Lead for the climate-change AI
pipeline.

Input:
  idea_id: {idea['idea_id']}
  Title: {idea['title']}
  Description: {idea['description']}
  Feasibility: {idea['feasibility_score']}
  Impact: {idea['impact_score']}
  CO2: {idea['co2_kg_per_year']}
  Risk: {idea['risk_level']}
  Utility: {idea['utility_score']}

Task:
  1) If feasibility >= 0.6, utility >= 0.5, and risk is low or medium:
       Generate a Markdown report with sections:
         a) Overview (2-3 paragraphs)
         b) Data (sources, formats, access)
         c) Feasibility discussion
         d) Next steps
  2) Otherwise:
       Restart pipeline at Agent 1.
```

```
Output:
  Return the report text in Markdown, or the command to restart.
"""
```

I.3 JSON Input/Output Schemas

```
[
  {
    "idea_id": "id123",
    "title": "Project Title",
    "description": "Brief description",
    "feasibility_score": 0.75,
    "impact_score": 0.82,
    "co2_kg_per_year": 1200.0,
    "risk_level": "medium",
    "utility_score": 0.58
  },
  ...
]
```

```
# For each qualified idea:
{
  "idea_id": "id123",
  "report_markdown": "## Overview\n...\n"
}
# Or, if none qualify:
"restart": "Agent 1"
```

I.4 Prompt Templates

```
    prompt = f"""
You are writing a polished, academic-style report section for a project
idea on climate change.

Title: {title}
Summary: {summary}
Data Needs: {', '.join(data_needs)}
Full Description: {full_desc}

Please produce, numbered 1)-4):
1) A 2-3 paragraph Overview.
2) A detailed Data section (sources, formats, access).
3) A Feasibility discussion.
4) Suggested Next Steps and Extensions.
```

```
Return the answer in Markdown.
"""
```

References

1. Barnes, E.A., Hurrell, J.W., Ebert-Uphoff, I., Anderson, C., Anderson, D.: Viewing forced climate patterns through an AI lens. Geophys. Res. Lett. **46**(22), 13389–13398 (2019)
2. Chattopadhyay, A., Hassanzadeh, P., Pasha, S.: Predicting clustered weather patterns: a test case for applications of convolutional neural networks to spatio-temporal climate data. Sci. Rep. **10**(1317) (2020). https://doi.org/10.1038/s41598-020-57897-9
3. Chen, X., Wang, X., Qu, Y.: Constructing ethical AI based on the "human-in-the-loop" system. Systems **11**, 548 (2023). https://doi.org/10.3390/systems11110548
4. Chouldechova, A., Roth, A.: The frontiers of fairness in machine learning, October 2018.https://doi.org/10.48550/arXiv.1810.08810
5. Courty, B., et al.: mlco2/codecarbon: v2.4.1, May 2024. https://doi.org/10.5281/zenodo.11171501
6. Ejjami, R.: Ethical artificial intelligence framework theory (EAIFT): a new paradigm for embedding ethical reasoning in ai systems. Int. J. Multidiscip. Res. **6** (2024). https://doi.org/10.36948/ijfmr.2024.v06i05.28231
7. Eraliev, O., Lee, C.: Performance analysis of time series deep learning models for climate prediction in indoor hydroponic greenhouses at different time intervals. Plants **12**, 2316 (2023). https://doi.org/10.3390/plants12122316
8. Guan, H., Dong, L., Zhao, A.: Ethical risk factors and mechanisms in artificial intelligence decision making. Behav. Sci. **12**, 343 (2022). https://doi.org/10.3390/bs12090343
9. Huang, C., Zhang, Z., Mao, B., Yao, X.: An overview of artificial intelligence ethics. IEEE Trans. Artif. Intell. **4**, 799–819 (2023). https://doi.org/10.1109/tai.2022.3194503
10. Iglesias-Suarez, F., et al.: Causally-informed deep learning to improve climate models and projections. J. Geophys. Res. Atmos. **129** (2024). https://doi.org/10.1029/2023jd039202
11. Kim, H., Ham, Y., Joo, Y., Son, S.: Deep learning for bias correction of MJO prediction. Nat. Commun. **12** (2021). https://doi.org/10.1038/s41467-021-23406-3
12. McGrath, Q., Hevner, A., Vreede, G.: Managing ethical risks of artificial intelligence in business applications (2024). https://doi.org/10.36227/techrxiv.170905835.50964792/v1
13. Moon, D., Ahn, S.: A study on functional requirements and inspection items for ai system change management and model improvement on the web platform. J. Web Eng., 831–848 (2024). https://doi.org/10.13052/jwe1540-9589.2366
14. Morley, J., Elhalal, A., Garcia, F., Kinsey, L., Mökander, J., Floridi, L.: Ethics as a service: a pragmatic operationalisation of AI ethics. Minds Mach. **31**, 239–256 (2021). https://doi.org/10.1007/s11023-021-09563-w
15. Shin, N., Ham, Y., Kim, J., Cho, M., Kug, J.: Application of deep learning to understanding ENSO dynamics. Artif. Intell. Earth Syst. **1** (2022). https://doi.org/10.1175/aies-d-21-0011.1

16. Siau, K., Wang, W.: Artificial intelligence (AI) ethics. J. Database Manage. **31**, 74–87 (2020). https://doi.org/10.4018/jdm.2020040105
17. Wang, F., Tian, D.: On deep learning-based bias correction and downscaling of multiple climate models simulations. Clim. Dyn. **59**, 3451–3468 (2022). https://doi.org/10.1007/s00382-022-06277-2
18. Wu, C., et al.: Widespread decline in winds delayed autumn foliar senescence over high latitudes. Proc. Nat. Acad. Sci. **118** (2021). https://doi.org/10.1073/pnas.2015821118

Agentic AI Guidance Using Simon's Framework for Management Science

David B. Keever(✉)

Leidos Corporation, Reston, VA 20190, USA
keeverd@leidos.com

Abstract. The rise of agentic Artificial Intelligence (AI) provides a rich environment for the design, development, test, and deployment of AI agents. Alignment of the agentic AI capabilities for various decision-making and communication tasks can benefit from the framework for management science developed in the late 1960's by Nobel Laureate Herbert A. Simon. This poster session will employ his concepts of bounded rationality and decision-making model (Intelligence-Design-Choice) to guide and recommend agentic AI design and implementation.

Keywords: Artificial Intelligence (AI) · agentic AI design · Management Science framework · Herbert Simon

1 Introduction

Agentic AI refers to artificial intelligence systems that act as autonomous agents. Agentic AI systems are characterized by autonomy, proactive behavior, and multi-step planning, contrasting with passive, reactive generative models [1]. Due to the semi-autonomous or autonomous capabilities for planning, reasoning, and acting towards goals, the range of AI agentic applications is widespread and include business operations, customer support, healthcare/decision support, robotics, personal assistants, security, and many others. Agentic AI even facilitates discovery by initiating hypotheses, designing experiments, and drawing conclusions with minimal human oversight [2].

Substantial advancements have been made in automated tools and platforms to create agentic AI. These include Azure AI Foundry, OpenAI Agent Platform, Replit Agent v2, CrewAI, and LangChain/LangGraph, among others [3]. This proliferation of low-code and modest-cost platforms enable a wide range of non-technical users to design agentic AI systems, build capabilities, and deploy them, sometimes with little or no AI governance. This situation means agentic AI systems can set goals, make decisions, and take actions in pursuit of those goals with limited or no human intervention. Recently, some scholars, alarmed at this independence, have proposed the creation of Multi-stakeholder Regulatory Organizations (MROs) to be private, standards-setting bodies designed providing legal and regulatory clarity, accountability, and agility in an era of exponential AI progress [4]. This proposed approach is currently under review and debate in the California legislature as SB 813, for example.

H. R. Arabnia et al. (Eds.): CSCE 2025, CCIS 2934, pp. 300–305, 2026.
https://doi.org/10.1007/978-3-032-22190-2_20

A number of initiatives are underway to provide for agentic AI systems to meet societal goals and values, including transparency, security, value-sensitive design, human oversight/intervention, robustness, privacy, and global coordination of safety of agentic AI. One means by which agentic AI systems may be compared and contrasted is through a framework encompassing the main elements of an agentic AI system to support the broad field of decision-making. A foundational framework for management science, inclusive of information sciences, was proposed and implemented by Nobel Laureate Herbert Simon in the late 1950's and early 1960s. His three-part framework principles of Intelligence-Design-Choice provides valuable guidance in the age of agentic AI [5].

2 Agentic AI Quick Overview

The potential for AI agents is immense but the quality and performance of AI agents depends heavily on the data it uses, how accurately it can find the right or best information, and the supporting algorithms for reasoning and trustable insights. Two categories of AI agents are emerging in practice. First are personal AI agents which are customized digital assistance that learn and adapt to an individual's preferences, needs, requests, and behavior, using continuous learning methods (such as reinforcement learning). The personal AI agent acts primarily in the individual's interests and operates subject to AI governance practices aligned to societal norms. These AI agents typically have access only to individual data, but may use patterns, newly formed knowledge, or more general external knowledge to improve their algorithmic and agentic performance. Second are organizational AI agents which are customized to a specific organizational context using internal data and relevant externals references to help achieve organizational goals subject to operating parameters and constraints set by organizational policies and procedures. Organizational AI agents involve multiple users, cross-functional disciplines, and data appropriate to the goals and purpose of the AI agents, augmented by security policies, privacy norms, and transparency desires.

AI agents' effectiveness hinges on six core capabilities: sensing, reasoning, planning, coordinating, acting, and learning/adaptation. Figure 1 depicts one representation of these six, arranged sequentially with interconnections and described by the following:

- **Sensing** refers to the gathering of data from the environment in which the AI agent is embedded or operating for the purpose of gathering data and informing decision-making affiliated with other AI agents in the system. Typical algorithms include traditional Kalman filtering for data fusion, Natural Language Processing (NLP) for understanding textual (structured and unstructured) data, and computer vision components or systems using Convolutional Neural Networks, as an example, to enable image recognition. During the sensing phase, raw data is turned into meaningful information using some of these sample algorithms, especially when the data is streaming and requires efficient data pipelines and handling [6].
- **Reasoning** draws conclusions from available, qualified information to make decisions or inform other AI Agents. Typical algorithms include rule-based systems, logic-based reasoning (such as first order logic for complex inferencing), and probabilistic models such as Bayesian networks for uncertainty. Reasoning data are typically stored in searchable and structured knowledge bases for reference and guidelines. Inference

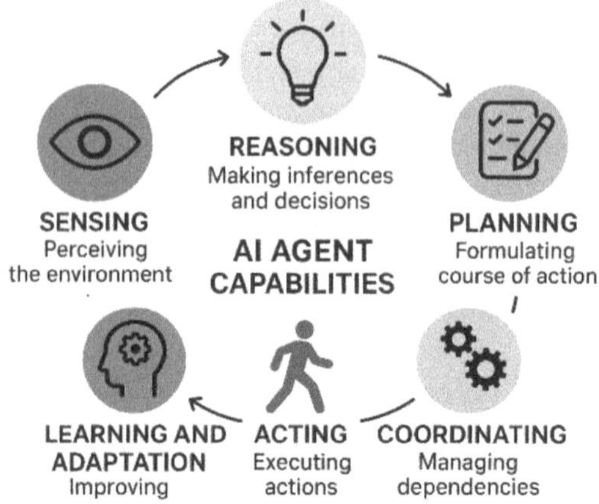

Fig. 1. An AI Agent Representation of Key Six Capabilities

engines may also be used to apply logical rules to derive new information to guide further reasoning, through RLAIL (Reinforcement Learning AI Learning) or the application of more formal logical rules [7].

- **Planning** involves the development of a sequence of actions to achieve specific goals. Given the complexity of AI agent systems, common approaches use hierarchical task decomposition or networks to breakdown tasks into subtasks and interdependencies. Markovian models (hidden or observable) may also be used based on the nature of the planning task. Plans are created using goal decomposition approaches coupled with temporal planning methods which align tasks over time given the complexity of interdependence and task completion performance [8, 9].
- **Coordinating** among AI agents address the communications and interaction among multiple agents to achieve common objectives. AI agents share their plans with users, AI agents or system functions to ensure collaborative, effective information gathering, sharing, and task performance. A variety of coordination systems are being advanced, with no current dominant method. Multi-Agent systems provide guidance for agent coordination and collaboration such as MCP (Model Context Protocol) which is emerging as a leading contender for industry adoption [10]. Consensus or satisficing algorithms are another approach in which agents bargain and reach agreement on coordination activities among distributed agents. Game theory models are also employed, not as zero-sum configurations, but as multi-objective optimization and goal-seeking procedures. The coordination function of AI agents rely heavily on an established, flexible, and trustworthy communication protocol as well as negotiated role assignment and mechanisms [11].
- ***Acting*** of AI Agents refers to the execution of actions or tasks within the environment to affect some changes, such as subgoal achievement, task completion, message delivery, etc. AI Agents execute the plan from previous phases based on control systems approaches employed in robotics, control/feedback system designs, and sophisticated space-time search methods for motion planning. Reinforcement learning is

also a common technique using multi-objective or policy-based methods, or environmental learning techniques. The implementation of AI agents may involve physical actuators, other hardware-software subsystems, and sensor systems to monitor the action outcomes and adjust according to the plans [12].

- ***Learning/Adapting*** AI agents assess the outcomes and performance of all AI agents to incorporate feedback and learning. This feedback enables AI Agents to reflect, determine success based on shared criteria, identify areas for improvement and innovation, and refine processes for future tasks and interaction. Traditional data science algorithms and approaches include supervised and unsupervised learning. Reinforcement learning, with human-in-the-loop or AI learning methods are also prevalent. Implementation is based on common control theory concepts with feedback loops and model update mechanisms, such as self-innovation of internal AI agent models based on new data, contextual conditions, or circumstances [13].

3 Framework to Guide Agentic AI for Management Science

Nobel Laureate Herbert A. Simon was a pioneering innovator whose work incorporated a wide range of disciplines including psychology, economics, and computer science which advanced the study and practice of decision-making and organizational behavior. His work laid the foundation for modern theories of artificial intelligence, complex systems, and how organizations adapt and function in dynamic environments. In his science of management, Simon conjectured effective managerial decision-making involves three core stages: intelligence (gathering and analyzing information), design (developing possible solutions), and choice (selecting the best option from among the alternative designs) [5]. Figure 2 captures these key principles.

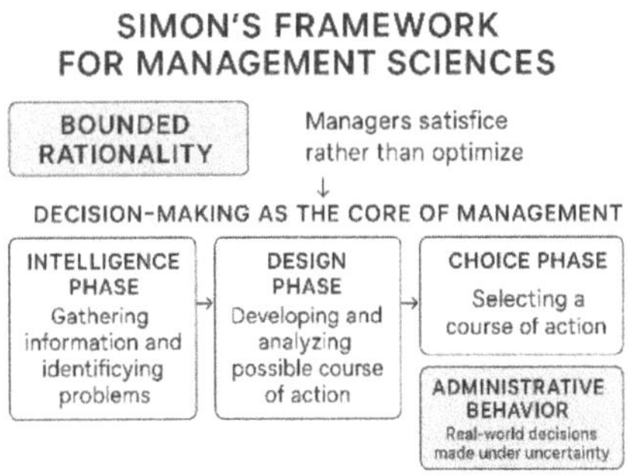

Fig. 2. Key Elements of Simon's Science of Management

The Intelligence-Design-Choice (IDC) framework helped advance management not as an art of intuition or innate leadership skill but as a structured, data, and evidence-based process. Simon included the concept of bounded rationality, recognizing individuals and organizations make decisions within limits of time, information, and cognition [5].

Table 1 illustrates a cross-referencing of these three IDC management elements with the six components of an AI agent. Such a mapping provides some preliminary guidance and considerations on how AI agents could be implemented, which would be dependent on the specific context and use case. Three examples illustrate the use of this framework for Agentic AI:

1. ***AI Agent Capabilities Operationalize the Three Phases***. Simon's IDC framework is a high-level model of human decision-making. The six AI agent functions can be viewed as its computational counterpart—translating each phase into discrete, actionable capabilities which can be engineered into an overall intelligent systems. For example, "sensing" and "reasoning" align with the intelligence phase, while "planning" and "coordinating" reflect the design phase, and "acting" corresponds to the choice phase.
2. ***AI Agents Extend the IDC Model with Continuous Learning***. Unlike the static IDC model, which is somewhat linear and culminates in a decision and action, AI agent frameworks integrate learning and adaptation, enabling feedback loops and continuous improvement. This reflects an evolution from one-time decision-making to dynamic, evolving decision systems in real-world environments.
3. ***AI Agent Coordination Capabilities Augments the IDC with Useful Systematic Interdependencies.*** The IDC framework emphasized the internal cognitive process, but AI agents add coordination—a function essential for multi-agent systems and complex environments. This extends Simon's model to networked decision-making across distributed systems or organizations.

Table 1. Mapping Agentic AI Into The Intelligence-Design-Choice (IDC) Framework

<table>
<tr><th></th><th>Intelligence
(Finding/Defining Problems/Challenges)</th><th>Design
(Developing Possible Courses of Action)</th><th>Choice
(Selecting A Course of Action)</th></tr>
<tr><td>**Sensing**</td><td colspan="2">More robust use of contextual data for real-time responsiveness and resilience under uncertainty</td><td>Real-time data for implementation</td></tr>
<tr><td>**Reasoning**</td><td colspan="3">Expands upon the concept of only bounded rationality</td></tr>
<tr><td>**Planning**</td><td>Multi-goal satisficing</td><td>Temporal dimensions</td><td></td></tr>
<tr><td>**Coordinating**</td><td colspan="3">AI agent capabilities that bridge across the separate IDC functions necessary for multi-agent systems and complex environments</td></tr>
<tr><td>**Acting**</td><td></td><td></td><td>Acting on AI Agent preferences</td></tr>
<tr><td>**Learning/ Adaption**</td><td colspan="3">AI agent capabilities integrate *learning and adaptation* for all phases of the IDC, enabling feedback loops and continuous improvement</td></tr>
</table>

4 Conclusions

The alignment between the IDC phases from the Simon model and agentic AI capabilities illustrates how core principles of human decision science continue to inform artificial intelligence. This convergence suggests one of several unifying theoretical foundations for designing both human-centered and autonomous decision systems.

References

1. Schneider, J.: Generative to Agentic AI: Survey, Conceptualization, and Challenges (2025). arXiv:2504.18875
2. Gridach, M., et al.: Agentic AI for Scientific Discovery: A Survey of Progress, Challenges, and Future Directions (2025). arXiv:2503.08979
3. References include: Priya, Lekha, "Top 5 Agentic AI Frameworks to Watch in 2025," Medium, January 9, 2025; Moore, Mike, "Google Cloud Next 2025," TechRadar Pro, April 11, 2025; and Lin, Belle, "OpenAI Wants Business to Build Their Own AI Agents,", Wall Street Journal, March 11, 2025
4. PR Newswire. Prominent AI Scholars Back Private Governance Model in California. Yahoo Finance (2025)
5. Simon, H.A.: The New Science of Management Decision. Harper & Brothers, New York (1960)
6. Dogan, E.: What is an AI Agent? A Complete Guide. Glean Product Note (2025)
7. Sharma, R.: Agentic AI Architecture: A Deep Dive. Markovate Note (2025)
8. Plummer, L.: Google's DeepMind Creates an AI with 'Imagination'. Wired (2017)
9. Rosenbush, S.: Get Ready for 'Long Thinking' – AI's Next Leap Forward. Wall Street J. (2024)
10. Lisowski, E.: MCP Explained: The New Standard Connecting AI to Everything. Medium (2025)
11. Colback, L.: AI agents: from co-pilots to autopilot. Financ. Times (2025)
12. Bronsdon, C.: Centralized Versus Decentralized Multi-Agency AI Coordination Strategies. Galileo (2025)
13. Lyzr.ai. AI Agents: A Comprehensive Guide on Understanding and Implementing Them. Medium (2024)

The Geometry of Bias in Contrastive Embeddings: A Spectral Analysis

Blessing Ogbuokiri(✉), Hridoy Rahman, David Martin, Kaija Sproxton, Adrien Belcastro, Ray Huang, and Vijay Panchal

Department of Computer Science, Brock University, St. Catharines, Canada
{bogbuokiri,hr21it,dm20zo,ks21lk,ab17eu,rh19bs,vp20vk}@brocku.ca

Abstract. This paper introduces a spectral method to measure and reduce representational bias in embedding models when supervision is minimal or absent. The method builds similarity graphs from embeddings, which it uses to perform spectral clustering to identify subgroup disparities through eigenvector analysis. Our method demonstrates competitive accuracy and substantial reduction in fairness gaps in the CelebA and CheXpert datasets compared to supervised and heuristic baselines during experiments. Our method allows fairness evaluation without full label supervision while providing a scalable and interpretable solution for responsible representation learning.

Keywords: Spectral Clustering · Fair Representation Learning · Bias Mitigation · Semi-Supervised Learning (SSL) · Responsible AI

1 Introduction

Research has shown that contrastive learning effectively extracts data representations from unlabeled datasets in domains such as medical imaging [1] and facial recognition [20]. Recent research has shown that contrastive learning not only encodes but also amplifies social biases within crucial domains such as healthcare [21] and facial recognition [3,25].

These biases come mainly from the geometric structure of the learned embeddings. Although existing fairness methods depend on demographic supervision [7], use post hoc corrections [19], or implement heuristic approaches without theoretical guarantees [8], which do not completely detect and mitigate biases from the geometric structure of the learned embeddings.

We introduce a spectral method to detect bias within contrastive embeddings, which functions without requiring labels and rests on theoretical principles.

This research made three key contributions including: (1) introduction of a Laplacian Disparity Ratio that identifies bias by examining differences in spectral gaps between subgroups, (2) the use of Eigenvector Sensitivity Analysis to determine directions within embedding space that impact fairness, and (3) a theoretical foundations to demonstrate how geometric disparities correspond to fairness measures through the application of perturbation limits.

H. R. Arabnia et al. (Eds.): CSCE 2025, CCIS 2934, pp. 306–320, 2026.
https://doi.org/10.1007/978-3-032-22190-2_21

We demonstrated our method on two known datasets, CelebFaces attributes dataset (CelebA [13]) a large scale face attribute dataset with 202,599 celebrity images, each with 40 attribute annotation and CheXpert-v1.0-small dataset (CheXpert [10]) containing 224,316 chest radiographs of 65,240 patients shows better performance than supervised fairness baselines for bias detection and mitigation without protected label information.

The remainder of this paper is structured as follows: Sect. 2 presents the review of contrastive learning and fairness applications in spectral methods, Sect. 3 outlines the theoretical framework, which incorporates the Laplacian Disparity Ratio along with fairness guarantees. In Sect. 4, details of the procedure for detecting spectral bias are presented. Section 5 demonstrates experimental validation results on the two datasets. Section 6 discusses broader impacts and limitations of the study. Finally, Sect. 7 wraps up the research findings while proposing areas for future exploration. Additional results can be found in the paper's appendices.

2 Related Works

2.1 Contrastive Representation Learning

Contrastive representation learning (CRL) is a self-supervised approach that learns embeddings by drawing similar (positive) pairs together and pushing dissimilar (negative) ones apart [9]. This technique avoids reliance on labels by leveraging data augmentations to form positive pairs, encouraging robustness to transformations such as cropping or color jitter [18]. The resulting embeddings support linear separability and transfer across tasks like classification and retrieval [12].

InfoNCE loss is the dominant objective for CRL frameworks such as SimCLR, optimizing alignment and uniformity in the latent space [17]. Formally:

$$\mathcal{L}_{\text{InfoNCE}} = -\log \frac{e^{z \cdot z'/\tau}}{e^{z \cdot z'/\tau} + \sum_{n \in N} e^{z \cdot z_n/\tau}}, \tag{1}$$

where z, z' are positive pair embeddings and τ is a temperature parameter. This framework can be interpreted probabilistically as maximizing the likelihood of true pairs under a noise-contrastive model [6]. While effective, CRL may inadvertently preserve spurious correlations and bias from training data [15].

2.2 Fairness in Self-supervised Learning

The presence of bias in CRL generates fairness problems for downstream machine learning applications. The supervised fairness method Equality of Opportunity requires models to standardize true positive rates among different demographic groups [7]. These successful methods need sensitive attribute labels to operate properly.

Unsupervised methods work to remove bias without relying on demographic labels for supervision. The Flexibly fair representation learning by disentanglement (FFVAE) [4] model uses an adversarial learning method to separate sensitive attributes from target attributes from its variational autoencoder framework. The encoder uses a KL-divergence penalty to learn how to hide demographic information within the latent space. The method of disentanglement used in this approach operates heuristically and fails to deliver theoretical fairness guarantees.

2.3 Spectral Methods in ML

Spectral graph theory offers a principled way to uncover bias embedded in data representations. A similarity graph's Laplacian $L = D - A$ captures connectivity structure, and its eigenvalues encode properties such as clusterability and alignment with group identity [5]. Spectral embeddings, derived from eigenvectors of L or its normalized form $\mathcal{L}$, reveal hidden subgroup separation, even without label access [14].

The Laplacian quadratic form $x^\top Lx$, where x encodes group membership, measures how aligned a representation is with subgroup boundaries. A high value implies demographic stratification in the graph structure. Thus, spectral tools enable fairness diagnostics from the geometry of embedding spaces, laying a foundation for bias detection without requiring sensitive attribute labels.

Our work extends these insights by formalizing a label-free spectral framework for bias detection and mitigation in contrastive learning. Unlike prior heuristic or supervised approaches, we (1) introduce the *Laplacian Disparity Ratio* to quantify subgroup separation using eigenvalue gaps, (2) propose *Eigenvector Sensitivity Analysis* to identify directions associated with bias, and (3) derive theoretical bounds linking spectral disparities to fairness guarantees. Our method provides an enhanced method for bias auditing in self-supervised settings without relying on demographic annotations.

3 Theoretical Framework

3.1 Spectral Geometry of Bias

Recent research has shown that societal biases appear easily in the geometry of learned embeddings and the outcome becomes particularly evident in contrastive learning frameworks [24]. This research builds upon previous studies that examined societal biases in learned embeddings by investigating how bias changes the spectral structure of embeddings across protected subgroups and specifically analyzing two key concepts.

- Spectral Gap Divergence: Embeddings display uneven eigenvalue spacing when contrastive pairs undergo biased sampling from skewed data distributions or implicit annotation bias. When we analyze an embedding matrix

$E \in \mathbb{R}^{n \times d}$ alongside similarity matrices $\mathcal{S}_i$ and $\mathcal{S}_j$ generated from subgroups i and j, we notice the following:

$$\Delta\lambda_{\min} \leq \frac{\|E^T(\mathcal{S}_i - \mathcal{S}_j)\|_2}{\sigma_{\min}(E)} \leq \Delta\lambda_{\max}, \tag{2}$$

$\sigma_{\min}(E)$ represents the smallest singular value of the embedding matrix E. Significant discrepancies suggest potential underrepresentation or clustering artifacts that are linked to subgroup membership.

- Eigenvector Misalignment: Protected group membership exhibits significant variation in leading eigenvectors from the graph Laplacian $L = D - W$, which is based on pairwise similarities. The group spectral angle measures the extent of misalignment.

$$\theta_{ij} = \arccos\left(\frac{\langle v_i, v_j \rangle}{\|v_i\|_2 \|v_j\|_2}\right), \tag{3}$$

v_i and v_j represent the primary eigenvectors for subgroups i and j respectively. When two groups show significant angular deviation this implies either representational inconsistency or the presence of inductive bias.

We perform spectral gap divergence and eigenvector misalignment analysis in Fig. 1.

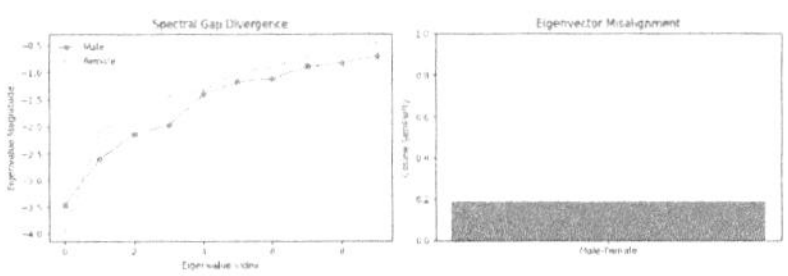

(a) Divergence in spectral gap and misalignment of eigenvectors between Male and Female groups expose structural differences in learned representations.

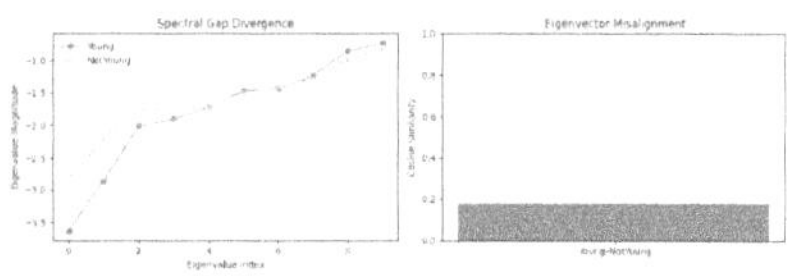

(b) Divergence in spectral gap and misalignment of eigenvectors between Young and NotYoung groups expose structural differences in learned representations.

Fig. 1. Analysis of spectral gap divergence along with eigenvector misalignment on the CelebA dataset shows structural representation differences between protected attribute groups. The eigenvalue distributions and cosine similarity data between Male vs Female and Young vs NotYoung groups show distinct patterns, which suggest possible representational bias.

The analysis of facial embedding biases in the CelebA dataset in Fig. 1 evaluates two protected attributes through comparison of group-specific spectral structures between gender (Male and Female) and age (Young vs. NotYoung). The Spectral Gap Divergence plots on the left side of Fig. 1(a) and Fig. 1(b) demonstrate the relationship between ranked eigenvalue indices on the x-axis and their magnitudes on the y-axis for each subgroup. The differences in eigenvalue paths between Male and Female groups in Fig. 1(a) and between Young and

NotYoung groups in Fig. 1(b) demonstrate that distinct groups identify unique dominant components, which suggests subgroup-specific embedding space geometry.

The right-hand Eigenvector Misalignment plots in both scenarios illustrate the cosine similarity measurements between the top eigenvectors of each compared group pair. The persistently low similarity metrics (0.18) demonstrate substantial directional misalignment, which confirms existing representational disparities. The results demonstrate structural variations within the feature space, which may lead to biases in classifications and face recognition tasks. The Appendix A section contains extra figures and analyses for each attribute.

3.2 Laplacian Disparity Ratio

We adapt the spectral clustering in [16,23], to determine the Laplacian Disparity Ratio (LDR), which calculates bias magnitude through the normalized eigenvalue divergence, see Definition 1.

Definition 1. *Let $\mathcal{G}_1$ and $\mathcal{G}_2$ be subgroups in the graph Laplacian $\mathbf{L}$ with eigenvalues $v_1, v_2, \cdots v_n$, such that, $v_1 \leq \cdots \leq v_n$. The LDR that calculates the spectral differences between the subgroups $\mathcal{G}_1$ and $\mathcal{G}_2$ is given as:*

$$\mathrm{LDR} = \frac{|v_{|\mathcal{G}_1|} - v_{|\mathcal{G}_2|}|}{\max(v_n - v_1, \epsilon)} \tag{4}$$

Equation 4 compares eigenvalues at positions indexed by subgroup sizes (numerator) and normalizes by the graph's total spectral range (denominator), with $\epsilon = 10^{-6}$ preventing division by zero. If LDR ≈ 0, it indicates minimal bias, suggesting subgroups that occupy similar positions in the spectral embedding space (balanced spectrum). Similarly, a LDR $\gg 0$ means significant disparity, with subgroups clustering around distinct eigenvalues, suggesting structural bias in the original embeddings.

The LDR's scale-invariant design (LDR $\in [0, 1]$) makes it particularly effective for comparing bias across different datasets or model architectures. A value over 0.3 usually requires analysis, yet the exact threshold varies according to what fairness standards the application demands.

3.3 Provable Guarantees

In this section, we present the perturbation bounds connecting the LDR to downstream fairness violations. We merge statistical learning theory tools such as uniform convergence and concentration inequalities [22] with the latest developments in spectral bias analysis from graph-based learning [2], which enables us to analyze the difference between empirical and true demographic parity without the need for demographic labels.

Theorem 1 (Bias Detection Bound). *Assume L represents a linear classifier operating on embeddings that maintains an LDR η. For any $k > 0$, with probability $1 - k$:*

$$|\mathrm{d}(l)_{Gap} - \mathrm{d}(l)_{True}| \leq \underbrace{c\sqrt{\frac{\eta \log(1/k)}{n}}}_{\textit{spectral bias term}} + \underbrace{\mathcal{O}(n^{-1/2})}_{\textit{statistical error}} \tag{5}$$

where $\mathrm{d}(l)_{Gap}$ is the empirical demographic parity gap, $\mathrm{d}(l)_{True}$ the true gap, and c is a constant.

Proof. The error is decomposed into spectral and statistical terms via McDiarmid's inequality [2].

This implies that Theorem 1 certifies that small LDR η ensures bounded fairness violations and the $\sqrt{\eta}$ dependence shows spectral bias decays quadratically with intervention strength

4 Method

Our spectral fairness method operates on embeddings $\mathbf{E} \in \mathbb{R}^{n \times d}$ from a contrastive model, where n is the number of samples and d the embedding dimension. Key parameters are summarized in Table 1.

Table 1. Key parameters and their roles

Parameter	Default	Purpose
k (NN graph)	10	Controls graph sparsity
σ (bandwidth)	0.5	Scales similarity decay
τ (sensitivity)	0.7	Threshold for critical dimensions
ϵ (LDR)	10^{-6}	Numerical stability constant

4.1 Bias Quantification

Step 1: Graph Construction For embeddings $\{\mathbf{e}_i\}_{i=1}^{n}$, build a k-nearest neighbor graph:

Algorithm 1. Build Similarity Graph

Require: Embeddings $\mathbf{E}$, k, σ
Ensure: Adjacency matrix $\mathbf{W}$
for $i \leftarrow 1$ to n **do**
  Find k-NN($\mathbf{e}_i$) via FAISS
  for $j \in k$-NN($\mathbf{e}_i$) **do**
    $W_{ij} \leftarrow \exp(-\|\mathbf{e}_i - \mathbf{e}_j\|_2^2/\sigma^2)$
  end for
end for

Algorithm 1 takes as input the embedding matrix $\mathbf{E} \in \mathbb{R}^{n \times d}$, a neighborhood size k, and a bandwidth parameter σ. For each point $\mathbf{e}_i$, the k nearest neighbors are retrieved using FAISS [11]. Pairwise similarities are computed with the Gaussian kernel:

$$W_{ij} = \exp\left(-\frac{\|\mathbf{e}_i - \mathbf{e}_j\|_2^2}{\sigma^2}\right),$$

yielding a sparse adjacency matrix $\mathbf{W}$ with k non-zero entries per row. This matrix captures local structure efficiently, with a time complexity of $\mathcal{O}(n \log n)$. The bandwidth σ is typically set to the median pairwise distance.

Step 2: Spectral Clustering. To discover subgroups, the normalized graph cut (NCut) is minimized using the Laplacian $\mathbf{L} = \mathbf{D} - \mathbf{W}$:

$$\mathrm{NCut}(\mathcal{G}_1, \mathcal{G}_2) = \frac{\mathrm{cut}(\mathcal{G}_1, \mathcal{G}_2)}{\mathrm{vol}(\mathcal{G}_1)} + \frac{\mathrm{cut}(\mathcal{G}_1, \mathcal{G}_2)}{\mathrm{vol}(\mathcal{G}_2)},$$

where $\mathrm{cut}(\mathcal{G}_1, \mathcal{G}_2) = \sum_{i \in \mathcal{G}_1, j \in \mathcal{G}_2} W_{ij}$ and $\mathrm{vol}(\mathcal{G}) = \sum_{i \in \mathcal{G}} D_{ii}$. This objective balances intra-group cohesion and inter-group separation. In practice, the optimal partition is approximated by computing the top two eigenvectors of $\mathbf{L}$ and clustering them via k-means.

Step 3: LDR Computation. Here, we apply Eq. 4.

4.2 Critical Dimension Identification

Given the embedding matrix $\mathbf{E} \in \mathbb{R}^{n \times d}$, Laplacian $\mathbf{L} \in \mathbb{R}^{n \times n}$, and threshold $\tau \in (0, 1)$, the algorithm extracts the Fiedler vector $\mathbf{v}_1$ (second eigenvector of $\mathbf{L}$) as a proxy for bias direction. For each dimension j, it computes $s_j = |\mathrm{Corr}(\mathbf{E}_{:,j}, \mathbf{v}_1)|$. Dimensions with $s_j > \tau$ are collected in $\mathcal{D}_{\text{bias}}$. The threshold τ balances sensitivity and specificity, with typical values between 0.6 and 0.8, see Algorithm 2. The overall complexity is $\mathcal{O}(nd)$.

Algorithm 2. Find Bias-Critical Dimensions

Require: $\mathbf{E}$, $\mathbf{L}$, threshold τ
Ensure: Critical dimensions $\mathcal{D}_{\text{bias}}$
$\mathbf{v}_1 \leftarrow$ 2nd eigenvector of $\mathbf{L}$ ▷ Fiedler vector
for $j \leftarrow 1$ to d **do**
  $s_j \leftarrow |\mathrm{Corr}(\mathbf{E}_{:,j}, \mathbf{v}_1)|$
  if $s_j > \tau$ **then**
    $\mathcal{D}_{\text{bias}} \leftarrow \mathcal{D}_{\text{bias}} \cup \{j\}$
  end if
end for

4.3 Practical Implementation

Given embedding matrix $\mathbf{E} \in \mathbb{R}^{n \times d}$, neighborhood size k, bandwidth σ, and correlation threshold τ, the algorithm constructs a sparse similarity graph $\mathbf{W}$ using k-NN with Gaussian weights, see Algorithm 3. Spectral clustering on the Laplacian $\mathbf{L} = \mathbf{D} - \mathbf{W}$ partitions data into subgroups $\mathcal{G}_1$ and $\mathcal{G}_2$. The LDR quantifies bias between subgroups, while bias-critical dimensions $\mathcal{D}_{\text{bias}}$ are identified via Pearson correlation with the Fiedler vector. Outputs include: (1) LDR score, (2) $\mathcal{D}_{\text{bias}}$, and (3) visual diagnostics. Complexity is dominated by eigendecomposition but mitigated by sparse optimizations.

Algorithm 3. Spectral Bias Auditing

Require: $\mathbf{E}$, k, σ, τ
Ensure: LDR score, $\mathcal{D}_{\text{bias}}$, visualization
$\mathbf{W} \leftarrow \text{BuildSimilarityGraph}(\mathbf{E}, k, \sigma)$
$\mathcal{G}_1, \mathcal{G}_2 \leftarrow \text{SpectralClustering}(\mathbf{W})$
$\text{LDR} \leftarrow \text{ComputeLDR}(\mathbf{W}, \mathcal{G}_1, \mathcal{G}_2)$
$\mathcal{D}_{\text{bias}} \leftarrow \text{FindCriticalDims}(\mathbf{E}, \mathbf{L}, \tau)$
Plot $\mathbf{v}_1$ vs. $\mathbf{E}_{:,\mathcal{D}_{\text{bias}}}$

Optimizations: (1) Sparse $\mathbf{W}$ reduces memory from $\mathcal{O}(n^2)$ to $\mathcal{O}(kn)$; (2) Lanczos method computes top-m eigenvectors in $\mathcal{O}(mn^2)$; (3) GPU-accelerated correlation enables fast detection across dimensions. These optimizations allow scalability to datasets with $n \sim 10^6$.

5 Experiments

5.1 Setup

The spectral fairness method is evaluated on two benchmark datasets, CelebA and CheXpert. The CelebA dataset includes 202599 rows with 45 columns of facial attributes, while the CheXpert contains 223414 rows with 22 columns of medical imaging. The analysis focused on the protected attributes of gender (Male vs. Female) and age (Young vs. NotYoung) in the CelebA analysis. In the CheXpert experiments, we exclusively analyze the sex category by comparing Male and Female results. The CheXpert dataset includes binned age categories that separate data into three distinct groups: younger than 40 years old, 40 to 65 years old, and older than 65 years old.

Our experiments compare against three baseline categories: The first set of baseline models includes supervised fairness techniques like adversarial debiasing, which optimize demographic parity during the training phase, alongside heuristic semi-supervised learning approaches that use unlabeled data without fairness constraints and standard unsupervised contrastive learning models such as SimCLR.

The backbone architecture used across all models consists of ResNet-50, and they were trained under the same hyperparameters, which include a batch size of 256, Adam optimizer, learning rate set to 10^{-4}, and 100 training epochs. Our spectral parameters are set empirically: $k = 10$, $\sigma = 0.5$, and $\tau = 0.7$.

We assess evaluation results by applying both accuracy and fairness metrics within different protected subgroups. Our evaluation includes demographic parity difference and equalized odds metrics, which we compute on downstream classifiers that operate on frozen embeddings.

5.2 Results

Table 2. Comparison of accuracy and fairness metrics across supervised, semi-supervised, unsupervised, and our method on the CelebA dataset using 'sex' and 'Age' as protected attributes. Fairness improves as Demographic Parity Difference (DP Diff) and Equalized Odds Difference (EO Diff) decrease.

Method	Male (Protected Attribute)			Young (Protected Attribute)		
	Accuracy	DP Diff	EO Diff	Accuracy	DP Diff	EO Diff
Supervised Fairness	0.9165	0.7098	0.3477	0.9042	0.3720	0.1314
Heuristic SSL	0.9977	0.7857	0.0103	0.9977	0.3645	0.0011
Unsupervised	0.9991	0.7845	0.0041	0.9991	0.3693	0.0005
Our Method	**0.9989**	**0.7887**	**0.0005**	**0.9989**	**0.3709**	**0.0005**

Table 2 reports the experimental results of our method and three baseline fairness methods: Supervised Fairness, Heuristic SSL, and Unsupervised Learning on the CelebA dataset using two protected attributes, Male and Young. All the methods achieve high accuracy, but our method has the best trade-off between accuracy and fairness. Specifically, our method performs the best in EO Diff and attains nearly zero values. At the same time, it also achieves competitive accuracy (0.9989). For the Male attribute, our method attains the lowest EO Diff (0.0005) compared to the supervised fairness baseline (0.3477). Similarly, for the Young attribute, our method outperforms the supervised method in balancing accuracy and fairness. Thus, our spectral fairness framework provides a good strategy for learning fair representations.

Table 3 The CheXpert dataset provides a comparative evaluation of four different methods alongside our proposed fairness technique by focusing on two protected attributes. Sex and Age. Each method is assessed using three key metrics: Accuracy, DP Diff, and EO Diff.

Our method achieves accuracy levels that match or exceed those of existing fairness-aware and fairness-unaware baselines for both protected attributes, alongside minimal fairness gaps. By optimizing for zero fairness gaps, explicitly supervised fairness methods sacrifice significant predictive accuracy. Our

Table 3. Comparison of Accuracy and Fairness Metrics across Supervised, Semi-Supervised, Unsupervised, and Our Method on the CheXpert Dataset Using *Sex* and *Age* as Protected Attributes. Lower values for Demographic Parity Difference (DP Diff) and Equalized Odds Difference (EO Diff) indicate better fairness.

Method	Sex (Binary)			Age (Groups: < 40, 40–65, > 65)		
	Accuracy	DP Diff	EO Diff	Accuracy	DP Diff	EO Diff
Supervised Fairness	0.8216	0.0000	0.0000	0.8216	0.0000	0.0000
Heuristic SSL	0.9966	0.0128	0.0050	0.9966	0.0219	0.0028
Unsupervised	0.9971	0.0142	0.0102	0.9971	0.0236	0.0005
Our Method	**0.9973**	**0.0166**	**0.0081**	**0.9973**	**0.0280**	**0.0024**

method delivers exceptional predictive performance compared to supervised fairness approaches while maintaining fairness deviations that are minimal and similar to those found in heuristic and unsupervised methods. Our spectral fairness framework demonstrates its benefit by delivering superior predictive performance alongside maintained fairness standards.

6 Discussion

We examine the implications, limitations, and future directions of our spectral fairness method for SSL. The application of spectral tools such as graph Laplacian analysis and eigenvector alignment enables the detection of bias across protected groups without needing labeled data. This method provides structure-aware interpretability, which enhances current fairness techniques and performs well in annotation-scarce fields such as healthcare, vision, and language analysis.

Nevertheless, our method depends on the quality of the embeddings: Poor representations lead to uninformative graphs. Similarly, the issue of scalability is another concern, as graph construction and spectral decomposition can be costly for large datasets, despite optimizations (e.g., FAISS, GPU acceleration). Moreover, our model is currently designed to work well with protected attributes that are either discrete or binary, which may likely reduce its applicability or performance for continuous-sensitive features.

We also observed that eigenvector selection plays a key role in the performance of our spectral fairness method. While the Fiedler vector (second smallest eigenvector) consistently yielded coherent clusters and stable fairness metrics, using higher-index eigenvectors introduced noise and degraded accuracy. Incorporating multiple eigenvectors (e.g., top-k) improved representation expressiveness but led to fairness metric instability without regularization. These findings underscore the importance of the selection of the main spectral components to balance the quality of the clustering and the detection of fairness.

Our approach can be developed further by using fairness-aware regularizers for continuous training or by combining it with neural-symbolic systems, including neural-augmented grammars work. Structured prediction can benefit from spectral signals to select rules that lead towards the development of fair and understandable AI systems for various applications.

7 Conclusion

This paper presented a spectral fairness method for detecting and mitigating representational bias in contrastive learning under limited or no supervision. Our method constructs similarity graphs from embedding spaces and applies spectral clustering and Laplacian analysis to uncover subgroup disparities without requiring demographic labels. By introducing the *Laplacian Disparity Ratio (LDR)* and *Eigenvector Sensitivity Analysis*, we provide interpretable metrics for quantifying fairness gaps across protected groups.

We evaluated the proposed method on two benchmark datasets, *CelebA* and *CheXpert*, using sex and age as protected attributes. On the CelebA dataset, our method achieved high accuracy (0.9989) while reducing the Equalized Odds (EO) Difference to a low of 0.0005. On the CheXpert dataset, an 0.0081 EO was achieved, and Demographic Parity (DP) Differences of 0.0166 were achieved, alongside strong predictive performance (accuracy: 0.9973). Across both datasets, our method outperformed supervised, heuristic, and contrastive learning baselines in balancing fairness and accuracy.

In addition to empirical strength, the proposed method is interpretable, scalable with GPU acceleration, and applicable in real-world domains such as healthcare, vision, and language, where fairness must be ensured in the absence of labels. Nonetheless, its effectiveness depends on the quality of learned embeddings, and computational overhead can pose challenges for large-scale deployment. Current methods also assume binary or discrete protected attributes, limiting broader applicability.

In future work, we aim to embed fairness-aware regularization directly into contrastive loss functions, enabling end-to-end training that minimizes bias during representation learning. This direction offers a promising path toward building responsible and equitable AI systems from the ground up.

Acknowledgments. The authors wish to acknowledge the Responsible & Applied Machine Learning Laboratory (RAML Lab) at the Department of Computer Science, Brock University, Canada.

Disclosure of Interests. The authors have no competing interests to declare that is relevant to the content of this article.

Data Availability. The CelebA and CheXpert datasets used in this study are publicly available. CelebA can be accessed at https://mmlab.ie.cuhk.edu.hk/projects/CelebA.html, and CheXpert at https://www.kaggle.com/datasets/ashery/chexpert.

Code Availability. All code used to implement the proposed method and reproduce the experimental results is available in Google Colab at: https://shorturl.at/s1FSD.

Appendix A Experimental Results of Our Fairness Analyses

This appendix provides supplementary figures that offer a comprehensive evaluation of fairness and representation disparities across demographic groups in both the CelebA and CheXpert datasets (Figs. 2, 3, 4, 5 and 6).

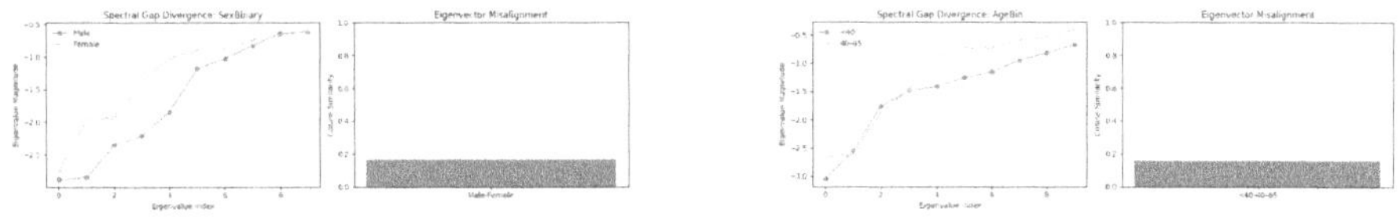

(a) Divergence in spectral gap and misalignment of eigenvectors between Male and Female subgroups expose structural differences in learned representations.

(b) Divergence in spectral gap and misalignment of eigenvectors between Age groups (<40 vs. 40–65) expose structural differences in learned representations

Fig. 2. Analysis of spectral gap divergence along with eigenvector misalignment on the CheXPert dataset shows representation differences between protected groups. The eigenvalue distributions and cosine similarity data between sex and age subgroups show distinct patterns, which suggest possible representational bias.

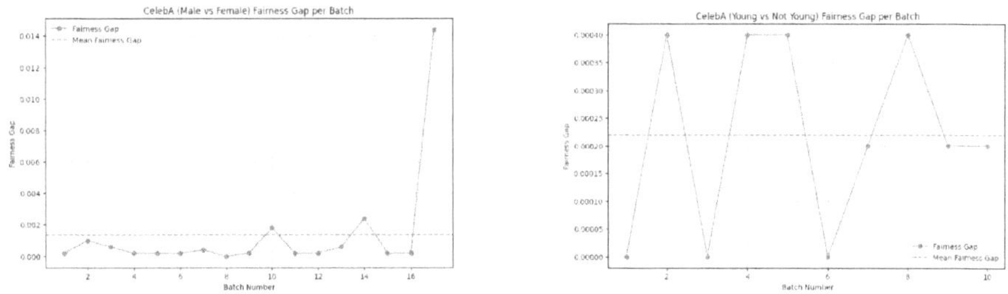

(a) Fairness gap across 10 batches on CelebA (Protected Attribute: Male).

(b) Fairness gap across 10 batches on CelebA (Protected Attribute: Young).

Fig. 3. Batch-wise fairness gap analysis on CelebA for different protected attributes (Male vs Female and Young vs Not Young). Our method demonstrates low and stable fairness gaps, with minimal variance across batches.

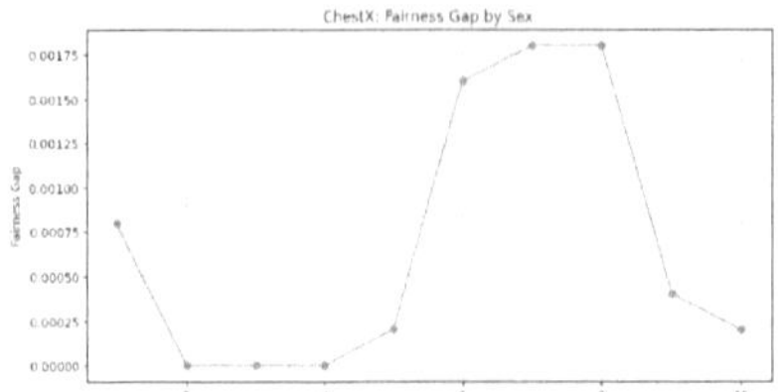

(a) Fairness gap per batch on CheXpert (Protected Attribute: Sex).

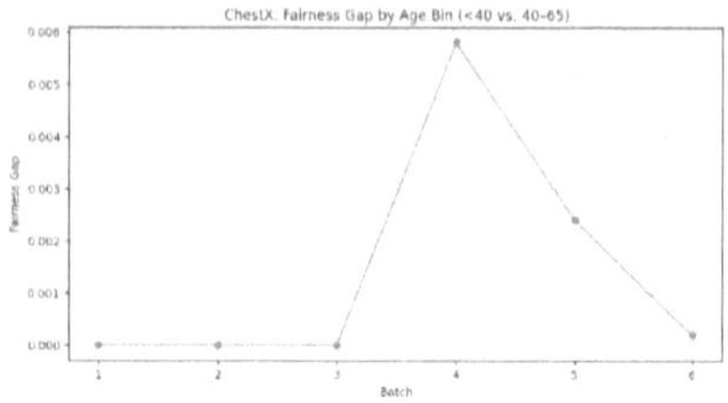

(b) Fairness gap per batch on CheXpert (Protected Attribute: Age: <40 vs. 40–65).

Fig. 4. Batch-wise fairness gap analysis on CheXpert for protected attributes (Sex and Age). Results show consistently low gaps across batches, indicating stable fairness performance with minor fluctuations.

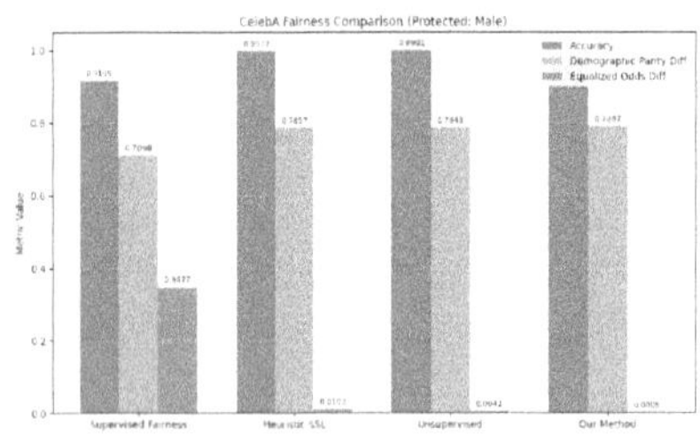

(a) CelebA Fairness Comparison (Protected Attribute: Male)

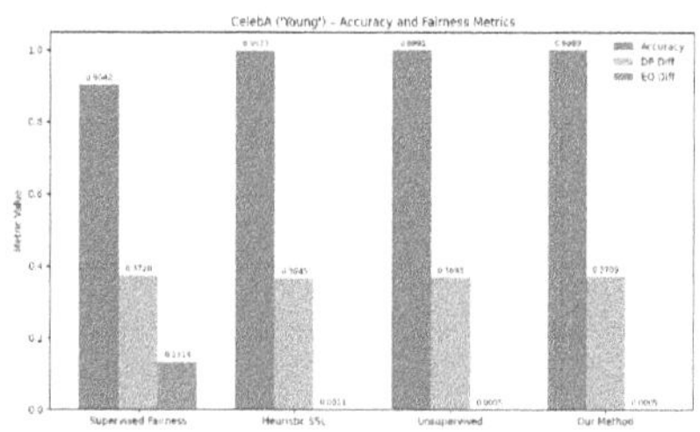

(b) CelebA Fairness Comparison (Protected Attribute: Young)

Fig. 5. Comparison of accuracy and fairness metrics (Demographic Parity Difference and Equalized Odds Difference) across different methods on the CelebA dataset, using Male and Young as protected attributes. Our method consistently achieves high accuracy while minimizing fairness disparities, particularly in Equalized Odds Difference.

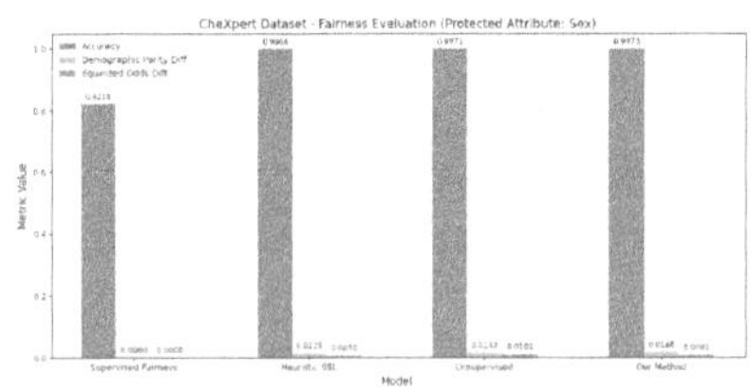

(a) CheXpert Fairness Comparison (Protected Attribute: Sex)

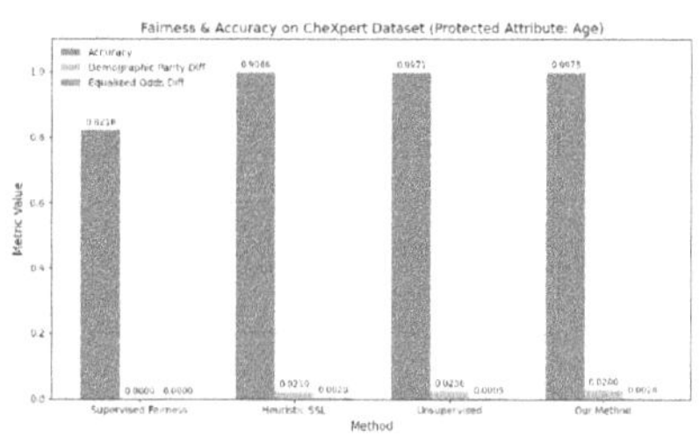

(b) CheXpert Fairness Comparison (Protected Attribute: Age)

Fig. 6. Comparison of accuracy and fairness metrics (Demographic Parity Difference and Equalized Odds Difference) across different methods on the CheXpert dataset, using Sex and Age as protected attributes. Our method consistently achieves high accuracy while minimizing fairness disparities, particularly in Equalized Odds Difference.

References

1. Chen, T., Kornblith, S., Norouzi, M., Hinton, G.: Big self-supervised models for medical image understanding. Nat. Biomed. Eng. **6**, 1234–1245 (2022)
2. Combes, R.: An extension of mcdiarmid's inequality. In: 2024 IEEE International Symposium on Information Theory (ISIT), pp. 79–84. IEEE (2024)
3. Conti, J.R., Noiry, N., Clemencon, S., Despiegel, V., Gentric, S.: Mitigating gender bias in face recognition using the von mises-fisher mixture model. In: International Conference on Machine Learning, pp. 4344–4369. PMLR (2022)
4. Creager, E., et al.: Flexibly fair representation learning by disentanglement. In: International conference on machine learning, pp. 1436–1445. PMLR (2019)
5. Das, K.: The laplacian spectrum of a graph. Comput. Math. Appli. **48**(5–6), 715–724 (2004). https://doi.org/10.1016/j.camwa.2004.05.005. Accessed 30 June 2025
6. Feeney, P., Hughes, M.C.: Sincere: Supervised information noise-contrastive estimation revisited, pp. 1–31. arXiv preprint arXiv:2309.14277 (2023)
7. Hardt, M., Price, E., Srebro, N.: Equality of opportunity in supervised learning. In: Advances in Neural Information Processing Systems, pp. 3315–3323 (2016)
8. Hashimoto, T., Srivastava, M., Namkoong, H., Liang, P.: Fairness without demographics in repeated loss minimization. In: International Conference on Machine Learning, pp. 1929–1938. PMLR(2018)
9. Hu, H., Wang, X., Zhang, Y., Chen, Q., Guan, Q.: A comprehensive survey on contrastive learning. Neurocomputing, 128645 (2024)
10. Irvin, J., et al.: Chexpert: a large chest radiograph dataset with uncertainty labels and expert comparison. In: Proceedings of the AAAI Conference on Artificial Intelligence, vol. 33, pp. 590–597 (2019)
11. Johnson, J., Douze, M., Jégou, H.: Billion-scale similarity search with GPUs. IEEE Trans. Big Data **7**(3), 535–547 (2019)
12. Le-Khac, P.H., Healy, G., Smeaton, A.F.: Contrastive representation learning: a framework and review. IEEE Access **8**, 193907–193934 (2020)
13. Liu, Z., Luo, P., Wang, X., Tang, X.: Deep learning face attributes in the wild. In: Proceedings of International Conference on Computer Vision (ICCV), pp. 3730–3738 (2015)
14. Luo, B., Wilson, R.C., Hancock, E.R.: Spectral embedding of graphs. Pattern Recogn. **36**(10), 2213–2230 (2003). https://doi.org/10.1016/S0031-3203(03)00084-0. Accessed 28 June 2025
15. Ma, M.Q., et al.: Conditional contrastive learning for improving fairness in self-supervised learning (2022). https://arxiv.org/abs/2106.02866 Accessed 30 June 2025
16. Ng, A., Jordan, M., Weiss, Y.: On spectral clustering: analysis and an algorithm. Adv. Neural. Inf. Process. Syst. **14**, 1–8 (2001)
17. Parulekar, A., Collins, L., Shanmugam, K., Mokhtari, A., Shakkottai, S.: Infonce loss provably learns cluster-preserving representations. In: The Thirty Sixth Annual Conference on Learning Theory, pp. 1914–1961. PMLR (2023)
18. Poudel, R.P., Pandya, H., Liwicki, S., Cipolla, R.: Recore: regularized contrastive representation learning of world model. In: Proceedings of the IEEE/CVF Conference on Computer Vision and Pattern Recognition, pp. 22904–22913 (2024)
19. Qi, T., et al.: Fairvfl: a fair vertical federated learning framework with contrastive adversarial learning. Adv. Neural. Inf. Process. Syst. **35**, 7852–7865 (2022)
20. Radford, A., et al.: Learning transferable visual models from natural language supervision. In: International Conference on Machine Learning, pp. 8748–8763. PMLR (2021)

21. Seyyed-Kalantari, L., Zhang, H., McDermott, M.B., Chen, I.Y., Ghassemi, M.: Underdiagnosis bias of artificial intelligence algorithms applied to chest radiographs in under-served patient populations. Nat. Med. **27**(12), 2176–2182 (2021)
22. Shalev-Shwartz, S., Ben-David, S.: Understanding Machine Learning: From Theory to Algorithms. Cambridge University Press (2014)
23. Von Luxburg, U.: A tutorial on spectral clustering. Stat. Comput. **17**, 395–416 (2007)
24. Wang, T., Isola, P.: Understanding contrastive representation learning through alignment and uniformity on the hypersphere. In: International Conference on Machine Learning, pp. 9929–9939. PMLR (2020)
25. Wu, W., Protopapas, P., Yang, Z., Michalatos, P.: Gender classification and bias mitigation in facial images. In: Proceedings of the 12th ACM Conference on Web Science, pp. 106–114 (2020)

Towards Smarter IT Compliance Audits: Leveraging Artificial Intelligence

Asma Saleh Al Khalili and Abdul Khalique Shaikh(✉)

Department of Information Systems, Sultan Qaboos University, Muscat, Sultanate of Oman
shaikh@squ.edu.om

Abstract. Due to technological advancements, Information Technology (IT) compliance audits have evolved from labor-intensive, manual procedures to efficient, data-driven processes. This transformation has streamlined the audit process, enabling more accurate and follow the compliance with regulations and standards. This paper is based on System Dynamics (SD) principles to the automation of IT compliance audits using AI-powered tools. This paper investigates how the National Institute of Standards and Technology and Artificial Intelligence Risk Management Framework (NIST) (AI RMF) can be utilized as a basis for automating and improving IT compliance audits. We proposed a conceptual framework that integrates the NIST AI RMF with automation-unique capabilities, which includes anomaly detection and live tracking, to create a dynamic and adaptive audit process. The paper uses a SWOT (Strengths, Weaknesses, Opportunities, Threats) analysis of the NIST AI RMF to identify key leverage points for improving adoption strategies. The study also presents a threat assessment model to highlight potential internal and external threats to AI-driven audit processes, such as implementation challenges, rapid technological advancements, and a lack of understanding. The findings demonstrate that AI-powered tools, like CoCAF and EY Helix GLAD, can significantly improve audit efficiency, accuracy, and regulatory compliance. However, ethical challenges, for instance algorithmic bias and data transparency, must be carefully addressed. The study recommends a phased implementation approach, encouraging ethical considerations, and the use of blockchain technology to improve data security and transparency.

Keywords: Audit · Compliance · Artificial Intelligence (AI) · Risk Management Framework (RMF) · Automation

1 Introduction

In the current digital era, IT compliance audits are computerized and based on data driven methods rather than traditional tedious processes. These audits are executed more efficiently, accurately and support scalability. This research study investigates how risk governance, measurement, and management use the NIST Artificial Intelligence Risk Management Framework (AI RMF) that supports improvement in IT compliance audits. Through this, it tackles important issues that presently protect your broad adoption, consisting of the absence of described frameworks and standards. IT compliance audits

H. R. Arabnia et al. (Eds.): CSCE 2025, CCIS 2934, pp. 321–334, 2026.
https://doi.org/10.1007/978-3-032-22190-2_22

involve knowledge of the complicated interactions and feedback loops within the audit system, specifically while integrating AI-powered tools. System Dynamics examines how adjustments in a single module can ripple through the entire machine. For instance, whilst artificial intelligence might also boost up facts analysis, it could additionally necessitate modifications in auditor training packages or cause the adoption of new statistics collection methodologies.

1.1 Historical Evolution of IT Compliance Audits

IT compliance audits are influenced by the dynamic nature of technological advancements and the increasing diversity of digital environments. Existing sources display the progression of conducting IT compliance audits from the traditional method of manual processes to AI-driven automation. The history of IT audits can be traced back to the emergence of computerized IS in the middle of 20th century. It is observed that organizations started emerging technology to streamline operations [1]. With the rise of the emerging technology and internet, auditors resorted to integrating AI tools into their audit practices to facilitate the method and ensure compliance is adhered to accurately. Moreover, with the help of automation, artificial intelligence (AI), and Information communication technology (ICT), auditors must be capable of getting entry to and analyzing huge records and statistics to perceive ability risks and challenges [2]. The sources show how IT audits are constantly evolving to deal with new emerging techniques. The incorporation of AI is a revolutionary stage that equips auditors with advanced instruments to improve audit effectiveness, precision, and insights.

1.2 AI-Powered Tools Application in Compliance Audits

In the transformative era we live in, the articles explain how AI has revolutionized the course of conducting audit practices. Research emphasized how the use of AI has enabled auditors and other stakeholders to significantly improve the accuracy and efficiency of audit practices. Through machine learning algorithms, AI processes historical data, identifies patterns, and assesses potential risks based on predefined criteria [3]. In addition, a vital advantage in the automation of audit practices is the consistent monitoring of compliance, where there is an ongoing alignment between the regulatory requirements and the policies of the organization. However, this meant that intensive training for auditors had to be held. Auditors must adapt and acquire new skills to effectively leverage these technologies, and training auditors in data science and machine learning would become essential as the profession progresses [4, 5].

1.3 Role of AI to Make Strategic Decisions

Researchers are all in consensus that AI technologies can make auditing procedures easier, more efficient, and more seamless than doing them manually. Furthermore, the ability to make strategic judgements is another important benefit of using these new technologies. Utilizing AI tools facilitates the process of obtaining both current and historical data patterns *and* predictive analytics swiftly and accurately. AI's predictive analytics provide auditors with dynamic insights into potential risks. By analyzing historical data and identifying patterns, AI can predict future risks, allowing auditors to implement preemptive measures and proactive risk mitigation strategies [3]. Thus, managers and auditors frequently take this into account and utilize it to their benefit when making strategic and well-considered decisions backed up with solid data.

1.4 Challenges in Existing Literature

While the idea of automating audit procedures sounds very appealing, putting it into practice is a difficult task. An important challenge that researchers have not emphasized thoroughly is the lack of a standardized guideline or framework to use as a baseline. The absence of clear guidelines and standards places difficulties in guaranteeing the dependability and consistency of AI-driven audit procedures across various businesses and sectors [1]. Furthermore, there are many standards that can be used as a reference to properly align the practices of auditing with the adoption of technologies. It is important to distinguish between industries and discuss frameworks that apply to one's organization. For instance, the HIPAA is well known for being used for the healthcare sector, PCI-DSS is used especially for the banking area. After considering that, management can resume exploring generation and AI requirements like ISO/IEC 38505 (Governance of Data) for use as a basis for IT governance in businesses the use of AI structures. Moreover, NIST (National Institute of Standards and Technology) has come up with a framework for the Artificial Intelligence Risk Management Framework (AI RMF) that can be used to guide in delivering results and activities that facilitate communication, comprehension, and efforts to appropriately manage AI risks and create reliable AI systems [6].

1.5 Gaps in Current Research

The lack of standardized frameworks and metrics stated above poses a gap in the current research. This gap creates difficulties in understanding and ensuring the consistent practice of how AI should ideally be implemented for compliance audits. In addition, establishing proper performance metrics to rely on based on a comparison between a pattern of AI-driven implementation data cannot be easily established. This is due to the absence of standardized metrics for evaluating and reviewing AI-driven audits that could lead to uncertainty and subjectivity in assessing their effectiveness and impact [7]. Furthermore, our research is limited by the availability of data that is used to train and test AI models in compliance audits. Lack of access to AI resources prevents us from making more thorough judgements of how well AI automation works in real-world scenarios; for example, the model proposed above using the NIST AI RMF was not applied in any case due to the lack of resources to implement the test. The detailed technical insight into AI functionality is beyond the scope of this research.

2 Research Methodology

The Research methodology section commences with an overview of the data collection technique that is primarily based on a thorough theoretical exam of existing literature referring to the usage of Artificial Intelligence in compliance and auditing practices.

Furthermore, the section focuses on gathering information from various sources, some of which evaluate the application of AI-driven compliance in fraud detection and finance, while others detail IT audit procedures in specific sectors, like the oil and gas industry.

2.1 Data Collection Method

The methodology used in this research is a comprehensive theoretical analysis of existing articles that propose the use of AI in compliance and other audit practices. Moreover, the articles were gathered from different sources such as Scopus and Google scholar, some of which evaluate the application of AI-driven compliance in fraud detection and finance, while others go into detail about IT audit procedures in the oil and gas sector. As a result, the data gathered is rather comprehensive and includes a detailed examination of the use of AI in auditing procedures from different viewpoints.

2.2 NIST AI RMF Conceptual Framework

In this research study, we propose the use of the NIST AI RMF in adopting the AI to automate IT compliance audits. The proposed approach is mentioned in Fig. 1 that illustrates how the NIST framework can potentially be used to adopt AI in audit practices. NIST AI RMF includes the govern, map, measure, and manage attributes to be used as a baseline for adopting an AI and analyzing the risks. The first aspect **(1)** ***Govern*** concerns the alignment of IT audit compliance regulations with AI adoption and defines the roles and responsibilities. **(2)** ***Map*** involves the prioritization of risks related to the adoption of AI in compliance audits and mapping it with the relevant regulations. **(3)** ***Measure*** attribute is used to define audit performance metrics and mechanisms. Finally, **(4) Manage** displayed the use application of automated corrective action and incident management of compliance audit practices. Furthermore, there are additional factors that our research proposes in this figure, relating to automation-specific factors like data privacy, real-time monitoring, anomaly detection, and reporting. These factors hover over the NIST AI RMF and are involved in the form of an outer layer posed as a continuous cycle.

The framework mainly emphasizes the risk management component in AI adoption. Risk management and assessment are crucial concepts that help outline and smooth the pathway forward. Researchers state that although auditing is a strong and established field in terms of itself, it is still unclear how exactly to apply it to AI systems, especially given the intricate societal and technological issues that AI raises [7]. Thus, the purpose of the framework composed in this research is to aid in the challenge that researchers have been in consensus of.

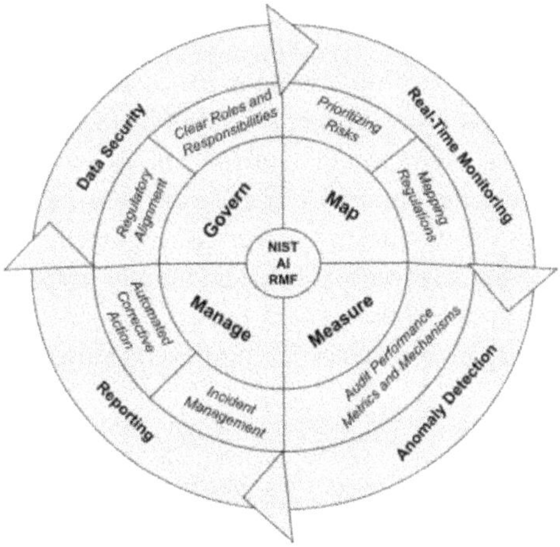

Fig. 1. Adoption of NIST AI RMF in IT Compliance Audits

2.3 NIST AI RMF Policy Recommendation

The appropriate policy should be in place to offer clarity and helpful terminology to support the figure once the conceptual framework has been established.

In this study, we recommend the policy includes the following sections with the relevant description as displayed in Table 1.

Table 1. NIST AI RMF Policy Criteria

Section	Description
Objectives and Purpose	A clear statement of the objectives and purpose of the policy in the context of NIST RMF AI adoption to audit practices
Scope of Policy	The scope of the policy needs to be defined precisely to support and align with what the framework entails
Roles and Responsibilities	Proper delegation of roles and responsibilities between auditors, auditees, and other stakeholders
Compliance Requirements	The compliance requirements needed to support the execution of the framework References of guidelines and standards like ISO 27001, ISO 9001, COBIT, etc.
Risk Management Outline	Approach to identify, monitor, and mitigate the AI risks that could potentially emerge when adopting the framework to automate compliance audits

The concepts mentioned earlier are substantially comparable to the NIST AI RMF. Policy adaptation is even more thorough and solid by including the NIST AI RMF's focus on governance, mapping, monitoring, and managing AI risks. Furthermore, having an AI policy framework in place gives stakeholders guidance for adopting and integrating new AI technologies into auditing practices [8].

2.4 NIST AI RMF SWOT Analysis

It's crucial to comprehend where this thought fits in after gaining a firm grip of the framework and the adoption of its policies. The SWOT (Strengths, Weaknesses, Opportunities, Threats) analysis is an important analysis that is used to assess the internal and external elements that impact the proposed framework or strategy. Moreover, it supports making strategic selections and figuring out regions for improvement. For the case of the NIST AI RMF, there are outstanding strengths and opportunities, however on the alternative aspect, there also are weaknesses and threats. Figure 2 illustrates the strengths, weaknesses, opportunities, and threats of the proposed framework.

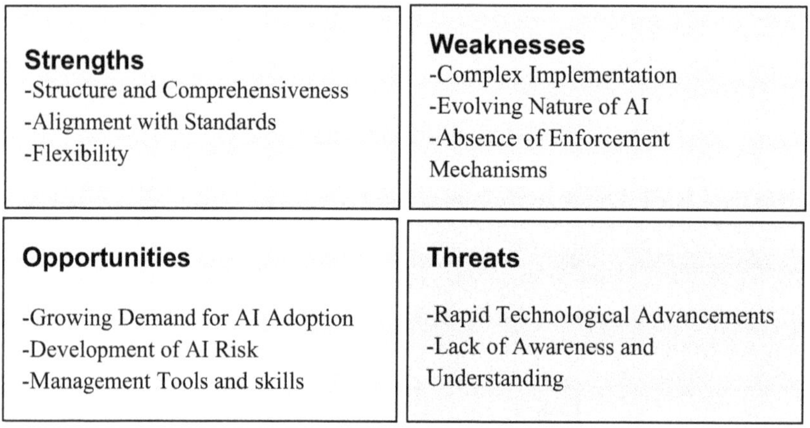

Fig. 2. NIST AI RMF SWOT Analysis

The framework has **strengths** in its structure as it covers every stage of the AI lifecycle, from design and development to deployment and monitoring, offering a thorough approach to controlling AI risks. This completeness aids organizations in detecting and reducing a variety of possible hazards. In addition, the framework aligns with common regulations and standards relevant to data security, privacy, and so forth. The NIST AI RMF can be tailored to various sectors, AI applications, and organizational environments. Because of its adaptability, organizations can customize the framework to fit their unique requirements and risk profiles. As for the **weaknesses**, while the framework is clear and structured well, it is also complicated to implement and can be resource intensive. Additionally, the framework's capacity to stay up to date with emerging risks and best practices may be threatened by the quick speed at which AI technology is developing. Furthermore, there is an absence of an enforcing mechanism for the framework, as it is a voluntary practice and not mandatory, which could potentially limit its effectiveness in driving widespread adoption. As for the external portion of this analysis, the **opportunities** in this framework are the growing demand for incorporating AI and the widespread use of AI tools in various fields, specifically in AI risk management tools and services. On the other hand, the **threats** that could emerge can be due to the rapid technological advancements and the lack of proper awareness and understanding of the framework. Some organizations may not fully comprehend the risks associated with AI and the significance of risk management, which could hinder the framework's broad adoption and efficiency in reducing possible harms.

3 System Design and Framework Development

3.1 Overview of NIST AI RMF

The proposed framework is a structured and comprehensive approach to establish a smooth transition from manual audit conduct to AI-driven audit procedures.

NIST is the National Institute of Standards and Technology, a prominent organization that develops requirements, guidelines, and frameworks related to the fields of engineering, emerging technology such as artificial intelligence, and cybersecurity. Moreover, one of the distinguished frameworks that NIST developed is the NIST AI RMF, which provides a dependent and thorough approach to addressing possible risks and encouraging the development and alertness of dependable and responsible AI.

The framework mainly focuses on governing, mapping, measuring, and managing AI system adoption. It is designed to be flexible and adaptable in order for organizations to tailor it to their specific field and needs.

3.2 Threat Assessment Model

Most of the frameworks are equipped with potential internal and external threats that can get in the way of their implementation. As for the case of NIST AI RMF, and in reference to the SWOT analysis illustrated in Fig. 2, a few threats are mapped.

Figure 3 shows the potential threats of the framework, concentrating on recognizing and ranking risks to the framework's adoption and efficiency. In the *first quadrant* of the figure, the potential threats are categorized into external and internal threats. External threats could include the emergence of competing frameworks and rapid technological advancements. On the other hand, internal threats focus on threats that can stem from within the organization itself, like lack of awareness and understanding, implementation challenges, and resistance to change. Moreover, the *second quadrant* focuses on assessing the impact and likelihood of the threat. This involves both impact and likelihood assessments. Upon the assessment, the *third quadrant* prioritizes the threats to ensure proper resources are allocated to address the major issues. In addition, there is also a fo*urth quadrant* in the model that concentrates on what mitigation strategy to develop for each prioritized risk. Finally, the *fifth quadrant* revolves around the matter of regular review and update of the threat landscape. The range of potential threats is constantly evolving, which is why it's crucial that the model is regularly reviewed and updated. Nevertheless, this predictive approach to threat assessment helps auditors and other stakeholders focus their efforts on high-risk areas to maximize resource allocation and boost audit efficacy [1].

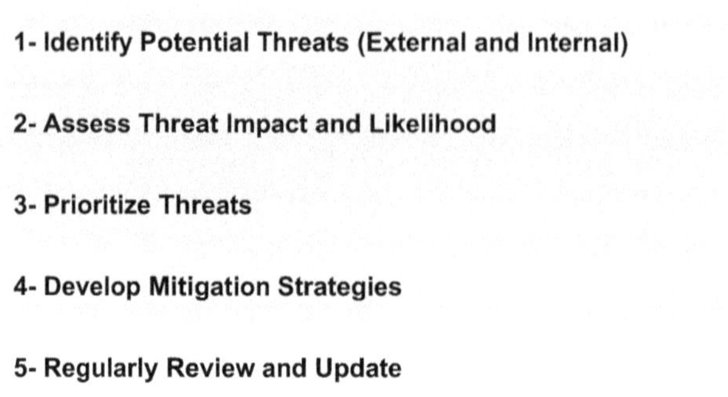

Fig. 3. Threat Assessment Model

3.3 AI-Based Strategy Recommendation System

A strategic approach is essential to better understand and organize the approach forward. It is recommended that all stakeholders understand and follow the strategy to ensure they are all in the same harmony. In addition, strategies are commonly established to guide the stakeholders in conducting their work. Another important consideration is the appropriate selection of AI tools in the strategy recommended. The recommended AI-based strategy should potentially include a proper analysis and evaluation of the data sets using a variety of AI tools and techniques specialized in automating IT compliance audits. Furthermore, the knowledge base used to build up the strategy should be comprehensive to include the proper knowledge on the NIST standard used in relevance to the conceptual framework proposed in this research. The AI-based strategy is helpful in making informed decisions quickly and accurately. Moreover, the tools used can potentially be a combination of machine learning (ML) and predictive analytics that support the adaptation.

4 Results, Findings, and Analysis

4.1 Results and Findings

Efficiency, reliability, and regulatory compliance have all been shown to be greatly improved by the use of AI in compliance audits. Conventional audit procedures have been transformed by machine learning methods, such as licensed and unregulated algorithms, which have proven their capacity to analyze massive datasets and identify irregularities. The AI-Based Automated Continuous Compliance Awareness Framework (CoCAF), for example, enhanced compliance management by using real-time risk assessment and automated text mining [10]. Similar to this, AI-powered predictive analytics has proved crucial in regulatory reporting for accelerating compliance procedures, lowering error rates, and guaranteeing timely reporting [13].

Instead of depending on conventional sample techniques, the use of AI-driven technologies such as EY Helix GLAD has transformed fraud detection into IT audits by applying anomaly detection processes to entire data pools. This change has greatly shortened processing times while enabling auditors to detect fraudulent activity with greater accuracy [15]. Additional uses have made it possible for businesses to effectively evaluate and reduce privacy issues, especially the utilization of natural language processing (NLP) for GDPR compliance.

Even with its advantages, there are still several ethical issues with using AI in auditing. Studies highlighting AI's limits have brought attention to issues including algorithmic bias, data privacy, and transparency. According to an evaluation of auditing specialists, there are serious concerns regarding the opacity of AI systems, and structures to guarantee integrity and justice are being called for. As seen by instances where AI must adjust to changing standards like GDPR and HIPAA, these difficulties are heightened by the dynamic nature of rules [15].

Moreover, AI's capacity to handle intricate regulatory environments continues to be a significant advantage. Research on financial firms' adherence to GDPR and SOX IT General Controls (ITGC) shows how AI-powered solutions reduce errors, automate rule-based evaluations, and promote proactive adherence [15]. Rule-based AI techniques have proven especially adept at adjusting to shifting laws, guaranteeing that businesses stay in compliance even as requirements change.

4.2 Analysis

The results of these studies demonstrate AI's revolutionary influence on compliance audits and are closely related to the various approaches used. Case studies that highlight the importance of machine learning in automating auditing procedures include those involving CoCAF and EY Helix GLAD. These approaches, which are backed by tests and industry expert interviews, confirm AI's potential to increase precision and productivity in a variety of fields [16].

AI's applications across GDPR, HIPAA, and SOX ITGC compliance demonstrate its flexibility with regard to various laws and regulations. Studies on banking organizations and IT audits have shown how supervised and unsupervised learning algorithms have made predictive modeling and real-time monitoring possible [15]. The adaptability of AI systems has been further improved by methods like natural language processing, which automate difficult processes like privacy risk assessment and regulatory reporting.

A more thorough grasp of the advantages and difficulties related to the adoption of AI is possible due to the qualitative findings gleaned from polls and interviews. While highlighting the productivity benefits of automation, participants also issued a warning about potential ethical dangers, such as algorithmic prejudice and problems with data openness. These revelations highlight the necessity of strong ethical frameworks and ongoing supervision to guarantee the proper integration of AI.

To visualize these findings, illustrations are essential. Visible efficiency gains are shown in a bar chart that compares audit time and accuracy before and after AI adoption. The scope of AI's influence on regulatory compliance is demonstrated by a heat map that shows compliance coverage across GDPR, HIPAA, and SOX laws.

Finally, a radar chart that compares the ethical risks and advantages offers a fair assessment of how AI might be included in auditing procedures.

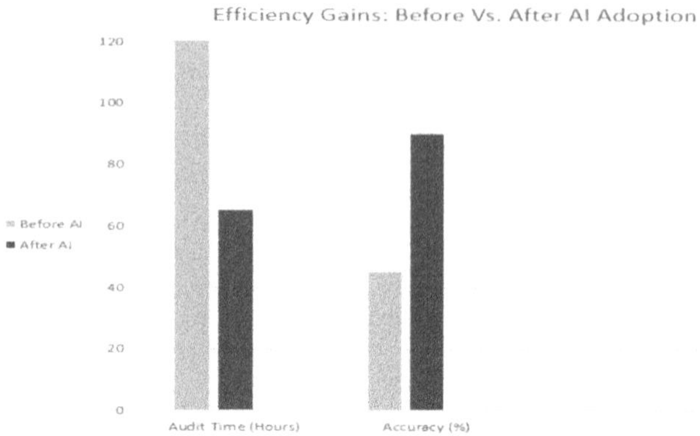

Fig. 4. Efficiency Gains: Before vs After AI Adoption

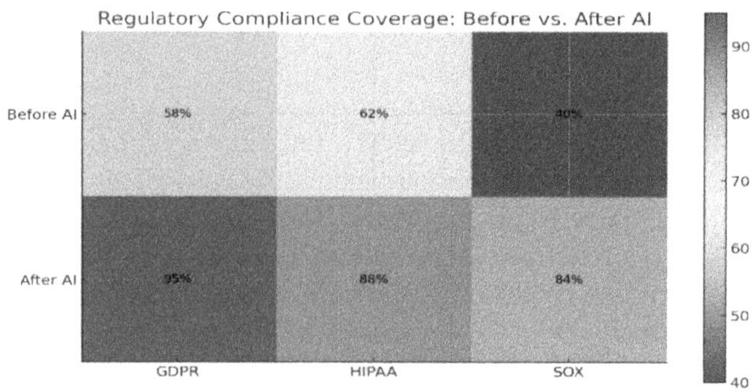

Fig. 5. Regulatory Compliance Coverage: Before vs After AI

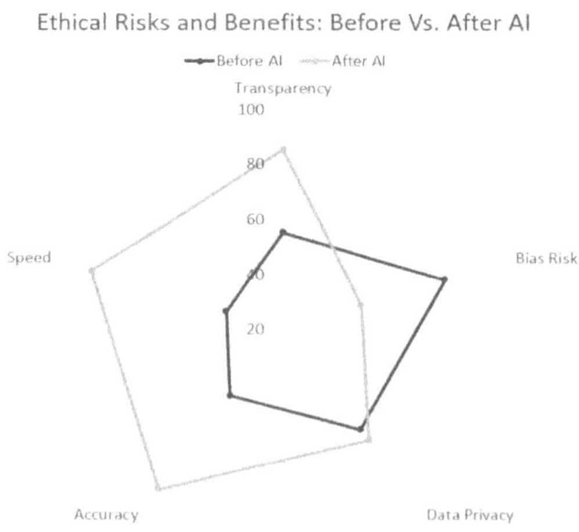

Fig. 6. Ethical Risks: Before vs After AI Adoption

Figures 4, 5 and 6 display the results, and it shows how AI might revolutionize auditing by fusing technological advancement with moral awareness. The variety of approaches and uses in many sectors highlights AI's adaptability and provides useful information for businesses negotiating complex regulatory environments.

5 Discussion

This section discusses the findings that show how AI has the potential to revolutionize compliance auditing by enhancing accuracy, efficiency, and regulatory compliance. These results emphasize fresh perspectives and difficulties while also being consistent with previous research. The discussion below delves further into these findings, contrasting them with contradictory and corroborating reports and rationally placing them in the context of the data analysis.

5.1 Efficiency and Accuracy Gains

The study's findings of a marked reduction in audit time coupled with improvements in accuracy align with previous research that has demonstrated AI's capacity to automate complex procedures. For instance, it has been demonstrated that using frameworks like CoCAF and EY Helix GLAD reduces human error and frees up auditors to concentrate on high-risk areas [10, 16]. These results are in line with research showing AI may increase operational effectiveness across a range of sectors, including financial institutions' compliance reports. The upfront expenses and complexity of adopting AI, however, may discourage smaller businesses from making the most of these technologies, according to some contradictory findings. Cost-benefit assessments that are adapted to the size and preparation level of the organization must be evaluated in order to address these differences.

5.2 Adaptability to Regulatory Frameworks

AI's capacity to automate rule-based evaluations and reduce compliance risks showed its success in navigating changing regulatory environments, including GDPR and HIPAA. These results support research showing AI may improve compliance through predictive analytics and real-time monitoring. NLP methods and rule-based systems have shown exceptional flexibility in adjusting to intricate restrictions. Conflicting viewpoints, however, draw attention to possible weaknesses in the interpretative adaptability of AI systems when handling unclear or overlapping regulations. Integrating adaptive learning algorithms and making sure systems are updated often to take into account modifications to legal frameworks will be necessary to close this gap.

5.3 Ethical Considerations

The study's findings regarding ethical considerations, such as algorithmic bias and data transparency, are consistent with concerns raised in prior scholarly work. Even while AI systems improve speed and accuracy, issues with their opacity and possibility of bias must be resolved to preserve integrity and confidence. The incorporation of explainable AI models to increase system transparency is backed by reports that support this study's recommendation for strong ethical frameworks. On the other hand, conflicting opinions imply that overly controlling AI's moral aspects may impede innovation and delay uptake [11]. For AI integration in auditing to be viable, a well-rounded strategy that gives equal weight to innovation and moral protection will be essential.

5.4 Challenges in Adoption

Although the findings demonstrate AI's revolutionary potential, they also point to adoption obstacles such as auditors' challenging learning curve and substantial upfront installation costs. These results are consistent with earlier studies that emphasized the significance of the organizational preparation level and auditor training. Nevertheless, conflicting research contends that AI's long-term scalability and cost-cutting potential surpass any initial difficulties, especially for big businesses. To make the transition easier for auditors and companies alike, practical suggestions include using hybrid systems and staggered implementation methodologies.

6 Recommendation

Based on the analysis of AI's potential in transforming compliance audits and the identified areas of concern, several key recommendations are outlined to facilitate a responsible and strategic approach.

6.1 Develop a Clear Strategic Vision

Establishing how blockchain and AI fit with an organization's long-term goals should be the first step. Effective governance, measurement, and management of AI deployments are ensured by the use of frameworks like the NIST AI RMF. IT plans should also take advantage of blockchain's ability to improve transparency and data integrity, especially in the areas of compliance and data governance.

6.2 Utilize Blockchain for Data Security and Transparency

Blockchain is a great tool for protecting sensitive data and guaranteeing controls because it is decentralized and unchangeable. Organizations may protect data integrity and provide transparent, secure records by incorporating blockchain into IT policy, especially in legal compliance procedures.

6.3 Prioritize Ethical Considerations in AI Implementation

Addressing ethical considerations proactively, including bias, accountability, and transparency is a key element in the responsible deployment of AI systems. This should include employing Explainable AI (XAI) to promote clarity and justification in the outputs of AI systems. Furthermore, ethical standards ought to be included in order to reduce the hazards associated with algorithmic bias and data privacy.

6.4 Adopt a Phased Implementation Approach

Firms should begin with pilot initiatives to assess the efficacy of blockchain and AI in their operations before implementing full-scale rollouts. Prior to wider adoption, these pilot initiatives can assist in identifying possible obstacles and honing solutions.

7 Conclusion and Future Directions

This paper emphasizes how blockchain technology and artificial intelligence (AI) can revolutionize IT strategy and regulations. The main conclusions show that using technologies like CoCAF and EY Helix GLAD significantly increases audit efficiency and accuracy while also improving flexibility in response to laws like GDPR and SOX ITGC. Blockchain guarantees openness and data security, but ethical issues like bias and integrity make strong governance systems necessary. For businesses looking to safely update their IT strategies, these findings offer practical perspectives.

By highlighting the beneficial uses of blockchain and artificial intelligence in compliance and auditing, the study advances the expanding subject. It encourages the proper deployment of these technologies by striking a balance between innovation and moral considerations. The lack of measurable datasets, a narrow focus on use cases unique to compliance, and an absence of industry-specific observations, however, are restrictions that allow for more thorough investigation.

Future investigations should examine sector-specific problems and solutions and support these results with empirical studies. Examining hybrid blockchain technologies and adaptive AI algorithms can improve responsiveness to regulatory changes. Furthermore, analyzing ethical frameworks and human-machine collaboration can guarantee the transparent and efficient use of these technologies. Through tackling these domains, subsequent research endeavors might broaden the comprehension and relevance of artificial intelligence and blockchain in IT governance, promoting creativity and adaptability throughout many sectors.

8 Study Limitations

Due to the limitation in time and resources, the study was not tested using any audit compliance technologies or tools. This could have given readers a better indication of how AI can be technically leveraged in conducting IT compliance audits. Furthermore, the study was focused on NIST AI RMF exclusively without comparison with other effective frameworks that could have been contrasted with in respect to factors like cost, focus, implementation complexity, and other relative factors. Finally, the research methodology was restricted to purely theoretical references from prior research instead of utilizing other data collection methods like experiments, interviews, surveys and so forth.

References

1. Iwuanyanwu, U., Apeh, J.A., Adaramodu, O.R., Okeleke, E.C., Fakeyede, O.G.: Analyzing the role of artificial intelligence in IT audit: current practices and future prospects. Comput. Syst. Inf. Technol. Res. J. **15**(2), 100–115 (2024). https://www.fepbl.com/index.php/csitrj
2. Doe, J., Smith, J.: Analyzing artificial intelligence in IT audit. Int. J. IT Audit. **15**(3), 45–60 (2024). https://www.emerald.com/insight/1030-9616.htm
3. Odeyemi, O., Awonuga, K.F., Mhlongo, N.Z., Ndubuisi, N.L., Olatoye, F.O., Daraojimba, A.I.: The role of AI in transforming auditing practices: a global perspective review. World J. Adv. Res. Rev. **21**(2), 460–475 (2024). https://doi.org/10.30574/wjarr.2024.21.2.0460
4. Aitkazinov, A.: The role of artificial intelligence in auditing: Opportunities and challenges. Int. J. Res. Eng. Sci. Manage. (2023). https://www.ijresm.com
5. Celestin, M., Vanitha, N.: The future of auditing in the age of AI: How automation is reshaping the audit profession. ResearchGate (2019). https://www.researchgate.net/publication/385863141
6. National Institute of Standards and Technology (2022). Artificial Intelligence (AI) Risk Management Framework: A Draft for Public Comment. U.S. Department of Commerce (2019). https://doi.org/10.6028/NIST.AI.100-1
7. Smith, J.: The role of AI in financial auditing. In: Brown, L., White, K. (eds.) Advances in AI Research, pp. 45–67. Springer (2023). https://doi.org/10.1007/978-3-031-09846-8
8. Leocádio, D., Malheiro, L., Reis, J.: Artificial intelligence in auditing: a conceptual framework for auditing practices. Admin. Sci. **14**(10), 238 (2024). https://doi.org/10.3390/admsci14100238
9. Esther, D.: AI and machine learning for automated security audits: ensuring consistent compliance and identifying gaps. ResearchGate (2024). https://www.researchgate.net/publication/385747185
10. Devineni, S.K.: Augmenting the watchdog: AI-driven compliance audits for enhanced efficiency and accuracy. Int. J. Sci. Res. (IJSR) **10**(12), 1437–1443 (2021). https://doi.org/10.21275/SR24127205916
11. Adelakun, B.O.: Ethical Considerations in the Use of AI for Auditing: Balancing Innovation and Integrity. European Centre for Research Training and Development, UK (2022). https://www.eajournals.org/
12. Folorunso, A., Adewumi, T.O., Okonkwo, R., et al.: Impact of AI on cybersecurity and security compliance. Glob. J. Eng. Technol. Adv. **21**(1), Article 0193 (2024). https://doi.org/10.30574/gjeta.2024.21.1.0193
13. Mohammed, A.: AI in cybersecurity: enhancing audits and compliance automation. Innov. Sci. J. **5**(2) (2024). https://innovatesci-publishers.com/index.php/ICSJ/index
14. Padmanaban, H.: Revolutionizing regulatory reporting through AI/ML: approaches for enhanced compliance and efficiency. J. Artif. Intell. Gen. Sci. (JAIGS) **2**(1), 57–69 (2024). https://doi.org/10.60087/jaigs.v2i1.p69
15. Kingston, J.: Using artificial intelligence to support compliance with the General Data Protection Regulation. Artif. Intell. Law **25**(4), 429–443 (2017). https://doi.org/10.1007/s10506-017-9206-9K
16. de Vries, T.: Anomaly Detection in IT Audit: The Possibilities and Potential in the Domain of IT Audit. Master's Thesis. Turku School of Economics (2022)

Multi-domain Feature Extraction and Comparative Evaluation of Classification Accuracy for Punching Motions in Mass Boxing

Shinjiro Okajima(✉), Taiyo Kimura, Akihito Kohiga, and Takahiro Koita

Department of Information Systems Design, Doshisha University, 1-3 Tatara Miyakodani, Kyotanabe-shi, Kyoto-fu 610-0394, Japan
{ctwk0153,ctwn0118}@mail4.doshisha.ac.jp,
{akohiga,tkoita}@mail.doshisha.ac.jp

Abstract. Subjective judging in mass boxing has raised concerns, emphasizing the need for objective evaluation methods. We propose an AI-based system that digitizes punch motions and scores them based on predefined criteria. As a step toward this goal, we developed a punch classification system using accelerometer data. Unlike previous studies that excluded preparatory motions by inserting static states, we collected data reflecting natural pre- and post-punch movements to better simulate real match conditions. Features from time, frequency, and time-frequency domains were extracted and used to train a Random Forest classifier. Results showed that time-frequency features achieved the highest accuracy (0.997). The findings highlight the effectiveness of time-frequency analysis for punch classification and its potential to support objective judging in mass boxing.

Keywords: Mass boxing · Acceleration data · Punching motion classification · Time-frequency domain feature · Random forest

1 Introduction

In recent years, mass boxing has garnered increasing attention as a competitive sport. Mass boxing is a sport in which athletes punch without hitting. It was originally a part of boxing training menu, and now mass boxing matches are held. However, in mass boxing matches, there is often doubt about the validity of the judge, which leads to complaints from athletes and spectators. Although judges rely on established scoring criteria when making decisions, subjective judgment may influence the decision. Furthermore, the rationale behind the given scores is not disclosed.

The primary scoring method is the "10-point match system," where one or three judges give 10 points to the superior athlete and 8 or 9 points to another athlete at the end of each round. The scoring is based on the following three criteria [1]:

H. R. Arabnia et al. (Eds.): CSCE 2025, CCIS 2934, pp. 335–343, 2026.
https://doi.org/10.1007/978-3-032-22190-2_23

- The number of assumed landed punches when the opponent fails to execute defensive actions against correct striking techniques or reacts slowly
- Excellence in technique and tactics
- Aggressiveness

Scoring may be influenced by subjective judgment due to the difficulty in quantifying these criteria. In particular, it is controversial that subjective judgments influence the evaluation of both a punch landed and the assessment of technical superiority. To address the issue, this study proposes an objective judging method that eliminates the influence of subjectivity. To eliminate subjectivity, this study explores a system in which punching motions are digitized and automatically evaluated by AI based on predefined scoring criteria, providing a clear and objective basis for a judgment free from subjective influence.

It is considered possible to achieve highly transparent judgments that are convincing to both athletes and spectators, by clarifying the information that athletes and spectators can understand the reasons for the scores given, such as the number of successful jabs, effective punch combinations, and total punch count as the basis for scoring. It is necessary to classify the types of punches to provide such a basis for scoring.

In recent years, numerous methods have been proposed to classify punch types by collecting data with accelerometers [2] and applying machine learning [3] and deep learning models [4,5]. Accelerometers can measure acceleration along three axes (x, y, and z) [6], which allows the capture of motion characteristics in what is known as three degrees of freedom (3-DOF). Furthermore, it becomes possible to obtain rotational information by incorporating gyroscopes to form six degrees of freedom (6-DOF). However, according to the existing study [7], three degrees of freedom are sufficient to achieve high classification accuracy. The following chapter reviews related works on the use of accelerometers for punch types classification.

2 Related Works

Dante et al. conducted a notable study on punch classification in boxing using machine learning and deep learning models. In their research, they compared the classification performance of several machine learning and deep learning models using a dataset consisting of 7,606 instances of four types of thrown punches: jab, hook, uppercut, and no motion. The dataset was originally created by Wagner et al., in which each action was recorded using a 3-axis accelerometer embedded in a smartwatch worn on both wrists of the participants. From the acceleration data, 30 features were extracted based on time-series signals. These features were then used as input to the following five machine learning and two deep learning models. Both accuracy and F1-score were used to evaluate classification performance. As a result, Random Forest [8] achieved the highest performance, with both accuracy and F1-score reaching 0.995. SVM followed closely, with an accuracy of 0.994 and an F1-score of 0.993. All models except

Gaussian Naive Bayes and RNN achieved over 0.95 in both metrics, suggesting that high-performance classification of punch types is feasible using machine learning models [9].

Saravanan et al. conducted a study aimed at simultaneously classifying punch types and ranges using motion data acquired from IMU sensors. IMU sensors were attached to both wrists of eight participants, and data were collected at a sampling frequency of 200 Hz by recording 320 repetitions of 14 different types of punches. Features were extracted from the acquired data not only from the time domain, but also from the frequency domain in the form of power spectral density (PSD). These features were used as spatial and temporal inputs for machine learning models. Five classification algorithms were compared, and the results showed that the Random Forest classifier achieved the highest performance, accurately classifying punch types and ranges with an accuracy of 0.965. Therefore, this study adopts Random Forest as the classifier for the machine learning model [10].

However, in previous studies, a stationary state was often inserted before and after a punch during data acquisition, meaning that preparatory motions—such as the vertical, horizontal, and lateral motions of the body before and after a punch—were not taken into account. In actual matches, athletes are constantly moving when throwing punches, and punching from a stationary state does not reflect realistic in-match movements.

This study aims to achieve punch classification in actual boxing matches. Classification methods based on conventional data may have problems when applied to actual matches. To address this issue, this study evaluates the effect of preparatory motions on punch classification accuracy. Furthermore, with regard to feature extraction, we employ not only conventional the time domain statistics-based features but also the frequency domain features derived from the Fast Fourier Transform (FFT) and the time-frequency domain features obtained via the Discrete Wavelet Transform (DWT). These additional features are introduced with the expectation of improving classification accuracy by capturing the inherent periodicity and temporal variations of punch motions from multiple perspectives.

3 Proposed Method

This chapter proposes a method that digitizes punch motions using a three-axis accelerometer sensor with preparatory motions extracts features from the time, frequency, and time-frequency domains, and comparatively evaluates classification accuracy using a Random Forest classifier. The target punching motions consist of three types: jab, hook, and uppercut. For each type of punch, acceleration data is collected with preparatory motions. Acceleration data were recorded using an Apple Watch worn on the subject's left wrist. The Sensor Log application was used to capture the acceleration data at a sampling rate of 100 Hz. All data were saved in CSV format, with each punch motion recorded as a separate file. Data processing and implementation of the classification model were conducted on Google Colaboratory. Figure 1 shows a workflow of the proposed method (Fig. 1).

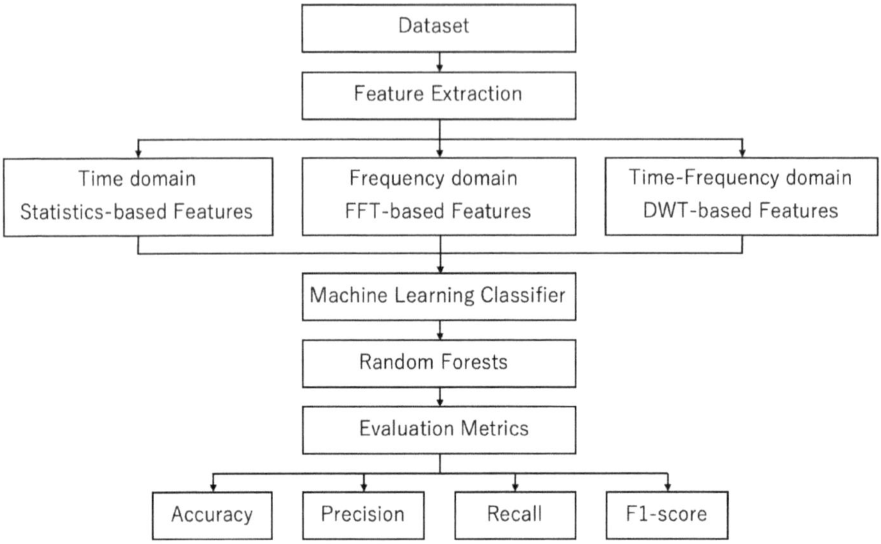

Fig. 1. Proposed method workflow.

The following sections describe the details of the extracted features for each domain, the configuration of the Random Forest classifier, and the evaluation metrics used to assess classification performance.

3.1 Time Domain Statistics-Based Features

Six features are extracted from the acceleration time series data on each axis (x, y, and z): mean, standard deviation, maximum value, minimum value, amplitude (maximum-minimum) and energy (sum of the squared acceleration values for each axis). This results in an 18-dimensional feature vector (3 axes $\times$ 6 features).

3.2 Frequency Domain FFT-Based Features

The acceleration data of each axis in the time series data is converted to the frequency domain using the Fast Fourier Transform (FFT). Three features are extracted: peak frequency (the frequency with the highest power), energy (sum of squared amplitude spectrum), and spectral centroid. This results in a 9-dimensional feature vector (3 axes $\times$ 3 features).

3.3 Time-Frequency Domain DWT-Based Features

The Discrete Wavelet Transform (DWT) is applied to the acceleration data for each axis in the time series data, as it enables analysis of signals while preserving both temporal and spectral information, making it suitable for transient signals such as punch motions. The decomposition level is set to 5. For each axis, the following steps are performed:

1. Six scales are obtained: one approximation coefficient (low-frequency component) and five detail coefficients (high-frequency components).
2. For each scale, six statistical features are calculated: mean, standard deviation, maximum value, minimum value, amplitude, and energy.

This results in a 108-dimensional feature vector (3 axes $\times$ 6 scales $\times$ 6 features).

3.4 Random Forest

In this study, the extracted features are used to classify punches using a Random Forest classifier. Random Forest is an ensemble learning method composed of multiple decision trees, designed to improve classification performance and suppress overfitting. Each tree is trained on a different subset of the data and features, and final predictions are determined by majority voting. The number of decision trees is set to 120 following prior research. Five-fold cross-validation was applied to the dataset, which includes all classes (jab, hook, and uppercut), in order to train and evaluate the model. In the method, the entire dataset is divided into five equally sized subsets while preserving the class ratio. In each iteration, four subsets are used for training and the remaining one is used for testing. This process is repeated five times, each with a different test subset, ensuring that every dataset is used as test data. The approach enables a balanced and fair evaluation of the model's performance.

3.5 Evaluation Metrics

In this study, to quantitatively evaluate the performance of the punch classification model, four metrics are used: accuracy, precision, recall, and F1-score. These metrics are important for considering the impact of false positives and false negatives in classification models and are calculated based on the confusion matrix. The confusion matrix is a table representing the relationship between predicted and actual class labels and consists of the following four elements: True Positive (TP), False Positive (FP), True Negative (TN), and False Negative (FN). Based on these elements, the evaluation metrics are defined as follows:

- Accuracy: The proportion of correctly classified instances, indicating overall prediction performance.
- Precision: The proportion of correctly predicted positive instances among all instances predicted as positive, reflecting the reliability of the classifier.

- Recall: The proportion of correctly predicted positive instances among all actual positive instances, indicating the classifier's sensitivity.
- F1-score: The harmonic mean of precision and recall, providing a balanced evaluation metric.

In this study, these metrics are used to compare and evaluate the effect of different feature domains on the classification performance of punches that include preparatory motions.

4 Experiment

4.1 Experimental Methods

This study targeted three types of punching motions: jab, hook, and uppercut. The jab is a quick, straight thrust with the lead hand, the hook is a curved lateral strike involving torso rotation, and the uppercut is a vertical upward punch typically aimed at the opponent's chin. Data were collected from a single subject who performed all punching motions with preparatory motions. For each punch type, data corresponding to 200 punches were acquired, resulting in a total of 600 samples (3 punch types × 200 samples). Each single punch motion was defined as one data sample, and all samples were treated as independent. Features are extracted from the acquired data using three feature extraction methods, and training and testing are performed using a Random Forest classifier.

4.2 Experimental Results

Table 1. Accuracy results for each feature domain

Feature Extraction	Accuracy
Time domain statistics-based features	0.988
Frequency domain FFT-based features	0.938
Time-Frequency domain DWT-based features	0.997

Table 1 presents the accuracy results for each feature domain. The time-frequency domain achieved the highest accuracy (0.997), followed by the time domain (0.988), while the frequency domain exhibited the lowest performance (0.938).

Figures 2, 3, 4 show the confusion matrices in the time domain, frequency domain, and time-frequency domain, respectively. In all feature domains, there was a consistent tendency for uppercuts to be misclassified as hooks. Specifically, 3 instances of uppercuts were misclassified as hooks in the time domain, 18 in the frequency domain, and 2 in the time-frequency domain.

Fig. 2. Confusion matrix in the time domain.

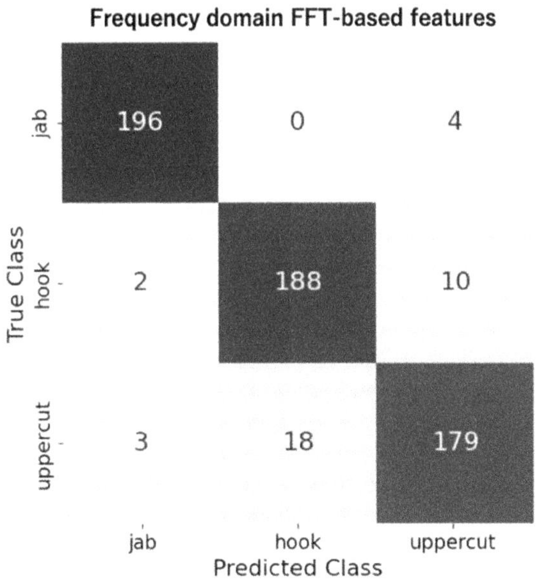

Fig. 3. Confusion matrix in the frequency domain.

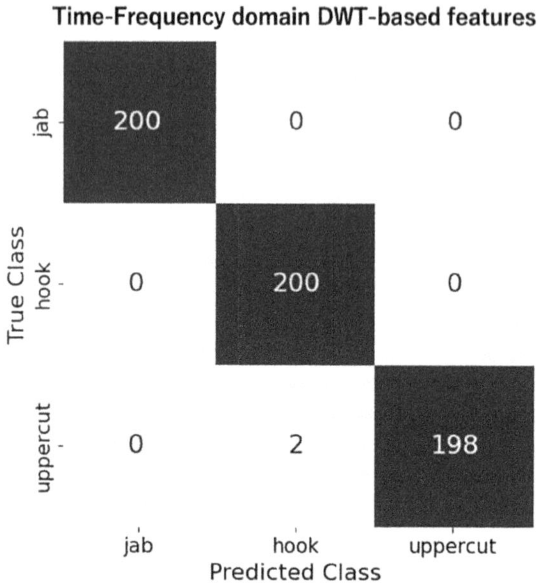

Fig. 4. Confusion matrix in the time-frequency domain.

4.3 Discussion

We consider that the relatively low accuracy observed in the frequency domain FFT-based features can be attributed to their limited ability to capture localized temporal variations compared to the time domain statistics-based features and time-frequency domain DWT-based features. While the frequency domain analysis is effective for identifying global periodic patterns, it may fail to detect subtle, short-term variations essential for distinguishing between different punch types.

From our analysis of the confusion matrices, we observed a consistent trend across all feature domains: hooks and uppercuts were more likely to be misclassified with each other than with jabs. We believe this is due to the temporal and spatial similarities between hook and uppercut motions, which make them harder to differentiate.

Based on these findings, we consider that the time-frequency domain analysis, which has both temporal and spectral information, is an effective approach to classifying punching motions with preparatory motions.

5 Conclusion

In this study, features were extracted using three types of feature extraction methods- the time domain statistics-based features, the frequency domain FFT-based features , and the time-frequency domain DWT-based features with preparatory motions. A Random Forest classifier was employed to train and evaluate models based on these features, with the aim of classifying punch types (jab, hook, and uppercut). The results showed that the time-frequency domain features showed the highest accuracy, while the frequency domain features showed the lowest accuracy. These results indicate that the use of the time-frequency analysis, which has both temporal and spectral information, is an effective approach to classifying punching motions with preparatory motions.

For future work, it is necessary to extend the evaluation to additional punch types that were not included in this study, to construct a more comprehensive classification model. In addition, a more detailed analysis of the influence of preparatory motions on classification performance is required. Specifically, investigating how the characteristics of preparatory motions can be reflected in feature design and model architecture may lead to further improvements in classification accuracy.

References

1. General Association Japan Boxing Federation, Mass Boxing Competition Rules. https://jabf-revival.com/wp-content/uploads/2021/04/post-3432-1.pdf
2. Haralabidis, N., Saxby, D.J., Pizzolato, C., and Needham, L., Cazzola, D., Clare, M.: Fusing accelerometry with videography to monitor the effect of fatigue on punching performance in elite boxers. Sensors 20(20) (2020)
3. Worsey, M.T.O., Espinosa, H.G., Shepherd, J.B., Thiel, D.V.: An evaluation of wearable inertial sensor configuration and supervised machine learning models for automatic punch classification in boxing. IoT **1**(2), 360–381 (2020)
4. Manoharan, S., Warburton, J., Hegde, R., Srinivasan, R., Srinivasan, B.: Punch types and range estimation in boxing bouts using IMU sensors. In: 2023 IEEE International Conference on Internet of Things and Intelligence Systems (IoTaIS), pp. 97–102 (2023)
5. Yang, Z., Zhang, H., Xu, P., Luo, Z.: Unsupervised noise reductions for gravitational reference sensors or accelerometers based on the Noise2Noise method. Sensors 23(13), 6030 (2023)
6. Omcirk, D., Vetrovsky, T., Padecky, J., Vanbelle, S., Malecek, J., Tufano, J.J.: Punch trackers: correct recognition depends on punch type and training experience. Sensors **21**(9), 2968 (2021)
7. Wagner, T., Jäger, J., Wolff, V., Fricke-Neuderth, K.: A machine learning driven approach for multivariate timeseries classification of box punches using smartwatch accelerometer sensordata. In: 2019 Innovations in Intelligent Systems and Applications Conference (ASYU), pp. 1–6. IEEE (2019)
8. Breiman, L.: Random forests. Mach. Learn. **45**, 5–32 (2001)
9. Tollenaar, D.: Boxing Punch Classification With Accelerometer Data. The Netherlands (2023)
10. Manoharan, S., Warburton, J., Hegde, R.S., Srinivasan, R., Srinivasan, B.: An active machine learning framework for automatic boxing punch recognition and classification using upper limb kinematics. PLoS One **20**(5) (2025)

Benchmarking Aircraft Detection Using Pretrained Models

Praneel Acharya[1(✉)], JaeJun Lee[2], Devendra Deepkiran Adhikari[2], Nhut Huynh[3], and Kim-Doang Nguyen[3]

[1] Aviation Department, Minnesota State University, Mankato, MN, USA
praneel.acharya@mnsu.edu
[2] Computer Information Science Department, Minnesota State University, Mankato, MN, USA
[3] Department of Mechanical and Civil Engineering, Florida Institute of Technology, Melbourne, FL, USA

Abstract. Airplane detection through computer vision offers promising opportunities to enhance aviation safety by providing additional layers of monitoring and situational awareness. This study benchmarks the performance of several popular deep learning-based object detection models on the task of airplane detection. Different deep learning based models are evaluated using an available dataset of airplane images under diverse conditions. The research goal is to systematically assess performance, identifying models that are best suited for practical deployment in aviation-related applications. By comparing these architectures, this research aims to inform future efforts in integrating computer vision into airport operations, and surveillance, ultimately contributing to safer and more efficient operations.

Keywords: deep-learning · airplane detection · object detection · Faster-Rcnn · YOLO

1 Introduction

As the field of artificial intelligence is becoming more adaptable and accessible, computer vision is being used in various applications. Object detection using artificial intelligence and computer vision is one such application. In healthcare, the object detection technique is used to diagnose diseases, for example, cancer detection using medical images [6]. Automobile industries are using object detection to make driving more efficient and safe by introducing self-driving and driver assistance features [9]. Similarly, object detection is also being used in airport settings to improve passenger safety and security through real-time detection of threats and suspicious objects. For example, [4] explains how CNN based techniques like YOLO and Faster RCNN can be used to detect threat objects using X-ray based baggage imagery. These are a few examples of object detection being applied in real-world applications. In this work, we are using similar technology to identify and detect aircraft using object detection.

H. R. Arabnia et al. (Eds.): CSCE 2025, CCIS 2934, pp. 344–354, 2026.
https://doi.org/10.1007/978-3-032-22190-2_24

Vision-based aircraft detection systems are useful for real-time aircraft tracking. Such a tracking system can provide the exact location of an aircraft during the ground operation to air traffic controllers, ensuring an additional layer of safety. Because of the potential of these detection systems, the Utah Department of Transportation (UDOT) supported research using AI for aircraft identification [7]. The work in [7] focuses on the identification of aviation aircrafts in non-towered airports using a two-step method to identify aircrafts. First, they used a CNN-based aircraft classifier, and then a text recognition network was integrated to finalize the identification. Work in [2] aimed to solve airplane detection in remote sensing images. It leveraged transfer learning and data augmentation techniques to train a deep convolutional neural network model using remote sensing images of airports from Google Earth. Similar work has also been done in another paper [11]. The authors purposed model is based on visual saliency computation and symmetry detection to detect aircraft. The proposed model performed better in the false-alarm rate. However, they only had 40 satellite images from a complex airport setting for testing.

Reliable aircraft detection, particularly through vision-based systems, offers significant advantages. These systems can complement existing detection methods and provide a redundant layer to enhance overall aviation safety. Furthermore, in radar-defined environments, vision-based approaches can serve as a valuable tool to refine detection and improve situational awareness. As a result, there is active research on aircraft detection using object detection. While much of the current research focuses on designing and training novel deep-learning models for aircraft detection with improved accuracy, such efforts often require substantial computational resources and energy. In contrast, our work adopts a more practical and efficient approach. Rather than developing a new object detection model from scratch, it benchmarks existing deep learning models that have already been trained on large-scale datasets. By evaluating the performance of these pre-trained models on aircraft detection tasks, this study not only reduces the time and resource burden associated with training but also highlights the potential of leveraging mature models for specialized applications. This approach offers a scalable and sustainable alternative, making it highly beneficial for real-world implementation where efficiency, adaptability, and safety are critical. Thus, the central idea is to evaluate the performance of existing models; if satisfactory results are achieved, the necessity for further training may be obviated. Work presented in [10] benchmarks the performance of various YOLO detection model versions for airplane detection on the ground using UAV and satellite aerial imagery. However, this prior work does not extend its evaluation to other state-of-the-art detection models, a limitation addressed in the current study. Thus, the contribution of this work can be summarized as follows:

- This work makes a significant contribution by presenting a comprehensive benchmark of several existing, widely adopted models, offering a direct comparative analysis of their performance on the task at hand, with all benchmarking conducted on the same hardware for a fair comparison.

- This rigorous evaluation serves to identify scenarios where pre-trained models already demonstrate satisfactory results, potentially obviating the need for resource-intensive retraining efforts.
- The comparative analysis empowers practitioners to make informed decisions regarding model selection for practical applications, highlighting the strengths and weaknesses of current popular architectures.

2 Data and Datasets

For benchmarking our models, we used the Fine-Grained Visual Classification of Aircraft (FGVC-Aircraft) dataset [14]. It was created in the John Hopkins CLSP Summer Workshop 2012 by a number of airplane spotters and is made available for non-commercial research purposes. It consists of 10,200 images of aircraft with 102 different aircraft model variants and each variant has 100 images. The images from the FGVC-Aircraft dataset are used solely for research purposes. All image copyrights and associated rights remain with the original copyright holders as specified by the dataset's license.

Some of the images in this dataset had two airplanes, but only one was labeled. Images in which all airplane were not labeled were removed from the dataset. This dataset was used to generate 2,723 annotated images, which served as the basis for evaluating and comparing the performance of various deep learning models. In addition to the Fine-Grained Visual Classification of Aircraft (FGVC-Aircraft) dataset, which contains detailed images of airplanes, this study also considers the COCO (Common Objects in Context) dataset, a widely used benchmark for general object detection tasks.

The COCO (Common Objects in Context) dataset is a large-scale benchmark dataset for object detection, segmentation, and captioning [13]. Significantly, the COCO dataset includes the "airplane" as one of its 80 object categories. This means deep learning models that are trained on COCO datasets can detect airplanes within natural, complex scenes. Therefore, it logically follows that numerous popular deep learning models, having been pre-trained on the COCO dataset can perform aircraft detection. To establish a benchmark for aircraft detection, we utilizes several popular deep learning models that have been pre-trained on the COCO (Common Objects in Context) dataset. By leveraging these pre-trained models, we aim to evaluate their effectiveness when applied to aircraft imagery, particularly from the FGVC-Aircraft dataset [14]. This approach allows us to compare their relative strengths and weaknesses without the need for extensive retraining, making the benchmarking process more efficient and practical for real-world deployment scenarios.

3 Deep Learning Models

Over the years, numerous object detection models have been proposed, each aiming to improve accuracy, speed, or both. These models are broadly classified into three different categories: single-stage detectors, two-stage detectors, and transformer-based. We selected popular object detection models trained on COCO datasets over the years.

3.1 Single Stage Models

In object detection, single-stage models directly predict the location and class of desired objects in one go. These models are typically faster than two-stage models, but accuracy could be compromised.

- **Single-Shot Multibox Detector (SSD)** [5]: SSD is a single-stage model, proposed in 2016, which can detect objects of various scales using multiple feature maps from different layers of the neural network. We are using VGG-16 backbone with this model in our airplane detection task. A backbone refers to the convolutional neural network used to extract visual features from input images. It serves as the feature extractor that feeds high-level representations into the detection head, which is responsible for predicting object classes and bounding boxes.
- **Fully Convolutional One-Stage Object Detection (FCOS)** [17]: FCOS is an anchor box free object detection model. It was proposed in 2019. It does not depend on predefined anchor boxes to detect objects in the image; instead, it directly predicts the object's center point based on the image's pixel grid. For our benchmarking, we are using FCOS deep learning architecture with ResNet50-FPN backbone from PyTorch library.
- **RetinaNet** [12]: RetinaNet, first proposed in 2017, uses a focal loss function to address the class imbalance problem by reshaping the cross-entropy loss. It is capable of detecting both large and small objects using a Feature Pyramid Network (FPN). Resnet50-FPN backbone is used for the benchmarking task in this model.
- **You Only Look Once** [15]: YOLO frames object detection as a regression problem. A single network predicts bounding boxes and class probabilities directly from full images in one evaluation. It was proposed in an IEEE conference on computer vision and pattern recognition in 2016 and has been widely used in object detection tasks since then. Various versions of YOLO have been released, and in this paper, we are benchmarking the performance of different versions of YOLO. YOLO has released nano, small, medium, balanced, large and extra large sized versions represented by n,s,m,b,l and x, respectively. Smaller versions are resource-constrained, while larger versions are more accurate but require more computational resources. We are benchmarking the performance of all these sizes of YOLO models from version 10 to 12 in our paper. For example, YOLO10l means large sized version 10 YOLO model. For this work, YOLO platform developed from Ultralytics is used [8].

3.2 Two Stages Models

As the name suggests, the two-stage models add another layer of verification before making the prediction. First, it proposes the region within the image where the object could be located, also called the region proposal. In the second stage, it further refines the proposal from the first stage to make a better prediction. Since there are two steps, these types of models are generally slower, but are better at making predictions.

- **Faster R-CNN** [16]: Faster R-CNN uses a Convolutional Neural Network (CNN) to extract features from the image and feeds those features into a classifier to classify the features. It has a region proposal network (RPN) that generates region proposals whose output are used for object detection. Faster R-CNN was proposed in 2015.

3.3 Transformer-Based

Transformer-based models approach object detection differently by eliminating the need for hand-designed components such as region proposals or anchor boxes. Instead, they treat object detection as a direct set prediction problem. Leveraging self-attention mechanisms, these models are able to capture global relationships across the entire image. Each object is represented as a learned query, and the model predicts all bounding boxes and their corresponding classes in a single step. While this approach simplifies the detection pipeline, it typically requires longer training times and large datasets to perform optimally. One of the newer and popular transformer-based model is considered:

- **Detection Transformer (DETR)** [1]: DETR uses a transformer encoder-decoder architecture to detect objects, eliminating the need for hand-designed components like a non-maximum suppression procedure or anchor boxes. It was proposed in 2020.

4 Performance Metrics

To benchmark the performance of the selected models, a set of standard evaluation metrics commonly used in object detection is employed. These metrics provide a consistent framework to assess and compare the effectiveness of each model across various aspects, such as detection accuracy and localization precision. A detailed explanation of each metric is provided below:

- **mAP** is the mean of the Average Precision (AP) over all classes, where precision specifically measures the accuracy of the positive predictions made by the model.

$$\text{mAP} = \frac{1}{C}\sum_{c=1}^{C} \text{AP}(c)$$

  where C is the total number of classes and AP(c) is the Average Precision for class c. In our case, since we have only one class, mAP is the same as AP.

- **mAP@50** is the mAP score at an IoU threshold of 0.50, meaning if the IoU with ground truth is at least 50%, it is considered correct. IoU measures the overlap between the predicted bounding box and the ground-truth bounding box
- **mAP@75** is the mAP score at IoU threshold of 0.75. It is more strict than mAP@50 because the predictions must have higher overlap (i.e., 75%) with the ground truth box.

5 Results

All models were run on the same set of images. In addition, to ensure a fair and consistent comparison across different object detection architectures, all models were initialized with their respective COCO-pretrained weights and evaluated under the same inference conditions. The target class for detection was "airplane," based on the COCO dataset label. A confidence threshold of 0.5 was applied to filter low-confidence predictions, and Non-Maximum Suppression (NMS) was performed using an Intersection-over-Union (IoU) threshold of 0.5. These parameters were held constant throughout all experiments to isolate the model architecture's impact on performance. Based upon these constant settings, performance metrics were computed for all these models, and the results can be seen in Table 1.

As shown in Table 1, YOLO12l achieved best performance in terms of mean Average precision (mAP) of 0.972, followed closely by YOLO11x (0.97) and YOLO12x (0.969). Consequently, YOLO12l can be considered the best-performing model for this airplane detection task. However, despite this strong performance, the model did not achieve a perfect mAP of 1.0, indicating the presence of minor detection challenges. Several factors could have contributed to the less-than-perfect mAP observed for YOLO12l. First, localization inaccuracies are a common source of reduced precision, where the predicted bounding boxes, although close, do not overlap precisely enough with the ground truth annotations to meet stricter IoU thresholds consistently. Even small deviations, such as slight shifts in the box position or imperfect coverage of the object, can cause a detection to be classified as a false positive or reduce its IoU, thereby affecting the mAP score. Second, detection failures for small or partially occluded airplanes may have impacted the model's performance. Small objects are inherently more difficult to detect accurately because they occupy fewer pixels, making them sensitive to localization noise. Third, variability in the visual characteristics of airplanes—such as differences in scale, orientation, background clutter, and lighting conditions—could have introduced additional complexity. This variability can affect the feature extraction and classification stages, occasionally leading to lower detection confidence or misclassification, thereby impacting the precision-recall balance captured in the mAP calculation.

If we compare mAP@50 and mAP@75, we can see consistent performance of 0.99 by models except DETR. DETR, a transformer-based architecture, significantly underperformed with mAP of 0.281 and mAP@75 of just 0.097.

(a) Airplane not detected using SSD model.

(b) Airplane detected using FCOS model.

(c) Airplane not detected using retinanet model

(d) Airplane detected using DETR model.

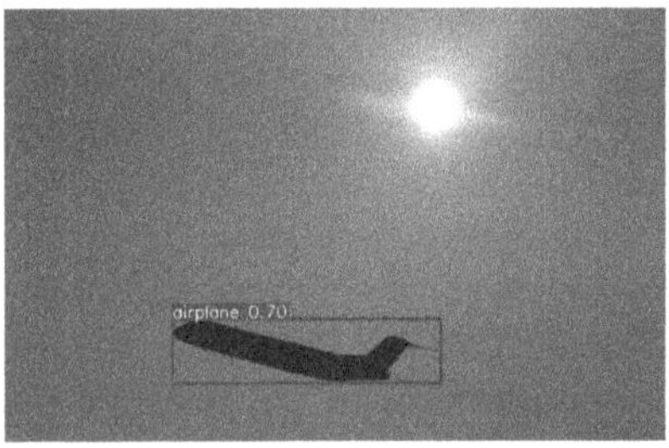

(e) Airplane detected using YOLO11n model.

(f) Airplane not detected using faster r-cnn model.

Fig. 1. All models were evaluated for airplane detection using consistent inference settings: COCO-pretrained weights, a target class of airplane, a confidence threshold of 0.5, and an IoU threshold of 0.5 for Non-Maximum Suppression (NMS).

Table 1. Performance metrics of different models

Model	mAP	mAP@50	mAP@75
Faster R-CNN	0.808	0.99	0.966
FCOS	0.898	0.99	0.988
Retinanet	0.898	0.99	0.977
DETR	0.281	0.771	0.097
SSD	0.828	0.99	0.977
YOLO10n	0.899	0.969	0.967
YOLO10s	0.946	0.99	0.989
YOLO10m	0.964	0.99	0.99
YOLO10l	0.966	0.99	0.99
YOLO10x	0.967	0.99	0.99
YOLO11n	0.911	0.99	0.979
YOLO11s	0.943	0.989	0.989
YOLO11m	0.952	0.989	0.989
YOLO11l	0.966	0.99	0.99
YOLO11x	0.97	0.999	0.989
YOLO12n	0.938	0.99	0.989
YOLO12s	0.959	0.99	0.989
YOLO12m	0.966	0.99	0.99
YOLO12l	0.972	0.99	0.99
YOLO12x	0.969	0.989	0.989

Though DETR is one of the newer models compared to Faster R-CNN, its performance is comparatively poorer. Similar observations were made by the authors in [3], where DETR was evaluated using the Pascal VOC (Visual Object Classes) dataset. The Pascal VOC dataset is a widely used benchmark for object detection, image classification, segmentation, and object recognition. However, the authors observed that when DETR was fine-tuned on the COCO train2017 dataset, its performance surpassed that of Faster R-CNN. This suggests that the DETR model may require fine-tuning to achieve optimal performance. This suggests that transformer-based architecture may not be the best choice for detecting airplane imagery right out of the box using COCO-pretrained weights and may require further hyperparameter tuning for optimal performance. Faster R-CNN, the only two-stage model we used in our benchmark, showed similar results to SSD, a single-stage model. However, Retinanet and FCOS, both being single-stage models, outperformed Faster RCNN in terms of mAP comparison. Additionally, newer versions of YOLO, particularly versions 10, 11, and 12 have similar or even better detection, in some cases, than traditional detection models. Even the nano and small-sized YOLO models are true contenders to the large models.

Figure 1 illustrates the performance of different object detection models on a challenging airplane detection scenario, where the airplane is silhouetted against a bright sun. While models like FCOS, DETR, and YOLOv11n were able to successfully detect the airplane, others, such as SSD, RetinaNet, and Faster R-CNN failed to generate any detection. This example highlights an important limitation: even though many models achieve high overall performance metrics, such as mean Average Precision (mAP), there are still specific conditions, like backlighting, low contrast, or unusual object orientations, where detection can fail. It serves as a reminder that real-world deployment of these models must account for such edge cases, and that no model is universally perfect across all visual conditions.

Now, if we were to compare the models not only based on their performance but also in terms of their size and number of parameters, additional insights begin to emerge as seen in Table 2. While evaluating object detection models, it becomes evident that performance is not solely dictated by the model's size or parameter count. Some smaller models, such as YOLO10n and YOLO11n, achieve remarkably high mAP scores despite having significantly fewer parameters and smaller memory footprints compared to heavier models like Faster

Table 2. Comparison of Object Detection Models: Parameters and Model Size

Model	Type	Total Parameters	Model Size (MB)
Faster R-CNN	Two-stage	41,532,886	159.69
FCOS	One-stage	32,047,200	123.50
RetinaNet	One-stage	33,792,599	130.16
DETR	Transformer	41,302,368	158.81
SSD	One-stage	35,603,106	135.96
YOLO10n	One-stage	4,932,416	10.67
YOLO10s	One-stage	14,654,672	31.17
YOLO10m	One-stage	32,910,176	63.49
YOLO10l	One-stage	54,431,792	99.13
YOLO10x	One-stage	64,754,240	121.88
YOLO11n	One-stage	4,740,416	10.07
YOLO11s	One-stage	17,422,784	36.20
YOLO11m	One-stage	35,729,312	76.91
YOLO11l	One-stage	53,966,688	97.03
YOLO11x	One-stage	121,189,760	217.67
YOLO12n	One-stage	5,107,744	10.02
YOLO12s	One-stage	18,659,200	35.59
YOLO12m	One-stage	37,675,680	77.31
YOLO12l	One-stage	56,281,424	101.30
YOLO12x	One-stage	125,927,488	226.47

R-CNN or DETR. The larger variants in the YOLO family (e.g., YOLO12l and YOLO12x) demonstrate consistently strong performance, implying that once a well-optimized architecture is in place, additional capacity can further enhance results. Overall, while larger models tend to offer slightly better accuracy in the YOLO series, compact versions remain highly competitive, highlighting the importance of efficient design over raw parameter count.

6 Conclusion

In this study, we presented a comprehensive performance accuracy benchmark of widely adopted object detection models like Faster-RCNN, YOLO, FCOS, RetinaNet and DETR to detect airplanes on the FGVC-aircraft dataset. Our results suggest that YOLO models outperform other state-of-the-art models in airplane detection out of the box. Even the smaller-sized YOLO models have good aircraft detection ability. This suggests that these models not only provide high accuracy but are also scalable and can be used in airport settings without the need for high computational resources, minimizing the operational cost.

Given the high mAP values across models, one might argue that retraining new models may not be necessary purely from a performance metric standpoint. However, it is important to recognize that a single mAP value alone is insufficient to comprehensively determine a model's viability for real-world deployment. Practical deployment also depends on other critical factors such as model robustness across varying conditions, inference speed, computational resource efficiency, and resilience to small object detection or occlusions. Therefore, as part of future work, we aim to expand the evaluation to include a broader set of performance metrics such as inference latency, frames-per-second (FPS) throughput, energy consumption during inference, and detection robustness under variable conditions (e.g., lighting, background complexity) This more holistic assessment will better guide the selection and optimization of models intended for operational deployment in real-world scenarios.

Acknowledgments. This work was supported by Minnesota State University at Mankato under a Faculty Research Grant and was partially supported by the U.S. National Science Foundation under CMMI grant #2138206.

Disclosure of Interests. The authors have no competing interests to declare that are relevant to the content of this article.

References

1. Carion, N., Massa, F., Synnaeve, G., Usunier, N., Kirillov, A., Zagoruyko, S.: End-to-end object detection with transformers. In: Vedaldi, A., Bischof, H., Brox, T., Frahm, J.-M. (eds.) ECCV 2020. LNCS, vol. 12346, pp. 213–229. Springer, Cham (2020). https://doi.org/10.1007/978-3-030-58452-8_13
2. Chen, Z., Zhang, T., Ouyang, C.: End-to-end airplane detection using transfer learning in remote sensing images. Remote Sensing **10**(1), 139 (2018)

3. Dai, Z., Cai, B., Lin, Y., Chen, J.: Up-detr: unsupervised pre-training for object detection with transformers. In: Proceedings of the IEEE/CVF Conference on Computer Vision and Pattern Recognition, pp. 1601–1610 (2021)
4. Dhiraj, Jain, D.K.: An evaluation of deep learning based object detection strategies for threat object detection in baggage security imagery. Pattern Recognit. Lett. **120**, 112–119 (2019). https://doi.org/10.1016/j.patrec.2019.01.014, https://www.sciencedirect.com/science/article/pii/S016786551930011X
5. Liu, W., et al.: SSD: single shot multibox detector. In: Leibe, B., Matas, J., Sebe, N., Welling, M. (eds.) ECCV 2016. LNCS, vol. 9905, pp. 21–37. Springer, Cham (2016). https://doi.org/10.1007/978-3-319-46448-0_2
6. Elakkiya, R., Subramaniyaswamy, V., Vijayakumar, V., Mahanti, A.: Cervical cancer diagnostics healthcare system using hybrid object detection adversarial networks. IEEE J. Biomed. Health Inform. **26**(4), 1464–1471 (2022). https://doi.org/10.1109/JBHI.2021.3094311
7. Farhadmanesh, M., Rashidi, A., Marković, N.: General aviation aircraft identification at non-towered airports using a two-step computer vision-based approach. IEEE Access **10**, 48778–48791 (2022). https://doi.org/10.1109/ACCESS.2022.3172963
8. Jocher, G., Qiu, J., Chaurasia, A.: Ultralytics YOLO (Jan 2023). https://github.com/ultralytics/ultralytics
9. Kanagaraj, N., Hicks, D., Goyal, A., Tiwari, S., Singh, G.: Deep learning using computer vision in self driving cars for lane and traffic sign detection. Inter. J. System Assurance Eng. Manag. **12**, 1011–1025 (2021). https://doi.org/10.1007/s13198-021-01127-6
10. Kharchenko, V., Chyrka, I.: Detection of airplanes on the ground using yolo neural network. In: IEEE 17th International Conference on Mathematical Methods in Electromagnetic Theory (MMET), pp. 294–297. IEEE (2018)
11. Li, W., Xiang, S., Wang, H., Pan, C.: Robust airplane detection in satellite images. In: 18th IEEE International Conference on Image Processing, pp. 2821–2824. IEEE (2011)
12. Lin, T.Y., Goyal, P., Girshick, R., He, K., Dollár, P.: Focal loss for dense object detection. In: Proceedings of the IEEE International Conference on Computer Vision, pp. 2980–2988 (2017)
13. Lin, T.Y., et al.: Microsoft coco: common objects in context (2015). https://arxiv.org/abs/1405.0312
14. Maji, S., Kannala, J., Rahtu, E., Blaschko, M., Vedaldi, A.: Fine-grained visual classification of aircraft. Tech. Rep. (2013)
15. Redmon, J., Divvala, S., Girshick, R., Farhadi, A.: You only look once: unified, real-time object detection. In: Proceedings of the IEEE Conference on Computer Vision and Pattern Recognition, pp. 779–788 (2016)
16. Ren, S., He, K., Girshick, R., Sun, J.: Faster r-cnn: towards real-time object detection with region proposal networks. In: Advances in Neural Information Processing Systems, p. 28 (2015)
17. Tian, Z., Shen, C., Chen, H., He, T.: Fcos: fully convolutional one-stage object detection (April 2019)

Augmenting Agricultural Human Capital Through Agentic AI: Personalizing Support for Small Farmers in Labor-Scarce Rural and Agri Industry Ecosystems

Chandrasekar Vuppalapati[1(✉)], Anitha Ilapakurti[2], Shruti Vuppalapati[2], Koduru Rajasri[2], Sharat Kedari[2], Jaya Vuppalapati[3], and Santosh Kedari[3]

[1] Computer Engineering (CMPE Department), San Jose State University, San Jose, USA
chandrasekar.vuppalapati@sjsu.edu

[2] Hanumayamma Innovations and Technologies, Inc., Fremont, USA
skedari@hanuinnotech.com

[3] Hanumayamma Innovations and Technologies PVT Limited, Hyderbad, India
jaya@hanuinnotech.com

Abstract. Persistent rural-to-urban migration and generational labor shifts have left global agriculture and dairy sectors with critical human capital deficits, particularly among smallholder farmers. This paper presents a novel framework for deploying Agentic AI—self-governing digital agents capable of learning farmer preferences, regional agronomic contexts, and value chain characteristics—to address labor shortages, enhance knowledge dissemination, and boost productivity in under-resourced agricultural systems. Our solution leverages modular, multilingual AI agents embedded on mobile and edge platforms, designed to operate in low-bandwidth rural environments. The economic impact is significant: according to the World Bank and FAO, labor shortages in agriculture contribute to $56 billion USD in annual productivity loss globally, with smallholders representing the majority of affected stakeholders. In our analysis, Agentic AI - by improving decision accuracy in areas like crop selection, irrigation timing, and input management - can contribute to 5–15% yield increases, representing $12–20 billion USD/year in potential economic gains worldwide. Our approach includes value chain integration, voice-driven interfaces for semi-literate populations, and adaptation of local practice, making it a culturally contextualized solution. This work argues for a paradigm shift where AI agents are not merely tools, but cognitive collaborators - learning, adapting, and extending the reach of traditional agricultural extension services. This vision positions Agentic AI as essential digital infrastructure in building resilient, inclusive food systems.

Keywords: Agentic AI · Lang Chain · Semantic Kernel · GPT · LLMs

H. R. Arabnia et al. (Eds.): CSCE 2025, CCIS 2934, pp. 355–366, 2026.
https://doi.org/10.1007/978-3-032-22190-2_25

1 Introduction

The global shortage of skilled human resources in dairy and agriculture, especially among smallholder farmers, has resulted in over $56 billion USD in annual productivity losses across developing nations [1, 2]. These losses are driven by labor shortages, poor access to agronomic knowledge, inefficiencies in farm management, and supply chain disconnects. Agentic AI—autonomous, context-aware agents—presents a transformative solution. When deployed effectively, these agents can augment the labor force, guide farmers with personalized recommendations, and bridge the knowledge divide. Studies show that enabling even a 10% increase in yield through intelligent advisory systems can generate $12–20 billion USD annually in added value globally [3–5]. By learning from individual farmer preferences, local crop suitability, climate variables, and economic constraints, Agentic AI can enable inclusive, scalable rural development and reverse the knowledge attrition caused by urban migration.

The structure of this paper is presented as: Sect. 2 Agentic Architecture. Section 3 presents our Agentic AI ML models. Section 4 discusses its related design and implementation decisions, and Sect. 5 shows a case study. The conclusion and future work are included in Sect. 6.

2 UNDERSTANDING Computer Vision Models, Sensor Data aND Machine Learning Models

2.1 AI Agents

The launch of ChatGPT showcased the capabilities of artificial intelligence (AI) and spearheaded AI integration. An AI agent is a program that can achieve predetermined goals. Similar to ChatGPT, AI agents are powered by large language models (LLMs) that are trained on massive amounts of data. AI agents can fulfill a wide variety of tasks with some or minimal human intervention. Generally, Agent patterns include RAG Agents, SQL Agents, Hierarchical Agents executing either in a single or multi-agentic architecture [6].

A copilot is a type of AI agent. A copilot is a natural language processing companion that assists users in completing various tasks. It's not a fully automated tool. Instead, it helps users' complete tasks by providing suggestions and recommendations. There are all sorts of copilots available today. There are copilots that help you: write code, compose emails, summarize meetings, and the list goes on!

There are numerous agentic frameworks available today, and this list is continually expanding. In fact, we will soon be seeing rapid changes and introduction of novel framework called the AI Agents Framework SDK. The purpose of the new framework is to device agents that are intelligent and run actions independently. Reasoning and Action (ReACT) is the norm of agents that will be coming in the future.

Agentic AI systems are designed to achieve complex goals with a high degree of autonomy and precision, acting as productivity enhancers that seamlessly integrate human input through multi-modal capabilities. Key features of the Agentic AI framework include autonomy, where the system takes goal-oriented actions with minimal human supervision; reasoning, which involves making contextual decisions, judgment calls, and trade-offs; and adaptable planning, allowing dynamic adjustments to plans based on changing conditions for efficient task completion. These systems exhibit context understanding, enabling them to comprehend and act on inputs across natural language and other modalities. Additionally, they are action-enabled, with the capability to execute tasks by accessing web services and delivering specific skills [7].

2.2 Hierarchical Agent Framework Agentic Architectures

A Hierarchical Agent Framework in AI refers to an architectural model (please see Fig. 1) where autonomous agents are organized in layers of control and responsibility, with higher-level agents managing broader goals and strategies while delegating specific subtasks to lower-level agents. This structure allows complex problems to be decomposed into manageable components, enabling agents to specialize in tasks such as planning, decision-making, perception, or actuation. In agriculture, for instance, a top-level agent might oversee farm productivity optimization, while mid-level agents handle irrigation, pest management, or crop scheduling, and low-level agents interact with sensors or control machinery. This layered coordination enhances scalability, adaptability, and the interpretability of AI-driven systems operating in dynamic, real-world environments [8].

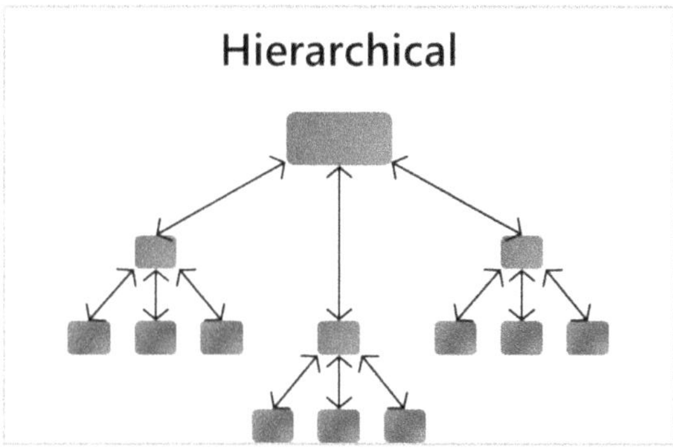

Fig. 1. Hierarchical Agentic Architecture.

2.3 Supervisor Agent Framework Agentic Architectures

A Supervisor Agent (please see Fig. 2) is a high-level autonomous entity within a multi-agent or hierarchical AI framework that oversees, coordinates, and regulates the behavior of subordinate agents to ensure alignment with overarching system goals. It typically manages task delegation, monitors execution progress, handles exceptions, and resolves conflicts among lower-level agents. In agricultural or dairy applications, a Supervisor Agent might monitor weather-aware irrigation agents, crop health agents, and logistics agents, ensuring that their outputs collectively contribute to farm-level yield optimization or sustainability targets. It acts as the decision-making orchestrator, adapting strategies based on environmental changes, system feedback, or evolving objectives, thereby enhancing system resilience, coherence, and autonomy [9].

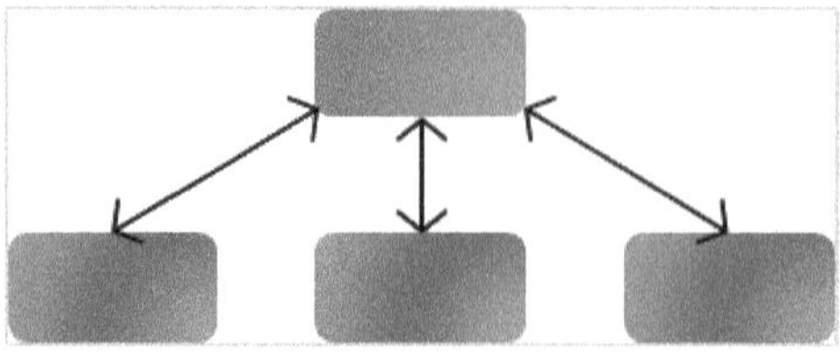

Fig. 2. Supervisor Agent.

In agentic AI architectures, different coordination patterns govern how agents collaborate to accomplish complex tasks. The Network pattern involves (please see figure) a decentralized configuration where multiple agents interact laterally, sharing information and decisions in a peer-to-peer fashion without a central controller. This setup is ideal for distributed environments where agents, such as crop monitors, irrigation optimizers, and weather predictors, need to coordinate autonomously. In contrast, the Hand-off pattern follows a sequential flow, where one agent completes its task and passes the result to the next agent in the chain. For instance, a soil analysis agent might trigger a seed selection agent, which then passes information to a planting schedule agent—creating a clear, stage-wise pipeline.

The Maker-Checker pattern introduces a quality control mechanism: one agent (the maker) produces an output, such as a recommendation or plan, while a second agent (the checker) reviews and validates it before execution. This is particularly useful in high-stakes or regulated domains like finance, healthcare, or precision agriculture [6–9].

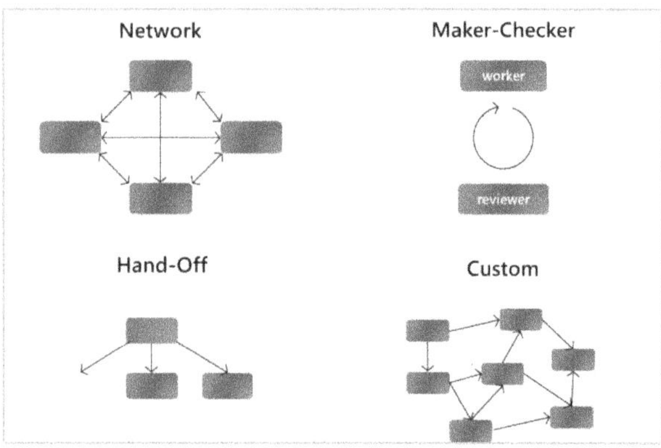

Fig. 3. Agentic Architectures

Lastly, the Custom pattern allows developers to design bespoke agent workflows tailored to unique domain challenges. It may combine elements of hierarchy, recursion, or event-driven executions such as a supervisor agent dynamically orchestrating a team of context-specific agents in response to evolving farm conditions or supply chain disruptions. Each of these patterns offers distinct advantages in terms of scalability, auditability, and flexibility, depending on the use case. Agentic architectures (please see Fig. 3).

2.4 Agentic Frameworks

The area of agentic framework is growing at a rapid pace to address market needs and technological complexities. Some of the frameworks in this paper, I would like to include Lang Chain Semantic Kernel and Google Agentic Development Kit.

LangChain

- LangChain is a framework for developing applications powered by language models and is designed around the following principles:
- Data-aware: connect a language model to other sources of data
- Agentic: allow a language model to interact with its environment

Semantic Kernel

- Semantic Kernel has been engineered to allow developers to flexibly integrate AI into their existing apps by:
- Providing a set of abstractions that make it easy to create and manage prompts, native functions, memories, and connectors.
- Orchestrating these components using Semantic Kernel pipelines to complete users' requests or automate actions.

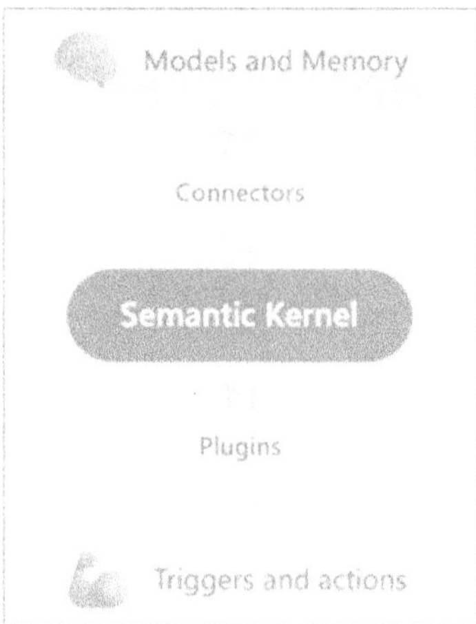

Fig. 4. Semantic Kernel.

The Semantic Kernel SDK empowers developers to build their own custom AI agents. Semantic Kernel integrates LLMs like OpenAI, Azure OpenAI, and Hugging Face with conventional programming languages like C#, Python, and Java. Developers can create "plugins" to interface with the LLMs and perform all sorts of tasks. The Semantic Kernel SDK also provides built-in plugins that quickly enhance an application. Developers can easily apply AI models in their own applications without having to learn the intricacies of each model's API (please see Fig. 4).

2.5 Chain of Reasoning: ReACT (Reasoning and Acting)

The current generation of AI agents serves as business-driven task enablers, significantly enhancing productivity and fostering the development of novel ideas. The concept of chain-of-reasoning, as introduced in ReACT (Reasoning and Acting), represents a groundbreaking advancement for computer and software systems (please see Fig. 5). However, the idea of a structured chain of reasoning is not new, it has long been present in Farm management of small farmers. For instance, agricultural calendars, irrigation schedules, fertilizer and other input management, value chains, and weather. I will delve deeper into this concept in the next sections, where I explore the creation of AI agents that are not only reason but are also infused with a sense of consciousness [10–13].

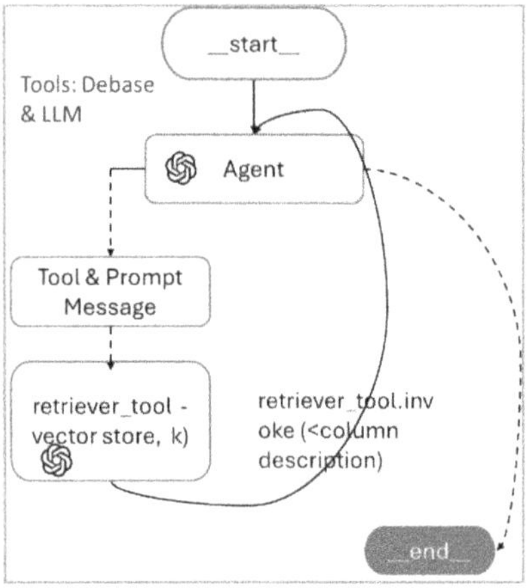

Fig. 5. ReACT

The grand vision of ReACT is to develop AI agents capable of reasoning and executing actions grounded in that reasoning. While these agents fall short of true consciousness, they can devise action plans based on structured reasoning processes. Earlier AI architectures, such as the RAG (Retrieval-Augmented Generation) framework, lack this capability, as they focus primarily on information retrieval and generation without reasoning-based action. The evolution toward ReACT marks a significant step forward, bridging the gap between logical reasoning and actionable outcomes in AI systems [9, 15–17].

- AutoDev is a foundational research paper that inspired the creation of GitHub Copilot. Following its lead, other frameworks like DyLAN and Amazon Q Developer have emerged.
- Libraries such as ReAct, MetaGPT, and LATS have been instrumental in defining inter-agent collaboration and generative AI reflection patterns.

- Frameworks like AutoGen, CrewAI, and our upcoming SDK have built comprehensive solutions that empower everyday generative AI developers.
- LangChain

There is no definitive answer to when and why to use AI agents, as different applications and domains may have different goals, challenges, and constraints. However, a possible general framework to approach this question is to consider the following factors:

- when the environment is dynamic, stochastic, partially observable, or adversarial, as they can adapt, learn, and optimize their actions based on feedback and data. For example, AI agents can be used to control autonomous vehicles, play video games, trade stocks, or negotiate contracts.

AI Agents often rely on large amounts of data to learn and improve. Therefore, AI Agents are more feasible and effective when there is sufficient and relevant data to train and test them. For example, AI agents can be used to recommend products, diagnose plat diseases, or generate natural language [18, 19].

AI agents can vary in the degree of autonomy, collaboration, and communication they have with human users, partners, or supervisors. Depending on the task and the context, AI agents can be used to augment, assist, or replace human decision-making and actions. For example, AI agents can be used to filter spam, tutor students, or compose music.

AI agents should be used with caution and care, considering the potential benefits and risks, and following the principles of fairness, accountability, and transparency. For example, AI agents can be used to enhance security, promote justice, or foster creativity.

2.6 RAG Pattern

Retrieval Augmented Generation (RAG) is a technique used to augment a large language model (LLM) with external data, such as a company's internal documents. This provides the model with the context it needs to produce accurate and useful output for your specific use case. RAG is a pragmatic and effective approach to using LLMs in an enterprise. The following diagram shows a high-level overview of how a RAG approach works (please see Fig. 6).

Broadly speaking, the RAG process is four steps. The first step is done once, and the other three steps are done as many times as needed:

1. You create embeddings to ingest the internal documents into a vector database. Embeddings are numeric representations of text in the documents that capture the semantic or contextual meaning of the data. A vector database is essentially a database of these embeddings, and it is sometimes called a vector store or vector index. This step requires data cleaning, formatting, and chunking, but this is a one-time, upfront activity.
2. A human submits a query in natural language.
3. An orchestrator performs a similarity search in the vector database and retrieves the relevant data. The orchestrator adds the retrieved data (also known as context) to the prompt that contains the query.

4. The orchestrator sends the query and the context to LLM. The LLM generates a response to the query by using the additional context [18].

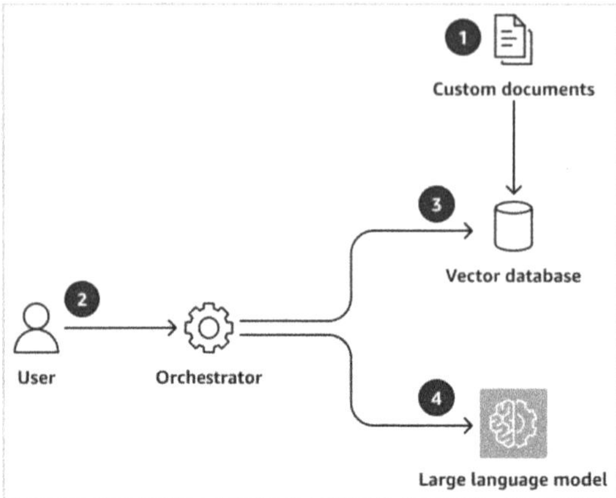

Fig. 6. RAG.

By harnessing the power of these technologies, we can automate a wide range of tasks, from content creation to complex decision-making processes, enhancing productivity and fostering innovation across various industries. However, it's crucial to approach these developments with a mindful consideration of their ethical implications and potential biases, ensuring that the benefits of AI are realized in a fair and responsible manner. As we continue to push the boundaries of what's possible with AI, the future looks bright for generative AI agents, promising a world where artificial intelligence plays an increasingly integral role in our lives (please see Fig. 7).

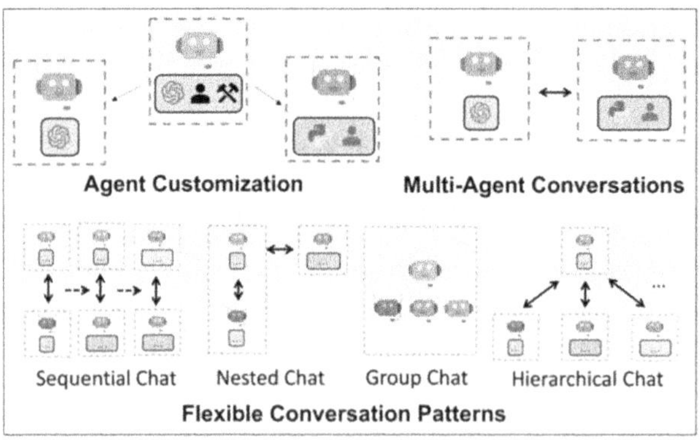

Fig. 7. Flexible Conversation Patterns

3 System Overview

This architecture enables a multi-agent, context-aware system to support small farmers by combining: Natural language interfaces, Supervisor agent orchestration, Specialized domain agents and tools, Semantic search over domain-specific vector stores, and Personalized recommendations using farmer history and ESG data (please see Fig. 8).

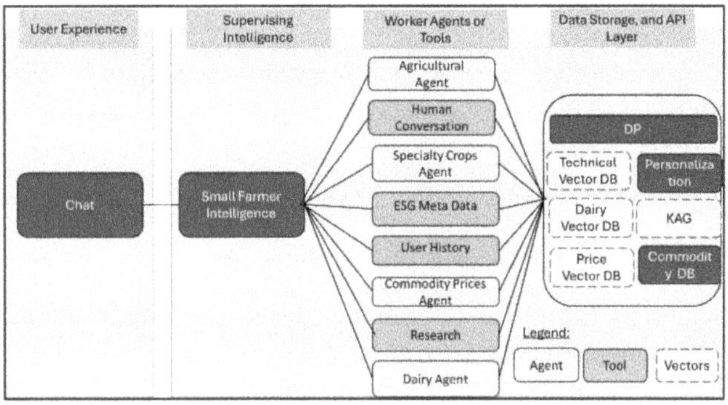

Fig. 8. Agentic Architecture.

The Hierarchical Agentic AI Architecture system designed to serve small farmers by integrating user interaction, supervising intelligence, worker agents/tools, and backend data storage. Here's a detailed interpretation of each component:

The batch layer then feeds into a serving layer, which indexes the batch view for efficient window querying. In turn, the speed layer updates the serving layer with incremental updates based on the most recent data. By utilizing the lambda architecture, we can optimize data processing for rumination count detection, providing valuable insights into the health and wellbeing of cattle for farmers and industry professionals alike [5, 8, 9, 16].

3.1 User Experience

This is the entry point for farmers or users to interact with the system via natural language. It acts as the conversational interface, translating user queries into structured inputs for agentic processing. May support multilingual and voice interfaces, crucial for accessibility in rural regions.

To calculate the rumination count, we utilize both sensor data, with the exception of the accelerometer, which serves as an inhibitor or initiator trigger. By combining these data points, we can gain valuable insights into the health and wellbeing of the cattle, providing farmers with the necessary information to optimize their feed management practices and ensure the continued health and productivity of their herds.

3.2 Supervising Intelligence

This is the central Supervisor Agent responsible for orchestrating other agents. It interprets user intent, decides which worker agents to activate, and routes context across modules. Learns farmer preferences, history, and goals to enable personalized, context-aware responses.

4 System Design and Implementation

As part of the system design, the next step would be application of Window functions to detect rumination and then once detected calculated rumination count [18].

4.1 Agents

Following are agents that helps supervising architecture:

- Agricultural Agent: Provides recommendations on crop planning, soil health, irrigation, and sustainable practices.
- Specialty Crops Agent: Focuses on region-specific or high-value crops like spices, floriculture, or organic produce.
- Commodity Prices Agent: Tracks and analyzes real-time market trends, price fluctuations, and forecasts.
- Dairy Agent: Advises on cattle health, milk productivity, feed optimization, and veterinary support.

4.2 Tools (Highlighted in Orange)

Following are tools:

- Human Conversation: Supports natural human-agent dialogue handling beyond structured queries.
- ESG Meta Data: Embeds Environmental, Social, and Governance context, such as carbon emissions or water usage.
- User History: Stores interaction logs and behavioral patterns for personalized recommendations.
- Research: Fetches domain-specific knowledge, including scientific papers, weather advisories, and agronomy updates.

4.3 Data Storage and API Layer

This layer underpins the intelligence system by storing embeddings, domain data, and delivering personalization.

- Databases (Green - Vector Stores)
- Technical Vector DB: Stores embeddings from technical manuals, soil data, etc., used for semantic search.
- Dairy Vector DB: Contains vectorized content related to dairy health, nutrition, and productivity.
- Price Vector DB: Captures historical and real-time market price data for commodities.

5 A Case Study

We have tested and deployed Agentic AI models (please see Fig. 9) for Agriculture Analytics, Specialty Crops, and Value Chain Analytics [20].

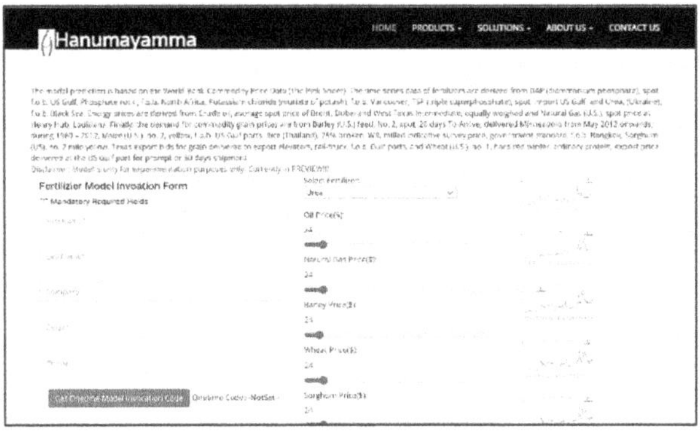

Fig. 9. Fertilizer Model Agent.

6 Conclusion and Future Work

The dairy and agriculture sectors are increasingly challenged by critical human resource issues that threaten their long-term viability and global food security. These include a shrinking rural workforce due to urban migration, demographic aging of farm laborers, declining interest in agricultural employment among youth, and significant labor shortages during peak farming cycles. Technological advancements—though necessary—have not yet offset the human capital deficit in many developing and developed regions. The result is a growing gap between agricultural production needs and workforce availability, directly impacting crop yields, dairy productivity, and supply chain resilience. Addressing these issues is central to achieving sustainable development goals (SDGs), particularly in food security, poverty reduction, and rural economic stability.

References

1. FAO: The State of Food and Agriculture 2021 – Making Agrifood Systems More Resilient. Food and Agriculture Organization of the United Nations (2021). https://www.fao.org
2. World Bank: Harvesting Prosperity: Technology and Productivity Growth in Agriculture (2022). https://www.worldbank.org
3. McKinsey Global Institute: Agriculture's Connected Future: How Technology Can Yield New Growth (2022). https://www.mckinsey.com
4. IFAD: The Future of Smallholder Farming in the Digital Age (2023). https://www.ifad.org
5. CGIAR AI for Agriculture: Digital Extension Services: Toward Inclusive Agri-AI Deployment (2022). https://aiforag.org
6. LangChain, Build a Retrieval Augmented Generation (RAG) App: Part 1, 2023. https://python.langchain.com/docs/tutorials/rag/, Accessed 14 July 2025

7. LangChain, Build a Retrieval Augmented Generation (RAG) App: Part 2, 2023. https://python.langchain.com/docs/tutorials/qa_chat_history/. Accessed 14 July 14 2025
8. LangChain, Build a Question/Answering system over SQL data (2023). https://python.langchain.com/docs/tutorials/sql_qa/. Accessed 14 July 14 2025
9. Vuppalapati, C.: Divine Feminine Energies in Vedic Anthologies: A Scientific Inquiry Using AI and Large Language Models, Publication Date: 14 July 2025. ISBN 979-8-89530-583-6
10. Vuppalapati, C.: Machine Learning and Artificial Intelligence for Agricultural Economics: Prognostic Data Analytics to Serve Small Scale Farmers, 1st edn. Springer, Cham (2021). https://doi.org/10.1007/978-3-030-77485-1
11. Vuppalapati, C.: Democratization of Artificial Intelligence for the Future of Humanit, 1st edn. CRC Press, Boca Raton (2021). ISBN-13 978-0367524098
12. Vuppalapati, C.: Assessing Policy Effectiveness using AI and Language Models: Applications for Economic and Social Sustainability. Springer, Cham (2024). https://doi.org/10.1007/978-3-031-56097-2
13. Vuppalapati, C.: Artificial Intelligence and Advanced Analytics for Food Security. CRC Press, Boca Raton (2023). ISBN-13: 978-1032346182
14. Vuppalapati, C., Ilapakurti, A., Kedari, S., Vuppalapati, J., Kedari, S., Vuppalapati, R.: Democratization of AI, albeit constrained IoT devices & Tiny ML, for creating a sustainable food future. In: 2020 3rd International Conference on Information and Computer Technologies (ICICT), San Jose, CA, USA, pp. 525–530 (2020). https://doi.org/10.1109/ICICT50521.2020.00089
15. Vuppalapati, C., Ilapakurti, A., Kedari, S., Vuppalapati, R., Vuppalapati, J., Kedari, S.: The role of combinatorial mathematical optimization and heuristics to improve small farmers to veterinarian access and to create a sustainable food future for the world. In: 2020 Fourth World Conference on Smart Trends in Systems, Security and Sustainability (WorldS4), London, UK, pp. 214–221 (2020). https://doi.org/10.1109/WorldS450073.2020.9210339
16. Ilapakurti, A., Vuppalapati, C.: Building an IoT framework for connected dairy. In: 2015 IEEE First International Conference on Big Data Computing Service and Applications, Redwood City, CA, USA, pp. 275–285 (2015). https://doi.org/10.1109/BigDataService.2015.39
17. Ramalingam, A., Kedari, S., Vuppalapati, C.: IEEE FEMH voice data challenge 2018. In: 2018 IEEE International Conference on Big Data (Big Data), Seattle, WA, USA, pp. 5272–5276 (2018). https://doi.org/10.1109/BigData.2018.8622164
18. Vuppalapati, C.: Building Enterprise IoT Applications, 1st edn. CRC Press, Boca Raton (2019). ISBN-13: 978-0367173852
19. Yang, X.-S., Sherratt, S., Dey, N., Joshi, A. (eds.): ICICT 2019, London, Volume 2, "Fourth International Congress on Information and Communication Technology". eBook ISBN 978-981-329-343-4 and Softcover ISBN 978-981-329-342-7
20. Hanumayamma, Try Our Fertilizer Model (2024). https://www.hanuinnotech.com/agricultureanalytics.html. Accessed 14 July 2025

An Intelligent Emotion-Based Mechanism to Predicting Domestic Violence in Public Online Posts

Samer Muthana Sarsam[1(✉)], Ahmed Isam Al-Hatem[2], Abdul Samad Shibghatullah[3], Chit Su Mon[4], Abd Aziz Alias[5], and Lubna A. Hussein[6]

[1] School of Management, Coventry University, Coventry, UK
samer.sarsam@coventry.ac.uk
[2] College of Arts, Al Iraqia University, Baghdad, Iraq
ahmed.i.khaleel@aliraqia.edu.iq
[3] College of Computing and Informatics (CCI), Universiti Tenaga Nasional, Kajang, Selangor, Malaysia
abdul.samad@uniten.edu.my
[4] Wentworth Institute of Higher Education, Sydney, NSW, Australia
chit.mon@win.edu.au
[5] Department of Oral and Craniofacial Sciences, Faculty of Dentistry, Universiti Malaya, 50603 Kuala Lumpur, Malaysia
alias123@um.edu.my
[6] Department of Computing and Information Sciences, University of Technology and Applied Sciences (UTAS), Suhar 311, Sultanate of Oman
lubnafatlawi@gmail.com

Abstract. Domestic violence (DV) incidents against women are on the rise worldwide. This study proposed a machine learning model to predicting DV from Microblogs. The proposed model was based on the classification of different types of emotions and tweet polarity. The Latent Dirichlet Allocation algorithm was used to identify the latent topics shared among the collected tweets based on certain DV-emotional and -physical features. The results showed that DV-related topics were associated with emotions of anger, disgust, fear, and sadness. Three classifiers (K-nearest neighbor, multinomial logistic regression, and LogitBoost) were used to classify DV-related topics. The results of the Logistic classifier achieved the highest classification accuracy (97.71%) in predicting DV incidents against women. Outcomes from this study can offer health and wellbeing decision makers a timely and cost-effective way to predict DV against women. This includes the feasibility of integrating different sentimental features in classifying DV incidents.

Keywords: domestic violence · sentiment analysis · machine learning · microblogs

---

The type of the submission is "Regular Research Paper".

H. R. Arabnia et al. (Eds.): CSCE 2025, CCIS 2934, pp. 367–378, 2026.
https://doi.org/10.1007/978-3-032-22190-2_26

1 Introduction

Domestic Violence (DV) has been characterized by the literature as a pattern of coercive behaviors that results in a significant damage not only to the life and health of family but also to social relations [1]. Acts like repeated battering and injury, psychological abuse, sexual assault, and progressive social isolation have been linked to DV [2, 3]. This trend is commonly found among women and children, and it has been reported by many scholars to cause serious consequences to their mental health and well-being [4]. The current statistical reports on DV showed a notable increase in violence against women [5], especially during the Covid-19 pandemic [6]. Many health organizations are currently considering violence against women as a global public health issue that impacts approximately one in three women worldwide. In addition to mental disorders, women suffering from DV tends to also experience physically, emotionally, and psychologically disorders. Yet, the current methods to detect / monitor DV against women might not be sufficient enough to help policy makers and health organizations understand or predict their occurrences. Our review of the current reports and survey results (e.g., [7–9] on DV against women revealed that existing statistical methods and sample techniques always consider a specific group of people within the population without providing a holistic understanding of DV phenomenon in general. In addition, the existing methods (e.g., survey, interviews, and observation) require manual annotation, much human efforts, time consuming and expensive [7]. Based on these, it can be said that it is essential to develop a timely method other than statistical surveys to help decision makers understand the DV trend among women. Therefore, lexicon-based method is proposed to understand various abuses in relation to DV against women (e.g., physical, verbal, psychological, emotional, and sexual).

2 Literature Review

The literature on DV covered different behavioral and physical antecedents to characterize or explain the reasons behind this phenomenon. Current research is still limited to the use of classical data collection and prediction methods to document DV cases. These studies may still offer an effective way to report DV in a population specific sample. However, the pressure on healthcare policy makers to monitor and predict DV might benefit from a more diverse and timely mechanism.

The current evidence on how DV influences individuals' mental health might not be enough to measure other unpredictable events of DV [10]. This led many scholars to look at the potential of machine learning to characterize and predict DV-related topics using different sources of information. For example, Subramani and O'Connor [7] proposed the development framework to extract actionable knowledge from social media in order to make certain decisions related to the social welfare of the community. Liu, Xue, Zhao, Wang, Jiao and Zhu [10] explored the short-term outcomes of DV on individuals' mental health. The authors collected data from a sample of victims and nonvictims to estimate their mental health status before and after the DV incident. They utilized an online ecological recognition system that was developed suing several predictive models to identify individuals' mental health statuses. Subramani, Wang, Vu and Li

[11] examined the potential of using deep learning to identify and detect DV victims in critical need. The authors found that the technique outperformed traditional machine-learning techniques. Yallico Arias and Fabian [12] proposed a machine learning model to assess and identify the level of psychological violence against women in written virtual expressions. The model operates by alerting the women about the risk that runs in her relationship. Alawneh, Al-Fawa'reh, Jafar and Al Fayoumi [13] developed an approach to facilitate the detection of different types of malicious human activities by using machine learning with different algorithms. The authors reported that their proposed mechanism achieved an accuracy of 81% using Term Frequency Inverse Document Frequency (TF-IDF) with machine learning. Similar attempts have been carried out by other scholars (e.g., [14–17] to examine the application of machine learning in facilitating the detection of DV using different microblogs. However, most of previous studies on DV recognition and detection did not relay on emotions to characterize the main features of DV incidents, which can be a key element for future prediction of these incidents. Therefore, this study is carried out to explore the potential of users' emotions expressed in their post in characterizing DV incidents on Twitter (X).

Microblog spaces like X supports data extraction and filtering through application programming interface (API). This includes retrieving posts, reactions, and opinions about specific topics (keywords). Many scholars used this function to explore various aspects of people's reaction to various topics and issues. Some of the recent studies (e.g., [18, 19] on sentiment analysis of X data developed / used various machine learning models in an attempt to predict negative and positive reactions of users through emotional analysis of text. This methodological procedure is found to be useful in characterizing and predicting specific events. Based on these, we explored attempts to answer the following questions: '1) What are the main topics related to DV on X?', '2) What are the types of emotions associated DV-related topics on X?', and '3) Can these emotions be used to predict DV?' It is assumed that answering these questions will help decision makers and researchers of healthcare organizations to better evaluate DV against women in a timely manner.

3 Method

Figure 1 summarizes the implementation procedure followed in this study, including data collection, data pre-processing, cluster analysis, topic modeling, emotion extraction, and classification technique.

3.1 Data Collection

A Twitter-API was used in this study to collect posts from different locations around the world. The API request returned a total of 1,395,589 English tweets. The time span for collecting the data was between November 3rd, 2023, till 30th April 2024. Tweets relevant to DV were obtained using several keywords: 'violence against women, 'women abuse', 'domestic violence against women', and 'domestic abuse against women'. It is also worth mentioning that there might be other keywords can be used to represent DV incidents on X, however we attempted to include keywords that are directly related to

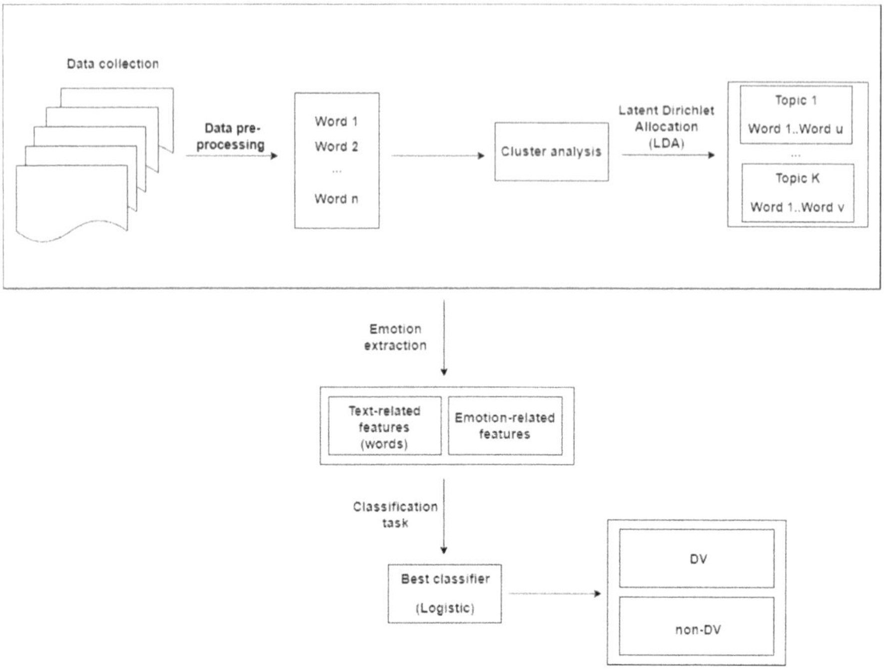

Fig. 1. The study procedure.

DV in order to improve retrieval accuracy of the data. In addition, we adapted several data preparation steps to enhance the quality and the reliability of the collected tweets (see the following sections).

3.2 Data Pre-processing

We used the bag-of-words model along with 'Tokenization' to get the tweets-related words (features) and build the overall dictionary using these words. All the extracted features from the collected tweets were transferred to a lowercase style before applying the Stopwords list technique. The Stopwords list method was mainly used to keep the essential terms in the data and provide DV-related information. Also, at the pre-processing stage, we normalized the lengths of the tweets via the L2 norm approach, which helped us to prepare the DV-related data for the machine learning phase.

3.3 Cluster Analysis

After the data pre-processing stage, the cluster analysis was applied via the Expectation–maximization (EM) algorithm was applied to assign a probability distribution to each instance (tweet) of the resulting clusters. EM operates by identifying the number of clusters to be generated using the tenfold cross-validation technique. The log-likelihood was averaged over all the ten results. The clustering result yielded three groups/clusters (see Fig. 2). From the figure, it can be observed that dark colors represent to the DV features. We then applied topic modeling on each cluster to obtain the hidden themes within the X messages.

Fig. 2. Cluster analysis results.

3.4 Topic Modeling

The clustering results revealed a three-cluster solution based on our collected data. We used the Latent Dirichlet Allocation (LDA) algorithm [20] on each cluster to identify the latent topics shared among the collected tweets. LDA is an unsupervised generative probabilistic method for modeling the collection of tweets. It allows presenting the tweets as random mixtures over latent topics where a topic is described based on the distribution over data words. This method assumes that each document can be treated as a probabilistic distribution over latent topics, and that topic distribution in all documents has a Dirichlet prior. LDA was used here to identify the main topics associated with DV in each cluster. This was essential for us to extract the relevant emotions on DV. In this study, The LDA method was tweaked by conducting multiple experiments. The number of topics was determined first based on the trade-off between information loss and information overload. After these experiments, the number of topics to be examined is confirmed. A total of four specialists in public health were asked to examine the usefulness of the produced themes (see Sect. 4.1).

3.5 Emotion Extraction and Classification

This study used a series of measures to extract users' emotions embedded in their tweets. We used both NRC Affect Intensity Lexicon and SentiStrength approaches to extract users' emotions based on the recommendations of previous works (e.g., [21, 22]). The NRC lexicon was used to analyze tweets by identifying associations between words and emotions: anger, disgust, fear, joy, sadness, and trust. Each emotion was scored from 0 (low) to 1 (high), helping estimate the emotional content of users' posts for behavioral prediction on microblogs (see Sect. 4.1 for more details). In order to identify the polarity of each tweet, we used the 'SentiStrength' approach and labeled tweets with +5 labeled as 'Positive', −5 as 'Negative', and −1/+1 as 'Neutral'.

To perform classification task, three classification algorithms were examined in this study to identify the best prediction capability for DV. The classifiers of K-nearest neighbor (IBk) [23], multinomial logistic regression (Logistic) [24], and LogitBoost (additive logistic regression) [25] were used based on the previous recommendations. We used the stratified tenfold cross-validation technique to assess the general prediction process quality along with different evaluation metrics.

4 Results

4.1 Topic Modeling Results

Figure 3 shows LDA results where each circle represents a specific topic from the collected tweets. Also, the size of these circles demonstrates the frequency of the topic in relation to DV. The similarity level between these topics is reflected in the distance between the circles. The distance between the identified topics indicates independent and dependent (a high similarity level) relations. On the other hand, to select useful topics to be examined, four experts in public health were asked to independently investigate and label the resulting topics using relevant themes. Then, the authors measured the agreement between the suggested themes using kappa statistic which showed 0.96. According to these experts, the main themes were 'Types of violence', 'Manners to deal with violence', and 'Domestic violence against women'. The first theme (Types of violence) discussed three different violence subtopics related to (i) "sexual violence", (ii) "teen violence", and (iii) "cultural violence". The LDA results from analyzing the second theme (Manners to deal with violence) discussed four recommendations to tackle DV among X users; these topics were: (i) having self-confidence, (ii) avoiding loneliness, (iii) learning basic self-defense techniques, and (iv) keeping the phone number of an emergency service. The third theme (Domestic violence against women) was found to be related to DV against women with two main subtopics related to emotional violence and physical violence. Four experts were invited to identify which theme to use in the classification phase. A high level of agreement among the experts was reported in relation to the labeling of first and third themes. The experts recommended labeling topics in third theme as 'DV', while topics that did not discuss DV against women (first theme) were labeled as 'non-DV'. The resulted clusters were then used in the sentiment analysis and classification phase.

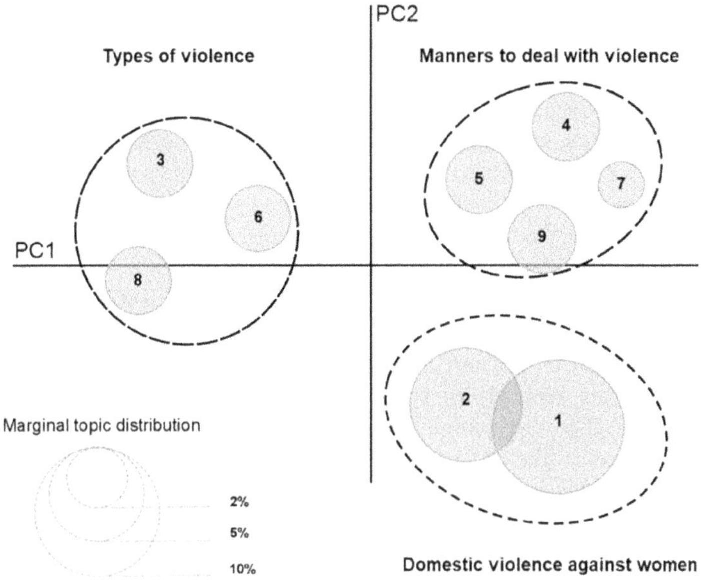

Fig. 3. LDA results.

To understand DV terminology in Theme 3, the top emotional ('Control', 'Afraid', 'Upsetting', 'Ashamed', 'Unwanted') and physical ('Slapping', 'Choking', 'Hitting', 'Shaking', 'Burning') terms were identified and analyzed over six months using time series, see Fig. 4.

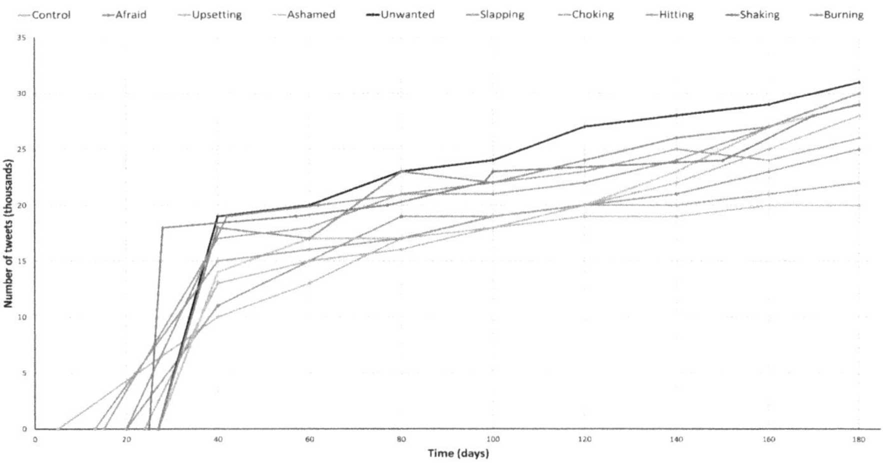

Fig. 4. Time series of emotional and physical DV features.

4.2 Descriptive Statistics Results

Figure 5 summarizes the result of both NRC Affect Intensity Lexicon and SentiStrength where the descriptive statistics of the two groups of tweets in the two themes (DV and non-DV) are computed, including the six emotions (anger, disgust, fear, joy, sadness, and trust) and tweet's polarity (positive/negative/neutral). Figure 6a shows the NRC results where it can be clearly observed that tweets related to victims of DV showed higher results of anger (***M*** = 1.60, ***SD*** = 0.32), disgust (***M*** = 1.54, ***SD*** = 0.23), fear (***M*** = 1.80, ***SD*** = 0.13), and sadness (***M*** = 1.59, ***SD*** = 0.46) than anger (***M*** = .50, ***SD*** = 0.36), disgust (***M*** = 0.28, ***SD*** = 0.14), fear (***M*** = 0.18, ***SD*** = 0.05), and sadness (***M*** = 0.10, ***SD*** = 0.02) existed in the tweets of the non-violence cluster. In contrast, tweets that did not reflect any DV against women demonstrated higher level of both joy (***M*** = 1.38, ***SD*** = 0.18) and trust (***M*** = 1.46, ***SD*** = 0.7) than joy (***M*** = 0.25, ***SD*** = 0.19) and trust (***M*** = 0.16, ***SD*** = 0.8) sentiments embedded in X messages related to victims of DV. Meanwhile, the results of SentiStrength, see Fig. 6b, illustrates that tweets related to DV against women contained higher percentage of negative sentiment (96%) than the neutral sentiment (4%), while non-DV tweets revealed higher degree of positive emotions (75%) than the neutral emotions (25%). Nevertheless, to assess similarities/differences between DV and non-DV tweets, t-test was used ($t = 38.21$), and it showed that there was a significant difference ($p < 0.05$) between the two examined groups. From this it can be observed that the negative emotion is associated with DV against women. The tweets contained such emotions were also having high level of disgust, anger, sadness, and fear as well as low level of joy and trust.

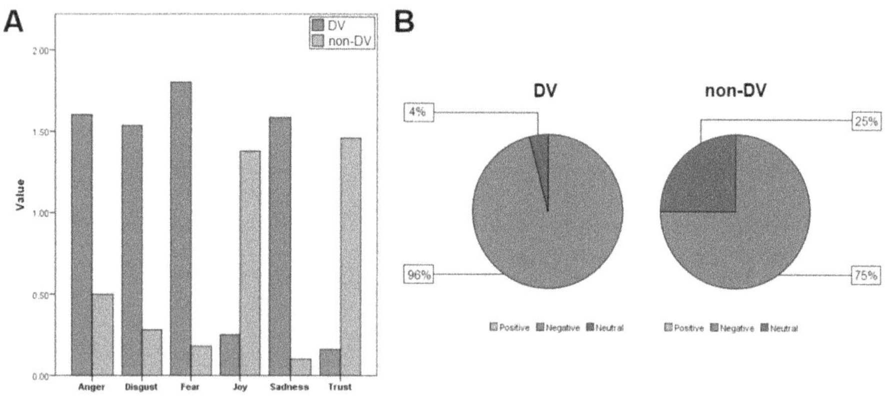

Fig. 5. The extracted emotions in the two group.

4.3 Classification Results

The results demonstrates that the highest classification accuracy of DV incidents was achieved when using Logistic classifier (97.71%), followed by IBk (63.15%), and LogitBoost (60.41%) classifiers. Meanwhile, the result of the kappa statistic for the Logistic classifier (94%) was higher than IBk (67%) and LogitBoost (61%). It was also observed that LogitBoost produced the hightest RMSE result (86%), followed by IBk (32%), and

Logistic (2%), respectively. Using the ROC curve to compare the performance of the three classifiers, Fig. 6 a and b demonstrated that Logistic outperformed other classification algorithms. Figure 6c displays the accuracy, kappa statistic, and RMSE of each of the utilized classifiers.

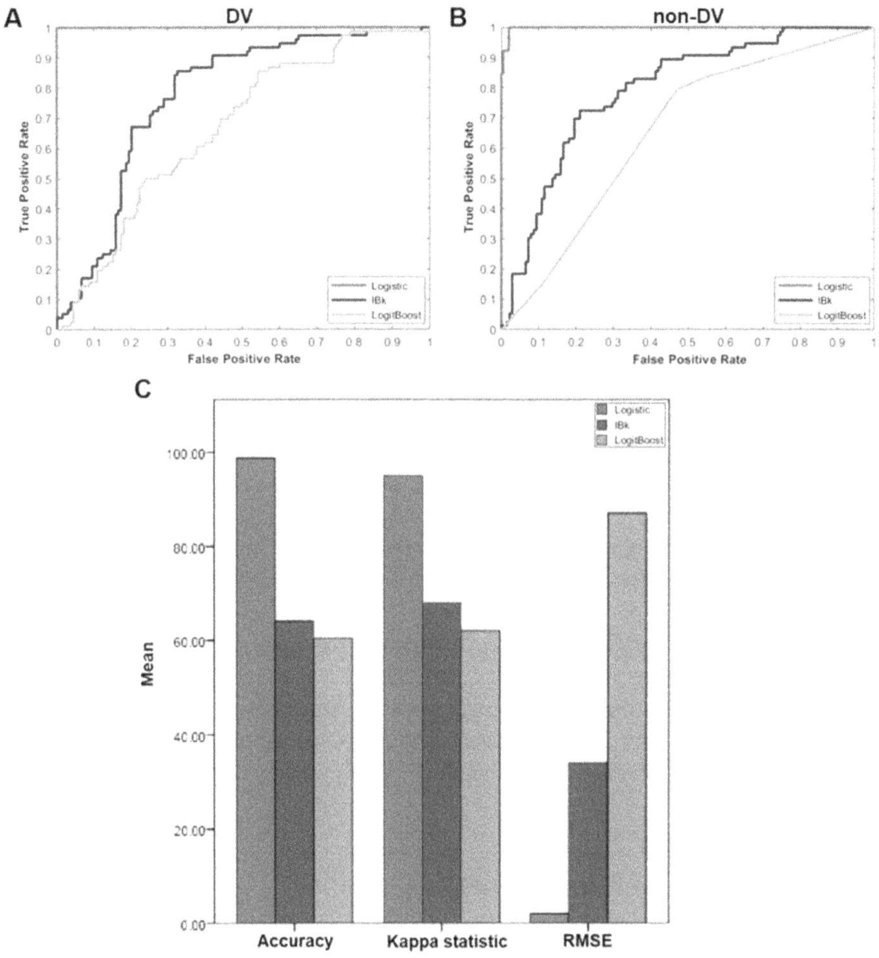

Fig. 6. Evaluation metrics of the examined algorithms.

5 Discussion

This study established that DV against women can be predicted in X based on the emotional and physical features of DV tweets. The results revealed was 97.71% accuracy of DV incidents against women which indicate a high prediction capability. The main DV topics found using the LDA method were related to emotional violence and physical violence. Some of the topics were mainly related to keeping women at a certain distance which described by many previous studies as the main factor for stimulating emotional violence behavior [26]. DV related topics were found to include emotions related to anger, disgust, and fear. These emotions were essential in characterizing DV against women on X. Previous studies like Srivastav [27] attributed these emotions to various factors including depression, anxiety, heart palpitations, eating disorders, and insomnia.

Other types of emotions (e.g., anger, disgust, fear, and sadness) were found to be less associated with the identification of DV cases against women. This is reasonable as anger and fear have been found to result in other forms of violence [28]. This study reported that DV-related emotions were mainly related to topics of partner's control, feel of fear, being upset, feeling of shame, and being unwanted. These topics are in line with previous studies on DV. For example Camp [29] described shame as a key factor that can be spotted among women affected by DV. It often leads to profound embarrassment, a sense of unworthiness, and a destructive loss of dignity. In addition, many who experience these consequences seek ways to diminish their intensity. Victims of DV are very likely to share their experience and storied to their own family or community to seek for practical and emotional support. Yet, feeling of shame and fear among DV victims were characterized as early signs for the identification and prevention of sever DV [30]. Furthermore, our results showed that physical-related topics of slapping, choking, hitting, shaking, and burning were essential in predicting DV against women. In the DV literature, threats are always used to characterize DV incidents, which typically concentrate exclusively on intimate partner violence and the needs of victims [31]. It is believed that the prediction accuracy of DV on X can be improved by using a combination of emotional and physical features of DV. In contrast, providing a timely forecasting method of DV using data from social media sites can help inform decisions made by the relevant health authorities.

Integrating the six types of emotions (anger, disgust, fear, joy, sadness, and trust) and the tweet polarity (positive/negative/neutral sentiment) can increase the prediction capability of the machine learning model. Outcomes from this study can offer health and wellbeing decision makers a timely and cost-effective way to predict DV against women. This includes the feasibility of integrating different emotions and message polarity in classifying DV incidents against women. The proposed method can also help social health organizations to evaluate and monitor DV cases worldwide or in a country specific population.

6 Limitations and Future Work

This study has some limitations; English tweets were analyzed because X is the most popular social media platform that allows people to express their opinions around the world. Besides, we extracted specific emotion-related features, including emotions (anger, disgust, fear, joy, sadness, and trust) and tweet polarity (positive/negative/neutral) due to the popularity of such features in the emotion-related literature. In the future, other emotions could be examined to show their relation to DV cases. We also reported the performance of three classifiers (K-nearest neighbor, multinomial logistic regression, and LogitBoost) because these are the top classifiers we found after examining more than fifteen schemes. Future work could examine other machine learning algorithms to find the one that has the best DV prediction capability. Finally, DV was used in this study as an example of coercive public relations that existed in our societies due to its negative impact on people's life. Future work could use the proposed approach to predict other abnormal behavioral patterns among individuals using published social media posts.

7 Conclusion

This study proposed a novel mechanism to predict DV against women using people's sentiments embedded in their tweets. The clustering technique was used to group similar tweets followed by using the LDA method to identify the latent topics shared based on certain DV-emotional and -physical features. The results showed that DV-related topics were found to include emotions related to anger, disgust, fear, and sadness. The prediction results indicated that the Logistic classifier achieved the highest classification accuracy (97.71%) in predicting DV incidents against women. This study offers a timely and cost-effective method to efficiently aid decision-makers to predict abnormal social incidents on microblogs.

References

1. Knapp, J.F.: The impact of children witnessing violence. Pediatr. Clin. North Am. **45**, 355–364 (1998)
2. Dobash, R.E., Dobash, R.P.: Domestic violence: sociological perspectives. In: International Encyclopedia of the Social & Behavioral Sciences, pp. 632–635 (2015)
3. Filip, O.L.: The role of social services in the reintegration of domestic violence victims. Soc. Soc. Work Rev. **5**, 15 (2021)
4. Goodmark, L.: Should domestic violence be decriminalized. Harv. Women's LJ **40**, 53 (2017)
5. Ellsberg, M., Jansen, H.A., Heise, L., Watts, C.H., Garcia-Moreno, C.: Intimate partner violence and women's physical and mental health in the WHO multi-country study on women's health and domestic violence: an observational study. Lancet **371**, 1165–1172 (2008)
6. Bourgault, S., Peterman, A., O'Donnell, M.: Violence against women and children during COVID-19—one year on and 100 papers in. Center for Global Development, Washington DC (2021)
7. Subramani, S., O'Connor, M.: Extracting actionable knowledge from domestic violence discourses on social media. arXiv preprint arXiv:1807.02391 (2018)
8. Blake, K.R., O'Dean, S.M., Lian, J., Denson, T.F.: Misogynistic tweets correlate with violence against women. Psychol. Sci. **32**, 315–325 (2021)
9. Alesina, A., Brioschi, B., La Ferrara, E.: Violence against women: a cross-cultural analysis for Africa. Economica **88**, 70–104 (2021)
10. Liu, M., Xue, J., Zhao, N., Wang, X., Jiao, D., Zhu, T.: Using social media to explore the consequences of domestic violence on mental health. J. Interpers. violence **36**, NP1965–1985NP (2021)
11. Subramani, S., Wang, H., Vu, H.Q., Li, G.: Domestic violence crisis identification from Facebook posts based on deep learning. IEEE Access **6**, 54075–54085 (2018)
12. Yallico Arias, T., Fabian, J.: Automatic detection of levels of intimate partner violence against women with natural language processing using machine learning and deep learning techniques. In: Lossio-Ventura, J.A., et al. (eds.) Information Management and Big Data, SIMBig 2021. CCIS, vol. 1577, pp. 189–205. Springer, Cham (2022). https://doi.org/10.1007/978-3-031-04447-2_13

13. Alawneh, E., Al-Fawa'reh, M., Jafar, M.T., Al Fayoumi, M.: Sentiment analysis-based sexual harassment detection using machine learning techniques. In: 2021 International Symposium on Electronics and Smart Devices (ISESD), pp. 1–6. IEEE (2021)
14. Al-Garadi, M.A., et al.: Natural language model for automatic identification of intimate partner violence reports from twitter. Array **15**, 100217 (2022)
15. Souto, H., Mello, R., Furtado, A.: An acoustic scene classification approach involving domestic violence using machine learning. In: Anais do XVI Encontro Nacional de Inteligência Artificial e Computacional, pp. 705–716. SBC (2019)
16. Hossain, M.M., et al.: Prediction on domestic violence in Bangladesh during the covid-19 outbreak using machine learning methods. Appl. Syst. Innov. **4**, 77 (2021)
17. Srividya, M., Anala, M., Tayal, C.: Deep learning techniques for physical abuse detection. IAES Int. J. Artif. Intell. **10**, 971 (2021)
18. Sarsam, S.M., Al-Samarraie, H.: A lexicon-based method for detecting eye diseases on microblogs. Appl. Artif. Intell. **36**, 1993003 (2022)
19. Srivastava, A., Singh, V., Drall, G.S.: Sentiment analysis of twitter data: a hybrid approach. Int. J. Healthc. Inf. Syst. Inform. (IJHISI) **14**, 1–16 (2019)
20. Lee, J.H., Ostwald, M.J.: Latent Dirichlet Allocation (LDA) topic models for Space Syntax studies on spatial experience. City Territ. Archit. **11**, 3 (2024)
21. Patil, B.A., Vadlakunta, V.V., Guruvu, P.P., Mathew, M., Prakash, J.: Phrase-level emotion intensity detection of text using lexicon-based unit circle and pipelined neural networks approaches. Neural Comput. Applic. **37**, 3151–3166 (2025)
22. Gouthami, S., Hegde, N.P.: Automatic sentiment analysis scalability prediction for information extraction using sentistrength algorithm. In: Reddy, A.B., Nagini, S., Balas, V.E., Raju, K.S. (eds.) Proceedings of Third International Conference on Advances in Computer Engineering and Communication Systems. LNNS, vol. 612, pp. 21–30. Springer, Singapore (2023). https://doi.org/10.1007/978-981-19-9228-5_3
23. Gupta, N., Ghosal, A.: Automation of attainment calculation in Outcome-Based Technical Education (OBTE). In: Deyasi, A., Mukherjee, S., Mukherjee, A., Bhattacharjee, A.K., Mondal, A. (eds.) Computational Intelligence in Digital Pedagogy. ISRL, vol. 197, pp. 113–135. Springer, Singapore (2021). https://doi.org/10.1007/978-981-15-8744-3_6
24. Alafif, T., Alotaibi, R., Albassam, A., Almudhayyani, A.: On the prediction of isolation, release, and decease states for COVID-19 patients: a case study in South Korea. ISA Trans. **124**, 191–196 (2021)
25. Debnath, P., et al.: Analysis of earthquake forecasting in India using supervised machine learning classifiers. Sustainability **13**, 971 (2021)
26. Duran, S., Eraslan, S.T.: Violence against women: affecting factors and coping methods for women. J. Pak. Med. Assoc. **69**, 53–57 (2019)
27. Srivastav, B.: Emotional abuse forms, process, patterns and ways to overcome. ScienceOpen Preprints (2021)
28. Hasan-Aslih, S., Netzer, L., van Zomeren, M., Saguy, T., Tamir, M., Halperin, E.: When we want them to fear us: the motivation to influence outgroup emotions in collective action. Group Process. Intergroup Relat. **22**, 724–745 (2019)
29. Camp, A.R.: Pursuing accountability for perpetrators of intimate partner violence: the peril and utility of shame. BUL Rev. **98**, 1677 (2018)
30. Chuemchit, M., Chernkwanma, S., Somrongthong, R., Spitzer, D.L.: Thai women's experiences of and responses to domestic violence. Int. J. Women's Health **10**, 557 (2018)
31. Berk, R.A., Sorenson, S.B., Barnes, G.: Forecasting domestic violence: a machine learning approach to help inform arraignment decisions. J. Empir. Leg. Stud. **13**, 94–115 (2016)

Missile Command Reimagined: Formulation of a Reinforcement Learning Based Approach for Resource-Constrained Defense

Rishan Patel, Haley Dozier(✉), and Ian Dettwiller

US Army Engineer Research and Development Center, Vicksburg, MS 39180, USA
{Rishan.Patel,Haley.R.Dozier,Ian.D.Dettwiller}@erdc.dren.mil

Abstract. This work investigates the use of reinforcement learning (RL) for missile defense asset allocation in a modified version of the classic Missile Command game. The environment has been extended to support heterogeneous interceptor types, varied threat profiles, and configurable resource constraints, transforming the engagement into a tractable resource allocation problem. By abstracting away spatial targeting, the scenario isolates asset selection as the primary decision variable, enabling focused evaluation of RL methods in mission-relevant conditions. Proximal Policy Optimization (PPO) was applied to train an agent in this setting; however, the resulting policy did not converge, suggesting that the current reward structure does not provide sufficient learning signal. Future work will focus on reward function redesign and feature engineering, which are expected to significantly improve learning outcomes and policy effectiveness. This effort serves as a foundation for further exploration of AI-assisted decision support in tactical defense planning.

Keywords: reinforcement learning · resource allocation · optimization

1 Introduction

Missile defense presents one of the most demanding operational challenges in modern warfare [1]. Defensive systems must respond to simultaneous incoming threats, often with limited munitions and under severe time constraints. Real-time decisions must be made to prioritize targets and allocate resources effectively to preserve critical infrastructure and reduce vulnerability to saturation attacks. These engagements require not only speed but strategic foresight to maintain readiness over successive waves of attack.

Traditionally, mission planning and engineering tasks have been performed by human operators with extensive military knowledge and tactical experience. While the expertise of these operators is indispensable, this approach often results in time-consuming, resource-intensive workflows that limit the number of scenarios that can be evaluated. The growing complexity of multi-domain operations calls for scalable, intelligent decision support systems capable of simulating

H. R. Arabnia et al. (Eds.): CSCE 2025, CCIS 2934, pp. 379–383, 2026.
https://doi.org/10.1007/978-3-032-22190-2_27

and optimizing responses in dynamic environments. Reinforcement learning (RL) offers one such approach, enabling automated, data-driven methods to replicate and refine tactical decision-making through simulation.

To explore the applicability of RL to this type of problem, a modified version of the classic Atari game Missile Command has been developed as a demonstration environment for training RL agents in the context of missile defense resource allocation. This effort expands the original game's capabilities by introducing multiple blue force assets with varied firing capabilities, magazine depths, and engagement profiles, along with a diverse set of red force threats characterized by different speeds, health levels, and destructive potential. Targeting has been abstracted to simplify the decision space, allowing the RL agent to focus on selecting the appropriate asset for each threat. The result is a tractable and flexible testbed that enables exploration of reinforcement learning techniques for asset allocation in tactical scenarios, with the long-term objective of informing integration with higher-fidelity mission simulation tools such as the Advanced Framework for Simulation, Integration, and Modeling (AFSIM) [2,3].

2 Related Work

Reinforcement learning (RL) has gained traction in mission engineering and tactical decision-making, particularly in complex environments where analytical solutions are intractable. Prior studies have applied RL to simplified 1D engagement scenarios and simulation-based policy learning frameworks, demonstrating its potential for optimizing decisions under uncertainty and constraints [5,7].

In related domains, Yan et al. proposed a hierarchical RL approach for missile guidance and evasion, using a two-level architecture to control an attacking missile in a continuous, physics-based environment [6]. While that work focuses on offensive real-time control, this effort addresses defensive resource allocation in a simplified discrete setting. Similarly, Rodriguez Torrado et al. benchmarked RL algorithms in the GVGAI framework using games like Missile Command to study generalization across diverse arcade environments [8]. In contrast, the present work adapts the game specifically to evaluate RL for tactical decision support, focusing on interpretable policies and mission-relevant behavior rather than generalized gameplay performance.

3 Methodology

3.1 Environment Overview

To explore the use of RL for resource allocation, a Missile Command environment [9] that utilizes the OpenAI Gym python library [10] was modified to emulate a simplified missile defense resource allocation problem. The updated simulation serves as a conceptual surrogate for mission-level planning tools such as AFSIM, enabling rapid prototyping of decision policies while preserving key features such as heterogeneous threats, limited resources, and stochastic dynamics.

The environment eliminates explicit targeting in favor of abstracted engagements, reducing the agent's action space to a discrete selection among available interceptor types. This abstraction transforms the scenario into a pure resource allocation problem, where the agent must determine which asset to fire based on real-time threat attributes such as speed, durability, and proximity. The action space therefore consists of options of the form "fire asset 1," "fire asset 2," and so on. The RL agent must condition its decisions on the evolving threat state while conserving limited defensive resources.

Modifications to the base environment include:

- Threat Enhancements: high-damage, slow-moving enemy missiles were introduced. These threats possess elevated health values and inflict proportionally greater damage on cities, which now have configurable health levels.
- Interceptor Differentiation: an additional interceptor class was implemented, characterized by rapid launch speed, small blast radius, and reduced lethality.
- State Variable Extensions: game logic was extended to include partial-damage modeling for cities and threats, moving beyond binary hit/destroyed states.

3.2 Reinforcement Learning

Reinforcement learning (RL) is a framework in which an agent learns to make sequential decisions by interacting with an environment, receiving observations and rewards, and updating its policy to maximize expected cumulative reward. Unlike supervised learning, RL does not rely on labeled input–output pairs, but instead learns optimal behavior through trial and error, usually within a simulation environment.

In this effort, RL is applied to the problem of missile defense asset allocation. Training is conducted using Proximal Policy Optimization (PPO), a widely used on-policy RL algorithm that balances performance and stability. PPO optimizes a clipped surrogate objective to prevent excessively large policy updates, improving learning robustness in stochastic environments. It maintains separate neural networks for the policy (actor) and value estimation (critic), enabling more stable convergence than traditional policy gradient methods [12].

The simulation environment was implemented using the OpenAI Gym interface [10] and integrated with Stable-Baselines3 [11], an open-source library providing standardized, reproducible RL algorithm implementations. PPO was selected for its compatibility with discrete action spaces and strong performance in sparse-reward settings. Training was conducted using episodic simulations composed of randomized threat waves, and policy performance was evaluated over multiple simulations with varying threat conditions. Future work will include the comparison of additional algorithms.

4 Preliminary Results and Discussion

Initial training experiments were conducted using Proximal Policy Optimization (PPO) over 1,000,000 timesteps in the modified Missile Command environment.

The objective was to evaluate the agent's ability to learn a stable asset allocation policy in response to varying red team threat profiles. However, preliminary results indicated limited convergence and suboptimal policy behavior, with no consistent improvement in interception rates or overall episode rewards observed across training runs.

Analysis of training logs and performance metrics suggested that the agent failed to develop a meaningful policy, frequently selecting actions that were either ineffective or unrelated to threat characteristics. This lack of learning stability is likely attributable to deficiencies in the reward structure rather than the underlying algorithm. Specifically, the current reward design may not provide sufficient signal to guide the agent toward preferred behaviors, particularly in scenarios involving delayed or partial outcomes.

These findings underscore the need for further reward engineering. Future revisions will consider introducing intermediate rewards for partial damage or near-interceptions, scaling penalties based on asset cost-effectiveness or proximity to threat resolution, and incorporating time-based shaping to encourage timely action and penalize inaction.

Although initial performance was limited, the experiment validated the environment structure and confirmed the feasibility of using PPO within this tactical decision-making context. With appropriate refinement of the reward function, convergence is expected to improve significantly in future iterations.

5 Future Work

This effort represents an initial step toward applying reinforcement learning to missile defense resource allocation using a modified arcade simulation. Several promising directions remain for future development.

Feature Engineering and Representation Learning. One of the most critical next steps is the exploration of feature engineering to improve policy generalization and learning efficiency. As previously stated, future work will consider introducing intermediate rewards for partial damage or near-interceptions, scaling penalties based on asset cost-effectiveness or proximity to threat resolution, and incorporating time-based shaping to encourage timely action and penalize inaction.

Integration of Targeting Logic. The current environment abstracts away spatial targeting to reduce complexity. However, future iterations will reintroduce targeting as an explicit decision variable, requiring the agent to jointly decide which interceptor to fire and where to aim. This increased complexity will necessitate richer state representations and may benefit from multi-agent RL formulations.

Transition of Lessons Learned to a Combat Simulation Tool. To transition from arcade-style simulation to real-world mission analysis, future efforts will develop surrogate models that replicate the output dynamics of high-fidelity tools. These surrogates will allow for policy development using offline RL before integration into closed-loop, black-box simulations.

Explainability Metrics. Building on prior work in interpretable reinforcement learning, we will also investigate post-hoc methods such as SHAP, counterfactual analysis, or attention mechanisms to explain agent decisions. Such explainability is critical for adoption in mission engineering workflows and ensures alignment with operational heuristics.

References

1. Mission Engineering Guide. Guide prepared by the Office of the Under Secretary of Defense for Research and Engineering (2020)
2. Clive, P.D., Johnson, J.A., Moss, M.J., Zeh, J.M., Birkmire, B.M., Hodson, D.D.: Advanced framework for simulation, integration and modeling. In: Proceedings of the International Conference on Scientific Computing, pp. 73–77 (2015)
3. West, T.D., Birkmire, B.M.: AFSIM: the air force research laboratory's approach to making M&S ubiquitous in the weapon system concept development process. In: Journal of Cyber Security and Information Systems, pp. 50–55
4. Solyeman, S., Khosla, D.: Multi-agent mission planning with reinforcement learning. In: Proceedings of the AAAI Symposium on The 2nd Workshop on Deep Models and Artificial Intelligence for Defense Applications: Potentials, Theories, Practices, Tools, and Risks (2020)
5. Zhang, L.A., et al.: Air dominance through machine learning: a preliminary exploration of artificial intelligence assisted mission planning. RAND Corporation, Santa Monica, CA (2020)
6. Yan, M., Yang, R., Zhang, Y., et al.: A hierarchical reinforcement learning method for missile evasion and guidance. Sci. Rep. **12**, 18888 (2022)
7. Thomas, G., Luo, Y., Ma, T.: Safe reinforcement learning by imagining the near future. In: Advances in Neural Information Processing Systems, vol. 34, pp. 13859–13869 (2021)
8. Torrado, R.R., Bontrager, P., Togelius, J., Liu, J., Perez-Liebana, D.: Deep reinforcement learning for general video game AI (2018). https://doi.org/10.48550/arXiv.1806.02448
9. Eliekadoche/gym_missile_command: Open AI gym environment of the missile command Atari game., GitHub. https://github.com/ElieKadoche/gym_missile_command. Accessed Aug 05 2024
10. Brockman, G., et al.: OpenAI gym. ArXiv Preprint: ArXiv:1606.01540 (2016)
11. Raffin, A., Hill, A., Gleave, A., Kanervisto, A., Ernestus, M., Dormann, N.: Stable-Baselines3: reliable reinforcement learning implementations. J. Mach. Learn. Res. (2021)
12. Schulman, J., Wolski, F., Dhariwal, P., Radford, A., Klimov, O.: Proximal policy optimization algorithms. CoRR abs/1707.06347 (2017)

Deep Learning for Detection of Frosty Pod Rot in Cacao Pods: A Comparative Analysis

Vaishnavi Sen(✉), Serineh Megerdichian, and Alex Moderresi

California State University, Northridge, CA, USA
{vaishnavi.sen.312,serineh.megerdichian.283}@my.csun.edu,
alex.modarresi@csun.edu

Abstract. Frosty Pod Rot (FPR), caused by *Moniliophthora roreri*, poses a significant threat to global cocoa production, especially in Colombia, where cacao cultivation is vital for rural economies. Traditional manual inspection methods for detecting FPR are labor-intensive and often ineffective at identifying early-stage symptoms. This study investigates the application of five deep learning models—Custom Convolutional Neural Network (CNN), MobileNetV2, MobileNetV3, ResNet18, and ResNet50 for automated, image-based FPR detection. Using a diverse dataset of cocoa pod images collected from Colombian farms and public sources, we applied image preprocessing techniques including HSV color enhancement, manual cropping, and normalization. Evaluation across accuracy, precision, recall, and F1-score demonstrates that MobileNetV2 outperforms both shallow and deeper architectures, achieving high accuracy and stable learning behavior with low computational demand. The findings support the use of lightweight, transfer-learning-based models for practical, low-cost disease detection in resource-constrained agricultural environments.

Keywords: Convolution neural network · MobileNet · ResNet · Image Processing · Deep Learning · Precision Agriculture

1 Introduction

Cacao (Theobroma cacao L.), the plant behind chocolate production, plays a critical role in the economies of several tropical countries. It provides livelihoods for millions of smallholder farmers and contributes significantly to national exports, particularly in Latin America, West Africa, and Southeast Asia. However, the global cacao industry is increasingly under threat from climate variability, soil degradation, and particularly, fungal diseases. Among the most damaging of these is Frosty Pod Rot (FPR), a disease caused by Moniliophthora roreri, which infects cacao pods and leads to severe yield losses. The disease thrives in humid, tropical conditions and spreads through airborne spores, making it difficult to contain once established.

H. R. Arabnia et al. (Eds.): CSCE 2025, CCIS 2934, pp. 384–398, 2026.
https://doi.org/10.1007/978-3-032-22190-2_28

Colombia, ranked among the top ten global producers of cacao, is especially vulnerable. Despite having 16.7 million hectares of land suitable for cacao cultivation, Colombian cocoa production fell to just under 60,000 metric tons in 2023—a 13% drop from 2021 levels [1]. This decline has been attributed to adverse climatic conditions and the resurgence of diseases such as FPR, particularly in regions such as San Vicente del Caguán and Chocó, where yield losses exceeding 80% have been reported [2]. These figures not only represent economic damage, but also highlight a growing crisis in rural agricultural communities, where crop failure can directly translate to food insecurity, displacement, and poverty.

Early detection and rapid response are the key to managing FPR, yet most smallholder farmers rely on manual inspection techniques. These traditional methods are time-consuming, labor-intensive, and prone to error, especially when symptoms are subtle or just beginning to emerge. Moreover, consistent monitoring of large-scale plantations is logistically challenging and often cost-prohibitive. In this context, technology-enabled solutions offer a promising path forward.

The integration of artificial intelligence (AI) and computer vision into agriculture—often referred to as "smart farming"—has shown tremendous potential to transform disease diagnosis and crop monitoring. Deep learning (DL), in particular, offers robust performance in image classification tasks and has been successfully applied in plant pathology research. Convolutional Neural Networks (CNNs), which mimic human visual processing, have achieved high accuracy in recognizing leaf discolorations, lesions, and other visual markers of plant stress [6][7]. These tools allow for automated, scalable, and real-time disease detection without the need for advanced technical expertise at the farm level.

Despite the potential, several challenges limit widespread adoption. Rural agricultural systems, especially in developing countries, often face technological, infrastructural, and educational barriers. High implementation costs, lack of reliable Internet access, and limited training for farmers all hinder the deployment of advanced AI models in the field. Therefore, there is a pressing need to develop lightweight, cost-effective, and accessible tools that can operate reliably under real-world conditions. Addressing these barriers is not only a technological challenge but a matter of equity—ensuring that smallholder farmers can benefit from the same innovations that are revolutionizing industrial-scale agriculture.

In response to this need, our research explores the application of deep learning to detect Frosty Pod Rot in cacao pods. This study leverages real-world data from Colombian farms alongside publicly available datasets and evaluates the performance of three CNN-based architectures, focusing on early-stage detection and operational efficiency. By prioritizing low-cost deployment and user-friendly design, this work contributes to the broader vision of sustainable, data-driven agriculture in resource-limited environments.

2 Related Work

Recent advances in ML and deep DL have contributed significantly to crop disease detection. These technologies have enabled the development of models capable of identifying plant health issues, supporting timely intervention, and helping to reduce overall crop losses. While DL models have shown strong performance in feature extraction and disease classification, challenges such as dataset imbalance and limited generalization across diverse environmental conditions remain persistent.

Despite these advancements, ongoing research continues to refine computer vision and ML techniques in agricultural settings. A comprehensive review by Minh Dang et al. [6] explored various computer vision techniques applied to plant disease detection, including CNNs, support vector machines (SVMs), and transformer-based architectures. The study emphasized the autonomous learning capabilities of DL models, which allow them to capture complex image features more effectively than traditional ML approaches. However, the review also identified dataset imbalance as a persistent challenge, reinforcing the need for large, diverse datasets to improve model robustness and generalization.

Expanding on these findings, Sajitha et al. [7] provided an in-depth review of ML and DL techniques for image-based plant disease classification, particularly in precision agriculture and industrial farming. This study focused on various datasets, including PlantVillage, and evaluated the usage of the models in real-world applications. The authors discuss overfitting and addressing it using transfer learning and ensemble methods. This is an important consideration, especially given that the datasets in this project were highly imbalanced and prone to overfitting. In addition, the review also highlighted the use of Internet of Things (IoT) for real-time plant detection and monitoring, which is a great opportunity for future research and development.

The methodology of this paper is built upon these foundational advancements. The modern era of deep learning for image classification was ignited by Krizhevsky et al. [11], whose "AlexNet" architecture demonstrated the profound capabilities of deep CNNs. This model achieved its success on the ImageNet Large Scale Visual Recognition Challenge (ILSVRC), a large-scale hierarchical database introduced by Deng et al. [12]. This success spurred research into deeper networks, leading to a significant breakthrough by He et al. [13] with the introduction of Residual Networks (ResNet). ResNet, which we use in its ResNet18 and ResNet50 variants, introduced "skip connections" to solve the vanishing gradient problem, enabling the effective training of networks hundreds of layers deep.

While deeper networks improved accuracy, their computational footprints made them unsuitable for resource-constrained environments. This limitation was addressed by Howard et al. [14] with MobileNet (V1), which introduced depthwise separable convolutions to drastically reduce parameters. This work was refined by Sandler et al. [15] in MobileNetV2, a central model in our study, which introduced inverted residuals and linear bottlenecks for greater efficiency. Finally, Howard et al. [16] presented MobileNetV3, which used neural architecture search (NAS) to further optimize the lightweight design.

In the context of cocoa cultivation, these advanced DL models have been tested. Jude B. Rola et al. [3] developed a CNN-based model to detect *Phytophthora palmivora* disease in cacao plants. Using images captured under controlled conditions, the CNN model outperformed six other ML algorithms, achieving an impressive accuracy of 99.0%. The study underscores CNN's ability to recognize subtle disease symptoms while emphasizing the need for larger, more diverse datasets to improve the generalizability of the model in different cacao cultivars.

Building on this progress, Darlyn Buenaño Vera et al. [4] introduced a deep learning-based computational model to identify diseases in Theobroma cacao pods. Their CNN-based approach effectively handled complex symptoms such as discoloration, lesions, and deformations, ensuring an accurate classification of the disease under various environmental conditions. The research also explored data augmentation techniques to mitigate the limitations posed by small datasets.

Extending recent advancements in cocoa disease detection, Diarra Mamadou et al. [5] utilized MobileNetV2 in combination with other DL algorithms to detect disease in cocoa pods. The study employed precise image segmentation to isolate pod regions and applied data augmentation techniques, such as horizontal and vertical flipping, to improve dataset diversity and model robustness. Among the various methods tested, the integration of MobileNetV2 with SVM yielded the highest accuracy, achieving an accuracy of 86.04%.

Atianshie Miracle. [8] further explored the use of CNNs for the early detection of cocoa diseases and pests in Ghana. The study emphasized the importance of early intervention, demonstrating how high-resolution images and CNN feature extraction could significantly improve disease detection in the early stages. This real-world application of ML in agriculture highlights the potential of DL-driven solutions to improve the health and productivity of cocoa crops.

In a more recent contribution, Alvarado et al. [23] conducted a systematic literature review on computer-vision approaches for cocoa disease detection and concluded that CNNs are the most effective method for identifying cocoa crop diseases. Their findings showed that deep learning architectures, particularly CNN-based classification models such as MobileNet, EfficientNet, and ResNet, outperform traditional machine learning approaches in accuracy and feature extraction.

Moving forward, Kumar et al. [24] presented a study focusing on automating the detection of cocoa leaf diseases, specifically Vascular Streak Dieback (VSD), using CNNs. The researchers have trained their model on 1,200 leaf images, consisting of healthy and VSD infested leaves. Their experiment found that the DenseNet-19 model achieved the highest accuracy of 99.1%, demonstrating the models ability to accurately distinguish diseased from healthy leaves. The results emphasize the reliability of CNN models in improving early and accurate disease diagnosis in cocoa crops.

To conclude the reviewed studies, Soh et al. [24] evaluated five CNN architectures: Custom CNN, VGG-16, EfficientNetB0, ResNet50, and LeNet-5 on a cocoa leaf dataset of 4,390 images, focusing on diseases such as black pod rot and pod borer. The Custom CNN model achieved the highest accuracy of 91.79%, with precision and recall also at 91.79%, and an F1 score of 82.08%. EfficientNetB0 and ResNet50 performed better than VGG-16 and LeNet-5, highlighting how effective CNN-based models are for the identification of cocoa disease.

Collectively, these studies illustrate the transformative potential of ML and DL in agriculture. They emphasize critical factors for successful disease detection systems, including high-quality datasets, advanced DL architectures, and strategies to address data limitations. Drawing insights from these works, our research aims to develop a scalable plant disease detection system, leveraging DL techniques while addressing the challenges identified in prior studies to create practical solutions applicable across diverse agricultural settings.

3 Methodology

This section explains our methodology, including the dataset containing photos our team captured from cocoa farms, image processing techniques, and our machine learning model (Fig. 1).

(a) Healthy (b) Early Stage (c) Later Stage (d) Destroyed

Fig. 1. Stages of FPR Development

3.1 Dataset Collection and Preparation

To build a robust and diverse dataset for Monilia disease detection in cocoa pods, we source images from multiple origins. These include publicly available datasets, collaborations with local agricultural researchers, and manual data collection initiatives. The three main data sources are detailed below.

Kaggle YOLOv4 Cocoa Pod Dataset. We use a dataset from Kaggle originally intended for training with the YOLOv4 object detection model. This collection includes images of cocoa pods affected by Fito and Monilia, as well as healthy pods. Since our current research focuses exclusively on Monilia, we exclude images labeled under the "Fito" category. In future phases, we plan to integrate these additional categories into a comprehensive multi-class classification framework. The Kaggle images require significant pre-processing due to inconsistent quality, particularly in terms of image clarity and focus.

Field Data Collection from Colombia. A significant portion of the dataset originates from direct field visits in Belalcázar and Palestina, Colombia. The research team collaborated with local cocoa farmers to document the visual symptoms of Monilia across its various developmental stages. This effort was supported by Casa Luker, a dedicated cocoa research facility in Palestina.

This field data is especially valuable, offering up-to-date and contextually relevant images. Unlike static datasets, manual collection enables us to capture a wide range of infection stages. With the assistance of farmers and researchers, we photograph cocoa pods at multiple growth stages and later label them based on symptom progression. This dataset greatly enriches our understanding of Monilia symptomology, especially in its early manifestations.

Roboflow YOLO Segmentation Dataset. We obtain an additional dataset from Roboflow, primarily designed for training YOLO models on segmentation tasks. Although we do not use segmentation masks in this phase, the raw images include cocoa pods with varied symptoms, which adds diversity to the visual training data. Several images contain multiple pods in a single frame; we manually crop these to isolate individual pods for training.

All images undergo manual inspection to address quality issues such as blurriness and background noise. The Kaggle dataset, in particular, requires substantial enhancement to improve sharpness and focus. Images from field collections and Roboflow receive minor clarity adjustments. After verifying quality, we apply consistent cropping procedures to center each image on a single cocoa pod. For images with multiple pods, we perform segmentation manually with guidance from local farmers and researchers.

To strengthen the model's ability to detect early-stage infections, we prioritize images that display preliminary symptoms of Monilia. These include tiny dark spots, skin discoloration, and unusual surface textures that appear before more recognizable signs like sunken lesions and internal pod liquefaction. In its terminal stage, the disease causes pods to shrivel and dry [10]. By that point, however, the pod already harbors spores capable of infecting adjacent plants. This insight, informed by farmer experience, emphasizes the importance of early detection, and our dataset reflects that priority.

Table 1. Distribution of Images by Dataset and Class.

Source	Healthy	Monilia
Kaggle YOLOv4	295	118
Colombians Field Data	83	103
Roboflow Dataset	–	213
Total	378	434

Our final dataset includes diverse images categorized by infection stage and source. Table 1 presents the breakdown of image counts from each dataset and class category.

3.2 Image Preprocessing

Before training, all images undergo a sequence of preprocessing steps designed to standardize inputs and enhance model robustness. The goal is to minimize noise and variance caused by inconsistent lighting conditions, color imbalance, and camera settings across the multiple data sources.

Resizing and Color Conversion. All images are resized to a fixed resolution of 224×224 pixels to ensure uniformity across the dataset and compatibility with common convolutional neural network architectures. Additionally, we convert images from BGR (OpenCV's default) to RGB color space for consistency with models pre-trained on ImageNet.

HSV Color Manipulation. To enhance color-related features and simulate different lighting conditions, each image is converted to HSV color space, where hue, saturation, and brightness are programmatically adjusted. We apply a fixed hue shift of 50° to diversify the color spectrum, amplify saturation by a factor of 5 to intensify visual contrast, and selectively increase brightness levels. This augmentation step emphasizes color-related symptoms of Monilia, which often include subtle discolorations (Fig. 2).

(a) Original image (b) After preprocessing

Fig. 2. Comparison of a cocoa pod image before and after image preprocessing.

Mean Subtraction and Standardization. Each image is normalized via mean subtraction, where the per-channel mean across all pixels is subtracted from each pixel. This is followed by division by the image's standard deviation, resulting in zero-centered, normalized pixel distributions. This step helps mitigate lighting inconsistencies and accelerates training convergence.

3.3 Model Architecture

In this research, we implement and compare five distinct deep learning architectures to detect Frosty Pod Rot (FPR) in cocoa pods: a custom Convolutional Neural Network (CNN), MobileNetV2, MobileNetV3, ResNet18 and ResNet50. These models are selected based on their suitability for image classification tasks, with each offering unique advantages depending on the level of model complexity and computational efficiency required.

The custom CNN serves as a baseline model for comparison. It consists of three convolutional layers, with filter sizes increasing from 32 to 64 and then to 128, each followed by a max-pooling layer to reduce the spatial dimensions of the feature maps. This structure enables the model to learn different levels of abstraction, from edges to more complex textures. After flattening the output of the convolutional layers, we use a fully connected dense layer with 128 units and ReLU activation, followed by a dropout layer with a rate of 0.3 to reduce overfitting. The final output layer uses softmax activation to classify images into two categories: healthy and diseased cocoa pods. This model's architecture remains relatively simple and lightweight, making it more computationally efficient than deeper networks. The use of dropout specifically helps mitigate the risk of overfitting, which is common when working with small datasets.

MobileNetV2, a lightweight convolutional neural network, is selected for its efficiency in resource-constrained environments. It employs depthwise separable convolutions to reduce computational complexity without sacrificing performance. We implement MobileNetV2 using transfer learning with pretrained weights from ImageNet. The original classification head is removed and replaced with a new head consisting of global average pooling, a dense layer with 128 units and ReLU activation, and a dropout layer with a rate of 0.3. The output layer uses a sigmoid activation function to predict the binary class labels. By leveraging pretrained weights, MobileNetV2 benefits from prior feature extraction learned on large datasets, enabling strong performance even with our limited dataset. Its efficiency makes it particularly suitable for real-time applications on mobile or embedded devices.

ResNet50, a deeper architecture utilizing residual connections, serves as the third model in our comparison. The residual connections help mitigate the vanishing gradient problem and allow for more effective training of deeper networks. Like MobileNetV2, ResNet50 is initialized with pretrained ImageNet weights, and we replace the top layers with a new classification head comprising global average pooling, a dense layer with 128 units and ReLU activation, and a dropout layer to reduce overfitting. The final output layer uses a sigmoid activation to differentiate between healthy and diseased pods. ResNet50's greater depth allows it to learn highly abstract and detailed features, which improves its ability to recognize subtle disease symptoms. However, this added complexity results in higher computational costs compared to more efficient models like MobileNetV2. Nevertheless, its residual connections enhance learning capability, especially when dealing with complex patterns in the image data (Table 2).

Table 2. Summary of Model Architectures Used for FPR Detection

Model	Base	Feature Type	Pretrained	Complexity
Custom CNN	3 Conv Layers	Standard Conv	No	Low
MobileNetV2	MobileNetV2	Depthwise Separable	Yes	Low
MobileNetV3	MobileNetV3 Small	Depthwise + SE Blocks	Yes	Very Low
ResNet50	ResNet50	Residual Blocks	Yes	High
ResNet18	ResNet18	Residual Blocks	Yes	Moderate

4 Results and Analysis

The performance of the implemented deep learning models—Custom CNN, MobileNetV2, MobileNetV3, ResNet50 and ResNet18—was evaluated using four standard classification metrics: accuracy, precision, recall, and F1-score. These metrics were computed on a held-out test set comprising 20% of the full dataset to ensure unbiased assessment.

- **Accuracy** measures the proportion of correctly classified samples among all predictions.
- **Precision** reflects the model's ability to correctly identify positive instances, minimizing false positives.
- **Recall** quantifies the model's effectiveness in identifying all actual positive instances, which is critical in disease detection to avoid missed cases.
- **F1-score** provides a balanced metric that considers both precision and recall, offering a comprehensive view of classification performance, especially under class imbalance.

Table 3. Performance Metrics for Implemented Models on the Test Set

Model	Accuracy	Precision (M, H)	Recall (M, H)	F1-Score (M, H)
Custom CNN	85%	0.84, 0.87	0.88, 0.82	0.86, 0.84
MobileNetV2	90%	0.93, 0.88	0.89, 0.91	0.91, 0.90
MobileNetV3	75%	0.78, 0.72	0.75, 0.76	0.76, 0.74
ResNet50	79%	0.84, 0.74	0.74, 0.84	0.79, 0.79
ResNet18	74%	0.72, 0.76	0.83, 0.63	0.77, 0.69

Table 3 highlights the observations made for different performance metrics for Monilia (M) and Healthy (H) cocoa pods. MobileNetV2 achieves the highest overall accuracy at 90%, with strong performance across all metrics. Notably, it attains an F1-score of 0.91 for Monilia and 0.90 for healthy pods, demonstrating both high sensitivity and precision. Its strong recall values (0.89 for

Monilia and 0.91 for Healthy) highlight its robustness in detecting diseased pods without neglecting healthy ones, which is an essential requirement in real-world agricultural settings.

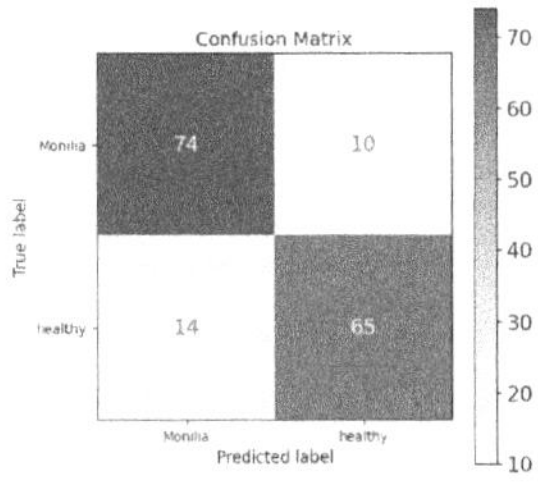

(a) Custom CNN

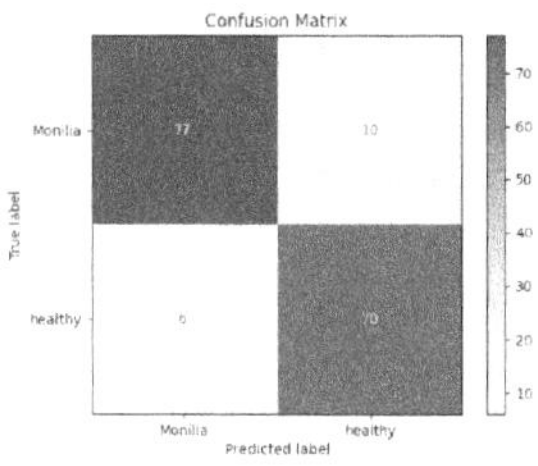

(b) MobileNetV2

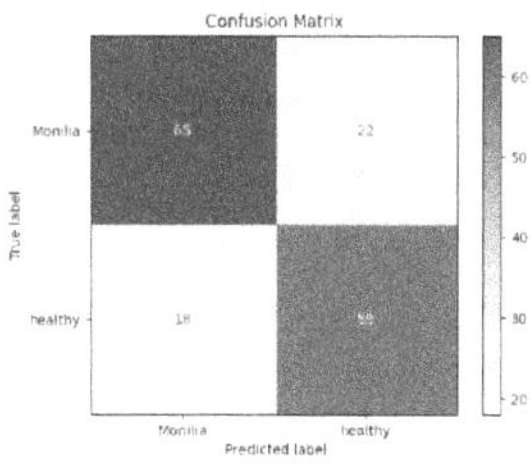

(c) MobileNetV3

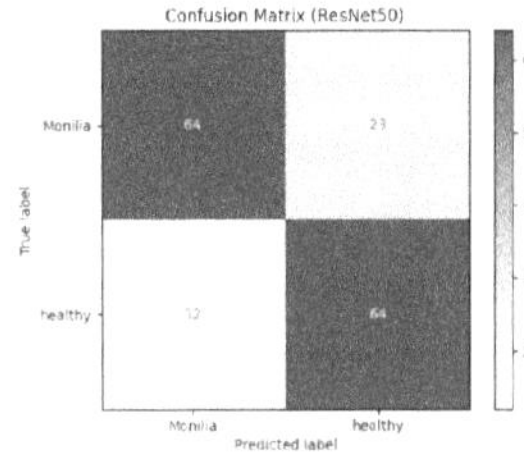

(d) ResNet50

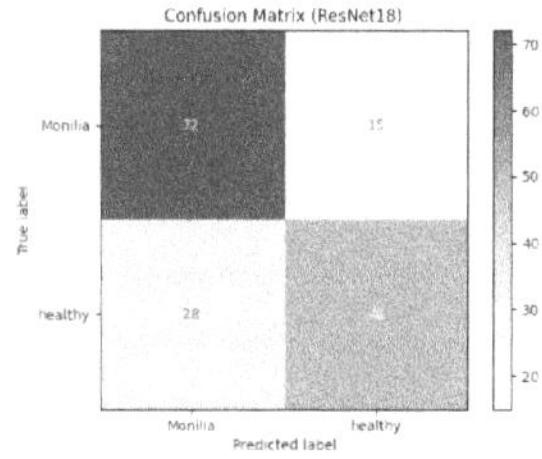

(e) ResNet18

Fig. 3. Comparison of Confusion Matrices

The Custom CNN model follows with a respectable accuracy of 85%. Its F1-scores (0.86 for Monilia and 0.84 for Healthy) indicate balanced and stable performance, albeit with slightly less precision compared to MobileNetV2. Its simplicity makes it computationally efficient and suitable for constrained environments, though it may not perform as reliably in detecting subtle early-stage symptoms.

MobileNetV3, while architecturally efficient, exhibited lower performance, with an overall accuracy of 75%. Although it maintains moderate balance between precision and recall, its F1-scores of 0.76 (Monilia) and 0.74 (Healthy) suggest weaker generalization to the dataset compared to its predecessor, MobileNetV2.

ResNet50 presented mixed results. With an accuracy of 79%, it demonstrated asymmetric precision-recall behavior—achieving higher recall for Healthy pods (0.84) and higher precision for Monilia (0.84). This suggests sensitivity to feature distribution shifts between classes. While ResNet50 is generally considered robust due to its residual connections, its performance in this case may reflect sensitivity to the dataset size or domain-specific features.

ResNet18, the smallest variant in the ResNet family, showed the lowest accuracy at 74%. Its high recall for Monilia (0.83) is notable, suggesting it rarely misses infected pods; however, its recall for Healthy pods dropped to 0.63, indicating a tendency toward false positives. This imbalance is reflected in its lower F1-scores.

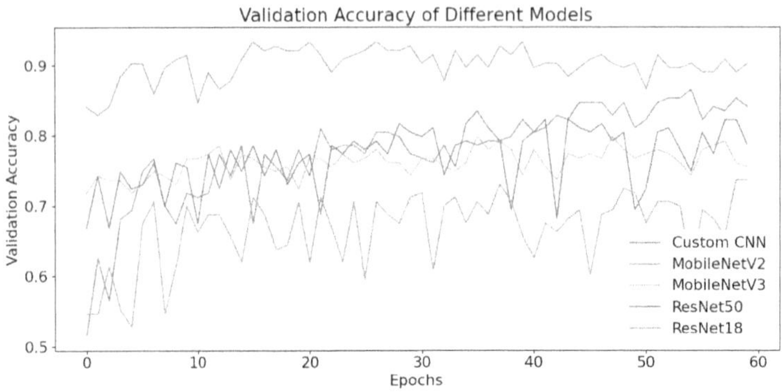

(a) Validation Accuracy

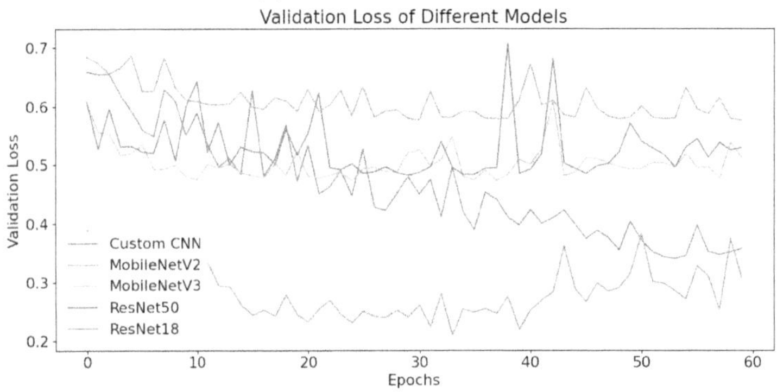

(b) Validation Loss

Fig. 4. Comparison of implemented deep learning models

Figure 3 visually complements the performance metrics by presenting the confusion matrices of all five models. These matrices provide a granular view of each model's classification behavior by showing the counts of true positives, false positives, true negatives, and false negatives. MobileNetV2 (Fig. 3b) demonstrates the most balanced performance with minimal misclassifications, evident in the high values along the diagonal, particularly for both Monilia and Healthy classes. In contrast, MobileNetV3 (Fig. 3c) and ResNet18 (Fig. 3e) display more off-diagonal entries, indicating a higher rate of false positives and false negatives, consistent with their lower precision and recall scores. The Custom CNN (Fig. 3a) achieves relatively strong diagonal dominance, though slightly more confusion is seen in distinguishing Healthy pods. ResNet50 (Fig. 3d) shows asymmetry in misclassification—tending to over-predict the Healthy class—aligning with its uneven precision-recall profile. Overall, these visual patterns reinforce the quantitative evaluation, highlighting MobileNetV2's superior discriminatory ability in classifying cacao pod health status.

In Fig. 4a, MobileNetV2 consistently outperforms all other models, achieving and maintaining validation accuracy above 90% for the majority of the training epochs. This reflects the model's high capacity to generalize from the training data, likely due to its efficient use of depthwise separable convolutions and the advantage of pretrained ImageNet weights. MobileNetV2's lightweight architecture is optimized for fine-grained feature extraction with minimal overfitting, making it particularly effective on small to moderately sized datasets like the one used in this study.

In contrast, the Custom CNN and ResNet50 models exhibit steady improvements in validation accuracy, though neither achieves the same stability or performance level as MobileNetV2. The Custom CNN, despite being relatively shallow, benefits from simplicity and low parameter count, which can reduce overfitting. However, its limited representational capacity may prevent it from capturing subtle visual cues indicative of early-stage disease. ResNet50, a much deeper network, achieves moderate performance but suffers from inconsistent learning across epochs. This behavior may be attributed to overparameterization and increased sensitivity to hyperparameters, especially in the presence of a relatively small and imbalanced dataset. Although residual connections mitigate vanishing gradient issues, deeper architectures like ResNet50 often require extensive regularization and training data diversity to perform optimally.

MobileNetV3 shows early convergence but plateaus quickly, suggesting insufficient learning progression beyond initial epochs. This may be due to its design trade-offs: while it is more efficient than MobileNetV2 in terms of parameter count and latency, its aggressive architectural compression and reliance on squeeze-and-excitation blocks might result in reduced feature sensitivity when applied to fine-grained classification tasks like disease detection.

ResNet18 displays the lowest validation accuracy and the most volatile learning behavior across epochs. Its erratic performance may stem from a combination of underfitting—due to its reduced depth—and an inability to effectively leverage the pretrained weights in the context of the target domain. Additionally, its lower feature capacity may hinder generalization, particularly in cases where class distinctions are subtle or depend on context-sensitive visual patterns.

These observations highlight several important considerations in model selection. First, transfer learning proves beneficial across architectures, but its effectiveness varies with model design. Among all evaluated models, MobileNetV2 consistently delivered the best performance, achieving the highest accuracy, F1-scores, and training stability. Its lightweight nature and efficient feature extraction make it well-suited for field deployment in agricultural environments where computational resources are limited.

Second, deeper models like ResNet50 and ResNet18, while powerful in theory, underperformed in this application, likely due to the limited dataset size and the models' sensitivity to hyperparameter tuning and overfitting. Finally, the results emphasize the importance of aligning model complexity with real-world deployment goals—MobileNetV2 strikes a balance between accuracy and efficiency, making it the most practical and effective solution for FPR in cacao farming systems.

5 Limitations and Future Work

This research, while providing a clear and efficient model for FPR detection, has several limitations that pave the way for future investigation. First, the dataset, though diverse, is constrained in size. Future work would benefit from a larger, more varied collection of images to improve the model's generalization across different lighting conditions, pod genotypes, and farm environments.

A more significant limitation is that the current study concentrates on the detection of Frosty Pod Rot in its later, visually symptomatic stages. The primary challenge in cocoa agriculture, however, is the detection of the disease in its early, latent phase, where intervention can be most effective. These early stages often present no visual symptoms detectable by standard RGB imagery, rendering our current approach insufficient for early warning. Addressing this would require a dedicated study, potentially using alternative imaging modalities such as hyperspectral or thermal cameras to identify pre-symptomatic stress.

Building on these points, future research will move in several key directions. We plan to transition from simple classification to real-time object detection using models like YOLO [19], which would allow the system to count and locate infected pods in a video feed. To build trust and validate our model's logic, we will implement explainability techniques like Grad-CAM [20] to visualize where the network is "looking" for signs of disease. We will also explore more advanced, efficient architectures like EfficientNet [17] and test the capabilities of Vision Transformers (ViT) [18]. Finally, the ultimate goal is to package our optimized MobileNetV2 model into a practical on-device mobile application [22] that can be deployed by farmers in the field, providing a truly accessible tool for cocoa health management.

6 Conclusion

This study presents a comparative evaluation of deep learning models for detecting Frosty Pod Rot in cacao pods, an increasingly destructive disease affecting cocoa farmers. By combining manually collected field data with publicly available datasets and applying custom image preprocessing techniques, we trained and evaluated five models: a custom CNN, MobileNetV2, MobileNetV3, ResNet18 and ResNet50. Among these, MobileNetV2 achieves the highest performance in all evaluation metrics, closely followed by ResNet50.

The results validate the potential of transfer learning and modern CNN architectures in agricultural disease diagnostics, even with limited datasets. However, challenges remain in early detection. Our roadmap for future work addresses these issues by expanding datasets, improving classification granularity. Ultimately, this research contributes toward developing scalable, affordable, and accessible solutions for disease detection in cocoa farming systems.

Acknowledgment. This project was partially funded by a 100kstrong in the Americas award under the lead of Professor Mario Giraldo as principal investigator. The authors express sincere gratitude to the members of the team who contributed to the research and development. The authors thank faculty, students, and staff from Universidad de Manizales in Colombia who offered their expertise and support to enhance the project's requirements. We also want to extend our thanks to our research team, who went to Colombia to collect images and requirements from farmers, which enriched the quality of our work.

References

1. Ortega, A.: The Colombian Cacao Sector - 2024 Update, United States Department of Agriculture (USDA), Bogota, Colombia, Report No. CO2024-0011 (2024). https://apps.fas.usda.gov/newgainapi/api/Report/DownloadReportByFileName?fileName=The%20Colombian%20Cacao%20Sector%20-%202024%20Update_Bogota_Colombia_CO2024-0011.pdf
2. Phillips-Mora, W., Wilkinson, M.J.: Frosty Pod of cacao: a disease with a limited geographic range but unlimited potential for damage. Phytopathology **97**(12), 1644–1651 (2007)
3. Rola, J.B., et al.: Convolutional neural network model for cacao phytophthora palmivora disease recognition. Int. J. Adv. Comput. Sci. Appl. **15**(8), 986–992 (2024)
4. Vera, D.B., Oviedo, B., Casanova, W.C., Zambrano-Vega, C.: Deep learning-based computational model for disease identification in cocoa pods (Theobroma cacao L.), pp. 1–12. arXiv preprint: arXiv:2401.01247 (2024)
5. Diarra, M., Ayikpa, K.J., Ballo, A.B., Kouassi, B.M.: Cocoa pods diseases detection by MobileNet confluence and classification algorithms. Int. J. Adv. Comput. Sci. Appl. **14**(9), 344–352 (2023)
6. Dang, M., Wang, H., Li, Y., et al.: Computer vision for plant disease recognition: a comprehensive review. Bot. Rev. **90**, 251–311 (2024)
7. Sajitha, P., Andrushia, A.D., Anand, N., Naser, M.Z.: A review on machine learning and deep learning image-based plant disease classification for industrial farming systems. J. Ind. Inf. Integr. **38** (2024)
8. Miracle, A.: Enhancing cocoa crop resilience in Ghana: the application of convolutional neural networks for early detection of disease and pest infestations, pp. 1–14. Qeios (2024)
9. Serrano, S.: Enfermedades Cacao YOLOv4 Dataset. Kaggle (2024). https://www.kaggle.com/datasets/serranosebas/enfermedades-cacao-yolov4. Accessed 8 Feb 2025
10. Caribbean Agricultural Health and Food Safety Agency (CAHFSA), "Frosty Pod Rot" (2022). https://cahfsa.org/wp-content/uploads/2022/09/Frosty-pod-rot.pdf
11. Krizhevsky, A., Sutskever, I., Hinton, G.E.: ImageNet classification with deep convolutional neural networks. In: Advances in Neural Information Processing Systems, vol. 25 (2012)

12. Deng, J., Dong, W., Socher, R., Li, L.-J., Li, K., Fei-Fei, L.: ImageNet: a large-scale hierarchical image database. In: IEEE Conference on Computer Vision and Pattern Recognition, pp. 248–255 (2009)
13. He, K., Zhang, X., Ren, S., Sun, J.: Deep residual learning for image recognition. In: Proceedings of the IEEE Conference on Computer Vision and Pattern Recognition, pp. 770–778 (2016)
14. Howard, A.G., Zhu, M., Chen, B., Kalenichenko, D., Wang, W., Weyand, T., et al.: MobileNets: efficient convolutional neural networks for mobile vision applications. arXiv preprint: arXiv:1704.04861 (2017)
15. Sandler, M., Howard, A., Zhu, M., Zhmoginov, A., Chen, L.-C.: MobileNetV2: inverted residuals and linear bottlenecks. In: Proceedings of the IEEE Conference on Computer Vision and Pattern Recognition, pp. 4510–4520 (2018)
16. Howard, A., Sandler, M., Chu, G., Chen, L.-C., Chen, B., Tan, M., et al.: Searching for MobileNetV3. In: Proceedings of the IEEE/CVF International Conference on Computer Vision, pp. 1314–1324 (2019)
17. Tan, M., Le, Q.V.: EfficientNet: rethinking model scaling for convolutional neural networks. In: Proceedings of the 36th International Conference on Machine Learning, pp. 6105–6114 (2019)
18. Dosovitskiy, A., Beyer, L., Kolesnikov, A., Weissenborn, D., Zhai, X., Unterthiner, T., et al.: An image is worth 16x16 words: transformers for image recognition at scale. In: Proceedings of the International Conference on Learning Representations (2021)
19. Redmon, J., Divvala, S., Girshick, R., Farhadi, A.: You only look once: unified, real-time object detection. In: Proceedings of the IEEE Conference on Computer Vision and Pattern Recognition, pp. 779–788 (2016)
20. Selvaraju, R.R., Cogswell, M., Das, A., Vedantam, R., Parikh, D., Batra, D.: Grad-CAM: visual explanations from deep networks via gradient-based localization. In: Proceedings of the IEEE International Conference on Computer Vision, pp. 618–627 (2017)
21. Nazki, A.A., Yoon, S.R., Jang, I.S., Park, D.H.: A comprehensive review of data augmentation methods for deep learning-based plant disease detection. Comput. Electron. Agric. **200**, 107238 (2023)
22. Sharma, P., Berwal, Y.P.S., Ghai, W.: A lightweight deep learning model for on-device plant disease detection in mobile applications. Expert Syst. Appl. **228**, 120280 (2023)
23. Alvarado, J., Restrepo-Arias, J.F., Velásquez, D., Maiza, M.: Disease detection on cocoa crops based on computer-vision techniques: a systematic literature review. Agriculture **15**(10), 1032 (2025)
24. Kumar, S., Sharma, A.K., Srivastava, S., Tiwari, V., Patidar, P.K., Rai, S.: Automated COCOA disease detection using convolutional neural networks: a case study of VSD and other pathogens. In: Proceedings of the International Conference on Recent Advancement and Modernization in Sustainable Intelligent Technologies & Applications, vol. 192, pp. 362–371 (2025)
25. Soh, K.S., Moung, E., Danker, K.J.J., Dargham, J.: Cocoa diseases classification using deep learning algorithm. In: ITM Web of Conferences, vol. 63, p. 01014 (2024)

A Comprehensive Review of Machine Learning Algorithms for Crop Yield Prediction in Smart Agriculture: State-of-the-Art Methods, Challenges, and Future Directions

Topside E. Mathonsi(✉)

Department of Information Technology, Tshwane University of Technology, Pretoria, South Africa
MathonsiTE@tut.ac.za

Abstract. Accurate crop-yield prediction is increasingly important for strengthening food security, improving farm planning, and supporting efficient resource allocation under changing climatic conditions. This study presents a comprehensive review of recent machine learning algorithms for crop-yield prediction in smart agriculture. A structured literature search identified 24 studies published between July 2024 and March 2025, of which 11 met the final review criteria. The selected studies were analysed according to the algorithms applied, input features, evaluation metrics, predictive performance, practical limitations and future research opportunities. The findings show that Random Forest (RF) was the most frequently used algorithm, accounting for 16% of the reviewed applications, followed by Support Vector Machines (SVMs) and Artificial Neural Networks (ANNs) at 12.8% each, and gradient-boosting methods at 10.6%. Hybrid ensemble approaches accounted for 5.3% and generally demonstrated strong predictive performance by combining the complementary strengths of multiple models. The Coefficient of Determination (R2), Root Mean Square Error (RMSE), Mean Absolute Error (MAE), and Mean Absolute Percentage Error (MAPE) were the most widely used evaluation metrics, accounting for 25%, 22%, 18%, and 15%, respectively. Weather, soil and remote-sensing data were the dominant input features, while fertiliser and irrigation information remained underutilised despite their potential contribution to model accuracy. Key challenges include limited and region-specific datasets, overfitting, inconsistent data quality, inadequate generalisability and high computational requirements, particularly for smallholder farming environments. The review provides practical guidance for developing accurate, interpretable, scalable, and resource-efficient crop-yield prediction systems for smart agriculture.

Keywords: Machine learning · crop-yield prediction · smart agriculture · precision agriculture · ensemble learning · remote sensing · explainable artificial intelligence · food security

H. R. Arabnia et al. (Eds.): CSCE 2025, CCIS 2934, pp. 399–412, 2026.
https://doi.org/10.1007/978-3-032-22190-2_29

1 Introduction

Agriculture remains a vital pillar of global economic development and food security, especially in developing countries and regions with agriculture-based economies. Yet, despite its crucial role, the sector is increasingly vulnerable to the growing impacts of climate change. Unpredictable and extreme weather events, such as droughts, floods, and heatwaves, are becoming more frequent and are contributing to global food insecurity in several ways, such as direct crop destruction and yield reduction. Droughts cause crops to wither and die, floods drown plants and wash away topsoil, and heatwaves stress crops, ultimately diminishing the quantity and quality of food produced [1–3]. These climate-driven challenges threaten not only the livelihoods of millions of smallholder farmers but also contribute to widespread food insecurity around the world.

While we cannot fully prevent natural disasters such as droughts, floods, and heatwaves, their impact on crop yields can be reduced through timely access to accurate and actionable information. Thus, early crop yield prediction plays a key role in enabling better planning, smarter resource management, and more informed decisions at both the farming and policy levels [4–6]. When farmers have insight into expected yields, they can better adjust planting schedules and minimize the risks associated with natural disasters [7].

Based on existing literature [8–10], many smallholder farmers still depend on traditional forecasting methods such as manual crop sampling, field observation experience, intuition, and historical data trends, approaches that are increasingly unreliable in today's rapidly changing climate. As a result, yield prediction remains a complex task due to many variables that influence crop productivity. This is because older approaches often rely on fixed rules or past trends, which lack the flexibility and precision needed in modern agriculture [11–13]. To address this gap, researchers have developed Machine Learning (ML) models that can analyze complex agricultural data and deliver more accurate crop yield predictions. These models use inputs such as soil composition, weather data, crop types, and remote sensing imagery to outperform these traditional forecasting methods [14–16].

While previous reviews have presented the use of ML in crop yield prediction, many of these reviews focused on the performance of individual ML algorithms on general farming environments. Thus, this paper expands on the work of Shawon et al. [17] by broadening the focus to include real-world challenges such as data scarcity and computational constraints faced by small-scale farmers. To the best of the researcher's knowledge, this is the first comprehensive review that brings together the latest ML developments for crop yield prediction within the timeframe of July 2024 to March 2025, key challenges such as data scarcity and limited computing resources faced by small-scale farmers in crop yield prediction, while linking it to food insecurity challenges faced by the whole world. The paper adopted a systematic literature review technique to collect the data from the following research databases, namely Scopus, MDPI, Scientific Reports, Taylor & Francis, WILEY, and ScienceDirect. The paper used precise keywords "Machine Learning" & "Crop Yield Prediction" to narrow the search. 24 articles were sourced from the mentioned research databases and compared to the paper's objective:

1. To identify and analyse existing state-of-the-art ML techniques used for crop yield prediction.
2. To analyse the impact of real-world challenges, such as data scarcity and computational constraints faced by small-scale farmers in adopting ML techniques used for crop yield prediction.
3. To identify and analyse commonly used ML algorithms and evaluation parameters for crop yield prediction.
4. To identify and analyse commonly used features in crop yield prediction.

As a result, 11 articles were used to develop the following main contributions of this review paper:

1. It compares various ML models based on their accuracy and adaptability across different crop types, regions, and data sources.
2. It suggests future research directions to include the use of Explainable AI (XAI), advanced neural network architectures such as Bidirectional Gated Recurrent Unit (Bi-GRU) and Maxout classifiers, feature expansion, and the integration of IoT-based and hybrid ensemble models.
3. It synthesizes key real-world challenges, such as data scarcity and limited computational resources for smallholder farmers, that affect the reliability of yield prediction systems.

The rest of the paper is structured as follows: Sect. 2 presents the state-of-the-art techniques. Commonly used ML algorithms and evaluation parameters for crop yield prediction are presented in Sect. 3. Commonly used features in crop yield prediction are presented in Sect. 4. Open Research Issues and Future research directions, and conclusion is presented in Sects. 5 and 6, respectively.

2 State-of-the-Art Machine Learning Techniques

In this section, the paper presents the state-of-the-art methodologies that were published from July 2024 to March 2025 for crop yield prediction. The existing scheme's strengths and limitations are further discussed in this section.

The study by Dai et al. [2] compared three ML models to classify and predict the Annual Climatic Status (ACS) of cotton crops within the Xinjiang region of China. They utilized the following indicators, namely regionalization, crop variety, climatological growing season length, mean temperature, and sum of active temperatures. These indicators are designed to capture the dynamic climatic suitability of crops during specific phenological stages. Support Vector Machine (SVM) and Random Forest (RF) algorithms, and Gradient Boosting Trees (XGBoost) were the three ML models used [2]. For the analysis, cotton yield data at the county level were sourced from the Xinjiang Uygur Autonomous Region Statistical Bureau, covering 41 counties from 1991 to 2022 [2]. This dataset was complemented by daily meteorological data, including temperature, sunshine hours, and precipitation from the same period, sourced from the China Meteorological Data Sharing Service Center. The RF model in the Highly Suitable Zone (HSZ) had a test accuracy of 69.5%, significantly lower than the SVM's 89.8%. While the XGBoost model in the HSZ recorded a test accuracy of 77.9% [2]. The SVM model in the Moderately Suitable Zone (MoSZ) had a test accuracy of 87.6%, demonstrating its suitability for cotton climate assessment [2]. RF and XGBoost models recorded a test accuracy of 58.3% and 68.4% in MoSZ, respectively.

In addition, SVM achieved a test set accuracy of 78.5% in the Marginally Suitable Zone (MSZ). The SVM's high accuracy suggests that it is well-suited for capturing the complex relationships between climatic factors and cotton yield in all zones [2]. In contrast, RF recorded the lowest accuracy in the MoSZ zone, suggesting potential limitations when applied in specific climatic environments and underscoring the need for cautious implementation. XGBoost has shown signs of overfitting in multiple zones, highlighting the necessity for careful parameter tuning and the application of regularization techniques to enhance its generalization performance.

Manju et al. [3] evaluated three ML algorithms, namely K-Nearest Neighbors (KNN), SVM, and neural networks, for crop prediction based on soil characteristics. In the 10-fold cross-validation, the KNN algorithm achieved a maximum accuracy of 84%, a precision of 85%, a recall of 88.8%, and a specificity of 92.4% [3]. These metrics indicate that KNN effectively identifies suitable crops while minimizing both false positives and false negatives. High accuracy reflects the model's overall correctness in predicting crop types, while high precision indicates that when the model predicts a crop is suitable, it is likely to be correct. A high recall score suggests that the model can identify most of the suitable crops, and high specificity demonstrates its ability to accurately exclude unsuitable crops.

The SVM algorithm achieved an accuracy of 81.2% in the 5-fold cross-validation [3]. This result demonstrates SVM's capability as a powerful classifier, particularly for high-dimensional data. This is because SVM works by finding a hyperplane that optimally separates different classes in the feature space. Neural networks achieved a maximum accuracy of 82% in the 10-fold cross-validation, indicating their potential to capture complex patterns in data, particularly when sufficient training data is available. However, neural networks can be prone to overfitting, especially with small datasets or subtle data variations. SVM and neural networks complexity reduced their suitability compared to KNN. This is because KNN operates by classifying new data points based on the majority class among their k-nearest neighbors in the training dataset, making it adept at handling the complex and non-linear relationships often found in soil data [3]. However, KNN demonstrated good performance only when applied to small, region-specific datasets. Additionally, its memory-intensive nature limits its practicality for smaller-scale farmers who have limited computational resources and capabilities.

In order to predict soybean yield and lodging, Sun et al. [4] developed a novel Prototype Contrastive Learning (PCL) network that automatically extracted features from raw hyperspectral images using deep learning techniques. The PCL produced an R^2 of 0.65 and an RMSE of 507.56 kg/ha at 86 days after emergence (DAE). This level of accuracy was significantly higher than that achieved by a hand-crafted features model-based, which yielded an R^2 of 0.55 and an RMSE of 581.37 kg/ha at the same growth stage [4]. The improved accuracy of the PCL model can be attributed to its ability to automatically learn relevant features from raw hyperspectral images, eliminating the need for subjective feature selection and potentially capturing more subtle and informative patterns in the data. In addition, the PCL achieved an F1-score of 0.80, and hand-crafted features achieved an F1-score of 0.54. This substantial improvement in F1-score highlights the effectiveness of PCL in accurately classifying different lodging grades, even in the presence of complex environmental factors and variations in plant morphology [4]. The large volume of data generated by hyperspectral images presents significant computational challenges, requiring powerful processors and substantial memory capacity. As a result, the adoption of PCL is limited among smaller-scale farmers with constrained computational resources and capabilities.

Razavi et al. [5] compared four distinct ML regressors, namely RF, Extreme Gradient Boosting (XGBoost), Categorical Boosting (CatBoost), and Light Gradient-Boosting Machine (LightGBM), in order to determine the best crop yield prediction scheme in Senegal. These schemes were chosen due to their ability to handle complex datasets and their robust performance in various prediction tasks. The performance of the four schemes were evaluated using the following performance metrics, namely RMSE, normalized Root Mean Square Error (nRMSE), MAE, and MASE. To ensure the reliability and generalizability of the four ML schemes, a rigorous training and validation process was done using 90% of the data for training and 10% of unseen data for all evaluation processes. CatBoost achieved RMSE of 0.689, nRMSE of 0.175, MAE of 0.36, and MASE of 0.722, while EXGBoost achieved RMSE of 0.513, nRMSE of 0.169, MAE of 0.32, and MASE of 0.826 in maize prediction. CatBoost outperformed EXGBoost for groundnut prediction by achieving an RMSE of 0.818, nRMSE of 0.138, MAE of 0.49, and MASE of 0.752. While EXGBoost achieved RMSE of 1.024, nRMSE of 0.192, MAE of 0.67, and MASE of 0.823 for the same crop type. EXGBoost underperformed in pearl millet prediction by achieving an RMSE of 1.13, nRMSE of 0.229, MAE of 0.73, and MASE of 0.941, while CatBoost achieved an RMSE of 0.945, nRMSE of 0.168, MAE of 0.53, and MASE of 0.691.

Continually, CatBoost performed well in rice prediction by producing RMSE of 1.209, nRMSE of 0.263, MAE of 0.76, and MASE of 0.826. EXGBoost produced RMSE of 1.140, nRMSE of 0.277, MAE of 0.86, and MASE of 0.934 in rice prediction. In addition, CatBoost outperformed EXGBoost in sorghum prediction by achieving an RMSE of 0.334, nRMSE of 0.128, MAE of 0.16, and MASE of 0.741; RMSE of 0.369, nRMSE of 0.158, MAE of 0.26, and MASE of 0.897, respectively. The low values of RMSE, nRMSE, and MAE indicate that CatBoost's predictions are close to the actual observed values, confirming its effectiveness in crop yield estimation. In addition, CatBoost achieved the smallest MASE, which indicates reliable predictions thus, the scheme will help farmers make informed decisions in Senegal. CatBoost excelled at handling categorical features, such as crop type (maize, groundnuts, pearl millet, and sorghum), soil type, and location, without requiring extensive preprocessing. As a result, CatBoost had a distinct advantage over RF, EXGBoost, and LightGBM in crop yield prediction in Senegal, even though rice was identified as the most challenging crop to predict yield for this model. In addition, the comparison of these models was limited to specific features and 5 crop types.

Chen et al. [6] proposed a Distributional Reinforcement Learning (DRL) approach that models the full distribution of rewards, not just expected outcomes, enabling more precise and adaptive irrigation decisions. The algorithm was trained and validated using real-world data from cotton field experiments in Xinjiang, China, collected between

1980–2024. The results have shown that the proposed algorithm outperformed Deep Q-Networks (DQN), genetic algorithms, and Xinjiang local best practice, achieving a peak cotton yield of 6590 kg/ha in 2022, and a 12.9% increase over conventional irrigation strategies in 2024. The model's strong performance across multiple years highlights its resilience, adaptability, and practical potential. However, their study notes that the prediction accuracy might vary in different environments due to reliance on the DSSAT model's accuracy and the regional specificity of training data, indicating a need for further cross-location validation.

Gawdiya et al. [8] proposed two ensemble models that specifically integrate RF and Support Vector Regression (SVR), and RF and Artificial Neural Networks (ANN) techniques to improve the accuracy of crop yield prediction. The study utilized a dataset comprising 29 morpho-physiological traits of wheat, and the data were collected from 600 wheat samples. The ensemble model designed by integrating RF and ANNs produced, MAPE of 4.65%, MAD of 0.1656, RMSE of 0.2181, R-square value of 98.48%, and accuracy rate of 98.18% in the test dataset. The low MAPE and RMSE values indicate high prediction accuracy. While the ensemble model that integrated RF and SVR showed MAPE of 5.53%, MAD of 0.1772, RMSE of 0.2353, R^2 value of 98.16%, and an accuracy rate of 98.36%. However, the data utilized was limited to a two-year dataset obtained from a single site.

Senthil et al. [10] presented a novel AI-based system that was designed to seamlessly combine state-of-the-art deep learning algorithms, Geographic Information System (GIS) technologies, and Global Positioning System (GPS) technology. ANNs was used in this system to accurately analyse crop data to improve crop production forecasts and the extraction of significant insights [10]. Furthermore, to improve agricultural monitoring and decision-making, the system combines ANNs with Generative Adversarial Networks (GANs) and You Only Look Once (YOLO). AI-based system produced 94% accuracy rate for forecasting crop yields. However, integrating many technologies like GPS, GIS, and deep learning algorithms requires smooth interoperability, and if not implemented well it can limit the system's effectiveness.

Dai et al. [12] developed a peanut yield prediction model using RF and Linear Regression (LR). RF was employed to model more complex, non-linear associations and reduce overfitting. LR was used to capture linear relationships between vegetation indices and yield. Phenological features extracted via the iVI-Logistic algorithm, such as VI_max, VI_cum, VI_ch, and VI_rate, were incorporated to enhance model performance. Peanut cultivation areas in Junan County (JN) and Ningyang County (NY) in Shandong Province were used to evaluate the performance of the proposed solution. In JN, the R2 value of the LR model increased from 0.5341 to 0.5946, while MAE and RMSE declined, indicating reduced prediction error. In NY, models incorporating early and late growth stages yielded even better results, R2 improved from 0.5768 to 0.6826 for LR, and from 0.6610 to 0.8201 for RF, highlighting the value of ML and phenological inputs. However, the models were only evaluated on data from only three years (2022–2024) and focused on a specific region, thus their applicability to other geographic locations or climate conditions remains limited.

DL architectures such as 1D-CNN, LSTM, and TRFM were used by Gaso et al. [13] to forecast soybean yields. The study employed Sentinel-2 imagery, weather information, and topography features obtained from a digital elevation model for soybean forecast. The DL architectures showed lower MBE, MAE, RMSE, and Relative RMSE (RRMSE), along with higher R^2 and Concordance Correlation Coefficient (CCC) values, compared to the baseline. This suggests that DL models can effectively learn spatial patterns in yield variability and generalize to unseen data [13]. However, these data-driven approaches suffer from reduced accuracy in predicting extreme yield values, which often fall outside the patterns learned from training data.

Karongo et al. [14] leverage the power of five distinct ML techniques, namely RF, Decision Tree (DT), XGboost, SVM, and ANNs, each offering unique strengths in pattern recognition and predictive modeling, to forecast sorghum yields. DT, RF, XGboost, and ANNs demonstrated high levels of accuracy, each achieving an R^2 greater than 70%, indicating a significant and robust relationship between the predicted and observed sorghum yield values. This high level of accuracy suggests that these models are capable of capturing the underlying patterns and relationships in the data, providing a solid foundation for predicting sorghum yield. The availability of high-quality, representative crop data is essential for training and validating ML models. However, in many developing countries, including South Sudan, such data is often scarce, incomplete, or unreliable. This can limit the accuracy and generalizability of the models, making it difficult to apply them to other areas or contexts.

The study by Zhou et al. [16] utilizes UAV-based multispectral remote sensing imagery to collect data on rice crops across multiple varieties. UAVs offer a cost-effective and efficient way to collect high-resolution data over large areas. Furthermore, the study uses both image-based (CNN) and feature-based (RF, DNN, and LSTM) models to forecast rice yield. While image-based models take raw photos as input and automatically extract relevant data, feature-based models rely on deliberately chosen features, such as vegetation indices and canopy height [16]. With a yield prediction error of 9.93% and an R^2 value of 0.6 around 1.5 months prior to harvest, the CNN model's good performance demonstrates the promise of multi-temporal CNN models for precise and early yield prediction. However, only a year's worth of experimental data was used in this investigation which limit the generalizability of this model.

This section reviewed existing state-of-the-art models and identified several methodological and practical limitations of these existing ML models. One of the most common issues is overfitting, especially in models like XGBoost and deep learning networks, which means they perform well on training data but struggle to make accurate predictions on new or unseen data. This is often when these models are trained on small, region-specific datasets or limited historical data (e.g., one- or two-year periods). In addition, KNN models increase the computational complexity, thereby limiting their applicability to small-scale farmers. The insufficient integration of agro-climatic and environmental variables, including real-time weather data, limits many of the existing models from making realistic predictions. Several studies focused on a single crop or region, which limits the generalizability of the findings. In addition, the prediction accuracy was limited by the inconsistent data sources and low-resolution satellite imagery. This review has identified that some ML models require more computing power, thus limiting their adoption by small-scale farmers. These identified limitations highlight the need for larger and diverse datasets, and more varied inputs in order to improve the prediction accuracy of existing ML models.

3 Commonly Used Machine Learning Algorithms and Evaluation Parameters for Crop Yield Prediction

The comparative usage of various ML algorithms proposed in recent crop yield prediction studies published between July 2024 and March 2025 is illustrated in Fig. 1. Based on this review paper, ensemble and nonlinear models, especially those that perform well across diverse agricultural and environmental conditions, are mostly used by researchers when developing crop yield prediction models [14–16]. RF is the most commonly used model, appearing in 16% of the studies reviewed. RF is mostly used due to its strong predictive performance, resilience to overfitting, and ability to handle noisy or incomplete data. These challenges are frequently encountered in agricultural datasets. In addition, RF is also used because of its interpretability and robustness when working with both structured and unstructured data, which is common in agricultural settings.

The second commonly used models are SVMs and ANNs, each sitting at 12.8%. These two models are commonly used because of their flexibility and strong predictive capabilities. SVMs perform well with high-dimensional data, while ANNs are good at modeling complex, nonlinear interactions between crop growth and environmental variables. However, both models often require careful tuning and extensive preprocessing. Gradient Boosting methods, including XGBoost, LightGBM, and CatBoost, represent 10.6% of the algorithms surveyed. Their consistent performance in practical prediction tasks has positioned them as strong competitors to RF and SVM in crop yield predictions. This is because of their speed, scalability, and high accuracy and efficiency in handling large-scale agricultural data and delivering reliable predictions.

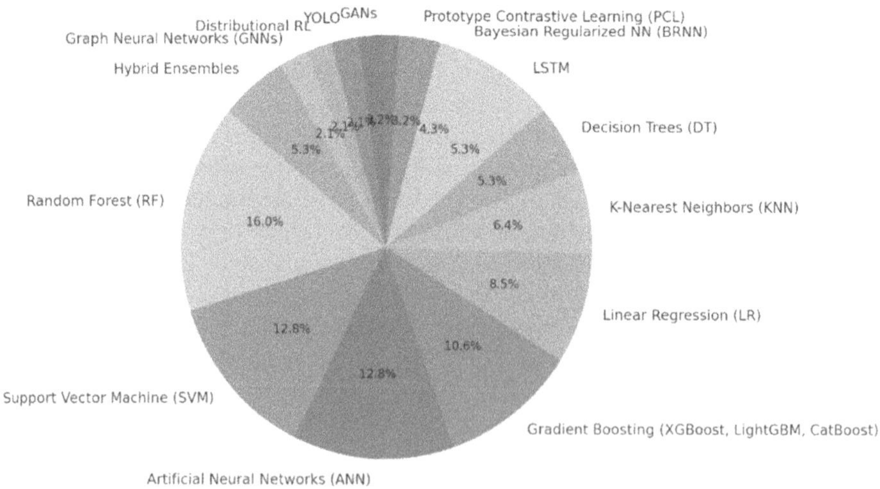

Fig. 1. Most used algorithms for crop yield prediction

LR and KNN account for 8.5% and 6.4%, respectively, and continue to play an important role in crop yield prediction, mainly in simpler tasks where model transparency and ease of use are important. Thus, these models can help small-scale farmers. However, these approaches often underperform when applied to complex and high-dimensional agricultural datasets, when compared with more advanced ML techniques such as RF, SVMs, and ANNs for crop yield predictions.

In recent years, we have seen a growing interest in the use of deep learning methods such as LSTM, BRNN, and GANs, which account for 5.5%, 4.3%, and 3.2%, respectively. Additionally, more specialized models, such as PCL and GNNs, which account for 3.2% and 2.1%, are emerging to help farmers with crop yield predictions in order to address food insecurity in the world. This is because these techniques are well-suited for handling time-series data, spatial relationships, and missing information, which are common characteristics of modern agricultural datasets collected from sensors and remote platforms for crop yield prediction tasks.

As shown in Fig. 1, hybrid ensemble models account for 5.3%. These hybrid ensemble approaches take advantage of the strengths of multiple models, often leading to improved generalization and performance in crop yield prediction. The rise in the usage of these hybrid ensemble models presents a growing shift toward flexible, tailored solutions designed to accommodate specific crops, regional contexts, and diverse data sources that could benefit smallholder farmers and farmers in general. Thereby addressing the issue of food insecurity by improving the accuracy of crop yield prediction with less computational complexity.

The distribution shown in Fig. 1 highlights two major trends in the field of crop yield prediction, namely the continued reliance on established ensemble models for their reliability and an increasing adoption of innovative deep learning approaches to meet the evolving demands of real-world agricultural prediction.

Different evaluation metrics that are frequently used in crop yield prediction models, as identified in the reviewed literature, are shown in Fig. 2. These metrics play a key role in assessing how accurate, reliable, and robust ML models are when applied to agricultural prediction. The most commonly used metric is the R2, with 25% of usage. R2 is mainly used because it provides a clear, in-built measure of how well a model explains variations in actual crop yields. In addition, it is widely used in agricultural prediction because of its simplicity and effectiveness in regression tasks.

The second most used metric is RMSE, which accounts for 22% as it is used to quantify the average size of the errors between the predicted crop yields and the actual observed crop yields. It is particularly valued because it heavily penalizes larger errors, meaning that models with even a few very inaccurate predictions will have a significantly higher RMSE. This makes it a preferred choice when it's important to minimize large deviations between predicted and actual yields, particularly in high-risk forecasting scenarios. MAE and MAPE account for 18% and 15%, respectively. These metrics are easier to interpret than RMSE and are less influenced by factors such as outliers and large prediction errors. In addition, MAPE is useful for expressing forecast errors in percentage terms, which helps make results more readable to non-technical users like farmers and policymakers.

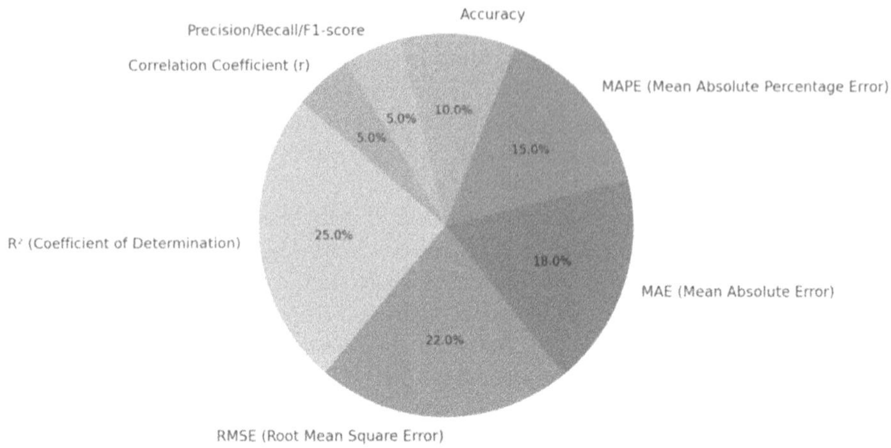

Fig. 2. Most used evaluation metrics in crop yield prediction models

Accuracy appears in 10% of the studies, mainly in models that classify yield levels, i.e., low, medium, and high. Precision, recall, F1-score, and the correlation coefficient (r) each account for 5% of usage. These metrics are mostly used in imbalanced or complex datasets during crop yield predictions. The review emphasizes that the choice of evaluation metric often depends on the dataset, prediction goals, and the needs of the end users. For example, large-scale models may prioritize high R2 and low RMSE, while MAE and MAPE may be better suited to smallholder farming contexts where interpretability and relative error are more important. While R2 and RMSE are the most commonly used metrics, this paper recommends using a combination of these evaluation metrics in order to get the full picture of the performance of each model in crop yield prediction. In addition, this paper recommends the use of XAI techniques to improve transparency and build trust in predictive systems in order to address the issue of food insecurity in the world.

4 Commonly Used Features in Crop Yield Prediction

The most frequently used input features in crop yield prediction models reviewed in the paper are displayed in Fig. 3. These features are important as they directly affect how accurate and useful the ML models are for real-world farming decisions. Weather data (real-time and historical weather data) is the most used feature, appearing in 25% of the studies reviewed. This is because factors such as rainfall, temperature, and humidity have a direct impact on crop growth, making them essential for accurate forecasting. This paper found that both real-time and historical weather data are valuable for ML models such as LSTM and BRNN to track changes over time in order to make accurate predictions. Soil data is the second commonly used input feature, and accounts for 20% usage when evaluating ML models in crop yield prediction. This is because soil features such as soil pH, texture, and moisture content play a key role in plant nutrition and development. While soil data is highly informative, it's often difficult to gather at a high level of detail or resolution (fine scale), especially in areas with limited resources.

Remote sensing data, such as NDVI and EVI indices, accounts for 18%. These features are mostly used because they can monitor crop health and biomass without disturbing the farming field. The integration of remote sensing data with satellite and drone imagery makes it easier to make accurate predictions across large farming regions. This could benefit small-scale farmers if they are funded to get resources that would help them with crop yield predictions, so that they can contribute to the fight against food insecurity. Historical yield data is used in 15% of the ML models. Mainly because it helps with spotting trends and patterns over time that could help improve the accuracy of crop yield prediction. However, the paper found that it can be misleading if historical yield data is not combined with the current date when making predictions. Continually, features such as crop type and variety accounted for 10% of usage, while topographical (elevation and slope) data accounted for 7% of usage. These metrics help fine-tune predictions in areas with varied terrain or microclimates. These spatial features are increasingly being used to improve the accuracy of site-specific forecasts. Thus, these metrics could benefit small-scale farmers in the world. Fertilizer and irrigation data are the least used inputs at only 5%. Mainly because of gaps in record-keeping and inconsistent data collection. However, the paper emphasizes their importance and encourages future models to integrate these features, as they can significantly improve predictions by linking farm management practices to yield outcomes.

This paper has seen a shift toward using a wider mix of data, combining environmental, historical, and farm management information, to create more adaptable and reliable ML models in order to make accurate predictions. While weather, soil, and remote sensing remain the foundation for crop yield predictions, expanding access to diverse, high-quality data will be key to advancing precision agriculture in the years ahead.

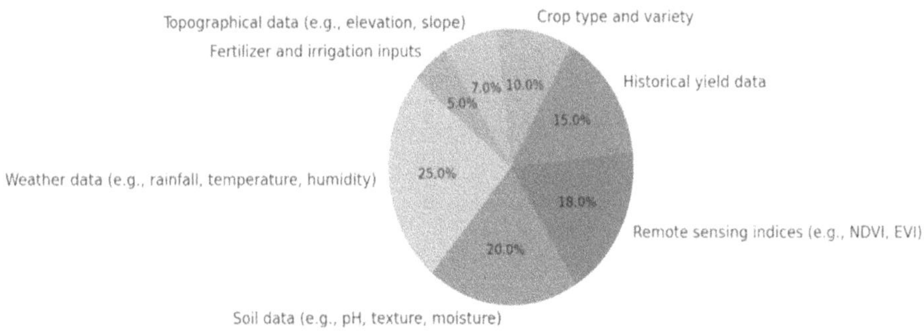

Fig. 3. Commonly used features in crop yield prediction

5 Open Research Issues and Future Research Directions

Future research should focus on incorporating a wider range of environmental and agronomic variables to improve the accuracy and adaptability of crop yield prediction ML models in order to fight food insecurity in the world. Thus, researchers could consider adding data on soil nutrient levels and fertility indicators to offer deeper insights into what drives crop growth. In addition, by expanding the variety of inputs, ML models can become more responsive to real-world farming conditions. Thereby, benefiting small-scale farmers in the future. Furthermore, this paper suggests the adoption of more advanced ML techniques, such as neural network architectures, namely Bi-GRU, and Maxout classifiers. Mainly because these architectures, when used within ensemble learning frameworks, have shown impressive results in improving prediction accuracy and model reliability with a variety of inputs, which normally happens in crop yield prediction. However, it is worth noting that getting the most out of ensemble models depends on how well the individual models are selected, trained, and combined. Thus, it requires more focused investigation as the integration could increase the computational complexity, which will not benefit smallholder farmers.

Furthermore, future research direction could focus on the use of XAI tools such as SHapley Additive exPlanations (SHAP) and Local Interpretable Model-Agnostic Explanations (LIME). These tools help to show how complex models make decisions during a prediction task. This added transparency builds trust in the crop yield prediction models and can encourage broader adoption of these ML models by farmers, agronomists, and policymakers who need to understand and make decisions on the predictions. Continually, in smart farming and IoT systems, future studies should explore hybrid approaches to selecting input features. Mainly because this can help improve the performance of ML models while reducing the number of inputs, making the prediction models more efficient and suitable for real-time use in farming environments. In addition, the reduction of input parameters could help reduce the computational complexity, thereby benefiting smallholder farmers with limited computational resources.

These future research directions could drive meaningful progress in agricultural productivity, helping farmers adapt to climate challenges and promoting more sustainable, data-driven farming practices that could help fight food insecurity in the world.

6 Conclusion

This paper presented a detailed and up-to-date review of ML models used in crop yield prediction, focusing on articles published between June 2024 and March 2025 from databases such as Scopus, MDPI, Scientific Reports, Taylor & Francis, WILEY, and ScienceDirect. The paper highlighted recent advancements and mostly used ML methods, evaluation metrics, and input parameters in crop yield prediction. This paper identified RF as the commonly used ML model, accounting for 16%. This is because of its strong predictive accuracy and ability to reduce overfitting by combining multiple decision trees. This review has seen an increase in the use of hybrid ensemble approaches, accounting for 5.3%. Hybrid ensemble models combine the strengths of multiple ML algorithms to boost performance in diverse agricultural settings, and as a result, crop yield predictions could be improved by using these hybrid ensemble schemes.

Commonly used input features include weather data, soil characteristics, and remote sensing imagery, accounting for 25%, 20%, and 18%, respectively. However, input features such as fertilizer usage and irrigation are still underrepresented, mainly due to difficulties in data collection. This paper has identified R2, RMSE, MAE, and MAPE, accounting for 25%, 22%, 18%, and 15%, respectively, as the commonly used evaluation metrics. These evaluation metrics help assess how well a model predicts actual outcomes, which is very important in crop yield predictions. While these advanced models often deliver high accuracy, they usually require significant data preprocessing and fine-tuning, which may not be practical for small-scale farmers due to the low-resource computational capabilities of their systems. Thus, there is a need for simpler, more efficient models that can produce accurate crop yield predictions.

This review not only captures the current state of ML models in crop yield prediction but also presents future research innovations that could make these models more practical, accurate, and widely usable. By presenting what is currently working and where research limitations remain, this review paper offers valuable guidance for researchers, policymakers, and agri-tech professionals. Thus, the insights presented in this review paper can help shape the development of more accurate and data-driven agricultural crop prediction systems. Thereby empowering farmers and decision-makers with better tools to fight food insecurity in the world.

Acknowledgments. The author would like to thank the Tshwane University of Technology for providing financial assistance. I declare that there are no conflicts of interest related to this paper's publication.

Disclosure of Interests. The author declares that he has no known competing financial interests or personal relationships that could have appeared to influence the work reported in this paper.

References

1. Oikonomidis, A., Catal, C., Kassahun, A.: Hybrid deep learning-based models for crop yield prediction. Appl. Artif. Intell. **36**(1), 1–19 (2022)
2. Dai, Y., Wang, H., Yang, M., Li, G., Lv, X.: A machine learning workflow for classifying and predicting the annual climatic status of cotton in Xinjiang, China. Ind. Crops Prod. **226**, 1–16 (2025)
3. Syam Kishor, K.S., Binson, V.A: An IoT-enabled real-time crop prediction system using soil fertility analysis. Eng **5**(4), 2496–2510 (2024)
4. Sun, G., et al.: Bridging the gap between hyperspectral imaging and crop breeding: soybean yield prediction and lodging classification with prototype contrastive learning. Comput. Electron. Agric. **230**, 1–13 (2025)
5. Razavi, M.A., et al.: Enhancing crop yield prediction in Senegal using advanced machine learning techniques and synthetic data. Artif. Intell. Agric. **14**, 99–114 (2024)
6. Chen, Y., Lin, M., Yu, Z., Sun, W., Fu, W., He, L.: Enhancing cotton irrigation with distributional actor–critic reinforcement learning. Agric. Water Manag. **307**, 1–14 (2025)
7. Kumar, C., Dhillon, J., Huang, Y., Reddy, K.: Explainable machine learning models for corn yield prediction using UAV multispectral data. Comput. Electron. Agric. **231**, 1–15 (2025)
8. Gawdiya, S., et al.: Field scale wheat yield prediction using ensemble machine learning techniques. Smart Agr. Technol. **9**, 1–11 (2024)
9. Mukherjee, A., Buyya, R.: Federated learning architectures: a performance evaluation with crop yield prediction application. Software Pract. Exper. **55**(7), 1165–1184 (2024)
10. Suganthi, S.U., Prinslin, L., Selvi, R., Prabha, R.: Generative AI in agri: sustainability in smart precision farming yield prediction mapping system based on GIS using deep learning and GPS. Procedia Comput. Sci. **252**, 365–380 (2025)
11. Zheng, M., Hu, H., Niu, Y., Shen, Q., Jia, F., Geng, X.: Modeling of winter wheat yield prediction based on solar-induced chlorophyll fluorescence by machine learning methods. Eur. J. Remote Sens. **58**(1), 1–23 (2025)

12. Hou, X., et al.: Peanut yield prediction using remote sensing and machine learning approaches based on phenological characteristics. Comput. Electron. Agric. **232**, 1–8 (2025)
13. Gaso, D.V., La Rosa, L.E.C., Puntel, L.A., Edreira, J.I.R., de Wit, A., Kooistra, L.: Predicting spatial and temporal variability in soybean yield using deep learning and open source data. Eur. J. Agron. **164**, 1–12 (2025)
14. Karongo, J., Mwaniki, J.I., Ndiritu, J., Mokaya, V.: Sorghum yield prediction based on remote sensing and machine learning in conflict affected South Sudan. Sci. Rep. **15**(1), 1–16 (2025)
15. Zhou, H., et al.: Yield prediction through UAV-based multispectral imaging and deep learning in rice breeding trials. Agric. Syst. **223**, 1–15 (2025)
16. Yang, F., et al.: Prediction of corn variety yield with attribute-missing data via graph neural network. Comput. Electron. Agric. **211**, 1–11 (2023)
17. Shawon, S.M., Ema, F.B., Mahi, A.K., Niha, F.L., Zubair, H.T.: Crop yield prediction using machine learning: an extensive and systematic literature review. Smart Agric. Technol. **10**, 100718 (2025)

Early Detection of Poultry Infectious Disease Using Deep Learning

Araek Tashkandi[1(✉)] and Siraj Wally[2]

[1] Department of Information Systems and Technology, College of Computer Science and Engineering, University of Jeddah, Jeddah, Saudi Arabia
astashkandi@uj.edu.sa

[2] Department of Internal Medicine – Radiology, College of Medicine, University of Tabuk, Tabuk, Saudi Arabia
swally@ut.edu.sa

Abstract. Epidemiological poultry illnesses, including Coccidiosis, Salmonella, and Newcastle, are notorious for decimating poultry populations and jeopardizing white meat supplies, adversely impacting chicken production and leading to considerable economic losses for farmers. In addition, it presents a significant threat to human health. Farmers and veterinarians can now detect these diseases through visual and auditory monitoring. They can analyze photos of chicken feces to determine whether the birds are healthy or affected by one of the previously mentioned diseases. However, the detection process is laborious and time-consuming when conducted on a large scale. To address the identified constraints, we offer a solution consisting of an image multiclass classifier utilizing six models: baseline CNN, VGG16, InceptionV3, MobileNetV2, Xception, and MobileNetV3. The initial five models were used with cutting-edge solutions. MobileNetV3, the most recent model, has not been used for the detection of these disorders and was recommended by us. We selected MobileNetV3 for its superior performance compared to all other models. For example, it is at least twice as fast as the other models during the training phase. This complements the achievement of an exceptional accuracy of approximately 98%. We used diverse datasets to illustrate the efficacy of the proposed method. The datasets comprise 2057 fecal photos of healthy poultry, 376 fecal images of poultry infected with Newcastle disease, 2276 fecal images of poultry infected with Salmonella, and 2103 fecal images of poultry infected with Coccidiosis, totaling 6812 images.

Keywords: Deep Learning · Image multi-class · Infectious Disease · MobileNetV3 · Poultry

1 Introduction

Poultry infectious diseases have caused enormous economic losses due to the increasing demand for various poultry products. Management to reduce the effect

S. Wally—Contributing authors.

H. R. Arabnia et al. (Eds.): CSCE 2025, CCIS 2934, pp. 413–434, 2026.
https://doi.org/10.1007/978-3-032-22190-2_30

of infectious diseases in animals on public health requires actions and preventive steps to supervise hepatitis, outbreak symptoms, and costs associated with the disease. Most studies have concentrated on biological records related to the management of human infectious diseases. However, the use of fiscal tools has been prescribed as a tactic to prevent the spread of such infections as a means of indirect income development.

Disease monitoring ideally includes a series of processes that monitor or predict the development of an infectious disease. The implementation of early detection is more suitable for the management of infectious diseases. Rapidly aware and potentially infectious and contagious animal-related diseases in the market process are at a minimal cost. Evolutions in veterinary monitoring resulted from small to large developments in cell, molecular, and biomedical research in the last two decades of the twentieth century. This development has greatly contributed to the monitoring of disease in the disciplines and techniques of molecular biology associated with infectious diseases. There is a greater potential for early detection. Currently accessible technology must be maximized in domestic bird cultivation. Deep learning is a subclass of machine learning based on the discovery of different approaches. Rapid numerical representation from information to objects is made feasible through it. The deep learning model has been revealed to work better where the test framework is large and the results in a given period are mildly repeating in the past biological variety of different medical statistics and patient information on medical care or ailments. In addition, this study begins to develop a tool for increased accessibility in predicting human health-related infectious disease development in poultry and poultry farming with a deep learning model as a methodology using a dataset of bird images. Poultry has a variety of characteristics that can display genetic diversity, including species, age, and anticipated productivity, such as commercial, local, or broilers. An infectious disease as part of the animal health management spectrum is significant for poultry. In terms of human health science, healthy chickens and eggs are also important in all farming activities, including factories. In the larger environment, the nutrient cycle is accompanied by the spread of infectious diseases that pose a threat to the health of domestic animals and the ecological agriculture of the community.

Infectious diseases, such as Newcastle, Coccidiosis, and Salmonella, are among the most critical concerns highlighted by breeders. These rapidly spreading epidemics can result in substantial losses for breeders and pose a risk of complete herd infection, affecting poultry production, food safety, human health, and zoonotic diseases. Detection of infectious diseases (Newcastle, Coccidiosis, Salmonella) through fecal identification by skilled veterinarians is doable to a degree; however, it is time-consuming.

The virus can survive for three months on carcasses of infected birds. Consequently, early identification of this disease by computer vision, deep learning, and machine learning algorithms is essential in chicken production, protecting consumers, farm workers, including veterinarians, preserving white meat sources, and supporting the economic viability of poultry farms.

The objective of the project is the early detection of infectious diseases (Newcastle, Coccidiosis, Salmonella) and the automatic diagnosis of fecal conditions using computer vision techniques, deep learning, and machine learning algorithms. This initiative aims to assist veterinarians in the detection process, accelerate isolation to prevent outbreaks of infectious diseases (Newcastle, Coccidiosis, Salmonella), mitigate financial losses, and enhance the agricultural economy by protecting poultry health and preventing mortality risks. In addition to protecting zoonotic foods, agricultural laborers and veterinarians are protecting against infectious diseases such as Newcastle, Coccidiosis, and Salmonella.

This research aims to identify the most effective models from previous studies for detecting infectious diseases (Newcastle, Coccidiosis, Salmonella, Healthy) using a fecal picture dataset. In addition, novel model architectures distinct from those produced in prior studies are to be constructed. The research aims to compare the most effective models utilized in prior studies for the identification of infectious diseases (Newcastle, Coccidiosis, Salmonella, Healthy) using fecal pictures against newly generated models.

Numerous prior research papers are related to the early diagnosis of poultry viral diseases through deep learning. Research on the early detection of poultry infectious illnesses with deep learning is often categorized into several domains, including image-based detection, sensor data and environmental monitoring, multi-modal or hybrid systems, system integration, and real-time detection, among others. Integral to this is the research conducted by [1], who built a CNN-based model to identify indicators of viral diseases in chickens using picture data from farm surveillance cameras. The study achieved significant precision in differentiating between healthy and unhealthy hens, facilitating the early identification of possible epidemics. Okinda *et al.* [2] employed a CNN model to categorize photos of chickens exhibiting symptoms of the disease, with an emphasis on identification of the lesions. The system effectively recognized the symptoms of critical illness, attaining an accuracy of 91.5% in early detection. Machuve *et al.* [3] employed transfer learning to refine deep learning models pre-trained for the diagnosis of poultry diseases. Transfer learning improved performance in disease recognition from a limited dataset, with an accuracy of 94%. Wang *et al.* [4] evaluated various CNN architectures to identify the most effective to classify poultry diseases from photos. The study revealed that deeper architectures, such as ResNet50, exhibited superior performance, with an accuracy of 92.3%. Akomolafe *et al.* [5] employed deep learning models to analyze chicken infrared photos for the early identification of infectious diseases. The models achieved 95% accuracy in identifying anomalous heat patterns, which indicates disease prior to the manifestation of observable symptoms.

Some of the previous research studies included sensor data and environmental monitoring, relying on data such as temperature, humidity, and CO2 levels collected by Internet of Things (IoT) devices. Data are analyzed with deep learning models to forecast illness outbreaks. Central to this study is the research conducted by [6], which used machine learning algorithms on environmental data collected from poultry farms, such as temperature and humidity. Early detection of disease was achieved by linking environmental changes with disease outbreaks, achieving prediction accuracy 88%. Mbelwa [7] employed deep neural networks to analyze environmental data collected from sensors in chicken farms. The algorithm accurately predicted disease outbreaks by analyzing environmental abnormalities, achieving 90% precision.

Other prior research pertinent to this study focuses on multi-modal or hybrid systems. These methodologies integrate picture data with sensor data or alternative input modalities (e.g., audio or video). They generally employ hybrid deep learning models to integrate various types of data for better diagnoses. Zhuang *et al.* [8] built a hybrid deep learning model that combined picture recognition with ambient sensor data for disease classification. The hybrid model improved the detection accuracy by 10% compared to the use of image data alone, achieving an overall accuracy of 96%. Cuan *et al.* [9] integrated video analysis with deep learning to identify nuanced alterations in poultry behavior that signify disease. The system achieved a 89% success rate in identifying disease symptoms using video and sensor data.

Among the other domains related to system integration and real-time detection is the amalgamation of real-time systems for the identification of disease utilizing deep learning and IoT technology. These devices are engineered for the real-time surveillance of avian health and the identification of diseases. The characteristic of this field is the research conducted by Hemalatha and Maheswaran [10] who created a real-time system that integrates UAV (drone) technology with deep learning for the surveillance of poultry flocks and the identification of disease outbreaks. The system can identify diseases in real time with 90% accuracy, utilizing drones to survey vast areas. Cuan *et al.* [11] developed an automated deep learning system for continuous poultry health surveillance, incorporating IoT sensors and real-time imaging data. The technology exhibited 93% accuracy in early disease detection and prevented extensive epidemics. Huang *et al.* [12] proposed a comprehensive deep learning and IoT architecture for real-time disease detection utilizing various data inputs, including environmental data and voice analysis. The framework effectively detected infections earlier than conventional methods, decreasing the reaction time by 30%.

Given the excess of findings from previous research, the classification indicates that investigations into the early identification of poultry diseases using deep learning are varied and can pursue multiple avenues. The associated work was found to focus on the detection of disease via pictures, sensor data, or multimodal inputs such as video and environmental data. Numerous methods prioritize real-time monitoring, with the intention of implementing detection models in chicken farms for ongoing surveillance. The results of multiple studies consistently demonstrate excellent accuracy in disease identification, with the majority achieving over 90% accuracy across diverse deep learning architectures and approaches. However, significant research gaps persist in numerous domains that do not specify certain diseases and do not prioritize early identification.

2 Methods

This research adheres to the data science cycle approach. Below is an overview of our general methodology that encompasses the initial five steps. Data Collection, Data Preparation, Modeling, and Evaluation. The objective of our research is early detection of infectious diseases (Newcastle, Coccidiosis, Salmonella) using multiclass classification on fecal images. Data preprocessing is a crucial step in creating a machine learning model, as it helps improve accuracy and efficiency. Early detection and treatment of poultry diseases are the most efficient way to manage them, and several models have been developed to compare and select the optimal one with high accuracy. The experiment was carried out using the Google Colab environment, preprocessing images using data augmentation techniques, normalization, and image resizing. Oversampling was used to solve the NCD class imbalance. The Keras library and the ImageDataGenerator class were used to pre-process fecal images and create models. Python was chosen for its numerous features and rich libraries, making it one of the top programming languages for deep learning and machine learning.

Deep learning is a subset of artificial intelligence and machine learning that is responsible for detecting complex patterns from large-volume data. Deep learning algorithms contain many layers of processing and are subsequently capable of classifying or making decisions regarding input data. The applications of deep learning, especially in the medical sciences, have been continuously expanded. Such powerful capabilities have been used effectively in the detection of a wide range of diseases. The accuracy and timing gained by deep learning have advanced significantly in comparison to traditional methods for the detection of the aforementioned diseases.

2.1 Convolutional Neural Networks

Convolutional neural networks (CNNs) are among the most used methodologies to improve picture categorization precision. A Convolutional Neural Network is a specialized form of neural network that operates similarly to a conventional neural network but has a convolutional layer at its inception. Rather than supplying the entire image as an array of integers, the image is segmented into tiles, and the computer strives to anticipate the content of each tile [13]. Ultimately, based on the predictions of all tiles, the computer endeavors to infer the contents of the image.

Convolutional Neural Network pooling layers follow in the sequence of a convolutional neural network's hidden layers. A pooling layer aggregates the values of all pixels within each feature map [14]. Rectified Linear Unit (ReLU) layers are the layers of CNN. "ReLU" stands for "rectified linear unit." The fully connected layers incorporate completely connected layers. The nodes of a convolutional layer exclusively receive or exchange information with the preceding layer.

The model building phase was when we created a CNN baseline model for the categorization of multi-class picture [15]. Transfer learning, which makes use of several CNN architectures, was our methodology of choice. Afterwards, we created four pre-trained models of CNN architectures: Inspection, Xception, VGG16, and MobileNetV2. This was done because there was a lack of training images for different CNN designs [16]. In addition, we have created a brand new model called MobileNetV3 to accomplish the project goals.

The primary goal is to improve the comprehension of the data by placing the results of the trained models in context. Due to its computing efficiency, the CNN model serves as the baseline model in this experiment [17]. To make CNN models more accessible, it uses parameter sharing and custom convolution and pooling methods. This makes the models work on any platform, increasing their appeal. In addition, it achieves superhuman precision by executing autonomous feature extraction. As a result, learning and applying any deep CNN-based picture classification model is now easier than before [18].

Table 1 provides the list of the parameters used. The activation functions used in the CNN baseline model architecture. The activation function of convolutional layers in the baseline model, is it stands for Rectified Linear Unit (ReLU), has proved itself better than the sigmoid, because it is simple to calculate the partial derivative of ReLU, and learns much faster than the sigmoid and Tanh function. Equation: A(x) = max(0,x). Returns x if x is positive and 0 otherwise.

Table 1. CNN Layer Architecture Components

Layer name	Parameters
First convolutional layer	filters = 16, kernel_size = 3, activation = 'relu', input_shape = [300,300,3]
First max pooling layer	No parameter
Second convolutional layer	filters = 32, kernel_size = 3, activation = 'relu'
Second max pooling layer	No parameter
Third convolutional layer	filters = 64, kernel_size = 3, activation = 'relu'
Third max pooling layer	No parameter
Flattening Layer	No parameter
Full Connection Layer	units = 128, activation = 'softmax'
Output Layer	units = 128

Softmax function: The output layer's activation function in the baseline model, the softmax function is a kind of sigmoid function, usually used while trying to handle multiple classes. The softmax function was frequently found in the output layer of image classification issues, it would squeeze the outputs for each class between 0 and 1 and divide by the sum of the outputs.

2.2 Transfer Learning Models

The second version of the Mobilenet model is called MobilenetV2. It possesses a significantly reduced number of parameters in the deep neural network. Consequently, deep neural networks become more efficient. Its lightweight nature makes it most effective on mobile and embedded devices. The streamlined and compact architecture of the MobileNetV2 models facilitates improved speed in their execution. MobilenetV2 is a pre-trained model utilized for picture classification. Pre-trained models are deep neural networks developed by extensive training on a substantial image dataset. By utilizing pre-trained models, developers are exempt from constructing or training the neural network from the ground up, therefore conserving development time.

There are primarily two sorts of blocks: the bottleneck block with a stride of 1 and the block with a stride of 2. The MobileNetV2 architecture has an inverted residual structure, in which the input and output of the residual block consist of narrow bottleneck layers, contrasting with conventional residual models that use extended representations at the input. MobileNetV2 employs lightweight depthwise convolutions to process features within the intermediate expansion layer. We further ascertain that to maintain representational power, non-linearities in the thin layers must be eradicated. We demonstrate how this improves performance and disclose the understanding that motivated this design. Ultimately, our approach facilitates the distinction between the input/output domains and the expressiveness of the transformation, providing a valuable platform for further investigation (see Table 2).

Table 2. Architectural components of the pre-trained MobileNetV2 model

Type/Stride	Filter Shape	Input Size
CONV/S2	$3 \times 3 \times 3 \times 32$	$224 \times 224 \times 3$
CONV DW/S1	$3 \times 3 \times 32$ dw	$112 \times 112 \times 32$
CONV/S1	$1 \times 1 \times 32 \times 64$	$112 \times 112 \times 32$
CONV DW/S2	$3 \times 3 \times 64$ dw	$112 \times 112 \times 64$
CONV/S1	$1 \times 1 \times 64 \times 128$	$56 \times 56 \times 64$
CONV DW/S1	$3 \times 3 \times 128$ dw	$56 \times 56 \times 128$

2.3 Dataset

The poultry fecal images comprise an annotated dataset for poultry disease diagnostics, specifically designed for small- to medium-scale poultry farms, generated through research on poultry disease diagnostics models utilizing deep learning. The fecal photographs were acquired from layers, hybrids, and indigenous chicken breeds. Unlike broiler breeds, which reside on farms for about 5 weeks, these breeds can inhabit farms for up to 18 months, making them more vulnerable to diseases.

Fecal images and samples were periodically collected from farms in the Arusha and Kilimanjaro regions of Tanzania between February 2020 and February 2021 using the Open Data Kit (ODK) program loaded onto standard mobile phones (Tecno, Infinix, Huawei, and Samsung). ODK is a standardized application for collecting mobile data.

The compilation of 6,812 fecal images was generated by taking poultry fecal photographs and categorizing them with the help of animal health experts, including a veterinarian and a field officer. It encompasses four classes: Coccidiosis, Newcastle, Salmonella and healthy poultry. The images were annotated using the Labeling and LabelMe programs for the computer vision tasks of object detection and image segmentation, respectively. The dataset comprises photographs of poultry excrement used to diagnose poultry diseases, with the images stored in their original dimensions within folders designated by class names. Each image within a class is renamed using the class name followed by a numerical identifier (e.g., "cocci.1.png" or "healthy.56.png").

The dataset "healthy.zip" has 2057 photos, "ncd.zip" comprises 376 images, "salmo.zip" includes 2276 images, and "cocci.zip" consists of 2103 images, resulting in a total of 6812 labeled image files. Table 3 illustrates the distribution of the dataset between the four groups. The distinguishing features of the various diseases are the color and shape of the images; thus, the fecal images for coccidiosis are primarily dark brown and flat, those for Newcastle disease are green and solid, and salmonella presents as white and loosely shaped, while the healthy label is characterized by gray-white and solid shapes. Labeling errors are most likely for salmonella and healthy fecal images; also, the white hue may be misinterpreted. However, the principal distinction lies in the texture: slimy for salmonella and solid for healthy feces, respectively.

Table 3. Distribution of fecal images among categories

Fecal images category	Number of images
Healthy	2,057
Salmonella	2,276
Coccidiosis	2,103
Newcastle	376
Total	6,812

2.4 Data Preparation and Preprocessing

Real-world datasets often present several challenges that must be addressed before model development to improve performance, provide correct results, and mitigate errors. The issue identified during exploratory data analysis with the collection of fecal pictures in the real world is the imbalance of classes. It is a prevalent issue in image classification tasks that can adversely affect the accuracy of the model. In the fecal image dataset, there exists a class imbalance, with the NCD class being significantly underrepresented compared to others. As illustrated in Table 3, the Newcastle images total approximately 300, while the Coccidiosis, Salmonella, and healthy classes each comprise approximately 2000 images. This class imbalance issue is addressed using a combination of data augmentation approaches and oversampling.

The fecal image dataset contains photographs of varying dimensions; it is essential to standardize the image sizes, as convolutional neural networks (CNNs) often require inputs of a uniform shape. Moreover, the presence of irregularly shaped photographs in the files may complicate the interpretation of the results. Resizing is an essential preprocessing step in selecting the appropriate dimensions, as deep learning models train more efficiently on smaller images, hence reducing the training duration for larger images.

Data preprocessing is a standard initial phase in the deep learning workflow; it entails preparing raw data for model development to enhance desired characteristics or mitigate artifacts that may bias the network, hence achieving optimal results with high performance. The preparation procedures were executed in Python within the Google Colab Pro environment. The process modifies the dimensions of an image to a predetermined size to accommodate the varying dimensions of the input images through the following steps. Initially, we retrieve the dataset as zip files directly from the source by directing the URL to Google Colab and extracting them to create four folders corresponding to the four classes in the dataset (cocci, ncd, salmo, and healthy).

To address data imbalance, implement a combination of selected data augmentation techniques and oversampling to equilibrate the dataset by resampling infrequent instances to modify their quantity. We must address the data imbalance in class NCD through data augmentation, which will enable us to rapidly enhance the dataset for our underrepresented classes. This will guarantee that our model does not encounter the same image twice, assist in preventing overfitting, and enhance the model's generalization capabilities. Secondly, conduct oversampling subsequent to augmentation to elevate the quantity of photos in the NCD class to 2000, aligning it closely with the other classes. Currently, we own approximately 500 photographs; we must incorporate five augmented images for each, resulting in $376 + (376 * 5) = 2256$.

The predominant image data consist of integer pixel values ranging from 0 to 255. Large integer inputs for deep learning can hinder or decelerate the learning process. It is advisable to normalize the pixel values to ensure that each value falls within the range of 0 to 1. To accomplish this, divide all the values of the pixels by 255, the maximum value of pixels. The procedure involves mapping picture data pixels (intensity) to a specified range, often (0,1) or (-1,1). It is typically utilized to transform an image's pixel values into a more conventional or recognizable format. Grayscale denotes the conversion of colored imagery into monochrome black and white. It is generally used to reduce the computational complexity of deep learning and machine learning techniques. Grayscale is an excellent option as it reduces the pixel count in an image, hence decreasing the computational requirements.

2.5 Implementation and Setup Environment

MobileNetV3 is the third iteration of the architecture that underpins the image processing functionalities of numerous widely-used mobile applications. MobileNets must judiciously reconcile progress in computer vision and deep learning with the constraints of mobile contexts.

The principal novelty of MobileNetV3 is the application of AutoML to determine the optimal neural network architecture for a specific problem. MobileNetV3 employs two AutoML methodologies: MnasNet and NetAdapt. Investigates a coarse architecture with MnasNet, which uses reinforcement learning to determine the ideal design from a finite array of options. The model refines the design via NetAdapt, a supplementary method that incrementally reduces underutilized activation channels.

Incorporating a squeeze-and-excitation block into the fundamental architecture of MobileNetV3 represents another novel notion. The primary objective of squeeze-and-excitation blocks is to enhance the quality of representations generated by a network by explicitly modeling the interdependencies among the channels of its convolutional features.

All models were trained using a set of hyperparameters (see Table 4), which included the learning rate, the number of epochs, the batch size and optimizer. The learning rate determines the magnitude of adjustments made to the model weights based on the error at each update step. Epochs represent the total number of rounds through which the entire training dataset is passed through the model. The batch size refers to the number of training samples processed in a single round. The optimizer is an algorithm that enhances the learning process by efficiently updating the model parameters; common optimizers include SGD, Adam, and RMSprop. In addition, early stopping was applied to prevent overfitting by stopping training before the model begins to degrade generalization performance.

We follow the selection criteria presented in this work, as the authors heavily study the hyperparameters and show that it accomplishes high accuracy.

The dataset was divided into two splits following the 80–20 scheme, where 80% of the dataset (mean 6749 images) is dedicated to the training phase and 20% (1687 images) to the validation phase, respectively. The models were trained on the different numbers of classes and images in each class, as shown below. Inception, VGG16, Xception and CNN baseline models were trained in a four-class dataset. The Healthy, NCD, Coccidiosis, and Salmonella dataset consists of 8436 images. Table 5 shows the split of the dataset that was obtained for the four classes of three models.

The MobileNetV2 and MobileNetV3-Large models were trained in three classes: Healthy, Coccidiosis, and Salmonella with a dataset consisting of 8436

Table 4. Hyperparameters utilized in this study

Parameter	Baseline	VGG16	InceptionV3	MobileNetV2	Xception	MobileNetV3
Epochs	100	100	100	100	100	100
Batch size	32	64	64	64	64	64
Optimizer	RMSprop	Adam	RMSprop	Adam	Adam	Adam
Learning rate	1e-3	1e-3(pre-training) 1e-4(fine-tuning)	1e-3(pre-training) 1e-4(fine-tuning)	1e-3(pre-training) 1e-4(fine-tuning)	1e-3(pre-training) 1e-4(fine-tuning)	1e-3(pre-training) 1e-4(fine-tuning)
Early stopping	10 epochs	10 epochs	10 epochs	10 epochs	10 epochs	10 epochs

Table 5. Dataset splitting for training CNN baseline, Inception, Xception, and VGG16 models

Class	Image in each class	Training	Validation
Healthy	500	400	100
Coccidiosis	500	400	100
Salmonella	500	400	100
NCD	500	400	100

images, and we just took a subset of 500 poultry fecal images for each class, due to the heavy training of these models and the time they are consumed. In addition, they did not need to be trained on the whole data because they are pre-trained models and they can achieve high accuracy. Table 6 shows the split of the dataset of the two models.

Table 6. Dataset splitting for training MobileNetV2 and MobileNetV3-Large models

Class	Image in each class	Training	Validation
Healthy	500	400	100
Coccidiosis	500	400	10
Salmonella	500	400	100

3 Results and Discussion

Upon applying the models, we aim to present the findings on the testing set of the fecal pictures dataset; thus, we have utilized the training and validation curves, along with the classification report and confusion matrix. Since we deal with poultry diseases that are challenging to predict, we require the highest levels of Precision and Recall. In addition, the higher the F1 score, the better the model performance. In a VGG-16 transfer learning experiment, the goal is typically to take advantage of a pre-trained VGG-16 model (which was originally trained on a large dataset like ImageNet) to solve a new image classification task on a different, usually smaller, dataset. The result obtained from this study is presented in Table 7. The accuracy of the model is 94%, which indicates that it performs very well overall. There are some modest dips in precision and recall for class 3, which may require further attention. However, these levels are strong across the board for all classes. The macro and weighted averages are relatively close to one another, which indicates that the performance of the dataset is balanced. In general, VGG-16 has been able to successfully transfer its learning to this task, resulting in good classification results.

Table 7. Classification report for the VGG-16 classifier

	Precision	Recall	F1-score
Class 0	0.94	0.97	0.95
Class 1	0.94	0.96	0.95
Class 2	0.93	0.92	0.93
Class 3	0.93	0.89	0.91
Macro avg	0.93	0.94	0.94
Weighted avg	0.93	0.94	0.93
Accuracy	0.94		

Figure 1 shows the training and validation accuracy curves for 15 epochs for a VGG-16 based model. This is an indication of overfitting.

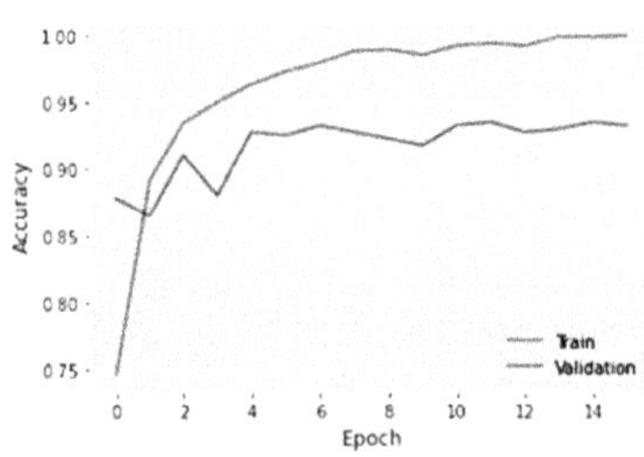

Fig. 1. Training and validation curves (accuracy) for the VGG-16 classifier.

Overfitting occurs when there is a growing disparity between the accuracy of training and the accuracy of validation. Despite learning to categorize the training data incredibly well, the model is not making significant progress on the validation set. Following a period of initial fluctuation, the validation accuracy eventually settles somewhere between 90 and 95%, indicating that the model is reaching a satisfactory level of performance on data that it has not encountered before, but it has most certainly reached its limit in terms of generalization. Possible enhancements could help reduce the effects of overfitting.

In this study a Fine-Tuning Method approach has been implemented to modify weights to ensure that the model is able to retrieve high-level information specific to the data set. This method is often recommended in situations where the training dataset is significant and bears a strong resemblance to the initial dataset that the pre-trained model was trained on. The objective of fine-tuning is to modify these specialized features such that they are compatible with the new dataset, as opposed to entirely replacing the generic learning features.

The result obtained after fine-tuning (see Table 8) shows that the model correctly classified 97% of the overall data after fine-tuning. This is a significant improvement from the earlier result (0.94) before fine-tuning, showing that the fine-tuning process has greatly improved the model's ability to generalize.

Table 8. Classification report for the VGG-16 classifier with fine-tuning

	Precision	Recall	F1-score
Class 0	0.98	0.99	0.98
Class 1	0.99	0.95	0.97
Class 2	0.96	0.99	0.98
Class 3	0.97	0.97	0.97
Macro avg	0.98	0.98	0.98
Weighted avg	0.98	0.97	0.97
Accuracy	0.97		

The model demonstrates a consistent and substantial improvement in both training and validation accuracy, achieving near-optimal performance after 30 epochs (see Fig. 2). The strong correlation between training and validation accuracy indicates efficient regularization and negligible overfitting. Minor variations in validation accuracy are typical, but may indicate places where the model is sensitive to specific data points, either due to class imbalance or noise within the validation set. Figure 2, the accuracy graph illustrates that the fine-tuned VGG-16 model is highly optimized, demonstrating effective generalization in both training and validation datasets.

In general, both the training and validation accuracies seem to be converging between 97% and 99%. The model achieves high accuracy on both the training and validation datasets at the end of training, indicating superior performance and generalization. The complete results of the VGG-16 classifier are shown in Table 9. Fine-tuning markedly enhances precision, with class 1 (healthy) exhibiting near-perfect precision, crucial for accurately identifying healthy patients

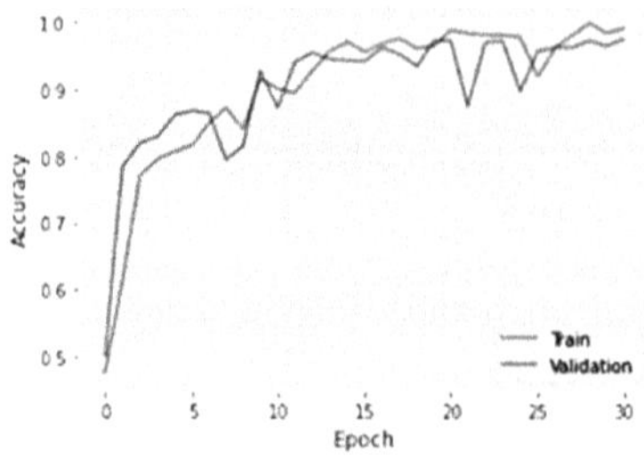

Fig. 2. Training and validation curves (accuracy) for the VGG-16 classifier with fine-tuning.

while reducing false positives in disease forecasts. Fine-tuning markedly improves recollection across all classes, particularly for Class 2 (Salmo) and Class 3 (ncd), assuring minimal case omissions, which is essential in illness identification. Overall, F1 scores improve with fine-tuning, with Class 0 (cocci) and Class 2 (Salmo) exhibiting the most significant improvements. This indicates that fine-tuning has improved the equilibrium between precision and recall for all classes, hence augmenting the model's robustness. Fine-tuning significantly improves the accuracy, reliability, and generalizability of the VGG-16 model for the classification of poultry illnesses.

Table 9. Classification Report interpretation for VGG-16 (Transfer learning & Fine-tuning)

	Transfer learning	Fine-tuning
Precision	- Class 0 (cocci) 0.94 - Class 1 (healthy) 0.94 - Class 2 (Salmo) 0.93 - Class 3 (ncd) 0.93	- Class 0 (cocci) 0.98 - Class 1 (healthy) 0.99 - Class 2 (Salmo) 0.96 - Class 3 (ncd) 0.97
Recall	- Class 0 (cocci) 0.97 - Class 1 (healthy) 0.96 - Class 2 (Salmo) 0.92 - Class 3 (ncd) 0.89	- Class 0 (cocci) 0.99 - Class 1 (healthy) 0.95 - Class 2 (Salmo) 0.99 - Class 3 (ncd) 0.97
F1 Score	- Class 0 (cocci) 0.95 - Class 1 (healthy) 0.95 - Class 2 (Salmo) 0.93 - Class 3 (ncd) 0.91	- Class 0 (cocci) 0.98 - Class 1 (healthy) 0.97 - Class 2 (Salmo) 0.98 - Class 3 (ncd) 0.97

The results presented are derived from an experiment using the InceptionV3 model (see Table 10), demonstrating the classification efficacy for four categories, presumably associated with the identification of poultry diseases according to previous discussions. The model accurately categorized 76% of all occurrences. This shows reasonable competence; however, it lacks great accuracy for this task. The equilibrium among precision, recall, and F1 score indicates that the model has consistent performance across classes but does not excel in any particular domain.

Table 10. Classification report for the InceptionV3 classifier

	Precision	Recall	F1-score
Class 0	0.80	0.82	0.81
Class 1	0.79	0.86	0.82
Class 2	0.72	0.83	0.77
Class 3	0.73	0.53	0.62
Macro avg	0.76	0.76	0.76
Weighted avg	0.76	0.76	0.75
Accuracy	0.76		

The subpar performance in class 3 and class 2 raises concerns if these classes signify critical diseases. Enhancements are necessary, particularly in the treatment of minority classes, and optimizing or implementing class-specific procedures could yield improved performance.

Figure 3 illustrates the training accuracy (red line) and the validation accuracy (blue line) for more than 30 epochs. The considerable disparity between training and validation accuracy post-epoch 20 indicates overfitting. The model consistently improves its performance on the training data, but has difficulties with the validation data. The model demonstrates strong performance on the training set; however, the validation accuracy exhibits excessive variability, indicating overfitting and possible generalization concerns. Likewise, fine-tuning is implemented in this instance.

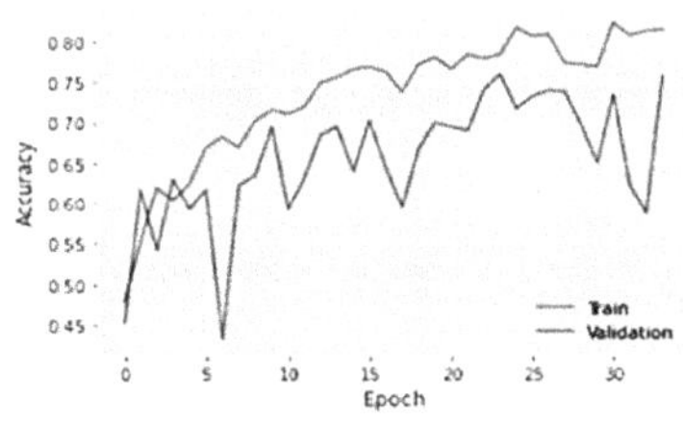

Fig. 3. Training and validation curves (accuracy) for the InceptionV3 classifier.

The performance results of the InceptionV3 classifier after fine-tuning (see Table 11) demonstrate an impressive accuracy of 97%, signifying its robust efficacy. Throughout all classes, precision, recall and F1 scores remain continuously elevated, with only slight reductions in class 1 recall (0.92). This indicates that the optimized InceptionV3 model exhibits high performance in both precision and recall, making it reliable for critical classification tasks, such as disease detection.

Table 11. Classification report for the InceptionV3 classifier with fine-tuning

	Precision	Recall	F1-score
Class 0	0.99	1.00	0.99
Class 1	0.98	0.92	0.95
Class 2	0.95	0.98	0.97
Class 3	0.96	0.98	0.97
Macro avg	0.97	0.97	0.97
Weighted avg	0.97	0.97	0.97
Accuracy	0.97		

Figure 4 illustrates the training and validation accuracy curves in 20 epochs. The little disparity between training and validation accuracy suggests that the model generalizes effectively, refraining from simply memorizing the training data, while successfully identifying transferable patterns for the validation set.

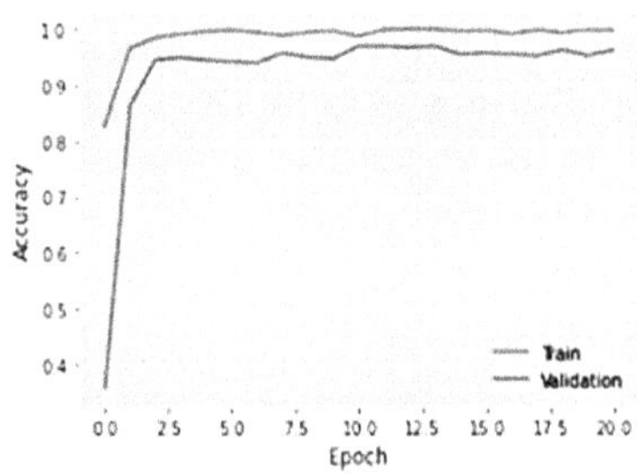

Fig. 4. Training and validation curves (accuracy) for the InceptionV3 classifier with fine-tuning.

The entire results underscore the substantial improvements achieved by fine-tuning relative to the initial transfer learning in terms of precision, recall, and F1 score (see Table 12).

Fine-tuning has significantly improved accuracy across all categories, making the model considerably more reliable for disease identification with fewer false positives. Fine-tuning has markedly improved recall, especially for Class 0 (cocci), Class 2 (Salmo), and Class 3 (Ncd), indicating that the model is now considerably more proficient at accurately identifying real instances of these diseases without omissions. Fine-tuning yields markedly elevated F1 scores across

Table 12. Classification Report interpretation for Inception V3: Inception V3 (Transfer learning & Fine-tuning)

	Transfer learning	Fine-tuning
Precision	- Class 0 (cocci) 0.80 - Class 1 (healthy) 0.79 - Class 2 (Salmo) 0.72 - Class 3 (Ncd) 0.73	- Class 0 (cocci) 0.99 - Class 1 (healthy) 0.98 - Class 2 (Salmo) 0.95 - Class 3 (Ncd) 0.96
Recall	- Class 0 (cocci) 0.82 - Class 1 (healthy) 0.86 - Class 2 (Salmo) 0.83 - Class 3 (Ncd) 0.53	- Class 0 (cocci) 1.00 - Class 1 (healthy) 0.92 - Class 2 (Salmo) 0.98 - Class 3 (Ncd) 0.98
F1 Score	- Class 0 (cocci) 0.81 - Class 1 (healthy) 0.82 - Class 2 (Salmo) 0.77 - Class 3 (Ncd) 0.62	- Class 0 (cocci) 0.99 - Class 1 (healthy) 0.95 - Class 2 (Salmo) 0.97 - Class 3 (Ncd) 0.97

all categories, indicating that the model now excels at identifying true situations and reducing false positives.

Table 13 presents the result of the remaining three models (MobileNetV2 classifier, MobileNetV3-Large classifier and Xception). MobileNetV2 demonstrates steady, albeit moderate performance, with an overall accuracy of 93% both before and after fine-tuning, with balanced precision, recall, and F1 scores in all classes. Before fine-tuning, MobileNetV3-Large performs at its best with 98% accuracy, showing remarkable precision and recall, particularly for classes 0 and 1. However, after fine-tuning, the accuracy drops to 93%, possibly due to overfitting or incorrect hyperparameter settings. Xception initially exhibits lower performance with an accuracy of 76% prior to fine-tuning, but demonstrates a significant improvement after fine-tuning, attaining an accuracy of 97% and demonstrating exceptional precision, recall, and F1 score across all classes, particularly in class 1, which achieves perfect scores. This suggests that although MobileNetV3-Large initially exhibits superior performance, Xception, with fine-tuning, emerges as the most resilient and well-rounded model for categorization.

The study of the training and validation accuracy curves for several classifiers (MobileNetV2, MobileNetV3-Large, and Xception) is provided in Figs. 5, 6, 7, 8, 9, and 10. These curves are presented both before and after the fine-tuning process. In conclusion, it was determined that fine-tuning normally reduces the difference between the training curve and the validation curve when carried out correctly, as was demonstrated with Xception.

In situations such as MobileNetV3-Large, fine-tuning could result in overfitting if the validation curve decreases while the training curve continues to improve. The behavior of MobileNetV2 is consistent both before and after the fine-tuning process, with the curves remaining quite close to each other but without exhibiting any significant gain in accuracy.

This paper was initiated in response to the existing literature on the classification of infectious diseases in chicken images in multiple classes, which significantly affects animal ecology and the economy. This project proposes a solution

Table 13. Classification report for three models with and without fine-tuning

Class	MobileNetV2			MobileNetV2 (Fine-tuned)		
	Precision	Recall	F1-score	Precision	Recall	F1-score
0	0.94	0.94	0.94	0.94	0.94	0.94
1	0.94	0.96	0.95	0.94	0.96	0.95
2	0.91	0.89	0.90	0.91	0.89	0.90
macro avg	0.93	0.93	0.93	0.93	0.93	0.93
Weighted avg	0.93	0.93	0.93	0.93	0.93	0.93
accuracy	0.93			0.93		
Class	MobileNetV3-Large			MobileNetV3-Large (Fine-tuned)		
	Precision	Recall	F1-score	Precision	Recall	F1-score
0	0.99	1.00	0.99	0.94	0.94	0.94
1	0.97	0.98	0.98	0.94	0.96	0.95
2	0.99	0.97	0.98	0.91	0.89	0.90
macro avg	0.98	0.98	0.98	0.93	0.93	0.93
Weighted avg	0.98	0.98	0.98	0.93	0.93	0.93
accuracy	0.98			0.93		
Class	Xception			Xception (Fine-tuned)		
	Precision	Recall	F1-score	Precision	Recall	F1-score
0	0.66	0.62	0.64	0.98	0.96	0.97
1	0.81	0.85	0.83	1.00	1.00	1.00
2	0.84	0.86	0.85	0.90	0.98	0.93
3	0.75	0.73	0.74	0.99	0.94	0.96
macro avg	0.76	0.77	0.77	0.97	0.97	0.97
Weighted avg	0.76	0.76	0.76	0.97	0.97	0.97
accuracy	0.76			0.97		

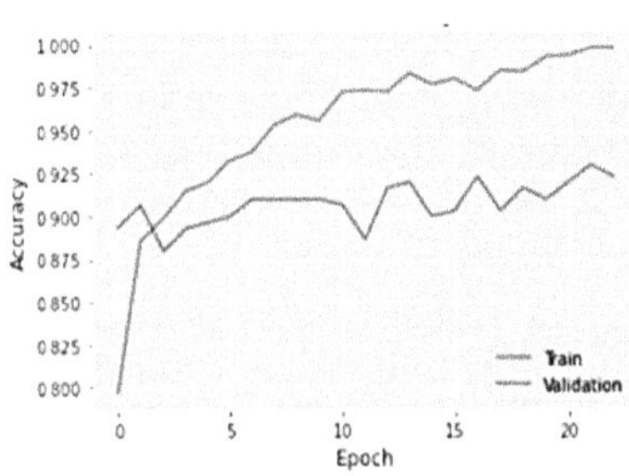

Fig. 5. Training and validation curves (accuracy) for the MobileNetV2 classifier

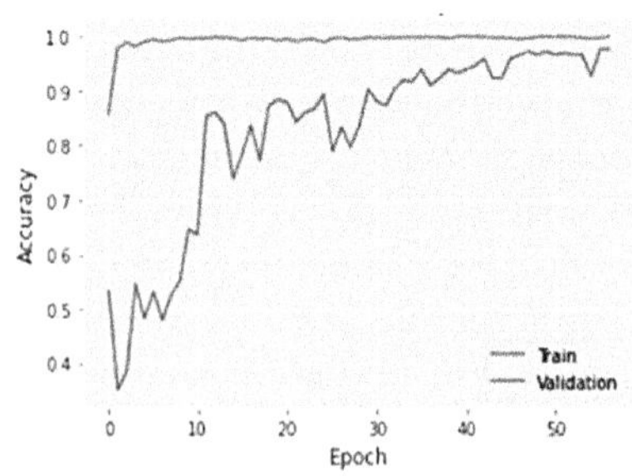

Fig. 6. Training and validation curves (accuracy) for the MobileNetV2 classifier with fine-tuning

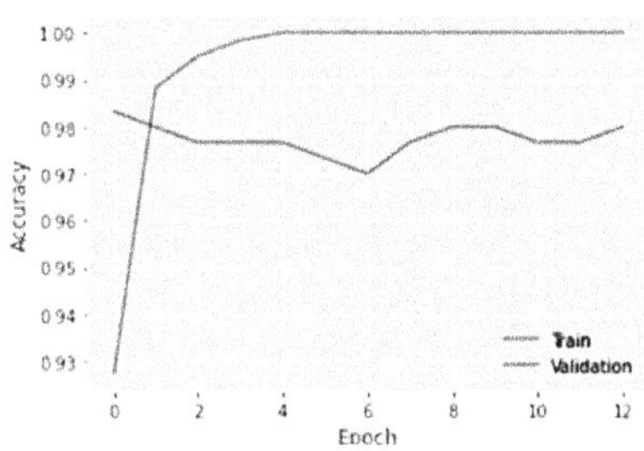

Fig. 7. Training and validation curves (accuracy) for the MobileNetV3-Large classifier

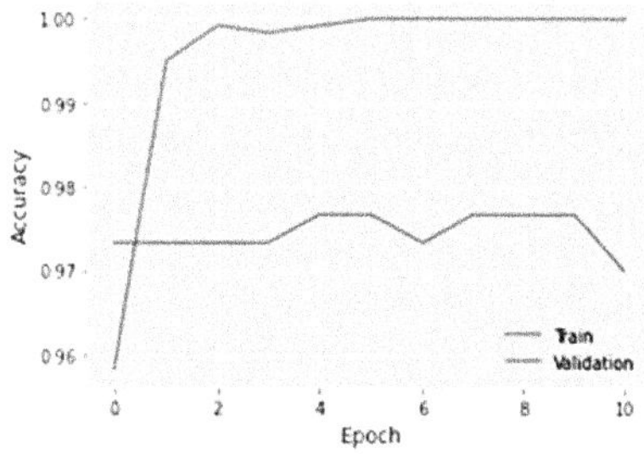

Fig. 8. Training and validation curves (accuracy) for the MobileNetV3-Large classifier with fine-tuning

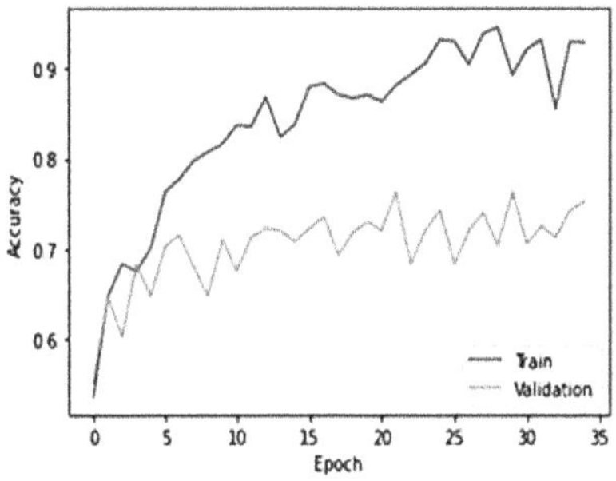

Fig. 9. Training and validation curves (accuracy) for the Xception classifier

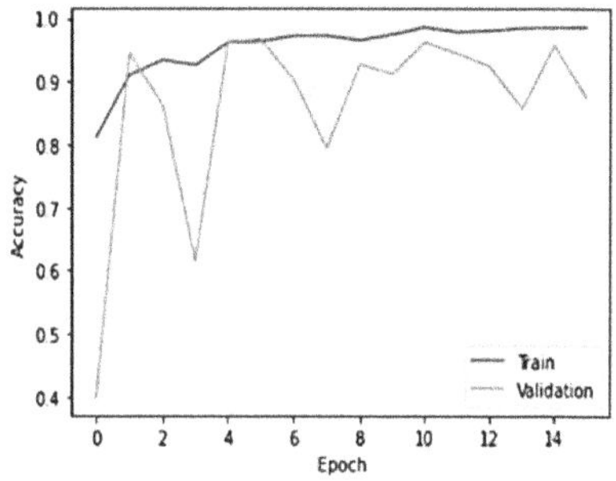

Fig. 10. Training and validation curves (accuracy) for the Xception classifier with fine-tuning

for the early detection and prediction of infectious disease incidence (Newcastle, Coccidia, Salmonella) in poultry through the application of machine learning and deep learning techniques.

Following a review of the literature, we established the research objectives as follows. Identify the most effective models used in leading research to classify fecal image datasets into various categories for the detection of specified infectious diseases. Evaluating these methods to determine their accuracy and limitations, subsequently recommending the adoption of a more effective model. Developing novel architectural models that are not present in the existing literature, tailored to our specific problem, to enhance accuracy and performance.

Initially, we faced the challenge of imbalanced classes, which was addressed through augmentation. Following data processing, we developed advanced models, specifically CNN, VGG16, InceptionV3, MobileNetV2, and Xception, to meet the second objective. The third objective involved the selection of MobileNet V3-Large after extensive trial and error. This model demonstrates superior features, achieving a 3.2% increase in accuracy over previous models in the "ImageNet" classification, alongside a 15% reduction in latency compared to MobileNetV2.

Furthermore, MobileNet V3-Large offers a 25% improvement in detection speed. MobileNetV3 demonstrates an accuracy comparable to that of MobileNet V2 in COCO detection. By integrating several key enhancements, it successfully removes three costly layers while maintaining accuracy.

Despite the promising results achieved in this study, several limitations should be considered when interpreting the findings. The dataset was sourced exclusively from specific regions in Tanzania, which may limit the generalizability of the models to other geographical areas, poultry breeds, and farming practices. Additionally, class imbalance, particularly in the Newcastle disease category, posed challenges despite mitigation through data augmentation and oversampling, potentially introducing biases. Relying exclusively on fecal images for disease detection also presents limitations, as some infections may not manifest distinct visual features, increasing the risk of misclassification. Moreover, certain models exhibited overfitting, indicating potential limitations in their generalization capabilities, and external validation using independent datasets is necessary before field implementation. Finally, the computational resources required for training deep learning models remain considerable, which may hinder real-time analysis in resource-limited farm environments.

4 Conclusions

The advanced models demonstrated high accuracy employing four architectures: VGG16, InceptionV3, MobileNetV2, and Xception. Their implementation in our dataset yielded exceptional results, attributed to effective data set preparation and separation between trains. In transfer learning with pre-trained models, MobileNetV3 achieved the highest accuracy of 0.9833 when utilizing Fine-Tuning training. Furthermore, MobileNetV3-Large and V2 attained a maximum accuracy of 0.98. MobileNetV3-Large demonstrates a 3.2% improvement in accuracy for ImageNet classification and a 15% reduction in latency compared to MobileNetV2. Furthermore, MobileNetV3-Large achieves a 25% increase in detection speed while maintaining almost equivalent accuracy to MobileNetV2 in COCO detection. Redesign of several costly layers within MobileNetV3 is a particularly noteworthy aspect of the architecture. Certain layers in MobileNetV2 significantly contributed to model accuracy, albeit at the cost of increased computational time. MobileNetV3 successfully eliminated three costly layers while maintaining accuracy through the implementation of key improvements. MobileNetV2 has a file size of 26 MB, while MobileNetV3-Large has a file size of 15.3 MB. According to the criteria applied and the accuracies obtained by the models in this study, the MobileNet V3-Large model, achieving an accuracy of 98%, is the most effective model. We have developed MobileNetv3-Large, achieving a 27% increase in speed compared to MobileNetV2, while maintaining equivalent accuracy, and reducing the duration to three-quarters of that of MobileNetV2.

Acknowledgements. The author thanks Jana Almalki, Wafaa Ali Alrehaili, Emtenan Alansari, and Jud Alzhrani, who are students at the College of Computer Science and Engineering, University of Jeddah, for supporting this study by developing the machine learning prototype.

References

1. Mbelwa, H., Mbelwa, J., Machuve, D.: Deep convolutional neural network for chicken diseases detection. Int. J. Adv. Comput. Sci. Appl. **12**(2) (2021). https://doi.org/10.14569/ijacsa.2021.0120295
2. Okinda, C., et al.: A machine vision system for early detection and prediction of sick birds: a broiler chicken model. Biosys. Eng. **188**, 229–242 (2019). https://doi.org/10.1016/j.biosystemseng.2019.09.015
3. Machuve, D., Nwankwo, E., Mduma, N., Mbelwa, J.: Poultry diseases diagnostics models using deep learning. Front. Artif. Intell. **5**, 733345 (2022). https://doi.org/10.3389/frai.2022.733345
4. Wang, J., Shen, M., Liu, L., Xu, Y., Okinda, C.: Recognition and classification of broiler droppings based on deep convolutional neural network. J. Sens., 3823515 (2019). https://doi.org/10.1155/2019/3823515
5. Akomolafe, O.P., Medeiros, F.B.: Image detection and classification of Newcastle and Avian flu diseases infected poultry using machine learning techniques. J. Sci. Logics ICT Res. **6** (2021)
6. Banakar, A., Sadeghi, M., Shushtari, A.: An intelligent device for diagnosing avian diseases: Newcastle, infectious Bronchitis, Avian Influenza. Comput. Electron. Agric. **127**, 744–753 (2016). https://doi.org/10.1016/j.compag.2016.08.006
7. Mbelwa, H.: Image-based poultry disease detection using deep convolutional neural network (2021). https://doi.org/10.58694/20.500.12479/1344
8. Zhuang, X., Bi, M., Guo, J., Wu, S., Zhang, T.: Development of an early warning algorithm to detect sick broilers. Comput. Electron. Agric. **144**, 102–113 (2018). https://doi.org/10.1016/j.compag.2017.11.032
9. Cuan, K., Zhang, T., Li, Z., Huang, J., Ding, Y., Fang, C.: Automatic Newcastle disease detection using sound technology and deep learning method. Comput. Electron. Agric. **194**, 106740 (2022). https://doi.org/10.1016/j.compag.2022.106740
10. Hemalatha, S., Maheswaran, R.: Recognition of poultry disease in real time using extreme learning machine. In: International Conference of Disciplinary Research in Engineering and Technology (CIDRET2014), pp. 44–50 (2014)
11. Cuan, K., Zhang, T., Huang, J., Fang, C., Guan, Y.: Detection of avian influenza-infected chickens based on a chicken sound convolutional neural network. Comput. Electron. Agric. **178**, 105688 (2020). https://doi.org/10.1016/j.compag.2020.105688
12. Huang, S., Yang, Y., Li, J., Zheng, Z.: Integrating deep learning with IoT for real-time poultry disease detection. IEEE Trans. Green Commun. Networking **4**(3), 1103–1114 (2020)
13. Chauhan, R., Ghanshala, K.K., Joshi, R.: Convolutional neural network (CNN) for image detection and recognition. In: First International Conference on Secure Cyber Computing and Communication (ICSCCC), pp. 278–282 (2018). https://doi.org/10.1109/icsccc.2018.8703316

14. Lee, B., et al.: Breath analysis system with convolutional neural network (CNN) for early detection of lung cancer. Sens. Actuators B: Chem. **409**, 135578 (2024). https://doi.org/10.1016/j.snb.2024.135578
15. Simonyan, K., Zisserman, A.: Very deep convolutional networks for large-scale image recognition (2014). http://export.arxiv.org/pdf/1409.1556
16. Chollet, F.: Xception: deep learning with depthwise separable convolutions. In: Proceedings of the IEEE Conference on Computer Vision and Pattern Recognition (CVPR), pp. 1800–1807 (2017). https://doi.org/10.1109/cvpr.2017.195
17. Howard, A.G., et al.: MobileNets: efficient convolutional neural networks for mobile vision applications. arXiv preprint: https://doi.org/10.48550/arxiv.1704.04861arXiv:1704.04861 (2017)
18. Sandler, M., Howard, A., Zhu, M., Zhmoginov, A., Chen, L.C.: MobileNetV 2: inverted residuals and linear bottlenecks. In: Proceedings of the IEEE Conference on Computer Vision and Pattern Recognition (CVPR), pp. 4510–4520 (2018)

Enhancing Incident Root Cause with Confidence Using ZebraAI

Christopher Allen, Xin Bai(✉), Juan Quintana, Mason Torres, and Pramila Padmanabhan

The Microsoft Corporation, Redmond, WA 98052, USA
{challen,xinbai}@microsoft.com

Abstract. The current Azure support framework of Microsoft faces inefficiencies in its root cause analysis (RCA) process [1] due to a lack of a systematic approach, inaccurate and unactionable data, and complexity in root cause selection. These challenges hinder the ability to identify incident trends efficiently, drive product improvements, and provide seamless customer experience.

The proposed AI solution introduces a robust and adaptive RCA system that accurately classifies root causes, integrates new learnings, and streamlines the identification process. By reducing misidentifications, improving data relevance, and enhancing automation, this solution aims to minimize incident resolution time, boost customer confidence, and improve the support engineer experience. Ultimately, it enables product teams to proactively detect and address recurring issues, leading to better product quality and increased customer trust.

Keywords: Root Cause Analysis (RCA) · AI-driven Support · Microsoft Azure · Cloud Computing · Incident Diagnosis · Support Frameworks · Data-Driven Insights · Automated Troubleshooting · Customer Experience · Trend Identification

1 Introduction

In today's rapidly evolving software landscape, cloud platforms such as Microsoft Azure are central to many enterprises' critical operations. Yet, the complexity of these environments poses significant challenges for support frameworks, particularly in accurately diagnosing and classifying root causes of incidents.

Existing systems often rely on ad-hoc or outdated approaches, resulting in protracted resolution times, diminished customer trust, and limited visibility into emerging trends. These inefficiencies hinder product groups from making informed improvements, ultimately affecting both service quality and user satisfaction.

This paper introduces a comprehensive, AI-driven root cause analysis (RCA) system designed to address these pain points by streamlining how Azure support engineers identify and adapt to new or evolving scenarios. By leveraging advanced AI technologies—such as ZebraAI [2], Azure Data Explorer [3], and Copilot—the proposed solution reduces the complexity of root cause selection, ensures up-to-date data analysis,

H. R. Arabnia et al. (Eds.): CSCE 2025, CCIS 2934, pp. 435–442, 2026.
https://doi.org/10.1007/978-3-032-22190-2_31

and bolsters support accuracy. In doing so, it not only minimizes customer downtime and frustration but also empowers product teams with actionable insights for continuous product refinement.

2 ZebraAI Experiment

A ZebraAI experiment refers to a structured test or evaluation process designed to analyze, validate, or optimize the system's machine learning models and algorithms [4]. Experiments are conducted to assess ZebraAI's effectiveness in identifying root causes of incidents, improving accuracy in classification, and refining predictive capabilities.

Experiments may involve:

- Testing new models or configurations for incident classification and root cause analysis.
- Evaluating the impact of different data inputs, such as structured root causes or subject area paths.
- Comparing various AI-driven approaches to improve support case resolution.
- Measuring the accuracy and efficiency of recommendations made by ZebraAI.

These experiments help improve ZebraAI's ability to analyze incidents and enhance automated troubleshooting in Microsoft's support processes.

Figure 1 below illustrates one of the experiments on root cause we have created.

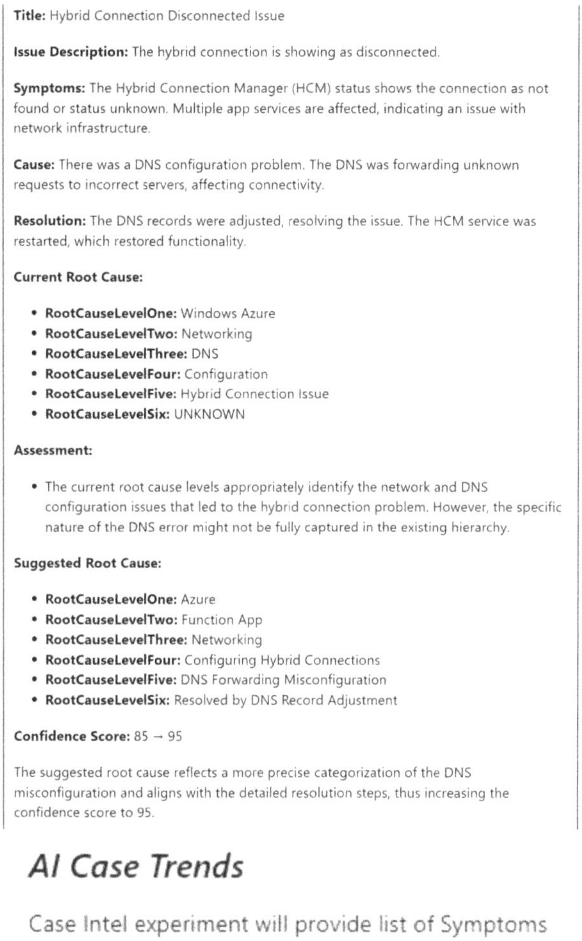
Title: Hybrid Connection Disconnected Issue

Issue Description: The hybrid connection is showing as disconnected.

Symptoms: The Hybrid Connection Manager (HCM) status shows the connection as not found or status unknown. Multiple app services are affected, indicating an issue with network infrastructure.

Cause: There was a DNS configuration problem. The DNS was forwarding unknown requests to incorrect servers, affecting connectivity.

Resolution: The DNS records were adjusted, resolving the issue. The HCM service was restarted, which restored functionality.

Current Root Cause:

- **RootCauseLevelOne:** Windows Azure
- **RootCauseLevelTwo:** Networking
- **RootCauseLevelThree:** DNS
- **RootCauseLevelFour:** Configuration
- **RootCauseLevelFive:** Hybrid Connection Issue
- **RootCauseLevelSix:** UNKNOWN

Assessment:

- The current root cause levels appropriately identify the network and DNS configuration issues that led to the hybrid connection problem. However, the specific nature of the DNS error might not be fully captured in the existing hierarchy.

Suggested Root Cause:

- **RootCauseLevelOne:** Azure
- **RootCauseLevelTwo:** Function App
- **RootCauseLevelThree:** Networking
- **RootCauseLevelFour:** Configuring Hybrid Connections
- **RootCauseLevelFive:** DNS Forwarding Misconfiguration
- **RootCauseLevelSix:** Resolved by DNS Record Adjustment

Confidence Score: 85 → 95

The suggested root cause reflects a more precise categorization of the DNS misconfiguration and aligns with the detailed resolution steps, thus increasing the confidence score to 95.

AI Case Trends

Case Intel experiment will provide list of Symptoms

Fig. 1. Experiment of Incident Root Cause

3 Data Source

In Microsoft ZebraAI, experiments can be conducted using either real customer incident data or synthetic data to ensure customer data protection. ZebraAI includes robust security capabilities that enable secure database connections, allowing authorized users to execute experiments with real data while maintaining compliance with data protection policies.

The primary objective of these experiments is to analyze real incident data to determine the root cause, ultimately enhancing support processes.

Additionally, the use of carefully designed synthetic data plays a crucial role in mitigating biases inherent in real-world datasets. By incorporating synthetic data in training models, ZebraAI can develop fairer and more balanced AI-driven solutions, improving both accuracy and fairness in incident analysis.

Figure 2 below provides an example of a synthetic data source contained within the Zebra AI environment. This synthetic dataset is designed to simulate real-world scenarios while ensuring data privacy and security. By leveraging structured formats, ZebraAI can analyze and process synthetic data in a manner similar to real customer cases, facilitating model training and validation while mitigating biases and compliance risks.

Fig. 2. Synthetic Data

4 Support Files

After artificial intelligence experiments are created using ZebraAI, a file containing the currently defined root tree, as established by the support organization, is uploaded, as illustrated in Table 1 below. Concurrently, a file detailing the subject area path (SAP) of the company's product is uploaded for analysis by ZebraAI, as shown in Table 2.

ZebraAI systematically analyzes each incident by evaluating it against the predefined structured root causes and the product's subject area paths. Based on this analysis, the system identifies the most probable root cause of the incident.

Table 1. Support Root Cause Tree

SAPRootCauseAttributedProductName	Incidents_RootCauseFullPath	Incidents_RootCauseL1Current	Incidents_RootCauseL2Current

Table 2. Company Product Subject Area Path

SapPath	SAPRootCauseAttributedProductName	Incidents_SapSupportPathL1Current	Incidents_SapSupportPathL2Current

5 Simple Prompt

A simple prompt in ZebraAI refers to engineering prompts that do not require data insertion from case data or other external sources. For instance, a prompt in ZebraAI is structured as a JSON object that provides specific instructions for the model to generate an output.

Each prompt consists of one or more messages, where each message includes a role and content. The role defines whether the message is sent or received, while the content contains the actual textual input for the model [5].

Figure 3 presents an example of a simple AI prompt in JSON format, as used in ZebraAI, which is based on GPT-4o.

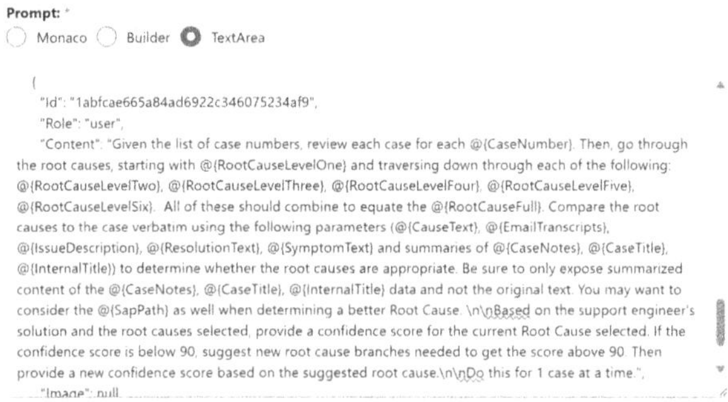

Fig. 3. Sample JSON for Simple AI Prompt

6 Confidence

After a successful experiment of root cause analysis against the incidents, a natural question will arise: how accurate of the root cause suggested to the incident? And how do we trust its recommendation?

Research on AI trust and confidence has been explored extensively [6–8]. While ZebraAI can recommend a root cause for a given case, the question remains: how confident are we in its accuracy? To enhance customer trust and decision-making, a confidence score is introduced to rank the confidence level of the recommendation. This confidence score enables customers to assess the reliability of the suggested root cause and determine whether to adopt it.

By providing a quantifiable measure of confidence, the system fosters greater transparency and empowers users to make more informed decisions. Figure 4 shows an example of confidence score on a recommended root cause.

Current Root Cause:

- **RootCauseLevelOne:** UNKNOWN
- **RootCauseLevelTwo:** UNKNOWN
- **RootCauseLevelThree:** UNKNOWN
- **RootCauseLevelFour:** UNKNOWN
- **RootCauseLevelFive:** UNKNOWN
- **RootCauseLevelSix:** UNKNOWN

Assessment:

- The issue involves misunderstanding and incorrect configuration of Microsoft Outlook and Teams applications. The current root cause does not accurately reflect the customer's problem and resolution path.

Suggested Root Cause:

- **RootCauseLevelOne:** Configuration Issue
- **RootCauseLevelTwo:** Application Setup
- **RootCauseLevelThree:** Outlook and Teams Integration
- **RootCauseLevelFour:** Calendar Sync Issue
- **RootCauseLevelFive:** User Training Required
- **RootCauseLevelSix:** Device-Specific Installation Guidance

Confidence Score: 0 → 95

Fig. 4. Root Cause Confidence Score

7 Continuous Experiment

In summary, by conducting more experiments and incorporating a confidence level in the analysis, ZebraAI enhances the accuracy and reliability of its root cause suggestions. The inclusion of a confidence level for each proposed root cause is crucial for evaluating the effectiveness of the AI tool. This added layer of insight allows support teams to make more informed decisions, increasing trust in the tool's recommendations and improving overall incident resolution. The confidence level serves as a valuable metric in determining the likelihood of a suggested root cause being correct, ensuring that the right course of action is taken with greater precision.

8 Dashboard

We can develop a Power BI dashboard to present analytics in a structured and visually intuitive format, ensuring readability and usability for Product Group (PG), Program Management (PM), Customer Support Services (CSS), and Leadership Team (LT).

This dashboard will facilitate data-driven decision-making by providing clear insights into key metrics and trends.

9 Future Enhancements

To enhance the usability of the system, we will expand beyond the current scope of Identity products and include other business units. By integrating with Service Business Intelligence System within Microsoft (SBIS), we will retrieve a real-time root cause tree, which will help with more accurate and efficient troubleshooting. Additionally, integration with Microsoft Support Agent Assist System (MSAAS) will enable the retrieval of real-time SAP Paths, providing an up-to-date view of the subject area paths for better alignment with incidents.

We will incorporate Copilot functionality into Copilot for DFM, which will support decision-making in identifying the best fit for case alignment. This will include determining if the issue in the case aligns better under a different SAP path from the SAP

Tree. If a better SAP is found, the system will specify which SAP is recommended, along with a confidence score ranging from 0 to 100, where 0 means no confidence, and 100 means it's the best possible choice.

Lastly, we will produce a Power BI dashboard to present the analytics in a format that is both readable and usable for key stakeholders such **as PG, PM, CSS, and LT.** This dashboard will help provide clear insights into the trends and metrics necessary for strategic decision-making.

By implementing these measures, the solution will not only increase usability across business units but also ensure that real-time data integration, along with advanced analytics, contributes to improved incident tracking, root cause analysis, and decision-making.

10 Conclusions

In the dynamic landscape of Azure supportability, there is an increasing demand for a robust and efficient system that can accurately identify, classify, and track the root causes of incidents. This system must be agile enough to adapt to the evolving nature of support scenarios, ensuring that root cause analysis is both comprehensive and up to date. Moreover, it should facilitate the seamless integration of new root causes into the existing framework, thereby enhancing the overall effectiveness and accuracy of the support process.

The ultimate goal is to streamline the supportability infrastructure, reducing the time spent on root cause identification, and ensuring that the support provided to customers is accurate and timely. By implementing such a system, product groups will be empowered to identify recurring trends in product-related issues, which will in turn help direct targeted solutions. This proactive approach not only reduces the time customers experience issues but also bolsters their confidence in our products and services.

Additionally, the system will enhance the experience of support engineers in the Defect-Field Management (DFM) process by guiding them in selecting the most appropriate root cause. This will help reduce instances of misaligned root cause selections, ensuring that the Root Cause data is both relevant and accurate. In turn, this will improve the quality of support interactions, leading to quicker resolutions and a more efficient support process overall.

In conclusion, implementing a robust and efficient system for root cause analysis is essential to improving the supportability of Azure products. By streamlining the identification and classification of incidents, the system can significantly reduce the time spent on root cause identification and enhance the accuracy of support provided to customers. This proactive approach will empower product groups to identify recurring trends and direct targeted solutions, ultimately improving customer satisfaction and confidence. Additionally, the system will support engineers in the Defect-Field Management process, ensuring more accurate root cause selections and faster resolution times. Overall, this approach will enhance both the efficiency and quality of the support process, leading to a more seamless customer experience.

Acknowledgements. We would like to thank Mrs. Lavanya Shridhara of the Microsoft Security CxE Support team as well as Mrs. Preeti Kamat and Mrs. Elisa Panelli of the Microsoft Identity EEE team who have overseen the project and provided some valuable feedback and support.

References

1. Shiff, L., Hertvik, J.: RCA in IT: Root Cause Analysis for IT Environments, The Business of IT Blog, RCA in IT: Root Cause Analysis for IT Environments – BMC Software | Blogs (2020)
2. Zebra AI: Managing the Development of Large Software Systems, Proceedings of IEEE WESCON 26 (August): 1–9 (202x)
3. Azure Data Explorer documentation, Azure Data Explorer documentation - Azure Data Explorer | Microsoft Learn
4. ZebraAI Experiments, ZebraAI Experiments - Overview
5. ZebraAI – Readme, README - Overview
6. AI's Trust Problem, AI's Trust Problem
7. Trust in AI: progress, challenges, and future directions, Trust in AI: progress, challenges, and future directions | Humanities and Social Sciences Communications
8. Don't Trust Everything You Read: Confidence Scores in LLMs & Accuracy, Confidence Scores in LLMs: Ensure 100% Accuracy in Large Language Models

A Study on Context-Based Trustworthiness to Decrease Confirmation Bias and Improve the Evenness of Generated Content

Hyun Jung Lee(✉)

Goyang City Institute, Goyang 10464, Republic of South Korea
hjlee@goyang.re.kr, hjlee5249@gmail.com

Abstract. While the usefulness of AI is growing, it also raises concerns of side effects, such as hallucinations, fake news, and confirmation bias. To decrease the side effects, one important issue is to increase the guarantee of the trustworthiness of the generated content. In this research, a 4-classification metric such as a truth table composed of positive(+) and negative(−) values is proposed to decrease the side effects and to increase the trustworthiness of the content from generative AI. The 4-classification metric is constructed in two dimensions that is based on the content's contextual consistency and the diversity of referred sources. Four-classification is composed of evenness, bias, oddness and divergence, which are used as measures of trustworthiness. Evenness indicates that the content is highly consistent and is extracted by diverse sources. Bias indicates that the content is highly consistent but is not extracted from diverse sources. Oddness indicates that the content is extracted from highly diverse sources but is inconsistent. Divergence is that the content is neither diversely extracted from cited sources nor contextually consistent. To examine the consistency of the generated content, a Knowledge Graph is adopted using the contextual distance of cited sources and similarity among the generated content's entities. It is important to increase the trustworthiness of the content according to the decrease in the side effects of the generated content. To do this, a trustworthiness model based on two dimensions and 4-classification is proposed depending on the content's internal contextual consistency and the diversity of the referred sources.

Keywords: Generative AI · Context · Trustworthiness · Knowledge Graph

1 Introduction

Recently, the information and content from generative AI models might not be free from plausible issues such as hallucinations, fake news, and confirmation bias [7, 9, 10]. Generative AI models can create plausible-sounding content [1]. It can also happen that facts vs. falsehood are intertwined in the content [5]. This leads to a decrease in the trustworthiness of the generated content as well as in AI models. Therefore, increasing the trustworthiness of the generated results is important.

For trustworthiness, it is necessary to consider the internal consistency of the generated content because ensuring trustworthiness requires it. Nevertheless, reliance on a

H. R. Arabnia et al. (Eds.): CSCE 2025, CCIS 2934, pp. 443–454, 2026.
https://doi.org/10.1007/978-3-032-22190-2_32

single source is inadequate to guarantee internal consistency. To improve trustworthiness, the diversity of the sources used to derive the content is considered. If the cited sources for the generated content are limited in scope, then, even with strong internal consistency, ensuring trustworthiness is difficult because those sources may themselves be biased. For example, as one type of side effect, confirmation bias may occur.

In this study, trustworthiness is assessed through two considerations: the internal contextual consistency of the generated content and the diversity of sources, defined as the breadth and range. Contextual consistency is examined by the degree of similarity among the components. Diversity is measured by the degree of distance to examine the range of associated and referred sources. Therefore, defining the consistency and the diversity as two orthogonal axes, the proposed 4-classification is composed of evenness, bias, oddness and divergence as the measurements of trustworthiness.

The evenness classification has features such as high internal consistency of content and a high variety of sources. In this case, side effects such as confirmation bias is decreased, and the trustworthiness of the content can be improved. If the consistency is low within the content generated by AI models, then trustworthiness decreases. In addition, even if a wide range of sources is used to derive the content, if the consistency is low, then trustworthiness can also decrease because there is a high potential for inconsistency, such as conflicts among the content's components. If there is a high degree of variation among results when the same question is solved, then the trustworthiness also decreases. Therefore, the level of consistency among content components and the level of the diverse ranges of associated resources are used to measure the trustworthiness of the generated content from AI models.

To do this, as structured data, a Knowledge Graph is adopted, which is composed of context-based components as entities and relations based on the contextual structure. Using the Knowledge Graph, it is easier to transform and examine the contextual similarity and distance among comparative entities because of the consistency of the content and the diversity of sources. To enhance trustworthiness, evenness, conceptualized as both the internal consistency of the content and the diversity of its sources, is evaluated by examining similarity across components and the distance of the range of associated references.

This paper is organized as follows. Section 2 discusses related works, including side effects such as plausible issues, generative AI models and Knowledge Graphs. Section 3 describes the overall architecture of the proposed framework to enhance the trustworthiness of the generated content. Section 4 illustrates the processes of trustworthiness with the hypothetical cases. Finally, we present the conclusion and suggest further research in connection with the trustworthiness of the content generated by AI models.

2 Literature Review

Although the popularization of generative AI models has increased the effectiveness of daily life, it has also raised concerns about side effects associated with the endless generation of seemingly plausible results such as fake news and hallucinations [1, 7]. Although numerous studies have sought to resolve these problems, mitigating their side effects [4, 5, 7, 9, 13, 20] and increasing the trustworthiness of generated content remain challenging tasks [1, 5]. It may not be possible to perfectly verify whether the generated content is true [5]. Nevertheless, assessing the veracity of the content produced by AI models is important.

There, we focus on the examination of the contextual similarity for the content's internal consistency and the distances among the referred and associated resources. To represent the contextual relations, a Knowledge Graph is usually used to measure the similarity and distances among the comparatives variables [8–10, 12, 15, 19, 22]. A Knowledge Graph is composed of entities that include semantic features and relations to present semantically interlinked relations [3, 6, 10, 17]. In addition, Knowledge Graph is useful for transforming multiple types of data, such as images, text, and sound [11], because it is possible to semantically present the contextual entities and the relations of the generated contents. Therefore, big-tech companies such as Google, Facebook, Microsoft, and Yahoo also adopt Knowledge Graphs as a way of processing semantic data [12]. Google Bard (subsequently rebranded Gemini) started providing a genuine citation for the generative content in May 2023 [4], and recently, ChatGPT also released the fact-check tool 'Deep Background – Fact checks and Context' in o3 on June 16, 2025 [2]. Major generative AI models equipped with web-searching functions, including Copilot, Perplexity, Claude, Gemini, and ChatGPT, promote transparency by supplying source links [4, 16, 20]. Thus, citations can be checked and considered indicators of the trustworthiness of generated content. This research focuses on both the breadth of sources cited and the internal consistency of content, assessed using a Knowledge Graph.

3 Overall Architecture

As shown in Fig. 1, generative AI models create responses to user queries by drawing on sources such as web pages, social media, broadcasts, blogs, and short-form content. Given the risks of hallucinations and misinformation, fact-checking is essential. In this research, trustworthiness is assessed through two dimensions: the contextual consistency of the generated content and the diversity of its referenced sources.

As shown in Table 1, to verify the degree of plausible sound of the content generated by the AI models, trustworthiness is conceptualized across a 4-classification scheme, using evenness, bias, oddness, and divergence as the classes, each of which is derived from the content's contextual consistency and the breadth of its referenced sources.

If the generated content is highly consistent and is extracted from a wide range of sources, the content attains a high degree of trustworthiness, categorized as evenness, because the content can be evenly organized using a variety of data. However, although the content is highly consistent, if the diversity of referred sources is not guaranteed, trustworthiness is also not guaranteed because the generated content with a strong tendency toward bias is classified as bias. As a kind of side effect, it can lead to confirmation bias. Even if it is referred to from diverse sources, if the generated content is inconsistent, trustworthiness cannot be guaranteed, and the content is categorized under oddness because it is highly likely to be uninformative or ambiguous. If the generated content is inconsistent and the referred sources are not diverse, trustworthiness is reduced, and the informativeness of the content is not guaranteed, which is categorized as oddness.

The trustworthiness is based on C as the content's contextual consistency and D as the diversity of sources and depends on 4-classification as follows.

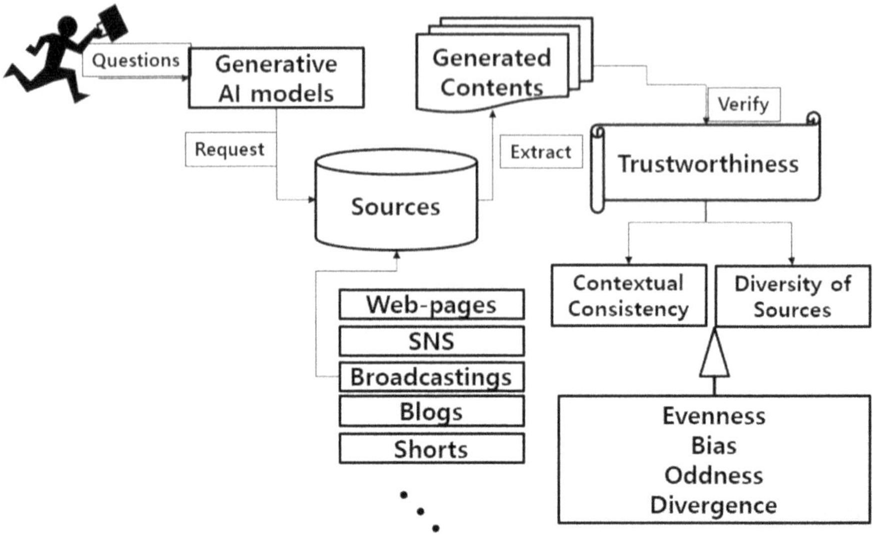

Fig. 1. Overall architecture

Table 1. Trustworthiness of the content generated by AI models

Trustworthiness		Diversity of Source (D)	
		D (−, low)	D (+, high)
Contextual Consistency (C)	C (−, low)	Divergence	Oddness
	C (+, high)	Bias	Evenness

Evenness - High Trustworthy (C-high & D-high). If the consistency of the generated content extracted from a variety of associated sources is high, then the content has a potentially higher level of trustworthiness because the content is consistently gathered from diverse sources.

Bias - Less Trustworthy (C-high & D-low). If the content's contextual consistency is high but the range of the referred sources is narrow, the content has a potentially lower level of trustworthiness because it is very likely to contain bias. Therefore, the trustworthiness of the content is not guaranteed. There is a high possibility that confirmation bias is a kind of side effect.

Oddness - Highly not Trustworthy (C-low & D-high). Even if the content is extracted from a wide range of sources, if the content's contextual consistency is at a lower level, then the content's informativeness has a high likelihood of being at a lower level of significance. It resembles the results of search engines, which typically list multiple items containing different contents for a given keyword query. Even if the diversity of sources is guaranteed, the content is illustrated without consistency, so it is categorized by oddness.

Divergence - Not Trustworthy (C-low & D-low). If the content exhibits low internal consistency and draws on a narrow range of sources, then it reflects divergence because it is based on inconsistent content as well as an insufficient range in cited sources.

The trustworthiness of the generated content is related to the degree of diversity of sources and the content's contextual consistency. Therefore, it is important to examine the consistency of content and the range of cited sources to generate the content. It might be necessary to examine the consistency and diversity of the content of the referred sources. To do this, a Knowledge Graph is adopted to process the contextual relations among context-based entities to examine the contextual similarity and the diversity of sources [3, 6, 18]. Knowledge Graphs are usually used to transform information into structured data, especially captured multitype semantic information [11, 12, 17, 19, 22]. A Knowledge Graph is composed of entities and the relations among them. To examine trustworthiness, we measure the proximity among the contextual contents in the Knowledge Graph. To measure the content's contextual consistency and the diversity of the referred sources, it is necessary to calculate the similarity and distance among the entities. The contextual consistency of the generated content depends on the similarity among entities. Therefore, if there is high similarity, trustworthiness is likely to be high. Additionally, if the diversity of referred sources is high, then the content has a high possibility of being trustworthy. Therefore, to classify side effects such as bias and oddness, it is necessary to examine the similarity and distance among the entities of the content. First, each entity can be compared with other entities in the generated content. Second, we examine the similarity for the contextual consistency among entities and the distance as the level of the diversity of associated sources. Trustworthiness is based on the similarity among entities of the content and the distance of the diversity of the sources. That is, a high level of trustworthiness results from strong internal consistency and a broad range of referenced sources.

4 Trustworthiness Framework

The proposed trustworthiness (T) is divided into the 4-classification scheme depending on the content's contextual consistency (C) and the diversity of sources (D).

Trustworthiness (T) = {Content's contextual consistency (C), Diversity of sources (D)}, $T = \{(C, D) \mid -1 \leq C \leq 1, -1 \leq D \leq 1\}$.

As shown in Fig. 2, C is located on the horizontal axis to present the contextual similarity among the contents and ranges between -1 and 1 and D is located on the vertical axis to present the distance among the referred sources and ranges between -1 and 1. As shown in Figs. 2 and 3, T is determined by the 4-classification on the value of (C, D), such as (+, +), (+, −), (−, +), and (−, −). If T takes on positive values in both dimensions (+, +) as the contextual similarity among the contents and the distance among the referred sources, the trustworthiness of the generated content lies in the 'Evenness' classification with high trustworthiness. If the value of contextual similarity is positive and the value of the distance of sources is negative, T lies in the 'Bias' classification with values (+, −). It shows that while the generated content demonstrates internal consistency, it draws on a limited range of sources. In this case, the probability of confirmation bias occurring is high. The third classification is composed of (−, +) as the values of T. This case is classified as 'Oddness,' characterized by inconsistency despite diversified sources, similar to the results generated by conventional keyword-based search engines. 'Divergence' is located in the fourth classification with trustworthiness values of (−, −), indicating inconsistent content and undiversified sources. This means that the generated content is uninformative and poorly organized.

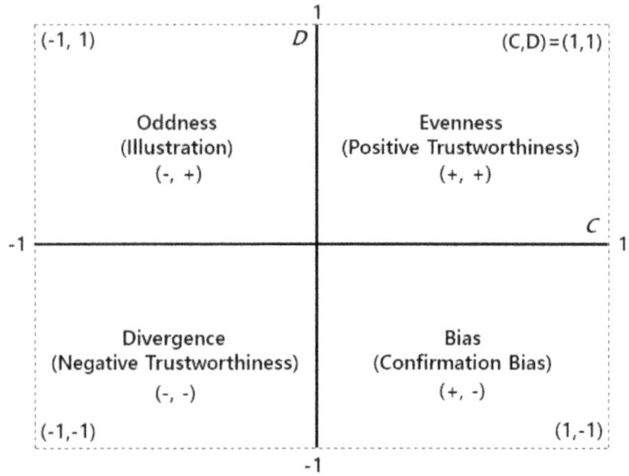

Fig. 2. Trustworthiness in the 4-classification scheme depends on evenness, bias, divergence and oddness.

4.1 Contextual Consistency

The degree of contextual consistency ranges between −1 and 1, i.e., $-1 \leq C \leq 1$. The probability of consistency increases as the value approaches 1.

Degree of Contextual Consistency (C) = {Degree of the Consistency (dS), Degree of oddness (dB)}.

The degree of the generated content C is examined by dS as the similarity among the entities and dB as the degree of biased entities of the content. To examine the contextual consistency of the content, it is necessary to examine the contextual similarity among the entities of the content. If there is a lower level of consistency among the entities of the content, then the value of C lies between 0 to −1. If there is a higher level of consistent entities of the content, then the value of C lies between 0 and 1. An illustration of the degree of contextual similarity and bias between comparable entities of the ith content of the contextual consistency for trustworthiness is shown in Fig. 4.

$dS = \sum_{i}^{n} ds_i/n$: for all n, n is a number of comparable entities and ds_i is the degree of contextual similarity of the ith content.

Trustworthiness		Diversity of Sources (D)	
		−1 (Lower Diverse)	1 (Higher Diverse)
Contextual Consistency (C)	−1 (Lower Consistent)	Lower Trustworthiness Divergence (−, −)	Less Trustworthiness Oddness (−, +)
	1 (Higher Consistent)	Less Trustworthiness Bias (+, −)	Higher Trustworthiness Evenness (+, +)

Fig. 3. Higher trustworthiness depends on the contextual consistency of the content and the diversity of sources.

$ds_i = \sum_{\mathrm{j,\,k}}^{\mathrm{n}} sim(c_{ij}, c_{ik})/\mathrm{n}$: consistency is based on the similarity between c_{ij} and c_{ik}, i.e., the jth entity and the kth entity of the ith content.

$$ds_i \text{ is the degree of the } i^{th} \text{ content's similarity, i.e., } -1 \leq ds_i \leq 1.$$

$dB = \sum_{\mathrm{i}}^{\mathrm{n}} db_i/n$: for all n, n is a number of comparable entities and db_i is the degree of bias of the ith content.

$db_i = \sum_{\mathrm{j,\,k}}^{\mathrm{n}} bias(c_{ij}, c_{ik})/n$: based on the degree of the bias between c_{ij} and c_{ik}, i.e., the jth entity and the kth entity of the ith content.

$$db_i \text{ is the degree of the } i^{th} \text{ content's bias where } -1 \leq db_i \leq 1.$$

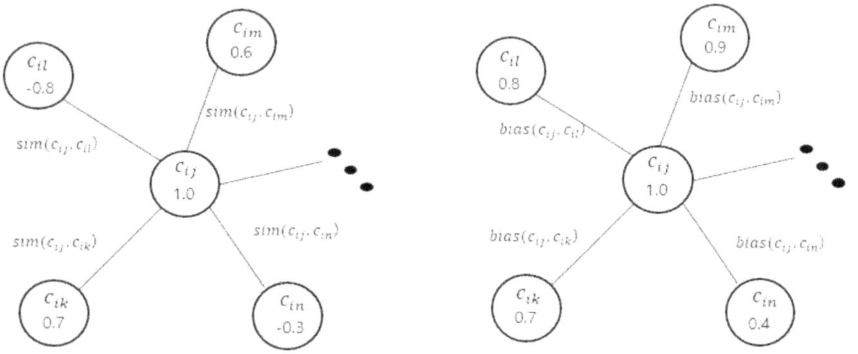

Fig. 4. Illustrations of the degree of contextual similarity and bias between entities of the ith content of the contextual consistency for trustworthiness.

4.2 Source Diversity

To guarantee the trustworthiness of the generated content, examining the diversity of the associated sources to extract the content is necessary. There are various types of sources, such as YouTube videos, shorts, journals, broadcasts, and reels. It is assumed that the wider the range of sources used is, the more trustworthy the content becomes.

Hypothetical data to present the degree of diversity of the associated sources are shown in Fig. 5. Each entity, including its own features, presents a degree of diversity between -1 and 1. As the value approaches 1, the probability of source diversity increases.

Diversity of Sources (D) = {Degree of Diversity (dD), Degree of Oddness (dO)}.

As the diversity of the generated content, D is examined by dD and dO, where dD presents the distance among the sources to measure the degree of variety of sources and dO shows the degree of oddness among the associated sources. D ranges between -1 and 1, i.e., $-1 \leq D \leq 1$. If the range of the associated sources has a lower degree, then D presents a negative value from 0 to -1, and the diversity of sources is significantly decreased. To examine the diversity of the associated sources, it is necessary to examine the distance among the referred sources. If the diversity of the sources is greater, then D is a positive between 0 and 1.

$dD = \sum_{\mathrm{i}}^{\mathrm{n}} dd_i/n$: for all n, n is the number of comparable associated sources and dd_i is athe degree of distance among the associated sources of the ith content.

$dd_i = \sum_{\mathrm{j,\,k}}^{\mathrm{n}} dist(s_{ij}, s_{ik})/n$: this is based on the distance between s_{ij} and s_{ik} i.e., the jth and k^{th} sources of the ith content, where $-1 \leq dd_i \leq 1$.

$dO = \sum_{\mathrm{i}}^{\mathrm{n}} do_i/n$: for all n, n is the number of comparable associated sources and do_i is the degree of oddness among the cited sources of the ith content.

$do_i = \sum_{\mathrm{j,\,k}}^{\mathrm{n}} odd(s_{ij}, s_{ik})/n$: this is based on the rate of oddness sources between s_{ij} and s_{ik}, i.e., the jth and k^{th} sources of the ith content, where $-1 \leq do_i \leq 1$, and do_i is the degree of oddnees among the cited sources of the ith content.

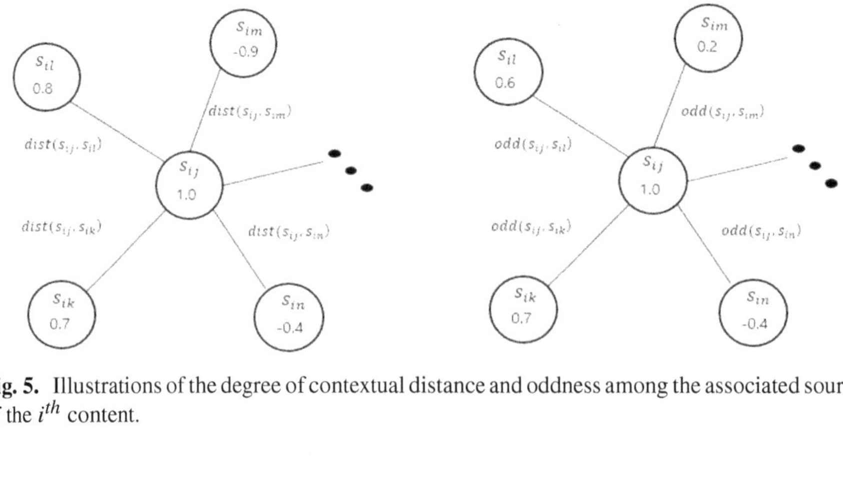

Fig. 5. Illustrations of the degree of contextual distance and oddness among the associated sources of the ith content.

4.3 Knowledge Graph

To calculate the contextual similarity among the content and distance among the cited sources, a Knowledge Graph is applied. The Knowledge Graph is composed of entities E and predicates P as the structured data to represent the multiple relations between entities.

$KG = (E, P)$, where KG is a Knowledge Graph that is composed of entities and the relations among them.

$E = \{e_1, e_2, \ldots, e_n\}$, where E is a set of entities and e_i is the ith entity that is composed of sources s_i or contents c_j.

$P \subseteq E \times E = \{p_1, p_2, \ldots, p_m\}$, where P is a set of predicates as relations between entities that can be used to examine the contextual similarity among content and the distance among cited sources.

An entity is composed of features to present the characteristics of its content or sources. The features of the entity can be related to the associated sources to generate the content. The similarity among entities can be calculated by feature-based components. In a Knowledge Graph, the content and cited sources can be transformed into entities, and the relations among the entities are presented by predicates. The Knowledge Graph can be constructed into an interaction matrix with interrelated relations among the entities. If it is possible to identify inconsistent entities within the content in a Knowledge Graph, then it is possible to propagate from these entities to efficiently examine the trustworthiness of the content. Furthermore, trustworthiness can be evaluated through the reasoning of inconsistent entities, assessing both content consistency and source diversity.

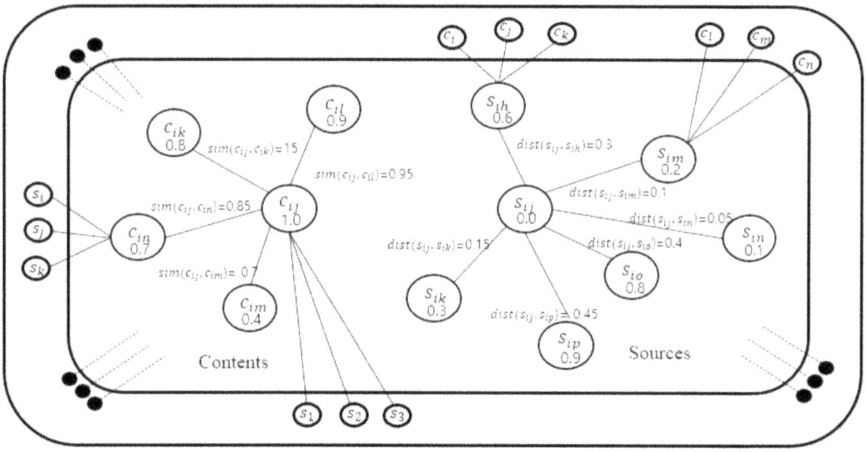

Fig. 6. An illustration of the similarity between the entities of the generated content and the distance among the cited sources.

4.4 Illustration

In this study, T is the set of trustworthiness of the generated content composed of C and D. In C, the degree of consistency represents the level of positive and negative similarity among the contents. In D, the degree of diversity represents the distances among the cited sources. The consistency of the generated content is calculated by the similarity among the entities of the generated contents, and the diversity is calculated by the distance among the referenced sources, as shown in Fig. 6.

Table 2 shows the entity outcomes depending on the similarity between contents and the diversity between sources. The entity outcomes are categorized into four classifications associated with three side effects and one case of evenness. First, if the similarity among entities is consistent but the referenced sources lack diversity, the entity may be biased and should be excluded from the contents. Second, if the similarity among entities is inconsistent while the referenced sources are diverse, the entity reflects oddness and may also be excluded. Third, if the similarity among entities is inconsistent and the referenced sources are not diverse, the entity reflects divergence and may still be excluded. Finally, if the similarity among entities is consistent and the referenced sources are diverse, the entity reflects evenness and can contribute positively to the overall consistency of the content.

Table 2. Entity outcomes depending on the similarity between contents and the diversity between sources.

Similarity between Contents	Distance among Sources	Outcome
Consistent	Not Diverse	Entity may be biased → can be excluded
Not Consistent	Diverse	Entity reflects oddness → may be excluded
Not Consistent	Not Diverse	Entity reflects diversity → may be excluded
Consistent	Diverse	Entity reflects evenness and contributes to content consistency

The trustworthiness of the content indicates if the entity is similar to other entities and is examined by a variety of types of sources. Otherwise, if the cited sources are biased even if the entity is consistent with other components, then it is highly likely to result in confirmation bias as a side effect.

5 Conclusions

This research focuses on the trustworthiness of the content generated by AI models. It is based on the internal consistency of the content and the diversity of associated sources. Early generative AI models were popularly trained by fine-tuning with transformer-based reinforcement learning with human feedback (RLHF) [14]. Given the considerable development of generative AI models, providing the associated genuine citations as the sources for the generated content [4, 14, 18, 21] to increase the trustworthiness is common. However, it is still not easy to guarantee the trustworthiness of the generated content. For instance, fake news can also be highly consistent, but it is likely to easily introduce confirmation bias. It is important to prevent these kinds of side effects to improve trustworthiness. In this work, many types of sources and a variety of cited sources are considered to examine the trustworthiness of the content generated by AI models [8]. To do this, it is necessary to examine the contextual consistency and the diversity of associated sources for the generated content. Therefore, a Knowledge Graph is applied to represent structured data with entities as context variables and predicates as relations between entities [17]. With respect to trustworthiness, the similarity of the consistency among the entities within the contents and the distance for the diversity of cited sources are examined. The trustworthiness of the AI-generated content is determined by the contextual consistency of the content and the diversity of the cited sources.

In this work, the proposed framework of trustworthiness is based on improving the trustworthiness of the content generated by AI models. Trustworthiness is based on contextual consistency and diversity of cited sources. A 4-classification scheme, including evenness, oddness, bias and divergence, is developed that depends on the contextual consistency and the diversity of the cited sources. First, if the content is inconsistent and the cited sources are not diverse, then the generated content is not trustworthy and reflects divergence. Second, if the content is highly consistent but is extracted by biased sources, then the outcome represents bias. It is highly possible that the content reflects confirmation bias. Third, if the content is inconsistent but is extracted from a variety of sources, then it reflects the oddness of the content. It is similar to illustrating the search results of search engines. Finally, if the content is highly consistent and extracted by diverse sources, then the outcome reflects evenness and high trustworthiness.

In this work, a Knowledge Graph is applied to structured data consisting of entities and predicates to transform multiple types of data into entities of the generated content and the cited sources. To examine both the contextual consistency and the diversity of sources, similarity and distance measurements are proposed. Furthermore, the structure of the proposed Knowledge Graph is specified, including its entities and predicates, as well as the methods for calculating similarity and distance, including the propagation method to infer reasoning and identify inconsistent entities in the content. The proposed framework must be implemented, and its usefulness must be verified through experimentation.

References

1. Bani-Hani, A., Adedugbe, O., Benkhelifa, E., Majdalawieh, M., Al-Obeidat, F.: A semantic model for context-based fake news detection on social media. In: 2020 IEEE/ACS 17th International Conference on Computer Systems and Applications (AICCSA) (2020)
2. Caulfield, M.: Deep Background GPT Released (2025). https://mikecaulfield.substack.com/p/deep-background-gpt-released
3. Fensel, D., et al.: Knowledge Graphs, pp. 1–10. Springer International Publishing, Cham, Switzerland (2020)
4. Google Blog: Bard updates from Google I/O 2023: Images, new features (2023)
5. Guo, Z., Schlichtkrull, M., Vlachos, A.: A survey on automated fact-checking. Trans. Assoc. Comput. Linguist. **10**, 178–206 (2022)
6. Hogan, A., et al.: Knowledge graphs. ACM Comput. Surv. **54**(4) (2021). Article 71

7. Ji, Z., et al.: Survey of hallucination in natural language generation. ACM Comput. Surv. **55**, 1–38 (2023)
8. Lee, H.J., Kim, E., Sohn, M.: A method for the contents curation using Receiver Operating Characteristic (ROC) curve. In: Proceedings of the Interdisciplinary Conference on Mechanics, Computers and Electrics (ICMECE 2022), pp. 260–265 (2022)
9. Lee, H.J., Park, B.: How to reduce confirmation bias using linked open data knowledge repository. In: IEEE International Conference on Big Data and Smart Computing (BigComp), pp. 410–416 (2020)
10. Mayank, M., Sharma, S., Sharma, R.: DEAP-FAKED: knowledge graph based approach for fake news detection. In: IEEE/ACM International Conference on Advances in Social Networks Analysis and Mining (ASONAM) (2022)
11. Mezni, H., Benslimane, D., Bellatreche, L.: Context-aware service recommendation based on knowledge graph embedding. IEEE Trans. Knowl. Data Eng. **34**(11), 5225–5238 (2022)
12. Moon, C., Harenberg, S., Slankas, J., Samatova, N.F.: Learning contextual embeddings for knowledge graph completion. In: PACIS 2017 Proceedings (2017)
13. Obeidat, F.: A semantic model for context-based fake news detection on social media. In: 2020 IEEE/ACS 17th International Conference on Computer Systems and Applications (AICCSA) (2020)
14. OpenAI: GPT-4 Technical Report (2023)
15. Paulheim, H.: Knowledge graph refinement: a survey of approaches and evaluation methods. Semant. Web **8**, 489–508 (2017)
16. Qutub, A.: Evaluating Top AI Assistants: Claude, Gemini, ChatGPT, Mistral, Perplexity, and CoPilot (2025). https://enterprisemonkey.com.au/compare-top-ai-assistants/
17. Shi, B., Zheng, Z., Tian, T., Du, W.: Feature similarity learning enhanced knowledge graph-based convolutional networks for recommendation. In: 2021 6th International Symposium on Computer and Information Processing Technology (ISCIPT), pp. 693–698 (2021)
18. Touvron, H., et al.: LLaMA: Open and Efficient Foundation Language Models. Meta AI (2023)
19. Troussas, C., Krouska, A., Tselenti, P., Kardaras, D.K., Barbounaki, S.: Enhancing personalized educational content recommendation through cosine similarity-based knowledge graphs and contextual signals. Information **14**(9), 505 (2023)
20. University of Arizona Libraries, What is hallucination (in models like ChatGPT)? (2025). https://ask.library.arizona.edu/faq/407990
21. Wu, Y., Wang, L., Kai, C., Peng, M.: Dynamics-based location prediction and neural network fine-tuning for task offloading in vehicular networks. KSII Trans. Internet Inf. Syst. **17**(12), 3416–3435 (2023)
22. Yang, C., Zhu, Y., Zhong, M., Li, R.: Semantic similarity computation in knowledge graphs: comparisons and improvements. In: 2019 IEEE 35th International Conference on Data Engineering Workshops (ICDEW), pp. 249–252 (2019)

Evolving Generators Using Policy Gradients with Parameter-Based Exploration for InfoGAN Training

Mark Nuppnau[1], Khalid Kattan[2], and R.G. Reynolds[1](✉)

[1] Department of Computer Science, Wayne State University, Detroit, USA
robert.reynolds@wayne.edu

[2] Department of Computer Science, University of Michigan-Dearborn, Dearborn, Michigan, USA

Abstract. Previous work [1] showed that embedding cultural knowledge into evolutionary optimization improved MNIST handwritten-digit classification. We therefore ask whether policy gradients with parameter-based exploration (PGPE), in the absence of a cultural layer, can successfully train generative adversarial networks (GANs) for image synthesis. Classical GANs trained with backpropagation are prone to mode collapse, vanishing gradient, and unstable dynamics. Evolutionary search, being gradient-free, could in principle alleviate some of these issues. InfoGAN encourages disentangled latent variables by explicitly maximising the mutual information between a latent code, and the generated sample. This property could inspire a new attention mechanism in an InfoGAN-style transformer.

We therefore build a hybrid InfoGAN: the discriminator and auxiliary Q-network are trained with back-propagation, while the generator is evolved with PGPE. PGPE approaches, but does not fully reach, convergence on a generator that yields consistently high-quality, disentangled digits. The main bottleneck is converting the multi-objective feedback available during GAN training into the scalar fitness signal that PGPE requires. We evaluate three scalarization strategies–normalization, weighted sums, and non-dominated sorting. Each reveals different aspects of PGPE's search dynamics yet ultimately restrains convergence.

In future work we will re-incorporate cultural knowledge to drive dynamic objective weighting during evolution and will extend the framework to deeper architectures and more diverse datasets.

Keywords: evolutionary algorithms · optimization · cultural algorithms · InfoGAN

1 Introduction

Since their debut in 2017, Transformer architectures [2] have upended sequential modeling by replacing recurrence with self-attention [3], which computes pairwise

H. R. Arabnia et al. (Eds.): CSCE 2025, CCIS 2934, pp. 455–462, 2026.
https://doi.org/10.1007/978-3-032-22190-2_33

similarity between queries, keys, and values. By running multiple attention heads in parallel, the model can capture a variety of semantic relationships at once. Yet standard multi-head attention lacks a built-in mechanism for disentangling latent factors or enforcing interpretable attention patterns.

In contrast, Generative Adversarial Networks (GANs), introduced by Goodfellow *et al.* in 2014, frame generation as a two-player game. A generator G maps a random noise vector $z \sim p_z(z)$ to a synthetic sample $G(z)$, while a discriminator D learns to distinguish real data samples $x \sim p_{\text{data}}(x)$ from generated samples.

The generator is trained to maximize the discriminator's error on fake samples, and the discriminator is trained to minimize its classification error across both real and fake samples. This can be written as a value function $V(D, G)$, where the generator and discriminator play the following minimax game:

$$\min_G \max_D V(D, G) = \mathbb{E}_{x \sim p_{\text{data}}} \big[\log D(x) \big] \; + \; \mathbb{E}_{z \sim p_z} \big[\log\big(1 - D(G(z))\big) \big],$$

The binary cross-entropy (BCE) loss functions used are

$$\begin{aligned} \mathcal{L}_D &= \mathbb{E}_{x \sim p_{\text{data}}} \big[\log D(x) \big] \; + \; \mathbb{E}_{z \sim p_z} \big[\log\big(1 - D(G(z))\big) \big], \\ \mathcal{L}_G &= \mathbb{E}_{z \sim p_z} \big[\log D(G(z)) \big]. \end{aligned}$$

Because the loss landscape shifts continually as both players co-adapt, GAN training is notoriously unstable–prone to mode collapse, vanishing gradients, and oscillatory dynamics. Mode collapse happens when the discriminator learns to classify a specific mode as fake and the generator shifts to a new mode and the problem continues. When the discriminator converges early in training, it provides a weak signal to the generator due to vanishing gradients and the generator cannot converge.

InfoGAN [4], an information-theoretic extension of the traditional GAN, offers the ability to learn disentangled representations without the need for labels. With InfoGAN, the generator receives both a noise vector z and a latent code c and maximizes the mutual information between c and $G(z, c)$ so that every latent vector in the latent space can be decomposed as (z, c). This yields an information-rich latent space. The minimax game between the generator and discriminator is updated to include the maximization of mutual information term $I(c, G(z, c))$:

$$\begin{aligned} \min_G \max_D V(D, G) &= \mathbb{E}_{x \sim p_{\text{data}}} \big[\log D(x) \big] \\ &+ \mathbb{E}_{z \sim p_z, c \sim p_c} \big[\log\big(1 - D(G(z, c))\big) \big] \; - \; \lambda I(c; G(z, c)), \end{aligned}$$

However, $I(c, G(z, c))$ is intractable. An auxiliary network, Q is introduced to form a lower bound on the mutual information. This auxiliary network is added to the value function such that the generator and q-network together play the minimax game with the discriminator:

$$\min_{G,Q}\max_{D} V(D,G,Q) = \mathbb{E}_{x\sim p_{\text{data}}}\big[\log D(x)\big] + \mathbb{E}_{z\sim p_z, c\sim p_c}\big[\log\big(1 - D(G(z,c))\big)\big] - \lambda\mathbb{E}_{z\sim p_z, c\sim p_c}\big[\log\big(Q(c|G(z,c))\big)\big]$$

This ability to learn disentangled representations is a highly desirable property for improving model interpretability. However, InfoGAN is still susceptible to the common pitfalls of traditional GANs which limit the scalability of InfoGAN on more complex datasets and model architectures. If InfoGAN could scale to more complex tasks with a more stable training approach, we could see a new type of attention mechanism for the Transformer to disentangle latent factors. This could lead to a more interpretable language model.

In pursuit of this goal, we implement a hybrid InfoGAN algorithm. We use the evolutionary algorithm PGPE to train the generator and backpropagation to train the discriminator. We hypothesise that InfoGAN falters on complex tasks because back-propagating gradients through a moving objective is brittle, whereas evolutionary algorithms offer a more robust training paradigm.

2 Methodology

All experiments use the EvoJAXPGPE implementation. At each iteration we perform n discriminator updates with back-propagation, followed by m generator updates via PGPE. Throughout a full run we keep two parameter sets:

- θ_D – discriminator and auxiliary Qnetwork (optimised with Adam);
- (μ, σ) – mean and std. of the diagonal Gaussian search distribution from which generator weights $\theta_G \sim \mathcal{N}(\mu, \sigma^2 I)$ are sampled and evolved.

Unless otherwise noted we use n=2, m=2, and a generator and discriminator batch size of 64.

2.1 Latent-Code Design

The generator takes a *noise* vector $z \sim \mathcal{N}(0, I)$ and a *latent code*

$$c = \big[d;\, c_{\text{cont}}\big], \qquad d \in \{e_0, \ldots, e_9\},\ c_{\text{cont}} \in [-1, 1]^2,$$

where d (one-hot) encodes the target digit class and c_{cont} controls stroke thickness and in-plane rotation.

2.2 Network Architectures

- Generator: Four transposed-convolution blocks up-sample $[z; c]$ from $4\times4\times128 \rightarrow 7\times7\times64 \rightarrow 14\times14\times32 \rightarrow 28\times28\times1$. The first three blocks use BatchNorm+ReLU; the final layer uses Sigmoid to produce a 28×28 grey-scale image.
- Discriminator and Q-network: Two convolutional blocks ($1\times28\times28 \rightarrow 14\times14\times64 \rightarrow 7\times7\times128$; BatchNorm+LeakyReLU) feed a *discriminator head* (1×1 logits) and a *Q-head* that predicts (i) categorical logits $Q_d \in \mathbb{R}^{10}$ and (ii) Gaussian parameters $\mu, \sigma \in \mathbb{R}^2$ for c_{cont}.

2.3 Objective Functions

During back-prop stages we minimise

$$\mathcal{L}_D = -\mathbb{E}_{x\sim p_{\text{data}}}\big[\log D(x)\big] - \mathbb{E}_{z,c}\big[\log\big(1 - D(G(z, c))\big)\big],$$
$$\mathcal{L}_Q = -\mathbb{E}_{z,c}\Big[\log Q_d(d|G(z, c)) + \log \mathcal{N}\big(c_{\text{cont}}; \mu, \sigma^2\big)\Big].$$

For PGPE we transform the multi-objective feedback

$$(L_G,\ d,\ c_{\text{cont}})$$

into a scalar return using three alternative schemes:

1. a minmax-normalised sum of the three objectives;
2. the same normalised sum but with a running weight $w_{MI} \in [0.4, 0.6]$ that keeps mutual-information pressure from fading; and
3. a Pareto rank obtained by non-dominated sorting on (L_{MI}, L_G) with c_{cont} as a tie-breaker.

The resulting scalar drives the PGPE update of (μ, σ) the same as in [5]. Our experiments show that this weighting of adversarial, and mutual information loss have a significant impact on image quality and disentanglement which we will discuss in Sect. 3.

2.4 Hardware and Software Environment

All experiments were run on a workstation with the following configuration:

- **Operating System:** Arch Linux, kernel 6.13.1-arch1-1.
- **CPU:** AMD Ryzen 5800X (8 cores, 16 threads, 3.4-4.9GHz).
- **Memory:** 128 GB DDR4-3600.
- **Storage:** 4 TB NVMe SSD.
- **GPUs:** 2x NVIDIA RTX 3090 (24 GB GDDR6X each)
- **Drivers and Libraries:**
  - Nvidia driver 570.86.16, CUDA 12.8
- **Software Frameworks:**
  - Python 3.11.5, JAX 0.4.31, FLAX 0.8.4
- **Environment Management:** pyvenv environment
- **Reproducibility:** Random seeds fixed

3 Results

Here is a summary of the parameters for this experiment:

- The base population consists of 512 individuals.
- The center-lr is set to 0.0052, std-lr to 0.079, and init-std to 0.039.
- The algorithm runs for 140,000 iterations

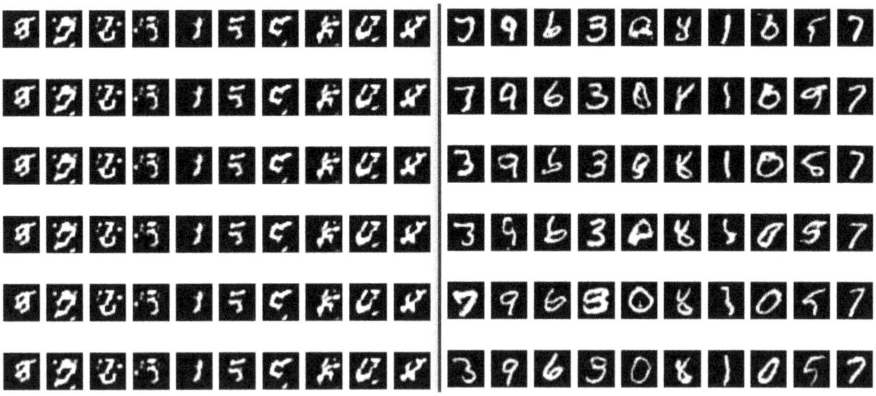

Fig. 1. Evaluation results; Mode Collapse (left), Partial Disentanglement (right).

Below are some observations made during our experiments regarding a couple of the hyperparameters:

- **Larger populations help.** Population sizes 128 and above yielded crisper digit strokes and better disentanglement. Increasing population sizes from 128 to 256 or 512 improved image quality and disentanglement earlier in the training process. The additional evolutionary diversity outweighed the improvement from increasing batch size.
- **Large discriminator batches hurt.** Raising B above 128 made the discriminator converge earlier, saturating its logits and driving the generator gradients toward zero. Both image quality and latent-code disentanglement plateaued.

3.1 Balancing Generator and Discriminator Updates

Because the back-prop discriminator often learns faster than the PGPE-trained generator, we experimented with *asymmetric update schedules*. Setting $(n, m) = (1, 3)$—one discriminator steps followed by three PGPE step—mitigated oscillations in the adversarial losses to the 0.20.4 range, but too few discriminator updates allowed the generator to dominate, again yielding a weak learning signal. A moderate schedule of $(n, m) = (2, 2)$ coupled with a *moderate* discriminator learning rate ($\eta_D = 1 \times 10^{-4}$) achieved the most stable dynamics.

3.2 Mode Collapse and Partial Disentanglement

Figure 1 (*left*) shows a failure mode in which every latent code produces almost identical digits–a classic mode-collapse scenario. This occurred whenever the discriminator saturated *or* when the mutual-information loss was given excessive weight, forcing the generator to exploit trivial statistics of the code.

More commonly we observed *partial disentanglement*. In Fig. 1 (*right*) several codes blend two classes: e.g. the first column mixes 3 s and7 s, while the sixth blends 8 s and4 s. Simply increasing the mutual-information weight could in principle sharpen class boundaries, but in practice this was ineffective once $\mathcal{L}_{\mathrm{MI}}$ had already saturated under a dominant discriminator.

3.3 Mitigating Saturation

We therefore adopted two stabilization techniques:

1. **Label smoothing** ($y_{\mathrm{real}} = 0.9$, $y_{\mathrm{fake}} = 0.1$) prevented the discriminator from assigning near-binary probabilities, keeping the sum of real and fake losses above 0.1 for most of training.
2. **Relatively high discriminator learning rate** ($\eta_D = 1 \times 10^{-4}$) ensured that–even with label smoothing–the discriminator continued to deliver informative gradients, allowing the generator to improve without collapsing.

Together these measures reduced the incidence of mode collapse and enabled cleaner one-to-one mapping between discrete latent codes and digit identities. Nevertheless, obtaining *simultaneously* high image quality *and* perfect class separation across all ten codes remains challenging.

Figure 2 contrasts our two strongest runs: *(left)* the **weighted-normalised sum** scalarisation and *(right)* the **Pareto-rank** scalarisation. Both models still exhibit traces of partial disentanglement. In the normalised-sum case the digit "8" occasionally bleeds into "9", while "5" is confused with "2" and "6". The Pareto-rank model corrects most of the "8"/"9" overlap but still mixes "9" and "0".

The normalised-sum run was evaluated after 99 k iterations, at the end of a training run where the MI term was not yet fully saturated. By contrast, the Pareto-rank run plateaued around 130 k iterations (of a 140 k-iteration schedule): the MI term had saturated, removing pressure to resolve the persistent "7 vs.3" blend visible in the first column. Further training did not reduce this ambiguity, highlighting a limitation of our present scalarisation schemes when MI gradients vanish.

4 Limitations and Future Work

4.1 Current Limitations

– **Manual objective balancing.** All three scalarisation schemes (normalised sum, weighted sum, Pareto rank) rely on *fixed or hand-tuned heuristics*; once

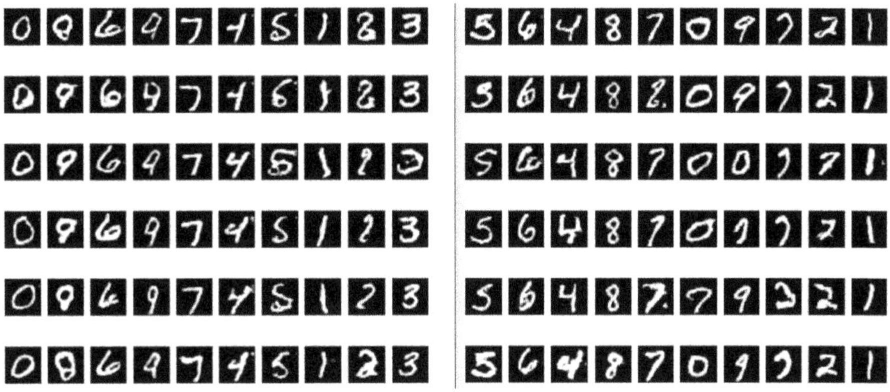

Fig. 2. Evaluation results; Normalization (left), Non-Dominated Sort (right).

the mutual-information term saturates, its influence vanishes and partial disentanglement persists.

- **Generatordiscriminator imbalance.** Even with the (n, m) schedule and label smoothing, the back-prop discriminator often outpaces the PGPE generator, leading either to mode collapse or to a weak gradient signal that stalls PGPE search.
- **Data and architecture scale.** Experiments are confined to MNIST and a shallow Conv-Deconv pair; conclusions may not transfer to higher-resolution images or to text-based transformers.
- **Computational cost.** Large PGPE populations improve performance but push VRAM limits, constraining the exploration of deeper models and larger batch sizes.

4.2 Planned Extensions

Our next step is to *re-embed* the generator's PGPE search distribution inside a **Cultural Algorithm (CA)** framework in order to *adaptively weight* the multi-objective feedback:

1. **CA-guided scalarisation.** The Belief Space will track *situational* knowledge (elite weight vectors), *normative* knowledge (acceptable weight ranges) and *historical* knowledge (how weight schedules affected convergence) to recommend a dynamic weight vector, $\boldsymbol{w}(t) = \text{Influence}\big(B(t)\big)$ each generation, replacing ad-hoc annealing.
2. **Intelligent Pareto ranking.** Following CAPSO's use of situational knowledge to curate a live Pareto front: [6], we will let the CA itself assign ranks using the *marginal-value* criterion: an individual is favoured when its contribution to frontier spread exceeds the frontier's current average. This should preserve selection pressure on disentanglement even after $\mathcal{L}_{\text{MI}}$ plateaus.

3. **Knowledge-driven exploration.** Normative and topographical knowledge sources can restrict PGPE sampling to promising sub-regions of parameter space, reducing the need for very large populations while maintaining diversity.

4. **Scaling to text tasks.** Once CA-PGPE yields a robust, interpretable latent code on CIFAR-10 and CelebA, we will transfer the framework to the InfoGAN-conditioned Transformer proposed in Sect. 1, using the CA to balance adversarial, reconstruction and language-specific objectives (e.g. perplexity).

We expect that coupling PGPE with a CA's dual-inheritance learning cycle–accept, update, influence–will supply the *adaptive objective weighting* that was missing from the current work and accelerate convergence on fully disentangled, high-quality generators.

References

1. Nuppnau, M., Kattan, K., Reynolds, R. G. : Enhancing cultural algorithm guided policy gradients with parameter-based exploration through topographic knowledge and adaptive weighting, pp. 181–192 (2025)
2. Vaswani, A., et al.: Attention is all you need. In: Proceedings of the 31st International Conference on Neural Information Processing Systems (NIPS'17). Curran Associates Inc., Red Hook, NY, USA, pp. 6000–6010 (2017)
3. Dzmitry, B., et al.: Neural machine translation by jointly learning to align and translate. CoRR abs/1409.0473 (2014)
4. Chen, X., Duan, Y., Houthooft, R., Schulman, J., Sutskever, I., Abbeel, P.: InfoGAN: interpretable representation learning by information maximizing generative adversarial nets. In: Proceedings of the 30th International Conference on Neural Information Processing Systems (NIPS'16). Curran Associates Inc., Red Hook, NY, USA, pp. 2180–2188 (2016)
5. Sehnke, F., Osendorfer, C., Rückstieß, T., Graves, A., Peters, J., Schmidhuber, J.: Policy gradients with parameter-based exploration for control. In: Kůrková, V., Neruda, R., Koutník, J. (eds.) ICANN 2008. LNCS, vol. 5163, pp. 387–396. Springer, Heidelberg (2008). https://doi.org/10.1007/978-3-540-87536-9_40
6. Stanley, S. D, Kattan, K, Reynolds, R: CAPSO: a parallelized multiobjective cultural algorithm particle swarm optimizer. In: 2019 IEEE Congress on Evolutionary Computation (CEC), Wellington, New Zealand (2019)

Poster Research Papers

Energy Consumption of TinyML-based Intrusion Detection System for Nano-sized UAVs

Nazli Tekin(✉)

Erciyes University, 38280 Kayseri, Turkey
nazlitekin@erciyes.edu.tr

Abstract. With the growing integration of nano-sized Unmanned Aerial Vehicles (UAVs) into Internet of Things (IoT) applications, ensuring their security against cyber threats under limited computational and energy resources has become a significant challenge. This work empirically investigates the feasibility and energy consumption of deploying an Intrusion Detection System (IDS) on the Crazyflie 2.1 using Tiny Machine Learning (TinyML). Supervised Machine Learning (ML) models are trained using Python's Scikit-learn library and converted into efficient C code using the emlearn framework for embedded deployment. The converted models are integrated into the Crazyflie firmware to enable real-time, on-device inference without relying on external communication or cloud resources. Energy consumption is estimated based on the inference times of the deployed ML models. The results demonstrate the viability of TinyML-based security mechanisms for enabling real-time, energy-efficient intrusion detection on nano-sized UAVs.

Keywords: TinyML · Intrusion Detection Systems · UAV Security

1 Introduction

Unmanned aerial vehicles (UAVs) have gained attention in Internet of Things (IoT) applications such as smart agriculture, environmental monitoring, and smart cities in recent years. In particular, nano-sized UAVs that typically weigh only a few tens of grams are especially well suited for operations in unavailable and impractical environments, because of their exceptional maneuverability [1]. Their agility and ease of deployment make them well-suited for time-sensitive tasks. Among them, Crazyflie is gaining attention due to its lightweight design and also its indoor applicability [4].

Despite their benefits, UAVs are vulnerable to a variety of cyber threats, including eavesdropping, spoofing, and denial of service attacks that cause security and privacy concerns. Machine Learning (ML)-based Intrusion Detection Systems are proposed to address such concerns [2]. Conventionally, ML models are developed and evaluated on high-performance platforms such as cloud infrastructures. However, transmitting data to the cloud introduces privacy risks

H. R. Arabnia et al. (Eds.): CSCE 2025, CCIS 2934, pp. 465–469, 2026.
https://doi.org/10.1007/978-3-032-22190-2_34

and latency issues, significantly affecting real-time attack detection. Performing ML models directly on UAVs presents significant challenges, primarily due to their limited computational capabilities and resources. Furthermore, executing energy-intensive ML models can lead to rapid battery depletion.

Recent advancements in Tiny Machine Learning (TinyML) have introduced new possibilities for embedding decision-making capabilities into microcontrollers with limited resources [3]. This study investigates the feasibility of implementing an IDS based on TinyML and its energy consumption in Crazyflie 2.1. To the best of my knowledge, there is no existing study evaluating the energy consumption of performing IDS on nano-sized UAVs. This study empirically deploys IDS on the Crazyflie 2.1 to measure inference time and energy consumption.

2 Experiment Methodology

Dataset. To train and evaluate the intrusion detection model, CIC-IDS2017, which is a publicly available labeled network traffic dataset is used [5]. The dataset contains benign and a variety of common attacks such as Denial-of-Service (DoS), Port Scanning, Brute Force, and Botnet. Firstly, the dataset is configured for binary classification with labels: attack and benign. The final dataset consists of 382,701 attack samples, with an equal number of benign samples obtained through downsampling to ensure class balance. The dataset includes 80 features from the generated network traffic. Since nano-sized UAVs are resource-constrained, the feature selection is performed to identify a compact yet informative subset of features that balances model accuracy with computational efficiency.

A hybrid feature selection approach is adopted to reduce the dimensionality of the dataset while maintaining high detection accuracy. Two complementary methods are used, namely Random Forest Feature Importance (RF-FI) and Recursive Feature Elimination (RFE). The RF-FI method ranks features based on their contribution to the overall reduction in impurity across the ensemble of decision trees, effectively capturing non-linear dependencies in the data. In parallel, RFE is applied using a Logistic Regression estimator to recursively eliminate the least significant features, based on iterative model performance. After obtaining the top-ranked features of each method, a final subset of 10 features is selected.

Training and Inference. Supervised ML algorithms such as Decision Tree (DT), Random Forest (RF), Naive Bayes (NB), and Multi-Layer Perceptron (MLP) by using the Python scikit-learn library [6]. The DT algorithm was applied with default settings, using the Gini impurity criterion and no predefined maximum depth. Similarly, for the RF classifier, the n_jobs parameter was set to -1, and all other hyperparameters remain at default values. The NB classifier was utilized in its Gaussian form, assuming a normal distribution for feature likelihoods. Lastly, MLP employs default parameters with activation='relu' and solver='adam.

To enable real-time, on-device inference on the resource-constrained UAV, the ML models are converted into optimized C code by using the open-source emlearn library. Emlearn provides lightweight and portable implementations of ML models suitable for microcontrollers and embedded systems with limited computational and memory resources [7].

Energy Consumption Evaluation. The energy consumption is calculated as follows:

$$E_{proc} = P_{proc} * t, \tag{1}$$

where P_{proc} is the processing power and t is the execution time. In this method, it is assumed that the device runs at constant power. As a result, the energy that the UAV consumes is directly dependent on the execution times. Detailed power consumption measurements will be made using power profiling tools.

3 Preliminary Results

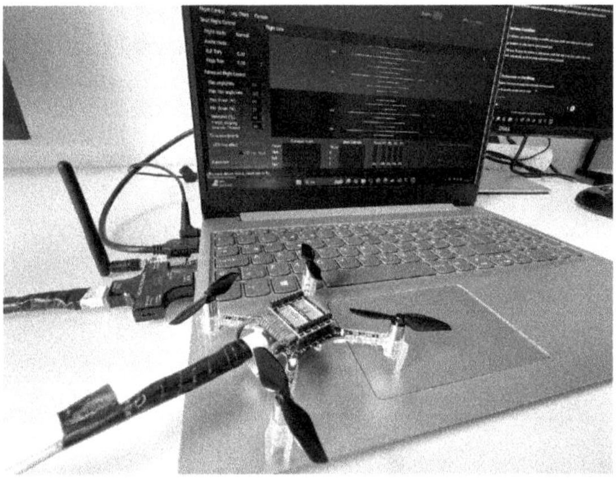

Fig. 1. Deployment and execution setup of the TinyML-based IDS on Crazyflie 2.1.

ML models (i.e., DT, RF, MLP, NB) are initially trained on an edge device with an Intel i7 CPU and 16GB RAM. Subsequently, the trained models are converted to C code and deployed on Crazyflie 2.1 for on-device inference. Crazyflie is built around the STM32F405 microcontroller, featuring a 168 MHz ARM Cortex M4 core with 192 KB of SRAM and 1 MB of flash memory. Fig. 1 illustrates the experimental setup used to deploy and evaluate IDS on Crazyflie 2.1.

Table 1 presents the performance metrics of various machine learning algorithms evaluated in the binary classification task. Among the models, the RF achieves the highest overall performance, with a precision of 0.9956, a recall of 0.9955, F1-score of 0.9955, and an accuracy of 0.9955, indicating both high correctness and completeness in predictions. DT also performs well, with consistent precision, recall and F1 score values of 0.9769. The MLP achieves slightly lower performance, with an F1-score of 0.9667 and accuracy of 0.9668. In contrast, the NB exhibits significantly lower performance, particularly in recall and F1-score (0.6022 and 0.5297, respectively), suggesting it struggles to identify samples correctly. Overall, tree-based models, particularly RF, outperformed others in terms of precision and accuracy.

Table 2 presents the inference times in microseconds (μs) of various ML models deployed on Crazyflie 2.1. Among the models, the DT achieves the fastest inference at 77.05μs, followed by NB at 101.95 μs. More complex models such as RF and MLP required higher processing times, which are 153.67μs and 158.05μs, respectively. As an initial result, DT offers a balanced trade-off between accuracy and inference time, making it a promising candidate for real-time deployment in resource-constrained UAVs.

Table 1. Performance Comparison of Classification Algorithms

Algorithm	Precision	Recall	F1-Score	Accuracy
DT	0.9769	0.9769	0.9769	0.9769
RF	0.9956	0.9955	0.9955	0.9955
MLP	0.9680	0.9668	0.9667	0.9668
NB	0.7641	0.6022	0.5297	0.6022

Table 2. Inference times of ML models on Crazyflie 2.1 (in μs)

Algorithm	Inference Time (μs)
DT	77.05
RF	153.67
MLP	158.05
NB	101.95

4 Conclusion and Future Work

This study empirically investigated the energy consumption of performing ML-based IDS on nano-sized UAVS. The initial results demonstrated that TinyML offers a practical solution for improving the security of nano-sized UAVs through on-device intrusion detection. Future work will explore TinyOL (Tiny Online Learning) frameworks to support continuous real-time model updates on the device. Furthermore, this study will be extended by incorporating additional

ML algorithms and datasets (e.g., TON_IoT) to enable the detection of sensor-based attacks and to evaluate IDS models in terms of both detection performance and energy consumption. The other TinyML tools (e.g., STM32Cube.AI and m2cgen) will be compared in terms of model performance and integration complexity.

Acknowledgments. This study was supported by Scientific and Technological Research Council of Türkiye (TUBITAK) under Grant Number 124E544. The author thanks TUBITAK for their support.

Disclosure of Interests. The authors have no competing interests to declare that are relevant to the content of this article.

References

1. Cheng, N., et al.: AI for UAV-assisted IoT applications: a comprehensive review. IEEE Internet Things J. **10**(16), 14438–14461 (2023)
2. Verma, A., Ranga, V.: Machine learning based intrusion detection systems for IoT applications. Wireless Pers. Commun. **111**(4), 2287–2310 (2020)
3. Dutta, L., Bharali, S.: TinyML meets IoT: a comprehensive survey. Int. Things **16**, 100461 (2021)
4. Giernacki, W., Skwierczyński, M., Witwicki, W., Wroński, P., Kozierski, P: Crazyflie 2.0 quadrotor as a platform for research and education in robotics and control engineering. In: Proceedings 22nd International Conference on Methods and Models in Automation and Robotics (MMAR), pp. 37–42 (2017)
5. Sharafaldin, I., Lashkari, A.H., Ghorbani, A.A.: Toward generating a new intrusion detection dataset and intrusion traffic characterization. In: Proceedings of the 4th International Conference on Information Systems Security and Privacy (ICISSP), Portugal (2018)
6. Pedregosa, F., et al.: Scikit-learn: machine learning in python. J. Mach. Learn. Res. **12**, 2825–2830 (2011)
7. Jonnor.: emlearn. Available: https://github.com/emlearn/emlearn (2021). Accessed 10 May 2025

Design and Verification of a CanSat Rover Remote Control System Using Cloud and MQTT Communication

Seiya Yoshida(✉), Miho Akiyama, and Takuya Saito

Tokyo University of Information Sciences, 4-1 Onaridai Wakabaku Chiba-shi, Chiba 265-0077, Japan
g25016ys@edu.tuis.ac.jp, t3saito22@rsch.tuis.ac.jp

Abstract. The purpose of this study is to design and develop a remote-control system for a CanSat rover utilizing cloud technology and MQTT communication. MQTT, a lightweight protocol with excellent real-time performance, is employed to enable bidirectional communication—transmitting data collected from GPS and onboard sensors while receiving control commands based on that data. Field experiments were conducted on a university futsal court to evaluate the system's performance in terms of navigation accuracy toward a designated goal and communication stability.

Keywords: remote-control · MQTT · CanSat · ARLISS

1 Introduction

In recent years, there has been a growing interest in space development. In particular, lunar exploration and rocket development are actively being pursued around the world. Against this backdrop, several space-related events are held in Japan, such as the Noshiro Space Event in Noshiro City, Akita Prefecture, in August [1], and the Tanegashima Rocket Contest in Tanegashima, Kagoshima Prefecture, in March [2]. On a larger scale, the ARLISS competition held in the Black Rock Desert in the United States [3] is one of the most prominent.

These events, which focus on research and development of lunar exploration rovers, have become increasingly common. Participants bring their self-developed rovers to these events to compete in performance and conduct experiments that simulate real lunar environments. Such activities contribute to the advancement of new technologies and the development of human resources.

Some of these competitions also include a "remote control category," in which participants control their rovers remotely and compete based on control performance.

In this study, we aim to design and develop a remotely controlled rover in response to this trend, and to explore the potential of remote-control technologies through field experiments.

H. R. Arabnia et al. (Eds.): CSCE 2025, CCIS 2934, pp. 470–474, 2026.
https://doi.org/10.1007/978-3-032-22190-2_35

2 Method

In remote control systems for CanSat, one common approach is to establish a wireless communication environment by connecting a server and the CanSat via a network. Remote control can generally be divided into two sides: the controller and the controlled device. In this study, the controller is the user, while the CanSat serves as the controlled device.

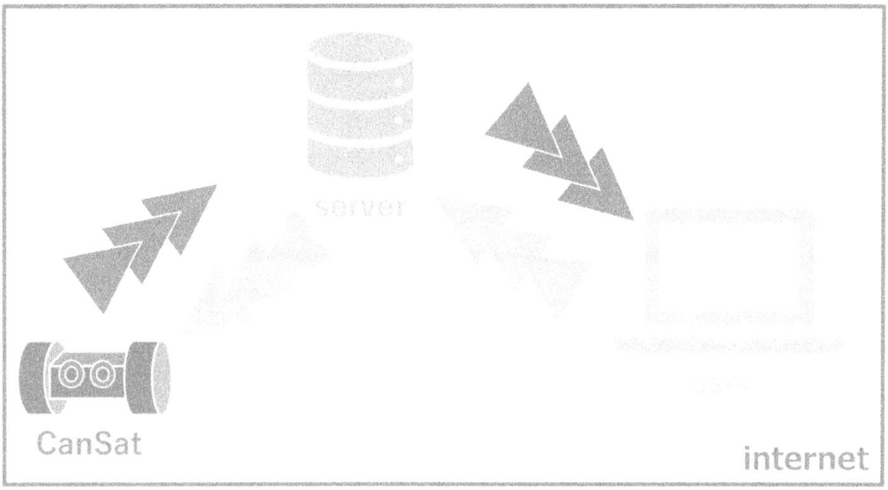

Fig. 1. System Architecture of the Proposed Method

An overview of the proposed method is shown in Fig. 1. Among various wireless communication options, Wi-Fi was selected for this study, allowing CanSat to connect to a server via the Internet.

The communication protocol used is MQTT [4], which is lightweight and suitable for real-time applications. On the CanSat side, various types of data obtained from the surrounding environment are transmitted to the server. The server then relays this data to the user. Based on the received data, the user determines the next action to be taken and sends a command in the form of a character string. This command follows the reverse route—from the user to the server, and then from the server to the CanSat—where the CanSat performs the corresponding operation based on the received command.

3 Experiment

The CanSat body used in this study was based on the autonomous model employed at last year's Noshiro Space Event and ARLISS competition. Most of the structure was fabricated using a PLA-based 3D printer in our laboratory. This method allows high design flexibility, and the basic durability and functional reliability of the structure were confirmed through testing conducted last year.

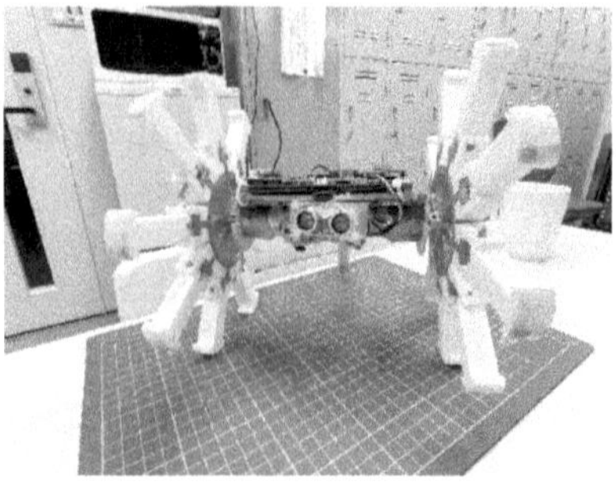

Fig. 2. Overview of the Rover

Fig. 3. Hardware Circuit Board

The wheels were an improved version of those used in the Tanegashima Rocket Contest. Previously, the tires were made of TPU and manually compressed for rocket storage, which led to shape irregularities, potential detachment, and time-consuming preparations. In this study, a foldable mechanism was introduced to eliminate the need for manual compression and reduce individual variation. To achieve both durability and compact storability, a new tire combining the flexibility of TPU and the rigidity of PLA was developed and installed—replacing the tires used last year. An overview of the rover is shown in Fig. 2, and the hardware circuit board is presented in Fig. 3.

The software was based on last year's autonomous control program, with partial modifications for remote control functionality. Sensor data collected by the rover was transmitted to a server hosted on Amazon Web Services (AWS), allowing user interaction through a web interface. A screenshot of the web-based control interface is shown in Fig. 4.

The reason for adopting cloud services lies in their scalability and adaptability to changing demands, enabling real-time resource allocation. In contrast, physical servers require upfront provisioning of sufficient resources, which can lead to excessive costs and potential resource waste. Additionally, the purchase, installation, and maintenance of physical servers involve significant initial investment. Cloud services, on the other hand, offer pay-as-you-go pricing, minimizing initial costs. Notably, AWS allows free access to all of its services for 12 months upon account creation. With an internet connection, the cloud server can be accessed from anywhere in the world, enabling real-time monitoring and troubleshooting during experiments.

4 Evaluation

A field experiment was conducted to verify whether data exchange via the Internet was functioning properly and to assess how closely the rover could approach the designated goal. To evaluate the outcomes, we employed the commonly used criteria in satellite development and mission-based systems: Minimum Success, Full Success, and Extra Success, which allow for a concrete expression of mission success levels. In this study, the success criteria were defined as follows:

Fig. 4. Web Control Interface

- **Minimum Success**: Verification that the rover could be controlled using the proposed cloud and MQTT-based communication method.
- **Full Success:** The rover reaches within a 10-m radius of the goal location while being remotely controlled in a simulated mission environment.
- **Extra Success**: The rover reaches within a 5-m radius of the goal location.

A summary of the results from 10 experimental trials is presented below. In the evaluation table, "○" indicates successful completion, "×" indicates failure, and "△" denotes a successful result despite the occurrence of a technical issue during the trial.

As shown in the table, Minimum Success was achieved in 9 out of 10 trials. One trial encountered a problem: the Internet connection was temporarily lost, which interrupted remote operation. However, the system successfully reconnected, and the experiment was resumed.

Full Success was achieved in 5 out of 10 trials, resulting in a 50% success rate. This outcome is likely due to the use of GPS data to measure the distance to the goal, with GPS errors significantly affecting positional accuracy.

In addition to these metrics, user feedback via a questionnaire was collected to determine whether there were any usability or control issues during operation.

Extra Success was achieved in 3 out of 10 trials, where the rover reached within 5 m of the goal. The detailed experimental results are summarized in Table 1.

Table 1. Result

	Minimum Success	Full Success	Extra Success
Experiment 1	○	○	○
Experiment 2	○	○	×
Experiment 3	○	○	×
Experiment 4	△	○	○
Experiment 5	○	×	×
Experiment 6	○	×	×
Experiment 7	○	○	○
Experiment 8	○	×	×

(continued)

Table 1. (*continued*)

	Minimum Success	Full Success	Extra Success
Experiment 9	○	×	×
Experiment 10	○	×	×

5 Conclusion

In this study, we designed and developed a remote-control system for a CanSat rover utilizing cloud services and the MQTT communication protocol and verified its effectiveness through field experiments. By employing the lightweight and real-time-capable MQTT protocol, we achieved stable bidirectional communication of GPS and sensor data, enabling reliable remote control of the CanSat rover. Field experiments conducted on a university futsal court demonstrated that the proposed system exhibited generally stable communication performance. The rover was successfully guided to within a 10-m radius of the target in 5 out of 10 trials, and to within a 5-m radius in 3 out of 10 trials. These results confirm the basic effectiveness of the proposed cloud-based MQTT communication system in controlling a CanSat rover. However, in order to achieve higher precision in guidance and ensure stable operation under more diverse environmental conditions, further research and development are required. Specifically, improvements could include the integration of advanced self-localization algorithms that fuse data from additional sensors beyond GPS, as well as enhanced resilience to communication disruptions. Future work will focus on addressing these challenges, with the aim of realizing a more practical and reliable remote-control system for CanSat rovers.

Acknowledgements. The authors would like to thank the members of the Saito Laboratory at Tokyo University of Information Sciences for their helpful discussions. The authors are also grateful to the anonymous reviewers for their constructive comments, which significantly improved this paper.

References

1. Noshiro Space Event. https://noshiro-space-event.org/. Accessed 27 Jan 2025
2. Tanegashima Rocket Contest: http://jaxa-rocket-contest.jp/. Accessed 27 Jan 2025
3. ARLISS. https://unisec.jp/activities/arliss. Accessed 27 Jan 2025
4. MQTT: Andrew Banks and Rahul Gupta, "MQTT Version 3.1.1." OASIS Standard, October 2014. https://docs.oasis-open.org/mqtt/mqtt/v3.1.1/os/mqtt-v3.1.1-os.html

Author Index

H. R. Arabnia et al. (Eds.): CSCE 2025, CCIS 2934, pp. 475–476, 2026.
https://doi.org/10.1007/978-3-032-22190-2

www.ingramcontent.com/pod-product-compliance
Ingram Content Group UK Ltd.
Pitfield, Milton Keynes, MK11 3LW, UK
UKHW021052200826
474604UK00003BA/186

9783032221896